The Umayyad Empire

EDINBURGH HISTORY OF THE ISLAMIC EMPIRES
Series Editor: Ian Richard Netton

Editorial Advisory Board

Professor John L. Esposito
Professor Carole Hillenbrand

Available titles

The Almoravid and Almohad Empires
Amira Bennison

The Fatimid Empire
Michael Brett

The Umayyad Empire
Andrew Marsham

The Mongol Empire
Timothy May

The Great Seljuq Empire
A. C. S. Peacock

edinburghuniversitypress.com/series/ehie

The Umayyad Empire

Andrew Marsham

EDINBURGH
University Press

For B.E.M.

Edinburgh University Press is one of the leading university presses in the UK. We publish academic books and journals in our selected subject areas across the humanities and social sciences, combining cutting-edge scholarship with high editorial and production values to produce academic works of lasting importance. For more information visit our website: edinburghuniversitypress.com

© Andrew Marsham, 2024

Edinburgh University Press Ltd
13 Infirmary Street
Edinburgh EH1 1LT

Typeset in 11/13pt Adobe Garamond Pro by
Cheshire Typesetting Ltd, Cuddington, Cheshire
and printed and bound in Great Britain

A CIP record for this book is available from the British Library

ISBN 978 0 7486 4301 1 (hardback)
ISBN 978 0 7486 4300 4 (paperback)
ISBN 978 1 3995 2739 2 (webready PDF)
ISBN 978 1 3995 2740 8 (epub)

The right of Andrew Marsham to be identified as author of this work has been asserted in accordance with the Copyright, Designs and Patents Act 1988 and the Copyright and Related Rights Regulations 2003 (SI No. 2498).

Contents

List of Box Text	vii
List of Illustrations	viii
List of Abbreviations	xi
Note on Dates, Transliteration and Names	xiii
Acknowledgements	xiv
Introduction	1

Part I The Formation of the Umayyad Empire

Introduction	29
1 The Origins of Arabian Empire	31
2 The Seventh-century 'World Crisis'	47
3 The 'Conquest Society' and the Defeat of Rome and Iran	64
4 The Emergence of the Umayyad Empire	78
5 The Succession to Mu'awiya and the Second Civil War	101

Part II The Marwanid Umayyad Empire, 692–750

Introduction	119
6 The Imperial Marwanid Caliphate	127
7 The Siege of Constantinople and the Short Caliphates of Sulayman, 'Umar II and Yazid II	162
8 Hisham b. 'Abd al-Malik: Renewal and Defeat	176
9 The Collapse of Umayyad Power	192

Part III Ecology, Economy and Society in Umayyad Times

    Introduction   211

10 Resources, Settlement Patterns and Commerce   213

11 Christians, Zoroastrians, Jews and Others in the Umayyad Empire   257

12 The Provinces, Government and Taxation   294

Afterword   328
Bibliography   332
Index   360

Abbreviations

Journals, Encyclopedias and Reference Works

BSOAS   *Bulletin of the School of Oriental and African Studies*
 CAH   *Cambridge Ancient History*
 DOP   *Dumbarton Oaks Papers*
   EI^1 *Encyclopaedia of Islam, First Edition*
   EI^2 *Encyclopaedia of Islam, Second Edition*
   EI3   *Encyclopaedia of Islam: THREE*
   E.Ir. *Encyclopaedia Iranica*
    EQ   *Encyclopaedia of the Qur'an*
 IJMES *International Journal of Middle East Studies*
  JAOS *Journal of the American Oriental Society*
 JESHO *Journal of the Economic and Social History of the Orient*
   JLA   *Journal of Late Antiquity*
  JNES   *Journal of Near Eastern Studies*
  JRAS   *Journal of the Royal Asiatic Society*
  JSAI   *Jerusalem Studies in Arabic and Islam*
   JSS   *Journal of Semitic Studies*
  NCHI   *New Cambridge History of Islam*
  ODLA   *Oxford Dictionary of Late Antiquity*
  PmBZ   *Prosopographie der mittelbyzantinischen Zeit Online*

Frequently Cited Texts and Translations

Baladhuri, *Ansab*   Aḥmad b. Yaḥyā al-Balādhurī, *Ansāb al-Ashrāf*, ed. M. Fardūs al-Aẓm (Damascus, 1997–2004).
Baladhuri, *Futuh*   Aḥmad b. Yaḥyā al-Balādhurī, *Futūḥ al-Buldān*, ed. M. J. de Goeje (Leiden, 1866).
History of the Patriarchs   B. Evetts (ed. and tr.), *History of the Patriarchs of the Coptic Church of Alexandria* (Paris, 1904–14).
Ibn 'Asakir   'Alī b. al-Ḥasan b. 'Asākir, *Ta'rīkh Madīnat Dimashq*, ed. 'Umar Gharāma al-'Amrawī (Beirut, 1995–2000).

Khalifa   Khalīfa b. Khayyāṭ al-ʿUsfurī, *Ta'rīkh Khalīfa b. Khayyāṭ*, eds Muṣṭafā Najīb Fawwāz and Ḥikma Kashlī Fawwāz (Beirut, 1995).

Kindi   Abū ʿUmar Muḥammad b. Yūsuf al-Kindī, *The Governors and Judges of Egypt* (= *Kitāb Wulāt Miṣr wa-Quḍātihā*), ed. Rhuvon Guest (Leiden, 1912).

Tabari   Abū Jaʿfar Muḥammad b. Jarīr al-Ṭabarī, *Ta'rīkh al-Rusul wa-l-Mulūk*, eds M. J. de Goeje et al. (Leiden 1879–1901).

Tabari, *History*   Abu Jaʿfar Muhammad b. Jarir al-Tabari, *The History of al-Tabari*, eds and trs Ehsan Yar-Shater et al. (Albany, NY, 1985–2007).

Theophanes   Cyril Mango and Roger Scott (eds and trs), *The Chronicle of Theophanes Confessor: Byzantine and Near Eastern History AD 284–813* (Oxford, 1997).

Theophilus   Robert G. Hoyland, *Theophilus of Edessa's Chronicle and the Circulation of Historical Knowledge in Late Antiquity and Early Islam* (Liverpool, 2011).

Yaʿqubi   Aḥmad b. Abī Yaʿqūb al-Yaʿqūbī, *Historiae* (= *Ta'rīkh al-Yaʿqūbī*), ed. M. J. Houtsma (Leiden, 1883).

Frequently Cited Secondary Studies

EIC   Fred M. Donner, *The Early Islamic Conquests* (Princeton, 1981).

IatMC   Michael G. Morony, *Iraq after the Muslim Conquest* (Princeton, 1984).

RoIM   Andrew Marsham, *Rituals of Islamic Monarchy: Accession and Succession in the First Muslim Empire* (Edinburgh, 2009).

SaMS   Petra M. Sijpesteijn, *Shaping a Muslim State: The World of a Mid-Eighth-Century Egyptian Official* (Oxford, 2013).

SIAOSI   Robert G. Hoyland, *Seeing Islam As Others Saw It: A Survey and Evaluation of Christian, Jewish and Zoroastrian Writings on Early Islam* (Princeton, 1997).

SoH   Patricia Crone, *Slaves on Horses: The Evolution of the Islamic Polity* (Cambridge, 1980).

WtaWC   James Howard-Johnston, *Witnesses to a World Crisis: Historians and Histories of the Middle East in the Seventh Century* (Oxford, 2010).

Languages

| Ar. | Arabic | Lat. | Latin | pl. | plural |
| Gk | Greek | pl. | plural | sing. | singular |

Note on Dates, Transliteration and Names

Except where noted otherwise, dates are given in the Common Era (CE) form (AD, or Anno Domini, in most older publications). BCE is used to mark Before Common Era (BC, Before Christ).

Where the Islamic lunar *hijrī* calendar is used, it is marked AH (Anno Hegirae). The Islamic lunar calendar begins with year 1 in mid-July 622 CE and each year is ten or eleven days shorter than the solar year.

Other than primary sources cited in the Bibliography, Arabic personal names and book titles are transliterated without the diacritical marks used by specialists. Only the markers for the letters *'ayn* and *hamza* have been retained (an opening and closing single quotation mark, respectively). Both are forms of glottal stop (arguably in the case of *'ayn*). Other Arabic words and phrases are italicised and transliterated according to a modified version of the scheme used in Brill's *Encyclopaedia of Islam: THREE*.

Only the most widely recognised name for each person is used after the first mention of them, where a fuller set of names is sometimes given.

In the Arabic sources, everyone is known by their own name (their *ism*) and those of their forefathers (their *nasab*). Hence, the famous Umayyad caliph 'Abd al-Malik is often known as 'Abd al-Malik b. Marwan – that is, 'Abd al-Malik the son of Marwan (*ibn*, abbreviated to b., being the word for son; *bint*, abbreviated to bt., the word for daughter). Sometimes an individual became best known by a patronym. For example, an early biographer of the Prophet, Muhammad b. Ishaq, is more usually known simply as Ibn Ishaq – 'Son of Ishaq', since this distinguishes him more effectively than his *ism*, Muhammad.

People had at least two other names: a *kunya*, or teknonym, usually derived from the name of their eldest child, and a *nisba*, relating to their tribe or place of origin. 'Abd al-Malik's *kunya* was Abu Sa'id – the father of Sa'id. One of 'Abd al-Malik's *nisba*s was al-Umawi, 'the Umayyad', after his great great-grandfather, Umayya b. 'Abd Shams. Someone could have more than one *kunya* and more than one *nisba*.

Acknowledgements

This book has been long enough in the making that I have incurred far more debts than it is possible to acknowledge individually here. I have attempted to single out some of the greatest, to institutions, groups and individuals. I apologise sincerely for oversights.

Much of the preliminary research for this book was supported by an Arts and Humanities Research Council (AHRC) Early Career Fellowship (grant no. 1026731/1) and further research and writing was facilitated by the universities of Edinburgh and Cambridge, as well as by Queens' College, Cambridge. I am most grateful to all four institutions.

I would like to thank the editor of the series, Ian Netton, and the staff at Edinburgh University Press, particularly Nicola Ramsey, Rachel Bridgewater, Eddie Clark and Lel Gillingwater. Early in the publishing process, the anonymous reviewers of the book proposal made helpful comments and criticisms, for which I am also most grateful.

I have benefited from numerous enjoyable conversations about the Umayyads and their empire with colleagues and students, especially in various forums at the universities of Cambridge, Edinburgh, Leeds, Hamburg, Tübingen and Paris. It is a great pleasure to express particular thanks to Katie Campbell, Ann Christys, Lauren Erker, Caroline Goodson, Hannah-Lena Hagemann, Geoffrey Khan, Sam Lasman, Marie Legendre, Petra Sijpesteijn and Philip Wood, all of whom gave generous advice and support of various kinds. Alain George is a long-standing collaborator and interlocutor on all things Umayyad, who also provided crucial moral support, while Amira Bennison, Harry Munt and Ed Zychowicz-Coghill read the book at various stages of its production; I am especially grateful to all four of them. All remaining errors in the book are of course my own.

Finally, I would like to record my thanks to my mother, Judith, my late father, Dennis, my brother, John, and my wife, Farrhat. My daughter arrived near the beginning of the process of writing this book, which is dedicated to her, with love.

6.1	The eastern frontier at the time of Qutayba b. Muslim	160
10.1	The main ecological zones of the Mediterranean and West Eurasia	215
10.2	Umayyad-era 'aristocratic settlements' (or 'desert castles') in Syria	236
10.3	Map depicting volume of imports in amphorae from a late seventh-century deposit at the Crypta Balbi, Rome	249
12.1	Late Sasanian and early Islamic Iraq	297
12.2	Late Roman and early Islamic Egypt	299
12.3	The military districts (*ajnād*) of Syria after the conquests	300
12.4	The 'Umayyad North' (the Caucasus and Mesopotamia)	302
12.5	Late Roman and early Islamic South Mediterranean and North Africa	304
12.6	The eastern lands of the Umayyad Empire in Marwanid times	306

10.1	Tiraz embroidered with 'God's Servant Marwan Commander of the Faithful … in the tiraz of Ifriqiya'	225
10.2	Plan of the Umayyad-era mosque-palace complex at Kufa, Iraq	227
10.3	The caliphal palace building at Qasr al-Hayr al-Sharqi, between Tadmur/Palmyra and Raqqa, April 1996	237
10.4	Bathhouse reception room floor mosaic at Khirbet al-Mafjar, near Jericho	238
10.5	Reconstructed façade of the gateway to the palace at Qasr al-Hayr al-Gharbi at the National Museum, Damascus, January 1993	239
10.6	Plan of the caliphal palace at Qasr al-Hayr al-Gharbi, between Damascus and Tadmur/Palmyra	240
10.7	Schematic plan of the site of Qasr al-Hayr al-Gharbi	241
11.1	St Catherine's Monastery at Mount Sinai in 2013	263
12.1	Milestone inscribed in Arabic in the name of 'Abd al-Malik, Commander of the Faithful, from Khan al-Hathrura, between Jerusalem and Damascus, 685–705 CE	309
12.2	Papyrus document in Arabic about a tax debt, dated Safar AH 91/December 709–January 710 CE	313

Charts

I.1	Simplified genealogy of the Prophet Muhammad, the first two caliphs, the Umayyads, the Abbasids and the Shi'i Imams	6
I.2	The caliphal branches of the Umayyads	16
2.1	Simplified genealogy of Quraysh	57
4.1	Simplified genealogy of the Hashimites and Zubayrids	81
4.2	Simplified genealogy of the Banu Kalb and their marriages to Umayyads	87
5.1	Simplified genealogy of Marwan b. al-Hakam and his Umayyad relatives	109
II.1	Simplified genealogy of the Marwanid caliphs	120

Maps

I.1	The Umayyad Empire at its greatest extent, in c. 740 CE	3
1.1	Rome and Iran in the fourth–fifth centuries CE and the neighbouring steppe, forest and desert zones	33
1.2	Relief map of the Arabian Peninsula and the Syrian Desert	36
1.3	Modern precipitation map of 'Greater Syria' (*Bilād al-Shām*) with some of the major late antique settlements	38
4.1	The Arabian conquests at c. 650 CE	79

Box Text

Chapter 2
The 'Late Antique Little Ice Age' and the 'Justinianic Plague'   51

Chapter 3
An Administrative Papyrus from the Conquest of Egypt, 642 CE   72

Chapter 4
The Inscription from Hammat Gader, 5 December 662   94

Chapter 5
The Rebellion of al-Mukhtar al-Thaqafi at Kufa, 685–7   105

Chapter 6
Medinan Scholars in the Orbit of the Marwanids   148

Chapter 7
Joining the Conquerors: *walā'* and *mawālī*   169

Chapter 8
Religious Leaders in Marwanid Basra and Kufa   184

Chapter 9
Factional Competition in the Umayyad Armies? 'Qays' and 'Yemen'   195

Chapter 10
Itinerant Monarchy: The Umayyads and the Syrian Landscape   242

Chapter 11
The Monastery at Mount Sinai in the Umayyad Era   264

Chapter 12
Chief Scribes and Tax Officials at the Syrian Umayyad Court   309

Illustrations

Figures

I.1	The three largest (upper curve) and single largest (lower curve) states through history	2
1.1	Sheep grazing on the Syrian steppe with Bedouin tents in the background, near Damascus, Syria, c. 1950–5	39
1.2	The Namara inscription	42
2.1	The Harran inscription, 568 CE	49
3.1	Receipt for sixty-five sheep, 25 April 643 CE	73
4.1	The Bathhouse inscription at Hammat Gader, 5 December 662 CE	94
6.1	Solidus of Justinian II, c. 690 CE	129
6.2	'Standing Caliph' dinar, Damascus mint, AH 77/696–7 CE	129
6.3	Dirham in the name of 'Qatari, Commander of the Faithful' (Middle Persian), Bishapur mint	134
6.4	Folio from the 'Fustat Umayyad codex' (after François Déroche)	139
6.5	Aniconic and epigraphic 'reform' dinar from Syria, dated AH 77/696–7 CE	140
6.6	Aerial view of the Old City of Jerusalem in winter, looking north-west	143
6.7	The Dome of the Rock, Jerusalem, from the north	144
6.8	The Dome of the Rock, Jerusalem, interior of the top of the inner arcade, looking north	145
6.9	Aerial view of the Umayyad Mosque at Damascus, looking south-east	155
7.1	Aerial view of the Old City of Istanbul in the early twentieth century, looking north	165
8.1	Near life-size stucco figure from the palace of Qasr al-Hayr al-Gharbi, between Damascus and al-Rusafa, probably depicting Caliph Hisham, c. 727 CE	177

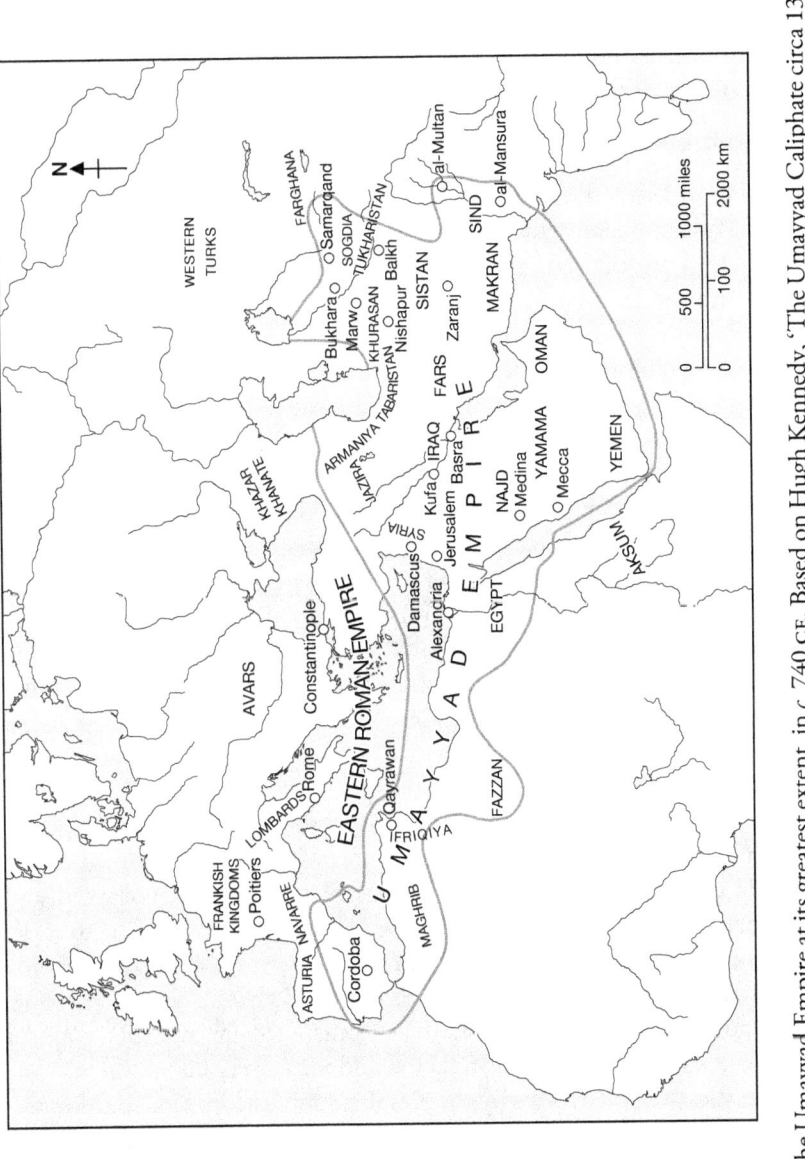

Map I.1 The Umayyad Empire at its greatest extent, in c. 740 CE. Based on Hugh Kennedy, 'The Umayyad Caliphate circa 132/750', in *An Historical Atlas of Islam*, edited by Hugh Kennedy. Brill. Consulted online on 25 April 2020.

Umayya, Muʻawiya's great-grandfather. The Umayyad Caliphate remains the largest ever Islamic empire in terms of land area, and the only trans-regional empire in history to be dominated by a military elite who came from the Arabian Peninsula and its northern extension, the Syrian Desert and Steppe. The Umayyad era was also the last occasion when the entire Islamic world was politically united – notionally at least – under one ruler; thereafter it began to fragment into separate emirates and, eventually, separate imperial caliphates.

Shiʻis, Sunnis, and the Reputation of the Umayyads

In order to understand why neither Muʻawiya's status as a Companion of the Prophet Muhammad, nor his political achievements and those of his dynasty, are enough to protect his name from the anger of modern vandals, we must look beyond the Umayyad period itself, at the history of the first 300 years of Islam and the formation of the two sectarian positions known today as Sunnism and Shiʻism. Ultimately, the ambivalent and sometimes negative image of Muʻawiya and his Umayyad successors among many (but by no means all) Muslims is a consequence of the close connection between political leadership and religious authority in the formative era of Islam.

In 622, the Prophet Muhammad had established a new community at the oasis now known as Medina (in modern Saudi Arabia). This community identified as 'faithful' (Ar. *muʼmin*, pl. *muʼminūn*) monotheists in the Jewish and Christian tradition, emphasising the idea of one God to the exclusion of all others, and the importance of loyalty to that God over other loyalties to family and tribe. By the time of Muhammad's death, in 632, his political influence reached across much of the Arabian Peninsula. Muhammad's immediate successors presided over the dramatic conquest of the Middle East, North Africa and western Central Asia. The two great empires that had dominated the temperate lands of West Eurasia for centuries – the Roman Empire in the Mediterranean and the Sasanian Empire of Iran – were overwhelmed in one decade, in the 630s and 640s. By 650, the Sasanian Empire had collapsed, and the Romans had surrendered control of Egypt and Syria. (According to widespread convention, Greater Syria – *Bilād al-Shām* in Arabic – is here simply called 'Syria', by which is denoted modern Syria, Lebanon, Israel, Palestine, Jordan and parts of southern Turkey.) The Romans fought hard for the North African lands west of Egypt, which they abandoned after 700.

With these vast conquests by the Arabian monotheists came bitter internal political conflict over resources and legitimate leadership. Because political leadership was also leadership of the new religious community, these conflicts generated passionate and often violent disputes that were at once political and religious. And because the leadership of the new empire of the 'Faithful' stayed in the hands of close relatives of the Prophet Muhammad, these religio-political

Introduction

Just to the south of the medieval circuit walls of the Old City of Damascus, in Syria, is the Bab al-Saghir Cemetery, where Damascenes have buried their dead for centuries. I visited the cemetery in 2010, about six months before the beginning of the horror of the Syrian War. I had come to see the tomb of the caliph Muʿawiya b. Abi Sufyan (r. 661–80 CE). Muʿawiya was a brother-in-law and distant cousin of the Prophet Muhammad, and is usually considered to be the founder of the Umayyad dynasty. Once an extra-mural burial ground, the cemetery was now surrounded by the modern city. It was full of densely packed gravestones, separated only by narrow paths. There were also larger monuments, visible across the fields of smaller grave markers. When I visited, one mid-week afternoon in blazing July heat, veiled women pilgrims surrounded the large domed tomb of the Prophet Muhammad's great-granddaughter, Fatima bt. al-Husayn.

Muʿawiya's grave was about 100m further along – a modern, pale, concrete cube, about 2m high, encased in green-painted railings and capped by a concrete dome decorated with religious invocations in the same green paint. An inscribed band of Arabic ran around the top of its four walls. The tomb stood in silence, with no visitors. When I got closer, I noticed a large hole broken in the modern inscription, through which the blue and white tiles of an older building showed. The gap seemed unlikely to be accidental damage, since it coincided exactly with Muʿawiya's name, all but the last syllable of which had been broken away.

As the damage to his tomb suggests, although Muʿawiya lived more than 1,300 years ago, he and his family still excite strong feelings – often ambivalent and sometimes fiercely negative. This may seem surprising, and not just because of the remote time in which he lived; Muʿawiya has the prestigious status of a Companion of the Prophet Muhammad – someone who is said to have met the founder of the Islamic religion, and converted to Islam while Muhammad still lived. Furthermore, in the ninety years between 661 and 750, Muʿawiya, and then thirteen of his relatives from the Umayyad clan, presided over an era of astonishing empire-building on a hitherto unknown scale.

No previous empire had ever been as geographically vast as that the Umayyads ruled, and none would be again until the conquests of Genghis Khan and the Mongols, half a millennium later, in the thirteenth century (Figure I.1).

During the ninety years of Umayyad rule, many of what were to become the core territories of Islam and the Arab world were conquered by commanders loyal to Muʿawiya or his Umayyad successors. By 711, the Umayyad Empire stretched from modern Spain and Morocco in the West to modern Afghanistan and Pakistan in the East; by 750, when the Umayyad dynasty fell from power, armies composed of the Arabians and their allies were fighting on imperial frontiers in the Caucasus, Central Asia, East Africa, South Asia and Europe (see Map I.1). The Arabic language had been established as the language of religion and imperial administration across much of the empire, and its governors and soldiers prayed in the mosques that had been built in its cities.

Members of the Umayyad family ruled all these lands as a single political entity. It is often referred to as the Umayyad Caliphate, after one of the titles used by its rulers – 'God's Caliph' (*khalīfat Allāh*), meaning 'God's Representative on Earth' – and after the name of their common ancestor

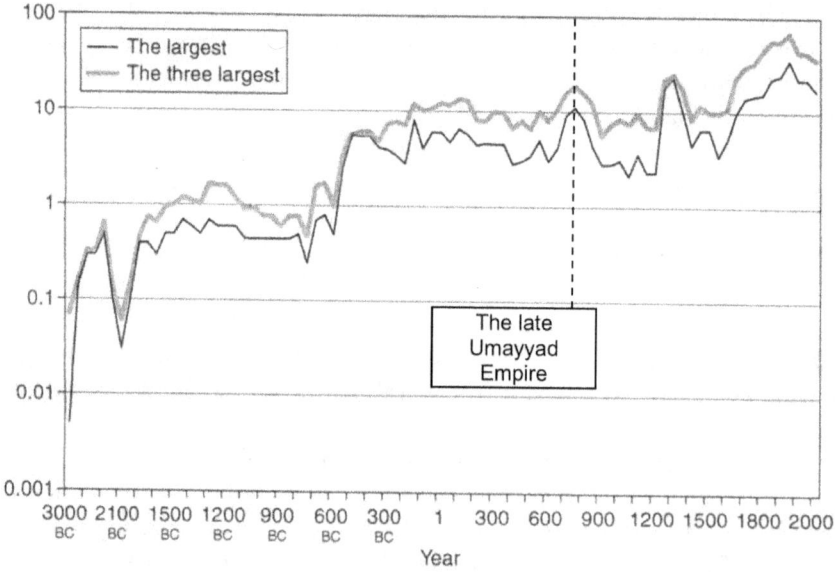

Figure I.1 The three largest (upper curve) and single largest (lower curve) states through history, measured in million square kilometres with a semi-logarithmic scale. The Umayyad Empire is marked at *c*. 740 CE. Based on a chart by J. Myrdal in Alf Hornborg, Brett Clark and Kenneth Hermele (eds), *Ecology and Power* (Routledge, 2012), 38.

Abbreviations

Journals, Encyclopedias and Reference Works

BSOAS *Bulletin of the School of Oriental and African Studies*
CAH *Cambridge Ancient History*
DOP *Dumbarton Oaks Papers*
EI^1 *Encyclopaedia of Islam, First Edition*
EI^2 *Encyclopaedia of Islam, Second Edition*
EI3 *Encyclopaedia of Islam: THREE*
E.Ir. *Encyclopaedia Iranica*
EQ *Encyclopaedia of the Qur'an*
IJMES *International Journal of Middle East Studies*
JAOS *Journal of the American Oriental Society*
JESHO *Journal of the Economic and Social History of the Orient*
JLA *Journal of Late Antiquity*
JNES *Journal of Near Eastern Studies*
JRAS *Journal of the Royal Asiatic Society*
JSAI *Jerusalem Studies in Arabic and Islam*
JSS *Journal of Semitic Studies*
NCHI *New Cambridge History of Islam*
ODLA *Oxford Dictionary of Late Antiquity*
PmBZ *Prosopographie der mittelbyzantinischen Zeit Online*

Frequently Cited Texts and Translations

Baladhuri, *Ansab*   Aḥmad b. Yaḥyā al-Balādhurī, *Ansāb al-Ashrāf*, ed. M. Fardūs al-Aẓm (Damascus, 1997–2004).
Baladhuri, *Futuh*   Aḥmad b. Yaḥyā al-Balādhurī, *Futūḥ al-Buldān*, ed. M. J. de Goeje (Leiden, 1866).
History of the Patriarchs   B. Evetts (ed. and tr.), *History of the Patriarchs of the Coptic Church of Alexandria* (Paris, 1904–14).
Ibn 'Asakir   'Alī b. al-Ḥasan b. 'Asākir, *Ta'rīkh Madīnat Dimashq*, ed. 'Umar Gharāma al-'Amrawī (Beirut, 1995–2000).

Khalifa	Khalīfa b. Khayyāṭ al-ʿUsfurī, *Taʾrīkh Khalīfa b. Khayyāṭ*, eds Muṣṭafā Najīb Fawwāz and Ḥikma Kashlī Fawwāz (Beirut, 1995).
Kindi	Abū ʿUmar Muḥammad b. Yūsuf al-Kindī, *The Governors and Judges of Egypt* (= *Kitāb Wulāt Miṣr wa-Quḍātihā*), ed. Rhuvon Guest (Leiden, 1912).
Tabari	Abū Jaʿfar Muḥammad b. Jarīr al-Ṭabarī, *Taʾrīkh al-Rusul wa-l-Mulūk*, eds M. J. de Goeje et al. (Leiden 1879–1901).
Tabari, *History*	Abu Jaʿfar Muhammad b. Jarir al-Tabari, *The History of al-Tabari*, eds and trs Ehsan Yar-Shater et al. (Albany, NY, 1985–2007).
Theophanes	Cyril Mango and Roger Scott (eds and trs), *The Chronicle of Theophanes Confessor: Byzantine and Near Eastern History AD 284–813* (Oxford, 1997).
Theophilus	Robert G. Hoyland, *Theophilus of Edessa's Chronicle and the Circulation of Historical Knowledge in Late Antiquity and Early Islam* (Liverpool, 2011).
Yaʿqubi	Aḥmad b. Abī Yaʿqūb al-Yaʿqūbī, *Historiae* (= *Taʾrīkh al-Yaʿqūbī*), ed. M. J. Houtsma (Leiden, 1883).

Frequently Cited Secondary Studies

EIC Fred M. Donner, *The Early Islamic Conquests* (Princeton, 1981).

IatMC Michael G. Morony, *Iraq after the Muslim Conquest* (Princeton, 1984).

RoIM Andrew Marsham, *Rituals of Islamic Monarchy: Accession and Succession in the First Muslim Empire* (Edinburgh, 2009).

SaMS Petra M. Sijpesteijn, *Shaping a Muslim State: The World of a Mid-Eighth-Century Egyptian Official* (Oxford, 2013).

SIAOSI Robert G. Hoyland, *Seeing Islam As Others Saw It: A Survey and Evaluation of Christian, Jewish and Zoroastrian Writings on Early Islam* (Princeton, 1997).

SoH Patricia Crone, *Slaves on Horses: The Evolution of the Islamic Polity* (Cambridge, 1980).

WtaWC James Howard-Johnston, *Witnesses to a World Crisis: Historians and Histories of the Middle East in the Seventh Century* (Oxford, 2010).

Languages

Ar.	Arabic	Lat.	Latin	pl.	plural
Gk	Greek	pl.	plural	sing.	singular

conflicts also had the character of family, or 'tribal', conflicts (see Chart I.1). In the wake of two major civil wars in the seventh century, in which they were victorious, and then a third war in 744–50, in which they were defeated and deposed from power, the reputations of Muʿawiya and his Umayyad relatives suffered especially badly. By the mid-tenth century, when most of the defining characteristics of the two main sectarian traditions in Islam – Shiʿism and Sunnism – had taken shape, the Umayyads' image was entirely negative for the Shiʿis, and often somewhat ambivalent even for Sunnis.

The Shiʿis had come to believe that things had gone very wrong from the moment of Muhammad's death, in 632. Muhammad should have been succeeded immediately by a son-in-law and cousin, named ʿAli, whom the Shiʿis believed had been nominated as heir by Muhammad himself. ʿAli was unique in that he was the father of the only male descendants of the Prophet who survived into adulthood, via his marriage to Fatima, one of Muhammad's daughters. Hence, had ʿAli led the Muslims, he might have established a ruling dynasty of male descendants of Muhammad. But, instead of ʿAli, three others of the Prophet's Companions had seized power in sequence. When the third of these was assassinated, in 656, ʿAli was able finally to claim his right as leader of the Faithful. However, the violent and controversial circumstances of his accession to the caliphate made him politically vulnerable, and he was never universally recognised.

Among those who had withheld their allegiance was Muʿawiya, claiming a right to avenge the murdered ruler's death. When ʿAli was in turn himself assassinated, in 661, Muʿawiya proclaimed himself caliph, intimidating one of ʿAli's sons, al-Hasan, into surrendering any claim to power. Twenty years later, when Muʿawiya died, the other of ʿAli's sons by Fatima, named al-Husayn, made a bid for power, only to be slaughtered alongside his family by a commander loyal to Muʿawiya's son Yazid. This massacre, which took place at Karbala in Iraq, is commemorated by Shiʿi Muslims every year during Muharram, the first month of the lunar Islamic year. Many of the tombs of al-Husayn's family are in the same Bab al-Saghir Cemetery as Muʿawiya.[1]

For the Shiʿis of the tenth century and after, the rightful leadership of the Muslims had resided in a line of leaders descended from ʿAli and the Prophet's daughter, Fatima. The line includes ʿAli himself, then the Prophet's grandsons, al-Hasan and al-Husayn. In the majority 'Twelver' Shiʿi tradition, there are nine more individuals, making twelve in all, one in each generation. These men are the true spiritual leaders of Islam, or Imams, though none after ʿAli held

---

[1] Stephennie Mulder, *The Shrines of the ʿAlids in Medieval Syria: Sunnis, Shiʿis and the Architecture of Coexistence* (Edinburgh, 2014), 114–85.

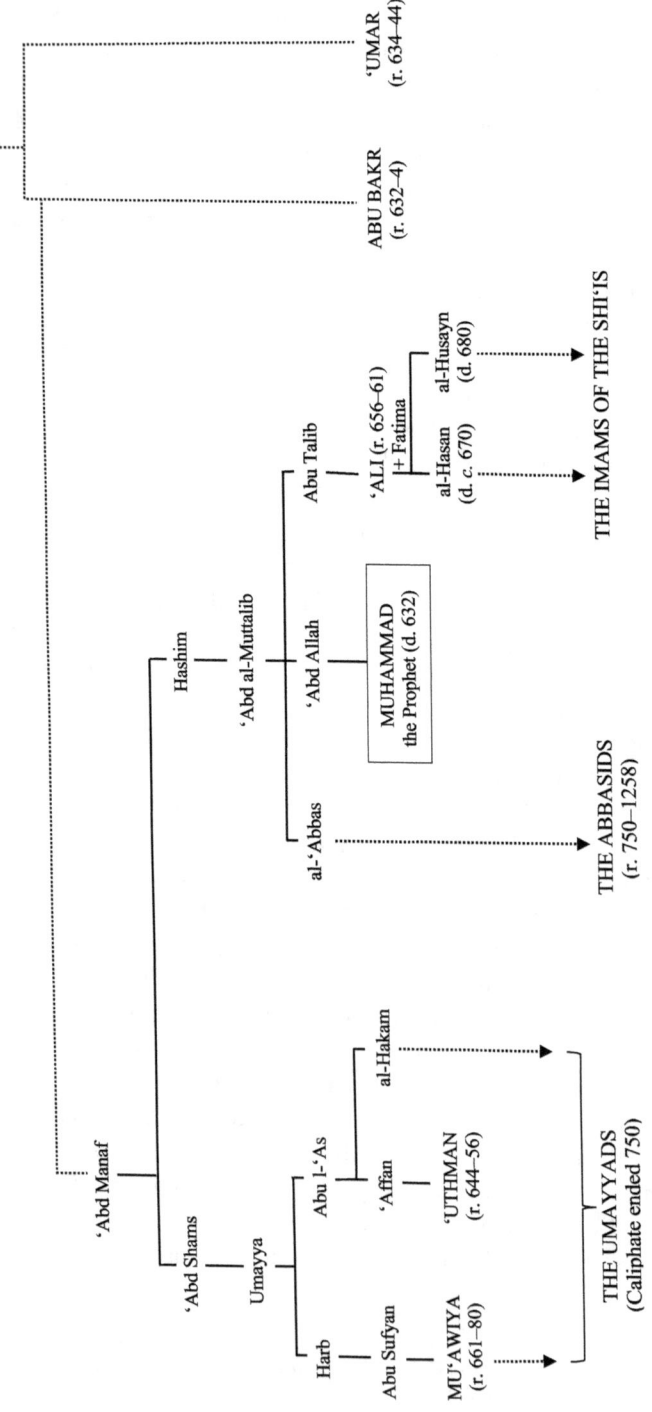

Chart I.1 Simplified genealogy of the Prophet Muhammad, the first two caliphs, the Umayyads, the Abbasids and the Shi'i Imams.

the caliphate. The twelfth of them, named Muhammad, disappeared in 874, to return – in much the same way as Christians believe Jesus will – at the end of time. All but this last of the twelve Imams are believed in the Shi'i tradition to have been murdered by the ruling caliphs. Mu'awiya's refusal to recognise the caliphate of 'Ali or his son al-Hasan (whom Shi'is believe he later assassinated), and Yazid b. Mu'awiya's association with the killing of al-Husayn, have given Mu'awiya, his son Yazid and the Umayyads in general a profoundly evil reputation in Shi'i thought.

For tenth-century Sunnis, in contrast, legitimate Islamic political leadership on earth was a reality, and existed in the form of the caliphate, which had been established by Muhammad's first successors and sustained first by the Umayyads and then by the Abbasid dynasty. The Abbasids were the branch of Muhammad's tribe who had replaced the Umayyads in a bloody revolution in 747–50. The Abbasids went on to hold the caliphate legitimately (in Sunni eyes) for over 500 years, until the sack of Baghdad by the Mongols in 1258.

The Abbasid caliphs had come to align themselves with Sunni religious scholars, opposed to the Shi'i understanding of authority in Islam. For these Sunni scholars, the caliph was the proper political leader of the Muslims, and necessary for legitimate (that is, divinely favoured) political organisation in Islam, but authority in matters of religion and law was to be found in the memory of the era of the Prophet Muhammad, as transmitted and interpreted by the religious scholars (*'ulama'*, sing. *'ālim*), and not in the person of any one Imam, or individual leader, of the later Muslims.

For Sunnis, the key point was that the majority of the Muslims had remained within a single religio-political community – a point emphasised in the longer name from which the label 'Sunni' derives, *ahl al-sunna wa-l-jamā'a* ('people of tradition and unity'). In contrast to Shi'i claims, the Sunnis held that the Companions of the Prophet had not acted in error when they chose their leaders. Among Sunnis, the special status of these first four caliphs, Abu Bakr (r. 632–4), 'Umar (r. 634–44), 'Uthman (r. 644–56) and 'Ali (r. 656–61) is marked by their being remembered collectively as 'The Rightly Guided Caliphs' (*al-khulafā' al-rāshidūn*).

This idea of the 'Rightly Guided Caliphs' can be seen as an attempt at détente with the Shi'i view of history, making retrospective sense of the violent conflicts of the Muslim past (see Chart I.1). The Shi'is were correct that 'Ali had been a legitimate leader, but they were wrong to claim that Muhammad had nominated him specially, and that the first three caliphs had been illegitimate. Criticism of 'Ali for taking advantage of the assassination of the third caliph, 'Uthman, in order to become caliph himself, was now overlooked; both 'Uthman and 'Ali had been rightly guided and were models for the present. Indeed, for the ninth- and tenth-century Sunnis, the contemporary Abbasid caliphs were legitimate political and military leaders, ruling with divine sanction. The Umayyads held a liminal and somewhat ambivalent status; they had successfully ruled the Muslims as caliphs, but Mu'awiya's accession marked the end of 'rightly guided' rule. Furthermore – almost as much for some Sunnis as for Shi'is – the killing of al-Husayn, the Prophet's grandson, together with many of his family, was a deep stain on the Umayyads' reputation.[2]

This Sunni idea of the 'rightly guided' caliphate being brought to an end by the assassination of 'Ali and the accession of Mu'awiya has continued to exert a powerful hold over the way that Umayyad history is perceived. For Sunni Muslims, Mu'awiya's place in history, and that of his Umayyad successors, has always been placed just beyond the line that divides the exceptional era of God's most important intervention in the world, through Muhammad and his leading Companions, from a more mundane historical time, where the caliphs were the legitimate dynastic political figureheads for the Muslims, but righteous authority in religious matters lay in looking back to the prophetic era. In contrast, for Shi'i Muslims, Mu'awiya and his son Yazid are emblematic of the tyrannical oppression of God's chosen righteous family and, by extension, of true, Shi'i, Islam. If the damage to Mu'awiya's tomb that I saw that summer was indeed something more than an accident or mindless vandalism it was probably an expression of Shi'i hostility to the man who had kept the Prophet's family out of power and so became a lasting symbol of injustice.

Re-framing the Umayyad Empire

Most of the Arabic narrative sources about these events were composed in their extant form in the ninth century or later. Hence, it is difficult to assess what we can know of how and why things happened at the time, in the seventh and eighth centuries, and how they were perceived by contemporaries. As we have seen, one question that concerned the compilers of our sources was whom among the Muslims' leaders had rightfully held power, and with whom religious authority rightfully resided. Associated with this question was the correct way to rule God's people, and so the personalities of leaders, their management of the affairs of state, and their interactions with men of religion, are all also prominent themes. So too is the question of their relationship to the proper interpretation of the religious tradition; as we have seen, the later Sunni and Shi'i perspectives on the Islamic past were quite different, and there were many other topics where the perspective of the scholar composing the text shaped the narrative. What most scholars shared was a focus on how God's

---

[2] On the 'four caliph thesis', see I-Wen Su, 'The Early Shi'i Kufan Traditionists' Perspective on the Rightly Guided Caliphs', *JAOS* 141 (2021), 27–47.

will had been manifested in the history of the Muslims. Above all, Islam was presented as a break with the misguided traditions of the past and – especially among Sunni scholars – the unity and coherence of the Muslims, and continuities within their history, tended to be emphasised over conflict, diversity, hybridity and discontinuity.

Until recently, the perspectives of the later Islamic tradition have shaped the treatment of early Islam in modern scholarship, and they still have significant influence today. The break with the pre-Islamic past is reflected in the tendency of many modern histories to begin with a short preliminary discussion of pre-Islamic Arabia and the Middle East, before turning to the narrative of the expansion of Islam from Mecca and Medina in Arabia and then development of the Caliphate. This can lead to the impression that the Islamic empire formed in something of a vacuum, with developments internal to it being far more important than the interaction of Arabians and Muslims with the world around them, and where the pre-Islamic history of the Middle East counted for little in the face of the new Arab culture and the religion of Islam.

Recent scholarship has broken with these teleological views by investigating continuities with the pre-Islamic past and the history of Islamic belief and practice before the consolidation of the Sunni and Shiʻi perspectives outlined above. Such reframing of early Islamic history is often expressed by the idea that early Islam belongs within the period of 'Late Antiquity' (often c. 200–750 CE). Late Antiquity was the era of the transformation of the power structures of the Roman Empire, including the adoption of Christianity as the empire's ruling ideology, together with the replacement of Roman rule by new elites from the margins of the former empire, who also took up Christianity as their legitimating belief system. Reframing the history of early Islam in this way has led to the questioning of many assumptions that might otherwise be adopted from the later source material, including the religious and ethnic identities of the rulers of the Umayyad Empire, and the power structures upon which they depended.[3]

This book similarly seeks to reframe the Umayyad Empire by moving beyond the narratives provided by the ninth- and tenth-century sources. It seeks to explain how the empire came into being and how it functioned, as well as the forces that brought about the fall from power of its ruling family and their allies. In so doing, it is necessary to uncover the social, economic, military and ideological forces that shaped the history of the Middle East, North Africa

---

[3] In English, the literature begins with Peter Brown's *World of Late Antiquity: From Marcus Aurelius to Muhammad* (London, 1971). For a recent discussion, see Harry Munt, 'The Transition from Late Antiquity to Early Islam in Western Arabia', in Andrew Marsham (ed.), *The Umayyad World* (London and New York, 2021), 357–73.

and western Asia in the sixth, seventh and eighth centuries. Vast new empires do not simply come into being because of the ideas of a single person, nor even because of the actions of a small group of people around them. Ideas and people do of course matter – and the case of Islam, where a tiny religious community was a crucial element in the formation of a new ruling elite, and ultimately of something that can be called a new civilisation, is a particularly eye-catching example of this. But ideas and people have their moment. Or, to put it another way, ideas have a context; social structures, economic patterns and, in the case of empire, the ability to marshal military force, must all be aligned to allow them to flourish. This book seeks to pay sufficient attention to all these dimensions of the era of the Umayyad Empire, and to take account of the long pre-Islamic context that gave rise to it and the forces that shaped its evolution.

What is perhaps hardest of all to recover is a full sense of contingency: in the seventh century, that Islam would both shape and be shaped by a lasting empire, let alone a huge world civilisation, was unknown to everyone; furthermore, Islam itself was different from what Muslims of later decades and centuries would know. Indeed, there is no evidence that the conquerors of Rome and Iran at the time of Muʿawiya usually called themselves 'Muslims', nor is the term 'Islam' widely attested. Rather, it was during the later Umayyad period that the label 'Muslims' (Ar. *muslimūn*) became a more prominent label for the group whose precursors seem more often to have called themselves the 'Faithful' (*muʾminūn*) or 'Emigrants' (*muhājirūn*); at the same time, this successful new community's religious tradition (or, rather, diverse competing versions of that tradition) changed and developed; by the latter decades of the Umayyad period, it becomes more straightforward to refer without qualification to various forms of 'Islam' as a religious tradition, as well as to 'Muslims', as its adherents. Although, even then, much of the doctrine and practice we consider intrinsic to Sunni and Shiʿi forms of Islam today had yet to take shape.[4]

Another anachronism in many modern narratives about the Umayyad Empire is the emphasis on the history of the Muslims, to the exclusion of other groups. This tendency reflects the concerns of medieval Muslim historians with the history of what they saw as their community – the Faithful of Arabian origin, who had conquered Rome and Iran. Of course, the Arabian armies were a tiny minority among the people they encountered in the territories

---

[4] For the idea of an early community of the 'faithful' as a more ecumenical 'believers movement', see Fred M. Donner, *Muhammad and the Believers: At the Origins of Islam* (Cambridge, MA, 2010). On *muhājirūn* and other labels, see Ilkka Lindstedt, 'Muhajirun as a Name for the First/Seventh Century Muslims', *JNES* 74 (2015), 67–73. See further on both points, below, Ch. 2, pp. 61–3.

they conquered – Romans, Persians, Aramaeans, Copts, Nabataeans, Kurds, Armenians, Albanians, Berbers, Khazars, Sogdians, Goths, Indians and Turks, according to some of the labels used in the sources. The languages, religions and cultures of these groups persisted far beyond the Umayyad period. Indeed, many still exist in in the Middle East of today.

While the conquering Arabian armies articulated their unity in religious terms, notably through pledges of allegiance made before God, they did not usually expect the populations they ruled to change their religious practices so long as they acknowledged the suzerainty of God and His community of the Faithful. Comparatively large-scale conversions to Islam among the conquered populations happened only towards the end of the Umayyad period and, even then, Muslims remained a tiny minority. By the best estimate, about 90 per cent of the empire's population at the very end of the Umayyad period were neither of Arabian heritage nor Islamic faith.[5] Conversion then accelerated significantly in the ninth century. Hence, most of the Muslim historians of the ninth and tenth centuries were descendants either of the conquered peoples or of both Arabian migrants and people from the lands they had conquered. Their ancestors had converted to Islam and adopted Arabic as the lingua franca of the world in which they lived. These shifts in identity were reflected in the concerns of their historical writing. When they discussed the histories of their own, non-Arabian, non-Muslim, ancestors they tended to do so within a framework provided by Islam – situating their people's preIslamic past in relation to God's creation of the world and the prophecy of Muhammad.

Thus, the Umayyad world was in many respects an as it were 'pre-Islamic' world, insofar as 'Islamic' is often shorthand for a majority-Muslim, Arab civilisation and its various Persian, Turkish and other successors. Instead, in Umayyad times a diverse conquering elite, led by a ruling group from West Arabia but composed from the various peoples of the Arabian Peninsula and the Syrian Desert, were dominant in the former lands of Rome and Iran. Like many of the other new elites of Late Antiquity, the conquerors' leaders articulated their political unity in religious terms. For the West Arabians, the example of the Prophet Muhammad and a sense of their own faith tradition as distinct from and superior to those of the conquered peoples were both important. However, much remained in contention, and many of the features of Islamic belief and practice that became core to the later tradition had yet to develop or gain widespread acceptance. Moreover, converts retained some previous beliefs

---

[5] Richard W. Bulliet, *Conversion to Islam in the Medieval Period: An Essay in Quantitative History* (Cambridge, MA and London, 1979).

and practices, which in turn shaped the development of Islam. Indeed, the context is still recognisably Roman and Sasanian: Greek, Latin, Syriac, Aramaic, Coptic, Middle Persian, Sogdian, Bactrian and other languages were employed by the diverse peoples of the empire and the ideas, structures and institutions of Roman and Iranian rule shaped those developed by the Arabian conquerors.

Among the peoples of the conquered territories were Christians, Zoroastrians, Jews, Buddhists and others, who attained high office in the service of the new imperial rulers or ruled themselves as allies of the new empire. Most definitions of empire depend upon the idea of a dominant ruling group, with a distinctive cultural or religious identity, exerting various forms of power over other, diverse, groups, but also co-opting some conquered peoples into the new hegemony. This definition holds true for the Umayyad era. The distinction between 'conqueror' and 'conquered' was often critical – with the former extracting tribute and taxes from the latter. The 'conquerors' defined themselves by shared faith, in God and one another, as 'the Faithful' or, increasingly, also as 'Muslims'. However, they also shared somewhat similar languages and cultures, as peoples from the Arabian Peninsula and its northern extension, the Syrian Desert and its steppe. Indeed, Arabian heritage and membership of a military elite were closely connected, and so non-Arabians serving in the army or the administration tended to be given a distinctive status as 'clients' (Ar. *mawālī*, sing. *mawlā*) of the Arabian person or group to whom they were affiliated.

However, just as much of what came to form the later Islamic religious tradition had yet to take shape, so too had some of the later ideas about 'Arabs'. The more geographical 'Arabians' is usually used here to describe the conquerors and their descendants instead of the ethnic 'Arabs'. This is because, 'the Arabs' (Ar. *al-'arab*) only began to gain widespread currency as a label for all the peoples who traced their heritage back to the Arabian Peninsula (or, alternatively, for all the people who spoke Arabic) during the Umayyad era. Out of the migration into the conquered territories came new questions of identity and belonging and it is in this context that 'the Arabs' began to gain its inclusive, but still contested, collective meaning among the migrants and the other members of the new imperial military elite. As a result, the term 'Arab' became inflected in some contexts with the idea of status and rulership; sometimes 'the Arabs' came to be used as a label for the imperial military elites of the Umayyad era. Meanwhile, many of the rebel movements in the later decades of Umayyad rule drew in part upon non-Arabs' resentments of the Arabs' privileges and power.[6]

---

[6] Peter Webb, *Imagining the Arabs: Arab Identity and the Rise of Islam* (Edinburgh, 2016), esp. 85–8, 126–56. See further below, Ch. 1, pp. 40–2. On 'Arabs' as the imperial elite, see Patricia Crone, 'The Significance of Wooden Weapons in al-Mukhtar's Revolt and the Abbasid

This is not to say, however, that there were not already some shared cultural characteristics among the various groups who comprised the first conquering armies. Indeed, the Arabian backgrounds of the West Arabian leadership and their armies are crucial to understanding the unique characteristics of their empire – a settled leadership, who could claim a sacred status by virtue of their association with the shrine at Mecca, led armies drawn primarily from nomadic pastoralist Peninsular and Syrian steppe groups. The strategic mobility of the pastoralists helps to explain the vast scale of their conquests, which anticipate in some respects the far larger thirteenth-century conquests of the Mongols. Moreover, the religious and governmental traditions established by the Meccan leaders, in combination with the Arabian backgrounds of their armies, meant that their empire developed a new and distinctive religious and cultural character. Much of this religion and culture took shape in new garrison settlements where many of the Arabian groups settled after the conquests, retaining and developing their sense of separateness from the non-Arabian populations around them.

An Umayyad Empire?

In what senses, then, can we speak of 'the Umayyad Empire'? Few, if any, Muslims in early Islamic times would have thought of the Muslim polity as an empire in the sense that the label is now used. Political power was described in more personal terms, as 'sovereignty' or 'kingship' (*mulk*). Where it was abstracted from a person, it was often simply the 'command', 'affair' or 'affairs' (*amr*, pl. *umūr*). Moreover, the conquering Faithful often deployed the rhetoric of suspicion of worldly power that was also widespread in Jewish and Christian cultures of the time. Indeed, the nascent religion of Islam came to be defined in part against the 'idolatry' (*shirk*) of Roman and Sasanian imperial rule. (Of course, the Roman and Sasanian rulers themselves had made very similar claims to divine sanction against the claims of their enemies.) The new political dispensation established by the Arabians was *amr Allāh* or *mulk Allāh* – the 'government', 'rule' or 'sovereignty' of God. In this, too, their language echoed that of their Roman and Sasanian opponents.[7]

From 661 at the latest, and quite possibly earlier, the ruler of the new empire used the formal title *amīr al-muʾminīn*, 'The Commander of the Faithful' (as noted above, 'the Faithful' is a more common term than 'Muslim'

Revolution', in Ian R. Netton (ed.), *Studies in Honour of Clifford Edmund Bosworth Volume I: Hunter of the East: Arabic and Semitic Studies* (Leiden, 2000), 178–80, 183–5.

[7] On *mulk*, see Sean W. Anthony, 'Prophetic Dominion, Umayyad Kingship: Varieties of *Mulk* in the Early Islamic Period', in Andrew Marsham (ed.), *The Umayyad World* (London and New York, 2021), 39–64.

for the adherents of Islam in early Arabic texts). 'Command' (*imāra*) was held by him (and hence the residence of the ruler or his governors was the *dār al-imāra*, 'the House of Command', or 'Government Palace'). Occasionally, in panegyric poetry, in some speeches and public letters, and on rare coins, the ruler was also *khalīfat Allāh*, 'God's Caliph' – that is, 'God's Deputy'. From this, a name for his office – the Caliphate (*khilāfa*) – came to be derived. ('Caliphate' did not tend to be used to refer to the territorial entity of his dominions, in the way that it is today.) He could also be described as a *malik* (king), but this was not a formal title, and is found only in the panegyric poems performed at the caliphal court, in some graffiti or informal inscriptions, and in Syriac Christian texts. Again, much of this political titulature echoes that of the Christian Roman emperors, who were the Umayyads' main rivals for dominance of the eastern Mediterranean and against whom the Umayyads came to define themselves.[8]

Thus, the Umayyads had much in common with their Roman and Sasanian imperial rivals. Moreover, there is a second reason for referring to the Umayyad Empire as an empire. This is to use the word empire not as a straightforward translation of a label that might have been used by its inhabitants, but rather as a term with analytical and descriptive utility. The vast domains of the Umayyads, comprising numerous religious, linguistic and ethnic groups, under the notional authority of a single monarch fits most modern definitions of empire. The exploitation of the resources of a conquered or subordinate population for the benefit of an elite or elites is another a defining feature of empire, and in the Umayyad Empire, tribute and taxation were collected for the benefit of a small ruling elite of Arabian conquerors and migrants and their descendants, together with their (often non-Arabian) administrators and allies. In the world of Late Antiquity, narratives of universal monarchy under universal divine sanction – Christian, Jewish or Zoroastrian – were the explanatory frameworks for such political arrangements. The institution of the caliphate and the religion of Islam developed as a distinctive iteration of this late antique pattern of imperial thought.[9]

---

[8] Andrew Marsham, '"God's Caliph" Revisited: Umayyad Political Thought in Its Late Antique Context', in Alain George and Andrew Marsham (eds), *Power, Patronage, and Memory in Early Islam: Perspectives on Umayyad Elites* (Oxford, 2018), 3–37; *EI3*, 'Commander of the Faithful' (A. Marsham).

[9] On defining empire, see Jane Burbank and Frederick Cooper, *Empires in World History: Power and the Politics of Difference* (Princeton, 2010), 8–22; Peter F. Bang, 'Empire – A World History: Anatomy and Concept, Theory and Synthesis', in Peter F. Bang et al. (eds), *The Oxford World History of Empire: Volume One: The Imperial Experience* (Oxford, 2021), 12–49.

The other element in 'Umayyad Empire' is dynastic. Dynasties – like other imagined human groupings – are established over time, and so the label 'Umayyad Empire' is to some extent retrospective. With hindsight, the period is indeed dominated by the political success of the Umayyad family. However, it was marked by persistent unrest, with two phases of prolonged internal conflict (656–61 and 680–92), between which Muʻawiya's long caliphate of 661–80 marks only a hiatus. Although Muʻawiya passed power to his son in 680, this was immediately contested, and it was only after 692 that ʻAbd al-Malik b. Marwan – from a different, sometimes rival, branch of the Umayyad clan than Muʻawiya – was able to establish his own family as more lasting leaders of the empire (see Chart I.2). Nonetheless, although no one at the time could have known for how long the various members of the Umayyad clan and their descendants would hold power, the Umayyads and their contemporaries all thought about politics in tribal terms and acted in ways that were demonstrably related to ideas about kinship connections. In these respects, the idea of an 'Umayyad dynasty' is not anachronistic.[10]

In attempting to think about history as it took place at the time, we should reconsider who we include in the Umayyad dynasty. Although Muʻawiya is often taken to be the first of the Umayyad dynasty, interconnections with the reign of the third caliph ʻUthman, who was also from the Umayyad clan, are emphasised here. ʻUthman's caliphate is rarely considered part of an 'Umayyad period'. Because later Sunni orthodoxy saw him as the third of four 'rightly guided caliphs', preceded by Abu Bakr and ʻUmar, and succeeded by ʻAli, ʻUthman's reign is usually separated from that of his second cousin Muʻawiya. Furthermore, whereas Muʻawiya definitely sought to establish dynastic succession by appointing his son as his heir, it is less clear what ʻUthman's intentions for the caliphate may have been before he was killed, and so for this reason too he is often not seen as part of the Umayyad dynasty. However, it is likely that ʻUthman had dynastic ambitions for his own sons. Moreover, ʻUthman was indubitably an Umayyad in that he was a grandson of the eponymous Umayya. He is remembered for having acted in a self-consciously clan-based manner, drawing upon kinship ties among the Umayyads and the wider clan of ʻAbd Shams. During ʻUthman's rule, crucial foundations were laid for the success about thirty years later of his cousin, ʻAbd al-Malik b. Marwan. Moreover, ʻUthman was claimed as a founding figure by later Umayyad caliphs: claims to legitimacy in the later Umayyad caliphs' public rhetoric often depended upon claims of rightful succession to him. When we include ʻUthman, we find that

[10] Andrew Marsham, 'Kinship, Dynasty, and the Umayyads', in Maaike van Berkel and Letizia Osti (eds), *The Historian of Islam at Work: Essays in Honor of Hugh Kennedy* (Leiden, 2022), 12–45.

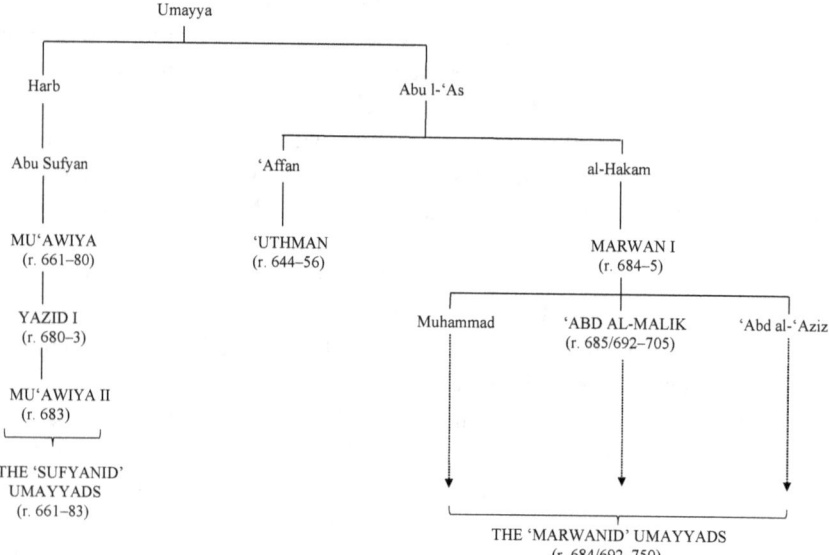

Chart I.2 The caliphal branches of the Umayyads.

members of the Umayyad clan claimed the caliphate for all but four of the 106 years between 644 and 750, albeit always facing rebels, rivals and challengers, and in a context of great turmoil for the periods 656–61, 680–92 and 744–50.[11]

The Sources and Modern Perspectives

As noted above, the formation of the Umayyad Empire can be seen as belonging to the latter part of the era often referred to as Late Antiquity (often c. 200–750 CE) or, alternatively, to the Early Middle Ages (often c. 500–1000 CE). While the use of these periodisations beyond Western Europe has been questioned, the histories of Europe, North Africa and the Middle East certainly share sufficient features to justify using them – advisedly – for the whole region. The character of the historical evidence is one consequence of these shared features. In Late Antiquity and the Early Middle Ages, Rome and Iran lost territory and power to groups from the empires' former frontier zones, or from regions beyond those frontiers. Only a much-reduced Eastern Roman Empire survived; the Western Empire collapsed in the fifth century, and Iran in the seventh. (The surviving Eastern Roman Empire, with its capital at Constantinople, is sometimes called the 'Byzantine Empire',

---

[11] Marshall G. S. Hodgson, *The Venture of Islam: Conscience and History in a World Civilization* (Chicago, 1974), I, 213; *EI*², 'Muʿawiya I' (M. Hinds); Marsham, 'Kinship'.

but this anachronistic label is avoided here – they and their neighbours still used 'Roman'.) In the West as in the East, new ethnic groups were formed as Roman and Iranian rule was replaced or challenged. In the West, these groups included the Goths, Franks, Angles and Saxons and, in the Eastern Roman Empire and Iran, the Slavs, Bulgars, Turks and Arabs. These peoples tended to be 'non-literate' – that is, their cultures depended primarily on the spoken word – although in many cases they were aware of writing and did use it for some purposes. One consequence of the predominantly oral nature of the culture of these new 'barbarian' (from a Roman perspective) elites is that the written historical record contemporaneous with the formation of their new polities within the lands of the old empires is often very thin indeed.[12]

This holds true for the Umayyad Empire. As noted above, most of the extant narrative sources date from the mid-ninth century and after – that is, from about 100 years after the fall of the Umayyads and 200 years after the death of the Prophet Muhammad. In contrast to the Latin West, where even the later sources are comparatively short, the later narrative sources in Arabic are extensive and detailed. However, they present significant problems of interpretation. After all, the whole Arabic written tradition has its origins in a social and cultural transformation on an epoch-making scale; in the space of three or four generations, the new Arabian polity went from being a small community of 'the Faithful' at an isolated oasis in the region of West Arabia known as the Hijaz to an imperial entity that outstripped Rome and Iran. As a result, the texture of life in the Hijaz at the turn of the sixth and seventh centuries is obscured in the extant tradition, which looks back across more than two centuries of empire-building to the memory of Muhammad as its founding figure. At the same time, the changing fortunes of the various descendants of the members of his original federation led to reworkings of the material that were favourable to the ancestors of the politically successful and critical of the losers. The extent of the transformation of the historical memory can be contested, but that significant transformation took place is beyond doubt.

A generation of so-called 'revisionist' or 'sceptical' historians, writing in the 1970s and 1980s, argued that the evidence for early Islam was uniquely problematic.[13] However, there is now a growing recognition that the evidential situation is not so dissimilar from that for the 'barbarian kingdoms' of the Latin West, which replaced the Roman Empire there in the fifth, sixth and seventh centuries CE, even if the volume of later Arabic material is far greater

---

[12] On Europe and the Middle East in this period, see Peter Sarris, *Empires of Faith: The Fall of Rome to the Rise of Islam* (Oxford, 2011).

[13] See, for example, Patricia Crone, *Slaves on Horses: The Evolution of the Islamic Polity* (Cambridge, 1980) [hereafter, *SoH*], 3–17.

than its Latin equivalent. In both regions, it was the adoption of scriptural religion by the 'barbarians' alongside their achieving political power that led to the production of narrative history writing about their peoples. This written tradition emerged only slowly, leaving a 'Dark Age' about which it can seem difficult to know much. However, in recent decades historians of both West and East have reappraised the most sceptical views. In the case of the history of very early Islam, three new perspectives have led to advances in historical understanding: first there are literary and source-critical approaches to the Arabic sources; second, the same kinds of approaches have been taken to relevant sources in languages other than Arabic; third, the value of material culture has received growing recognition, including its potential to address questions that the literary sources do not. These points are addressed in sequence in what follows.

The later Arabic chronicles and other narrative sources are now recognised as evidence primarily for the time in which they were composed, telling us about the interests and agendas of their authors and audiences; they cannot be taken as straightforward evidence for the past events they describe. Such an awareness of the socially constructed and literary character of these sources is crucial to accounting for their teleologies and omissions. However, although the extant texts were composed in the ninth and tenth centuries and after, they were largely compiled from earlier materials. Much of the extant material clearly derives from earlier texts composed at the very end of the Umayyad period and, more often, in the first decades of the Abbasid period. This brings us closer to the Umayyad era.[14]

Among the very earliest strata in the Arabic material are layers of information about people, their kin relations and their positions within the governing apparatus of the empire. Where they can be cross-checked with the surviving documentary materials such as coins and administrative documents, the narrative sources can be shown to be fairly accurate about people and their roles (but very far from complete, or completely accurate). Much of what follows in this book on the structures of power and the political history of the Umayyad Empire depends on these kinds of more reliable prosopographic ('relating to the person') material. Of course, these 'facts' are themselves also socially constructed, in that they were organised, recorded and remembered because they were important to the idea of the legitimate power of the Muslim empire. In particular, the extent of the central control exerted by the caliph, continuities

---

[14] On the character of the sources, see Antoine Borrut, *Entre mémoire et pouvoir: L'éspace syrien sous les derniers Omeyyades et les premiers Abbasides (v. 72-193/692-809)* (Leiden, 2011). For a recovered late Umayyad-era text, see Edward Zychowicz-Coghill, *The First Arabic Annals: Fragments of Umayyad History* (Berlin and Boston, 2021).

within institutions and their distinctive Islamic character all tend to be exaggerated. Nonetheless, the people, places and dates were not easily invented from nothing because they were easily falsifiable. Thus, they are vital evidence if one wants to understand the history of that empire, reflecting its structures of power.[15]

Furthermore, certain forms of Umayyad cultural production can be shown to have been remembered and transmitted more often and more carefully than others. Indeed, the scripture of Islam, the Qur'an, is in many respects an Umayyad document. A first compilation of the Qur'an as a single book (a 'codex') is said to have been presided over by 'Uthman, the third successor to Muhammad, and the first Umayyad to hold that office. How far his role may have been exaggerated in the later tradition is not clear. Complete large-format Qur'ans sponsored by the ruling Umayyad elite do survive from around the time of the Umayyad caliph 'Abd al-Malik (r. 685–705), and he and his allies made far more use of the Qur'an and its language in articulating their authority than their predecessors had done. Even then, other very slightly different Quranic recensions remained in circulation. The fact of the Umayyad elite's decisive role in the written compilation of the Islamic scripture is itself important evidence for the relationship between religious authority and political power, as well as for specific religious and political ideas among the Arabian Faithful.[16] While there are echoes of concern in the sources about the act of compiling of the Qur'an, the idea of 'the Book' (*al-kitāb*) succeeded quickly and comprehensively – probably because it resonated with the idea of the importance of 'writing', or 'scripture' (both also *kitāb* in Arabic) in religion, which was important in late antique Judaism and Christianity and is frequently echoed in the Qur'an itself.[17] Indeed, the other scriptures of the Jewish

---

[15] *SoH*, 16–17 is a statement of the potential of prosopography for the history of early Islam. A recent demonstration of Crone's historiographical ideas is Zychowicz-Coghill, *First Arabic Annals*. On some of the themes of the Islamic historical tradition, see Albrecht Noth and Lawrence I. Conrad, *The Early Arabic Historical Tradition: A Source-Critical Study* (Princeton, 1994); Fred M. Donner, *Narratives of Islamic Origins: The Beginnings of Islamic Historical Writing* (Princeton, 1998).

[16] On the compilation of the Qur'an, see below, Chs 4 and 6, pp. 86 and 137–8. On Quranic language, see Fred M. Donner, 'Qur'anicization of Religio-Political Discourse in the Umayyad Period', *Revue des mondes musulmans et de la Méditerranée* 129 (2011), 79–92.

[17] On traditions about the Qur'an's compilation, see Harald Motzki, 'The Collection of the Qur'ān: A Reconsideration of Western Views in Light of Recent Methodological Developments', *Der Islam* 78 (2001), 1–34. On the term *kitāb*, see *EQ*, 'Book' (D. Madigan). See also Angelika Neuwirth, *The Qur'an and Late Antiquity: A Shared Heritage*, tr. Samuel Wilder (Oxford, 2019), 65.

and Christian traditions were also accorded authority, both in the Quranic text itself and by members of the Faithful.[18]

Besides the Qur'an, no other books in the sense of bound texts for public use, whose contents were quite stable and repeatedly reproduced, are known to have been produced in Arabic in the Umayyad period. However, collections of non-Quranic religious and historical traditions had begun to be made in writing towards the end of the Umayyad period and some elements from these texts can be traced back to the early-to-mid eighth century. Versions of the poetry performed at the courts of caliphs and their allies are preserved in the much later Abbasid tradition, as are reports of famous speeches and – from the last three decades of the Umayyad era – public letters, issued for public promulgation by the caliph's senior scribes on his behalf. These poems, speeches and letters were often remembered for their literary merit and historical interest. Although the extant texts are very late, the character of the language of these materials and the world view and ideas they espouse tend to suggest that some of them reflect material that was composed in Umayyad times.[19]

Beyond Arabic and Islamic texts, there has been a growing recognition of the significance of sources composed in languages other than Arabic and by writers who were not Muslim. Materials composed in late antique and early medieval times in Greek, Syriac, Coptic, Armenian, Georgian, Middle Persian and Hebrew are susceptible to the same kinds of analyses as the Muslims' Arabic texts. There are also medieval Arabic texts composed by Christians living under Islamic rule and, after about 1000 CE, New Persian texts composed

---

[18] On the Bible and the Qur'an, see Neuwirth, *Qur'an*, 347–78. On Biblical material in the wider Islamic tradition, see Uri Rubin, *Between Bible and Qur'an: The Children of Israel and the Islamic Self-image* (Princeton, 1999).

[19] On the compilation of religious materials, see Gregor Schoeler, 'Oral Torah and *Hadit*: Transmission, Prohibition of Writing, Redaction', in Gregor Schoeler, *The Oral and the Writtten in Early Islam*, tr. Uwe Vagelpohl, ed. James E. Montgomery (London and New York, 2006), 111–41. On sermons, see Tahera Qutbuddin, '*Khutba*: The Evolution of Early Arabic Oration', in B. Gruendler and M. Cooperson (eds), *Classical Arabic Humanities in Their Own Terms: Festschrift for Wolfhart Heinrichs* (Leiden, 2008), 176–273; Tahera Qutbuddin, *Arabic Oration: Art and Function* (Leiden, 2019). On public letters, see Wadad al-Qadi, 'Islamic State Letters: The Question of Authenticity', in Averil Cameron and Lawrence I. Conrad (eds), *The Byzantine and Early Islamic Near East I: Problems in the Literary Source Material* (Princeton, 1992), 215–76; Wadad al-Qadi, 'The Religious Foundation of Late Umayyad Ideology and Practice', in Manuela Marín and Mercedes García-Arendal (eds), *Saber religioso y poder político en el Islam: Actas del Simposio Internacional…1991* (Madrid, 1994), 231–73. For two uses of poetry as a historical source, see Patricia Crone and Martin Hinds, *God's Caliph: Religious Authority in the First Centuries of Islam* (Cambridge, 1986), 30–42; Alain George, *The Umayyad Mosque of Damascus: Art, Faith and Empire in Early Islam* (London, 2021), 71–7.

by Muslims. These texts often interconnect with the Arabic-Islamic sources, through translation or shared bodies of orally transmitted knowledge; it is easy to underestimate the reach and volume of flows of information in the late antique and early medieval world.

Some of the non-Arabic sources were composed in the seventh and early eighth centuries and so offer contemporary perspectives on events. The most important of these are the Greek, Syriac, Armenian and Hebrew chronicles, saints' lives and religious treatises, written by Christians and Jews living in the lands conquered by the Arabians in the seventh and eighth centuries, or in lands adjacent to them. There are also important Greek narrative materials composed in Roman imperial court circles in the later eighth century, as well as materials in Middle Persian from later Zoroastrian contexts. Perspectives on the reach and character of the Umayyad Empire can also be gleaned from contemporaneous sources composed in more remote places that were nonetheless connected with it, notably the Kingdom of Northumbria, in northern Britain, and the Tang Empire, in China.[20]

Besides our written sources, the other crucial array of evidence about the early Islamic past, just as for other regions of the late antique and early medieval world, is the material evidence uncovered by archaeologists, specialists in documentary evidence and epigraphy, numismatists, and historians of art and architecture. Just as the development of a written historical tradition in Arabic reflects the development of a literate scholarly and scribal tradition among the rulers of the new empire, the production of a distinctive material culture reflects the marshalling of the resources of empire in the service of a new ruling class. The material evidence not only augments the evidence of the written sources but also provides data on subjects such as the environment, settlement patterns, the imperial administration and the economy that cannot be investigated in any detail through the literary material alone.

Umayyad History and the Structure of this Book

This book is arranged in three parts, which correspond with its main arguments. Because the Arabic historiography sees the coming of Islam in the early seventh century as a defining discontinuity, it tends to mask some of the underlying processes that brought about the success of Muhammad's community of

---

[20] On early sources composed by non-Muslims, see Robert G. Hoyland, *Seeing Islam As Others Saw It: A Survey and Evaluation of Christian, Jewish and Zoroastrian Writings on Early Islam* (Princeton, 1997) [hereafter, *SIAOSI*]. For the interconnections between the various traditions, see Borrut, *Mémoire et pouvoir*, 137–66; Robert G. Hoyland, *Theophilus of Edessa's Chronicle and the Circulation of Historical Knowledge in Late Antiquity and Early Islam* (Liverpool, 2011) [hereafter, *Theophilus*], 6–34.

the Faithful. In particular, the dynamics of political, religious and cultural change on the Arabian Peninsula and in its northern extension, the Syrian Desert and steppe, are beginning to be more fully understood. These processes are the focus of the first part of the book. While there is limited evidence that the peoples of Central and North Arabia thought of themselves collectively as 'the Arabs', there is evidence for the development of a shared culture in those regions. This culture is defined by the use of Old Arabic, which is the precursor to the Arabic language of later Islamic times, by a religious culture where Judaism and Christianity combined with local religious beliefs and practices, and by a political culture shaped by close interdependencies between nomadic and settled tribal groups.

The decline of the power of the South Arabian kingdom of Himyar, the dissolution of the Roman and Sasanian networks of alliance in the Syrian Desert, and war on an unprecedented scale between Rome and Iran brought about the circumstances for the political success of Muhammad's Meccan and Medinan followers. Long experience of maintaining networks of alliance with the nomadic pastoralist tribes of the western Arabian Peninsula made the Meccans and their Medinan allies well placed to take advantage of this 'world crisis'.[21] Muhammad's prophethood (c. 610–32) disrupted some of the more long-established local power structures in West Arabia but also catalysed West Arabian military and political expansion. While the well-established and locally influential Umayyad clan at Mecca are said to have initially lost out to Muhammad's network of followers, their participation in campaigns of the 630s and 640s secured them a place at the centre of the new religio-political federation. Muʿawiya's branch of the Umayyads took a leading role in campaigning against Roman forces in Syria and bringing the Arabic-speaking pastoralists of the Syrian steppe into alliance, while ʿUthman, one of the only early supporters of Muhammad from among the Umayyads, took the leadership of the federation in 644. This combination established the Umayyad clan as a powerful network within what was fast becoming an empire, uniting territories on the Arabian Peninsula with lands in Syria, Egypt and Iraq taken from Rome and Iran.

However, the interests of rival networks in the conquered territories led, in the 650s, to widespread support for alternative leaders than the Umayyads. Muʿawiya's victory against these rivals depended upon the pastoralist tribes of the former Roman desert frontier, which thereafter became the empire's military and political centre. Indeed, the empire after Muʿawiya might be

---

[21] For 'world crisis' see James Howard-Johnston, *Witnesses to a World Crisis: Historians and Histories of the Middle East in the Seventh Century* (Oxford, 2010) [hereafter, *WtaWC*], 6.

described as a 'Syro-Mesopotamian pastoralist' empire, insofar as the military forces that underpinned Umayyad rule were drawn largely from the pastoralists of the Syrian steppe and – after the 690s – also from the highland zones of Mesopotamia (modern eastern Turkey, northern Syria and northern Iraq). This is itself remarkable – the Umayyad Empire is the only large-scale, truly trans-regional empire in history whose monarchs resided in Syria.[22]

Ultimately, the long-term sustainability of Umayyad power was limited by this dependence on the resources of the Syrian steppe. However, in the short term, the re-centring of the empire in Syria had two important consequences for its subsequent evolution. First, as the rulers of post-Roman Syria, who contended directly with the Romans for territory and influence, Muʿawiya and the subsequent Umayyad rulers of the Arabian empire strove to replace their Roman rivals as God's chosen world rulers. This conflict further entangled the fortunes of the two empires and so shaped the articulation of Umayyad legitimacy and the character of the religion of Islam itself.

A second consequence of the Umayyads' dependence on the military support of the Romano-Syrian tribes was that they ruled from a predominantly Christian Syria, while most of migrants from the Peninsula and the greatest economic resources of the new empire were elsewhere, in the formerly Sasanian lands of Iraq. Muʿawiya ruled a large and decentralised 'conquest society', where military commanders in the other conquered territories wielded autonomous, but not completely independent, military and fiscal power in diverse post-Roman and post-Sasanian cultural contexts.[23] Groups from Iraqi garrisons had backed the Umayyads' rivals in the civil war and so Muʿawiya's death in 680, followed by the premature death of his son three years later, created the conditions for a second civil war. This second internal conflict again pitted the Umayyads against rivals from other branches of the Prophet's wider tribe of Quraysh, who again drew on the support of the Iraqi migrants. During the twelve-year war against these rivals, power structures in Syria were shaken; Muʿawiya's direct descendants lost the leadership of the Syrian tribes, who pledged allegiance instead to Muʿawiya's second cousin and former ally, Marwan b. al-Hakam.

The victory of Marwan and his son ʿAbd al-Malik in the second civil war in 692 marks an important break in many aspects of the empire's history and so it is where part two of the book begins. This second civil war took place

---

[22] Cases can of course be made for other Syrian polities. These would include the Ayyubids, who ruled from Greater Syria in the twelfth and thirteenth centuries, once again (briefly) uniting Egypt, Syria, the Hijaz, Yemen and Mesopotamia, but never reaching beyond these core territories.

[23] For 'conquest society', see *SoH*, 26.

when many of those who were adults at the time of the Prophet Muhammad had died. As a consequence, the era of the Prophet and his followers now became the focus of memorialisation, often in the context of competition for power. Furthermore, the demographic, economic and military structures of the empire were changing fast, with large communities of the Faithful established in new garrisons in the former Roman and Sasanian lands, and new frontiers for conquest developing in North Africa, Iran and Central Asia. It was among these communities, including Umayyad circles, that the religious and historical traditions of Islam began to be elaborated; some of the earliest written strands of that tradition can be traced back to around 700, making this post-692 era much more precisely delineated in the later Arabic literary sources than the seventh century.

Following his victory in 692, 'Abd al-Malik and other descendants of Marwan were able to assert an exclusive claim to leadership of the empire during the next fifty years. Collectively, this new ruling branch of the Umayyad clan – the first real dynasty in Islam – are known as the Marwanids. They ruled as collaborators and competitors, with competition between the different branches of the Marwanid clan being driven by their wider kinship connections and alliances. For the Marwanids, as for Mu'awiya before them, competition with the Roman Empire and the challenge of ruling Iraq from Syria were two primary concerns. However, unlike Mu'awiya, they sought to assert greater control over the provinces of the empire, aiming to bridge the institutional divide between the former lands of the Sasanian and Roman empires. In Iraq, they diverted the resources of the province to pay for Syrian soldiers to support their governors there, generating waves of resistance to their rule as a result. Conscious of the need to legitimate their rule beyond Syria, they promoted their authority through monumental architecture, on the precious metal coins and in other media, including huge parchment copies of the Qur'an. A consequence was a distinctive Marwanid horizon in the material evidence after c. 690, which reflects their efforts to assert leadership of a distinctive imperial religious tradition in direct competition with the Roman Empire, but also their need to address diverse audiences across what remained a huge and decentralised empire.

In the war with Rome, the Marwanids sponsored two further campaigns against Constantinople. The first culminated in a failed siege of the Roman capital in 717–18, and the second ended with defeats for the Muslims' armies in Roman Sicily and western Anatolia in 740. These defeats were damaging for the Marwanids, whose prestige depended on their status as competitors with the Roman Empire in the Eastern Mediterranean. However, Marwanid imperial power only unravelled when competition within the dynasty and between different tribal groups in Marwanid Syria turned violent at the same time as new forms of rebellion broke out on the western and eastern frontiers of their empire. Independent groups from North Africa challenged Umayyad rule in the name of Islam in the 740s, while a rebel movement in western Central Asia, retrospectively known as the 'Abbasid Revolution' (*al-dawla al-'Abbāsīya*) took advantage of the bloody succession crisis in Syria to march against the Marwanids and end their rule, founding a new caliphate led by their Abbasid relatives. Thus, Umayyad domination of the empire ended as it had begun, with the conquest of the empire by military groups from its frontiers.

The third part of the book steps back from the dynamics of politics and war to explore in more detail the geography, and economic, social and administrative history of the Umayyad era, in three chapters. The first is on ecology, settlement patterns and the economy. The second explores further the impact of the empire on the conquered religious communities. The third addresses the development of imperial administration and government. Together, the three chapters assess the character of environmental, economic, social and institutional change in the Middle East in the seventh and eighth centuries. The era of the Umayyad Empire was comparatively brief, but it sits at a hinge point in world history, brought into being by a unique combination of long-term and short-term processes of change and in turn bringing about a new Arab and Islamic world.

PART I
THE FORMATION OF THE UMAYYAD EMPIRE

Part I Introduction

Unlike the steppes of Central Asia, from where federations of pastoralists have repeatedly irrupted into the settled lands to their south, the Arabian Peninsula has only ever generated one episode of trans-regional conquest – the so-called 'Islamic conquests' or 'Arab conquests' of the 630s and 640s and after. Hence, this unique event presents a problem. Whereas some patterns can be discerned in the interaction between the predominantly nomadic peoples of the grasslands of Central Asia and the settled agrarian lands of Europe and Asia, no such pattern is immediately apparent in the interaction between the Arabian Peninsula and the world to the north. Nonetheless, this exceptional event is explicable. A dual perspective, which takes in the long-term interactions between the settled world and the steppe, together with the short-term context of the geopolitical circumstances of the later sixth and early seventh centuries, provides the best framework for understanding it.

In the first overview chapter, events in the Middle East until the beginning of the sixth century are set out. From the fourth century CE, interactions between the empires to the north and the peoples of the Syrian Desert led to new political formations among the Arabic-speaking pastoralists there, often in the context of the adoption of local forms of Christianity, distinct from those promoted in the Roman Empire. Meanwhile, in the far south of the Peninsula, the kings of Himyar promoted Judaic monotheism and built alliances with pastoralists in southern and central Arabia. In the second chapter, the escalating conflict between Rome and Iran and the weakening of Himyarite power are the immediate contexts that explain the expansion of the influence of the West Arabian region of the Hijaz in the late sixth century and the success of the mission of the Prophet Muhammad in the early seventh.

The third chapter shows how Muhammad and his allies reshaped the religious and political landscape of Arabia and how his immediate successors extended their influence into the Roman and Sasanian lands of Syria, Egypt, Iraq and western Iran. Members of the Umayyad clan, most of whom are said to have opposed Muhammad until his victory became inevitable, were leading participants in the wars of the 630s and 640s. In Syria, the sons of Abu Sufyan

b. Harb b. Umayya led the conquest of Roman territory, with the result that by the 640s Muʿawiya b. Abi Sufyan (g. c. 640–61) had become the leading West Arabian commander there. Muʿawiya built a close relationship with the tribe of Kalb in the Syrian Desert, fathering a son, Yazid, by the daughter of one their leaders. (Because the West Arabian conquerors practised polygamy and because Arabian women tended to retain close links with their birth family, marriage was an important mechanism by which a man could build alliances.[1])

Chapter Four begins with the accession of Muʿawiya's second cousin ʿUthman to leadership of the new Arabian empire in 644, which placed an Umayyad at the head of the whole conquest society. ʿUthman's rule led to the dominance of the empire by members of his wider kin-group, from the Umayyad clan and from the wider grouping of ʿAbd Shams. Then, in the 650s and 660s, the connections forged between Muʿawiya and the Syrian tribes, together with an alliance with the conqueror of Egypt, ʿAmr b. al-ʿAs, proved critical to Muʿawiya's taking over leadership of the empire.

Chapter Five shows how, after Muʿawiya's death, similar alliances underpinned the success of his relatives in regaining power over the empire in the face of challenges from others in the 680s and 690s. However, this second civil war within the Hijazi elite was fought with the resources of a more established empire. In turn, the war brought about further development of the structures of imperial power. Hence, with the victory of his second cousin ʿAbd al-Malik in 692, a new era in the history of the empire began. An Umayyad leader who had grown up in Medina in the era of ʿUthman imposed greater direct control over the provinces and used their revenues to express a distinctive vision of the Arabian conquerors' religion in order to legitimate his power.

---

[1] Marsham, 'Kinship'.

1

The Origins of Arabian Empire

The Middle East is a region where the some of the earliest empires began. The floodplains of the Nile, the Euphrates and the Tigris have sustained the production of food surpluses for millennia. Collected as taxation, at first in kind and later also in coin, these surpluses supported the armies upon which all empire ultimately depends, as well as the religious and political elites who create and maintain an empire's cultural and institutional identity. With the growth of long-distance trade – itself often stimulated by the dynamics of empire formation – revenues from control of trade routes and their entrepôts also became important. Ancient Middle Eastern societies became highly socially stratified: landowning and mercantile elites, and specialists in administrative, military and religious power, were dependent upon the great majority, the subsistence agriculturalists, who farmed the surrounding countryside. Military expansion, and the coercion of neighbouring groups into the provision of tribute and services or more complete incorporation into the empire's tax structure, was typical of these 'tributary empires'. By the beginning of the first millennium CE, much of the Middle East was ruled by two long-standing such empires. The Parthian Empire (247 BCE–*c.* 224 CE) was centred on the Iranian plateau, but also encompassed most of what is now Iraq, as well as modern Armenia and Azerbaijan. By the early first century CE, the neighbouring Roman Empire had encircled the Mediterranean, encompassing Gaul and Britain in the far north-west and Anatolia, Egypt and Syria in the east.[1]

In the third century CE, both the Iranian and Roman empires weathered major crises. In Iran, the Parthians were replaced by the Sasanian dynasty (r. *c.* 224–*c.* 650), a powerful landholding family from the highland region of Fars, in the south-west. The Sasanian Empire competed with Rome with

---

[1] For the earliest empires, see Michael Mann, *The Sources of Social Power Volume 1: A History of Power from the Beginning to AD 1760* (Cambridge, 1986), 73–104. For the same and the beginning of the first millennium, see the relevant chapters in Bang et al. (eds), *The Oxford World History of Empire Volume Two: The History of Empires* (Oxford, 2021), 1–157, 240–324.

renewed vigour, notably under Shapur I (r. c. 240–c. 270). At the same time, the Sasanian elite negotiated a new relationship with the priests of the Zoroastrian religious tradition of Iran, transforming diverse traditional practices into a more centralised, imperial cult (though not an exclusive one – the Sasanian Empire was multi-confessional, with large communities of Jews, Buddhists, Christians, Manichaeans and others subordinate to the Sasanian aristocracy).[2] In Rome, the 'third-century crisis' of invasions and civil wars prompted the reorganisation of the empire into two halves under Diocletian (r. 285–305) and then the sponsorship of Christianity as the favoured religion in the empire, under Constantine (r. 305–37). By the end of the fourth century, Christianity was the imperial cult of Rome. Roman Christianity had a more universalist character than the Zoroastrianism of Iran: minorities of other faiths were sometimes persecuted, as were adherents of variants of the Christian faith considered heretical.[3]

In both empires, these internal developments coincided with the formation of new political structures among the peoples of two of the great desert and steppe zones of Africa and Eurasia – the deserts of the Sahara and Arabia, to the empires' south, and the grasslands of the Central Asian steppe, to their north (see Map 1.1).

Neither the Sahara nor the Central Asian steppe supported the kinds of large-scale settled agriculture that were possible in the temperate zone. Instead, nomadic pastoralism was often the main means of supporting human life. Most of the inhabitants of the deserts and steppes herded animals, migrating between pastures seasonally to exploit the resources of the arid and steppe zones to their best advantage. Such pastoralist societies produced their own concentrations of social power and their own social hierarchies. Military specialists could acquire the wealth and prestige that allowed them to dominate other groups and to form federations, or steppe empires. Likewise, specialists in ritual and religion were often vital to the social functions of the steppe, servicing protected ceremonial spaces for trade and political negotiation. Shared

---

[2] Matthew P. Canepa, 'The Parthian and Sasanian Empires', in Peter F. Bang et al. (eds), *The Oxford World History of Empire: Volume Two: The History of Empires* (Oxford, 2021), 311–14; Albert de Jong, 'Religion in Iran: The Parthian and Sasanian Periods (247 BCE–654 CE)', in Michele Renee Salzman and Marvin A. Sweeney (eds), *The Cambridge History of Religions in the Ancient World* (Cambridge, 2013), 23–53. On Christians in the Sasanian Empire, see Richard E. Payne, *A State of Mixture: Christians, Zoroastrians, and Iranian Political Culture in Late Antiquity* (Oakland, CA, 2016).

[3] Peter F. Bang, 'The Roman Empire', in Peter, F. Bang et al. (eds), *The Oxford World History of Empire Volume Two: The History of Empires* (Oxford, 2021), 272–6.

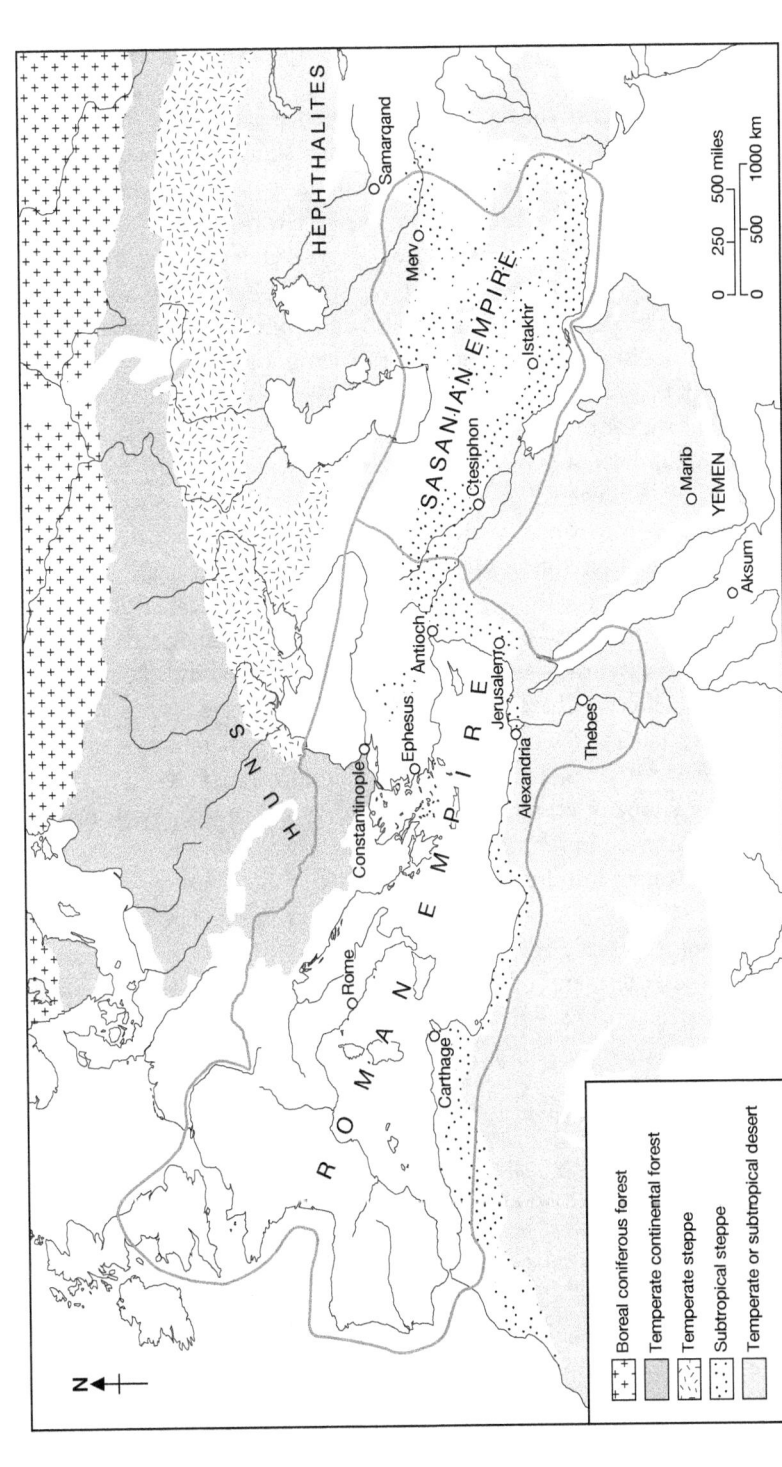

Map 1.1 Rome and Iran in the fourth–fifth centuries CE and the neighbouring steppe, forest and desert zones.

norms and customs underpinned the power of both military and religious aristocracies.[4]

Where the peoples of the desert and steppe encountered the settled zone, they traded the products of their herds and their skill as riders and soldiers, acting as middle-men and armed protection on long-distance overland trade routes, or as military allies of the settled powers. In turn, the pastoralists connected the settled empires to networks of long-distance economic exchange that those empires could not access directly, and supplied highly mobile warriors, who could be deployed against rivals or in policing the steppe frontier itself. The pastoralists could also pose a serious military threat to their settled neighbours. Of the two great desert and steppe regions, Central Asia generated far more problems for the settled world. This was because its grasslands could support large numbers of people and horses, and large and complex political organisations, with powerful cavalry armies. These interactions were at their most intense along the frontier with the Chinese empires to the east, but both Rome and Iran also had frontiers with the steppes of Central Asia.[5]

In contrast to the continuous formation of large political entities in the north and the frequent episodes of conflict between them and the empires of the temperate zone, the desert zone in the south tended to produce much smaller political effects. There is no equivalent to Attila the Hun or Genghis Khan from the Sahara Desert because its resources are far more meagre than those of the Asian steppes. The kingdom of Numidia (202 BCE–46 CE) was – to borrow the Romans' ethnic term for its elite – a 'Moorish' (Lat. *Mauri*) empire, encompassing much of western North Africa. Once it was incorporated into the Roman Empire, federations of 'Moorish' tribespeople from the desert did cause problems for Roman rule. However, these political formations were not on the scale of those in Central Asia.[6]

Beyond the eastern end of the Sahara, the Arabian Peninsula, including its northern extension, the Syrian Desert and its steppe, had also been barren

---

[4] On power structures in the Central Asian steppe, with a critique of some older perspectives, see David Sneath, *The Headless State: Aristocratic Orders, Kinship Society, and Misrepresentations of Nomadic Inner Asia* (New York, 2007).

[5] Nicola Di Cosmo, 'Ancient Inner Asian Nomads: Their Economic Basis and Its Significance in Chinese History', *Journal of Asian Studies* 53 (1994), 1092–1126. Cf. also Nicolai N. Kradin, 'Nomadic Empires in Inner Asia' and Nicola Di Cosmo, 'China-Steppe Relations in Historical Perspective', in Jan Bemmann and Michael Schmauder (eds), *Complexity of Interaction along the Eurasian Steppe Zone in the First Millennium CE* (Bonn, 2015), 35 and 68–9.

[6] For example, the early fifth century CE the Laguatan federation: D. J. Mattingly, 'The Laguatan: A Libyan Tribal Confederation in the Late Roman Empire', *Libyan Studies* 14 (1983), 96–108.

ground for the formation of major trans-regional imperial powers. So it would remain, with the single spectacular exception of the conquests of the seventh and eighth centuries CE. The explanation for this exceptional episode lies in long-term processes of social and political change on the Peninsula and in the Syrian Desert, catalysed, as was often the case elsewhere, by interactions between Arabian populations and settled polities on their peripheries. The unique consequences of these processes were a product both of the very specific conditions on the Peninsula and the exceptional short-term geopolitical circumstances of the early seventh century CE. As with the Central Asian steppe to the north, the starting point for considering these events, both long- and short-term, must be geography.

Arabian Geography and Ecology

The area of the Arabian Peninsula is more than 3,000,000km^2 – about the same size as the modern state of India.[7] Its predominantly hot, dry, climate supports a comparatively small population – one estimate has suggested that in the sixth century CE Arabia sustained perhaps one tenth of India's population at that time.[8] The Peninsula proper is almost rectangular, with its two long sides framed by the Red Sea in the west and the Gulf in the east. In the south-east, Oman (modern Oman and the United Arab Emirates) projects into the Gulf, coming within 40km of the Iranian coast where the narrow spike of the Musandam Peninsula forms the Straits of Hormuz (see Map 1.2). In the south-west, the straits of Bab al-Mandab put East Africa within 30km of the Arabian shoreline. In the far north, the top of the Peninsula segues into the Syrian Desert (parts of modern Jordan, Syria, Iraq and Saudi Arabia); this desert triangle is usually considered to be geographically part of Arabia, contiguous as it is with the Arabian deserts proper, which lie further to the south. In the west and north, the Syrian Desert becomes a steppe, where higher rainfall supports scrub and grazing animals, though the rain is too infrequent and light to support much settled agriculture.[9]

The highest land on the Arabian Peninsula is in the mountainous south-west corner (modern Yemen), and a range of hills projects north from there into the central West Arabian region known as the Hijaz. In the south-west of the

---

[7] John Misachi, 'Arabian Peninsula' and anonymous, 'Maps of India', in Oshimaya Sen Nag et al. (eds), *WorldAtlas*, <https://www.worldatlas.com/> (last accessed 22 August 2022).
[8] Colin McEvedy and Richard Jones, *Atlas of World Population History* (London, 1978), 144, 182.
[9] A useful survey of the geography and ecology of the Arabian Peninsula is Peter Magee, *The Archaeology of Prehistoric Arabia: Adaptation and Social Formation from the Neolithic to the Iron Age* (Cambridge, 2014), 14–45.

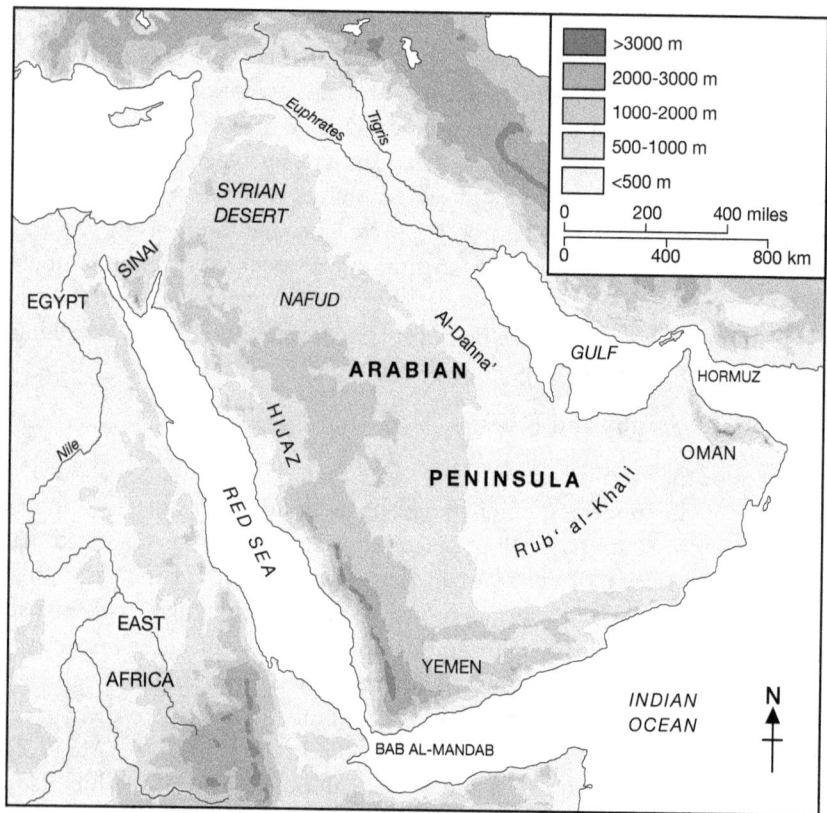

Map 1.2 Relief map of the Arabian Peninsula and the Syrian Desert. Based on Peter Magee, *The Archaeology of Prehistoric Arabia: Adaptation and Social Formation from the Neolithic to the Iron Age* (Cambridge, 2014), 15.

Peninsula the mountains reach heights of well over 3,000m, and are watered by monsoon rains, creating a tropical climate unique in Arabia, although significant rainfall also reaches the higher ground further north, facilitating small settlements there. In the east, the Hajar mountains of Oman catch some summer monsoon rain.[10] The Arabian interior is arid, with very low precipitation; settlements are found only where groundwater is accessible at oases or wells. Much of the land can be exploited only by nomadic pastoralism, where

---

[10] Stephen J. Burns et al., 'A 780-year Annually Resolved Record of Indian Ocean Monsoon Precipitation from a Speleothem from South Oman', *Journal of Geophysical Research: Atmospheres* 107, D20 (2002), 1–2. Cf. Magee, *Archaeology*, 25.

migrations follow the seasonal rains that support pasture for sheep, camels and other ruminant animals.[11]

There are two great sand-dune deserts, or ergs: the large Empty Quarter, which extends across most of the southern Peninsula, between the highlands of Yemen in the west and those of Oman in the east; the smaller northern sand-dune desert, the Nafud is at the top of the Peninsula. In pre-modern times, specific tribes of nomads monopolised the few routes across the sand deserts, using domesticated camels to make the crossing. The comparisons in pre-Islamic Arabic poetry between camels and ships are apt, not least because of the role that the deserts play in both uniting and dividing the region.[12] Like an inland sea, the deserts fragment the Arabian Peninsula into distinct regions, each with their own cultural and political traditions. On each side of the Peninsula its more densely populated edges face out, towards the economies and political networks that surround them: the Fertile Crescent, the Mediterranean, East Africa, the Indian Ocean and Iran. But at the same time the edges of the Peninsula are also linked together by the internal desert, and by the migrations of the pastoralists who inhabit it.

The desert and steppe zones that border the ergs do support plant and animal life, along with transhumant agriculture. In the far north, the Syrian steppe is watered by North Atlantic westerlies. There, the kingdoms of Nabataea and Palmyra flourished on its western side at the beginning of the first millennium CE. Both were built around urban oasis centres and the caravan trade, with Petra (in modern Jordan) being a leading Nabatean city, and Palmyra (in modern Syria) being the Palmyrene capital. Both were incorporated into the Roman Empire – Nabataea in the mid-first century CE and Palmyra at the beginning of the second. At this point, in 106 CE, the Roman province of Arabia was created. The Roman province is not to be confused with the Peninsula as a whole. Roman *provincia Arabia* was in the far north – roughly modern Jordan, the Sinai, Negev, and parts of southern Syria and northern Saudi Arabia. In this western arc of the Fertile Crescent, settled and pastoralist populations coexisted, exploiting different zones within the landscape where the 'desert' meets the 'sown' (see Map 1.3).[13] During the rainy autumn and winter, the pastoralists migrated south-east, into the drier steppe

---

[11] Nathaniel Miller, 'Seasonal Poetics: The Dry Season and Autumn Rains among Pre-Islamic Nagdi and Higazi Tribes', *Arabica* 64 (2017), 1–27.
[12] Michael Sells, 'The *Mu'allaqa* of Tarafa', *Journal of Arabic Literature* 17 (1986), 24–6.
[13] Zbigniew T. Fiema et al., '*Provincia Arabia*: Nabataea, the Emergence of Arabic as a Written Language, and Graeco-Arabica', in Greg Fisher (ed.), *Arabs and Empires before Islam* (Oxford, 2015), 373–86.

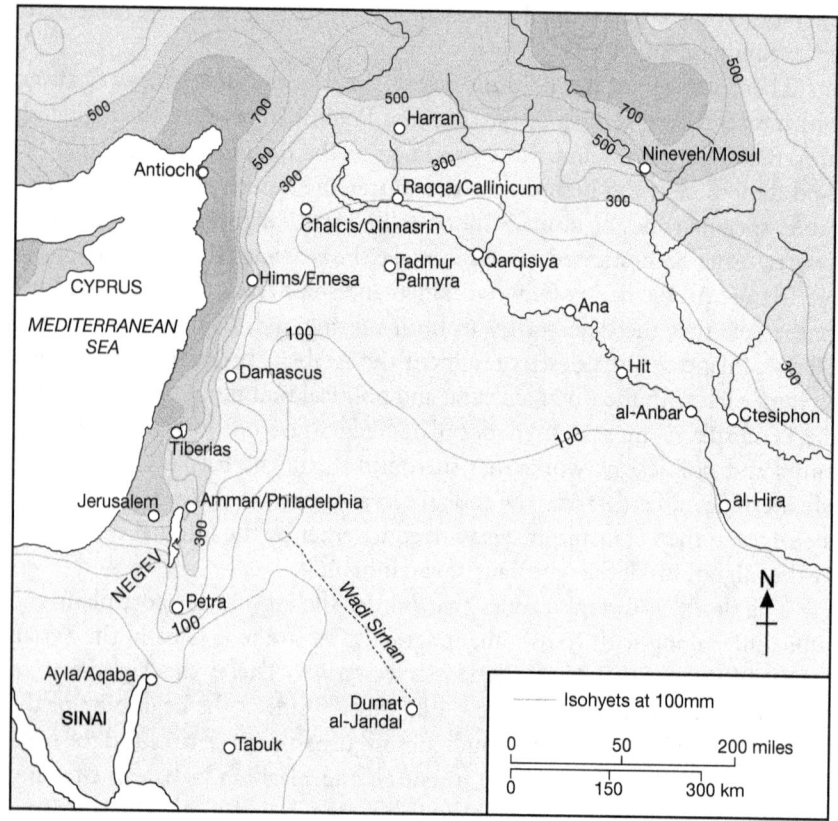

Map 1.3 Modern precipitation map of 'Greater Syria' (*Bilād al-Shām*) with some of the major late antique settlements. Isohyets at 100mm per year. Based on Reto Jagher, Hani Elsuede and Jean-Marie Le Tensorer, 'El Kowm Oasis, Human Settlement in the Syrian Desert during the Pleistocene', *L'Anthropologie* 119 (2015), 548.

regions, returning north-west towards better irrigated lands in the spring and summer, often grazing farmed lands after the summer harvest (Figure 1.1).[14]

At the opposite, southern, end of the Peninsula, oases on the south-western edges of the Empty Quarter also formed hubs for tribal federations that controlled overland trade. Just as the northern federations fell to Rome, these southern tribal groups tended to come under the influence of the settled

[14] E. B. Banning, 'Peasants, Pastoralists and "Pax Romana": Mutualism in the Southern Highlands of Jordan', *Bulletin of the American Schools of Oriental Research* 261 (1986), 25–50; Norman E. Lewis, *Nomads and Settlers in Syria and Jordan, 1800–1980* (Cambridge, 1987), 3–6.

Figure 1.1 Sheep grazing on the Syrian steppe with Bedouin tents in the background, near Damascus, Syria, c. 1950–5. Photograph by Clarence Woodrow Sorensen. Permission of American Geographical Society Library, University of Wisconsin-Milwaukee Libraries.

polities of the South Arabian highlands. Overland routes within the Peninsula passed through the western highlands and on north through a chain of oases, linking the oases on the edge of the Empty Quarter in the south with the entrepôts of Roman Syria, about 2,000km to the north. Other routes led diagonally west-to-east across the desert, from the southern oases to Oman and East Arabia's settlements and, from there, to Iran and the Indian Ocean, via the Gulf. Maritime trade also connected South Arabia to East Africa and the Indian Ocean, and ports on the Red Sea and Gulf coasts connected the Peninsula with the Mediterranean, Africa, Iran and India.[15]

The ebb and flow of political power among the groups that occupied the margins of the internal desert sea, and their interactions with the outward-facing settled polities on its edges, generated social and political change. In the middle centuries of the first millennium CE, the northern and southern poles of the great imperial powers, on the one hand, and the South Arabian kingdom, on the other, were particularly important, as they encroached more

---

[15] Daniel T. Potts, 'Trans-Arabian Routes of the Pre-Islamic Period', in F. E. Peters (ed.), *The Arabs and Arabia on the Eve of Islam* (Aldershot, 1999), 45–80.

closely on the peoples of the desert interior. Among these pastoralist groups and their settled neighbours at towns and oases, some shared cultural norms and practices had developed. The same period witnessed the formation of new federations of tribal groups. In the north, these federations were primarily influenced in their political culture by Rome and Iran, in the south by the settled kingdom of South Arabia.

Arab Ethnicity and Identity

Arabians have not always been Arabs. Like all ethnic identities, Arabness is socially constructed; that is, ethnic labels are a consequence of cultural, not genetic, phenomena, and their significance shifts with context, time and place. However – again like all ethnic identities – Arabness has at times been an important social and political resource, and so it is entirely real in this constructed, cultural, sense. The word 'Arab' first appears in Assyrian texts from the seventh century BCE. Simultaneously, it also occurs in a very early South Arabian inscription, from the sixth or seventh century BCE, and it is also found in the Bible. That 'Arab' occurs in the languages of many of Arabia's neighbours almost simultaneously tends to suggest that it reflected some indigenous Arabian term. It often seems to be used by the literate cultures on the Arabian periphery to refer to peoples practising nomadic pastoralism. What significances the term 'Arab' may have had in the first millennium BCE for peoples in the Arabian Peninsula itself, we do not know. Centuries later, in Late Antiquity, the Arabic word *al-aʿrab* (the plural of the singular *al-ʿarab*) refers to nomadic pastoralists, and the same root is also associated both with pledged loyalty and clarity of speech. *Al-ʿarab* in the collective sense – 'the Arabs' – rarely seems to have been in use in Arabic; where it was, its exact meanings are not clear.[16]

Identities are relational, reflecting social and political circumstances, and so a notion of 'the Arabs' as a single people would have made little sense in the absence of any political formations that encompassed all the peoples of this huge and culturally varied land. Ideas about an ethnic group, 'the Arabs' in the more inclusive sense of 'all Arabians' and the use of the collective noun *al-ʿarab* to denote it, are thus more a product of the formation of an Arabian empire than a cause.[17] Many Arabians already conceived of themselves as belonging to a patrilineal descent-group, or 'tribe' (Ar. *qabīla*, pl. *qabāʾil*), with a notional shared common male ancestor. Such groups reflected power structures and alliances and were reimagined in response to changing political arrangements. For example, the Banu Taghlib, a Central Arabian pastoralist

---

[16] Michael C. A. Macdonald, 'Arabs, Arabias and Arabic before Late Antiquity', *Topoi* 1 (2009), 277–332. Cf. Webb, *Imagining the Arabs*, 23–59.

[17] Macdonald, 'Arabs', 306; Webb, *Imagining the Arabs*.

grouping in the fifth and sixth centuries, are said to have been descendants of Taghlib b. Wa'il, while some other groups in the same region – often Taghlib's rivals – were said to have been sons of Taghlib's brother, Bakr b. Wa'il.[18] By the sixth century CE, many of the tribal groups living in the western and central Arabian Peninsula had also come to identify as belonging to a wider grouping, named Ma'add, after an ancestor imagined as having lived six generations earlier than Wa'il. Such a larger-scale group identity is suggestive of the greater connectivity across the Peninsula that may have developed in the middle centuries of the first millennium CE.[19]

All the languages of the Arabian Peninsula were Semitic, belonging to the same overall family as Hebrew, used by Jewish communities across Africa and Eurasia, and the various forms of Aramaic – including Syriac – used in the Fertile Crescent, as well as Ethiopic languages, such as Ge'ez, used in East Africa. However, the languages and dialects of the northern and central Arabian peoples are different from the languages of the southern Arabians and are classified as two separate branches of Semitic languages. The classical Arabic language derives from 'Old Arabic', which was becoming dominant among the tribes of the Arabian interior and in the north by the middle of the first millennium CE. Epigraphic South Arabian – the language used for inscriptions in South Arabia down to the sixth century CE – and other South Arabian languages are classified as 'South Arabian'.[20]

Perhaps the best-known early instance of written Old Arabic comes from the Namara inscription, now in the Louvre, Paris, but originally from what is now southern Syria (Figure 1.2). It was inscribed in 328 CE and is important evidence for the connection between changing political and ethnic structures in North Arabia and interactions with the Roman and Persian empires. While the words, carved in basalt stone, are Old Arabic, they are not recorded in Arabic script, which had yet to develop from the Nabataean letters that are used in the inscription. It is an epitaph, originally installed at a tomb near the Roman frontier fortress at Namara, in the desert about 100km south-east of Damascus.

---

[18] *EI²*, 'Taghlib b. Wa'il' (M. Lecker); Heinrich Ferdinand Wüstenfeld, *Genealogische Tabellen der arabischen Stämme und Familien. In zwei Abtheilungen* (Göttingen, 1852–3), II, Tab. A, B.

[19] Peter Webb, 'Ethnicity, Power and Umayyad Society: The Rise and Fall of the People of Ma'add', in Andrew Marsham (ed.), *The Umayyad World* (London and New York, 2021), 66–71.

[20] On Old Arabic, see Macdonald's and Al-Jallad's contributions in Fiema et al., '*Provincia Arabia*', 395–433. On Semitic languages, see Aaron Rubin, *A Brief Introduction to Semitic Languages* (Piscataway, NJ, 2010).

Figure 1.2 The Namara inscription. 173cm × 45cm. The Louvre, Paris. <https://collections.louvre.fr/en/page/cgu> (last accessed 12 July 2022). © Musée du Louvre / Maurice et Pierre Chuzeville.

> This is the funerary monument of Mara'-l-Qays son of 'Amrw, king of all 'Arab [?], who bound on the crown, and ruled the two Syrias and Nizaru and their kings, and fought with Madhhij, until he struck with his spear on the gates of Najran, the city of [the Himyarite king] Shammar. And he ruled Ma'addu and gave his sons [rule over] the (settled) peoples, and they were made proxies for Persia and Rome. And no king could match his achievements. Thereafter, he died in in the year 223 on the 3rd day of Kislul [328 CE] ... [?].[21]

The inscription is testament to the interconnectedness of the Arabian Peninsula. Mara'-l-Qays (sometimes Imru' al-Qays) is buried on the northern edge of Arabia, where he claimed authority: 'all 'Arab' probably refers to part of the steppe regions of Greater Syria and Mesopotamia, while the 'two Syrias' are probably Mesopotamia and Palestine; Nizar is a tribal group associated with that region. However, Mara'-l-Qays's military success had also taken him far to the south: as we have seen, Ma'add is a tribal label associated with Arabia's central regions, as is Madhhij; Najran is a settlement in the northern highlands of South Arabia, more than 1,600km from Namara. The Shammar to whom the inscription refers is Shammar Yuhar'ish (r. c. 270–c. 315), the founder of the kingdom of Himyar, which dominated the whole of South Arabia at this time. The location of the epitaph adjacent to a Roman military centre is suggestive: very likely, Mara'-l-Qays was an ally of the Romans, from whom he probably received the 'crown' mentioned early in the inscription. The tomb and its inscription are not just evidence for politics and identity on the Peninsula, but also for the intensification of interactions between the

---

[21] Macdonald, in Fiema et al., *'Provincia Arabia'*, 405–6, with further references.

Roman and Iranian empires and the pastoralists of the Arabian Peninsula during and after the third century CE.

Arabia, Rome and Iran in the Third, Fourth and Fifth Centuries CE

With the incorporation of Palmyra and Nabataea into the empire over the course of the second and third centuries CE, the former client states ceased to mediate the Romans' relationship with the pastoralist Arabian groups further south. Instead, the Roman authorities were drawn into direct engagement with Peninsular peoples. At the same time, the renewal of conflict between Rome and Iran – the latter reinvigorated under the leadership of the Sasanians after 224 CE – put increased pressure on the frontier between the two empires and stimulated a need for troops who were adept at negotiating the desert. The empires offered economic, political and military support to Arabian groups that came into alliance with them, leading to the formation of new political entities in northern Arabia. Meanwhile, the expansion of the South Arabian kingdom of Himyar during the third century CE generated similar processes in the south and drew both northern imperial powers into the politics of the whole Peninsula, and not just its northern frontiers.

By the fourth century, the Romans had come to depend upon alliances with various tribal groups from the Syrian steppe. The use of federated allies (Lat. *foederati*, Gk *symmachoi, hypospondoi*) by the Romans was not unique to their Syrian desert frontier.[22] Rather, it was typical of the increased employment of peoples the Romans called 'barbarians' on Roman frontiers after the fourth-century reorganisation of frontier defences. ('Barbarian' is the Anglicisation of the Latin and Greek terms for non-Roman peoples: *barbari* and *barbaroi*.) In Syria, these groups secured the Romans' desert frontier and served in the Roman field armies in battle against the Sasanians.[23] Similar processes were also taking place on the Iranian desert frontier. A Persian inscription from 293 CE, at Paikuli (in modern Iraqi Kurdistan), lists one 'Amru, king of the Lakhmids' among the allies of the Sasanian king, Narseh.[24]

---

[22] On the terms in the East, see Lucas McMahon, 'The Foederati, the Phoideratoi, and the Symmachoi of the Late Antique East (ca. AD 400–650)', Masters Dissertation, University of Ottawa (2014).

[23] Irfan Shahid, *Byzantium and the Arabs in the Fourth Century* (Washington, DC, 1984), 175–6.

[24] Helmet Humbach and Prods O. Skjaervo, *The Sassanian Inscription of Paikuli Part 3.1: Restored Text and Translation by Prods Skjaervo* (Wiesbaden, 1983), §92; Michael Macdonald et al., 'Arabs and Empires before the Sixth Century', in Greg Fisher (ed.), *Arabs and Empires before Islam* (Oxford, 2015), 60–1.

The North Arabian tribes' increasing military and political significance to the Romans may be reflected in changes in the Romans' labels for them. Both *arabes* (Arabs) and *nomades* (nomads) are found in the Eastern Roman sources from as early as they had encountered Arabians. However, from the second century CE *saraceni* and *saracenoi* (Saracen) begin to occur, becoming the main terms for them in subsequent centuries. The label probably derives from the name of one Arabian tribal group. In Syriac, the Arabian nomads are often called *tayyaye*, which derives from a specific tribal group in central and north-east Arabia.[25]

New labels coincided with new military, social and political circumstances. Barbarians were now present inside the empire in numbers in their capacity as Roman soldiers and Roman allies. Saracen leaders allied with Rome benefited from military assistance and the resources of the Roman tax system, but retained their connections with the steppes, from where they drew their military support. These Saracens tended to become Christian, under local religious leadership.[26] However, in Roman Syria, as elsewhere in the empire, barbarian allies negotiated their alliances to retain or enhance their own status and power. Their adoption of local forms of Christianity often at odds with the imperial church, their distinctive culture and their continued connections with people beyond the settled zone contributed to the potential for conflict. The Roman authorities appear to have been conscious of the risks of allowing any one barbarian group to become too powerful, maintaining a balance of alliances with a variety of tribes.

In the 370s a Roman miscalculation triggered a dramatic demonstration of the risks in the provinces that bordered the Syrian Desert. Following the death of 'the king of the Saracens' – perhaps a leader of the tribe of Tanukh – the emperor Valens (r. 364–78) sought to dissolve the alliance with the king's followers. The result was a revolt led by the king's widow, Mawia, who 'began to rock the towns and cities on the borders of Palestine and Arabia with fierce attacks, and to lay waste the neighbouring provinces'.[27] These military successes placed Mawia in a strong negotiating position: the treaty of alliance with her tribe was renewed; her daughter was married to the senior commander in

---

[25] Fergus Millar, *The Roman Near East, 31 BC–AD 337* (Cambridge, MA and London, 1993), 140; Greg Fisher et al., 'Arabs and Christianity', in Greg Fisher (ed.), *Arabs and Empires before Islam* (Oxford, 2015), 355.

[26] Greg Fisher, 'From Mavia to al-Mundhir: Arab Christians and Arab Tribes in the Late Roman Near East', in Kirill Dimitriev and Isabel Toral-Niehoff (eds), *Religious Culture in Late Antique Arabia* (Piscataway, NJ, 2017), 166–8.

[27] Rufinus, *The Church History of Rufinus of Aquileia: Books 10 and 11*, tr. Philip R. Amidon (Oxford, 1997), Book 11.6.

the East; and her demand that a hermit from the Syrian steppe, named Moses, be appointed as bishop for her tribe was fulfilled.

Mawia's formal adoption of Christianity may have been part of the peace deal with the Roman authorities, as was often the case elsewhere. However, it is notable that the new bishop, Moses, subscribed to what Rufinus and others called 'orthodox' Christianity – that is, to the Nicene version which claimed to look back to the religion as it had been established under Constantine. The reigning emperor at the time of the revolt, Valens, was a so-called 'Arian' Christian – that is, he followed a non-Nicene Christian tradition that was also popular among some of the barbarian groups in the Western Roman Empire. It seems likely that Mawia would have been conversant with Christianity and its political significance, and aware of the benefits of insisting upon adopting a non-imperial strand of the religion, indigenous to Syria.[28]

Hence, at the end of the fourth century, a federation on the northern steppe borders of the Arabian Peninsula had been able to put significant pressure on the Roman authorities and to extract concessions from them. Some of the Saracens were now integrated into the Roman frontier defences as *foederati* and had 'kings' – and sometimes 'queens' – who owed their status to Roman sponsorship and who could intermarry with the Roman elite. At the same time, Christianity, mediated by the charismatic authority of Syrian desert hermits, was gaining ground among those Arabians who were in close contact with the Roman world but had already also become a means of expressing a cultural identity distinct from that emanating from Constantinople. Although contemporaneous source material is far less plentiful for the Iranian side of the Fertile Crescent, it appears that similar processes were also taking place there: the Nasrid allies of the Persian kings managed tribal alliances from their base at al-Hira, on the Euphrates.[29]

At the southern end of the Arabian Peninsula, where agrarian wealth had long supported powerful settled kingdoms, the political landscape was also changing. An inscription dated 409 of the Himyarite era (299 CE), describes how the Himyarite king mentioned in the Namara inscription, Shammar Yuhar'ish, had conquered the other South Arabian kingdoms, declaring himself, 'king of Saba and Dhu Raydan [that is, of Himyar] and of Hadramawt

---

[28] On Mawia's revolt, see Glen W. Bowersock, 'Mavia, Queen of the Saracens', in Werner Eck et al. (eds), *Studien zur antiken Sozialgeschichte. Festschrift Friedrich Vittinghoff* (Vienna, 1980), 477–95; Shahid, *Byzantium and the Arabs in the Fourth Century*, 138–202, 532–44.

[29] On the early Nasrids, see Greg Fisher, *Between Empires: Arabs, Romans, and Sasanians in Late Antiquity* (Oxford, 2011), 64–9.

and Yamanat'.³⁰ Like Rome and Iran in the north, Himyar's expansion had also entailed the need to secure its desert frontier. Epigraphic South Arabian inscriptions indicate ongoing relations between the Himyarite kings and the southern tribal grouping of Kinda who controlled the oasis emporium of Qaryat al-Faw, among other centres. By the mid-fifth century, the Hujrid branch of Kinda led a Central Arabian federation of tribes, backed by Himyarite support – a South Arabian manifestation of the relationship between a settled state and a nomadic tribal elite.³¹

As in the north, religion in South Arabia was inextricably linked to politics. The Roman church historian Philostorgius (*fl. c.* 430) describes the mission of one Theophilus the Indian, despatched to South Arabia and Aksum (Ethiopia) by the emperor Constantius (r. 337–61).³² However, in *c.* 380 the Himyarite kings adopted not Christianity but a form of Judaism. No doubt the decision was in large part political, driven by the desire to retain autonomy from the neighbouring East African Christian kingdom of Aksum. Himyar's adoption of Judaism also led to its further diffusion within the Arabian Peninsula. Judaism had probably first arrived with Jewish exiles from Syria in the wake of the Roman suppression of the Jewish revolt in the second century CE, but it was now linked to the prestige of the Himyarite kings and their Hujrid allies in a form that has been called 'Judaeo-monotheism'.³³ Hence, in the south, as in the north, by the fifth century CE, Judaic and Christian monotheisms were inextricably entangled with political identities. Then, in the sixth century, relations between Rome and Iran deteriorated, triggering economic, demographic and social changes that were exacerbated by sudden changes in the climate and a prolonged pandemic. The northern and southern Arabian political formations collapsed, creating the space for new religious and political identities and alliances on the Peninsula and its northern peripheries.

---

³⁰ Robert G. Hoyland, *Arabia and the Arabs: From the Bronze Age to the Coming of Islam* (London and New York, 2001), 47. Cf. Christian Julien Robin, 'Himyar, Aksum, and Arabia Deserta in Late Antiquity: The Epigraphic Evidence', in Greg Fisher (ed.), *Arabs and Empires before Islam* (Oxford, 2015), 127.

³¹ Christian Robin, 'Le royaume hujride, dit «royaume de Kinda», entre Himyar et Byzance', *Comptes-rendus des séances de l'Académie des Inscriptions et Belles-Lettres* 140 (1996), 665–714; Robin, 'Himyar, Aksum, and *Arabia Deserta*', 137–45.

³² Photius, *Epitome of the Ecclesiastical History of Philostorgius*, tr. Edward Walford (Oxford, 1855), Book 3.4–6.

³³ Christian Robin, 'Ḥimyar et Israël', *Comptes-rendus des séances de l'Académie des Inscriptions et Belles-Lettres* 148 (2004), 831–908; Robin, 'Himyar, Aksum, and *Arabia Deserta*', 129–37.

2

The Seventh-century 'World Crisis'[1]

At the beginning of the sixth century, the Eastern Roman emperor, more confident of his security on his northern frontiers, began behaving in a more belligerent fashion towards his counterpart in Sasanian Iran. Violent conflict began in 502 and escalated during the rest of the century. Slow-moving siege warfare in the Fertile Crescent alternated with truces, while proxy conflicts continued at each end of the frontier. These hostilities drew both powers deeper into the Arabia Peninsula, with three important consequences. The first was the continued expansion of the Arabian federations in the north of the Peninsula, on the empires' desert frontiers. The second was further heightening of the political importance of religion, with various forms of Christianity and Judaism being markers of identity and political affiliation. Third, escalating conflict between the two powers led, at the end of the century, to the collapse of the northern federations and contributed to the weakening of Himyar. These events were the context for the expansion of the influence of West Arabian groups and the formation in the early seventh century of a new religious and political community under the leadership of the Prophet Muhammad.

Arabia, Rome and Iran in the Sixth Century

In the sixth century, the Romans replaced a balance of alliances on their Syrian Desert frontier with the sponsorship one ruling clan, the Jafnids, and their allies, known collectively as the Banu Ghassan, or 'Ghassanids'. This change in Roman policy was probably a response to the military effectiveness of the Sasanians' alliance with the Nasrid kings of al-Hira, in Iraq. In about 530, Emperor Justinian (r. 527–65) promoted the Jafnid al-Harith b. Jabala to 'the dignity of a king', in the sense of a local ruler, acknowledged by the Romans. Papyrus documents from Petra, in modern Jordan, show that members of the Jafnid elite were significant figures on the Roman frontier, called upon to

---

[1] The phrase is from *WtaWC*. See above, Introduction, n. 21.

arbitrate in local disputes.² Greek inscriptions show that the Jafnids participated in the wider political culture of the Roman Empire while asserting their own religious and cultural autonomy. For example, al-Harith's son's construction of a martyrium – a shrine for the relics of a Christian saint – at al-Burj, east of Damascus, is commemorated using formal epithets for high-ranking Roman officials. However, while the Greek of the Eastern Roman Empire remained the predominant language of epigraphy in the province of Arabia, there are a few instances of the Arabic language being used, in a distinctive new Arabic script, in short inscriptions on rocks that often amount to graffiti.

Moreover, Greek and Arabic are combined in one formal inscription, at Harran, also in southern Syria (Figure 2.1). Sharahil b. Zalim, who is otherwise unknown, dedicated a martyrium there in 568, recording the event in a carefully executed letters.

> [Greek text] Asaraël, son of Talemos, the phylarch founded this martyrion of St John in the first year of the indiction in year 463 (568 CE). May the writer be remembered. ☩

> [Arabic text] I, Sharahil son of Zalim, built this martyrion [in] the year 463, after the rebellion of Khaybar by one year.³

This occasional use of Arabic language and script – though rare – is notable because it is a break with the customary practice of inscribing public texts in Greek. Furthermore, the Arabic part of the Harran inscription (but not the Greek), also includes the dating 'after the rebellion [or destruction?] of Khaybar by one year', suggesting an Arabic-speaking constituency, to whom a conflict at a small oasis in Central Arabia, hundreds of kilometres to the south-west – and beyond the direct control of the Roman Empire – was a significant event against which other dates might be indexed.⁴ Both the language and this detail suggest a strong degree of cultural and political agency on the part of the Jafnids, who were composing texts that asserted a local identity, distinct from that expressed in the Greek lingua franca of the empire.⁵

---

² On the documents, see Zbigniew T. Fiema, 'The Byzantine Military in the Petra Papyri – a Summary', in Ariel S. Lewin and Pietrina Pellegrini (eds), *The Late Roman Army in the Near East from Diocletian to the Arab Conquest* (Oxford 2007), 313–19. Quotation from Procopius, *History of the Wars*, ed. and tr. H. B. Dewing (Cambridge, MA, 1914–28), Book 1.17.
³ Fisher et al., 'Arabs and Christianity', 349–50.
⁴ Fiema et al., '*Provincia Arabia*', 414–15.
⁵ See, for example, Robert G. Hoyland, 'Late Roman Provincia Arabia, Monophysite Monks and Arab Tribes: A Problem of Centre and Periphery', *Semitica et Classica* 2 (2009), 132–3.

Figure 2.1 The Harran inscription, 568 CE. Courtesy of Christian Robin.

So too do later versions of Arabic praise poems that were said to have been performed at their courts.[6]

The distinctive identity of the Jafnids was not just linguistic and cultural, it was also religious. This was the second consequence of the conflict between the great powers – a heightened salience for Judaism and Christianity as expressions of political identity. By the sixth century, the Chalcedonian form of Christianity tended to be propounded by the Constantinopolitan elite. The label Chalcedonian derives from the Council of Chalcedon, convened on the Asian shore of the Bosphorus by Emperor Marcian in 451 CE. The definition of the Trinity arrived at there remains in use by Roman Catholic, Greek and Russian Orthodox, and Protestant churches today. However, many long-standing Christian communities in Africa, the Middle East and Asia did not accept the precise language in which the Council had defined Jesus' status as both man and God. Versions of this miaphysite position, which emphasised the indissoluble unity of Christ's divine and human nature, held sway in Aksum (Ethiopia) and much of Roman Egypt and Syria. In the Sasanian lands and points east, the 'Church of the East' held to a standpoint which, like Chalcedonianism, was dyophysite, asserting greater distinction between Christ's divine and human natures, but remaining separate from Chalcedonian Christianity. These doctrines are maintained by many African, Middle Eastern and Asian churches today.[7]

Like Mawia in the fourth century, the Jafnid leaders of the sixth century affiliated themselves with a prevalent local variant of the imperial faith. For Mawia, this had been Nicene Christianity; for the Jafnids, this was now the miaphysitism prevalent in Roman Syria. The literary evidence from the miaphysite (also called 'Jacobite') church historian, John of Ephesus (*fl. c.* 580), who emphasises the role of the Jafnids in defending what he and they saw as orthodox religion, is supported by a document which lists the attendees

---

[6] Irfan Shahid, *Byzantium and the Arabs in the Sixth Century* (Washington, DC, 1995), II, i, 220–305, II, ii, 306–30.
[7] See further, below, Ch. 11, pp. 259–61, with references.

at a local church council convened at Bostra in 569 by al-Harith b. Jabala. Numerous churchmen from the Roman province of Arabia are named, as well as others from just beyond its borders. Hence the list appears to reflect Jafnid association with a miaphysite church organisation centred on the province of Arabia, with its capital at Bostra, but with some influence in other neighbouring provinces, too.[8] The Jafnids maintained their distance from their imperial patrons by cultivating a distinctive, local, religious identity.

At al-Hira, on the other side of the frontier between Rome and Iran, the Nasrids' relationship with Christianity was probably more fraught. Both literary evidence and some limited archaeological work indicate the presence of churches and monasteries. These were probably dyophysite, in line with the dominant form of Christianity in the Iranian world. However, it is not clear that the Nasrids themselves formally subscribed to Christianity; as Greg Fisher puts it, they may deliberately have created 'an indistinct and flexible picture of institutional religious affiliation', as they sought to triangulate mutually beneficial relations between the Sasanian elite, who adhered to the Zoroastrian religion of Iran, local religious cults, and the increasing prevalence of Christianity in the countryside around al-Hira and in the steppe to its south and west, which was dominated by the tribal groups collectively labelled as Bakr b. Wa'il.[9]

The success of Christianity placed the Sasanians at something of an ideological disadvantage against Rome. Christian communities were scattered across Iraq and Iran, as well as along the East Arabian Gulf coast. One Sasanian response was to seek to co-opt the non-Chalcedonian forms of the religion.[10] Another was to support Judaism as an expression of resistance to Christian Rome. There is some evidence, albeit deriving from much later sources, of Sasanian support for Jewish populations in the centre of the Peninsula, at the oases of Tayma', Khaybar and Yathrib (this latter later known as Medina).[11] However, the clearest example of Iranian support for Jewish allies against Rome's Christian supporters is the proxy conflict that took place in South Arabia in the middle decades of the century.

---

[8] Hoyland, 'Late Roman Provincia Arabia'; cf. Fergus Millar, 'Christian Monasticism in Roman Arabia at the Birth of Mahomet', *Semitica et Classica* 2 (2009), 97–115. 'Jacobite' is after Jacob Baradeus (d. 578), the miaphysite bishop of Antioch.

[9] Fisher, *Between Empires*, 64–70, quotation at 70; Isabel Toral-Niehoff, 'Late Antique Iran and the Arabs: The Case of al-Hira', *Journal of Persianate Studies* 6 (2013), 115–26; *EI*², 'Irak. iii. History (b) From the Arab Conquest to 1258' (D. Sourdel).

[10] Payne, *State of Mixture*, *passim* and esp. 133–74.

[11] M. J. Kister, 'Al-Hira: Some Notes on Its Relations with Arabia', *Arabica* 15 (1968), 143–69; Michael Lecker, 'The Levying of Taxes for the Sasanians in Pre-Islamic Medina', *JSAI* 27 (2002), 109–26.

In East Africa and South Arabia, Judaism and Christianity had also become the language of politics and identity. In *c*. 520, the East African kingdom of Aksum had invaded Himyar and installed a Christian king over Himyar's Jewish elite. The Himyarites rebelled almost immediately, replacing the Aksumites' appointment with their own monarch. In response, Aksum sponsored a second invasion, installing Abraha (r. *c*. 535–*c*. 565) as king of Himyar. Abraha and his sons appear to have presided over an era of political and military endeavour: inscriptions in Epigraphic South Arabian record Abraha's reception of embassies from Aksum, Rome, Iran, the Nasrids and the Jafnids, as well as various Central Arabian groups; they also record military expeditions against the same Central Arabians, notably in 552. Abraha presided over the Christianisation of the kingdom; a cathedral was constructed at Sanʿaʾ (usually the capital of modern Yemen) in about 550.[12]

Opposition to the rule of Abraha in South Arabia coalesced around the restoration of Judaism. In this, the Sasanians saw an opportunity to counter Roman diplomatic success in the region. In the early 570s, the Sasanian king is said to have sent an army of freed prisoners to South Arabia, who installed one Sayf ibn Dhi Yazʾan as a Jewish client king, perhaps alongside a Persian governor and troops. However, this era of Iranian dominance appears to have been a period of sudden and rapid decline in Himyarite power, exacerbated by drought and the spread of bubonic plague. Dated inscriptions in Epigraphic South Arabian ceased after 560; conflicts between the nomadic tribes of the interior and the South Arabians escalated; the great Maʾrib dam, upon which the agriculture of the heartlands of the state depended, collapsed in about 580 and was not rebuilt.[13]

The 'Late Antique Little Ice Age' and the 'Justinianic Plague'

The so-called 'Late Antique Little Ice Age' was one of the more significant recent fluctuations in the climate before the present era of unprecedented, disastrous anthropogenic global heating. It was caused by some large volcanic eruptions in either Iceland or North America, beginning in 536.

---

[12] Robin, 'Himyar, Aksum, and *Arabia Deserta*', 145–71.
[13] Iwona Gajda, 'L'Arabie du Sud unifiée par Himyar' and Mikhaïl B. Piotrovsky, 'Les causes d'une disparation', in Vogt Burkhard and Christian Robin (eds), *Yémen: au pays de la reine de Saba': exposition présentée à l'Institut du monde arabe du 25 octobre 1997 au 28 février 1998* (Paris, 1997), 190–2, 218; Hoyland, *Arabia and the Arabs*, 51–7; Yohannes Gebre Selassie, 'Plague as a Possible Factor for the Decline and Collapse of the Aksumite Empire: A New Interpretation', *ITYOPIS* 1 (2011), 36–61; Dominik Fleitmann et al., 'Droughts and Societal Change: The Environmental Context for the Emergence of Islam in Late Antique Arabia', *Science* 376 (2022), 1317–21.

The volcanic dust veil cooled the Northern Hemisphere suddenly, by an average of about 1° Celsius in less than a decade. Temperatures remained low until about 560 and the climate remained significantly cooler than it had been in antiquity until about 750. This cooling contributed to the conditions for an outbreak of bubonic plague (*yersinia pestis*), which probably began in East Africa in about 540 CE and continued for about two centuries.[14]

In 541–3 the plague spread quickly through the Mediterranean basin, East Africa, South Arabia and Iran, recurring at intervals of decades thereafter down to 750, and spreading into northern Europe and possibly into other regions, such as China. Sixth- and early seventh-century outbreaks in the Middle East and North Africa after 543 are recorded at Constantinople, Spain, North Africa, and various locations in Egypt, Syria, Mesopotamia and Iraq. The uneven literary evidence suggests that the plague became endemic in many densely populated areas, recurring regularly in regions such as Syria and Iraq, and frequently spreading beyond these reservoirs into less densely inhabited zones. Both long-established trade routes and, especially, the movement of people associated with the Roman–Persian wars contributed to its spread.[15]

The plague's impact was varied and localised, as with other outbreaks of diseases carried by fleas or other arthropods. Evagrius (*fl.* mid-to-late sixth century), who survived the plague at Antioch in northern Syria, but lost many family members, says:

> Whereas some cities were stricken to such an extent that they were completely emptied of inhabitants, there were parts where the misfortune touched more lightly and moved on ... there were places where it affected one part of the city but kept clear of the other parts, and often one could see in a city that was not diseased certain households that were comprehensively destroyed ... I lost many of my offspring and my wife and other relatives, and numerous estate dwellers ...[16]

---

[14] Ann Gibbons, 'Why 536 Was "the Worst Year to Be Alive"', *Science: News: Archaeology* 15 November 2018 <doi: 10.1126/science.aaw0632>; Peregrine Horden, 'Climate and Social Change at the Start of the Late Antique Little Ice Age', *The Holocene* 30 (2020), 1643–8.

[15] Lester K. Little (ed.), *The Plague and the End of Antiquity: The Pandemic of 541–750* (Cambridge, 2007); Peter Sarris, 'Viewpoint: New Approaches to the "Plague of Justinian"', *Past & Present* 254 (2022), 315–46.

[16] Evagrius, *The Ecclesiastical History of Evagrius Scholasticus*, tr. Michael Whitby (Liverpool, 2000), 4:29.

The account is corroborated by other sources for later outbreaks. They suggest a high mortality rate, concomitant with the much later medieval bubonic plague, known as the Black Death. While the overall impact of the first century of the Justinianic Plague remains difficult to assess, it seems reasonable to conclude that the prolonged pandemic would have stressed some populations and caused labour shortages in some places, while perhaps simultaneously easing pressure on some resources.[17] It is also possible that the plague contributed to a shift in the balance of population between the steppes of Arabia and the villages and cities of the settled regions to the north and south, and so might be seen as a contributory factor in the success of the Arabians' conquests.[18]

Himyar's decline is part of a wider pattern of destabilisation along the frontier between Rome and Iran in the last decades of the sixth century. Both powers sought to rearrange their relations with their North Arabian clients, wary of their respective reliance on a single, powerful client. At some point after 573 and 602 respectively, both the Jafnids and the Nasrids were deposed by their imperial patrons.[19]

Hence, at the end of the sixth century the Arabian Peninsula was in turmoil. In the north, the Jafnids and Nasrids had been deposed and their federations dispersed; in the south, the once-mighty kingdom of Himyar was in decline. In the competition between Rome and Iran on the Peninsula, Iran probably still had the upper hand. In East Arabia and Oman, the Sasanians sponsored client rulers; likewise, in Himyar they had backed the group who had ousted the new Aksumite rulers. There is also some evidence for Iranian agents operating in the centre and west of the Peninsula, although the collapse of the Nasrids' federation may have weakened Sasanian influence there.[20]

The 'World Crisis' of 610–30

In 589, a succession crisis in Sasanian Iran created an opening for a Roman military intervention on the side of a pretender to the Sasanian throne, who became the Sasanian King Khusro II Parvez (r. 591–628). Just over a decade

---

[17] *Theophilus*, 193, 231; Sarris, 'Viewpoint'.
[18] Anastasius of Sinai (d. *c.* 700) notes that the plague left West Arabia untouched: Simon Pierre, 'Can We Flee the Plague? A Theological, Moral and Practical Issue in the Early Islamicate World', *Journal of Islamic Ethics* 5 (2021), 11–13.
[19] *WtaWC*, 437–9. Cf. Fisher, *Between Empires*, 173–86, and Greg Fisher, 'Emperors, Politics, and the Plague: Rome and the Jafnids 570–585', in Denis Genequand and Christian Robin (eds), *Les Jafnides: des rois arabes au service de Byzance* (Paris, 2015), 223–8.
[20] See above, n. 11.

later, in 602, a coup at Constantinople gave Khusro II the opportunity he needed to restore his strategic position when he launched a series of invasions, claiming to avenge his deposed Roman patron.[21] Khusro II's campaigns met with gradual and then accelerating success.[22] By 609–10, the Sasanian armies had moved south from Armenia, reaching the Euphrates. At this point they were aided by a second coup in Constantinople, which installed the former governor of Roman Africa, Heraclius (r. 610–41), as the new emperor. Taking advantage of the confusion, a Sasanian naval raid was made on Constantinople itself, and armies pushed on into Roman Syria and Anatolia. In 614 Jerusalem, the holiest city in the Roman Empire, was sacked and the relic of the True Cross, on which Christ was believed to have been crucified, was looted. Two years later, in a clear statement of intent by Khusro, the members of a Roman embassy suing for peace were executed. Alexandria, the capital of Roman Egypt, fell in 619, and the whole province was under Sasanian control by 621. With Syria and Egypt secured, the Sasanians concentrated on Anatolia, co-ordinating their efforts with the Avar nomad federation in the Balkans.

The turning point came with the failure of a siege of Constantinople in 626. Surrounded by the Sasanian army and their Avar allies, the Roman capital was saved by its highly defensible location, its extensive fortifications, and – in the minds of its people at least – by the direct intervention of the city's heavenly patron, Mary, the Mother of God. Meanwhile, Heraclius had remained in the field rather than returning to the capital. He recruited Armenian support with emergency issues of silver coins, funded by the melting-down of church plate from across the empire, and by preaching a doctrine of the remission of all sins and immediate salvation through martyrdom on the battlefield. This message would have resonated among the Armenians, who already subscribed to a tradition of martial Christianity, in which warrior saints were venerated. Then, in the autumn of 627, Heraclius negotiated an alliance with the Western Turks, at Tiflis (in modern Georgia). While the Turks ravaged the Iranian Caucasus, Heraclius and his army headed south, into the lowlands of Iraq, defeating the Sasanian army at Nineveh. This defeat within reach of the Sasanian capital of Ctesiphon prompted the fall of Khusro II and then internecine conflict within the Sasanian elite. Heraclius was able to negotiate generous surrender terms, restoring the favourable borders from before 602.

At Easter of 629 or 630 Heraclius entered Jerusalem in ceremonial triumph, restoring the relic of the True Cross, looted by the Sasanians, to its place in the Church of the Holy Sepulchre, before returning to the capital of

---

[21] Sarris, *Empires of Faith*, 232–43.
[22] For this and what follows, see *WtaWC*, 436–60.

Constantinople. Heraclius was conscious of the eschatological resonances of his triumphal pilgrimage to Jerusalem: he was asserting the renewal of a victorious Christian kingdom after a war of annihilation against Iran, associating himself with the kingship of David and Solomon as it was remembered in the Bible, and as it prefigured the eternal kingship of Christ that he as emperor represented on Earth.[23]

The Formation of the Hijazi Polity

Both the material consequences of the war and its millenarian resonances reverberated far beyond the Roman Empire's political frontiers.[24] With hindsight, the most important of the groups affected were the inhabitants of the arid valley settlement of Mecca, in the region of western Arabia known as the Hijaz. At the time, however, it is unlikely that anyone in Rome or Iran would have predicted that this would be the case. The Quraysh of Mecca were only of importance within Arabia and perhaps not of great importance even there; the absence of both Quraysh and Mecca from contemporaneous sources suggests that the town lay below the horizons of literate elites in the settled empires to the north; indeed, the permanent settled population of Mecca was probably only in the hundreds.[25] Nonetheless, there is some evidence, deriving from the later Islamic tradition, that the decline of long-standing federations in the north and south of Arabia in the latter part of the sixth century had allowed the Qurashis to begin to build up their own position, founded on their control of sacred space and the associated pilgrimages and markets, as well as long-distance trading connections. The wealth and political influence acquired from these activities in turn further secured the network of alliances with other tribal groups in West Arabia upon which these activities depended.

According to these later traditions, Quraysh's commercial activities reached as far as Hadramawt in the south and Syria in the north, with gold, leather and textiles among the main items they traded. In South Arabia,

---

[23] *WtaWC*, 16–35, 48, 149–51, 167–9, 421–2; Constantin Zuckerman, 'Heraclius and the Return of the Holy Cross', in Constantin Zuckerman (ed.), *Travaux et Mémoires 17: Constructing the Seventh Century* (Paris, 2013), 197–218.

[24] On Iran's Christians, see John W. Watt, 'The Portrayal of Heraclius in Syriac Historical Sources', in B. H. Stolte (ed.), *The Reign of Heraclius (610–541): Crisis and Confrontation* (Leuven, Paris and Dudley, MA, 2002), 64–72. On Armenia, see R. W. Thomson and James Howard-Johnston, *The Armenian History Attributed to Sebeos* (Liverpool, 1999), I, 57–94, II, 193–231. For the Franks, see Steven H. Wander, 'The Cyprus Plates and the "Chronicle" of Fredegar', *DOP* 29 (1975), 346.

[25] Majied Robinson, 'The Population Size of Muhammad's Mecca and the Creation of the Quraysh', *Der Islam* 99 (2022), 10–37. Cf. W. Montgomery Watt, *Muhammad at Mecca* (Oxford, 1953), 170–9.

alliances were made with individuals from Kinda and with Hadramawtis. In the north, Abu Sufyan b. Harb (d. c. 653), who was a leading Qurashi from the Umayyad kin-group, is said to have owned land at an (unidentified) place called Qubbash, in al-Balqa', in modern Jordan, from where he traded with Roman Syria. There were also links with Roman Egypt and with the kingdom of Aksum, across the Red Sea.[26] At Mecca itself, Quraysh controlled markets and a shrine, the Ka'ba, with the associated *ḥaram* around it. The *ḥaram* was a taboo zone, where custom prohibited armed conflict at certain times of the year. Mecca's *ḥaram* was the focus of pilgrimages, with their attendant political and commercial benefits for the Qurashis. Thus, Quraysh were a local aristocracy whose association with their shrine allowed them to build alliances with the settled and pastoralist groups in the regions around Mecca. Most probably the *ḥaram* grew in significance in parallel with the growth of Meccan pilgrimage and trade. But both probably mattered more to the Qurashis and the pastoralist and settled groups in West Arabia than anyone else.[27]

By the early seventh century, there appear to have been three main groups within Quraysh, who collaborated and competed in the management of the shrine town and in their commercial enterprises. The wealthiest and most powerful group were probably led by Umayyad members of the larger clan of 'Abd Shams, while Makhzum and Hashim were also prominent tribes (see Chart 2.1). Property, alliances and claims about descent and sacred offices at the *ḥaram* were all important elements in the status of these groups. There were also close ties with the Banu Thaqif, of the neighbouring town of al-Ta'if, who were particularly close to the Meccan tribe of 'Abd Shams, including the Umayyads.[28]

---

[26] M. J. Kister, 'Some Reports Concerning Mecca from Jahiliyya to Islam', *JESHO* 15 (1972), 61–93 summarises some of the later Arabic tradition on some connections with South Arabia, Aksum ('Abyssinia'), Syria and Egypt. Ella Landau-Tasseron, 'Alliances among the Arabs', *Al-Qantara* 26 (2005), 162–3, mentions alliances with Daws and Hadramawt. See also Fred M. Donner, *The Early Islamic Conquests* (Princeton, 1981) [hereafter, *EIC*], 86 and 96, respectively. For Abu Sufyan's land and trading expeditions to Syria, see Ahmad b. Yahya al-Baladhuri, *Futuh al-Buldan*, ed. M. J. de Goeje (Leiden, 1866) [hereafter Baladhuri, *Futuh*], 129, and Ibn Hisham, Abu Muhammad 'Abd al-Malik, *Kitab Sirat Rasul Allah: Das Leben Muhammed's nach Muhammad Ibn Ishak*, ed. Ferdinand Wüstenfeld (Göttingen, 1859–60), 428.

[27] Patricia Crone *Meccan Trade and the Rise of Islam* (Cambridge, 1987); Paul Heck, '"Arabia without Spices": An Alternate Hypothesis', *JAOS* 123 (2003), 547–76; Patricia Crone, 'Quraysh and the Roman Army: Making Sense of the Meccan Leather Trade', *BSOAS* 70 (2007), 63–88; Robinson, 'Population Size'.

[28] Watt, *Muhammad at Mecca*, 4–11; *EI²*, 'Kuraysh' (W. M. Watt); Landau-Tasseron, 'Alliances'; Marsham, 'Kinship', 17, 21–6. On Central Asian 'house societies', see Sneath, *Headless State*, 111–19. On Thaqif, see Rasheed Hosein, 'Tribal Alliance Formations

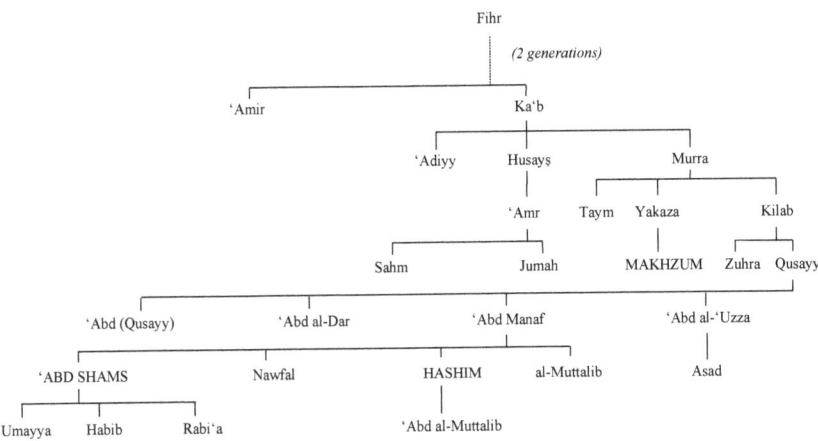

Chart 2.1 Simplified genealogy of Quraysh.

Among the Banu Hashim was a man now known as Muhammad (and occasionally Ahmad – both names may have originally been honorifics). Born at some point in the middle decades of the sixth century, Muhammad is said to have taken to retreating to the hills above Mecca in his late middle age.[29] There he is said to have experienced visions that prompted him to proclaim a message of warning about the impending Day of Judgement, which would be presided over by the one true God of Abraham, Moses and Jesus. This was probably in about 610, or a little later, just as news of the dramatic Iranian victories against Rome would have reached the Arabian interior. Although Muhammad gathered a small following at Mecca, many of the most influential figures there, including Abu Sufyan and most of his wider Umayyad clan, are said to have seen his message as threatening. This hostility from relatives and neighbours may have been what prompted some of Muhammad's associates to set out for the court of the Christian King of Aksum, across the Red Sea. A few years later, in 622, Muhammad himself and some of his other followers left for the oasis of Yathrib (later Medina), 300km to the north. This move is said to have been at the

and Power Structures in the Jahiliyah and Early Islamic Periods: Quraysh and Thaqif (530–750 CE)', PhD Dissertation, University of Chicago (2010); Marsham, 'Kinship'.

[29] On Muhammad's age, see Lawrence I. Conrad, 'Abraha and Muhammad: Some Observations apropos of Chronology and Literary Topoi in the Early Arabic Historical Tradition', *BSOAS* 50 (1987), 225–40. For a narrative account of Muhammad's life, see Watt, *Muhammad at Mecca* and W. Montgomery Watt, *Muhammad at Medina* (Oxford, 1956). On the sources and their interpretation, see Sean W. Anthony, *Muhammad and the Empires of Faith: The Making of the Prophet of Islam* (Oakland, 2020).

invitation of some of the Yathribis. There, Muhammad and his Meccan followers (who became known as the Muhajirun, or Emigrants) joined with elements of the two main Yathribi tribes (who became known as the Ansar, or Helpers) to form a new community under Muhammad's leadership. Muhammad articulated his role in religious terms, as the prophet of the one true God; membership of the new polity was predicated on recognition of this authority.

The later sources describe how Muhammad, the Muhajirun and the Ansar launched raids against Mecca from their new base at Yathrib/Medina. In 624, in response to the gathering military confrontation with Mecca, Muhammad is said to have preached martyrdom in battle as a direct route to Paradise – the same year that Heraclius proclaimed a similar doctrine as he recruited his armies in Armenia.[30] Conflict escalated, culminating in a failed Meccan siege of the oasis, conventionally dated to 627. At the same time as taking on Meccan hegemony in the wider region, Muhammad, the Muhajirun and the Ansar extended their grip on Yathrib/Medina itself. The tradition describes a series of conflicts with Jewish tribes, some of whom were expelled, and some killed, with the women and children being enslaved; other Yathribi tribal groups waited to see who emerged victorious, joining the federation as Muhammad's opponents were outmanoeuvred.

Having consolidated his control of Yathrib/Medina and having established alliances with neighbouring West Arabian pastoralist groups during the 620s, Muhammad negotiated the surrender of Mecca itself in 629–30. The Umayyad Abu Sufyan is said to have taken the lead among the Meccans in these negotiations; he had come to recognise that accommodation presented the best chance for survival. With the incorporation of Mecca into the new polity, Quraysh and their allies – who had been split by the message of Muhammad – were now reunited. A few of Muhammad's bitterest Meccan opponents are said to have left Mecca for neighbouring al-Ta'if, notably the Umayyad al-Hakam b. Abi l-As and his sons. Nonetheless, the surrender seems to have been negotiated as an agreement of mutual benefit to Muhammad and his allies and most of the old Meccan elite who had resisted them. This dramatic coup prompted many groups from across the Peninsula to join Muhammad's federation, during a year remembered as the 'year of delegations' (630–1). The political reach of Muhammad's new federation, established in a formerly marginal region of western Central Arabia, was beginning to resemble that of the former kings of Himyar at the height of their power.

Eighteen months later, in June 632, Muhammad died, and leadership passed to one of his closest associates, Abu Bakr. Abu Bakr (r. 632–4)

---

[30] *WtaWC*, 446–7.

consolidated the gains made by Muhammad, waging the 'Wars of Apostasy' (*ḥurūb al-ridda*), in which political control over Arabia was reasserted and extended. During these conflicts, some of the tribes of northern and Central Arabia began to follow their own prophets, while others simply refused to pay tribute to Medina, but after nearly two years of fighting these movements were subdued. Raids north into Roman Syria followed up on similar northern forays that had been made during the last years of the Prophet's life, and attacks are also said to have been made on Sasanian Iraq. By the end of the decade, under Abu Bakr's successor, 'Umar b. al-Khattab (r. 634–44), major victories would be won against both empires. However, there was no indication of such successes before 632: Muhammad appears to have died before his polity extended its military and political reach beyond the Arabian Peninsula.[31]

Such, in briefest outline, is the conventional account of Muhammad's prophetic career and his foundation of a new monotheist polity in the Hijaz, as it can be derived from the later Islamic tradition. Most of the tradition took shape in the eighth century and was compiled in its extant forms in the ninth. Despite the evidential problems presented by such late sources, some of the bare outline set out above is likely to be correct. Some of it is corroborated by seventh-century material from elsewhere in the Middle East; other elements appear to have become fixed features of the narrative at least by the early eighth century. Many of the genealogical details about the personalities involved are also probably accurate. Although genealogical memory in a tribal political context is flexible, to accommodate changing political allegiances, the identities of leading personalities in the formative era of Islam were often remembered quite precisely because they continued to have importance among subsequent generations and so could not easily be falsified.[32]

Besides the outline of events discernible in the later Islamic tradition, what is known of the wider Arabian milieu can be brought to bear on the question of the expansion of the Hijazi polity under Muhammad's leadership. So, too, can the text of the Qur'an. The Qur'an was certainly compiled in something very close to its current form before *c.* 700 and quite possibly by *c.* 650. Moreover, it appears to preserve much material that had been circulating within the Hijazi

---

[31] *EIC*, 75–220. Attempts to date some of the extra-Arabian conquests to Muhammad's lifetime are not convincing: Mehdy Shaddel, 'Periodisation and the *futūḥ*: Making Sense of Muhammad's Leadership of the Conquests in Non-Muslim Sources', *Arabica* 69 (2022), 96–145.

[32] On all this, with further references, see Anthony, *Muhammad*. On genealogy and prosopography, see Watt, *Muhammad at Mecca*, xiv–xv; *SoH*, 17; Majied Robinson, *Marriage in the Tribe of Muhammad: A Statistical Study of Early Arabic Genealogical Literature* (Berlin and Boston, 2019).

monotheist community during Muhammad's lifetime.³³ Hence, although many of the details remain obscure, the formation of a new West Arabian polity, the political identity of which was articulated in terms that resemble those found in late antique Jewish and Christian texts, fits well with the wider pattern of events in the Middle East. Viewed in long historical perspective, the rise of the Hijazi federation appears as part of a pattern deriving from the interaction of the settled world with the steppes; tribal federations were nothing new in Arabia. However, the Hijazi federation was also unique, in its geographical location and in its distinctive religious and cultural character.

Indeed, the formation of such a confederation centred upon the West Arabian highlands was unprecedented – the north and south of the Peninsula had historically been the loci of state formation. The shift was because Mecca was already benefiting from the turmoil generated by the decline of Himyar and the fall of the Jafnids and Nasrids; the Quraysh were now a minor power in West Arabia and had forged connections that reached into Roman Syria and Egypt and into South Arabia, as well as Aksumite East Africa. At Yathrib/Medina a crisis of leadership generated by the fall of the Nasrids, who had previously exercised some power over the oasis, may have contributed to Muhammad's gaining the support he needed to challenge established Meccan power structures. Six years later, and just as Mecca was increasingly isolated by Muhammad's new federation, Rome's crushing defeat of the Sasanian Empire appears to have pushed other former Sasanian allies in eastern and southern Arabia into diplomatic contact with Muhammad. The result was a growing West Arabian federation, centred on the settlements of Yathrib/Medina and Mecca, and led by settled tribespeople, but uniting Central and West Arabian nomadic pastoralist tribes, as well as groups from South Arabia and Oman and the Syrian Desert.³⁴

---

³³ For *c.* 650, see Motzki, 'Collection'; Nicolai Sinai, 'When Did the Consonantal Skeleton of the Quran Reach Closure?', *BSOAS* 77 (2014), 273–92, 509–21; Marijn van Putten, '"The Grace of God" as Evidence for a Written Uthmanic Archetype: The Importance of Shared Orthographic Idiosyncrasies', *BSOAS* 82 (2019), 271–88. For a more sceptical assessment dating the Qur'an's compilation to *c.* 700, see Stephen Shoemaker, *Creating the Qur'an: A Historical–Critical Study* (Oakland, 2022), with further references.

³⁴ *EIC*, 37–49; Jan Retsö, 'The Road to Yarmuk: The Arabs and the Fall of Roman Power in the Middle East', in L. Rydén and J. O. Rosenqvist (eds), *Aspects of Late Antiquity and Early Byzantium* (Istanbul, 1993), 31–41; Michael Lecker, 'Were Customs Dues Levied at the Time of the Prophet Muhammad?', *Al-Qantara* 22 (2001), 27–32. For dominion over Oman, see Abu Ja'far Muhammad b. Jarir al-Tabari, *Ta'rikh al-Rusul wa-l-Muluk*, ed. M. J. de Goeje et al. (Leiden 1879–1901) [hereafter, Tabari], I, 1560–1, 1600–1; Abu Ja'far Muhammad b. Jarir al-Tabari, *The History of al-Tabari*, ed. and tr. Ehsan Yar-Shater et al. (Albany, NY, 1985–2007) [hereafter, Tabari, *History*], VIII, 99 and n. 430 (Michael

The West Arabian Federation: A Covenant of the Faithful

Muhammad's articulation of his authority over this federation reflects his participation in the wider political culture of the wider Middle East. By the sixth century, Syriac miaphysite Christianity was closely associated with the Jafnids' federation in the north of the Peninsula. In Aksum and elsewhere in East Africa miaphysite Christianities were also prevalent. Meanwhile, Syriac dyophysite Christian communities were present in Iraq and along the Arabian Gulf coast and there were also Christians at Najran, in South Arabia.[35] In the Arabian interior, Judaic traditions predominated. This was largely because a distinctive form of Judaism had been articulated by the Himyarite monarchs since the early fourth century (briefly supplanted by Aksumite Christianity in the middle decades of the sixth) but also because of the long-standing presence of Jewish communities in the settlements of the west and north of the Peninsula.[36] More isolated groups in the Arabian interior followed polytheistic religious traditions, although these were being reshaped by the influence of monotheism.[37]

The 'Faithful' (*mu'minūn*, sing. *mu'min*) – was the term by which the first followers of Muhammad and their successors commonly identified themselves, that is, as a community of sincere faith with one another, as well as with God and His Prophet. *Mu'min* is analogous to the Greek *pistos* and the Syriac *mhaymna*, as they were used by late antique Christians who also thought of themselves in covenantal language as people of faith.[38] *Mu'min* is found in the Qur'an in more than 200 places, as well as in the earliest Arabic documentary

---

Fishbein). For the delegations from the Syrian Desert and from South Arabia, in c. 630–1, see Ibn Hisham, *Sira*, 946–57, 958–62.

[35] Stuart C. Munro-Hay, *Aksum: An African Civilisation of Late Antiquity* (Edinburgh, 1991), 202–13; Christopher Haas, 'Mountain Constantines: The Christianization of Aksum and Iberia', *JLA* 1 (2008), 101–26; Fisher et al., 'Arabs and Christianity', 281–3, 286–7, 313–50. On Najran, see Jack Tannous, 'Arabic as a Christian Language and Arabic as a Language of Christians', in A. S. Ibrahim (ed.), *Medieval Encounters: Arabic-speaking Christians and Islam* (Piscataway, NJ, 2022), 6–11, 19–21.

[36] *EI²*, 'Khaybar' (L. Vecca Vaglieri); Gordon D. Newby, *A History of the Jews of Arabia: From Ancient Times to their Eclipse under Islam* (Columbia, SC, 1988), 33–78; Michael Lecker, 'Judaism among Kinda and the Ridda of Kinda', *JAOS* 115 (1995), 635–50; Michael Lecker, *Muslims, Jews and Pagans: Studies on Early Islamic Medina* (Leiden, 1995); Robin, 'Himyar, Aksum and *Arabia Deserta*'.

[37] Nicolai Sinai, *Rain-giver, Bone-breaker, Score-settler: Allah in Pre-Quranic Poetry* (New Haven, 2019); Ahmad Al-Jallad, *The Religion and Rituals of the Nomads of Pre-Islamic Arabia: A Reconstruction based on the Safaitic Inscriptions* (Leiden, 2022).

[38] Jack Tannous, *The Making of the Medieval Middle East: Religion, Society, and Simple Believers* (Princeton, 2018), 87–8.

evidence for the conquest movement, which dates from the 640s onwards.[39] A closely related category, 'Muslims' (*muslimūn*, sing. *muslim*) – 'those who submit' or 'those who pledge themselves' – is found in the Qur'an in more than forty places.[40] However, aside from the Qur'an, 'Muslim' first appears in Arabic documentary evidence only about eighty years later, in an inscription of 725–6; it also becomes more prominent in the literary evidence for the early eighth century.[41]

Just as *muslim* had yet to supplant *mu'min* as the usual name for a member of the community Muhammad led, *islām* had most likely not yet gained currency as a label for a distinct religious tradition. In its embryonic form, very early 'Islam' probably resembled the earliest phases of many other religious movements, which have often positioned themselves within an existing tradition before a hardening of doctrinal and communitarian boundaries as mutual incompatibilities and political consequences become fully apparent.[42] Nonetheless, some aspects of a distinctive communal religious identity do seem to have taken shape during Muhammad's lifetime; in Late Antiquity, political and religious identities tended to be closely intertwined, as articulated in Quranic verses asserting that loyalty to God entailed military and political loyalty to Muhammad. Furthermore, the Quranic text appears to preserve some early elements of what later Islamic orthodoxies developed more fully – the idea of the restoration of true, uncorrupted Abrahamic (indeed, ultimately Adamic) monotheism, incorporating much distinctively West Arabian religious belief and practice.

One of the Qur'an's most salient features is the recurrent emphasis on God's Judgement. Its militant aspects – where martyrdom on the battlefield leads to salvation – likewise echo material found among Christian communities further to the north, notably in the contemporaneous speeches of

---

[39] Muhammad Fu'ad 'Abd al-Baqi, *Mu'jam al-Mufahras li-alfaz al-Qur'an al-Karim* (Cairo, 1945), s.v.; Lindstedt, '*Muhajirun*'.

[40] 'Abd al-Baqi, *Mu'jam*, s.v. On *muslim*, see Andrew Marsham, *Rituals of Islamic Monarchy: Accession and Succession in the First Muslim Empire* (Edinburgh, 2009) [hereafter, *RoIM*], 40–56; Nadia Jamil, *Ethics and Poetry in Sixth Century Arabia* (Cambridge, 2017), 24–9; Juan Cole, '*Paradosis* and Monotheism: A Late Antique Approach to the Meaning of *Islam* in the Quran', *BSOAS* 82 (2019), 405–25.

[41] Lindstedt, '*Muhajirun*', 67; Ilkka Lindstedt, 'Arabic Rock Inscriptions up to 750', in Andrew Marsham (ed.), *The Umayyad World* (London and New York, 2021), 429.

[42] For two contrasting interpretations, see Donner, *Muhammad*, and Aziz Al-Azmeh, *The Emergence of Islam in Late Antiquity: Allah and His People* (Cambridge, 2014). The former emphasises evidence for an ecumenism that could include Jews and Christians in the early community; the latter makes the case for the importance of a local Arabian deity, Allah, in a context where Judaism and Christianity had had less impact.

Heraclius.[43] Much else also recalls the customs and scriptural traditions of Jewish and Christian communities elsewhere in the Middle East. Such evidence as there is suggests that the Bible had yet to be translated into written Arabic; in an era when Judaism and Christianity were religions of the book written in others' languages, Muhammad was held to have brought an 'Arabic Liturgy' or 'Arabic Recitation' – *qur'ānan 'arabiyyan*, as the Qur'an itself puts it – to Arabic-speaking people. This suggests a degree of shared cultural and linguistic identity among the Arabian Faithful. Indeed, although the Qur'an often echoes late antique Jewish and Christian material, it is of course distinctive for being expressed in Arabic, for its many references to local, West Arabian beliefs and cultural practices, including animal sacrifice, and for its distinctive style, including many passages in 'rhymed prose' (*saj'*), which seems to have been typical of the speech of charismatic religious leaders in West Arabia. Crucially, Muhammad and his immediate successors retained the practice of pilgrimage to Mecca, which helped to sustain the authority of Quraysh, Mecca's guardians, in the new religio-political dispensation.[44]

---

[43] *Wta WC*, 445–8; Stephen J. Shoemaker, '"The Reign of God Has Come": Eschatology and Empire in Late Antiquity and Early Islam', *Arabica* 61 (2014), 514–58; Tommaso Tesei, 'Heraclius' War Propaganda and the Qur'an's Promise of Reward for Dying in Battle', *Studia Islamica* 114 (2019), 219–47. But cf. Adam J. Silverstein, 'Q 30: 2–5 in Near Eastern Context', *Der Islam* 97 (2020), 11–42.

[44] Emran Eqbal El-Badawi, *The Qur'an and the Aramaic Gospel Traditions* (London and New York, 2014); Neuwirth, *Qur'an*; Holger Zellentin, *The Qur'an's Reformation of Judaism and Christianity: Return to the Origins* (London and New York, 2019); Holger Zellentin, *Law beyond Israel: From the Bible to the Qur'an* (Oxford, 2022). See also Silverstein, 'Q 30: 2–5'. For a more positive assessment of possible Biblical material in pre-Islamic written Arabic, see Tannous, 'Arabic'. For 'an Arabic Qur'an' see Q. 12:2, Q. 13:37, Q. 20:113, Q. 39:28, Q. 41:3, Q. 42:7, Q. 43:3. On animal sacrifice, see Guy Stroumsa, *The End of Sacrifice: Religious Transformations in Late Antiquity* (Chicago, 2012); Al-Jallad, *Religion and Rituals*. For early non-Arabian attestations of the Arabians' beliefs and practices, see *SIAOSI*, 545–73 and *passim*. On *saj'*, see Qutbuddin, *Arabic Oration*, 101–2.

3

The 'Conquest Society' and the Defeat of Rome and Iran

Movements advocating social or political action in the name of religion or ideology are often founded by charismatic individuals. Where the movement survives, and the founder's charisma is gradually appropriated by institutional structures (or 'routinised'), claims about the memory of his or her example become crucial to the legitimation of those same institutions. The Qur'an and other seventh-century sources suggest that Muhammad's authority had depended above all upon his claim to direct access to God, that is, to 'prophecy' (*nubuwwa*) and to being a 'messenger' (*rasūl*). Such direct divine inspiration was always perceived as threatening by established religious authorities and so most (but not all) prophets in the late antique Roman and Sasanian world before Muhammad had come to be remembered merely as 'false prophets' or 'heretics'.[1] However, Muhammad's prophetic authority was perpetuated by members of the community of the Faithful who not only survived him but prospered. As a result, his legacy became the focus of intense political competition.

One consequence of Muhammad's prophetic authority was the importance of close association with him as the basis for a claim to lead the Faithful. Muhammad's first four successors are all said to have joined him in the 610s, before the emigration to Yathrib/Medina, and they were all related to him by marriage – the first two as fathers-in-law, and their successors as sons-in-law.[2] However, there is no evidence for prophecy being attributed to any of them in the same way that it had been for Muhammad.[3] This suggests that some aspects

---

[1] Guy Stroumsa, *The Making of the Abrahamic Religions in Late Antiquity* (Oxford, 2015), 59–69. An important exception is Mani (d. c. 274 or 277), see further below, Ch. 11, pp. 282–3.
[2] Abu Bakr and 'Umar were the fathers of 'A'isha and Hafsa, respectively: Tabari, I, 1767–71. 'Uthman married two of the Prophet's daughters, Ruqayya and Umm Kulthum, while 'Ali married another, Fatima: Tabari, I, 3055–6, 3470.
[3] The epithet 'al-Faruq', associated with Muhammad's second successor, 'Umar b. al-Khattab, may be a vestige of early charismatic authority: Suliman Bashear, 'The Title "Faruq" and Its Association with 'Umar I', *Studia Islamica* 72 (1990), 47–70. Another rare and late

of the process of 'routinising' Muhammad's prophetic authority were widely accepted by the first leaders of the Faithful.[4] God did not speak directly to leaders after Muhammad, but they did retain authority as military commanders, as judges of disputes and as moral exemplars. This 'routinisation' was probably bound up with the Meccans' determination to retain control of Muhammad's movement after his death – prophecy is an inherently destabilising force.

Besides the legacy of the charismatic authority of Muhammad himself, three further features of the early political history of his movement stand out. The first is the dynamic of military and political expansion upon which the unity of the wider federation depended. The second and third points are noted above: the political power of the Meccan relatives of Muhammad – the Quraysh – was dominant from the outset and Muhammad's legacy was politically central. Although many of the leading figures in the conquests appear to have owed their position to their pre-existing political power at Mecca, others were long-standing associates of Muhammad or were his close relatives. Moreover, even those with pre-existing power and status had to reframe their claims to authority with reference to Muhammad's monotheist mission. Shared political interests facilitated competitive collaboration among the leading figures from Mecca, where continued Meccan power depended upon tribal alliances funded by political and military expansion.

The Conquests and their Meccan Leadership

Loyalty to the expanding federation had growing material benefits for those who served it, while resistance was increasingly dangerous. The armed force for the campaigns depended initially upon the peoples of the Arabian Peninsula, secured through the spoils of conquest and through payments from revenues collected from the conquered regions. A language of conquest, migration and settlement is prominent in the unique documentary evidence of the Egyptian papyri and in the text of the Qur'an. The papyri include receipts for payments in kind made to the Arabian armies in the 640s. These texts reflect the importance of 'emigration' – using the Greek *magaritai*, which echoes the Arabic *muhājirūn*, 'emigrants'.[5] In the Qur'an, these and related terms usually appear in association with the category of 'the Faithful' (*al-mu'minīn*) and 'faith' (*imān*) and are associated at Q. 4:100 with 'God's path' (*sabīl Allāh*) in

---

exception is a fifteenth-century Ibadi text: Josef van Ess, *Theology and Society in the Second and Third Centuries of the Hijra: A History of Religious Thought in Early Islam*, tr. John O'Kane and Gwendolin Goldbloom (Leiden, 2017–20), I, 5.

[4] For prophets among other Arabian tribes, defeated by the Medinans, see M. J. Kister, 'The Struggle against Musaylima and the Conquest of Yamama', *JSAI* 27 (2002), 1–56.

[5] See further, Box Text, below, pp. 72–5. For *muhājirūn*, see Lindstedt, 'Muhajirun.'

the sense of military service. Hence, emigration is also linked to the 'pledged loyalty' (*bay'a*) and 'covenant' (*'ahd*) that bound soldiers to their commander. 'Emigrants' also appears in the later literary texts, as a term for those who moved to the new urban centres of the community – to Yathrib/Medina in the time of Muhammad, and then to the garrison camps (*amṣār*, sing. *miṣr*), in the time of the conquests. Thus, this third label for the followers of Muhammad emphasises their obligation to migrate to a community of the faithful, often in the context of the obligation to participate in divinely sanctioned warfare.[6]

The importance of the Meccan Quraysh is notable: despite the traditions that describe many of Quraysh initially opposing Muhammad, once their town was incorporated into the federation in 630, many of the same Meccans came to hold leading positions within it. For example, Abu Sufyan b. Harb and 'Ikrima b. Abi l-Hakam, who were leading members of, respectively, the 'Abd Shams and Makhzum clans of Quraysh and are said to have once been among Muhammad's most prominent antagonists, held governorships in Najran, in South Arabia, and over the tribe of Hawazin, in the Hijaz.[7] Meanwhile, the Ka'ba and its environs were secured as a sacred enclave (*ḥaram*), and as sites for pilgrimage rituals.[8] The nearby settlement of al-Ta'if surrendered shortly afterwards. Again, most of its tribe of Thaqif, many of whom had been allied with members of the 'Abd Shams branch of Quraysh, joined the new polity on favourable terms. While the later sources say that their idol to the female deity Allat was destroyed, the Ta'ifis' pastures were said to have been secured as a protected enclave, or *ḥimā*'.[9]

Many of the commanders sent out to reassert and extend the influence of the Hijaz in the wake of Muhammad's death were also drawn from among the later Meccan converts and their allies. Perhaps the most famous is Khalid b. al-Walid (d. 642), from the clan of Makhzum, who led campaigns against the tenacious opposition of the Banu Hanifa in Central Arabia, but there are numerous other examples of Qurashi commanders playing a leading role in the consolidation of the Medinans' political authority. Others were not Qurashi but are said to have been their allies or associates: Shurahbil b. Hasana, who fought alongside Khalid b. al-Walid, was from the South Arabian tribe of Kinda, but had lived in Mecca as an ally of the Qurashi Banu Zuhra; al-'Ala'

---

[6] 'Abd al-Baqi, *Mu'jam*, s.vv.; Patricia Crone, 'The First-century Concept of *Higra*', *Arabica* 41 (1994), 352–87; *RoIM*, 96–110.
[7] Watt, *Muhammad at Medina*, 75.
[8] *WtaWC*, 409–14, where it is suggested that the importance of Mecca was a result of the negotiating position of the Meccan Quraysh.
[9] *EI*², 'al-Ta'if' (M. Lecker); Hosein, 'Tribal Alliance', 158–9, 228–36.

b. al-Hadrami, from Hadramawt, in southern Arabia, who fought in Bahrayn (East Arabia), was an ally of the Umayyad branch of 'Abd Shams.[10]

Despite the incorporation of so many powerful Meccans and their allies into the new Hijazi polity, those who had joined Muhammad before Mecca's surrender retained prestige and influence: both Abu Bakr and his successor, 'Umar b. al-Khattab, were fathers-in-law of Muhammad who had emigrated with him from Mecca to Yathrib/Medina, and both were from relatively minor branches of Quraysh – that is, their authority appears to have depended primarily upon their position within the new monotheist group and not upon pre-existing status. That said, it is notable that no members of the Ansar – the Yathribi/Medinan hosts of the Meccan Emigrants – ever held overall leadership of the Faithful. Kinship with the Prophet and membership of the Meccan clans associated with the *haram* carried political weight; very probably, the large cohort of late converts among the Meccan contingent of the Faithful, who had been won over only by the unopposable success of Muhammad, were also keen to have one of their own lead the new federation.[11]

The Campaigns in Syria, Iraq and Egypt

Probably, there was not a highly centralised command structure, but rather competitive collaboration within the relatively small group of leading Meccans and their allies. Campaigns in 633 and early 634 appear to have been directed at bringing the pastoralist, Arabic-speaking, somewhat Christianised, populations of the Syrian Desert and southern and western Sasanian Iraq into allegiance to Yathrib/Medina. The new federation's reputation for success no doubt went before it, making it easier to begin to reconfigure alliances in these regions its favour; furthermore, the Quraysh are said to have had long-standing connections with some of these tribal groups. According to some accounts, the first major urban centres in the north to fall to the armies of the Faithful were the capital of the Roman province of Arabia, Bostra (Ar. Busra), and the former Nasrid capital in Sasanian Iraq, al-Hira. The leading commander in the Syrian campaigns was the Umayyad Yazid b. Abi Sufyan, accompanied by both his brother Mu'awiya and his father, Abu Sufyan. The Umayyads' leadership of the campaigns in Roman Syria probably reflects their existing connections with the region. At some point Yazid was joined by the Meccan early convert Abu 'Ubayda b. al-Jarrah.[12]

---

[10] *EIC*, 86–7, 110–11; *EI²*, 'Khalid b. al-Walid' (P. Crone); 'al-Walid b. 'Ukba' (C. E. Bosworth).
[11] For a detailed assessment of the traditions, see Wilferd Madelung, *The Succession to Muhammad: A Study of the Early Caliphate* (Cambridge, 1997).
[12] *EIC*, 112–19, 129, 146–8, 179–80; Madelung, *Succession*, 45–6; *EI²*, 'Kuda'a' (M. J. Kister). On Umayyad connections to Syria, see above, Ch. 2, pp. 55–6.

In August 634 Muhammad's first successor, Abu Bakr, died. Dynastic succession within a patrilineal group appears to have been out of the question, presumably because of the strength of the positions of Muhammad's closest associates. Instead, another father-in-law of Muhammad, 'Umar b. al-Khattab, took up the leadership. 'Umar's accession does not seem to have interrupted the advance into Roman Syria. Rather, expansion accelerated and became a campaign of direct confrontation with Roman imperial authority. Jerusalem, which probably held great symbolic importance for the Arabians, as for the Romans, fell in about 635. Arabian forces then advanced into the Golan Heights and on to Damascus, capturing it and the other major urban centres of the province of Phoenice Libanensis, including Heliopolis (Ar. Ba'albak) and Emesa (Ar. Hims) in the mid-630s.[13] In these conflicts, Quraysh, and southern and eastern Arabian tribes are named among the Arabian armies, together with some groups from northern Arabia and the Syrian Desert, including Lakhm and Quda'a. However, many other pastoralist groups, including some from the Ghassanid federation that the Jafnids had led, allied with the Romans.[14]

The Romans responded to the Arabians' successes with a campaign to reassert their control. A handwritten note, inscribed in the margin of a seventh-century Syriac gospel book, which is now in the British Library, records the witness of an observer at the time – most probably a local monk or priest:

> And at the turn of the year the Romans came; on the twentieth of August in the year nine hundred and forty-seven [636 CE] there gathered in Gabitha ... the Romans and a great many people were killed of the Romans, some fifty thousand ...[15]

The anonymous monk was right to think that he was witnessing an event worth noting down. A Roman army, comprising elite troops from Asia Minor and Armenia, as well as those local Syrian frontier troops still loyal to Constantinople, had marched south, retaking the three major cities that had just fallen to the Arabians. As the monk describes, the Arabians intercepted the Romans in August 636 at Yarmuk, near Gabitha, in the hills east of Lake Tiberias. The prolonged engagement, said in many accounts to have lasted six

---

[13] *EIC*, 146; *WtaWC*, 465–7. The Islamic tradition, which dates Jerusalem's fall a few years later, is probably misleading on this point: *WtaWC*, 380–1, with further references.

[14] *EIC*, 147–8, 356–60.

[15] Andrew Palmer et al., *The Seventh Century in the West Syrian Chronicles* (Liverpool, 1993), 3; Michael Philip Penn, 'Monks, Manuscripts, and Muslims: Syriac Textual Changes in Reaction to the Rise of Islam', *Hugoye: Journal of Syriac Studies* 12 (2009), 240.

days, ended in the rout of the Roman army. Now almost totally unobstructed, the Arabians fanned out across the rest of Syria.[16]

The occupation of southern and central Sasanian Iraq appears to have been complete before 642. The Arabians took advantage of chaos and unrest in Sasanian lands after their defeat by the Romans. Nonetheless, there were setbacks. Following the capture of al-Hira, the Faithful and their Arabian allies suffered defeat at the 'Battle of the Bridge'. This is usually dated to 634 or 635, but may in fact have taken place as late as 637.[17] 'Umar is then said to have appointed a new commander, Sa'd b. Abi Waqqas al-Zuhri.[18] Sa'd met the main Sasanian field army at al-Qadisiyya, near al-Hira, and won the day; the Sasanian capital, Ctesiphon (Ar. al-Mada'in) fell soon afterwards. The Sasanians regrouped at Jalula, west of the Zagros mountains, only to be defeated again. Meanwhile, other West Arabian commanders took the cities of southern Iraq. From there they headed east, into the highlands of Ahwaz (modern south-west Iran).[19]

The surrender of the cities of Syria and southern and central Iraq made the Arabians into a new ruling military class in their conquered territories. Central Iraq seems to have remained under Sa'd b. Abi Waqqas (g. *c.* 637–*c.* 647), while the senior commanders in southern Iraq were al-Mughira b. Shu'ba al-Thaqafi (g. *c.* 637–*c.* 638), from al-Ta'if, and then the South Arabian Abu Musa al-Ash'ari (g. *c.* 638–*c.* 650).[20] In Syria, an outbreak of plague in 639 killed both Yazid b. Abi Sufyan and Abu 'Ubayda, bringing two new men to power, Mu'awiya b. Abi Sufyan and 'Umayr b. Sa'd al-Ansari. Mu'awiya had come to Syria as the subordinate of his elder brother, Yazid. When Yazid died, Mu'awiya seems to have taken over the southern and central parts of Syria, including Damascus and Jerusalem.[21] The Medinan 'Umayr, newly despatched to the region, seems to have taken responsibility for Hims/Emesa and the northern frontier with Rome.[22] Meanwhile, the Qurashi 'Amr b. al-'As, who had also survived the plague, led some members of the Syrian federation

---

[16] *EIC*, 131–4, 140; *WtaWC*, 466–7.

[17] *EIC*, 129–31, 190–2.

[18] *EI²*, 'Sa'd b. Abi Wakkas' (G. Hawting). Sa'd is remembered as a Qurashi in the tradition, although his genealogy is unusually obscure, which suggests that he was not: Robinson, *Marriage*, 39–41.

[19] *EIC*, 202–17; *WtaWC*, 468.

[20] *EI²*, 'Sa'd b. Abi Wakkas' (G. R. Hawting); *EI²*, 'al-Mughira b. Shu'ba' (H. Lammens); *EI²*, 'al-Ash'ari, Abu Musa' (L. Vecca Vaglieri).

[21] Madelung, *Succession*, 61.

[22] Baladhuri, *Futuh*, 136–7; Tabari, I, 2866–7; cf. Khalifa b. Khayyat al-'Usfuri, *Ta'rikh Khalifa b. Khayyat*, ed. Mustafa Najib Fawwaz and Hikma Kashli Fawwaz (Beirut, 1995) [hereafter, Khalifa], 89.

of Qudaʿa, together with recent migrants from South Arabia, west, along the coast and into Roman Egypt, where he was joined by the Prophet's maternal cousin al-Zubayr b. al-ʿAwwam al-Asadi.[23]

These provincial commanders (*umarāʾ*, sing. *amīr*) acted with much autonomy. It would probably have been difficult for ʿUmar not to acknowledge Muʿawiya as his brother's replacement in southern and central Syria, and the sources suggest that ʿAmr acted independently in attacking Egypt.[24] Al-Mughira b. Shuʿba was deposed from the command of southern Iraq, and replaced by Abu Musa in *c.* 638, but perhaps only in response to criticism of him by the Iraqi settlers themselves.[25] ʿUmar does seem to have sought to distribute additional commands in order to limit the power of any one individual: the despatch of ʿUmayr and al-Zubayr to Syria and Egypt, respectively, was probably an attempt to counterbalance the power of Muʿawiya and ʿAmr.[26] ʿUmar is also credited with instigating institutional and administrative changes. There is clearly some basis for ʿUmar's reputation: the decade of conquests in the settled Roman and Sasanian Middle East over which he presided was critical for the future evolution of what now amounted to an embryonic empire. The most important development was the placing of garrison camps in the conquered territories, which became centres for the collection of taxes and their distribution as payments to the emigrant soldiers.[27]

These 'outposts' or 'forward bases' (*amṣār*, sing. *miṣr*) included Basra, which was established near the Sasanian Gulf port of Ubulla, and Kufa, just to the north of the old Nasrid centre of al-Hira.[28] Both camps are said to have been founded at some point between 636 and 639. In Egypt, the camp outside Roman Babil/Babylon, established by ʿAmr in about 643, became the kernel of a similar outpost, named Fustat (Gk *fossaton*, 'camp'), which now lies within modern Cairo. These Iraqi and Egyptian camps continued the principle of *hijra* ('emigration'), which is said to have been established by the Prophet himself: tribespeople were expected to make *hijra* to a *dār al-hijra* ('house', or 'place', of 'migration'), where they would settle, separated both from their old homelands and from the populations they now ruled, and so

---

[23] Madelung, *Succession*, 61–2.

[24] On Egypt, see Marek Jankowiak, 'P.Lond. I 113.10, the Exile of Patriarch Kyros of Alexandria, and the Arab Conquest of Egypt', in Phil Booth and Mary Whitby (eds), *Travaux et Mémoires 26: Mélanges James Howard-Johnston* (Paris, 2022), 287–314.

[25] *EI²*, 'Abu Musa al-Ashʿari (L. Veccia Vaglieri).

[26] Cf. Madelung, *Succession*, 60–2.

[27] Fred M. Donner, 'Centralized Authority and Military Autonomy in the Early Islamic Conquests', in Averil Cameron (ed.), *The Byzantine and Early Islamic Near East III: States, Resources and Armies* (Princeton, 1995), 355–7.

[28] On the early definition of *miṣr*, see *EI²*, 'Misr B.' (C. E. Bosworth).

with a stake in the continued success of the new polity. Many emigrants from Arabia remained outside the direct control of Quraysh and the Ansar, but the garrisons represented their coordinated effort to maintain political influence in the former lands of Rome and Iran.[29] Although there were small garrisons in Syria, the province was something of an exception to the pattern, perhaps because Muʿawiya recognised that his power depended upon the support of local Syrian tribal groups who were well established in the steppe and would not have accepted resettlement in new garrisons.[30]

Written registers (*dawāwīn*, sing. *dīwān*) of male members of the polity are said to have been created at the provincial garrisons, allowing for the management of regular stipends (*ʿaṭāʾ*) for the armies, drawn from the revenues of the conquered territories, which were also recorded in registers. A principle of 'precedence' (*sābiqa*) was said to have been the basis for the payment of those enrolled – early conversion and emigration being the basis for a claim to a larger payment. The later sources note various exceptions to this principle: powerful groups and individuals who came late to the conquests often received larger stipends, as did Roman and Sasanian elite troops who joined the conquerors. ʿUmar is also said to have insisted on the principle – building on established customs of war in the Middle East – that the conquerors allowed land to remain in the hands of those who surrendered without a fight, receiving their income as tax and tribute from the conquered.[31] Meanwhile, the position of leader of the Faithful may have begun to assume a more institutional identity. The later sources say that ʿUmar was the first to adopt 'Commander of the Faithful' (*amīr al-muʾminīn*) as a title. (The epithet 'caliph' (*khalīfa*), meaning 'deputy' or 'successor' of God or Muhammad respectively, seems only to

---

[29] On *hijra*, see Crone, 'First-century Concept'. On the date of the foundation of the *amṣār*, see *EIC*, 227, 229. On the name Fustat, see Jelle Bruning, *The Rise of a Capital: Al-Fustat and Its Hinterland, 18/639–132/750* (Leiden, 2018), 3 and n. 9. For some conquests outside Medinan control, see Robert G. Hoyland, *In God's Path: The Arab Conquests and the Creation of an Islamic Empire* (Oxford, 2015), 56–7.

[30] For garrisons in Syria, see Donald Whitcomb, 'Amsar in Syria? Syrian Cities after the Conquest', *ARAM* 6 (1994), 13–33.

[31] On the surrender agreements, see Milka Levy-Rubin, *Non-Muslims in the Early Islamic Empire: From Surrender to Coexistence* (Cambridge, 2011), 21–32. On the *dīwān*, see Marie Legendre, 'The Translation of the *Diwan* and the Making of the Marwanid "Language Reform": Secretarial Agency, Economic Incentives, and Regional Dynamics in the Umayyad State', in Antoine Borrut et al. (eds), *Navigating Language in the Early Islamic World: Multilingualism and Language Change in the First Centuries of Islam* (Turnhout, forthcoming).

have gained prominence a few decades later, in the specific political context of the end of the seventh century.[32])

While the later narratives about 'Umar's authority, the garrisons and the payment of the armies evidently simplify more complex and devolved processes, there is good evidence that they do reflect aspects of administrative developments from the time. In Egypt and Iraq, the conquerors were indeed concentrated in garrisons and there was not widespread settlement of the land. There are also documentary attestations for distinctive administrative practices, such as the use of a lunar calendar dated from Muhammad's migration from Mecca to Yathrib/Medina in 622, which 'Umar is said to have promulgated; such dates do indeed first occur in Arabic inscriptions and documents from the 640s.[33]

An Administrative Papyrus from the Conquest of Egypt, 642 CE

Before the introduction of paper made from pulped cloth in the middle of the eighth century, papyrus (made from reed and papyrus leaves) and parchment (made from sheepskin) were two of the main materials used for written documents in the Middle East. The arid Egyptian climate has preserved thousands of pieces of papyrus from the late Roman and early Islamic period. As functional pieces of writing they reflect life 'on the ground', as opposed to the later chronicles and other literary or religious texts, which were composed with a wider audience in mind. Their potential is only just beginning to be tapped, not least because of the significant difficulties posed by editing and interpreting them. Umayyad-era documents are also extant in much smaller numbers from Nessana, in the Negev, and Khirbet al-Mird, near the Dead Sea, and from Iran and western Central Asia.[34]

The example in Figure 3.1, below, was composed towards the end of April 643 in Greek and Arabic by two different scribes, John (Gk Yohannes) and Ibn Hadidu. The Greek material is indicated by italics in the translation.

The document is a dual-language receipt for goods handed over to the Arabian forces at Ihnas (Herakleopolis), about 100km south of Fustat (modern Cairo).

---

[32] Marsham, "'God's Caliph'"; *EI3*, 'Commander of the Faithful' (A. Marsham).
[33] Petra Sijpesteijn, *Shaping a Muslim State: The World of a Mid-eighth-century Egyptian Official* (Oxford, 2013) [hereafter, *SaMS*], 64, 65, 77–8.
[34] *SaMS*, 1–6.

In the name of God.
I, Abdellas, amir, to you, Christophoros and Theodorakios, pagarchs of Herakleopolis. I have taken over from you for the maintenance (probata) *of the Saracens being with me in Herakleopolis, 65 sheep, sixty-five only, as evidence thereof I have written this receipt for you. Written by me, Yohannes, notary and deacon, on the 30th of Pharmouthi of the first indiction [April 643].*

In the name of God, the Compassionate, the Merciful.
This is what 'Abd Allah b. Jabir and his companions have taken from the sheep of Ihnas. We have taken from the representative of Tudhuraq, the younger son of Abu Qir, and from the representative of Istafan, the elder son of Abu Qir, fifty of the sheep for slaughter and fifteen other sheep. He gave them for slaughter to his companions – his sailors and soldiers – in the month of Jumada al-awwal of the year twenty-two [March–April 643]. And Ibn Hadidu was the scribe.[35]

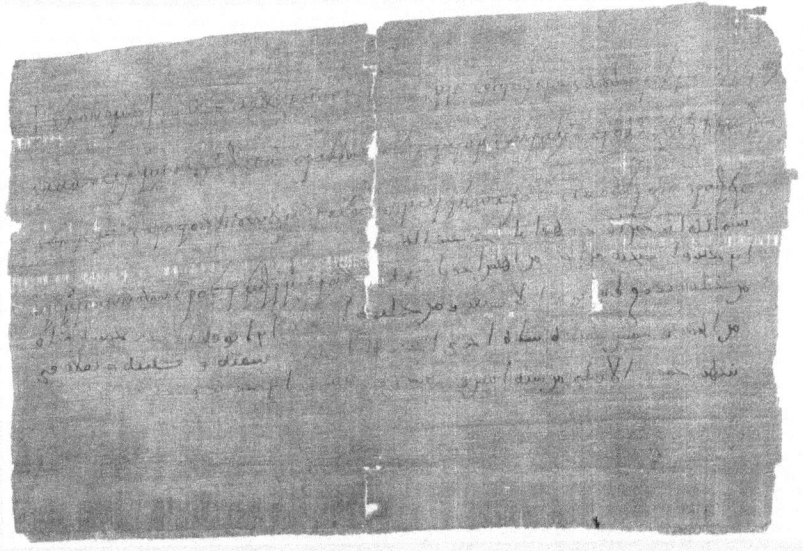

Figure 3.1 Receipt for sixty-five sheep, 25 April 643 CE. Recto from the Katalog der Papyrussammlung, Österreichische Nationalbibliothek, Inventory No. G 39726 Pap. 23cm × 36cm. © Österreichische Nationalbibliothek.

---

[35] Translation after Adolf Grohmann, *From the World of Arabic Papyri* (Cairo, 1952), 113–14; *SaMS*, 67–8.

The outside of the papyrus (*verso*, not in the photograph above) is marked with a description of the contents, in Greek:

Receipt regarding the sheep delivered to the Magaritai [Muhajirun] and others, moving upstream, in fulfilment of the public taxes.[36]

Herakleopolis was a sizeable late Roman settlement in the southern Fayyum, irrigated by a branch of the Nile. The pagarchy to which it gave its name was within the larger administrative region of Arcadia. (There were sixty pagarchies in Egypt divided between four larger administrative regions.) The receipt is issued to two pagarchs, Christopher and Theodorakios (transliterated as Istafan and Thudhuraq), which may reflect the division of the pagarchy immediately at the time of its conquest.[37] It records the transfer of sixty-five sheep to Arabian forces, led by one 'Abd Allah b. Jabir. The Arabian soldiers were travelling by boat, as is indicated by the mention of 'Abd Allah's sailors (*aṣḥāb sufunihi*), as well as his soldiers (*katā'ibihi*). That they were 'moving upstream' likely indicates that they were heading south after the capture of Babil in about 641 and Alexandria in later 641 or 642. It is one of several early papyri and other texts that record the Arabian armies living 'off the land', requisitioning food, horses and equipment.[38]

Besides the insights into the process of the conquest in the Fayyum, and relations between the local Egyptians and the Arabian forces, the document reveals much about administrative practice and language.[39] First, it shows that the Arabians brought with them Arabic-language scribal practices. Furthermore, it is among the earliest evidence for the Muslims' use of the lunar calendar counting years from the 'emigration', or *hijra*, of 622, which is said to have been commanded by 'Umar in 638.[40] It is also an early documentary attestation of the *basmala* – the formula, 'in the name of God, the Compassionate, the Merciful' (*bismillah al-rahmān al-rahīm*), with which the Arabian conquerors began most of their writings, and with which all but one of the *sūras* of the Qur'an begin. Such dedicatory formulae were ubiquitous in the late antique Middle East. A common Greek Christian equivalent opens the Greek portion of the text, 'in the name of

---

[36] Grohmann, *Arabic Papyri*, 114.
[37] *SaMS*, 139.
[38] Petra Sipesteijn, 'The Arab Conquest of Egypt and the Beginning of Muslim Rule', in Roger S. Bagnall (ed.), *Egypt in the Byzantine World, 300–700* (Cambridge, 2007), 440.
[39] See also *SaMS*, 66–8. On the conquest dates, see Bruning, *Rise*, 2–3.
[40] *SaMS*, 65. Cf. Mathieu Tillier and Naïm Vanthieghem, 'Recording Debts in Sufyanid Fustat: A Reexamination of the Procedures and Calendar in Use in the First/Seventh Century', in John Tolan (ed.), *Geneses: A Comparative Study of the Historiographies of the Rise of Christianity, Rabbinic Judaism and Islam* (London and New York, 2019), 148–88.

God' (*en onomati tou theou*).⁴¹ The spelling of the scribe's name, with a final *waw* ('u'), is an archaic feature, found in other early Arabic texts.⁴²

The text is also a record of linguistic change in Greek. The Arabic term *amīr* ('commander') is transliterated into Greek, rather than translated (later the Greek *symboulos* became a synonym for *amiras*). The Greek *probata* is used in a new way, not seen before the conquests, in describing the purpose of the sheep that are requisitioned. The Arabian conquerors themselves are described in two ways in Greek, as *sarakenoi* in document itself, and as *magaritai* on the label. The former term – 'Saracens' – had become a widespread term in Greek for Arabians during the fifth and sixth centuries and was now used of the conquerors; the latter, *magaritai*, was a transliteration of an Arabic term – *muhājirūn*, or 'emigrants' – which the conquerors brought with them and used of themselves, during the seventh and early eighth centuries (*mu'minūn*, 'faithful' being another).

The Egyptians' and Arabians' divergent scribal traditions are also in evidence: the Greek text is composed in the first person, as a declaration from the *amīr* 'Abd Allah to the pagarchs. In contrast, the Arabic begins as a declaration in the third person, 'This is what 'Abd Allah b. Jabir and his companions have taken ...', before switching to the first-person plural, 'We have taken ...', and then reverting to the third person again, 'He gave them for slaughter ...'. Naming customs also diverge, with the Arabic noting both names and patronyms (that is, the names of the fathers), and the Greek giving names and titles: *amīr*, pagarchs, notary and deacon.⁴³ The Greek refers to the pagarchy as Herakleopolis, in contrast to the Arabic scribe's use of the Coptic name, Ihnas. Furthermore, the two scribes record different information about the transaction itself: the Greek text simply records 'Abd Allah's acknowledgement that he has received sixty-five sheep, whereas the Arabic notes for what they were used and whom they fed, and that the sheep were handed over by the pagarchs' representatives. Whereas the divergences in form indicate two different scribal traditions, the differences in content suggest the functions of the two parts of the text: the former as proof of payment, the latter as a record of how the payment was used, and who made it.

---

⁴¹ On the *basmala*, see Andrew Marsham, 'The Pact (*amana*) Between Mu'awiya Ibn Abi Sufyan and 'Amr Ibn Al-'As (656 or 658 CE): "Documents" and the Islamic Historical Tradition', *JSS* 57 (2012), 76, with further references.

⁴² Ahmad Al-Jallad and Hythem Sidky, 'A Paleo-Arabic Inscription on a Route North of Ṭā'if', *Arabian Archaeology and Epigraphy: Early View* (2021), 7.

⁴³ *SaMS*, 67–8. For 'This is what ...' as an opening phrase in Arabic 'dispositive documents', see Marsham, 'Pact', 76–7, with references.

Such documents, together with the literary sources, attest to the formation of what amounted to a new empire, incorporating the Arabian Peninsula and the wealthy settled lands of Roman Egypt and the southern ends of the Roman and Iranian Fertile Crescent. In the process of the conquests, many of the Arabic-speaking tribespeople of the Syrian Desert and the Roman steppe frontier had been won over. However, the armies' senior commanders were mostly from the West Arabian region known as the Hijaz – and primarily from the Quraysh of Mecca, alongside some men from neighbouring al-Ta'if, from Yathrib/Medina, and from South Arabia. At lower levels, *ashrāf* – tribal notables from the groups from which the armies were assembled – held leadership positions.[44] Among the commanders, some of whom had been among Muhammad's closest associates, the monotheism preached by Muhammad was an important aspect of political culture. Meanwhile, the political unity of the wider federation of disparate Arabian groups depended upon continued military success, which furnished the wealth with which the leaders of the Faithful rewarded their armies.

In the conquered provinces of Rome and Iran, the migrants were a tiny minority – probably a few tens of thousands of migrant tribespeople among the millions inhabiting the wealthy cities and countryside of Syria, Iraq and Egypt. Many were garrisoned in the camps of Kufa, Basra and Fustat, although tribespeople continued to migrate into northern Iraq, and others 'abandoned their *hijra*' (*ta'arraba*), leaving the garrisons for an independent existence in the steppe zones of the Fertile Crescent.[45] Although most of the tribal names are attested for pre-conquest times, the composition of these groups was probably significantly altered by the conquests and settlements.[46] In Kufa, which was probably the largest and most diverse settlement at this point, a slight majority of the settlers were from southern and eastern Arabian groups. In Basra, the dominant groups were from northern Arabia, alongside some south-easterners.[47] In Alexandria and Fustat, many of the soldiers were South

---

[44] *EIC*, 225; Michael G. Morony, *Iraq after the Muslim Conquest* (Princeton, 1984) [hereafter, *IatMC*], 57–8.

[45] For the verb *ta'arraba*, see Clifford E. Bosworth, 'A Note on *Ta'arrub* in Early Islam', *JSS* 34 (1989), 355–62; *RoIM*, 97–8, 108–9; Webb, *Imagining the Arabs*, 122.

[46] Hugh Kennedy, 'From Oral Tradition to Written Record in Arabic Genealogy', *Arabica* 44 (1997), 542; *EI3*, 'Azd' (P. Webb). But cf. Brian Ulrich, *Arabs in the Early Islamic Empire: Exploring al-Azd Tribal Identity* (Edinburgh, 2019), esp. 75–8.

[47] *EIC*, 215–20, 227–9. See also the comments of Yahya K. Blankinship, *The End of the Jihad State: The Reign of Hisham Ibn 'Abd al-Malik and the Collapse of the Umayyads* (Albany, 1994), 57–8.

Arabians, who had participated in the conquest of Syria before heading to Egypt; others were from the Syrian Desert.[48]

Syria was exceptional in that the migrants were a minority among their allies from the post-Roman Syrian pastoralists and did not settle in large new garrisons. As described in Chapters One and Two, Arabic-speaking, Christian, Romano-Syrian tribes had long lived alongside the settled populations of the towns and villages and had become somewhat integrated into the economic, political and religious life of Roman Syria. They now became the foundation of the military power of the new rulers of Syria and, at least initially, seem to have expressed their membership of the new elite through pledged loyalty and military service more than the adoption of new beliefs and practices. Thus, the old Roman desert frontier – formerly a remote space to be managed and policed on behalf of the imperial authorities – had now become the military centre of the new province. Indeed, the pastoralists of the southern and central Syrian Desert formed what was probably one of the largest populations of fighting men in the new empire. Furthermore, with Muʿawiya b. Abi Sufyan as its senior commander, Syria was unique in the conquered territories in being led by someone from among the leading clans of Quraysh, the Prophet's tribe.[49]

---

[48] A. R. Guest, 'The Foundation of Fustat and the *Khittah*s of That Town', *JRAS* (1907), 49–83; *EI*², 'Khawlan' (A. Grohmann and A. K. Irvine).

[49] Baladhuri, *Futuh*, 144–6, 181–3; Blankinship, *End of the Jihad*, 49–50; Ignacio Arce, 'Romans, Ghassanids and Umayyads. The Transformation of The *Limes Arabicus*: From Coercive and Deterrent Diplomacy towards Religious Proselytism and Political Clientelarism', in Guido Vannini and Michele Nuccioti (eds), *La Transgiordania nei secoli XII–XIII e le 'frontiere' del Mediterraneo medieval* (Oxford, 2012), 53–72. See further, below, Ch. 10, pp. 231–2 and 235–45.

4

The Emergence of the Umayyad Empire

As their respective commanders secured Syria, Iraq and Egypt in the 640s, forays were made into the wealthy Iranian centres of Sistan and Khurasan and into the Roman Mediterranean, Asia Minor and North Africa (see Map 4.1). In part because of the marine and mountain barriers that protected it, Roman Constantinople escaped the fate of Sasanian Ctesiphon. Whereas the Sasanian king was killed in 651, and the surviving royal family were driven across the Oxus river to seek refuge with the Hephthalites in Central Asia, geography favoured the Romans. Both the distance to Constantinople and the shelter of the Mediterranean Sea and Anatolian highlands gave the Romans, led by the young Constans II (r. 641–c. 668/9), time to organise an effective defence of what remained of Roman territory and fiscal resources.

The Romans were also saved by the deep divisions within the Arabian armies. Like most conquerors, the Arabian Faithful saw themselves as rightfully separate from the defeated, tax-paying peoples. This distinction was expressed in the Arabian Faithful's sense of themselves as especially favoured by God and their sense of their cultural difference, in customs and language, as well as in their specific economic rights to the wealth of the conquered lands. However, this sense of difference, whether expressed in religious, cultural or fiscal terms, did not in itself confer political unity. The Arabian conquerors, the migrants who followed behind them, and the pastoralists of the Syrian Desert who had joined them, often found themselves competing with one another for resources and power. In this competition, both existing kinship connections and new associations brought about by the conquests and migrations produced shifting factional interests.[1]

Furthermore, the Arabians' Hijazi leaders were not themselves united, and so divisions in the armies aligned with conflicts among their leaders over control of the empire and its resources. Among the Hijazis, contention focused

---

[1] On 'migration' (*hijra*) to the garrisons and pay, see Crone, 'First-Century Concept'. On factional interests, see Patricia Crone, 'Were the Qays and Yemen of the Umayyad Period Political Parties?', *Der Islam* 71 (1994), 1–57.

EMERGENCE OF THE UMAYYAD EMPIRE | 79

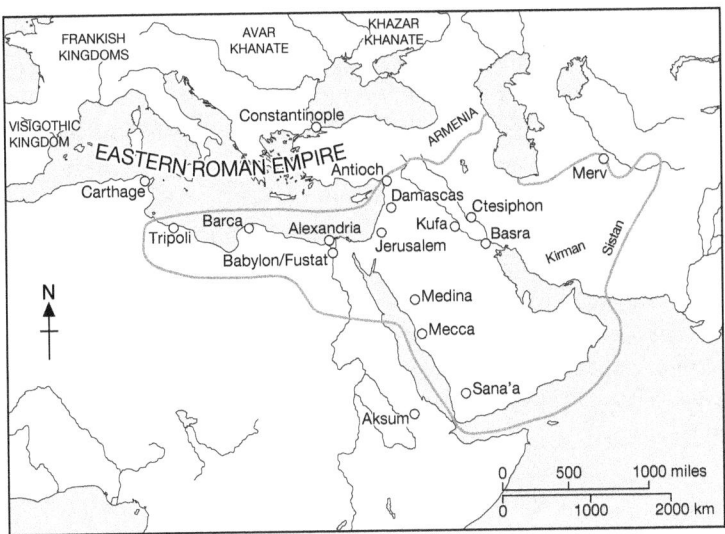

Map 4.1 The Arabian conquests at *c.* 650 CE. Based on Hugh Kennedy, 'Early Muslim Conquests', in *An Historical Atlas of Islam*, edited by Hugh Kennedy. Brill. Consulted online on 25 April 2020.

on whom among the Meccan grouping of Quraysh should lead the empire. Between 644 and 692 there were two particularly violent episodes. The first, in 656–61, was fought between men who were younger contemporaries of the Prophet Muhammad himself; the second, in 680–92 (also often given as 683–92) was fought between their sons and other close relatives. These wars are remembered in much of the later Arabic tradition as 'trials' or 'temptations' (dual, *fitnatān*, pl. *fitan*, sing. *fitna*). Other tribal groups besides Quraysh expressed alternative views and claims, including secessionist ones. However, Quraysh's privileged access to the growing wealth and organisational power of the empire, coupled with their ideological advantage through kinship with the Prophet Muhammad and association with the sacred space of Mecca, helped them to suppress these challenges and retain some authority over swathes of the conquered lands despite their own internal divisions.

After the 630s and 640s, no one could aspire to claim authority over the nascent empire without gaining control of some of its main armies and revenue sources. The tax revenues of the wealthy floodplains of Egypt and Iraq were critical. Coercive force was also now concentrated beyond the Peninsula, in the new frontier territories. The largest numbers of Arabian migrants were in the new settlements of Kufa and Basra in Iraq, with Egypt having been conquered by relatively small armies from Syria. However, the extensive migrations into the Iraqi centres also made these towns volatile, as leaders among the diverse settlers jostled for advantage in the new political context. In contrast, Syria was still occupied by the same pastoralist populations who had lived there in Roman times; immigration was mostly from a small number of South Arabian groups and was comparatively limited. As a result, the Syrian tribes were both more united and more familiar with the politics of empire, in which many of them had long participated. Winning over the Arabic-speaking pastoralists of Syria had been crucial to the Arabians' victories in the 630s and 640s; now their loyalties became equally critical to the new Arabian imperial politics.[2]

The close ties of the Umayyad branch of Quraysh with the Syrian tribes were crucial to their ability to secure power. Of the forty-eight years between 644 and 692, members of the Umayyad clan led the new empire for about thirty-five of them. That four of the five Umayyads who held power during this period died of natural causes, whereas none of their rivals did, is also testimony to Umayyad dominance of the new imperial polity and the success of their alliances in post-Roman Syria. However, the Umayyad kin-group was not itself united, with leadership of the empire being contested between rival Umayyad clans. Furthermore, opposition to the Umayyads from other Qurashi groups was fierce and Umayyad authority was rarely completely secure outside Syria. The most successful opposition external to the Umayyad clan derived from two other branches of Qurasyh, who found support in the former Sasanian territory of Iraq. The first was the kin-group descended from Hashim, the Prophet Muhammad's grandfather, including 'Ali and his sons al-Hasan and al-Husayn, who were grandsons of the Prophet via their mother, Fatima. The second group were maternal relatives of the Prophet and the first caliph, Abu Bakr, known collectively as the Zubayrids (see Chart 4.1).

'Uthman b. 'Affan and the First Civil War

The second man to succeed Muhammad in leading the Faithful, 'Umar b. al-Khattab (r. 634–44), was assassinated in early November 644. As with most such killings, the motives behind it are now obscure.[3] In somewhat legendary accounts that narrate a continuity of leadership among the Prophet's

---

[2] On settlement in Syria, Egypt, and Iraq see above, Ch. 3, nn. 45–9. Himyaris, Hadramis, and Kindis are prominent alongside Syrian tribespeople in Mu'awiya's appointments in Syria. See Khalifa, 141; Simon Gundelfinger and Peter Verkinderen, 'The Governors of al-Sham and Fars in the Early Islamic Empire – A Comparative Regional Perspective', in Hannah-Lena Hagemann and Stefan Heidemann (eds), *The Early Islamic Empire at Work. Volume 1, Transregional and Regional Elites – Connecting the Early Islamic Empire* (Berlin, 2020), 263, 297.

[3] Sean W. Anthony, 'The Syriac Account of Dionysius of Tell Mahre Concerning the Assassination of 'Umar b. al-Khattab', *JNES* 69 (2010), 209–24. Cf. Madelung, *Succession*, 68–70.

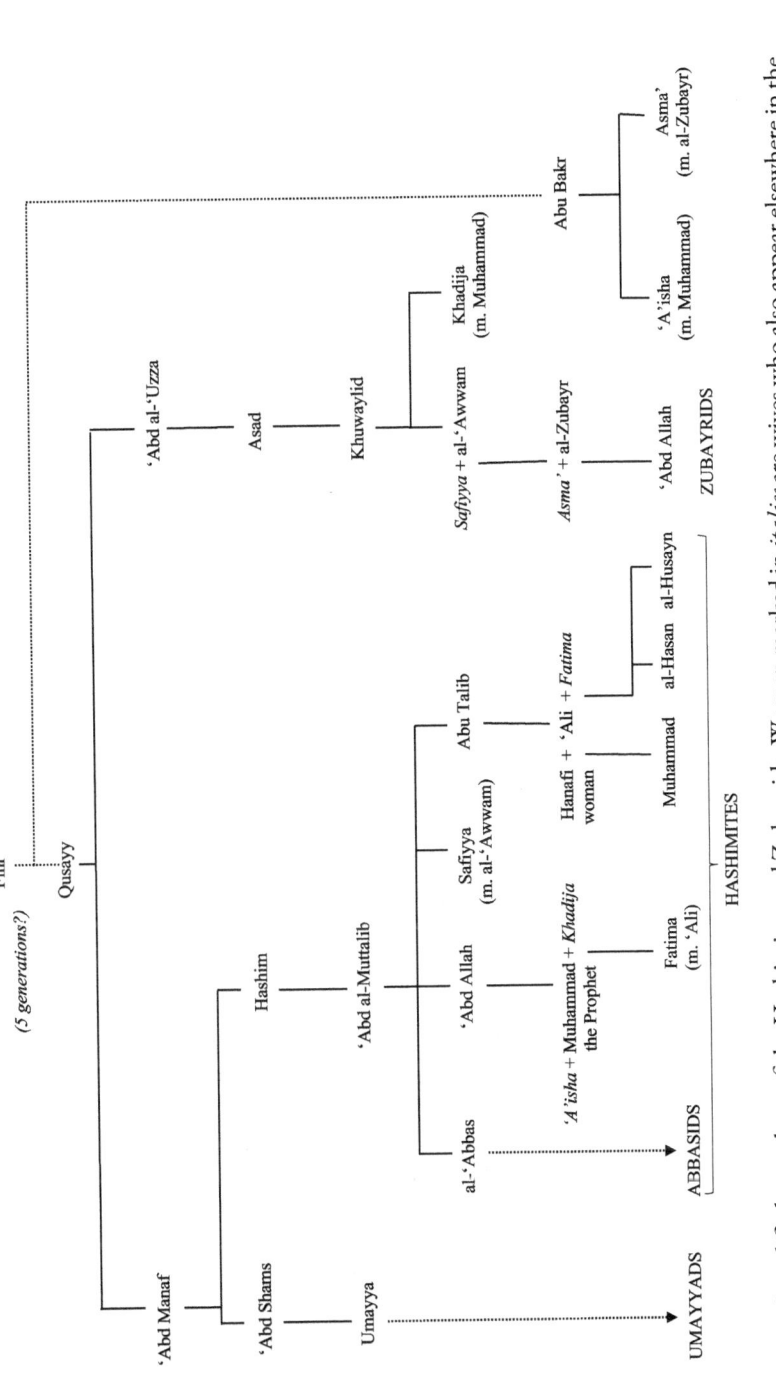

Chart 4.1 Simplified genealogy of the Hashimites and Zubayrids. Women marked in *italics* are wives who also appear elsewhere in the chart as daughters.

Companions, the dying ruler is said to have lived long enough to convene a conclave (*shūrā*) of six or seven leading Companions of the Prophet. The *shūrā* were to choose a new leader from among their number. Such a conference would have had precedents in the consensus-based politics of Mecca. However, discussions now took place among the new political elite of the Faithful at Yathrib/Medina. The exact membership lists of the *shūrā* vary but always include some of the key figures in the new elite.[4]

Whatever took place to decide on him, 'Uthman b. 'Affan became the new leader. 'Uthman seems to have been the first influential member of the old Meccan elite to have followed Muhammad; he is said to have joined the Prophet in about 610 and to have married one of the Prophet's daughters (Ruqayya, d. c. 624; he later married a second, Umm Kulthum). 'Uthman's early conversion is unusual because he was not only said to have been a wealthy and successful merchant but was also a first cousin once removed of Abu Sufyan (d. c. 653–5), a grandson of another Umayyad patriarch, Abu l-'As (*fl. c.* 600), and so a nephew of Abu l-'As's son al-Hakam (d. c. 651–2). All three of these men are said to have been powerful figures in late sixth- and early seventh-century Mecca and to have led opposition to Muhammad. While Abu Sufyan had changed his stance after 627 and had taken a lead role in negotiating Mecca's surrender, Abu l-'As is said never to have reconciled with Muhammad. His son al-Hakam went into exile near al-Ta'if and appears only to have regained political influence with 'Uthman's taking up leadership of the Faithful in 644. 'Uthman's contrasting and unusual early conversion is probably explicable through his maternal relationship to the Prophet. 'Uthman's mother, Arwa bt. Kurayz, was the Prophet's aunt, making 'Uthman the Prophet's first cousin once removed. Nonetheless, 'Uthman's accession may have marked something of a restoration of the old pre-prophetic Meccan leadership, albeit in a political context dramatically reshaped by the events of the past three decades.[5]

Changes to power structures soon extended far beyond the leadership of the Faithful. By about 650, 'Uthman had come to rely heavily upon his Umayyad cousins and other more distant relatives, descended from Umayya's father, 'Abd Shams, with whom he had connections by marriage or adoption. In Syria, his second cousin Mu'awiya b. Abi Sufyan, who was already governor of Damascus and points south, now gained overall authority for the whole province, including the northern frontier with Rome. At around the same time, 'Uthman replaced the conqueror of Roman Egypt, 'Amr b. al-'As al-Sahmi, with his own foster brother, 'Abd Allah b. Sa'd. In Iraq, Kufa was also

---

[4] Patricia Crone, '*Shura* as an Elective Institution', *Quaderni di Studi Arabi* 19 (2001), 3–9. Cf. Madelung, *Succession*, 70–3.
[5] Marsham, 'Kinship', 21–5, 27–9.

transferred into the hands of 'Uthman's relatives: first to 'Uthman's 'Abshami maternal half-brother al-Walid b. 'Uqba, and then to his 'Abshami son-in-law and brother-in-law, Sa'id b. al-'As. ('Abshami is an adjectival form derived from the name 'Abd Shams.) Basra was given to 'Uthman's young 'Abshami maternal first cousin, 'Abd Allah b. 'Amir b. Kurayz. A much younger paternal first cousin, and son of the rehabilitated al-Hakam b. Abi l-'As, named Marwan b. al-Hakam, served as 'Uthman's scribe and advisor, and was also appointed to commands on the new frontiers in North Africa and Fars, in southern Iran, while one of Marwan's brothers, al-Harith b. al-Hakam, was appointed to campaigns in North Africa and over the markets of Medina.[6]

The Umayyad and 'Abshami allies of 'Uthman made use of their new appointments and their proximity to the new ruler to build up their own alliances. One way this is reflected in the sources is in their choices of marriage partners. After marriage, Arabian women retained close links with their birth kin, making marriage an effective mechanism for alliance. Because a man could marry multiple wives, he could forge links with a variety of other groups through marriages. The future caliph Marwan b. al-Hakam was probably only about twenty years old at the time of 'Uthman's accession. His two sons who would become respectively the caliph and the governor of Egypt in the mid-680s, 'Abd al-Malik and 'Abd al-'Aziz, were born in the mid-640s. The former's mother was a paternal first cousin of Marwan and the latter's a Syrian woman who is said to have been from the same tribe as Mu'awiya's Syrian wives. In all, Marwan fathered an exceptional twenty or so children, including at least five sons and one daughter by a daughter of 'Uthman.[7] Likewise, 'Uthman's governor in Kufa, the Umayyad Sa'id b. al-'As, married two daughters of 'Uthman in succession, as well as a sister of 'Uthman's Syrian wife, and a daughter of Marwan's father, al-Hakam b. Abi l-'As.[8]

These Umayyad and 'Abshami governors pursued further raids and campaigns of conquest: west, from Egypt, into Roman Byzacena (modern Tunisia), and south into the kingdoms of Nubia (modern Sudan); north, from Syria and Iraq, into Roman Asia Minor and Armenia; and east, from Iraq,

---

[6] Khalifa, 92–3, 94, 106; Baladhuri, *Futuh*, 226; Tabari, I, 2813–19; *EI*², "Abd Allah b. Sa'd' (C. H. Becker); *EI*², 'Marwan I b. al-Hakam' (C. E. Bosworth); Martin Hinds, 'The Murder of the Caliph 'Uthman', *IJMES* 3 (1972), 453. On the *āmil al-sūq* ('market inspector'), see below, Ch. 12, pp. 315–16.

[7] Marsham, 'Kinship', 15–19, 33–4.

[8] Abu 'Abd Allah al-Mus'ab b. 'Abd Allah al-Zubayri, *Kitab Nasab Quraysh* (Cairo, 1953), 159; Ahmad b. Yahya al-Baladhuri, *Ansab al-Ashraf*, ed. M. Fardus al-Azm (Damascus, 1997–2004) [hereafter, Baladhuri, *Ansab*], IV, 13, 23, V, 253; 'Ali b. al-Hasan b. 'Asakir, *Ta'rikh Madinat Dimashq*, ed. 'Umar Gharama al-'Amrawi (Beirut, 1995–2000) [hereafter, Ibn 'Asakir], LXX, 137, §9435.

into the Iranian plateau. In Iran, the wealthy regions of Sistan and Khurasan – respectively on the south-western and northern edges of the mountains of Afghanistan – were the main targets. These were the ends of trade routes leading to India, via the Indus valley and, via Sogdia, into China; Khurasan was also a highly productive agricultural region, as was the Zaranj Delta, in Sistan. In this eastern expansion, the Arabians were aided by the fragmentation of the Central Asian federations of the Hephthalites and Western Turks. In the west, the Roman provinces that comprise what is now modern Tunisia were among the wealthiest remaining regions of the Roman Empire, and within striking distance of Egypt.[9]

Naval campaigns were launched in the Roman Mediterranean for the first time, using a fleet constructed in the shipyards of Alexandria; a naval raid was also sent across the Red Sea, against Aksum. By the early 650s, the Romans had been defeated at the battle of Sbeïtla (Ar. Subaytila, Lat. Sufetela), in Byzacena, and the large and strategically important island of Cyprus had been captured; a raid in 653 is said to have reached the Bosphorus near Constantinople.[10] In the same year the Roman commander in Armenia, Theodore Rshtuni, surrendered to Muʿawiya.[11] Later, Muʿawiya developed his alliance with Grigor Mamikonean (r. 658–82), who is remembered both for successful warfare against the Khazar Turks in the lands north of the Caucasus and for his patronage of Armenian Christianity.[12]

Various Arabian tribal groups had migrated into the region of northern Iraq known in Arabic as the Jazira (Mesopotamia).[13] In Iran, the highland towns of Fars, in the south-west, and their capital, Istakhr, had fallen to armies based in the garrison of Basra, and raids had been launched into Khurasan and Sistan, at the north-eastern and eastern edges of the Iranian plateau.[14]

[9] See further below, Ch. 10, pp. 214–17 and 247–55. On the Turks and Hephthalites, see relevant chapters in Bemmann and Schmauder (eds), *Complexity of Interaction*.
[10] Khalifa, 91– 8; Ahmad b. Abi Yaʿqub al-Yaʿqubi, *Historiae* (= *Taʾrikh al-Yaʿqubi*), ed. M. J. Houtsma (Leiden, 1883) [hereafter, Yaʿqubi], II, 191–5. For the raid on Aksum, see Tabari, I, 2865. For Nubia, see Stefan Jakobielski, *A History of the Bishopric of Pachoras on the Basis of Coptic Inscriptions* (Warsaw, 1972), 27, 29; Giovanni Ruffini, *Medieval Nubia: A Social and Economic History* (Oxford, 2012), 6. On the Bosphorus, see Khalifa, 97; Yaʿqubi, II, 195.
[11] Sarris, *Empires of Faith*, 284.
[12] Nina Garsoïan, *Interregnum: Introduction to a Study on the Formation of Armenian Identity (ca 600–750)* (Leuven, 2012), 29–37.
[13] Baladhuri, *Futuh*, 178. Such accounts overstate the extent of control from Syria: Chase F. Robinson, *Empire and Elites after the Muslim Conquest: The Transformation of Northern Mesopotamia* (Cambridge, 2000), 34–62. Al-Jazira means 'the island' in Arabic, just as Mesopotamia means 'the land between the rivers' in Greek.
[14] Khalifa, 91–8; Baladhuri, *Futuh*, 392–5; Yaʿqubi, II, 191–5; Tabari, *Taʾrikh*, I, 2819, 2828–9, 2830–1. See Martin Hinds, 'Kufan Political Alignments and their Background in

The Sasanian king, Yazdgird III (r. 632–51), had been pursued across Iran to the capital of Khurasan, at Marw (in modern Turkmenistan), where he is said in some accounts to have been betrayed and killed by Marw's Sasanian governor. Shortly afterwards, the city came to terms with 'Abd Allah b. 'Amir's army in return for a huge tribute payment to the Arabians. In the same year, the Tang Chinese annals record the first embassy from 'the Arab State' to the Tang court, suggesting awareness on the part of the Arabian conquerors of the prestige and influence of China in Central Asia.[15]

Whereas the prosopography of military leadership and the narratives of military campaigns during 'Uthman's rule appear plausible, the material about his interventions in religious and political authority are harder to assess. This is not least because of 'Uthman's later importance as a source of legitimation for later Umayyad rulers. Many of 'Uthman's actions anticipate those of his Marwanid Umayyad successors, raising the possibility that they are later inventions that bolster their claims. Like his Marwanid successors, 'Uthman is said to have shown great interest in sacred spaces, the pilgrimage and the Qur'an.

'Uthman's first major act of architectural patronage as caliph is said to have been the development of the Meccan sanctuary. In 646–7, he is said to have ordered the rebuilding of the Ka'ba and its courtyard as well as the restoration of the stone markers around Mecca's *ḥaram*, or sacred enclave.[16]

Meanwhile, 'Uthman's more quotidian authority was displayed at Medina. The main public building at Medina was the mosque where 'Uthman had been acclaimed as leader in 644 and it was where he routinely led the prayers and gave speeches. As with the Ka'ba and its environs at Mecca, the Medinan mosque is said already to have been enlarged by 'Umar; in 649–50 'Uthman is said to have further expanded and ornamented the building.

> Gypsum [for stucco decoration] was brought from Batn Nakhl [between Medina and Mecca]. He built it with cut stone, making its pillars out of blocks of stone with lead [joints] and constructing its roof from teak. He made it 160 cubits long and 150 cubits wide (perhaps *c.* 90m × 80m).[17]

---

the Mid-Seventh Century AD', *IJMES* 2 (1971), 355–6 on successes in southern and eastern Iran, but setbacks in the north.

[15] Tabari, I, 2862–4, 2872–88. On the embassy of 25 August 651, see Hans Bielenstein, *Diplomacy and Trade in the Chinese World, 589–1276* (Leiden, 2005), 356–7.

[16] Tabari, I, 2810–1; tr. Tabari, *History*, XV, 14–15 and nn. 24, 25 (R. S. Humphreys); cf. Khalifa, 91; Ya'qubi, II, 189–90.

[17] Tabari, *Ta'rikh*, I, 2833; tr. Tabari, *History*, XV, 38 (R. S. Humphreys). Cf. Khalifa, 94; Baladhuri, *Futuh*, 6–7; Ya'qubi, II, 191. On Batn Nakhl, see Hamd-Allah Mustawfi, *The Geographical Part of the* Nuzhat al-Qulub, tr. Guy Le Strange (Leiden, 1919), 165. On the cubit, see *EI²*, 'Dhira"' (W. Hinz).

Such accounts are later literary formulations. However, these stories about 'Uthman's rebuilding of the mosque at Medina suggest that competition between Medina and provincial centres may already have been expressed through architectural patronage.[18]

'Uthman is also widely reputed to have led the first compilation of the Qur'an as a book. Earlier efforts at collecting the Qur'an as a single document are associated in the tradition with his predecessors, Abu Bakr and 'Umar, but the reports about 'Uthman suggest a more systematic attempt at asserting authority over scripture. 'Uthman is said to have had a group of the Prophet's associates (*ṣaḥāba*, 'Companions') agree upon a single text. Some other versions are said to have been destroyed, and the new recension, often now referred to as the 'Uthmanic Codex, is said to have been sent out in written copies to the provincial capitals. These reports echo the better-attested actions of the later, Marwanid, Umayyads at the time of 'Abd al-Malik and so may at least in part reflect later justification of their actions by association with the patriarch of their dynasty. Certainly, in 'Uthman's time the Arabic script was not yet developed enough to produce a definitive, unambiguous Quranic text. Moreover, the decentralised political structures of the conquest society would have made imposing a single text across its territories impossible and the evidence of the early Qur'an manuscripts bears this out. Nonetheless, the stories of the Qur'an's dissemination to the other major urban centres of the growing empire fits with the pattern of greater political centralisation under his rule, in alliance with his Umayyad relatives, and so cannot easily be completely dismissed.[19]

Both this ideological centralisation and 'Uthman's appointment of relatives would have been a severe provocation to the rest of the Quraysh and the Ansar. Moreover, there was by now a further connection between 'Uthman in Medina and Mu'awiya in Damascus, of which other Qurashis would have had reason to be wary; both men had marriage connections in Syria (see Chart 4.2). Indeed, a Syrian Kalbi group identity may have developed in part as a result of conquests and association with the Umayyads (as may the wider federation of Quda'a, to which Kalb in turn belonged). Mu'awiya had married Maysun bt.

---

[18] On the problems of the literary evidence for the seventh century, see Thallein M. Antun, *The Architectural Form of the Mosque* (Oxford, 2016), esp. 50–70, 96–8.
[19] On the traditions about the collection, see Motzki, 'Collection'. See also above, Ch. 2, pp. 59–60, and n. 33. For a speech attributed to 'Abd al-Malik about 'Uthman, and the Qur'an, see Ibn Sa'd, *Kitab al-Tabaqat al-Kabir = Ibn Saad Biographien Muhammads, seiner Gefährten und der späteren Träger des Islams bis zum Jahre 230 der Flucht*, ed. Eduard Sachau et al. (Leiden, 1904–40), V, 173. Cf. Anthony, *Muhammad*, 91–2. For sceptical assessments, see Chase F. Robinson, *'Abd al-Malik* (Oxford, 2005), 100–4; Shoemaker, *Creating the Qur'an*.

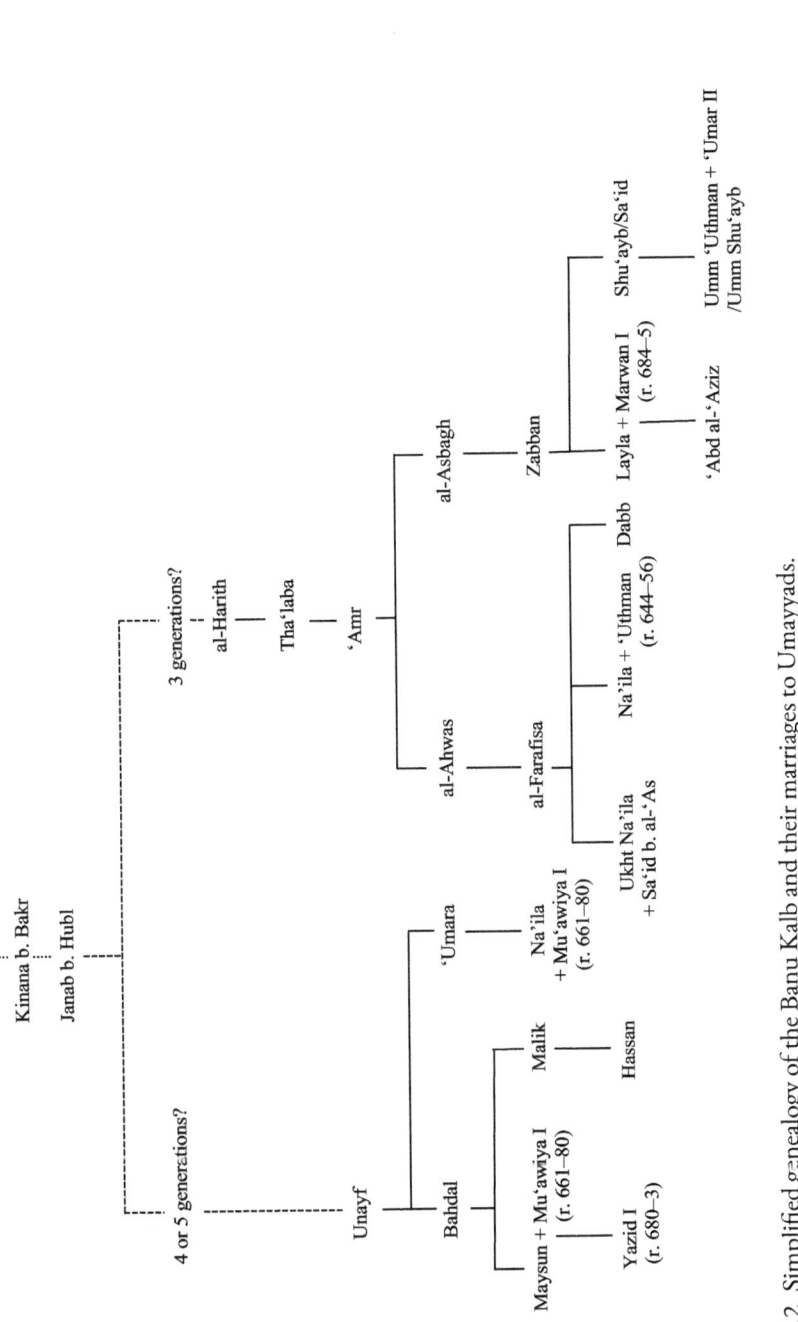

Chart 4.2 Simplified genealogy of the Banu Kalb and their marriages to Umayyads.

Bahdal, who was the daughter of a leading Kalbi chief, and her paternal cousin, Na'ila bt. 'Umara. 'Uthman married Na'ila bt. al-Farafisa, from another branch of the same tribe, perhaps in 648–9. That 'Uthman might have had intentions to pass power to a son, whom he had married to a daughter of Mu'awiya, is mentioned in the sources. The evidence of these and his other marriages suggests both that he indeed had such ambitions, and that he was both collaborating and competing with his second cousin Mu'awiya.[20]

Military failures in the latter years of 'Uthman's rule may have diminished his prestige: an ill-advised attack on the Khazar Khaganate in 652 ended with the slaughter of an army; worse, the war against Rome had stalled when an assault on Constantinople in 654 failed; in the East, the Kufan garrison struggled in the highland zones of northern Iran and Azerbaijan.[21] Meanwhile, resentment at 'Uthman's appointments of his men to the commands over the garrisons of Iraq and Egypt, as well as tensions over the allocation of resources, prompted unrest in the provinces.[22] In c. 655, the Kufans blocked 'Uthman's governor, Sa'id b. al-'As, from entering the garrison on his return from the *hajj*; Abu Musa al-Ash'ari, 'Umar's former governor of Kufa, was installed in his place. Shortly afterwards, 'Uthman's cousin 'Abd Allah b. 'Amir fled Basra in the wake of unrest there, leaving the garrison without a commander. In Egypt, rebels deposed and replaced 'Uthman's foster-brother, 'Abd Allah b. Sa'd, who departed for Syria.[23]

By 656 only Syria remained stable, under its long-serving Umayyad governor, Mu'awiya, and his allies among the Banu Kalb. Elsewhere, those excluded from power had rebelled, drawing support from disaffected elements within the provincial armies. In Iraq and Egypt, opposition is said to have been expressed in religious terms: 'Uthman's misrule made it legitimate to depose him and his appointees. Likewise, defences of 'Uthman's actions are also articulated in pious language.[24] When the rebels converged on Medina itself, in 656, 'Uthman is said to have been outnumbered and confined to his house

---

[20] Marsham, 'Kinship', 18, 29–30. On Maysun and the two Na'ilas, see Ibn 'Asakir, LXX, 130–4, 135–41, §9432, §9434, §9435. For the date of 'Uthman's marriage to Na'ila bt. al-Farafisa, see Khalifa, 92.

[21] Hinds, 'Kufan Political Alignments', 355–6; EI², 'Khazars' (W. Barthold–P. B. Golden); *WtaWC*, 377–8, 474–81; Nathaniel Miller, 'Dear Mu'awiya: An "Epistolary" Poem on a Major Muslim Military Defeat during the Mediterranean Campaigns of AH 28-35/649–56 CE', *Al-Usur al-Wusta* 31 (2023), 45–76.

[22] Hinds, 'Murder'.

[23] Tabari, I, 2927, 2930–1, 2934–6, 2999, 3057; EI², 'al-Ash'ari, Abu Musa' (L. Veccia Vaglieri).

[24] See, for example, the exchange between 'Uthman and his accusers in Tabari, I, 2951–4. See further on the context Hinds, 'Murder'; Madelung, *Succession*, 113–40.

by the crowd. After a prolonged period of negotiation, the house was stormed and 'Uthman was killed. A relief army, sent by Mu'awiya from Syria, is said to have turned back when it became clear it had arrived too late. Meanwhile, 'Uthman's supporters at Medina, largely comprising his Umayyad clan, had fled for Mecca. The provincial rebels and the Ansar now controlled the capital. They appointed the Prophet's cousin and son-in-law, 'Ali b. Abi Talib, as the new Commander of the Faithful.[25]

'Ali's accession in the wake of 'Uthman's killing exposed him to challengers. In the words of his opponents 'Ali was at best benefiting directly from the murder and sheltering 'Uthman's killers; at worst he was behind the assassination. Moreover, 'Ali had become the focus for the aspirations of groups who had felt excluded by the Quraysh's new political dispensation; the Ansar and some of the early migrants among the 'southern' tribal groups of Yemen at Kufa were among his most prominent supporters.[26] This would have made his accession threatening to those Qurashi clans who had held power before 656. That 'Ali, uniquely, had two living sons by one of the Prophet's daughters would have made him still more so, since he was well placed to establish dynastic power – sons who were direct descendants of the Prophet might easily be seen to embody the continuation of prophetic charisma.

In Iraq, the tribal armies were divided about how to respond to the killing of 'Uthman. The envoy 'Ali sent to govern Kufa was turned away, but 'Ali was still able to secure the garrison's allegiance by recognising the rebels' choice of governor, Abu Musa al-Ash'ari. At Basra, 'Ali's Ansari appointee enjoyed only partial support within a restive garrison. In Egypt, the conquering forces were also split. Many in Fustat were willing to recognise 'Ali and his governor. Others near the former Roman port of Alexandria held out in the name of 'Uthman. Another group gave their allegiance to the Romans.[27] On the Peninsula, 'Ali successfully installed a new governor in Sana'a, the former capital of Himyar, but Mecca – being the town of the Quraysh – quickly became a centre of opposition to him.[28] Damascus, held by Mu'awiya, and by 'Uthman and Mu'awiya's relatives by marriage from the Banu Kalb, was where many of 'Uthman's Umayyad relatives had gathered; they also withheld allegiance from 'Ali.[29]

---

[25] Tabari, I, 2950–3025, 3066–80.
[26] Tabari, I, 3039–40, 3080, 3082–5, 3255–6; Madelung, *Succession*, 141–7, 155–7.
[27] Tabari, I, 3087–9; Tabari, *History*, XVI, 27, n. 169 (A. A. Brockett); Madelung, *Succession*, 151–2.
[28] Madelung, *Succession*, 147–8, 155–7. For the faction that joined the Romans, see Thomson and Howard-Johnston, *Armenian History*, I, 154; *SIAOSI*, 559, n. 63.
[29] al-Tabari, I, 3089–91; Madelung, *Succession*, 147–8.

At Mecca, opposition to ʿAli rallied around two members of the family of the first caliph, Abu Bakr. Al-Zubayr b. al-ʿAwwam was Abu Bakr's son-in-law as well as the Prophet's cousin and a nephew by marriage (Chart 4.1, above).[30] Talha b. ʿUbayd Allah was another of Abu Bakr's sons-in-law, from the same Taymi branch of Quraysh as the first caliph.[31] ʿAʾisha, a daughter of Abu Bakr, the Prophet's youngest widow, and a sister-in-law of al-Zubayr, publicly backed their resistance to ʿAli. With Syria firmly in the hands of Muʿawiya, and Egypt split, al-Zubayr, Talha and ʿAʾisha decided to begin by wresting the Iraqi garrisons from ʿAli's fragile control. They made for Basra, where they took charge without much difficulty. However, ʿAli had also immediately left the Hijaz for Iraq, gathering support from Kufa. At the 'Battle of the Camel' near Basra in December 656 – so called because ʿAʾisha observed the fighting from her camel – ʿAli was victorious. His two Meccan rivals were killed and ʿAʾisha was forced to end her public backing for her relatives' political claims.[32]

At Damascus, ʿUthman's Syrian governor, Muʿawiya, is said to have displayed ʿUthman's bloodstained shirt and the severed fingers of Naʾila bt. al-Farafisa, Uthman's Syrian Kalbi widow, cut off as she sought to protect him from the rebels' blows.[33] The relic-like objects symbolised the united interests of ʿUthman's immediate kin – including Muʿawiya and the tribes of southern Syria. Muʿawiya was joined by ʿAmr b. al-ʿAs, the conqueror of Roman Egypt, who had been dismissed by ʿUthman in *c.* 646–7 and now saw alliance with Muʿawiya as a means to recover his conquered territory. Muʿawiya, ʿAmr and the Syrian tribes marched to meet ʿAli's forces and the two armies confronted one another at Siffin, on the Euphrates, in 657. The tradition records that a prolonged series of skirmishes were inconclusive, and a truce was called with a view to opening negotiations.[34]

This truce at Siffin and the subsequent negotiations were a turning point. ʿAli is said to have conceded ground, perhaps even agreeing implicitly to a new conclave to decide the question of the leadership of the Faithful. If so, this decision probably reflected the position of some of the tribal leaders among his supporters, who were willing to come to terms to secure their existing privileges. However, others appear initially to have lent ʿAli their support precisely because they resented the higher status accorded to powerful tribal leaders over earlier migrants. Some of this latter group now abandoned ʿAli. They became

---

[30] al-Zubayri, *Nasab*, 276–7; Baladhuri, *Ansab*, I, 103.
[31] *EI*[2], 'Talha' (W. Madelung).
[32] Tabari, I, 3091–233; Madelung, *Succession*, 159–76.
[33] Tabari, I, 3255.
[34] Tabari, I, 3249–341; Martin Hinds, 'The Siffin Arbitration Agreement', *JSS* 17 (1972), 93–113.

known as Kharijites (from the Arabic verb *kharaja*, 'to go out', and hence 'to depart from allegiance' or simply 'to rebel') or as Haruris (after the village of Harura where they had gathered).[35] Although he won an initial victory over these rebels, 'Ali could not regroup effectively against Mu'awiya because he faced further rebellions. A former supporter, al-Khirrit b. Rashid al-Naji, brought some of the conquered population of the highlands of Ahwaz and the tribes of north-east Arabia into rebellion alongside his own followers from Basra, and there were also rebellions in the highlands of southern and western Iran – in Fars, Kirman and Jibal.[36] Further to the east, 'Ali's attempts to impose his authority in Khurasan and Sistan were disrupted by the presence of more rebel groups, including allies of the Sasanian Piruz, son of Yazdgird III, who later established himself in Sistan.[37]

The unrest in Iraq, Iran and Arabia, and a truce bought from the Romans in exchange for tribute payments in gold, horses and slaves, allowed Mu'awiya to exert growing pressure on 'Ali.[38] At the same time, Mu'awiya's ally, 'Amr b. al-'As, invaded Egypt, delivering control of the Egyptian grain supply and taxes, and the naval resources and pro-'Uthmanid garrison of Alexandria, to Mu'awiya.[39] However, Mu'awiya still held back from a second direct confrontation with 'Ali, perhaps unsettled by Roman military activity in Asia Minor and then, in 660, the arrival of a Roman army in the Caucasus and north-west Iran.[40] Instead, he fomented rebellion against 'Ali at Basra and launched raids into the eastern Syrian Desert and northern Arabia and the Hijaz. At the annual *hajj* in the spring of 660 a stand-off between representatives of 'Ali and Mu'awiya at Mecca probably reflects the weakening of 'Ali's position; Syrian raids deeper into Iraq and into the Hijaz and South Arabia followed later in the year.[41]

What might have become a protracted and bloody conflict over Iraq was forestalled by 'Ali's assassination. A former supporter who had joined 'Ali's Kharijite opponents stabbed him to death as he led the prayers at Kufa. As with the death of 'Uthman about four years earlier, and 'Umar twelve years before

---

[35] Hinds, 'Kufan Political Alignments'; Hinds, 'Siffin'. Cf. Hannah-Lena Hagemann, *The Kharijites in Early Islamic Historical Tradition: Heroes and Villains* (Edinburgh, 2021), 11, 41–4, 135–64.

[36] Tabari, I, 3418–43, 3449–50; *EI*², 'Al-Khirrit' (Ch. Pellat).

[37] Baladhuri, *Futuh*, 395–6. For Piruz, see Patricia Crone, *The Nativist Prophets of Early Islamic Iran* (Cambridge, 2012), 4.

[38] Cyril Mango and Roger Scott (eds and trs), *The Chronicle of Theophanes Confessor: Byzantine and Near Eastern History ad 284–813* (Oxford, 1997) [hereafter, Theophanes], 484, s.a. 657–8. Cf. *Theophilus*, 149, n. 372.

[39] Tabari, I, 3396–413.

[40] *WtaWC*, 484–5.

[41] Tabari, I, 3413–18, 3444–8, 3450–52; McMillan, *Meaning*, 42–4.

that, any possible involvement of other actors is now impossible to discern. 'Ali's death is usually dated to the middle of the holy month of Ramadan in the fortieth year since Muhammad's emigration to Yathrib/Medina (January 661). Although there is good reason to doubt such a symbolic date, it is clear that his killing took place at about this time and that it presaged a Syrian victory over Iraq; the already fractious coalition of Iraqis ranged against Mu'awiya was now mortally weakened. 'Ali's son and successor, al-Hasan, surrendered to Mu'awiya a few months later – probably in the spring of 661.[42]

Mu'awiya b. Abi Sufyan

During the closing stages of the conflict with 'Ali, Mu'awiya had staged a triumphal accession ceremony at Jerusalem, which caught the attention of a local Christian observer:

> [M]any Arabs (*tayyaye*) gathered at Jerusalem and made Mu'awiya king and he went up and sat down on Golgotha; he prayed there, and went to Gethsemene and went down to the tomb of the blessed Mary to pray in it ... In July of the same year (*c.* 661) the emirs and many Arabs gathered and proffered their right hand to Mu'awiya. Then an order went out that he should be proclaimed king in all the villages and cities of his dominion and that they should make acclamations and invocations to him. He also minted gold and silver, but it was not accepted, because it had no cross on it. Furthermore, Mu'awiya did not wear a crown like other kings in the world. He placed his throne in Damascus and refused to go to Muhammad's throne.[43]

The ceremonial reveals Mu'awiya's sources of power and the balancing act he performed to secure them. In the decision to make Damascus, rather than Medina, his capital, Mu'awiya acknowledged that his fortunes were tied to the tribes of the former Roman desert frontier. By backing Mu'awiya in the conflict of 656–61 the Syrian tribes had succeeded in placing themselves at the centre of the new empire. By then, Mu'awiya had already been in alliance with many of them for over twenty years and had married two women from Banu Kalb. The nephew of one of these wives was his senior military commander in the lands around Lake Tiberias and Jerusalem.[44] Mu'awiya's senior scribe and tax official, Sarjun b. Mansur al-Rumi ('Sergius the Roman'), was a

---

[42] Tabari, I, 3456–64, 3467–70, II, 1–9. Al-Tabari overlooks that al-Hasan's surrender was in some accounts said to have been for only for a *shūrā* – consultation on the choice of leader: Tabari, *History*, XIX, xi–xii (I. K. A. Howard).
[43] Palmer et al., *Seventh Century*, 31–2.
[44] The military districts, or *junds*, of al-Urdunn and Filastin, respectively, were under Hassan b. Malik b. Bahdal. See Gundelfinger and Verkinderen, 'Governors', 297.

Chalcedonian Christian son of a former Roman tax official. Many of the other leading Syrian figures at his court are said to have been 'Ghassanids', from the same tribal group who had been Roman allies in the previous century. An attempt to rule from Medina (or, for that matter, Iraq) would have been to rule as an occupying power in a region where support for other branches of the Hijazi elite remained strong. Although Muʿawiya and other Umayyads owned extensive estates in the Hijaz, Mecca and Medina remained bastions of the wider tribe of Quraysh and of the Ansar, respectively. In Iraq, the Kufan garrison had supported ʿAli and generated the Kharijite rebellions; Basra had backed Abu Bakr's relatives Talha and al-Zubayr. In one later source, Muʿawiya is said to have increased the pay of the Syrians and reduced that of the Iraqis. This may well reflect a real economic change; certainly it symbolises the lasting shift in the balance of power between Iraq and Syria after Muʿawiya's accession.[45]

The importance of the Syrian pastoralists is also suggested by the details of the eyewitness's account of the accession ceremony. The ritual is seen as something primarily for the 'Arabs' (Syr. *tayyaye*) in the Christian chronicle. Many of the pastoralist tribespeople of the Syrian steppe followed Christian beliefs and practices, for all that they were perceived as outsiders by their settled Christian neighbours. Thus, Muʿawiya's veneration of the holy sites of Mary's tomb, Gethsemene and Golgotha, reflects the expectations of the audiences for his accession – the Christian or recently Christian armies from the Syrian steppe who had gathered at Jerusalem, but also the Syriac and Greek-speaking Christian populations of Jerusalem itself, to whom he may have sought to present himself as the legitimate successor to the Roman emperor; Muʿawiya's actions at Jerusalem recall Emperor Heraclius' triumphant pilgrimage in March 629 or 630, which was well within living memory. However, Muʿawiya was certainly not simply presenting himself as a Christian emperor; Muhammad's importance to 'the Arabs' is noted by the chronicler, and the attempt to have a coinage without crosses on it accepted suggests the tentative public promotion of anti-Trinitarian doctrine. Moreover, the comment about the absence of a crown suggests a response to the expectations of his nomadic pastoralist followers.[46]

---

[45] For scribes and officials, see Khalifa, 141, and Box Text, pp. 309–12. On estates, see Saleh El-Ali, 'Muslim Estates in Hidjaz in the First Century AH', *JESHO* 2 (1959), 247–61; Harry Munt, 'Caliphal Estates and Properties around Medina in the Umayyad Period', in Alain Delattre, Marie Legendre and Petra Sijpesteijn (eds), *Authority and Control in the Countryside: From Antiquity to Islam in the Mediterranean and Near East (6th–10th Century)* (Leiden, 2019), 432–63. On pay, see Theophanes, 485 and 486, n. 2; cf. *Theophilus*, 149–50; Crone, 'Qays and Yemen', 44.

[46] Andrew Marsham, 'The Architecture of Allegiance in Early Islamic Late Antiquity: The

The Inscription from Hammat Gader, 5 December 662

An inscription carved for the renovation of a large bathing complex near Lake Tiberias a year or two after Muʿawiya's accession reflects the distinctive character of post-Roman Syria at the beginning of Muʿawiya's securing rule over the new empire (Figure 4.1).

> ☩ In the days of *abdalla* Maavia *amēralmoumenēn* (God's Servant Muʿawiya Commander of the Faithful) the *clibanus* of the (baths) here was cleared and renewed by Abdalla son of Abouasemou ('Abd Allah b. Abi Hashim, or Abi ʿAsim), the governor (Gk *symboulos*); in the month of December; on the fifth day, Monday, in the 6th (year) of the indiction, in the year 726 of the colony, according to the Arabs (*arabas*) the 42nd year; for the healing of the sick, under the care of John the Gadarene, the steward.

The inscription is carved in Greek, beginning with a cross, according to the established conventions of the eastern Roman Empire at the time, but for the local Arabian governor, ʿAbd Allah b. Abi Hashim/ʿAsim. Muʿawiya's

Figure 4.1 The Bathhouse inscription at Hammat Gader, 5 December 662 CE. Marble, 50cm × 80cm. Photograph by Dirk Kossman of Corpus Inscriptionum with thanks to Robert Hoyland.

Accession of Muʿawiya in Jerusalem, ca. 661 CE', in Alexander Beihammer, Stavroula Constantinou and Maria Parani (eds), *Court Ceremonies and Rituals of Power in Byzantium and the Medieval Mediterranean: Comparative Perspectives* (Leiden, 2013), 87–112.

title, 'Commander of the Faithful', is transliterated, rather than translated, from Arabic, which suggests that it was usually heard in Arabic, like the Arabic personal names. In contrast, the position of 'governor' (Ar. *amīr*) is translated into Greek, as *symboulos*, and the exact date – 5 December 662 – is given according to the Roman calendar, with the *hijrī* lunar calendar year 'of the Arabs' given afterwards.

Thus, the inscription is in many ways both a Roman and a Christian artefact, and one in which the administrative power of the Roman Empire is present in the use of the Roman calendar. It conveys the sense of a Christian Roman society continuing uninterrupted in some respects, but now under the rule of 'the Arabs' (*arabas*), with prestige public writing still being inscribed according to Roman conventions. This continuity is reflected in the use of the bathing complex, the restoration of which it commemorates. It was a major public building which had been in use since the second century CE but had been rebuilt following an earthquake in the fifth century, and new floors had been laid at the end of the sixth. It continued in use throughout the Umayyad period, as inscriptions in Arabic and numerous small finds of pottery, glass, lamps and coins attest. Like many other public buildings in Syria, it collapsed in a large earthquake in 749, shortly before the fall of the Umayyads.[47]

Mu'awiya had publicly proclaimed his legitimate leadership over the newly conquered lands of the Faithful, asserting the same claim in opposition to Heraclius' successor, Constans II (r. 641–c. 668/9). Victory would not only secure Mu'awiya's position as the ruler in Syria, it would be proof of divine favour for his imperial authority, and so Constantinople's capture remained a priority throughout his reign.[48] However, Mu'awiya's imperial ambitions were difficult to achieve. The naval defeats of the 650s had already indicated the difficulties of subduing Constantinople. Now the civil war of 656–61 had provided the Romans with a hiatus in which their forces had been strengthened and reorganised. The manpower and the mountain passes of the Caucasus had proved critical to Heraclius' defeat of Khusro in the 620s, and Constans II sought to reconstitute a similar alliance when he visited the region in 660 and 661. Then, in 662, Constans II headed to Italy – now in the control of the barbarian Lombards – making the first visit to Rome by a Roman emperor in two

---

[47] Yizhar Hirschfeld et al., *The Roman Baths of Hammat Gader: Final Report* (Jerusalem, 1997); tr. after Leah Di Segni at 237–40; Rachel Stroumsa, 'Greek and Arabic in Nessana', in Alexander Schubert and Petra Sijpesteijn (eds), *Documents and the History of the Early Islamic World* (Leiden, 2014), 153–4.

[48] *WtaWC*, 488–9.

centuries in 663. From there, he went on to Syracuse, in Sicily. Sicily had proved crucial to the Romans' reconquest of North Africa from its Vandal rulers in the previous century, and it seems likely that Constans II was planning to use it as a secure base for efforts to drive back North Africa's Arabian assailants.[49]

Muʿawiya's response to the Romans' manoeuvres was to return immediately to the offensive. Raids were launched against Roman North Africa in 660 and 661. In the following year, the Syrian coastal towns of Tyre and Acre were fortified. Then, as soon as he had secured control of Iraq and the Hijaz, Muʿawiya sent overland raids into the Caucasus and, in 663, into Asia Minor. In 664, a naval raid was launched against Constans II's new base in Sicily. These efforts were combined with a diplomatic offensive, through which the Albanian ruler Juansher (d. c. 669) was lured away from his allegiance to the Romans, perhaps by suggestions that recent Arabian victories in the Caucasus made them better able to protect the Albanians from the raids of the Khazar Khaganate which dominated the steppes to their north. These diplomatic efforts preceded a major campaign, led by Muʿawiya's son Yazid, deep into Roman Asia Minor, in 667–9. In 668, Yazid's army reached Chalcedon, just across the Bosphorus from Constantinople, before withdrawing to overwinter inland at Amorion, in western Asia Minor.[50]

With timing that may not have been coincidental, Constans II was assassinated in Sicily, in July 668 or 669. As his son and successor, Constantine IV (r. c. 669–85) sought to secure power against a rival claimant to the imperial throne, the Arabians returned to the offensive against Constantinople. A sustained land campaign in North Africa began in 670. Meanwhile, in 670–1, the Arabian fleet overwintered in on the Cyzicus Peninsula, on the south coast of the Sea of Marmara, about 100km from the Roman capital. The pressure was sustained, with land raids in Asia Minor in 671 and 672 and naval assaults in 673 and 674. However, the Romans' resistance strengthened once Constantine IV secured his position. There were Roman counter-attacks in 672–4 and the Arabian naval raid of 674 met with disaster, when the army it landed on the south-west coast of Asia Minor was repulsed and its boats

---

[49] *WtaWC*, 483–6; Sarris, *Empires of Faith*, 281–4. On the Roman army, see John Haldon, 'Military Service, Military Lands, and the Status of Soldiers: Current Problems and Interpretations', *DOP* 47 (1993), 1–67; John Haldon, *The Empire That Would Not Die: The Paradox of Eastern Roman Survival, 640–740* (Cambridge, MA, 2016), 266–82.

[50] *WtaWC*, 118–20, 489–9; Marek Jankowiak, 'The First Arab Siege of Constantinople', *Travaux et Mémoires 17: Constructing the Seventh Century* (Paris, 2013), 237–320. On North Africa, see *EI²*, s.v. Muʿawiya b. Hudaydj (C. Pellat). For the coast, see Antoine Borrut, 'L'espace maritime syrien au cours des premiers siècles de l'Islam (VIIe–Xe siècle): le cas de la région entre Acre et Tripoli', *Tempora* 10–11 (1999–2000), 1–34.

destroyed at sea by 'Greek Fire' – a newly devised weapon based on naphtha. After this setback, naval warfare continued, but the Arabians were unable to seal off Constantinople as they had done at the turn of the decade, nor were they able to regain the momentum of the campaigns of the 660s.[51]

In 677 or 678, rebellion against Muʿawiya's rule broke out within Syria itself. The insurrection began near Mount Amanus, close to Antioch (modern Antakya, in south-east Turkey), but spread south through the Lebanese mountains, reaching the Golan Heights and Lake Tiberias. The Syriac sources refer to the insurgents as Mardaites (that is, simply 'rebels'); in the Arabic texts they are *jarājima* (after Garguma, a town near Mount Amanus). The core members of the insurrection were probably Maronite Christians from Mount Amanus, but, as with most such rebellions, the sources describe 'slaves, captives and natives' augmenting their numbers.[52] It is possible that the growing pressure on Muʿawiya led to his concluding a truce with the Romans – the evidence is unclear. What is certain is that by the late 670s, his ambition to replace the Roman emperor as the leader of the monotheist world had been thwarted. Roman military reorganisation, begun under Heraclius and consolidated under Constans II and Constantine IV, had made the most of existing natural advantages: Constantinople was far from Muʿawiya's main bases in Syria and Egypt, sheltered behind the highlands of Asia Minor and the waters of the Mediterranean and the Bosphorus. A Roman field army based on the distribution of land rather than payment in coin had been the response to the disastrous loss of revenue suffered in the first half of the seventh century. This army, and a navy equipped with the new Greek Fire, had effectively stalled the Arabians' advance.[53]

On other fronts, however, the West Arabians' dominion had been consolidated and expanded. In the wealthy garrison provinces of Iraq and Egypt, and their dependent territories, Muʿawiya had adopted a policy of delegating authority to single governors, who then held the post for life. In Iraq, this policy is exemplified by the appointments of al-Mughira b. Shuʿba, Ziyad b. Sumayya and ʿUbayd Allah b. Ziyad. Al-Mughira was governor of Kufa until his death in about 669; Ziyad governed Basra from 665, and then, after al-Mughira's death, both Basra and Kufa and their dependent territories in the East until his own death in 673. In 675 – after a brief experiment with local tribesmen and an Umayyad – Ziyad was replaced at Basra by his son,

---

[51] *WtaWC*, 226–7, 390, 489–95; Jankowiak, 'First Arab Siege', 316–17.
[52] *Theophilus*, 169–70; *WtaWC*, 226–7, 262, 302–4, 494–5; Jankowiak, 'First Arab Siege', 316–17.
[53] Haldon, 'Military Service'; *WtaWC*, 494–5; Jankowiak, 'First Arab Siege'. For the possible truce, see Theophanes, 496, s.a. 676–7, and n. 3.

'Ubayd Allah (g. 675–83), who held the post until shortly before his own death. In Egypt, Muʿawiya at first had to acknowledge his main Qurashi ally in the civil war, ʿAmr b. al-ʿAs, as governor. However, ʿAmr died in about 664, and by 667 Muʿawiya had appointed one of ʿAmr's former officials, Maslama b. Mukhallad al-Ansari (g. 667–82).

The creation of life-long commanders, all of whom already had strong existing connections within their provinces before their appointment, was potentially dangerous and may reflect the limits of Muʿawiya's control over the wider empire. Muʿawiya's confidence in his provincial commanders' loyalty appears to have been founded upon their being personally beholden to him, their lacking the necessary political status to claim the leadership of the whole empire, and their own interests being served by their control of their governorships. Al-Mughira was a brother-in-law of Muʿawiya from among the Thaqafi allies of ʿAbd Shams and had served as a governor in Iraq for ʿUmar. However, he had fallen from favour in the late 630s, and had held no post under ʿUthman or ʿAli. Ziyad was even more of an outsider. The son of a slave woman who was said to have belonged to someone other than his father (whence two of his names, Ibn Sumayya, 'the son of Sumayya' and Ibn Abihi, 'the son of his father'), Ziyad had risen from a minor position in the Basran administration in the 630s to become ʿAli's acting governor of the garrison. In 665, four years after Ziyad had fled to a stronghold in south-west Iran, Muʿawiya is said finally to have obtained his surrender by a combination of threats against his family in Basra and an agreement that Muʿawiya would adopt him as a brother (whence Ziyad's third name, Ibn Abi Sufyan). In Egypt, Maslama b. Mukhallad was a member of the Ansar who had joined ʿAmr's initial conquest of the province, was closely connected to the conquering troops and had supported Muʿawiya's cause alongside ʿAmr. As a member of the Ansar he was, like al-Mughira and Ziyad, from outside the Qurashi elite, and he served first Muʿawiya and then his son and successor Yazid loyally until his death in 682.[54]

These regional governors sought to maintain the momentum of the raids and conquests, using the distribution of the spoils to augment the tax revenues that underpinned the loyalty of their armies. The main targets of Kufa and Basra remained Sistan and Khurasan, at the eastern frontiers of what had been the Sasanian Empire. Both regions lay on valuable trade routes: the fertile river delta and arid passes of Sistan gave access to the Afghan highlands and beyond them to the wealthy Indus valley, while Khurasan – a wealthy agricultural

---

[54] *EI²*, 'Maslama b. Mukhallad' (Ed.), 'al-Mughira b. Shuʿba' (H. Lammens), 'Ziyad b. Abihi' (I. Hasson). For al-Mughira's kinship with Muʿawiya, see al-Zubayri, *Nasab*, 126; Baladhuri, *Ansab*, I, 529–30.

region – lay at the western end of trade routes that passed through the valleys of Sogdia and on into China. In the attacks on both territories, Basra seems to have supplied more troops and to have benefited from more of the spoils.

In Sistan the main Iraqi garrison was at Zaranj, where the lower river Helmand flowed into Lake Zirih (now Lake Sistan). There, the Iraqi troops competed for dominance with local warlords and independent Arabian groups, while campaigns were also sent against Hephthalite principalities in the highlands of south-west Afghanistan. In Khurasan, the former Sasanian centre of Marw had been captured in 651. In the wake of the civil war, a series of campaigns were fought to reassert control there and in Sistan, where Piruz's attempt to restore Sasanian rule was ended. Then, in 671, 50,000 troops and their families are said to have been sent from Basra and Kufa by the Iraqi governor, Ziyad, to settle in western Khurasan. This planned migration made Khurasan the part of Iran most densely settled by Arabian migrants. In the 670s, the Khurasanian settlers are said to have raided Quhistan, south of Khurasan, to have temporarily wrested control of the entrepôt of Balkh, in Tukharistan (modern northern Afghanistan), from the Hephthalites, and to have raided across the Oxus river for the first time, reaching Paykand, Bukhara and Samarqand, in Sogdia (modern Uzbekistan).[55]

Whereas the garrisons of Iraq faced east, confronting the remnants of Sasanian power and the borders of the Hephthalite Empire, Egypt was a flank in the ongoing war against the Romans. Shortly after Egypt came back under 'Amr b. al-'As' control in c. 659, raids into Roman North Africa resumed, but no permanent settlement seems to have been established before 'Amr's death. Then, in 670, an attack under a Qurashi commander and nephew of 'Amr, 'Uqba b. Nafi', led to the foundation of a permanent garrison and headquarters at al-Qayrawan (Ar. 'the garrison camp') in modern Tunisia. This more sustained attack came immediately in the wake of Constans II's assassination in 668 or 669 and coincided with the land and naval campaigns against Constantinople that had begun in 668 and continued into the early 670s. 'Uqba is said to have had an army of 10,000 Arabians, augmented by

---

[55] On Sistan and Khurasan, see Clifford E. Bosworth, *Sistan Under the Arabs, from the Islamic Conquest to the Rise of the Saffarids (30–250/651–854)* (Rome, 1968), 13–45; *EI*², 'Khurasan' (C. E. Bosworth); Robert Haug, *The Eastern Frontier: Limits of Empire in Late Antique and Early Medieval Central Asia* (London and New York, 2019). For the settlement in 671 and the campaigns: Baladhuri, *Futuh*, 410–13; Tabari, II, 155–6, 169–70, 178–80; Saleh S. Agha, 'The Arab Population in Hurasan during the Umayyad Period: Some Demographic Computations', *Arabica* 46 (1999), 211–29; Hugh Kennedy, *The Armies of the Caliphs: Military and Society in the Early Islamic State* (London, 2001), 43–4 and n. 180; Étienne de la Vaissière, 'The Abbasid Revolution in Marw: New Data', *Der Islam* 95 (2018), 119–21. On Piruz, see Crone, *Nativist Prophets*, 4–5; Haug, *Eastern Frontier*, 92–3.

the African Luwata nomads of Roman Libya (north-west Egypt), and to have captured tens of thousands of slaves. By 678, under 'Uqba's successor, Abu l-Muhajir, alliances with the Romans' former allies among the Christian Awraba tribespeople had confined the Romans to the coastal centre of Carthage (modern Tunis).[56]

Whereas Mu'awiya relied on outsiders with local connections in Egypt and Iraq, in the Hijaz he appointed his own Umayyad family. The Hijaz was militarily insignificant but ideologically vital, as the home of the Quraysh and the Ansar and their descendants, the first centre of the Prophet's community, the site for the annual pilgrimage and the location of 'Uthman's killing. Hence, the Hijaz could more safely be entrusted to men with status independent of their links with Mu'awiya, because it would be hard to launch a military bid for the whole empire from there. However, it was also important to retain close ties to the region via trusted allies.[57] The former capital, Medina, was the most important Hijazi governorship, and was consistently entrusted to Umayyad relatives of 'Uthman who were also allies of Mu'awiya. For about twelve of Mu'awiya's twenty years in power, 'Uthman's cousin, son-in-law, scribe and advisor (and Mu'awiya's second cousin), Marwan b. al-Hakam, governed Medina (g. *c.* 662–*c.* 669 and *c.* 674–*c.* 677). Then, in the last years of Mu'awiya's life, Medina was passed to Mu'awiya's nephew, al-Walid b. 'Utba b. Abi Sufyan (g. *c.* 677–*c.* 682). This change was perhaps to ensure that the governorship of the former capital was in the hands of a close relative who was unlikely to oppose the succession of Mu'awiya's son, Yazid. Leadership of the *hajj* was usually, but not always, entrusted to this Medinan governor. When it was not, Mu'awiya emphasised the primacy of his own family, by having his brothers, and probably on at least one occasion, his son, lead it.[58]

---

[56] *EI²*, 'Kayrawan' (M. Talbi), 'Maslama b. Mukhallad', 'Mu'awiya b. Hudaydj' (Ch. Pellat), "Uqba b. Nafi" (V. Christides); Hugh Kennedy, *The Great Arab Conquests: How the Spread of Islam Changed the World We Live In* (London, 2007), 209–12. *Theophilus*, 164, says 80,000 slaves were captured in 670.

[57] On Mu'awiya and the veneration of the Prophet and 'Uthman, see McMillan, *Meaning*, 43–5, 57–8.

[58] McMillan, *Meaning*, 45–7, 51–61. The one exception is said to have been the *hajj* of April 661, led by al-Mughira b. Shu'ba.

5

The Succession to Muʿawiya and the Second Civil War

For Muʿawiya's immediate family and their Syrian allies to sustain their dominant position in the empire, it was critical that they establish the means to retain power after Muʿawiya's death. Muʿawiya's son Yazid became the focus of these efforts. Yazid was a son by the sister of a Kalbi leader and so was the only one of Muʿawiya's three sons with the necessary tribal lineage to secure support in Syria.[1] Yazid's appointment to command the campaign in Asia Minor in 668–9 and his leadership of the annual pilgrimage to Mecca in 670 or 671 were directed at enhancing his prestige with the frontier armies and at seeking the support of the Hijazis for the succession.[2] Muʿawiya had many of the most powerful figures in the empire publicly pledge their allegiance to Yazid, often in return for substantial payments. While these and other efforts were effective in persuading most of the wider Umayyad clan, other groups were less pliable. Muʿawiya was particularly concerned with the threat posed by support for ʿAli's family in Kufa and in the Hijaz and sought to intimidate and confront them. Muʿawiya is said to have instituted the cursing of ʿAli at Friday prayers in Kufa and to have publicly cursed ʿAli's name at the *hajj* in *c.* 670 or 671. Then, in 672, Muʿawiya had fourteen of the most vocal Kufan partisans of ʿAli sent to Syria and executed eight of them, including the Companion Hujr b. ʿAdi al-Kindi.[3]

When Muʿawiya died in the spring of 680, the scene was set for the sons of the main participants in the civil war of 656–61 to revive their respective claims to power. At Kufa, where many had backed Muhammad's cousin and son-in-law ʿAli b. Abi Talib during the civil war, aspirations now focused on al-Husayn b. ʿAli. Al-Husayn was both ʿAli's son and the Prophet Muhammad's sole surviving grandson, via Fatima, a daughter of the Prophet. (Al-Husayn's full brother, al-Hasan, who had surrendered to Muʿawiya in 661, had died in *c.* 670;

---

[1] Marsham, 'Kinship', 29–30.
[2] McMillan, *Meaning*, 51–9.
[3] *EI3*, 'Hujr b. ʿAdi l-Kindi' (Wilferd Madelung); McMillan, *Meaning*, 50–1 and n. 51.

some sources imply that Muʿawiya had him poisoned.⁴) During Muʿawiya's reign, al-Husayn had remained at Medina and is said to have avoided confrontation with the Umayyads, despite various efforts by Kufans to persuade him to revolt. Only when it became known at Medina that Muʿawiya had died did al-Husayn flee to Mecca, from where he sent an emissary to Kufa to assemble support in preparation to resist Yazid. However, Yazid knew of the Kufans' restiveness and is said to have sent his Basran governor, ʿUbayd Allah b. Ziyad, to take control of Kufa, too. There, ʿUbayd Allah violently suppressed the nascent revolt. He was also in time to send scouts to intercept al-Husayn's own advance from Mecca to Kufa. A larger force then confronted al-Husayn's caravan at Karbala, about 80km north of Kufa. The Arabic tradition recounts that, after some failed efforts at negotiation, a series of skirmishes culminated in the killing of al-Husayn and the massacre of almost all his family.⁵

Shock at the killing of the Prophet's surviving grandson reverberated throughout the new imperial elite. It could not but have repercussions. At Kufa, movements seeking 'blood vengeance for al-Husayn' (*talab dam al-Ḥusayn*) formed, going to war against the Syrians and Umayyads in 685. The figure of al-Husayn as a martyr to the true religion, wrongfully killed by impious tyrants, became a powerful focus of religious and political feeling, generating beliefs and practices that shaped Shiʿi Islam.⁶ However, from the point of view of Yazid, in 680, al-Husayn's revolt was probably seen as having been suppressed relatively quickly and easily. Supporters willing to go to war in the name of ʿAli's family were confined to a few thousand predominantly South Arabian tribespeople from Kufa, as well as a growing number of Kufa's non-Arabian population.

In contrast, the relatives of the first caliph, Abu Bakr, who were now represented by Abu Bakr's grandson, ʿAbd Allah b. al-Zubayr (r. 683–92), were a more serious threat. Ibn al-Zubayr and his allies were able to mobilise many of the wider Qurashi imperial elite against Umayyad leadership, together with large sections of the Basran and Egyptian armies. Ibn al-Zubayr was not only closely related to the Prophet by kinship and marriage but was also the son of one of the leaders of the Meccan coalition that had opposed ʿAli at the Battle

---

⁴ Khalifa, 128 and n. 3. See, for example, Yaʿqubi, II, 266, 271, where al-Hasan's death is connected with the pledge to Yazid b. Muʿawiya.
⁵ *EI*², '(al-) Husayn b. ʿAli b. Abi Talib' (L. Vecca Vaglieri).
⁶ On these movements, see Baladhuri, *Ansab*, VI, 28–37. The events at Karbala are the central tragedy of Shiʿi Islam, when the Prophet's grandson and his family were unjustly slaughtered. Ashura, the tenth day of Muharram, the first month of the Islamic lunar year, is a day of mourning and repentance in the Shiʿi tradition: *EI3*, 'Ashura (Shiʿism)' (K. S. Aghaie). On Ashura in Sunnism, see *EI3*, 'Ashura (Sunnism)' (M. H. Reid).

of the Camel in 656 and of the sister of another – his mother, Asma', being the sister of 'A'isha bt. Abi Bakr, one of the Prophet's widows. (See Chart 4.1, above.) Furthermore, Ibn al-Zubayr, who was now in his late sixties, was an experienced commander, who had fought in Egypt, North Africa and Iran. Just as many of Quraysh who had opposed 'Ali in 656 had seen al-Zubayr, Talha and 'A'isha as the focus of their aspirations, many of the Faithful in 680 who supported neither Yazid nor al-Husayn saw Ibn al-Zubayr as the best candidate for the leadership; resentment of Syrian and Umayyad domination of the empire supplied him with extensive support.[7]

Like al-Husayn, Ibn al-Zubayr fled to Mecca when news of Mu'awiya's death reached Medina. However, unlike al-Husayn, he remained there, gathering a group of supporters and outmanoeuvring attempts to compel him to pledge allegiance to Yazid. Ibn al-Zubayr's opposition to Yazid is said to have been articulated as opposition to Mu'awiya's imposition of Yazid as nominated successor; Ibn al-Zubayr is said in some reports to have taken pledges of allegiance on the basis that he would initiate a *shūrā* – a consultation among the Hijazis about the choice of leader. In 680 or 681, Ibn al-Zubayr and his supporters successfully repulsed a force sent against them from Medina. By 682, resistance to Yazid and the Umayyads had spread through the Hijaz, and the Umayyad clan were driven from Medina. In response, in 683, Yazid sent a Syrian army south to recapture Medina and then march on Ibn al-Zubayr in Mecca. The army, led by two of Mu'awiya's most trusted former commanders, defeated the Medinans at the Battle of the Harra in August 683 and then pressed on south to besiege Mecca. However, after some months of fighting, news of Yazid's sudden and early death reached the Hijaz. For the Syrian forces at Mecca this made a return to Syria urgent, since their absence would mean losing any influence over the succession.[8]

Yazid's son Mu'awiya b. Yazid (r. 683–4) is said to have been chosen as a successor but to have died within a few months of his accession; he does not seem to have had time even to consolidate his rule much beyond Damascus.[9] This second death of an Umayyad leader within a few months broke the Umayyads' grip on the empire. By the summer of 684, the Hijaz was under Ibn al-Zubayr's control and Zubayrid governors were in place in Egypt and Iraq.[10] Even the Syrian tribes were split, with many of those groups who were not as closely tied to the Umayyad dynasty as the Banu Kalb now supporting

---

[7] *EI²*, "Abd Allah b. al-Zubayr' (H. A. R. Gibb); *EI3*, "Abd Allah b. al-Zubayr' (S. Campbell).
[8] Tabari, II, 219–27, 272–8, 395–9, 402–3, 405–32. The detail about the *shūrā* is in al-Baladhuri, *Ansab*, IV, 338, but not in al-Tabari's version.
[9] *EI²*, 'Mu'awiya II' (C. E. Bosworth).
[10] Tabari, II, 465–7.

Ibn al-Zubayr. Many of them had migrated to Syria from southern and central Iraq after the Battle of the Camel in 656, and so their decision to back Ibn al-Zubayr may reflect long-standing connections with the house of Abu Bakr.[11] Only the Syrian district of al-Urdunn, around Lake Tiberias, remained entirely loyal to the Umayyads, under the leadership of the Kalbi chief, and maternal cousin of Yazid, Hassan b. Malik b. Bahdal (usually simply known as Hassan b. Bahdal, or Ibn Bahdal).[12]

However, although Ibn al-Zubayr was best placed to claim leadership of the empire by the mid-680s, the years of conflict after Mu'awiya's death had created opportunities for other actors to reassert their independence or make bids for greater power. On the Arabian Peninsula, in the highlands of eastern Iraq and western Iran, and in the contested frontier territories of North Africa, northern Iraq and the Caucasus, local political actors were resurgent.

In North Africa, 'Berber' and Roman forces took advantage of the conflict among the Arabians. In 681, Kusayla (or Kasila, d. 688), leader of the Awraba federation of North African tribes broke his alliance with the Arabians. Kusayla inflicted defeats on the Arabians in the early 680s and by 683 he had made the former Arabian garrison of Qayrawan into his capital.[13] In the East, when news of Yazid's death reached Khurasan and Sistan, Yazid's governor faced widespread rebellion among his army and fled to the Hijaz, where he joined Ibn al-Zubayr. Competing elements in the Khurasani armies and Hephthalite leaders campaigning out of the Afghan highlands then fought over Khurasan's resources, with a commander sent by Ibn al-Zubayr joining the conflict in 683–4.[14] In the Caucasus, the Khazars and the Romans waged campaigns in 685 and 686, taking advantage of the absence of Arabian imperial authority.[15]

Much of the unrest in the later 680s presented particular challenges to Ibn al-Zubayr in the Hijaz and his paternal half-brother Mus'ab in Iraq. On the Arabian Peninsula, the Banu Hanifa, who had fought against Medina in the so-called 'Ridda Wars' fifty years earlier, produced two leaders, Nafi' b. al-Azraq (d. 685) and Najda b. 'Amir (d. 692–3), who both lent some support

---

[11] *SoH*, 105–9.
[12] Tabari, II, 467–71.
[13] Abu l-Qasim Ibn 'Abd al-Hakam, *Kitab Futuh Misr wa-Akhbariha (= The History of the Conquest of Egypt, North Africa and Spain)*, ed. Charles C. Torrey (New Haven, 1922), 198–200; Muhammad Ibn 'Idhari al-Marrakashi, *Al-Bayan al-Mughrib fi Akhbar al-Andalus wa-l-Maghrib*, ed. G. S. Colin and E. Lévi-Provençal (Beirut, 2009), I, 28–34; *EI²*, 'Kusayla' (M. Talbi).
[14] Haug, *Eastern Frontier*, 101–6.
[15] *WtaWC*, 496–7; Alison Vacca, 'The Umayyad North (Or: How Umayyad was the Umayyad Caliphate?)', in Andrew Marsham (ed.), *The Umayyad World* (London and New York, 2021), 223.

to Ibn al-Zubayr before breaking with him and asserting their own independent religious and political authority. Nafiʿ and Najda were based in southern Iraq and eastern Arabia, respectively, with followers from the dominant tribal groups in those regions – from their own Banu Hanifa, from the wider grouping of the Bakr b. Waʾil, and from Tamim.[16] Also in southern Iraq, there was a rebellion among the African agricultural slaves, who worked lands near Basra.[17]

Further north, Kufa had remained restive after the killing of al-Husayn. The ire of al-Husayn's supporters was initially directed towards the Syrians and the Umayyads – in 685 the Kufan 'Penitents' (*tawwābūn*) movement marched against the Syrians after a pilgrimage to al-Husayn's grave at Karbala, seeking 'blood vengeance for al-Husayn', but were defeated and killed by Syrian troops.[18] However, pro-ʿAlid feeling also inspired movements that challenged Ibn al-Zubayr's authority. After the defeat of the Penitents, al-Mukhtar al-Thaqafi (d. 687) proclaimed a summons at Kufa for allegiance to Muhammad b. al-Hanafiyya (d. 700–1), who was a son of ʿAli by a slave woman. The charismatic and prophet-like al-Mukhtar announced Muhammad b. al-Hanafiyya as a saviour figure (*mahdī*). Al-Mukhtar's supporters were different from the Penitents, in that they comprised many of the non-Arabians in Kufa to whom he promised a share of tax revenues, alongside his other, mostly South Arabian, supporters. The millenarian ideas promoted by al-Mukhtar united both groups in their opposition to the current power structures in the empire, but Ibn al-Zubayr's Basran governor, Musʿab b. al-Zubayr, defeated and killed al-Mukhtar and many of his followers in 687.[19]

The Rebellion of al-Mukhtar al-Thaqafi at Kufa, 685–7

For the medieval Arabic historians as for modern ones, al-Mukhtar's revolt of 685–7 was intriguing and somewhat exotic. Moreover, some of its distinctive social, political and religious features presaged the Abbasid Revolution of 747–50 that overthrew Umayyad rule. Certainly, the details in the Arabic accounts are suggestive about the social, political and religious

---

[16] *EI3*, 'Azariqa' (K. Lewinstein); *EI²*, 'Katari b. Fujaʾa' (G. Levi Della Vida), 'Nadjadat' (R. Rubinacci), 'Nafiʿ b. al-Azrak (A. J. Wensinck); Hannah-Lena Hagemann and Peter Verkinderen, 'Kharijism in the Umayyad Period', in Andrew Marsham (ed.), *The Umayyad World* (London and New York, 2021), 489–517.
[17] Baladhuri, *Ansab*, VI, 414; *EI²*, 'al-Zandj. 2. The Zandj revolts in Irak' (A. Popovic); Alexandre Popovic, *La Révolte des esclaves en Iraq au IIIe, IXe siècle* (Paris, 1976), 62–3.
[18] Baladhuri, *Ansab*, VI, 28–37.
[19] *EI²*, 'Muhammad b. al-Hanafiyya' (Fr. Buhl), 'al-Mukhtar b. Abi ʿUbayd' (G. Hawting). For the promise of tax revenues to the non-Arabians, see Tabari, II, 650–1.

dynamics at Kufa in the 680s, fewer than fifty years after the foundation of the garrison.[20]

According to the later Arabic narratives, al-Mukhtar was from a branch of the Banu Thaqif, a tribal group from al-Ta'if near Mecca who were closely allied with Quraysh. Al-Mukhtar's sister was married to a son of the second caliph, 'Umar I (r. 634–44), and his father had fought the Sasanians in Iraq, where he had been killed in the mid-630s. Thereafter, al-Mukhtar was brought up by an uncle, who was later 'Ali b. Abi Talib's governor of al-Mada'in/Ctesiphon. After the destabilisation of the empire on the death of Mu'awiya in 680, al-Mukhtar moved between Kufa and Mecca, apparently attempting to keep his political options open between the Umayyads, Zubayrids, and 'Alids. He was imprisoned twice at Kufa, by Yazid I's governor in 680 and then by Ibn al-Zubayr's governors in 684 but was released on each occasion at the intercession of his brother-in-law.

At Kufa, al-Mukhtar was critical of Sulayman b. Surad's (d. 685) weak leadership of the Penitents (*al-tawwābūn*), who had rebelled in 684 the name of vengeance for al-Husayn (d. 680), and by *c.* 685 he was preparing to revolt himself. He claimed to have a letter from Muhammad b. al-Hanafiyya, a son of 'Ali by a slave woman, designating him as the trusted representative (*amīn* and *wazīr*) of the Imam. Al-Mukhtar's speeches were delivered in the rhythmic rhyming prose (*saj'*) of the Qur'an and the West Arabian 'soothsayers' (*kuhanā'*, sing. *kāhin*), signalling a claim to sacred or inspired knowledge.[21] His supporters comprised some of the Kufan South Arabians sympathetic to 'Ali's family, as well as non-Arabians, who had originally come to Kufa as captives (*mawālī*, sing. *mawlā*, 'freed slaves'). Because some of his poorer recruits carried wooden clubs instead of expensive metal weapons, they are referred to as *khashabiyya* ('club bearers', lit. 'wood people'). They are also called *kaysāniyya* ('followers of Kaysan', lit. 'Kaysan people'), which became a term referring to groups who held that true leadership of the Muslims had passed from 'Ali to Muhammad b. al-Hanafiyya. Kaysaniyya is derived from the name of the head of

---

[20] On the revolt, see *EI²*, 'al-Mukhtar b. Abi 'Ubayd' (G. Hawting). For a literary analysis of the Arabic tradition, see Najam Haider, *The Rebel and the Imam: Explorations in Muslim Historiography* (Cambridge, 2019), 26–114.

[21] Qutbuddin, *Arabic Oration*; Hasan Al-Khoee, 'Functions of Arabic Public Speeches in Early Islam: The Evidence from the Second Civil War (64–70/683–689)', PhD Dissertation, SOAS, University of London (2020).

al-Mukhtar's personal guard (*ḥaras*), who comprised freed slaves of Iraqi and Iranian heritage.[22]

Between autumn 685 and summer 686, al-Mukhtar contested power with Ibn al-Zubayr's allies, achieving sufficient success to appoint his own commanders in Armenia, Azerbaijan, Mosul, al-Mada'in/Ctesiphon, Bihkuban and Hulwan. However, al-Mukhtar only comprehensively defeated his local opponents in July 686, after which he carried out executions in vengeance for the death of al-Husayn, sending some of the heads to Ibn al-Hanafiyya in Mecca, and sending men to spring him from the house arrest under which Ibn al-Zubayr had put him. Ibn al-Hanafiyya, however, seems to have been cautious about al-Mukhtar, going only to neighbouring al-Ta'if rather than to Kufa.

Al-Mukhtar now faced two attempts to retake Kufa, by the Umayyads and Zubayrids. On the river Khazir, near Mosul, he fought 'Ubayd Allah b. Ziyad, the Umayyad commander who had killed al-Husayn at Karbala. Al-Mukhtar brought to the battlefield a chair made from tamarisk wood that he claimed had belonged to 'Ali. It was carried on a mule and draped in cloth. While some of the sources are disparaging of this idolatrous 'Golden Calf', the presence of numinous talismanic objects on the battlefield was commonplace in Late Antiquity, as was veiling sacred objects under valuable textiles – the problem for the chair's detractors was that they considered it bogus and its owner false (*kadhdhāb*), not that they disapproved of proper talismanic objects. Indeed, the chair recalls the Christian icons and banners displayed by Roman armies, the display of the Qur'an pages at the Battle of Siffin in 657, or even the presence of the living 'A'isha, the Prophet's widow, in a howdah on a camel at the 'Battle of the Camel' in 656.[23] At the Battle of the Khazir, al-Mukhtar defeated and killed 'Ubayd Allah, but then marched south to face Ibn al-Zubayr's commander. The latter inflicted heavy defeats on al-Mukhtar, who fled to Kufa, where he was killed in the spring of 687. Many of his followers were executed.

Al-Mukhtar's revolt is an early example of a social movement comprising both migrant Arabians and freed slaves and their descendants acting in the name of the Arabians' monotheist religion. It shows the potential for the idea of leadership by 'Ali and his family to unite disparate social and

---

[22] On wooden weapons and the social context of the revolt, see Crone, 'Significance', 174–87. On the name 'Kaysaniyya', see *EI²*, 'Kaysaniyya' (W. Madelung).

[23] On banners, relics and 'Ali's chair, see Elizabeth Key Fowden, 'Shrines and Banners: Paleo-Muslims and their Material Inheritance', in Lorenz Korn and Ivrem Çiğden (eds), *Encompassing the Sacred in Islamic Art* (Wiesbaden, 2020), 5–24. For 'A'isha at the Battle of the Camel, see above, p. 90.

religious groups in opposition to the rule of the other Meccan clans who had benefited the most from the conquests – the Umayyads and Zubayrids and their allies. Indeed, the Kaysaniyya movement continued among the Kufan *mawālī* after al-Mukhtar's death. After Muhammad b. al-Hanafiyya died in 700–1, some Kaysaniyya believed he remained alive and would return as the Mahdi; others believed he would return from the dead (*rajʿa*). Still others looked to his son, Abu Hashim (d. *c.* 718–19), for leadership, and then to people they claimed the childless Abu Hashim had designated to lead after him – a claim later picked up by the Abbasids.[24]

The Coming of the Marwanids and the Defeat of Ibn al-Zubayr

Before the beleaguered Syrian tribes and Umayyads could confront their Zubayrid opponents, they needed a new leader and so they gathered near Damascus to decide. Muʿawiya's second cousin Marwan b. al-Hakam (r. 684–5) prevailed over Muʿawiya's immediate descendants: that is, the succession passed from the descendants of Muʿawiya's grandfather, Harb b. Umayya, and back to the descendants of ʿUthman's grandfather, Abu l-ʿAs b. Umayya (see Chart 5.1).

Much of the tradition represents Marwan b. al-Hakam as the pragmatic choice, based on age, experience and proven ability, albeit provoking grievances within Muʿawiya's family.[25] In 684 Marwan was probably about sixty years old. In his youth he had fought on many of the empire's frontiers and had also placed himself at the centre of Umayyad networks, having served as a scribe and leading confidant of his cousin ʿUthman, before becoming Muʿawiya's governor in the former imperial capital of Medina for most of the 660s and 670s. Marwan's wives included a daughter of ʿUthman, a woman from the Qurashi clan of Makhzum, and a cousin descended from his grandfather, Abu l-ʿAs. Like both Muʿawiya and ʿUthman, he also married into the Banu Kalb of Syria. These marriages speak to his own and his father's efforts to develop political connections.[26]

Meanwhile, other Syrian tribal groups who had decided instead for Ibn al-Zubayr had also gathered just outside Damascus, under the leadership of Muʿawiya and Yazid's former governor of the city, the Qurashi al-Dahhak b. Qays al-Fihri, who had pledged allegiance to Ibn al-Zubayr and been recognised

---

[24] *EI²*, 'Kaysaniyya' (W. Madelung). On the revolt and the Abbasid Revolution, see Crone, 'Significance'; Saleh S. Agha, *The Revolution Which Toppled the Umayyads: Neither Arab nor ʿAbbasid* (Leiden, 2003), xxxiii–vi, 6–38, 53–4 n. 13.
[25] Tabari, II, 473–7, 481–2, 487; *EI3*, 'Khalid b. Yazid' (R. Foster).
[26] *EI²*, 'Marwan I b. al-Hakam' (C. E. Bosworth); Marsham, 'Kinship', 27–31, 33–4.

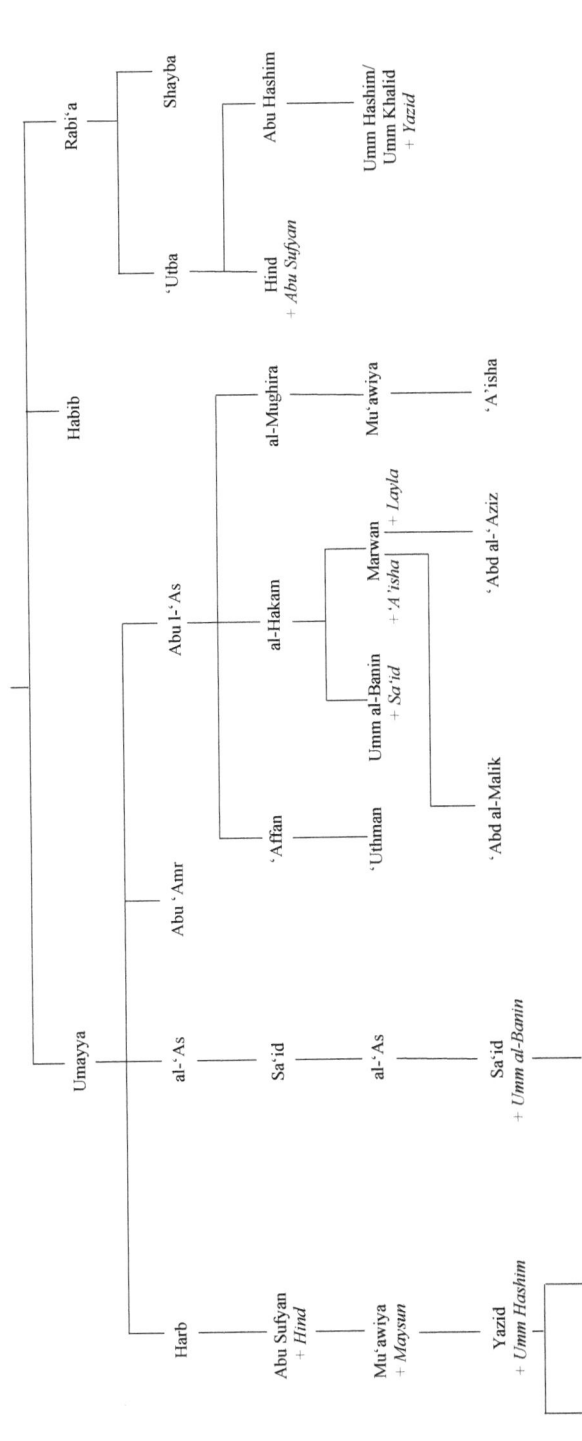

Chart 5.1 Simplified genealogy of Marwan b. al-Hakam and his Umayyad relatives. People marked in *italics* are spouses who also appear elsewhere in the chart as sons or daughters (except for Maysun and Layla, who appear in Chart 4.2, above).

as his governor in Syria. After some skirmishes, Marwan and al-Dahhak met in battle in August 684 at Marj Rahit ('the meadow of Rahit'), just to the east of Damascus. Had al-Dahhak won the day at Marj Rahit, he would almost certainly have extinguished the Umayyad claim to the caliphate forever. Instead, victory fell to Marwan and his Kalbi allies. With southern Syria regained, they could begin to reassert their claims against Ibn al-Zubayr more widely.[27]

As in the crisis of 656–61, access to the resources of Egypt was a priority for the Umayyads; Marwan is said to have gone there in person, together with his son 'Abd al-'Aziz and his sister's son, 'Amr b. Sa'id al-Ashdaq. Marwan then appointed 'Abd al-'Aziz (g. c. 684–704) as Egypt's governor.[28] A few months later, the same 'Amr al-Ashdaq who had gone to Egypt headed the army that repulsed efforts by Ibn al-Zubayr's brother Mus'ab to invade southern Syria. Two further expeditions were launched by Marwan, against the Hijaz and Iraq, the latter led by the province's former governor, 'Ubayd Allah b. Ziyad. However, these first counter-attacks against Ibn al-Zubayr were interrupted by the relatively elderly Marwan's illness and death in the spring of 685.[29]

Although Marwan's death came less than a year after he had taken power, he is said to have made efforts on his deathbed to prepare for a smooth succession, taking pledges to two sons by different women, 'Abd al-Malik and 'Abd al-'Aziz. 'Abd al-Malik was to take the leadership first. As a descendant on both sides from Marwan's grandfather, Abu l-'As, he was an ideal choice to consolidate the grip of Marwan's immediate family on the caliphate. However, were 'Abd al-'Aziz, newly appointed as governor of Egypt, to outlive 'Abd al-Malik, then he was to succeed him. Most likely, 'Abd al-'Aziz was nominated as 'Abd al-Malik's successor in order to secure the continued loyalty of the Kalb, who would have seen 'Abd al-'Aziz, with his descent from a Kalbi mother, as their guarantee of continued access to power after the end of Mu'awiya's ruling line.[30]

Despite Marwan's preparations, 'Abd al-Malik had inherited a precarious situation from his father. First, he had succeeded to power only in southern Syria and Egypt. Elsewhere, Ibn al-Zubayr was now widely recognised as caliph. Of Marwan's two expeditions against Iraq and the Hijaz, the first

---

[27] Tabari, II, 471–4, 477–81, 482–6.
[28] Abu 'Umar Muhammad b. Yusuf al-Kindi, *The Governors and Judges of Egypt* (= *Kitab Wulat Misr wa-Qudatiha*), ed. Rhuvon Guest (Leiden, 1912) [hereafter, Kindi], 42–5; Baladhuri, *Ansab*, VI, 25; Tabari, II, 481.
[29] Tabari, II, 476, 481, 576–8.
[30] Marsham, 'Kinship', 33. Some reports have Marwan having taken power on the agreement that he would be succeeded by Khalid b. Yazid or 'Amr al-Ashdaq, or both. In some accounts, this agreement was superseded by the plan for Marwan's sons to succeed him: Baladhuri, *Ansab*, VI, 25–6; al-Tabari, II, 476, 487, 576; *RoIM*, 117–18.

had returned to Syria on the news of Marwan's death and the other had been defeated outside Medina. Tribes in northern Syria also remained loyal to Ibn al-Zubayr and, although northern Iraq had recently been lost by its Zubayrid governor, this was limited comfort since the rebellions there were in the name of the family of 'Ali and al-Husayn, not the Umayyads.[31] Second, and perhaps most ominously, the Romans sent an army into the Caucasus in 686, who are said to have extracted tribute across the whole region and to have reached north-west Iran. At the same time, Roman support was given to renewed Mardaite rebellions in the mountains of northern and western Syria. Third, 'Abd al-Malik's own accession had provoked some resentment among some of the Banu Kalb who, for the first time since the reign of 'Umar, were not closely related to the caliph (leaving aside 'Ali, whom they had not acknowledged).

At first, 'Abd al-Malik sought to engage Ibn al-Zubayr directly. However, an expedition launched against Iraq was defeated by the pro-'Alid al-Mukhtar and his Kufan soldiers. The expedition's commander, 'Ubayd Allah b. Ziyad, was killed and some of its former members now joined the Zubayrid cause in northern Syria and Iraq.[32] This setback, together with the Roman and Khazar presence in the Caucasus, appears to have prompted a change in strategy. Just as the circumstances of the Umayyads in many ways now resembled those in 656–61, 'Abd al-Malik's response now came to resemble Mu'awiya's patient methods. Rather than attacking Ibn al-Zubayr head-on, he instead concentrated on negotiating a truce with the Romans and consolidating his position within Syria, while making tentative forays into northern Iraq and seeking to foment rebellion in the south. As in the first civil war, this incremental approach was made possible by disunity within the rival territories – particularly in Kufa, where the pro-'Alid insurrection was ongoing – but also elsewhere in Iraq and Arabia, where widespread unrest threatened the Zubayrids.[33]

Agreement with the Romans was probably reached at some point between 686 and 689. The resources of Egypt had given 'Abd al-Malik something with which to bargain. For their part, the Romans were probably also happy to come to terms, since they faced pressure in the Balkans from the newly formed Bulgar federation.[34] The agreement may have been drawn

---

[31] See above pp. 105–8.
[32] Tabari, II, 574, 578, 642–3.
[33] On unrest in Iraq and Arabia, see above, pp. 104–8 and Tabari, II, 496–537; cf. Sebastian Brock, 'North Mesopotamia in the late seventh century: Book XV of John Bar Penkaye's *Rīš Mellē*', *JSAI* 9 (1987), 64–7. On 'Abd al-Malik's efforts to foment insurrection in Basra, see Tabari, II, 798–803.
[34] *WtaWC*, 497–9.

up along the lines of the agreement Muʻawiya had previously made:[35] the Romans would cease hostilities and withdraw support for the Mardaites in north-west Syria in return for regular payments of thousands of gold coins, as well as horses or mules, freed prisoners and silk garments – all prestigious and valuable resources in seventh-century warfare and politics. Some accounts mention that the tax revenues of Cyprus, in the Mediterranean, and Armenia and Georgia, in the Caucasus, were also now to be shared between the Umayyads and the Romans.[36]

In Syria, ʻAbd al-Malik not only faced the continued resistance of tribal groups loyal to Ibn al-Zubayr but also resentment within the Umayyad elite and their allies in the Banu Kalb. In 689, as he gathered an army against the Zubayrid loyalists, his paternal cousin, ʻAmr b. Saʻid al-Ashdaq, returned to Damascus and claimed the caliphate for himself. Al-Ashdaq asserted that the succession had been promised to him in 684 in return for his support for Marwan. Al-Ashdaq had indeed been instrumental in reconquering Egypt and in defending Syria from Musʻab b. al-Zubayr's attacks and so was well placed to press such a claim. Furthermore, like Marwan, he had governed Medina for Yazid. He was the son of Marwan's sister and had also married into the Banu Kalb, who were split by al-Ashdaq's claim. Two of their leaders supported him and others remained loyal to ʻAbd al-Malik.[37]

ʻAbd al-Malik's response combined ruthlessness and political acumen. Having besieged Damascus with the support of his remaining Kalbi allies, he offered al-Ashdaq a guarantee of security (*amān*) and then, having ended the siege and lured al-Ashdaq into an audience, betrayed the pact. According to one account, ʻAbd al-Malik's intention was to keep his own hands clean and compromise his half-brother ʻAbd al-ʻAziz, by having ʻAbd al-ʻAziz kill al-Ashdaq. However, when ʻAbd al-ʻAziz refused, ʻAbd al-Malik himself gave orders that the bound al-Ashdaq be thrown to the floor. Then, ʻAbd al-Malik 'sat on his chest and cut his throat'. Whether or not this vivid image of one cousin slaughtering another is literary embellishment, other reports – of payments to al-Ashdaq's supporters, the execution of other opponents and the

---

[35] Baladhuri, *Ansab*, VI, 142. The specific terms echo those attributed to Muʻawiya and are likely a literary topos: see above, p. 91.

[36] The Greek and Syriac traditions have the payment at 1,000 solidi per day, the Arabic traditions per week: Baladhuri, *Ansab*, 141–2; Tabari, II, 796; *WtaWC*, 497; *Theophilus*, 180–1.

[37] Baladhuri, *Ansab*, VI, 27–8, 30; Tabari, II, 783–5. On ʻAmr's ancestry, governorships, and claims about the succession, see al-Zubayri, *Nasab*, 178–9; Baladhuri, *Ansab*, V, 23–7. For his Kalbi wife, see al-Tabari, II, 786; cf. al-Zubayri, *Nasab*, 182 and n. 1.

imprisonment of al-Ashdaq's sons prior to an eventual reconciliation with some of them – seem plausible.[38]

With his throne more secure in southern and central Syria, 'Abd al-Malik returned to the campaign on the Euphrates in the north and east.[39] This took place in a Syrian political landscape that had been transformed by the Umayyad victory against Syrian Zubayrid loyalists at the battle of Marj Rahit, in 684. As in most societies in which political identities are expressed in terms of the membership of kinship groups, political changes were also expressed in the language of kinship. Many of the Syrian supporters of Ibn al-Zubayr were from tribes that had migrated into northern Syria from Iraq after 656. These groups looked back to a common legendary ancestor named Qays, notionally the ancestor of most of the tribes of northern and Central Arabia (whence their other title, 'northerners'). Because Qays was believed to have lived about seventeen generations ago – that is, about 500 years in the past – he could serve as a fictional common bond among the recent migrants.[40]

Prior to the battle at Marj Rahit, Kalb and the wider federation of Quda'a, who were loyal to the Umayyads and had prevailed in the battle, also appear to have considered themselves 'northern' descendants of Qays. However, in the wake of Marj Rahit, they now came to define themselves in opposition to the 'Qaysi', 'North Arabian' tribes, claiming a common descent with Kinda from southern Arabia, in order to make their claims about their kinship line up with a shared loyalty to the Umayyad clan. That is, Kalb and the wider Quda'a now became 'southerners', or 'Yemenis', alongside Kindi tribespeople, who had migrated to Syria in the 630s and 640s and also remained loyal to Umayyad rule. Hence, all the Umayyads' Syrian supporters were now identified as 'southern', or 'Yemeni', in distinction from those Qaysi, 'northern', Syrian tribes still loyal to Ibn al-Zubayr.[41]

Thus, the conflict in northern Syria pitted Umayyad 'Yemenis' against the Zubayrid 'Qaysis', or, to put it differently, it opposed an alliance of local Romano-Syrians and South Arabian migrants of the 630s and 640s against more recent migrants who had come from Iraq after 656. The most prominent leader of the Zubayrids' allies was Zufar b. al-Harith al-Kilabi, who had fled to Qarqisiya, on the Euphrates (Roman Circesium, modern Buseira, near

---

[38] Baladhuri, *Ansab*, VI, 27–39; Tabari, II, 785–96, 805; quotation at II, 791 (tr. M. Fishbein in Tabari, *History*, XXI, 162); Robinson, *'Abd al-Malik*, 27–8.
[39] Tabari, II, 797.
[40] Wüstenfeld, *Genealogische Tabellen*, II, 'Uebersichts-Tabelle der Isma'ilitischen Stämme'.
[41] Julius Wellhausen, *The Arab Kingdom and Its Fall*, tr. M. G. Weir (Calcutta, 1927), 180–2; Gerald R. Hawting, *The First Dynasty of Islam: The Umayyad Caliphate, A.D. 661–750* (London, 2000), 36; Crone, 'Qays and Yemen', 2–3, 45–8. See further, Box Text pp. 195–7.

Dayr al-Zur, in north-east Syria) after the defeat at Marj Rahit. However, Qarqisiya became an isolated outpost of Zubayrid power, encircled by Syrian tribes loyal to ʿAbd al-Malik. Early in 691, Zufar was persuaded to surrender. Unlike al-Ashdaq, Zufar was not himself a potential rival claimant to leadership of Quraysh and their empire, and so his safe conduct was respected. ʿAbd al-Malik merely required non-aggression from Zufar until Ibn al-Zubayr was killed, after which he wanted military service; in return Zufar was rewarded with wealth to divide among his supporters and the marriage of one of Zufar's daughters to one of ʿAbd al-Malik's sons.[42]

Having paid off the Roman Empire with gold and having detached the Qaysi tribes of northern Syria and Iraq from loyalty to the Zubayrids, ʿAbd al-Malik could move against Iraq itself with the full force of a united Syrian army. Ibn al-Zubayr's brother Musʿab, who governed Iraq, was vulnerable, having faced continual unrest, and ʿAbd al-Malik was able to exploit these divisions to bring some Iraqi tribespeople into allegiance. Musʿab made what he is said to have known would be his last stand in the Autumn of 691 at 'the Monastery of the Catholicos [of the Church of the East]' (Dayr al-Jathaliq, now Tel al-Dayr), about 150km north of Kufa. With Musʿab killed and his army routed, the way to Kufa was open. ʿAbd al-Malik marched south, camping just outside the garrison to receive the allegiance of the Kufans' leaders. The death of Musʿab also prompted the Basrans to surrender, exposing the Hijaz and Ibn al-Zubayr's capital at Mecca.[43]

Whereas ʿAbd al-Malik had taken personal command of the conquest of Iraq, he appointed one of his commanders, al-Hajjaj b. Yusuf al-Thaqafi, over the invasion of the Hijaz. As a Thaqafi, from al-Taʾif near Mecca, al-Hajjaj had allies among the tribes in the region and – bypassing Medina – he was able to secure al-Taʾif without fighting. From there he approached Mecca. According to the later tradition, ʿAbd al-Malik had explicitly forbidden al-Hajjaj from fighting in the Meccan sacred enclave (ḥaram) or bombarding the shrine within it. However, Ibn al-Zubayr's continued resistance prompted al-Hajjaj to write to the caliph seeking reinforcements and permission to violate the enclave. A stand-off during the pilgrimage of April 692 was followed by a prolonged siege, in which the Kaʿba itself was eventually bombarded. By November, promises of safe conduct had lured most of Ibn al-Zubayr's supporters to al-Hajjaj and

---

[42] Baladhuri, *Ansab*, VI, 140–1, 142–51, XIII, 87–90; Tabari, II, 480–1, 482–6, 784; Abd Al-Ameer Dixon, *The Umayyad Caliphate 65–86/684–705* (London, 1971), 89–95; Suzanne Pinckney Stetkevych, 'Umayyad Panegyric and the Poetics of Islamic Hegemony: Al-Akhtal's *Khaffa al-Qatinu* ("Those that dwelt with you have left in haste")', *Journal of Arabic Literature* 28 (1997), 89–122.

[43] Tabari, II, 753–83, 796, 798–818; *EI*², 'Dayr al-Djathalik' (A. A. Duri).

Mecca was overwhelmed. Ibn al-Zubayr's beheaded body was displayed publicly on a gibbet at Medina. The violent public humiliation was intended to reflect God's judgement on Ibn al-Zubayr's false claims to legitimate authority, and the righteousness of the Umayyad cause.[44]

---

[44] Tabari, II, 829–52. On such executions, see Andrew Marsham, 'Public Execution in the Umayyad Period: Early Islamic Punitive Practice and its Late Antique Context', *Journal of Arabic and Islamic Studies* 11 (2011), 101–36; Sean W. Anthony, *Crucifixion and Death as Spectacle: Umayyad Crucifixion in Its Late Antique Context* (New Haven, 2014).

PART II
THE MARWANID UMAYYAD EMPIRE, 692–750

Part II Introduction

'Abd al-Malik's reign after his victory in the civil war (692–705) marks a turning point in the political history of the new empire. Kinship had always been a powerful factor in the politics of the Quraysh, but no leader before 'Abd al-Malik had been succeeded by a son without violent opposition and no leader could be said to have successfully established a dynasty. In contrast, 'Abd al-Malik was succeeded peacefully by nine members of his family, in three generations – between 705 and 743 two of his sons, a nephew, and then two more of his sons and a grandson held power. Even when violent conflict broke out within the dynasty after 743, another two grandsons and then another nephew ruled, until the fall of the Umayyads in 750. For this reason, the period 684–750 is usually known as the era of the Marwanid Umayyads, or Marwanids, after 'Abd al-Malik's father and predecessor as caliph in Syria, Marwan b. al-Hakam (r. 684–5), the progenitor of all the subsequent Umayyad caliphs (see Chart II.1).

The ability to pass power relatively smoothly within the Marwanid branch of the Umayyad clan for fifty years reflects the comprehensive nature of the victory of 'Abd al-Malik and the Syrian tribes in the campaigns of 689–92. Thereafter, the main Qurashi tribal groups who had contended for leadership of the empire in the seventh century abandoned their efforts to take power, some permanently and some only temporarily. None of Abu Bakr's Zubayrid relatives sought power for themselves again, and many of his former supporters went over to the Marwanids or at least tolerated their rule. In contrast, the claims of the Prophet's tribe, the Banu Hashim, retained their political potency; when the Umayyad caliphate collapsed in 750, it was the Abbasid branch of Banu Hashim (that is, the descendants of the Prophet's and 'Ali's uncle al-'Abbas b. 'Abd al-Muttalib) who took power. However, no member of Hashim was the figurehead for a rebellion between 687 and 740; after the debacles of the killing of al-Husayn in 680, the massacre of the Penitents in 685 and the failure of al-Mukhtar's rebellion in the name of Muhammad b. al-Hanafiyya in 687, it took a particular set of circumstances for the ideological potential of close kinship with the Prophet Muhammad to again be realised in effective militant political action.

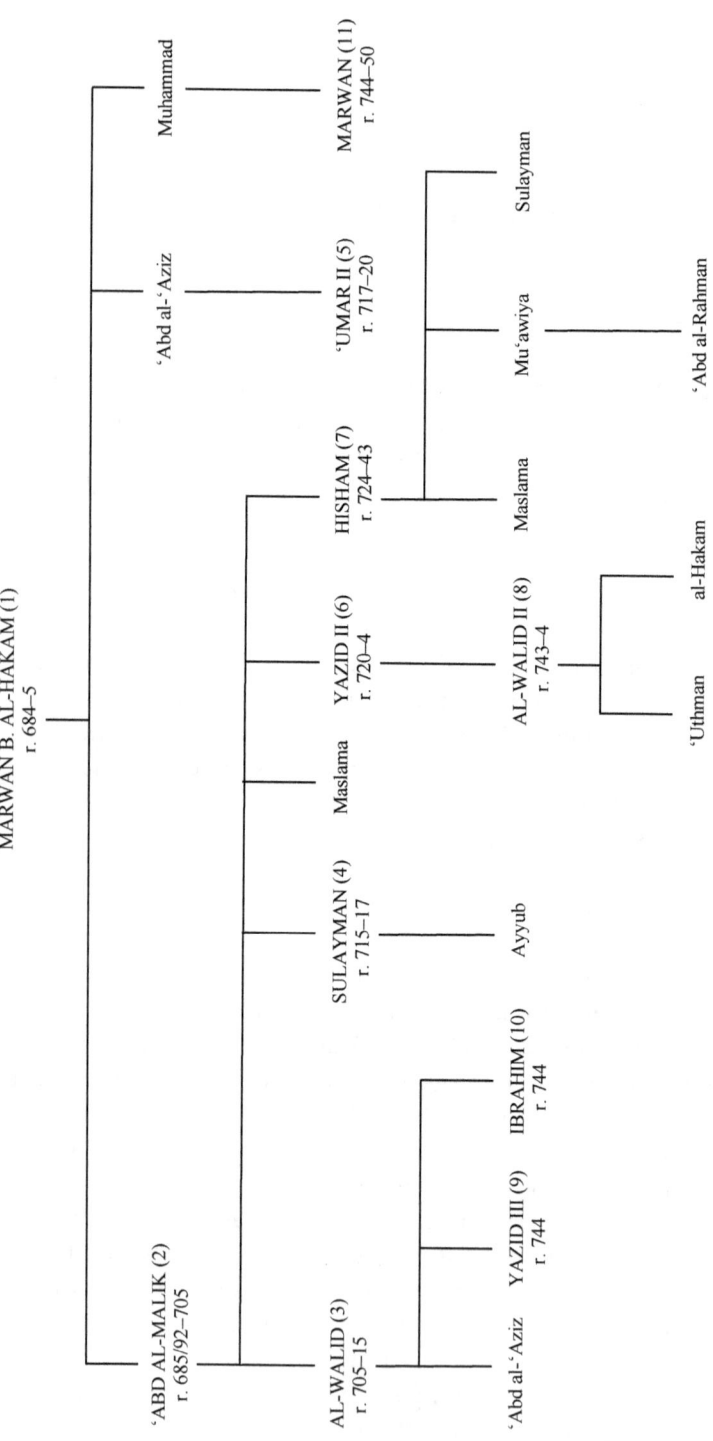

Chart II.1 Simplified genealogy of the Marwanid caliphs. Numerals in parentheses indicate the sequence of caliphal succession.

While their major Qurashi rivals had been suppressed by the mid-690s, the Marwanids still confronted the external opposition of the Roman Empire. Like Muʿawiya and Yazid before them, the Marwanids ruled from the Syrian and Mediterranean frontier, and competed directly with the Romans in these regions. The primary military objective of ʿAbd al-Malik's immediate successors was the Roman Empire's destruction, which looked like it might be within imminent reach at times in the later 700s and 710s. In a departure from the more ambiguous stance of Muʿawiya and Yazid, the Marwanids' war against Constantinople took place in the context of a policy of aggressive differentiation of Arabian monotheism from Christianity and amid mounting eschatological expectation. Indeed, from this period the evidence makes it more straightforward to refer to 'Islam' and 'Muslims'. This change reflects economic and social changes – Christian elites with long-standing local connections were beginning to be marginalised at the top of the Syrian and Egyptian military and tax system by Muslim ones in the Marwanid era. However, the new public language of Islam used by the Marwanid caliphs also reflects both the Marwanids' need to assert authority over the wider Arabian diaspora in the wake of the civil war and the demands of competing for authority with the Romans.

Difference from, and superiority to, the Christian Roman Empire was promoted in all the media available to the caliphs – in art and architecture, in coins and public inscriptions, and in poetry and sermons. In this cultural production, the symbolism of Roman and Christian authority was simultaneously invoked and rejected. As opposed to the Roman Emperor, the Marwanid ruler was the true 'Deputy of God' (Gk *hyparchos theou*, Lat. *vicarius dei*, Ar. *khalīfat Allāh*), ruling with true divine sanction and opposing the false doctrine of the incarnation. As for many of the Christian Roman emperors, victory had messianic resonances. Poets at the courts of ʿAbd al-Malik's three immediate successors proclaimed them as the *mahdī* – the 'rightly guided' saviour figure whose military success would be the final victory of true religion.[1] Apocalyptic materials about the defeat of the Romans also probably date from this period; the capture of Constantinople looked to be within reach, following on from the fall of Jerusalem, Antioch and Alexandria, which are often named in the same traditions.[2]

In leading the empire, the Marwanid clan were at once allies and potential rivals; each caliph relied on brothers and uncles for support but at the same time was wary of their political ambitions, especially as they conflicted with

---

[1] Crone and Hinds, *God's Caliph*, 36, and below, Chs 6 and 7, pp. 128–9, 138–47, 152–7 and pp. 163–4.
[2] David Cook, *Studies in Muslim Apocalyptic* (Princeton, 2002), 34–80 and below, Ch. 7, p. 163.

his own ambitions for his sons. The sons and grandsons of 'Abd al-Malik by women from Arabian allies, or from among the Umayyads, the Makhzum or Thaqif, each held a strong claim to the succession. However, claims were also made by the family of 'Abd al-Malik's half-brother, whose mother was from the powerful Syrian tribe of Kalb, as they had been by his cousin al-Ashdaq, whose wife had also been from Kalb. The Kalb lived on the former Roman–Sasanian frontier in the Syrian Desert, whereas tribal groups known collectively as Qays had settled further north and in eastern Anatolia and the Jazira (modern northern Syria, eastern Turkey and northern Iraq). 'Abd al-Malik's first two successors were sons by a Qaysi mother whose relatives held lands near Aleppo. However, after 'Abd al-Malik, the ruling Marwanid family avoided marriage into either of the powerful Syrian groups of Kalb or Qays, seeking to separate themselves as a ruling dynasty. Instead, new connections of clientship and military service were used to balance the interests of groups in the tribal armies. When the balance failed in the 740s, it contributed to the fall of the dynasty.[3]

While Syria and the Roman frontier provided the Marwanids' military power, and war with Rome their defining purpose, the greatest economic resources of the empire lay elsewhere. The agricultural lands around the Nile in Egypt and the Tigris and Euphrates in Iraq yielded by far the largest tax revenues. Of the two, Iraq was much the wealthiest. Under the Abbasids, in the later eighth century, Iraq's revenue was four times that of Egypt, and accounted for nearly a third of the revenue of the empire. In Umayyad times, Iraqi tax revenue was probably lower, but it was certainly the richest region in the empire.[4] The political dynamics of the two provinces were also quite different. Because Egypt had been conquered by armies from Syria, and because its garrison at Fustat was smaller than those in Iraq, it proved possible to control it more directly and to appropriate more of its tax revenue. Egypt was also strategically important in the war with Rome, through its provision of ship-building capacity at Alexandria and its oversight of conquests in Roman North Africa, to the west.

In contrast, Iraq had the largest new settlements in the empire, at Kufa and Basra, and these armies faced north and east, into the highland zones of the former Sasanian Empire, where there were smaller garrisons at centres like Mosul, Rayy, Istakhr and Isfahan. By Marwanid times Kufa and Basra had become very large cities, with populations that may have numbered 200,000 each. Any commander in Iraq had to manage these restive populations, but

---

[3] Marsham, 'Kinship', with further references. For the lands, see Baladhuri, *Futuh*, 146.
[4] Hugh Kennedy, 'The Decline and Fall of the First Muslim Empire', *Der Islam* 81 (2004), 11–12, 30. See further below, Chs 10 and 12, pp. 214–6, 221–2 and 317.

also benefited from access to Iraq's huge tax revenues and from further lucrative expansionist warfare. The Iraqi governor therefore risked becoming a threat to the caliph because of the resources available to him. At the same time, it was important that an effective governor was in place there precisely because of the huge resources of the province and the potential challenge that its garrisons and the tribal groups in their hinterlands could pose to Syrian power.[5]

The garrisons in Iraq and their hinterlands chafed under the governance of the Marwanids' appointees. 'Abd al-Malik and his Iraqi governor al-Hajjaj (g. 694–714) reorganised the payments to the descendants of migrants in the garrisons, removing pay from those not actively serving in the army. At the same time, Syrian troops were brought to Iraq to support Marwanid rule. These provocative decisions were prompted by the need for an outsider like al-Hajjaj to have a reliable military foundation in Iraq, by the need to pay those soldiers, and perhaps also by the need for tax revenue to support the caliph, his allies and his Syrian armies. The changes prompted violent resistance among tribal groups who resented this more centralised control and among the tribal notables (Ar. *ashrāf*, sing. *sharīf*) who had previously benefited from their role as intermediaries between the Iraqi governor and the groups in the garrisons.

In the wake of waves of resistance in Iraq, which culminated in a revolt led by a Kindi *sharīf* that nearly overturned al-Hajjaj's rule, a new permanent garrison of Syrian troops was founded between Basra and Kufa, at Wasit (meaning 'between'), in about 703 or 704. This marked a turning point, with Syrian troops becoming the main military force in the province, at the expense of the Kufans and Basrans. Afterwards, low-level unrest was near continuous, but the calculation that Syrian unity and military effectiveness could suppress any opposition from within Iraq proved correct. Waves of larger-scale violent resistance to Marwanid rule broke out among the armies of the Iraqi garrisons in each generation – in 720 and in 740. However, in these and other cases, the Syrians suppressed the Iraqi rebels. Indeed, despite these violent tensions within the empire, the period before the 740s saw the consolidation of an imperial administrative structure in the central lands of the caliphate and the further expansion of the empire's military reach, often with the support of troops from Syria.[6]

The governors of Egypt and Iraq sponsored further expansion west and east, benefiting from patronage of the commanders who led these expeditions

---

[5] On the dilemmas facing the Iraqi governor, see Tabari, II, 1306–7. On the garrison cities, see below, Chs 10 and 12, pp. 225–32 and 303–4.
[6] On the growing presence of Syrians in frontier provinces, see Wellhausen, *Arab Kingdom*, 248–9 and 248, n. 2; Kennedy, *Armies*, 34.

and the flows of loot and tribute that came from them. In the west, the first target was the reconquest of Roman Byzacena and Africa Proconsularis (Ar. Ifriqiya, modern Tunisia and eastern Algeria). This densely settled and well-connected region was rich in agricultural production and raw materials. It was also strategically vital in the Mediterranean war against the Romans. Ifriqiya's conquest drew the Arabians further into relations with the tribespeople of the North African countryside, steppe and mountain zones, some of whom paid valuable tributes of tens of thousands of slaves. Some of these North African groups, often referred to collectively in the Arabian sources as 'Berbers', joined the conquering armies and participated in further expansionist warfare in the West, crossing the straits of Gibraltar into Visigothic Hispania (Ar. al-Andalus) in 711.

In the East, much of the Iranian plateau beyond the western highlands of Jibal, Khuzistan and Fars (modern eastern Iraq and western Iran), remained outside the direct control of the Arabian conquerors. The main centres of settlement and further expansionist warfare were Khurasan, in the north-east, Sistan in the western highlands of Afghanistan and, latterly, Sind (modern southern and central Pakistan). Of the three, Khurasan was garrisoned by the largest number of migrants by far, who had moved from Basra and Kufa in 671, and this frontier remained a focus for further military expansion throughout the Marwanid era. Khurasan and the regions of Sogdia and Farghana to its east were densely settled and wealthy agricultural regions, as well as marketplaces on the trade routes from Tang China and Central Asia. As in North Africa, in western Central Asia the Arabians encountered a complex political environment, where militarily effective local powers competed with one another and with the Arabians, and so, as in North Africa, alliances had to be forged with local military actors.

Hence, new frontier societies emerged in North Africa and Central Asia, which had the potential to destabilise the whole empire. The conquests of the 700s had brought militarily capable, non-Arabian, groups from outside the borders of the old Roman and Sasanian empires into the new empire's orbit. Forms of Islam opposed to Marwanid or Qurashi rule that had developed in Iraq took root among some of these frontier groups and became a language that could unite disaffected Arabians with non-Arabians. These coalitions were inherently unstable, because many of the interests of their constituent parts did not align; a shared opposition to the status quo did not imply a shared vision of the future, with some Arabian groups expecting the perpetuation or restoration of their elite status, and non-Arabians often aspiring to replace existing Arabian imperial elites.

When the crisis came, it was because of the interaction of this frontier politics in North Africa and Central Asia with the failure of the Marwanids' commitment to replacing the Roman Empire in the Mediterranean. The Marwanids had successfully exploited a long period of instability in the Roman Empire between 685 and 717. However, an ambitious and determined attempt to take Constantinople failed disastrously in 718. The Roman usurper who defended the city became Emperor Leo III (r. 717–41), whose long reign was an era of religious and administrative reform and diplomatic and military success rather like that of Constans II in the seventh century. Hisham (r. 724–43), who was the last of 'Abd al-Malik's sons to rule the Umayyad Empire, built towards a second Marwanid campaign against the Roman capital in 740, but these expeditions failed in Sicily and in Anatolia without even reaching Constantinople. The defeats of 740 coincided with rebellions by Islamised Berber groups in North Africa, who inflicted further destruction on the caliph's Syrian forces. When a succession crisis on Hisham's death in 743 split both the Marwanid house and their Syrian armies, the way was open for rebels from the eastern frontiers to conquer the empire. Umayyad dominion ended suddenly and bloodily in 750, although many of the imperial structures they had developed survived.

6

The Imperial Marwanid Caliphate

The year 74 of the Hijri calendar (693–4) is sometimes referred to in the Islamic tradition by the name 'the year of unity' (*'ām al-jamā'a*). The years AH 40 or 41 (660–1 or 661–2) also sometimes have the same name. The label probably derives from Umayyad-era chronologies, celebrating the victories of Mu'awiya and then 'Abd al-Malik over their rivals in the first and second civil wars. Although 'Abd al-Malik had been acclaimed by the Umayyad clan and some Syrian tribesmen in 685 and had consolidated that claim by suppressing his cousin al-Ashdaq's bid for power in 689, it was only the victories of 691 and 692 that had extended his rule beyond Syria and Egypt, enabling him to appoint his own allies in other provinces. With Iraq and the Hijaz in the hands of men loyal to him, 'Abd al-Malik could now claim to rule the whole community of the Faithful.[1]

However, the challenge from Ibn al-Zubayr had exposed the Umayyads' vulnerability to opponents who could make effective claims to leadership and legitimacy beyond Syria and Egypt. It had also exposed the weaknesses of the vast and decentralised empire, where economic, military and political resources were concentrated in the hands of the provincial governors, and where the provincial armies remained volatile and difficult to control. In response, 'Abd al-Malik and his allies developed a programme of reforms to the tax systems of the provinces, to the military forces of the empire and to the promotion of the legitimacy of the caliph. Some of these policies had begun during the war with Ibn al-Zubayr, and some had first been developed by Ibn al-Zubayr himself. Others had precedents from the time of Mu'awiya. However, the scale and pace of change in the 690s was unprecedented. Meanwhile, as for

---

[1] Ibn 'Asakir, XII, 115, 197, §1217 (for 40/660–1); Khalifa, 123; Ibn 'Abd Rabbihi, *al-'Iqd al-Farid*, ed. Ahmad Amin, Ahmad al-Zayn and Ibrahim al-Abyari (Cairo, 1940–53), IV, 361, 362 (for 41/661–2); Baladhuri, *Futuh*, 467 (for 74/693–4). Cf. *Theophilus*, 183 and n. 487; Theophanes, 509, s.a. 689–90. The first embassy to China for twelve years, found only in the Chinese sources for 693, suggests a bid for external recognition at around the same time: Bielenstein, *Diplomacy and Trade*, 357.

all late antique monarchs, the most important pillar of 'Abd al-Malik's claim on power was that he was made victorious by God and so the war against Rome was pursued with vigour, alongside the ongoing struggle against internal opponents.

The War with Rome and Appointments in the North and West

As victory over Ibn al-Zubayr became imminent, the treaty made in the late 680s between 'Abd al-Malik and the Roman Emperor, Justinian II (r. 685–95, 705–11) broke down. The resumption of war came as both leaders sought to assert their divine right to rule to audiences within and beyond their empires. While the exact sequence and extent of direct interactions between the two rulers cannot be recovered, a consequence was heightened differentiation from one another, with Christology as a prominent marker of difference.[2] In 687, Justinian II had published a statement to the Church and the army emphasising his role as God's representative on earth. Probably in 690, he began to issue unusual new coins carrying the bust of Christ and the slogan 'Christ's Servant' (Lat. *servus Christi*; Figure 6.1). In 691–2, he convened a church council at the imperial palace, which again reinforced his claims to rule as Christ's servant and deputy. The Greek and Syriac traditions report that 'Abd al-Malik deliberately provoked the breakdown of the peace by paying the tribute agreed in the truce in a new type of coinage, unacceptable to the Romans, while Arabic sources also refer to a change in the protocols written on the papyri delivered from Egypt to Constantinople. Certainly, by the mid-690s, 'Abd al-Malik had begun to issue distinctive new coins (Figure 6.2), some of which carried the titles 'Commander of the Faithful' (*amīr al-muʾminīn*) and 'God's Deputy' (*khalīfat Allāh*).[3] Part of a long panegyric poem from *c.* 691 by the Christian court poet al-Akhtal (d. *c.* 710) emphasises 'Abd al-Malik's divinely sanctioned victories against his rivals:

> To a man whose gifts do not elude us, whom God has made victorious, so let him in his victory long delight!
> He who wades into the deep of battle, auspicious his augury, God's Caliph, through whom men pray for rain.[4]

---

[2] On the chronology and agendas, see Mike Humphreys, 'The "War of Images" Revisited: Justinian II's Coinage Reform and the Caliphate'", *Numismatic Chronicle* 173 (2013), 229–44; Mike Humphreys, *Law, Power, and Imperial Ideology in the Iconoclast Era, 680–850* (Oxford, 2014), 37–80; Haldon, *Empire*, 48; Marsham, '"God's Caliph"'.
[3] Changes to the coinage: *Theophilus*, 185–7; Theophanes, 509–12. Papyrus protocols: Baladhuri, *Futuh*, 240. Statement in 687: Haldon, *Empire*, 48. On the Council, see Humphreys, *Law*, 37–80.
[4] Stetkevych, 'Umayyad Panegyric', 103, 119, ll. 18–19 (with minor changes); *RoIM*, 102–4.

Figure 6.1 Solidus of Justinian II, *c.* 690 CE. Gold, 21mm diameter, 4.35g. © British Museum.

Figure 6.2 'Standing Caliph' dinar, Damascus mint, AH 77 /696–7 CE. Gold, 25.6mm diameter, 4.45g. © Ashmolean Museum.

As a Christian, al-Akhtal avoided specifically anti-Trinitarian imagery, while asserting his patron's claim to rule, like the Roman emperor, as God's delegate on earth.

Because the war against Rome was prosecuted in the arc spanning North Africa, the East Mediterranean, Anatolia and the Caucasus, these regions were not only crucial to 'Abd al-Malik's prestige but were also spaces where frontier armies operated close to the Syrian centre of the empire. This made the appointment of loyal allies to commands in these regions particularly critical. For most of his reign, 'Abd al-Malik delegated overall command in the frontier zone that has been called 'the Umayyad North' – Anatolia, Armenia, Azerbaijan and the Jazira – to his paternal half-brother Muhammad b. Marwan (d. 719–20).

As the son of a slave woman, Muhammad lacked maternal relatives and so was less well placed than some of his brothers to challenge for the caliphate or the succession. He was also a capable general, not only on the frontier with Rome but also in the East, where he suppressed internal revolts.[5] Moreover, his armies in northern Syria and the frontier comprised many 'Qaysi' or 'northern' tribespeople, as well as troops from the Caucasus, all of whom balanced the power of the Banu Kalb, whose heartlands were further south, in the Syrian Desert.[6]

This Qaysi support for Muhammad b. Marwan on the Roman frontier was important because Egypt was in the hands of 'Abd al-'Aziz (g. 684–704), a paternal half-brother of 'Abd al-Malik by a Kalbi mother. 'Abd al-'Aziz had a strong claim on succession to the caliphate, backed by his maternal Kalbi relatives. 'Abd al-Malik chose to leave 'Abd al-'Aziz in post, perhaps judging that he would be impossible to remove, given his kinship connections. Indeed, 'Abd al-'Aziz's replacement in 698 of the North African commander Hassan b. al-Nu'man with Musa b. Nusayr, who had fallen foul of 'Abd al-Malik, suggests his desire to develop the North African frontier as his own counter to Muhammad's strength in the north and a willingness to act provocatively towards his half-brother the caliph and his allies.[7]

Once war with Rome resumed, the Arabians quickly gained the initial advantage. However, there was no major advance on Constantinople to follow those of 654 and 668. Both the greater effectiveness of the Romans' defences and pressures elsewhere on 'Abd al-Malik's forces appear to have made this impossible. Instead, annual campaigns in Asia Minor saw the fortified cities of the western Armenian highlands and Cilicia (modern eastern and south-east Turkey) contested by the Arabian and Roman field armies. Two victories by Muhammad b. Marwan, at Sebastopolis, in about 692, and at Germanikeia (Ar. Mar'ash), in 694, coincided with the despatch of a large force led by the experienced Syrian commander Hassan b. al-Nu'man (d. 699–700) against Carthage, the Roman capital of North Africa.[8] One consequence of this renewed Arabian pressure appears to have been a coup at Constantinople in

---

[5] *EI²*, 'Muhammad b. Marwan' (K. V. Zettersteén). For the 'Umayyad North', see D. A. Spellberg, 'The Umayyad North: Numismatic Evidence for Frontier Administration', *American Numismatic Society Museum Notes* 33 (1988), 119–27; Vacca, 'Umayyad North'.
[6] *SoH*, 34; Robinson, *Empire*, 60–2; Vacca, 'Umayyad North', 223–5.
[7] On 'Abd al-'Aziz, see Joshua Mabra, *Princely Authority in the Early Marwanid State: The Life of 'Abd al-'Aziz ibn Marwan* (Piscataway, 2017); Marsham, 'Kinship', 33–4. For the appointment of Musa b. Nusayr, see Kindi, 52–3; Ibn 'Idhari, *Al-Bayan*, I, 38–40.
[8] Theophanes, 511–12, s.a. 691/2; Khalifa, 169, 171; Ibn 'Abd al-Hakam, *Futuh*, 200; Tabari, II, 853, 863. On Hassan and his campaigns, see *EI²*, 'Hassan b. al-Nu'man al-Ghassani' (M. Talbi).

695, which exiled Justinian II and installed in his place Leontius (r. 695–8).[9] However, thereafter the contest in Asia Minor reached a stalemate of annual raid and counter-raid.

In contrast, the conflict was more dynamic in the Caucasus and North Africa, with the reassertion and extension of Arabian power bringing local military elites into alliance. These allies were then used to apply pressure on Roman fortified centres in these southern and northern theatres. Muhammad b. Marwan fought regular campaigns in the Caucasus, violently suppressing an Armenian alliance with the Romans in the early 700s and contesting territory with Khazar forces raiding from the north. In the early 700s, the mint in the Caucasus was one of two mints striking Umayyad silver coins north and east of Damascus, reflecting the importance of this northern frontier army to Umayyad power and the status of its commander.[10] In North Africa, a coalition of tribal groups led by a charismatic female leader, known in the Arabic sources as 'al-Kahina' ('the Sorceress'), and the Roman reoccupation of Carthage were both defeated by Hassan b. al-Nu'man, in around 698;[11] two later raids west by the commander who replaced Hassan were remembered for the numbers of valuable slaves they yielded.[12] The distinctive gold coins struck in North Africa reflect the payment of local, predominantly Christian, troops.[13]

Iraq and the East

Whereas influence over groups in the Caucasus and North Africa had to be wrested from the Romans, while keeping an eye to the ambitions of the wider Marwanid family and their Syrian troops, Iraq and Iran posed different challenges. In the East, 'Abd al-Malik had to assert his authority over the diverse groups from among the Arabian conquerors who had formerly been loyal to Ibn al-Zubayr, or to the cause of 'Ali and his family, or who championed their own autonomy. 'Abd al-Malik appointed another half-brother, Bishr b. Marwan, over Kufa (g. *c.* 691–4), and then, having dismissed his first appointment to Basra almost immediately, over the southern garrison as well

---

[9] Theophilus, 190 and n. 510; Theophanes, 514–16, s.aa. 694–5, 695–6; *PmBZ*, 'Leontios', no. 4547/corr.

[10] Alison Vacca, *Non-Muslim Provinces under Early Islam: Islamic Rule and Iranian Legitimacy in Armenia and Caucasian Albania* (Cambridge, 2017), 36–8; Alain George, *The Rise of Islamic Calligraphy* (London, 2010), 71–3. On the coins, see further below, Ch. 12, pp. 324–6.

[11] Ibn 'Abd al-Hakam, *Futuh*, 201; Ibn 'Idhari, *Al-Bayan*, I, 35–8; *EI*², 'Hassan b. al-Nu'man al-Ghassani' (M. Talbi).

[12] Ibn 'Abd al-Hakam, *Futuh*, 204; Kennedy, *Conquests*, 222–3.

[13] See below, Ch. 12, pp. 325–6.

(g. 692–4). As with ʿAbd al-ʿAziz in Egypt, Bishr was both an ally and a potential dynastic rival.[14] When Bishr died within a few years of his appointment, ʿAbd al-Malik decided to transfer all of Iraq and the East to the young commander who had recently besieged Ibn al-Zubayr in Mecca and conquered the Hijaz, al-Hajjaj b. Yusuf (g. 694–714).[15]

Al-Hajjaj's tribe, Thaqif, had ties with the Umayyads and other Qurashi groups which predated the era of the Prophet, and Thaqafis had already governed the eastern provinces under Muʿawiya and Yazid. Al-Hajjaj owed his position to his having placed his considerable strategic and tactical acumen and his rhetorical and political abilities in the service of Marwan and ʿAbd al-Malik.[16] In this respect, his appointment resembled those made by Muʿawiya; al-Hajjaj was something of an outsider, whose fortunes were closely tied to the ruler. However, unlike Muʿawiya's governors, al-Hajjaj had no strong connection to the region over which he was appointed. Rather, he had previously served in Syria with ʿAbd al-Malik and now he used Syrian forces to assert greater centralised power over Iraq, including the use of Iraqi revenue to support his Syrian troops, provoking violent resistance from many of the leading Iraqi military commanders. Thus, ʿAbd al-Malik's appointment of al-Hajjaj marked a significant departure from the more decentralised model of rule over former Sasanian territories adopted by Muʿawiya.

Al-Hajjaj devoted his first four years to imposing control over the garrisons and countryside of Iraq. Many of the soldiers of Kufa and Basra had dispersed into the countryside and towns in the wake of the Marwanid victory in the civil war. Some of these groups of fighters led violent resistance to the assertion of al-Hajjaj's authority. Those who had stayed behind were often restive and reluctant to go on campaign. Al-Hajjaj is said to have used a combination of payments to loyal fighters, violent suppression of resistance and offers of safe conduct to secure some control.[17] Resistance in northern Iraq and the environs of Kufa was protracted, with one leader, Shabib b. Yazid al-Shaybani, being defeated and killed only in about 697, after repeated campaigns.[18] Another rebellion in the same region was led by a Thaqafi, Mutarrif, whose father, al-Mughira b. Shuʿba, had governed Iraq for ʿUmar and Muʿawiya. Mutarrif is said initially to have accepted a command in al-Madaʾin/Ctesiphon but then to have led a revolt against al-Hajjaj, in dismay at the ambitions of the

---

[14] Mabra, *Princely Authority*, 167–87.
[15] In 694 al-Hajjaj was probably in his mid-thirties: Ibn ʿAsakir, XII, 115, §1217.
[16] On Thaqif and Quraysh, see Hosein, 'Tribal Alliance'. On al-Hajjaj, see Baladhuri, *Ansab*, V, 343, XII, 330–1; *EI*², 'al-Hadjdjadj b. Yusuf' (A. Dietrich).
[17] Tabari, II, 863–74, 902–3, 913–14, 930–1, 1033.
[18] Tabari, II, 881–939, 940–1003; Robinson, *Empire*, 111–24.

new Syrian Marwanid regime.[19] This unrest in central Iraq extended into the less easily governed highland zones of northern and eastern Iraq and northern and western Iran – the Jazira, Jibal and Tabaristan.[20]

Beyond the violence in the rural hinterlands of the garrisons and their northern and eastern marches, there were three further challenges to Marwanid authority in Iraq and its borderlands. First, in the north-east Arabian Peninsula, there was a group known as the Najadat after their Hanafi leader, Najda b. 'Amir. This group are usually characterised as 'Kharijite' – that is, they accepted leadership of the Faithful by a non-Qurashi and are said to have taken a harsh attitude towards sinners. The Najadat were fragmenting by the early 690s. Nonetheless, they defeated a Basran army sent against them in Bahrayn (the eastern seaboard of Arabia) in 692 before they were decisively defeated in Bahrayn by a second expedition in 692–3.[21] Second, in the agricultural land around Basra, in southern Iraq, the African agricultural slaves rebelled again, and on a larger scale. This time their leader, who is named as Rabah Shir Zanji ('Rabah, the Black African Lion', d. c. 695), is said to have declared himself 'Commander of the Faithful'. This slave revolt was quickly suppressed in c. 695.[22]

The third, and most serious, threat came from a much larger independent political entity that had taken shape in south-east Iraq and south-west Iran during the civil war. The 'Kharijite' group known as the Azariqa, after their first leader, the Hanafi Nafi' b. al-Azraq, held the eastern bank of the Tigris and points further east, including the highlands of al-Ahwaz, Fars and Kirman. They had successfully repelled both Zubayrid and now Marwanid attempts to subdue them and made claims to rival 'Abd al-Malik himself; surviving post-Sasanian style silver coins from 694 show that their Tamimi leader, Qatari b. Fuja'a (r. 689–c. 698) controlled the mints in these regions and named himself 'Commander of the Faithful' in payments to his followers (Figure 6.3).

Campaigns against the Azariqa drove them out of Iraq and back to Kirman, in southern Iran. There, non-Arabians who had joined the Azariqa made a stand at Jiruft, and were defeated, while Qatari and his Arabian-heritage

---

[19] Baladhuri, *Ansab*, VI, 507–11, XII, 328–9; Tabari, II, 946–8, 979–1003.
[20] Baladhuri, *Ansab*, VI, 510–13; Tabari, II, 881–910, 941, 948, 972, 987–90, 1003; Robinson, *Empire*, 111–24.
[21] *EI²*, 'Najadat' (R. Rubinacci); Hagemann and Verkinderen, 'Kharijism'.
[22] Baladhuri, *Ansab*, VI, 414–15; 'Izz al-Din Ibn al-Athir, *Al-Kamil fi Ta'rikh*, ed. C. J. Tornberg (Leiden, 1853–71), IV, 314–15; *EI²*, 'al-Zandj. 2. The Zandj revolts in Irak' (A. Popovic); Popovic, *La révolte*, 62–3. The first rebellion had been suppressed by an Umayyad commander after the defeat of Mus'ab in 691, see the preceding references in this note, and above, Ch. 5, p. 105.

Figure 6.3 Dirham in the name of 'Qatari, Commander of the Faithful' (Middle Persian), Bishapur mint. The Arabic slogan in the obverse margin reads 'Judgement belongs only to God' (*lā ḥukma illā lillāh*). The imagery echoes Sasanian coins. Silver, approximately 33mm diameter, 4.14g. Stephen Album Rare Coins Auction 20 (18 September 2014) lot 115, <https://pro.coinarchives.com/> (last accessed 24 June 2023). Photograph courtesy of Stephen Album.

followers fled north into the highlands of Tabaristan, south of the Caspian Sea. However, Qatari failed to win the support of Tabaristan's inhabitants, who, though independent of Arabian rule, sought al-Hajjaj's support against the new arrival. The Syrian commander al-Hajjaj sent to Tabaristan killed Qatari in about 698 and then withdrew back to Iraq.[23]

Success in Iraq allowed al-Hajjaj to turn his attention to Iran, and particularly to the valuable frontier regions of Khurasan and Sistan, over which he was given direct authority by 'Abd al-Malik in *c*. 697.[24] Most of Khurasan had been taken from the control of former Zubayrid loyalists, but the province was still turbulent. Military intervention there would reduce opportunities for rivals to Marwanid power on the frontier, while directing the energies of the armies outwards and securing tribute to maintain their loyalty. Al-Hajjaj's appointee to Khurasan was the old and skilful Omani leader, al-Muhallab b. Abi Sufra, who had already had a forty-year career fighting in Iraq, Iran, Sistan and

---

[23] Tabari, II, 465–6, 513–20, 581–91, 821–9, 875–80, 1003–21, 1032; *EI²*, 'Katari b. Fuja'a' (G. Levi Della Vida), 'al-Muhallab b. Abi Sufra' (P. Crone); *EI3*, 'Azariqa' (K. Lewinstein); Charles Pellat, *Le Milieu basrien et la formation de Jahiz* (Paris, 1953), 41; Tabari, *History*, XXII, 165 n. 596 (E. K. Rowson); Hagemann and Verkinderen, 'Kharijism', 491, 496, 498–9 and fig. 23.1.

[24] Tabari, II, 1032, 1034.

Khurasan. Al-Muhallab chose to campaign against the Sogdian principalities of the upper Oxus, to the north-east of Marw. These campaigns were directed less at conquest than at the extraction of tribute from the competing Sogdian princes, who sought to use alliances with the Arabian raiders against their local political rivals. Al-Muhallab enjoyed significant success, temporarily capturing the entrepôt of Kish (Shahr, just south of Samarqand in modern Uzbekistan), and then using the town as a base for further campaigns. However, he avoided confronting a fellow former supporter of Ibn al-Zubayr who had established himself in exile in the east of the same region with Sodgian support.[25]

Sistan presented even more serious challenges. Many of the Arabian settlers there resisted the imposition of centralised authority, and Ibn al-Zubayr's governors and then 'Abd al-Malik's fought ongoing campaigns against these independent groups. At the same time, the opportunities for conquest and the extraction of tribute were more perilous. The highlands of southern and central Afghanistian were by the mid-660s ruled by rulers known as the Zunbils and the Kabul Shahs. These monarchs and their predecessors had paid substantial tributes in slaves and silver to Arabian raiders in the late 650s and 660s, but they were also adept adversaries, who made effective use of the precipitous Afghan mountains. 'Abd al-Malik's governors suffered defeats at their hands in the 690s, while a coin dated 694–5 suggests that Qatari's Azariqa briefly gained control of Zaranj. In 697–8, al-Hajjaj appointed a fellow Thaqafi to Sistan. However, this appointee died at his advanced base at Bust on the lower river Helmand in 698–9, having come to humiliating terms with the Zunbil and then losing most of his army on his retreat from the mountains.[26]

The Rebellion of Ibn al-Ash'ath and the Foundation of Wasit

Al-Hajjaj's next attempt to restore Arabian prestige in Sistan exposed the extent of resentment of Umayyad rule in Iraq and Iran. In 699, al-Hajjaj raised a large, well-equipped army from Kufa and Basra to send into Sistan. He appointed as its commander 'Abd al-Rahman b. Muhammad b. al-Ash'ath, who was known as Ibn al-Ash'ath, after his paternal grandfather, al-Ash'ath, from a leading

---

[25] Baladhuri, *Futuh*, 417; Tabari, II, 1033–5, 1039, 1040–2; Bosworth, *Sistan*, 49–50, 52–3; *EI²*, 'Al-Muhallab b. Abi Sufra' (P. Crone); Haug, *Eastern Frontier*, 106–10.

[26] Baladhuri, *Futuh*, 396–9; Tabari, II, 1032–5, 1036–9; Milton Gold, *Tarikh-e Sistan* (Rome, 1976), 66–90; Bosworth, *Sistan*, 34–5, 50–2, 53–5; *EI3*, "Abd al-Rahman b. Samura' (A. Marsham); Cameron Petrie, *Resistance at the Edge of Empires: The Archaeology and History of the Bannu Basin (Pakistan) from 1000 BC to AD 1200* (Oxford, 2017), 68–72, 92, 109–10, 200. For a coin dated AH 75/694–5 CE in the name of Qatari, see John Walker, *A Catalogue of the Arab-Sassanian Coins (Umaiyad Governors in the East, Arab-Ephthalites, 'Abbasid Governors in Tabaristan and Bukhara)* (London, 1941), 113, no. I. 47.

clan of the South Arabian tribe of Kinda. Ibn al-Ash'ath's father, Muhammad, had fought in the conquest of Iraq and Iran, while he himself had fought the Azariqa for Ibn al-Zubayr and then for al-Hajjaj. As the newly appointed commander in Sistan, Ibn al-Ash'ath made inroads against the Zunbil in 699 and overwintered at Bust. However, by late 700, Ibn al-Ash'ath and his army had turned against al-Hajjaj, and were marching back west. Al-Hajjaj's forces met the rebel army at Tustar, in the mountains of al-Ahwaz above Iraq, but were defeated.

The rebellion temporarily unified disparate interests in southern Iran and Iraq in opposition to Umayyad rule; by the time Ibn al-Ash'ath confronted al-Hajjaj in Iraq itself, his army is said to have numbered 200,000, augmented by elements of the local population. With the help of reinforcements sent from Syria by 'Abd al-Malik, al-Hajjaj drove Ibn al-Ash'ath out of Iraq in prolonged campaigns during 701. Ibn al-Ash'ath fled east, back to Sistan, and thence to the court of the Zunbil, where he is said eventually to have been betrayed and killed, or to have killed himself (c. 704). Meanwhile, the remnants of his rebel army were defeated in Sistan and Khurasan.[27]

Ibn al-Ash'ath's revolt became known as the revolt of the 'Peacock Army' (Ar. *jaysh al-ṭawāwīs*) because of the wealth of its leader and the extravagant equipment of his men. In explaining it, the sources emphasise the personal animosity between Ibn al-Ash'ath and al-Hajjaj, as well as al-Hajjaj's insistence that Ibn al-Ash'ath's army press on against the Zunbil during the winter of 699–700. It is certainly plausible that there was personal hostility between the two commanders, and an insistence on winter campaigning in the Afghan mountains might well have provoked an insurrection. Indeed, sending one's rivals on dangerous campaigns was a common tactic among pre-modern military elites.

However, the causes of the rebellion were also more profound. They are revealed in the make-up of the rebel army and the slogans associated with its leadership: Ibn al-Ash'ath is said to have proclaimed himself as the 'Qahtani' and the 'the Helper of the Faithful' (*nāṣir al-mu'minīn*). That is, he was asserting his descent from Qahtan, the legendary common ancestor of the 'southern' or 'Yemeni' Arabians, as opposed to the 'northern' Quraysh and Thaqif, who were thought to be descended from Mudar. The epithet also recalls the chiliastic report attributed to the Prophet that 'The Hour will not come until

---

[27] *EI²*, 'Ibn al-Ash'ath' (L. Vecca Vaglieri); Redwan Sayed, *Die Revolte des Ibn al-Aš'at und die Koranleser: Ein Beitrag zur Religions- und Sozialgeschichte der frühen Umayyadenzeit* (Freiburg, 1977); Muhammad Faruque, 'The Revolt of 'Abd al-Rahman ibn al-Ash'ath: Its Nature and Causes', *Islamic Studies* 25 (1986), 289–304; Michael Bates and Mehdy Shaddel, 'Note on a Peculiar Arab-Sasanian Coinage of Ibn al-Ash'ath', *JRAS* (2022), 1–10.

a man from Qahtan will come forth leading the people with his staff. At the same time, Ibn al-Ash'ath's use of the title 'Helper of the Faithful' suggests an assertion of his religious status, in implicit contrast to 'impious' Umayyad and Thaqafi rule over Iraq. Support for him among religious scholars from Basra and Kufa is noted in the sources; the rebels were expressing resentment of Iraq's subordinate status within the empire in religious terms. The presence of non-Arabians from Kufa, Basra and Sistan, the reputed size of his army, and the extent of the chaos in Iraq, suggests that other disaffected groups brought other grievances and expectations to the revolt.[28]

This near-fatal challenge to Umayyad authority in Iraq, which followed eight years of unrest there in the wake of the civil war, prompted the creation of a permanent garrison of tribespeople from Syria, loyal to the Marwanids and their Iraqi governors. A new walled city, established in 703 or 704, was constructed on the west bank of the Tigris, opposite the existing east bank Sasanian town of Kaskar. The new town was named Wasit ('the Middle'), situated as it was about midway between Kufa (on the Euphrates, about 180km to the west) and Basra (about 250km downriver, to the south). Wasit now became al-Hajjaj's headquarters, replacing Kufa and Basra. It remained the capital of Iraq until 715 and occasionally again after 720.[29]

With the creation of Wasit, 'Abd al-Malik and al-Hajjaj had moved to a policy of direct Syrian rule in central and southern Iraq. Wasit's foundation amounted to a recognition that Iraq was hostile territory for the Umayyads and that continued access to its revenues depended on soldiers from their home province of Syria, to whom much of Iraq's tax revenue was now diverted. For the next three years, the minting of coins in the eastern provinces was temporarily brought under the sole control of al-Hajjaj at Wasit, where a new design of coin echoed the proportions of the Arabic script also used in the inscriptions at 'Abd al-Malik's Dome of the Rock, in Jerusalem. At around the same time, in 704 or 705, al-Hajjaj is said to have sent copies (*maṣāḥif*, sing. *muṣḥaf*) of the Qur'an to the garrison cities in the other provinces, where these texts were publicly displayed in the congregational mosques. These were large-format

---

[28] *EI²*, 'Ibn al-Ash'ath' (L. Vecca Vaglieri), 'al-Mahdi. A. The Rightly-Guided One' (W. Madelung); Sayed, *Die Revolte*; Faruque, 'Revolt'; Tobias Andersson, *Early Sunni Historiography: A Study of the Tarikh of Khalifa b. Khayyat* (Leiden, 2019), 266–7. For the 'Peacock Army', see Tabari, II, 1046. For the idea that the campaign would rid al-Hajjaj of the Zunbil or Ibn al-Ash'ath, see Tabari, II, 1054. For the presence of non-Arabians and the size of the army, see Tabari, II, 1072, 1104. For wider unrest in Iraq, see Baladhuri, *Futuh*, 273.

[29] Baladhuri, *Futuh*, 290–1; Fu'ad Safar, *Wasit: The Sixth Season's Excavations* (Cairo, 1945); *EI²*, 'Wasit' (M. Sakhly); Antun, *Architectural Form*, 6–14.

parchment codices, some of which are almost one metre across when opened. The materials for their production would have been expensive and they drew upon the skills of highly specialist scribes who developed a distinctive new Arabic script. The composition of the Qur'ans also entailed at least some minor interventions in the Quranic text itself. Indeed, if it is accepted that the story of 'Uthman's compilation of the Qur'an is substantially exaggerated, it is even possible that it was al-Hajjaj who oversaw the systematic composition of the Qur'an as a book.[30] Thus, the foundation of Wasit seems to have heralded not just the longer-term presence of Syrian troops in the East, and the diversion of Iraqi resources to them, but also to have coincided with the further development of Marwanid assertions of their divinely sanctioned authority and the further promotion of a Marwanid imperial Islamic aesthetic.

Marwanid Imperial Islam

'Abd al-Malik and his allies have left behind the clearest horizon in the material evidence from the Arabian conquests and the early Islamic empire: a new imperial expression of faith, articulated in the language of the Qur'an, is visible across the archaeology from about 690. This horizon is found on coins and seals, in inscriptions and in Qur'an manuscripts (Figure 6.4), as well as in the surviving architecture sponsored by 'Abd al-Malik and his relatives and allies. The same imagery is found in the poetry which, while it is extant only in much later collections, probably echoes verse performed at the Marwanid court. These media proclaim God's rule, as brought by His Prophet and now represented by His deputy (*khalīfa*, or caliph) on earth. 'God's Caliph' was destined for victory over rebels and schismatics and over the Christian Roman Empire, with its erroneous Trinitarian belief in Jesus as God's son. A co-ordinated and coherent rhetorical programme was developed, with messages subtly judged for a range of audiences in different contexts. The most widely circulated were those on the coins. Monuments such as the Ka'ba and the Dome of the Rock were visible only to those who visited them, but reports about them could also spread much more widely. Panegyric poetry was performed for the caliph and his allies at their courts but could also circulate through memorisation and recitation.

The new coins issued in Syria and Iraq after 696–7 illustrate the boldness of this programme (Figure 6.5). Gold dinars and then silver dirhams (after 697–8) from these provinces ceased to carry images of the monarch

---

[30] George, *Calligraphy*, 72–89. For the date of al-Hajjaj's *muṣḥafs*, see François Déroche, *Qur'ans of the Umayyads: A First Overview* (Leiden, 2013), 139. On the extent of al-Hajjaj's intervention in the text, see the (maximalist) discussion in Shoemaker, *Creating the Qur'an*, 43–69.

IMPERIAL MARWANID CALIPHATE | 139

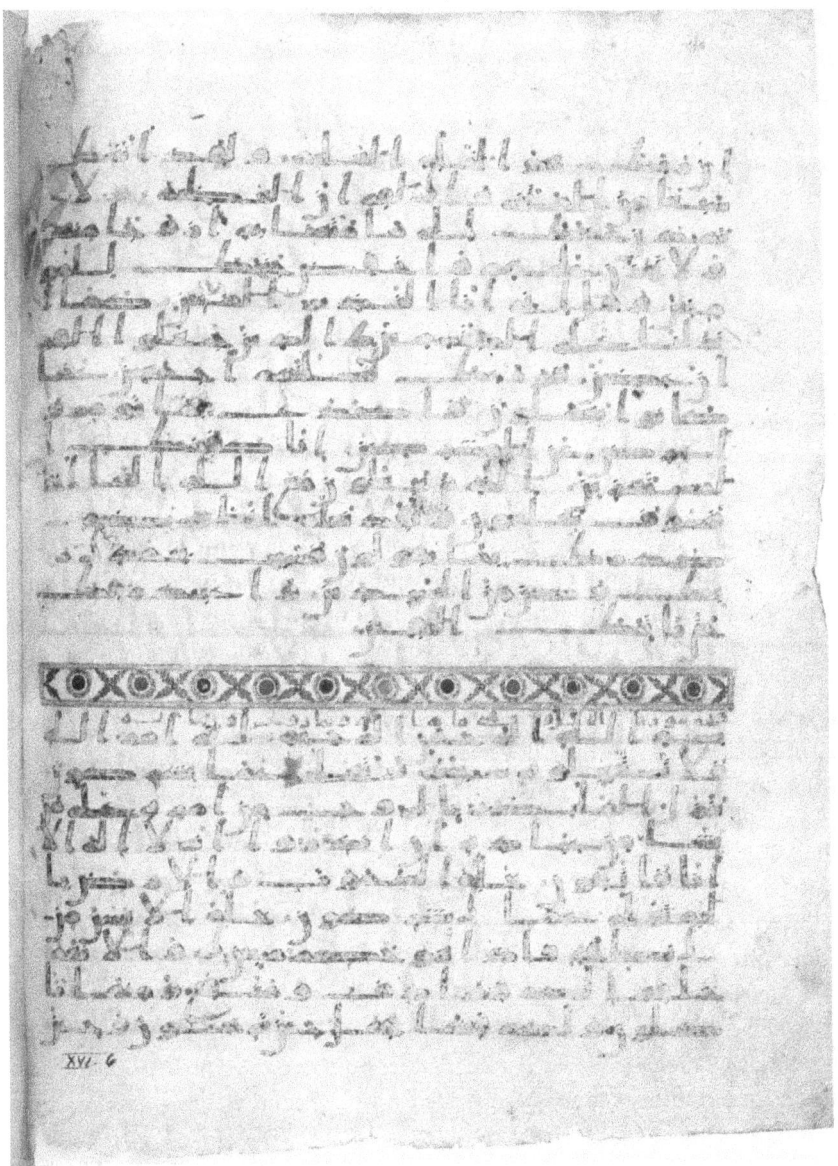

Figure 6.4 Folio from the 'Fustat Umayyad codex' (after François Déroche). The decorative band marks the end of the fifteenth *sūra* of the Qur'an and the beginning of the sixteenth. Ms. Paris, BNF, Arabe 330c, f. 12 verso. Writing surface: 27.5cm × 23.5cm. Bibliothèque nationale de France, public domain.

Figure 6.5 Aniconic and epigraphic 'reform' dinar from Syria, dated AH 77/696–7 CE. Gold, 19mm diameter, 4.25g. British Museum, no. 1874,0706.1.

derived from Sasanian and the Roman prototypes, or any other figural imagery. Instead, they carried only Arabic script, and made no mention of God's earthly representative. The central field of one side of the coin reads 'There is only one God, alone, He has no associate', echoing many Qur'anic verses.[31] The reverse reads 'God is one, God is eternal, He is not a father nor is He a son', which quotes from the first three of the four short verses of Surat al-Ikhlas (Q. 112). Around the margins of the obverse of the gold coins is 'Muhammad is God's Messenger, He sent him with guidance and the religion of truth, to proclaim it over all religion', which is an abbreviation of Surat al-Tawba (or al-Bara'a, Q. 9:33). Around the reverse is 'In the name of God, this dinar was struck in the year seventy-seven [696–7]'. The bigger circumference of the silver coins allowed for the inclusion of the mint name as well as the date and the completion of the Quranic quotation, 'even though those who associate others with God detest it.'[32]

The coins' aniconism is visually striking, while the eclipse on them of the monarch by God is at least as remarkable. Furthermore, the introduction of this stark monotheist message coincided with a weight reform – making these

---

[31] They combine Q. 6:163, which begins 'He has no associate', with the first part of the *shahada*, or 'declaration of faith', which is a variation on Q. 2:163, 255, 3:2, 3:18 et al.

[32] John Walker, *A Catalogue of the Arab-Byzantine and Post-reform Umaiyad Coins* (London, 1956), 84, no. 186, 104, no. Kh. 4; Michel G. Klat, *Catalogue of the Post-reform Dirhams: The Umayyad Dynasty* (London, 2002), 11, 36 nos 23a and 23b, 43 nos 45, 91 nos 200, 202, no. 539; Jere L. Bacharach, 'Signs of Sovereignty: The Shahada, Qur'anic Verses, and the Coinage of 'Abd al-Malik', *Muqarnas* 27 (2011), 16–19 and nn. 61 and 62; at 18 it is noted that from 698–9, the dirhams' marginal inscriptions are on the opposite sides of the coins to those on the dinars.

coins' value as bullion slightly lower than their post-Roman and post-Sasanian precursors. In the case of the dinars, this weight difference seems to have led to the Roman coins being replaced in circulation by the reformed ones, which were 'overvalued'; in the case of the dirhams, where the weight difference was much slighter, their users seem to have treated them more interchangeably. The systematic use of the date of issue and, on the silver, also the mint name, is suggestive of the organisational and religious intent behind the reforms. God's rule could now be proclaimed, God's soldiers paid, and God's taxes collected using the distinctive coins, on which the new so-called 'Kufic' Arabic script and the calendar of Arabian monotheism replaced the regal iconography of Rome and Iran.[33]

The rhetorical effects were no doubt carefully designed for the multiple audiences that they would reach within the empire and beyond it. The coins' primary audiences were the Arabian fighters in Syria and Iraq, to whom they were first issued. Some of these fighters were familiar with coins struck by Ibn al-Zubayr's commanders and by the Azariqa that included similar slogans in Arabic or Middle Persian alongside Sasanian-style images. The Arabic slogans on the Marwanid coins would have been easily recognised by many, and they appear to have been judged to resonate with the Arabians' expectations, making claims that emphasised the boundary between the 'in-group' of the Faithful (*al-mu'minūn*) and the 'out-group' of 'those who associate others with God' (*al-mushrikūn*). These latter could be anyone who was judged to be outside the new polity established by Muhammad and his followers – the verse from the ninth *sūra* of the Qur'an on the margin of the coins invokes Muhammad's prophethood and the victory of his religion over all others. Thus, the intention with respect to the payment of the armies appears to have been inclusion and consolidation. The slogans could unite Arabians in the wake of the civil war, especially in the context of the ongoing fighting against the various rebel groups in Iraq.[34] Other aspects of the coinage suggest concerns relating more to the Roman frontier, where the Roman and Arabian versions of faith were in military contention. The words in the central fields, with their reference to God being neither father nor son, imply a particular concern with drawing a distinction between the true faith and Christian Trinitarianism. This was a

---

[33] On the coin reforms, see Stefan Heidemann, 'The Merger of Two Currency Zones in Early Islam: The Byzantine and Sasanian Impact on the Circulation in Former Byzantine Syria and Northern Mesopotamia', *Iran* 36 (1998), 95–112, with 'Gresham's Law' at 97. See further, Bacharach, 'Signs of Sovereignty', 19–22. On the use of the date and mint, see Klat, *Catalogue*, 7.

[34] That the Kharijites of Iraq and Iran may have prompted earlier reforms is argued by Bacharach, 'Signs of Sovereignty'.

continuation of the symbolic competition with the Roman Empire begun by Muʻawiya but much advanced in the 680s and early 690s by ʻAbd al-Malik, who was proclaiming himself as the rightful representative of God, against false Roman claims and the false Roman faith.[35]

The same invocation and refutation of Roman and Christian imperium is made by the most famous by far of ʻAbd al-Malik's legacies – the Dome of the Rock, on the Temple Mount in Jerusalem. The Temple Mount was where Muʻawiya had received the pledge of allegiance in *c.* 661. It already had a mosque at its southern end, and a monumental entrance in the east, leading down to the Garden of Gethsemene and Mary's Tomb. However, the centre of the platform, where the Jewish Temple had once stood before its destruction by the Romans centuries earlier, remained empty. What ʻAbd al-Malik and his architects built there was not a mosque but a shrine – an octagonal sanctuary with a gold-plated dome. Its form echoed that of some East Roman churches, including the Holy Sepulchre, which was overlooked by the Temple Mount, about 500m to the west (Figure 6.6). Given its location, the new monument would have invoked not just the Holy Sepulchre but also traditions about Solomon's Temple. Moreover, as a pilgrimage shrine it was also a sort of counterpoint or companion to the Kaʻba, in Mecca.[36]

The Dome of the Rock still stands, with much of its original interior decorative design intact (Figures 6.6, 6.7 and 6.8). The whole building is only about 40m across and just over 30m high but is more imposing than these dimensions suggest because of the paved esplanade around it and its elevation above Jerusalem on the Temple Mount. It is just to the west of the centre of the Temple platform, on its own smaller raised platform, approached by steps and arches. Doors lead through the walls of the octagonal shrine at the four cardinal points of the compass. Inside, two colonnaded ambulatories divide up the space. At the centre a large, flat, rough-surfaced rock, more than 10m across, fills the floor beneath the high dome. The interior walls are clad in

---

[35] Marsham, "'God's Caliph'". *Amīr al-muʼminīn*, or 'Commander of the Faithful', is attested much earlier, from 661: *EI3*, 'Commander of the Faithful' (A. Marsham).

[36] There is an extensive literature. This and what follows depends in particular upon: Myriam Rosen-Ayalon, *The Early Islamic Monuments of al-Haram al-Sharif: An Iconographic Study* (Jerusalem, 1989); Jeremy Johns and Julian Raby (eds), *Bayt al-Maqdis: ʻAbd al-Malik's Jerusalem* (Oxford, 1992); Amikam Elad, *Medieval Jerusalem and Islamic Worship: Holy Places, Ceremonies, Pilgrimage* (Leiden, 1995); Oleg Grabar, *The Shape of the Holy: Early Islamic Jerusalem* (Princeton, 1996); Oleg Grabar and Said Nuseibeh, *The Dome of the Rock* (London, 1996); Jeremy Johns (ed.), *Bayt al-Maqdis: Jerusalem and Early Islam* (Oxford, 1999); Amikam Elad, "Abd al-Malik and the Dome of the Rock: A Further Examination of the Muslim Sources', *JSAI* 35 (2008), 167–226.

Figure 6.6 Aerial view of the Old City of Jerusalem in winter, looking north-west. The Dome of the Rock and the Aqsa Mosque on the Temple Mount are in the central foreground. The remains of Umayyad-era palaces are just to the south of the Aqsa Mosque, in the bottom left corner. The domes and tower of the Church of the Holy Sepulchre are about two-thirds of the way up, towards the left side of the picture. PhotoStock-Israel / Alamy Stock Photo.

opus sectile marble and in gold and green mosaics depicting unearthly combinations of vines, trees and jewels. Above the mosaic images, and just below the decorated wooden ceiling, the insides of the ambulatories are encircled by bands of Arabic in gold mosaic tiles on a blue-green background. In their content, these inscriptions resemble seventh-century Christian liturgy, with their allusions to, and quotations from, scripture (in this case the Qur'an) and their requests for God's mercy through intercession (appealing here to Muhammad). The main theme of the Quranic quotations is the unity, power and mercy of God, with the inner inscription explicitly addressing the false doctrine of the Trinity, 'O People of the Book! Do not go beyond the bounds of your religion and do not say about God except the truth ... do not say "three" ...' (Q. 4:171–2).

Figure 6.7 The Dome of the Rock, Jerusalem, from the north. Photograph by Andrew Marsham.

A separate inscription includes the date AH 72 (June 691–May 692). Whether this records the date on which the building was finished or begun remains an open question.[37] Whichever is the case, the date proves that the Dome's construction belongs to the era of 'Abd al-Malik's war against Ibn al-Zubayr and the resumption of the war with Rome. Like Mu'awiya at his accession in Jerusalem in c. 661, 'Abd al-Malik reasserted Syria's sacred status in the context of his conflicts with his Arabian rivals and the Roman Empire. The Dome's prominence above the city made it the most visible monument in the holiest city of Christianity, and this was how a tenth-century scholar remembered its purpose:

'Abd al-Malik, when he saw the greatness of the dome of the Church of the Holy Sepulchre' (*qubbat al-qumāma* [sic]) and its elegant shape, was

[37] For the current consensus that the Dome of the Rock was finished, and not started, in 692, see, for example, Robinson, *'Abd al-Malik*, 2–8. But cf. Sheila Blair, 'What is the Date of the Dome of the Rock?', in Johns (ed.), *Bayt al-Maqdis*, 59–87; George, *Umayyad Mosque*, 76.

Figure 6.8 The Dome of the Rock, Jerusalem, interior of the top of the inner arcade, looking north. B. O'Kane / Alamy Stock Photo.

distressed that it would hold great prestige in the hearts of the Muslims, so he set up over the rock the dome (*qubba*), which is seen today.[38]

This response to the monuments of Christianity would also have been an ideological challenge to the Roman Empire, which aligned with 'Abd al-Malik's military ambitions; the truce with the Romans had recently been broken and a victory won in Anatolia in 692.[39] Meanwhile, from an internal, Arabian, perspective the Dome's construction contributed to the prestige of Jerusalem as a holy site belonging to the conquerors and their religion. Indeed, one later tradition indicates that 'Abd al-Malik intended the city to supplant the Ka'ba as a site for pilgrimage while he did not control Mecca. Certainly the Dome's form as a sanctuary and its construction around a rock recall the Ka'ba and it may indeed have been a response extensive works on the Ka'ba carried out

---

[38] Shams al-Din Abu 'Abd Allah Muhammad b. Ahmad al-Muqaddasi, *Kitab Ahsan al-taqasim fi ma'rifat al-aqalim*, ed. M. J. de Geoje (Leiden, 1906), 159; first 1877 edition cited in Guy Le Strange, *Palestine under the Moslems: A Description of Syria and the Holy Land from AD 650 to 1500* (London, 1890), 117–18 and Grabar, *Shape*, 53. On *al-qumāma*, see Zakaria Mohammad, 'The Holy Sepulcher and the Garbage Dump: An Etymology', *Jerusalem Quarterly* 50 (2012), 108–12.

[39] See above, p. 130.

by Ibn al-Zubayr.[40] However, the Dome of the Rock was also the starting point for the *hajj* pilgrims who left Syria for the Hijaz once Mecca was under 'Abd al-Malik's control, linking the two sacred cities and Marwanid control of them. Once he had recaptured Mecca, 'Abd al-Malik immediately commenced building there too.[41]

In order to fully understand 'Abd al-Malik's works in Mecca, it is worth returning to the events of the 680s and the rhetoric of his opponent, Ibn al-Zubayr. The rituals of the pilgrimage and the memory of Muhammad associated with them had become a crucial focus of ideological competition. In 680, Ibn al-Zubayr had resisted giving the pledge of allegiance to Mu'awiya's son Yazid, calling himself 'the Seeker of Refuge in the House' (*al-ā'idh bi-l-bayt*). By taking up residence at Mecca, Ibn al-Zubayr had laid claim to the Prophet Muhammad's legacy, including the Meccan pilgrimage and the Ka'ba. At the *hajj* in August 682, Ibn al-Zubayr had refused to acknowledge Yazid's appointed leader of the pilgrimage and had led his own separate ceremony. In the following year, he led the *hajj* uncontested, while Yazid's army fought at Medina. In 684, after the Ka'ba had been damaged during the failed siege of 683, he rebuilt the shrine in a modified form, making the claim that he was instituting changes which had been planned by the Prophet himself, but had not been carried out:

> My mother, Asma' bt. Abi Bakr, told me that God's Messenger said to 'A'isha [her sister and the Prophet's widow]: 'If it were not that your people had only recently been in a state of unbelief, I would restore the Ka'ba on the foundations of Abraham and I would add to the Ka'ba part of the Hijr [the low semi-circular wall near the cubic shrine].'

During the next seven years, Ibn al-Zubayr continued to lead the pilgrimage in person, although in 686 and 688 he was unable to prevent rivals, including some of the Umayyads, from leading their own pilgrimages too.[42]

---

[40] Elad, "Abd al-Malik'; cf. Gerald Hawting, 'Ibn al-Zubayr, the Ka'ba and the Dome of the Rock', in Andrew Marsham (ed.), *The Umayyad World* (London and New York, 2021), 374–92.

[41] On the Dome of the Rock and the *hajj*, see Elad, "Abd al-Malik'; Alain George, 'A Builder of Mosques: The Projects of al-Walid I, from Sanaa to Homs', in Melanie Gibson (ed.), *Fruit of Knowledge, Wheel of Learning: Essays in Honour of Robert Hillenbrand* (London, 2022), 40–2.

[42] Khalifa, 146, 157–8; Baladhuri, *Futuh*, 46–7; Baladhuri, *Ansab*, IV, 386–7; Ya'qubi, II, 302, 309–11, 320; Tabari, II, 422, 592 (quotation translated after I. K. A. Howard, in Tabari, *History*, XIX, 218); McMillan, *Meaning*, 63–76. On the pledge of allegiance, see above, Ch. 5, p. 101. For the possibility that the focus on the Ka'ba in the *hajj* dates from this time, see Hawting, 'Ibn al-Zubayr', 378–9, 383–6.

However, in the Autumn of 692, Ibn al-Zubayr had been defeated and killed by al-Hajjaj. 'Abd al-Malik appointed al-Hajjaj over the Hijaz, entrusting him with re-establishing Umayyad authority there and the leadership of the *ḥajj*. Al-Hajjaj rebuilt the Ka'ba, which had been damaged in the siege, on 'Abd al-Malik's instructions. When the work was completed, in 694, 'Abd al-Malik extended al-Hajjaj's authority over the whole of the Hijaz and is said to have had him carry out punitive actions against some of the Prophet's Companions whom he accused of collaborating in the death of 'Uthman:

> Al-Hajjaj restored the structure of the Ka'ba. He gave it one door, as it had before Ibn al-Zubayr rebuilt it, and he removed from it what Ibn al-Zubayr had added near the *Hijr* [the low wall near the Ka'ba] – which was six – and had strengthened with lead, which he removed from it. He raised its door as it had been before and reduced its height, so that he made it how it is today. He completed its rebuilding in the year 74 (693–4). He sealed the necks of some of the Prophet's Companions, in order to humiliate them by this.[43]

In 694, with the Dome of the Rock constructed, and the Ka'ba rebuilt, 'Abd al-Malik briefly appointed his paternal uncle Yahya b. al-Hakam (g. c. 694) as governor of Medina before replacing him with the Medinan religious scholar and son of 'Uthman, Aban b. 'Uthman (g. c. 694–703). Together with the rebuilding of the Ka'ba and the public criticism of 'Uthman's opponents, these appointments emphasised the Marwanid victory and their claim to be the rightful successors of the murdered 'Uthman. Then, in March 695, 'Abd al-Malik led the *ḥajj* in person. This was a triumphant occasion, emphasising 'Abd al-Malik's role as the victor in the conflicts of the past decade, as leader of the Faithful and the proper guardian of the Meccan shrine. Reported fragments of 'Abd al-Malik's speeches at the Medinan mosque in the later sources are confrontational, criticising the Medinans for killing 'Uthman and warning them that he would not be diverted from power.[44]

Aban b. 'Uthman remained in post as governor until 703, when he was replaced by Hisham b. Isma'il (g. 703–6), from the Qurashi clan of Makhzum. Hisham b. Isma'il was a former supporter of Ibn al-Zubayr, who had quickly been brought into alliance with 'Abd al-Malik after Ibn al-Zubayr's defeat. One of Hisham's daughters, named 'A'isha, was married to 'Abd al-Malik and bore him a son in the early 690s. Thus, like Mu'awiya, 'Abd al-Malik placed

---

[43] Ya'qubi, II, 325. Cf. al-Baladhuri, *Futuh*, 47; Baladhuri, *Ansab*, VI, 240 (details about the sealing); Abu l-Walid Muhammad b. 'Abd Allah al-Azraqi, *Kitab Akhbar Makka*, ed. Ferdinand Wüstenfeld (Leipzig, 1858), 138–54.
[44] Khalifa, 170–1, 188; Tabari, II, 862, 873–7, 880–1; McMillan, *Meaning*, 84–5.

the Hijaz in the hands of Umayyads with connections to 'Uthman, and then replaced them towards the end of his life with a governor who was personally loyal to him and would not disrupt his succession plans.[45] As under Mu'awiya, these governors usually led the *hajj* and, as under Mu'awiya, the exceptions to this pattern were two pilgrimages led by the sons 'Abd al-Malik had named as his heirs, al-Walid and Sulayman.[46]

Medinan Scholars in the Orbit of the Marwanids

The city of Medina was dominated by the descendants of the Meccans who had moved there with the foundation of the city as the centre of the new religious community, alongside the descendants of the Ansar, the local Medinans who had hosted them. Consequently, it was an important centre of religious and political thought in the mid-seventh century and remained significant long afterwards.[47] 'Abd al-Malik had grown up in Medina and gained a strong reputation as a scholar of religion himself. Although many Medinans had backed his 'Alid and Zubayrid rivals in the 680s, expelling the Umayyads from the town, the status of the Medinans was such that in victory 'Abd al-Malik needed as far as possible to co-opt them. He enjoyed success with some of the former allies of Ibn al-Zubayr, including 'Urwa b. al-Zubayr (b. *c.* 642–3; d. *c.* 709–18) and Ibn Shihab al-Zuhri (b. *c.* 670–8; d. 742), while maintaining a cooler but nonetheless peaceful relationship with some of al-Husayn's relatives.

'Urwa b. al-Zubayr was a full brother of 'Abd Allah b. al-Zubayr who had reputation as a leading authority on law and custom (*sunna*) and the life and campaigns of the Prophet (*sira* and *maghāzi*). 'Urwa, who was about the same age as 'Abd al-Malik, had studied in Medina with the future caliph as a young man and was married to Abd al-Malik's paternal aunt. After the defeat and killing of his brother, 'Urwa continued to reside at Medina, travelling to Syria, it is said, only later, to offer his allegiance to 'Abd al-Malik's sons. This special journey in itself suggests that the public allegiance of this Zubayrid scholar was important to the Marwanids. Moreover, the

---

[45] Khalifa, 170–1; McMillan, *Meaning*, 90–3; Marsham, 'Kinship', 35–7.
[46] McMillan, *Meaning*, 77–9, 86–9.
[47] On some of the famous scholars of Medina, see *EI²*, 'Fukaha' al-Madina al-Sab'a' (Ch. Pellat). On the Umayyad court and religious scholars, see Steven C. Judd, *Religious Scholars and the Umayyads: Piety-minded Supporters of the Marwanid Caliphate* (London and New York, 2014); Mehmetcan Akpınar, 'Medinan Scholars on the Move: Professional Mobility at the Umayyad Court', in Mohamad El-Merheb and Mehdi Berriah (eds), *Professional Mobility in Islamic Societies (700–1750): New Concepts and Approaches* (Leiden, 2021), 15–39.

survival in the later sources of versions of correspondence about the life of the Prophet Muhammad exchanged between 'Urwa, 'Abd al-Malik and al-Walid shows that the caliphs attached a particular significance to 'Urwa's knowledge about the Prophet.

Alongside the Marwanids' building projects, which promoted a particular vision of religious legitimacy, effort was being made to promote religious knowledge that would also shore up their claims. This memory of Muhammad's life and times, which now lay beyond the lived experience of almost everyone, became crucial. Furthermore, the correspondence reflects a shared opposition on the part of the Marwanid caliphs and the Zubayrids to Hashimite, let alone 'Kharijite' (that is, effectively anti-Qurashi), interpretations of the past. As Sean Anthony notes, the version of the Prophet's life that 'Urwa sent to the caliphs was one in which, 'the most prominent figures ... are either from the Umayyad clan ... the Asad clan (to which the Zubayrids belonged), or 'Urwah's maternal relations, such as Abu Bakr ... and his daughters, Asma' and 'A'isha.' This emphasis on the Umayyads and Zubayrids contrasts with later traditions about the Prophet compiled under Abbasid patronage, where the Hashimites are more prominent.[48]

Muhammad b. Muslim al-Zuhri was probably about thirty years younger than 'Urwa. Al-Zuhri, who is also sometimes known as Ibn Shihab, was from a branch of Quraysh who had been allied with the Zubayrids. Traditions from al-Zuhri are prominent in later collections of reports (*aḥādīth*, sing. *ḥadīth*) about the Prophet and his Companions, as well as in *sīra* and *maghāzī* ('biography' and 'campaigns') materials about the life and times of the Prophet and may reflect a pro-Marwanid strand in the extant tradition. Al-Zuhri probably came to 'Abd al-Malik's court in the early 700s when he was in his twenties or early thirties. He remained in the orbit of the Marwanid rulers from then until his death in 742, shortly before the death of Hisham b. 'Abd al-Malik (r. 724–43). In 'Abd al-Malik's time, al-Zuhri is said to have served as a legal advisor (*qāḍī*) and to have gone to Egypt with 'Abd al-Malik's paternal half-brother and Egyptian governor, 'Abd al-'Aziz. Later, he is also said to have served as an army commander, again as a *qāḍī*, as the chief of the *shurṭa* (a senior military, administrative and judicial role) and then to have been a leading advisor to Hisham, and tutor to his sons.[49]

Whereas some former Medinan Zubayrids and their allies aligned themselves with Marwanid rule, the surviving descendants of al-Husayn kept more distance. Three generations were widely revered as religious

---

[48] Anthony, *Muhammad*, 94–128, quotation at 104.
[49] Michael Lecker, 'Biographical Notes on Ibn Shihab al-Zuhri', *JSS* 41 (1996), 21–63; Judd, *Religious Scholars*, 52–61; Akpınar, 'Medinan Scholars', 20–5, 28–35.

authorities, and by some as the true heirs to the Prophet. Al-Husayn's son 'Ali b. al-Husayn (d. 712–13) is remembered in later Shi'i tradition as 'Zayn al-'Abidin' ('The Ornament of God's Servants'), succeeded by his son, Muhammad al-Baqir (b. *c*. 675–7, d. *c*. 735–8), and in turn by his son, Ja'far al-Sadiq (b. *c*. 700–3, d. 765). Because these men are venerated in the later Shi'i tradition as the fourth, fifth and sixth imams and the true leaders of Islam after the Prophet and 'Ali, it is difficult to recover their doctrinal and political positions from the later sources. Indeed, they are also venerated as authoritative transmitters of stories about the Prophet and his Companions in later Sunnism. This ambiguity partly reflects their delicate political position in Marwanid Medina: relations with the Marwanids seem to have been cordial under 'Abd al-Malik, but they were no doubt perceived as a potential threat to Marwanid power.[50]

The Caliphate of al-Walid (I) b. 'Abd al-Malik

'Abd al-Malik died in October 705 and was succeeded by al-Walid (r. 705–15), a son by Wallada bt. al-'Abbas, from the 'northern', Qaysi tribe of al-'Abs.[51] In turn, al-Walid was to be succeeded by his full brother, Sulayman, should the latter outlive him. Support for these sons came from the governor of Iraq, al-Hajjaj, who would thereby cement his position as the most powerful provincial commander in the empire, and from the 'northern', or Qaysi, Syrian tribes, who had become crucial in warfare against the Romans in Anatolia and Armenia during the 690s and early 700s but were in competition with the 'southern' Kalbis for the patronage of the Marwanid elite. The Kalbis, who dominated southern and central Syria, had backed 'Abd al-'Aziz, 'Abd al-Malik's paternal half-brother and Egyptian governor, to whom some of them were closely related. The conveniently timed death of 'Abd al-'Aziz in 704 secured the succession of his nephews without having to test the solidarity of 'Abd al-Malik and his half-brother. It also further displaced the Banu Kalb from the leading position they had held under Mu'awiya and Yazid.[52]

---

[50] *EI²*, 'Dja'far al-Sadik' (M. G. S. Hodgson), 'Muhammad b. 'Ali Zayn al-'Abidin, Abu Dja'far, called al-Bakir' (E. Kohlberg), 'Zayn al-'Abidin' (E. Kohlberg). Tensions persisted with the Zubayrids. For religious and political conflict with a son of Ibn al-Zubayr under al-Walid I, see Ya'qubi, II, 339–40; Tabari, II, 1255.

[51] Marsham, 'Kinship', 35. There is also some indication in the sources that two other sons of 'Abd al-Malik by high-status mothers, Yazid and Hisham, were expected to succeed in due course: *RoIM*, 118. For Wallada's relatives' lands near Qinnasrin, see above, Introduction to Part II, p. 122 and n. 3.

[52] On 'Abd al-'Aziz's ambitions for the caliphate, see Mabra, *Princely Authority*. On his son, al-Asbagh, who also died in 704, see Baladhuri, *Ansab*, VI, 368, VII, 185; Ibn 'Asakir, IX, 169–71, §781.

Al-Walid's choice of governors reflects both the extent to which his caliphate was a continuation of that of his father, depending on similar alliances and networks, but also the ways in which the new caliph sought to develop his own power base. In Iraq, al-Hajjaj, who had played a crucial role in bringing about the new caliph's succession, remained in his post at Wasit until his death in June 714. Al-Hajjaj controlled the appointment of commanders to the dependent provinces east of Iraq, while one of al-Hajjaj's brothers, Muhammad (g. c. 692–715), kept the governorship of Yemen, which he had likewise already held under 'Abd al-Malik.[53] Al-Hajjaj is described as having a dominant role in al-Walid's caliphate, being consulted frequently by the caliph, and supporting the succession of al-Walid's son in place of his brother, Sulayman.[54] On the Roman and Caucasian frontiers, al-Walid's uncle Muhammad b. Marwan retained overall command until 710, when he was replaced by one of his nephews (and so al-Walid's paternal cousin), Maslama b. 'Abd al-Malik. Maslama, like Muhammad, was a caliph's son by a slave mother.

Al-Walid did make changes in the Hijaz and Egypt. In the Hijaz, Hisham b. Isma'il, who was the ally of one of al-Walid's paternal half-brothers and so potential rivals, was removed in favour of a cousin, 'Umar b. 'Abd al-'Aziz (g. 706–12). 'Umar was the maternal great-grandson of his namesake, the Prophet's second successor, 'Umar b. al-Khattab, and had an established reputation among the religious scholars of Medina. His appointment was probably also intended to conciliate the former supporters of his father, the late 'Abd al-'Aziz. In Egypt, al-Walid waited three years before replacing a half-brother with Qurra b. Sharik al-'Absi (g. 709–14). Qurra was from the same tribe as al-Walid's mother and may have previously served as a commander on the northern Roman frontier. Like the caliphal succession itself, the choice of Qurra reflected the growing power of the 'Qaysi', or 'northern' tribes in the frontier armies. It was also a departure from placing Egypt in the hands of a member of the Hijazi elite, reflecting a growing reliance on men from other tribes who had risen to prominence in the warfare of the later seventh century.[55]

The policies pursued by al-Walid and his allies also reflect some continuity from 'Abd al-Malik's time. The war with Rome and the consolidation of the institutional and ideological power of the Marwanid clan were old priorities, now taken up with renewed vigour and boldness. Meanwhile, Ifriqiya and Khurasan had become established garrisons, where soldiers who had made their fortunes in the conquests of the late seventh and early eighth centuries now pursued further expansionist warfare, generating huge revenues in loot

---

[53] Khalifa, 186, 198, 199; Tabari, II, 1274.
[54] EI², 'al-Hadjdjadj b. Yusuf' (A. Dietrich).
[55] Kindi, 58–66; EI², 'Kurra b. Sharik' (C. E. Bosworth).

and tribute, including slaves. In the East, this warfare was directed by al-Hajjaj, as he manoeuvred for the succession of al-Walid's son in place of his brother, just as he had worked for the succession for 'Abd al-Malik's sons over 'Abd al-'Aziz in the previous generation.

The War with Rome and the Articulation of Marwanid Legitimacy under al-Walid I

Whereas the war with Rome had become somewhat static in the later 690s and early 700s, unrest within the Roman Empire now allowed the Arabian commanders to regain the initiative. In 711, Justinian II, who had regained his throne in 705, was overthrown for a second time. The general Philippikos Bardanes (r. 711–13) replaced him. As in the coup of 695, this was achieved with Khazar support. Further years of internal conflict within the Roman Empire followed, with three more emperors taking power in the next six years.[56] Big Arabian military advances were made after the crises of 705 and 711. In 706, there were raids on Sardinia and in Anatolia. Then, in 707, Maslama b. 'Abd al-Malik crossed the Taurus, defeating a Roman field army and overwintering at Tyana (Ar. Tuwana). In 712 three separate armies crossed into the eastern Anatolian plateau and captured Amaseia and Sebasteia. The successes of 712 were interpreted as a sign of serious intent: a Roman embassy was sent to Damascus in 713, to investigate suing for peace, Constantinople was refortified and the Roman navy expanded. (Naval warfare had continued since the 690s and seems to have escalated after 705.)[57] The Roman offer of a peace treaty was rebutted; the Arabians instead began to prepare for an assault on Constantinople, while either Maslama or 'Abd-'Aziz b. al-Walid led the *hajj* at Mecca that Autumn.[58]

Just as victory against the Roman Empire remained essential for the continued prestige of the ruling house, al-Walid continued his father's policies of developing the institutional and ideological foundations of Marwanid power. Tax surveys in Egypt and the Jazira coincided with the appointment of new governors in these provinces and were directed at increasing revenues

---

[56] Theophanes, 527–45, s.aa. 710–17.
[57] Khalifa, 190–1, records a raid on Sardinia in 706. Tabari, II, 1201, records the capture of Khalid b. Kaysan, the sea commander (*ṣāḥib al-baḥr*), in 709 and his return to al-Walid. On the land campaigns, see E. W. Brooks, 'The Arabs in Asia Minor (641–750), from Arabic Sources', *The Journal of Hellenic Studies* 18 (1898), 191–4. Among other campaigns in the Caucasus, Maslama reached Bab al-Abwab (Darband) in 710 and razed it in 714; see Khalifa, 184, 191, 192, 193, 196. See also, *WtaWC*, 391, 508–9.
[58] For Maslama at the *hajj* in early Autumn 713, see Khalifa, 195. Cf. Tabari, II, 1266; McMillan, *Meaning*, 96, with further references. On the embassy and Roman preparations in 713–15, see Theophanes, 534; *WtaWC*, 243, 264, 301, with further references.

from two of the wealthiest parts of the empire.[59] Al-Walid also continued the development of a monumental Islamic architecture that 'Abd al-Malik had begun with the construction of the Dome of the Rock and other building projects at Mecca, Jerusalem and Wasit. As with 'Abd al-Malik's buildings, al-Walid's constructions were intended to monumentalise the religious and political authority of the Marwanid caliph, and particularly his twin roles of leader of the *hajj* and commander of the war with Rome. However, as with al-Walid's wars against Rome, these new building projects were carried out on an unprecedented scale.

Al-Walid's name is associated with the rebuilding and opulent decoration in marble and mosaic of seven mosques, as well as the sanctuary at Mecca. The three most prestigious mosques he rebuilt were the imperial congregational mosque in Damascus, the Aqsa congregational mosque on the Temple Mount, just to the south of the Dome of the Rock, and the congregational mosque at Medina. The four others were the main congregational mosques for the provinces of Egypt and Yemen, the congregational mosque at Hims, in Syria, and the mosque at Quba', at Medina, where the Prophet is said to have first prayed on his arrival from Mecca in 622. In cases where the construction work can be dated, it often began in the first few years of al-Walid's caliphate. The main exception is Fustat, which was begun in about 711 – that is, within about a year or so of Qurra b. Sharik's appointment to the province; the mosque at Sana'a, in Yemen, may also have been rebuilt at around the same time.[60]

Alain George has shown that al-Walid's buildings followed a consistent aesthetic, developed from the style and iconography of his father's constructions at the Dome of the Rock and the mosque at Wasit, and perhaps also from his works at Mecca and Jerusalem. Key features included opus sectile marble cladding, or dadoes, on internal walls, decorative wooden ceilings, extensive use of green and gold mosaic, and decorative pillars with gilded capitals. The four most prestigious buildings, at Damascus, Medina, Mecca and Jerusalem, had the most expensive and elaborate decoration, while Sana'a, Fustat and Quba', and probably also Hims, were simpler in style, with less use of mosaic and marble and, in most cases, stacked stone columns. The expansion of the mosques at Damascus and Medina and the redevelopment of the Ka'ba were all begun within about two years of al-Walid's accession and signalled the new caliph and his allies' intent to proclaim Islam's imminent victory over Roman Christianity and the righteousness of his own family's authority over

---

[59] See further below, Ch. 12, p. 322.
[60] George, 'Builder of Mosques'.

the Muslims. Indeed, they formed part of an aggressive diplomatic and propaganda campaign that coincided with the military assaults on Rome, and they provided the monumental stage for the ceremonial performances of al-Walid's legitimacy.

Al-Walid appointed oversight at Medina to his cousin, the respected religious scholar, and new Medinan governor, 'Umar b. 'Abd al-'Aziz, who in turn delegated much of the work to another Medinan scholar, Salih b. Kaysan (d. c. 758). The routes into Medina were improved and wells and a fountain constructed. The mosque itself was expanded to incorporate the Prophet's tomb, which was enclosed with a wall for the first time, as were the tombs of the Prophet's first two successors, Abu Bakr and 'Umar b. al-Khattab. The mosque was given four corner towers and decorated with gold and marble, some of which is said to have been requested as tribute from the Roman emperor, just as 'Abd al-Malik is said to have received columns for the Ka'ba from him. The development was controversial, in part simply because of its unprecedented scale, but also because of the memorialisation of the Prophet's tomb and because the houses of the Prophet's wives and of some of 'Ali's family were purchased and destroyed to make space for it.[61]

At Mecca, the new governor, Khalid al-Qasri, was likewise appointed to undertake the works on the Ka'ba and the surrounding enclosure, known as the Masjid al-Haram. The gates of the Ka'ba, its columns and the water-spout on its roof were all sheathed in gold, while the surrounding enclosure was also developed.

> He made [the enclosure] with [a single arcade of marble columns and] teak ceilings, and gilded the column capitals in sheets of the finest brass. He covered the inside of the mosque with marble and the spandrels with mosaics. He was the first to do this in the Masjid al-Haram. He provided the mosque with crenellations.[62]

These changes at Mecca appear to have been intended to bring the aesthetic of the Ka'ba and its enclosure into line with the new distinctive style of the mosques at Medina and Damascus and to reaffirm the Marwanids' association with the pilgrimage city.

At Damascus, the large enclosure at the centre of the city that surrounded the Church of St John the Baptist had up until 705 been shared with the Damascene Christians. Al-Walid ordered the compulsory purchase of the

---

[61] Harry Munt, *The Holy City of Medina: Sacred Space in Early Islamic Arabia* (Cambridge, 2014), 105–11, 138–9; George, *Umayyad Mosque*, 82–4; George, 'Builder of Mosques', 22–8.

[62] Al-Azraqi, *Akhbar*, 146; tr. George, 'Builder of Mosques', 29.

Figure 6.9 Aerial view of the Umayyad Mosque at Damascus, looking south-east. Photograph by Bernard Gagnon, CC BY-SA 3.0, Wikimedia Commons.

Christian church and its demolition, in order to make space to rework the whole enclosure as a single courtyard mosque, with a monumental prayer hall across its whole southern side (Figure 6.9).

The destruction of the church and construction of the mosque were deliberately confrontational. The demolition provoked outrage among the Christian population of the city and was a calculated gesture of diplomatic defiance directed at the Roman emperor. Whereas previous Umayyads in Syria had depended upon Christian administrators and soldiers, a new generation of converts to Islam now held the senior positions in the Damascene administration, and the leading Christian scribal families were becoming marginalised. At the same time, warfare in Anatolia and the Mediterranean was meeting with success, and the goal of capturing Constantinople was becoming a plausible war aim. Al-Walid is said to have demanded tribute payments from Justinian II to support the construction of the mosques at Medina and Damascus. For his part, Justinian II is said to have supplied craftsmen and materials for both projects. This seems plausible – the payment would have been intended to buy off the Arabians.

The renowned Tamimi poet Jarir (d. *c.* 728–9) performed a panegyric praising al-Walid as the 'Chosen Imam', whose 'banners flaunt victory and spoils', to whom 'kingship is given', and who defeats the 'slit-nosed' Justinian II – the latter a reference to the mutilation Justinian II had suffered when he had been deposed in 695:

> You leapt at the Christians – one bound; on landing,
>   it caused the mountains of Daylam to shake!
> The edifice of the church was razed by force;
>   there was a crushing defeat for the Slit-nosed [King]!
> The Lord showed you, when you broke their cross,
>   bright guidance; you knew what we did not ...[63]

The destruction of the church depended upon divine inspiration – 'you knew what we did not' is an echo of the Qur'an on God's knowledge about the merits of Adam's destructiveness (Q. 2:30).

Jarir's contemporary and rival al-Farazdaq (d. *c*. 728 or 730) emphasised the contrast between the truth of Islam and the idolatrous falsehoods of Christianity as well as the divinely inspired justice of al-Walid who, like David and Solomon, was a rightly guided saviour figure (*al-mahdī*):

> You divided Christians in their churches from those
>   who pray before dawn, and after dusk.
> Together at worship, faces turned
>   two ways: toward God, or toward the Idol.
> How should clappers struck by Acolytes of the Cross
>   intrude on Readers who do not sleep?
> *You were inspired* to rid them of these
>   with the wisdom, when they judged on the sheep and the tilth,
> Of David and [Solomon,] Right-guided King,
>   who awarded their lambs and the wool of the shear.[64]

The new monuments connected a narrative of divinely inspired imperial victory with the legitimacy of al-Walid and his family and their rightful leadership of the Muslims, whose separation from, and superiority to, Christians were emphasised.

The annual ritual of the *hajj* was a crucial venue where these claims could be made in public to audiences from across the empire, while the provincial mosques addressed their local populations. By 710 the Medinan mosque and the redevelopment of the Ka'ba and its precincts had been completed. The mosque at Hims, where one of al-Walid's sons, al-'Abbas b. al-Walid, was commander, had also probably been finished. Al-Walid's favoured son for the succession, 'Abd al-'Aziz b. al-Walid, who was a maternal grandson of 'Abd al-'Aziz b. Marwan, had been made governor of Damascus, where works on the congregational mosque were well under way. In the *hajj* season, which

---

[63] Tr. Nadia Jamil in George, *Umayyad Mosque*, 216.
[64] Tr. Nadia Jamil in George, *Umayyad Mosque*, 218–20.

fell in the autumn in 710, al-Walid himself made the pilgrimage. He stayed at Medina for a few days, where he held audiences, distributed slaves and bullion, and led the prayers at the recently completed mosque, before leaving for the pilgrimage rites at Mecca. These rituals were intended to present an image of al-Walid as the patron of the holy cities of Islam, associating his office of caliph with divinely sanctioned authority on earth.[65]

Although the sources are somewhat contradictory, it seems likely that ʿAbd al-ʿAziz b. al-Walid led the *ḥajj* in the early autumn of 712 and al-Walid's uncle and the leading general on the Roman frontier, Maslama b. ʿAbd al-Malik, led it in 713. In each case, these pilgrimages would have followed after the summer campaigning season in Anatolia, and in each case Maslama and al-Walid's sons had led successful raids into Roman territory. A third poem from this period, probably to be dated to 711–12, celebrates one of Maslama's victories, at Turanda in c. 709–11, and connects it to the construction of the Damascus mosque, which by now would have been nearing completion.[66]

> A hailstorm-strike disgraced Turanda;
>   troops not led by luckless fools.
> There blessed Maslama did stand
>   to pound her sides with boulder-rock;
> A clamorous host surrounding her,
>   as fibre rings the crowns of palm,
> To scale her wall from every side
>   till those within were stricken, grieved,
> Her folk between slain and despoiled,
>   and those whose arms were crossed with thongs.
> Steady you crop-nosed sniveller! Will the stroke
>   of your Lord, once aimed, be turned?
> The Christians pray for us, it seems –
>   but God knows best what ribs conceal.
> You plucked their church from out our mosque;
>   its rock was strewn across the earth.
> When People of the Book would pray,
>   the chanting bishops echoed back;
> Dissonance foreign, with pious acts;
>   like swallows chattering at dawn …[67]

---

[65] McMillan, *Meaning*, 95–106; Munt, *Holy City*, 105–15.
[66] George, *Umayyad Mosque*, 74–5; George, 'Builder of Mosques', 37–43. See also above, p. 152. On Medina: Tabari, II, 1192–4, 1232–4. On Turanda, see also *Theophilus*, 202 and n. 554.
[67] Tr. Nadia Jamil in George, *Umayyad Mosque*, 222.

Conquests in North Africa, Europe, Central and South Asia

Victories on the frontier with the Roman Empire in Anatolia were mirrored by similar military successes in the far West and East. However, whereas the war with Rome was prosecuted by leading members of the Marwanid dynasty, the western and eastern frontiers, in North Africa and Central Asia, were dependent upon Egypt and Iraq respectively. Hence, they were spaces where the Egyptian and Iraqi provincial governors could offer opportunities to their allies, including huge sums in tribute payments and loot. In both post-Roman North Africa and the post-Sasanian East, sons of the first conquerors, who had risen to prominence in the wars of the later seventh century, took the lead. These successful warlords now exploited the consolidation of Arabian power at Qayrawan and Marw to found local dynasties, whose wealth was based on the further extension of Arabian power in alliance with local military actors. They began by raiding for tribute, but more permanent political control followed, and new frontiers were opened.

In North Africa, Musa b. Nusayr (g. c. 698–714, d. 716) was probably the son of a tribesman from south-western Iraq. Although Musa had been appointed to North Africa by al-Walid's uncle and rival, 'Abd al-'Aziz, he was left in his post by subsequent governors, no doubt not least because removing him would have been very difficult; for his part, Musa wisely continued to acknowledge Egyptian authority, returning a share of the many slaves he captured to Fustat. By about 708, Musa had extended his influence over many of the so-called 'Berber' tribes of western North Africa, and had established a garrison at Tangier (Ar. Tanja, Lat. Tingis), just south of the straits of Gibraltar, which was placed under the leadership of a local client commander, Tariq b. Ziyad. In the summer of 711, Tariq led a raid north, across the straits, exploiting divisions in the Visigothic elite who ruled post-Roman Hispania (Ar. al-Andalus; modern Spain and Portugal); both King Roderic (r. c. 710–12) and Roderic's rivals within the Visigothic nobility were defeated within the year. Musa's decision to head for al-Andalus/ Hispania himself in 712 was no doubt motivated by a concern to wrest control of the newly conquered territories from Tariq; when Musa left, in 713 or 714, he appointed not Tariq but his own son as the acting governor.[68]

In the East, al-Hajjaj retained close control over frontier warfare as he sought to secure his position at the centre of al-Walid's caliphate. In Khurasan

---

[68] Khalifa, 174, 177, 193, 195, 196; Ibn 'Abd al-Hakam, *Futuh*, 203–11; David James, *A History of Early al-Andalus: The Akhbar Majmu'a* (London, 2012), 48–56; Ibn 'Asakir, LXI, 211–24, §7758; *EI²*, 'Musa b. Nusayr' (C. Lévi-Provençal), 'Tarik b. Ziyad' (L. Molina). On the narratives of the conquest of al-Andalus, see Nicola Clarke, *The Muslim Conquest of Iberia: Medieval Arabic Narratives* (London and New York, 2012).

and its dependent eastern provinces, al-Hajjaj had deposed the family of al-Muhallab b. Abi Sufra in 704 in favour of Qutayba b. Muslim al-Bahili (g. c. 705–15). Qutayba was from a tribe whose ancestors had migrated from Central Arabia into Iraq in the 630s or 640s. He had distinguished himself in the defence of Iraq against Ibn al-Ash'ath in 701 and had been rewarded in the following year with command over Rayy, in north-west Iran. The timing of Qutayba's promotion to Khurasan suggests that it was connected to the caliphal succession; al-Hajjaj and Qutayba were both leading proponents of the claims of al-Walid's son over those of his brother and named heir, Sulayman. The Muhallabids were deposed from Khurasan, Kirman and the office of chief of al-Hajjaj's *shurṭa* (approximately, 'urban guard' or 'police'). Al-Hajjaj also divorced his Muhallabid wife and imprisoned and tortured the members of the family sent to him by Qutayba.[69]

The new commander was energetic and successful. Having deposed the Muhallabids, Qutayba began a series of campaigns on the north-east frontier (see Map 6.1). Between 705 and 710, he consolidated and extended Arabian power in the highlands north and east of Herat, in modern northern Afghanistan, and across the river Oxus in the western fringes of Transoxiana – the region known in Arabic as *mā warā' al-nahr* ('what is across the river' – that is, modern southern Uzbekistan, western Tajikistan and northern Afghanistan). Qutayba joined forces with the Hephthalite ruler of the region, the Tarkhan Nizak. These military and diplomatic successes probably prompted the departure of Narseh, a grandson of the last Sasanian king Yazdgird III, from Transoxiana for China. However, by 709 relations with Nizak had deteriorated, and Qutayba captured and executed him in 710. Resistance to Qutayba's authority was violently suppressed; the sources describe the mass crucifixion of the 'bandits' who opposed Qutayba's rule in the wake of Nizak's defeat.[70]

The elimination of the Hephthalites of northern Afghanistan secured the town of Balkh and opened the valleys of the tributaries of the upper Oxus (western Tajikistan and southern Uzbekistan) to raids. The ruler of Samarqand, who had already come into alliance with the Arabians was overthrown by another Sogdian ruler known as Ghurak (r. c. 710–c. 738), whom Qutayba brought to terms in c. 711–12. In 711, Qutayba headed south to Sistan, to join his brother, 'Amr, for a successful raid on the Zunbil of Kabulistan, from whom they are said in one account to have extracted a tribute payment of 500,000 dirhams and 100 slaves. However, in 713 Qutayba was back in Transoxiana,

---

[69] Khalifa, 185, 187 198; Tabari, II, 1111–12, 1140–21, 1182; *EI²*, 'Muhallabids' (P. Crone); 'Kutayba b. Muslim' (C. E. Bosworth). See also the discussion in Crone, 'Qays and Yemen', 25–7. On the *shurṭa*, see further below, Ch. 12 pp. 312–16.
[70] Marsham, 'Public Execution', 131–2; Haug, *Eastern Frontier*, 93, 115–23.

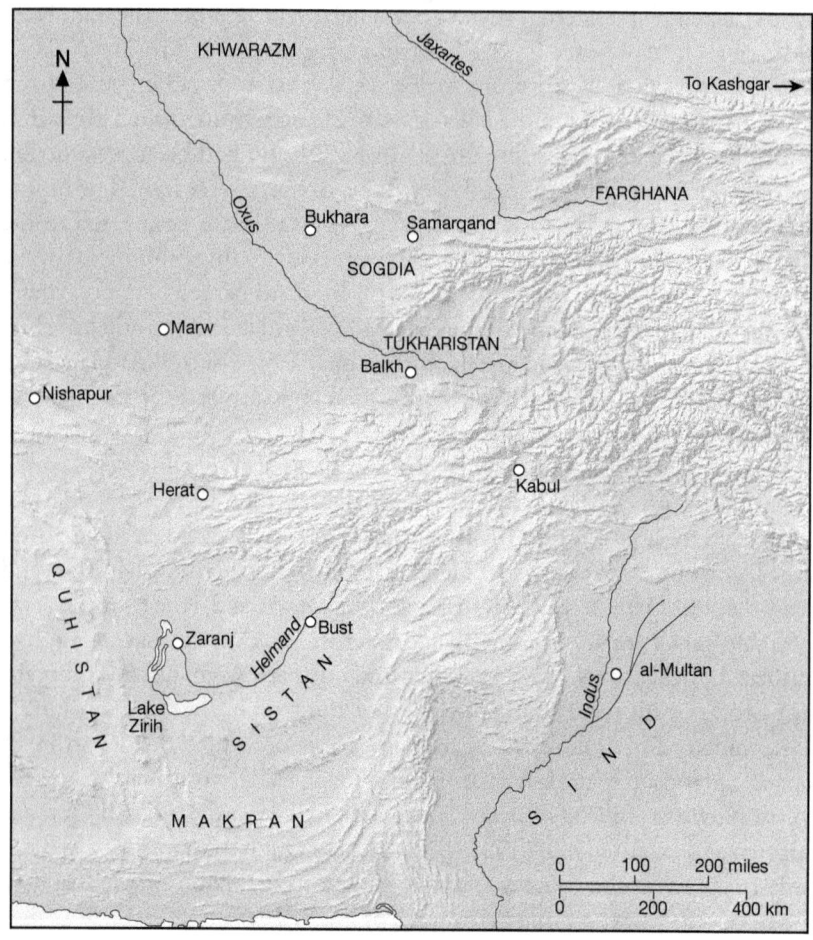

Map 6.1 The eastern frontier at the time of Qutayba b. Muslim.

raiding as far as the upper Jaxartes (southern Kazakhstan), with armies levied from Sogdia and Khwarazm alongside his troops from Khurasan. Then, in 714 and 715, he attacked the western termini (in modern western Kyrgyzstan) of the routes leading from Tang China, also held by Sogdian princes.[71] At around

---

[71] Khalifa, 187; Baladhuri, *Futuh*, 152; Ahmad b. A'tham al-Kufi (= Ibn A'tham), *Kitab al-Futuh*, ed. Muhammad 'Abd al-Mu'id (Hyderabad, 1968–75), VII, 234–48; Ya'qubi, II, 343–44; Tabari, *Ta'rikh*, II, 1227–30, 1235, 1236–53, 1256–7, 1267–8, 1275–6; Haug, *Eastern Frontier*, 111–12, 115, 122; *EI²*, 'Kutayba b. Muslim' (C. E. Bosworth). On aspirations to control Sogdian trade in Khurasan, see Haug, *Eastern Frontier*, 118; Arezou Azad, 'Ecology, Economy, and the Conquest of Khurasan', in Andrew Marsham (ed.), *The Umayyad World* (London and New York, 2021), 335.

this time Qutayba also sent an embassy to China. This was part of a pattern of more frequent embassies to the Chinese court between 711 and 725.[72]

At around the time that Qutayba and 'Amr were campaigning in Sistan, al-Hajjaj appointed Muhammad b. al-Qasim al-Thaqafi (g. 711–14), the young son of a paternal first cousin, to take command of the invasion of the lower Indus Valley (modern south-western Pakistan), 'attaching to him 6,000 troops from the Syrian army'.[73] Having reasserted Arabian control in Makran (south-eastern Iran and western Pakistan), Ibn al-Qasim marched south, into the territories of the Indian King Dahir (r. c. 679–712), who ruled Sind (modern southern and central Pakistan). Muhammad's campaigns are said to have yielded huge amounts of gold, slaves, elephants and buffaloes, as well as a series of tribute agreements.[74]

With his new appointments in the East and the demotion of the Muhallabids, al-Hajjaj was securing the grip of his own family over much of the wealth of the empire. Al-Hajjaj and his allies supported the demotion of al-Walid's brother Sulayman in the succession in favour of al-Walid's son by a Kalbi mother, 'Abd al-'Aziz b. al-Walid. Sulayman, meanwhile, had offered asylum to the Muhallabid leaders ousted by al-Hajjaj in 704. However, al-Hajjaj's death in summer 714 was followed only seven months later by the death of al-Walid. Sulayman duly acceded to the caliphate at Damascus, putting al-Hajjaj's appointees in the East into jeopardy. Qutayba had actively supported 'Abd al-'Aziz b. al-Walid against Sulayman and knew that the Muhallabids would certainly seek to avenge his treatment of them. He decided that revolt was preferable to this fate. However, much of Qutayba's army judged that he would eventually be defeated and refused to support him; he and many of his remaining supporters were killed by their former comrades near Samarqand in August 715.[75]

---

[72] Tabari, II, 1276–9. For the levies of troops, see Kennedy, *Armies*, 45. On diplomatic contact with China, see H. A. R. Gibb, 'Chinese Records of the Arabs in Central Asia', *BSOAS* 2 (1923), 619–22; Bielenstein, *Diplomacy and Trade*, 356–8. In this period of frequent contact there were embassies in 711, 713, 716, 719, 724 and 725. Some may perhaps be explained as accessional missions for Sulayman, 'Umar II and Hisham, but they also suggest an era of closer engagement between the two empires.

[73] Khalifa, 198; Ya'qubi, II, 345; *EI²*, 'al-Hadjdjadj b. Yusuf' (A. Dietrich). Quotation from Baladhuri, *Futuh*, 436.

[74] Khalifa, 193–5; Baladhuri, *Futuh*, 167–8, 292, 375, 435–40; Ya'qubi, II, 345–7; Francesco Gabrieli, 'Muhammad ibn Qasim ath-Thaqafi and the Arab Conquest of Sind', *East and West* 15 (1965), 281–95; André Wink, *Al-Hind, the Making of the Indo-Islamic World* (Leiden, 1991), 151–6, 201–7.

[75] Baladhuri, *Ansab*, VII, 28–30, 44; Tabari, II, 1283–1304.

7

The Siege of Constantinople and the Short Caliphates of Sulayman, ʿUmar II and Yazid II

The decade between 715 and 724 was a turning point both in the character of the Umayyads' empire and the fortunes of the dynasty itself. More than three generations away from the time of the Prophet, and two generations from the end of the first wave of conquests, the social structures within the empire were changing fast. These changes are reflected in language, with 'Muslims' (*muslimūn*) increasingly used alongside the 'Faithful' (*muʾminūn*), and with 'Migrants' (*muhājirūn*) disappearing from use. 'The Arabs' (Ar. *al-ʿarab*) begins to appear more often in the poetry and in the documentary evidence with a collective sense. At the same time, the incorporation of perhaps tens of thousands of enslaved women into the Muslim population, alongside male non-Arabian captives and migrants, was transforming the character of group identities within the garrisons.[1] From this period and after, anxieties about non-Muslims ruling over Muslims and conflicts about unequal treatment of recent converts become prominent features of the source material, as do pressures on tax revenue. These social and economic tensions coincided with an era of dynastic instability, with four caliphs dying in quick succession within the decade. As the caliphs' supporters jockeyed for power and influence, a major rebellion broke out in Iraq for the first time in a generation and new kinds of unrest appeared in North Africa and Khurasan. Moreover, these short caliphates came after the disastrous failure in 718 of the Marwanids' aspirations to conquer the Roman Empire and replace the Romans as the representatives of true monotheist faith. Defeat at the walls of Constantinople shook the ideological foundations which had been established by ʿAbd al-Malik and his son al-Walid.

---

[1] On the changing labels for the Arabian monotheists, see Lindstedt, *Muhajirun*. For early uses of 'the Arabs' in the later Umayyad era, see Webb, *Imagining the Arabs*, 85–8, 148–56. On enslaved women, see Robinson, *Marriage*, 86–125.

Sulayman b. 'Abd al-Malik and the Siege of Constantinople

The new caliph, Sulayman b. 'Abd al-Malik, installed his Muhallabid allies in Iraq and the eastern frontier provinces of Sind, Sistan and Khurasan.[2] Reprisals against their enemies continued; the former governor of Sind, Muhammad b. al-Qasim, and a number of other relatives of al-Hajjaj are said to have been tortured and killed at Wasit.[3] New frontier warfare also began; Yazid b. al-Muhallab, who was made governor in Iraq and Khurasan, set out with thousands of soldiers from Syria, Iraq and Jibal for Jurjan and Tabaristan, east and south of the Caspian (modern northern Iran). He took loot and tribute payments in silver, slaves and silk, and began to secure the northern routes across the Iranian plateau to Khurasan.[4] Among the main governorships elsewhere, al-Walid's men were left in post only in Egypt, where Qurra b. Sharik's two local successors retained power, and on the Roman marches, where the caliph's half-brother Maslama b. 'Abd al-Malik remained the senior commander over the predominantly Qaysi border tribes.[5]

Continuity in Egypt and on the Roman frontier was politically judicious, as well as necessary to sustain momentum in the war with Constantinople, where disarray in the Roman army and imperial elite allowed the Muslims to build on the advances of the previous decade. In the last years of al-Walid's caliphate, as the centenary of the Prophet's migration to Medina approached (Rabi' al-Akhir AH 100/November 718), preparations were already being made to besiege and capture the Roman capital.[6] Echoes of the millenarian terms in which the coming climactic war were understood in Syria and further afield can be seen in later texts that preserve the court poetry and a large corpus of apocalyptic Arabic traditions about the capture of Constantinople and other prominent Christian holy cities, including Rome.[7] Much was made in court poetry of the new caliph sharing his name with Solomon, the Quranic prophet-king, and of the idea that the caliph himself was the *mahdī* – the Saviour who prefigured the Day of Judgement. In these lines from a longer poem by Jarir, the *mahdī* illuminates God's path or way – a term often associated in the Qur'an with divinely sanctioned warfare. Moreover, salvation via God's covenant is achieved through him, as God's representative on earth.

---

[2] Khalifa, 203; Tabari, II, 1306–14; Crone, 'Qays and Yemen', 18.
[3] Baladhuri, *Futuh*, 441; Tabari, II, 1282; Gabrieli, 'Muhammad ibn Qasim', 290–1.
[4] Khalifa, 200–1; Baladhuri, *Futuh*, 335–8; Tabari, II, 1317–35.
[5] Khalifa, 203–4; Crone, 'Qays and Yemen', 17–18.
[6] For escalating campaigns in the 710s, see Theophanes, 525–35; *WtaWC*, 509.
[7] Cook, *Muslim Apocalyptic*, 34–80.

> The blessed Sulayman, whom you already know
> is the Saviour (*mahdī*) who has illuminated the path (*sabīl*).
> You redeem every soul from evils
> and bring about the Messenger's Covenant ...⁸

Likewise, in these lines from a poem by al-Farazdaq, the caliph and his son Ayyub (Jacob), who led campaigns in Anatolia before his death in 716–17, are compared with the two prophets David and Solomon:

> You are the most righteous of men in justice and fear of God
> and you are the dew which brings the earth to life, and cleanses it
> To which I awake ruling over us, like David and his son (Solomon),
> according to a right custom (*sunna*), by which those who follow its way
> are guided to salvation (*yuhdā bihā*) ...⁹

A few months after Sulayman's accession, in the summer of 715, the Muslim fleet captured Phoinix (probably modern Fenaket, on the mainland near Rhodes), to secure wood for shipbuilding ahead of an assault on Constantinople. The Romans' deposition of their new emperor followed in November of the same year. Then, in 716, two Muslim land armies reached western Asia Minor, under the overall leadership of Maslama, while a naval expedition was led by the Qaysi commander 'Umar b. Hubayra al-Fazari. Sardis and Pergamom, on the fertile western coastal plains of Asia Minor, fell to the Muslims, and Maslama and his army overwintered on the Asian side of the Bosphorus. A fifth Roman coup in fifteen years followed, in March 717, installing Leo III (r. 717–41), a native of Germanikeia (Ar. Mar'ash) on the Anatolian front.¹⁰ By August, the new emperor faced a Muslim army camped on the European side of the Bosphorus, west of the long land walls of Constantinople, and a Muslim fleet moored nearby (see Figure 7.1).¹¹

However, this fourth attack on Constantinople within a century failed, like its Sasanian and Arabian precursors. Both the city's location and near-impregnable fortifications as well as the vagaries of dynastic and climatic fortune were against the Muslims. Dynastic misfortune came with the death of the caliph, Sulayman, in northern Syria, in late September 717.

---

⁸ Jarir b. 'Atiyya b. al-Khatafa, *Sharh Diwan Jarir*, ed. Muhammad I. 'A. al-Sawi (Beirut, n.d.), 432; Crone and Hinds, *God's Caliph*, 36 and n. 81.

⁹ Abu Firas Tammam b. Ghalib al-Farazdaq, *Diwan al-Farazdaq*, ed. and tr. R. Boucher (Paris, 1870), I, 215. Cf. *RoIM*, 123–4. On Ayyub, see Khalifa, 204; Tabari, II, 1317, 1335.

¹⁰ *PmBZ*, 'Leon III', no. 4242.

¹¹ Theophanes, 535–45; *WtaWC*, 509–10; Rodolphe Guilland, 'L'Expédition de Maslama contre Constantinople (717–718)', in Rodolphe Guilland, *Études Byzantines* (Paris, 1959), 109–33.

Figure 7.1 Aerial view of the Old City of Istanbul in the early twentieth century, looking north. Topkapı Palace and the Aya Sofya mosque stand on the sites of the Roman Acropolis and the church of Hagia Sophia, respectively, at the eastern end of the isthmus, near the middle of the image. The Hippodrome is just to the south-west (left) of them, and the column of Constantine stands on the far left, about halfway up the picture. Wikimedia Commons, public domain.

Maslama and 'Umar b. Hubayra nonetheless persisted with the siege through a harsh winter, which devastated their forces. Meanwhile, the new emperor, Leo III, had forged an alliance with the Bulgar Khanate, trapping the Muslims between the Bulgars in Thrace and the walls of Constantinople. Having suffered heavy losses, Maslama and 'Umar finally withdrew in August 718, only for the fleet to be harried by the Romans and then destroyed by a storm in the Aegean Sea.[12]

> They embarked on their ships and set sail on the sea and the Romans did battle with them there and burned many of their ships. The survivors were caught at sea by a storm and most of the ships went down. Some were wrecked and thrown up on the barbarian coast. Such was the terrible fate of the Arab expedition after two years in Roman territory.[13]

---

[12] Theophanes, 545–50; Guilland, 'L'Expédition'; *WtaWC*, 509–10.
[13] *Theophilus*, 214–15.

In retrospect, the 717–18 siege of Constantinople marks the high point of Umayyad efforts to replace the Roman Empire in the Eastern Mediterranean; the stability and effectiveness of Leo III's long reign would make the possibility of ending the Roman Empire increasingly remote. No serious attempt on the Roman capital was made by Muslim forces for the next twenty years.

'Umar (II) b. 'Abd al-'Aziz and Yazid (II) b. 'Abd al-Malik

Sulayman is said to have nominated his successors on his deathbed in September 717: a cousin and brother-in-law, 'Umar b. 'Abd al-'Aziz, was to be Sulayman's first heir; a paternal half-brother of Sulayman, Yazid b. 'Abd al-Malik, was in turn to be 'Umar's successor. Whether or not the dying caliph truly ratified the arrangements, they do appear to reflect a negotiated agreement among the Marwanids and their most powerful supporters.[14] 'Umar's accession was a focus for the hopes of the Syrian and Egyptian 'southern' tribes, who had been sidelined first by 'Abd al-Malik's accession and then by the succession of his sons by a 'northern', or 'Qaysi', mother. Like his father, 'Abd al-'Aziz, 'Umar had married a 'southern', Kalbi wife. Moreover, 'Umar stood out among the Marwanids as a grandson in the maternal line of his namesake, the Companion and second successor to Muhammad, 'Umar b. al-Khattab, and for his reputation as a religious scholar with close ties to Medina. Thus, 'Umar II was an asset for the Marwanids in securing support in the Hijaz. The guarantor of the claims of 'Abd al-Malik's sons and their allies was the second successor in the arrangement, Yazid b. 'Abd al-Malik. Yazid had strong dynastic credentials: besides his descent from 'Abd al-Malik, he was the grandson of the former Umayyad caliph Yazid b. Mu'awiya in the maternal line (whence his name) and the husband both of a niece of al-Hajjaj, 'Abd al-Malik's governor of Iraq, and of a great-granddaughter of the first Umayyad caliph, 'Uthman b. 'Affan. These connections tied together the interests of several influential elements in the imperial elite.[15]

However, dynastic misfortune afflicted the succession arrangements. Like their predecessor Sulayman, who had died aged about forty, after a caliphate of only two years and seven months, neither 'Umar II (r. 717–20) nor Yazid II (r. 720–24) were long-lived rulers. 'Umar II died less than two and a half years after his accession, in February 720, aged thirty-nine or forty; Yazid II then reigned for just under four years, dying in late January 724, aged between thirty-three and forty. These short caliphates of 'Umar II and Yazid II are difficult to interpret in part because of their brevity. Both monarchs also have

---

[14] Baladhuri, *Ansab*, VII, 66; Tabari, II, 1340–7; *RoIM*, 118 and n. 26.
[15] Marsham, 'Kinship'. For poetry praising 'Umar II as 'the son of Layla bt. al-Asbagh', of the Banu Kalb, see al-Farazdaq, *Diwan*, I, 98–9, II, 264–5.

strong images in the later sources: 'Umar II is remembered as pious and concerned with just governance, and with converting both the conquered population and external rivals to Islam, Yazid II as handsome but dissolute and distracted by his appetites. These no doubt stylised caricatures may echo some real differences. 'Umar II had studied in Medina and had close links with the town's religious scholars; consequently, he is a prominent religious authority in the later Sunni tradition. Yazid II is criticised for sinful sex and drinking, and an excessive fondness for his concubines, the death of one of whom was said to have led directly to his own demise.[16]

While the images of the personalities of the two rulers are hard to evaluate, there are three recurrent themes in the evidence that indicate the main challenges they both faced as leaders of the empire. The first was the recent failure at Constantinople. Warfare in Late Antiquity was a measure of divine favour and the Umayyads had directed their efforts at replacing Rome and Roman Christianity from their base in Syria, on the frontier with the Roman Empire. Reassessment of strategy after the catastrophic defeat is very likely at least in part what lies behind 'Umar II's reputation for withdrawing from expansionist warfare. Indeed, 'Umar II and Leo III may have agreed a mutually beneficial truce in *c.* 718. Versions of diplomatic exchanges about religion are also recorded in the later sources.[17]

Second, the challenge of ruling Iraq remained the leading internal matter for both caliphs. Many of the commanders who had been fighting on the Roman frontier were redeployed to Iraq in this period, which may also have contributed to the lull in frontier warfare. The enormous resources of Iraq and the tribute and booty from its eastern frontier provinces were a prize that provoked conflict. Both caliphs fought hard to prevent the Muhallabid dynasty

---

[16] On 'Umar's appointment, see above, p. 166. On Yazid II's beauty, levity, singing-boys and girls, and concubines, see Baladhuri, *Ansab*, VII, 186–7, 195–206. Cf. Crone and Hinds, *God's Caliph*, 131. For 'Umar II and conversion, see, for example, Baladhuri, *Futuh*, 441; Mike Humphreys, 'First Iconoclasm, ca. 700–780', in Mike Humphreys (ed.), *A Companion to Byzantine Iconoclasm* (Leiden, 2021), 327–8 and below, pp. 168 and 174. For the images of these caliphs in the tradition, see further Borrut, *Mémoire et pouvoir*, 283–320; Luke Yarbrough, 'Did 'Umar b. 'Abd al-'Aziz Issue an Edict Concerning Non-Muslim Officials?', in Antoine Borrut and Fred M. Donner (eds), *Christians and Others in the Umayyad State* (Chicago, 2016), 173–206; I-Wen Su, 'Writing History under the Patronage: the Representation of Sulayman b. 'Abd al-Malik in the *Ansab al-ashraf* and Its Relation to the 'Abbasid Court Culture', *Foreign Language Studies* 24 (2016), 19–20; Antoine Borrut, 'The Future of the Past: Historical Writing in Early Islamic Syria', in Alain George and Andrew Marsham (eds), *Power, Patronage, and Memory in Early Islam: Perspectives on Umayyad Elites* (Oxford, 2018), 287–8.

[17] On the possible truce, see below pp. 172–3 and nn. 31 and 32. On the diplomatic exchanges, see *SIAOSI*, 490–501.

retaining control of the province after Sulayman's death; and both eschewed a return to appointing any of al-Hajjaj's relatives there. Indeed, concerns with securing tax revenues and with the social tensions driven by ethnic and religious differences in the provinces were pressing concerns for both caliphs; this was the third challenge, in Iraq and across the empire.

In the first decades after the conquests, being an Arabian member of the Faithful, or one of their descendants, had meant being both a tax-recipient and part of a military elite. Now there were many descendants of Arabian migrants who identified as members of the Faithful but who did not fight in the army, and there were many among the conquered non-Arabian populations who had joined the army or the administration or migrated into the garrisons for economic reasons, or who had arrived there as enslaved captives (or whose ancestors had done so). Moreover, on the new frontiers in Africa and Asia, non-Arabians had joined the armies in numbers and had begun to participate in the politics of the ruling military elite. As noted above, these changes in the demography of the empire may have contributed to the emergence of 'Muslims' (*muslimūn*) as a widely used label for the followers of the new Arabian faith. They may also have led to the beginning of a sense of 'the Arabs' as a collective category, also rooted in membership of the new military elite. The same changes generated new conflicts over taxation, social status and rights to the resources of the tax system; echoes of all these, however distorted by polemic, are prevalent in the sources for this period.[18] 'Umar II is often linked with taxation reform in the later tradition and both rulers are associated with legislating to restrict public expressions of status and identity on the part of Christians.[19]

---

[18] For resentments of unfair pay and tax, respectively, among non-Arabian Muslim soldiers and civilians in Khurasan in the late 710s, and 'Umar II's attempts to resolve them, see Tabari, II, 1353–4. For some comments on non-Arabians in the western and eastern frontier armies in the 710s, see Eduardo Manzano-Moreno, 'Conquest and Settlement: What al-Andalus Can Tell Us about the Arab Expansion at the Time of the Umayyad Caliphate', in Andrew Marsham (ed.), *The Umayyad World* (London and New York, 2021), 317–20.

[19] For two contrasting perspectives on the prospects for recovering 'Umar II's policies, see Milka Levy-Rubin, "Umar II's *Ghiyar* Edict: Between Ideology and Practice', in Antoine Borrut and Fred M. Donner (eds), *Christians and Others in the Umayyad State* (Chicago, 2016), 157–72, and Yarbrough, "Umar b. 'Abd al-'Aziz'. For the case that Yazid II issued an edict against images, see Christian Sahner, 'The First Iconoclasm in Islam: A New History of the Edict of Yazid II (AH 104/AD 723)', *Der Islam* 94 (2017), 5–56. On taxation, see below, Ch. 12, pp. 326–7.

Joining the Conquerors: *walā'* and *mawālī*

The conquering armies were formed from Arabian tribespeople and so where new political formations developed, they were most easily expressed using terms and practices deriving from the tribes' political practices. The later Arabic tradition describes outsiders being incorporated into tribal structures through *walā'* ('clientage', or, more broadly, 'loyalty'). Strangers to the group (either Arabians or non-Arabians), could join as a *mawlā* ('client', 'friend' or 'ally', pl. *mawālī*). In the seventh century, freed captives (that is, manumitted slaves) and those who had freely joined the conquering armies but were not members of the tribes that constituted them, were said to have been the main groups that became *mawālī*. Many of the Umayyads' courtiers are also said to have been *mawālī*, presumably often in something like this latter sense of 'client' – a person tied to a specific elite patron. The term *mawālī* is also sometimes used in the sources more loosely, of non-Arabians aspiring to join the Muslims, such as fugitive Iraqi peasants or rebellious Khurasanian landowners.[20] *Shākiriyya*, which is an Arabic term deriving from Sasanian usage (*chakir*, 'servant'), is sometimes used to describe the personal military following of a patron.[21]

The later tradition distinguishes between 'the clientage of manumission' (*walā' al-'itq*) and 'clientage of friendship' or 'clientage of assistance' (*walā' al-muwālāh*). A third category – or perhaps better a sub-category of the latter – is associated with conversion: 'clientage of Islam' or 'clientage of conversion' (*walā' al-islām*). It seems plausible that the first two categories have roots in the practice of the very earliest period of the West Arabian monotheist community and in the wider practices of clientage in the late antique Middle East. *Walā' al-'itq* created ties between a freedman and his former master, as client and patron respectively, where the patron stood to inherit from his client as a blood relative, although the precise nature of this relationship was debated. *Walā' al-muwālāh* allowed for clientage without conversion to Islam, which is congruent with the evidence for Christians and others in numbers among the conquering armies and their scribes and

---

[20] On this and what follows, see Ulrike Mitter, 'Origin and Development of the Islamic Patronate', in Monique Bernards and John Nawas, *Patronate and Patronage in Early and Classical Islam* (Leiden, 2005), 70–133. For the prominence of *mawālī* among the courtiers of the Umayyads, see the lists in Khalifa and Ibn 'Asakir. For some appointments of *mawālī* to commands and other prominent posts, and as soldiers, see Crone, 'Qays and Yemen', 12–14, 15–16. For the looser usage of *mawālī* for non-Arabians, see Crone, 'Qays and Yemen', 14–15; *EI²*, 'Mawla' (P. Crone).

[21] *EI²*, 'al-Shakiriyya' (K. Athamina); Khalil Athamina, 'Non-Arab Regiments and Private Militias during the Umayyad Period', *Arabica* 45 (1998), 347–78.

officials and with the absence of a strong sense of 'Islam' as a distinct religious category in the seventh century.[22]

Walā' al-islām may be a slightly later development, or perhaps a later rationalisation of outmoded earlier practices. It expresses the idea that a convert to Islam might choose – or, according to some, was required – to become a client of the man 'at whose hands' (*'alā yadayhi*) he had converted. *Walā' al-islām* appears to have slowly replaced *walā' al-muwālāh* as it gradually became expected that most members of the ruling elite would be Muslim. Tensions around the status of convert non-Arabians and of non-Muslims are evident in the edicts attributed to Marwanid caliphs regulating relations between Muslims and non-Muslims, in traditions against non-Muslims participating in caliphal government and in the provincial insurrections in the name of Islam in the 740s in which large numbers of converts of non-Arabian heritage participated.

In the institutions of clientage in the Umayyad period, therefore, we see another aspect of the transformation of the structures of power in the new empire. The conquests had brought together socially stratified armies, comprising various groups from the Arabian Peninsula, with diverse ethnic and cultural identities. One outcome of this was that the word 'Arab' began to acquire associations with personal status and ethnic and linguistic identity, as in the saying 'a person made tributary (*mufā'*) shall not rule over the one making him so (*mufiy*)' – idiomatically, 'a freed slave shall not rule over an Arab'.[23] However, at the same time, the associations between elite status, Islamic beliefs and practices, and Arab-ness were contested as groups of non-Arabian heritage sought to join the ruling classes. Resentment of Arab rule eventually became one of the main drivers of rebellion and unrest on the eastern and western frontiers.

Conflict in Iraq: The Revolt of Yazid b. al-Muhallab

On his accession in the autumn of 717, 'Umar II replaced most of Sulayman's appointees, retaining existing governors in only Mecca, Medina and Yemen, among the major posts in North Africa, Egypt, the Peninsula, Iraq and Iran. The Muhallabids' nascent patrimony in Iraq and the eastern provinces was broken up in favour of Qurashi and Syrian Qaysi governors of a partitioned

---

[22] For Christians in the conquering armies, see Wadad al-Qadi, 'Non-Muslims in the Muslim Conquest Army in Early Islam', in Antoine Borrut and Fred M. Donner (eds), *Christians and Others in the Umayyad State* (Chicago, 2016), 83–128. On seventh-century 'Islam', see above, Ch. 2, pp. 61–3.

[23] *EI3*, 'Fay'' (A. Marsham). See also *SoH*, 56.

East; 'Umar II may have balked at the risks inherent in leaving most of the revenues of the former Sasanian Empire in the hands of a family lacking specific ties of loyalty to him and with close ties within the East, preferring instead to channel the funds to relatives and Syrian allies.[24] However, the sudden illness and death of 'Umar II in February 720 gave the Muhallabids the opportunity to retake Iraq, no doubt in the hope of having their de facto authority recognised by the new caliph. Some Iraqi tribespeople had already revolted near Basra in 718–19, during 'Umar II's caliphate, but a much more widespread insurrection was triggered by the return to Iraq of Sulayman's former governor in the East, Yazid b. al-Muhallab (hereafter, Ibn al-Muhallab), early in 720. Having captured Basra, Ibn al-Muhallab sent envoys to his fellow Azdi tribesmen in the southern and eastern provinces of Iran, while heading north himself, taking control of Wasit and then advancing on Kufa, which was still held by 'Umar II's appointee.[25]

The Muhallabids feared the accession of the 'northern' al-Hajjaj's nephew-in-law, Yazid II. This rivalry with the Thaqafis was rooted in al-Hajjaj's brutal dismissal of his former associate from power in 704 and the revenge exacted by Ibn al-Muhallab against al-Hajjaj's family in 715.[26] As with the revolt of Ibn al-Ash'ath against al-Hajjaj twenty years earlier, there were also wider tensions in the empire behind the rebellion. Once again, many of the tribespeople of Iraq and its eastern frontier garrisons were willing to back a leader who could lead resistance to the Marwanids and their Syrian allies, whom they saw as having wrongfully appropriated the revenues of their home province. Indeed, many of Ibn al-Ash'ath's relatives were among the supporters of the Muhallabids.[27]

Unwilling to concede control of Iraq and the East to the Muhallabids, but unable to command the loyalty of the eastern armies, Yazid II despatched troops from the Syrian army to Iraq, led by two senior Marwanid frontier commanders – his own half-brother, Maslama b. 'Abd al-Malik, and his and Maslama's nephew, al-'Abbas b. al-Walid. Maslama and al-'Abbas had cooperated on several campaigns in Anatolia in the past fifteen years and now

---

[24] The dismissal of the Muhallabids is said to have been motivated by 'Umar II's dislike of tyranny (Tabari, II, 1350). However, his choice of a relative and a 'northern' ally as their replacements suggests more practical motivations. See further Khalifa, 198, 206; Baladhuri, *Futuh*, 426–7; Tabari, II, 1120, 1138–44, 1282, 1352–7, 1359–62; Ibn 'Asakir, XXXIV, 68, §3705; *EI²*, 'al-Djarrah b. 'Abd Allah' (D. M. Dunlop); Bosworth, *Sistan*, 67; Haug, *Eastern Frontier*, 125.

[25] Tabari, II, 1347–9, 1379–95.

[26] Tabari, II, 1359–62. See also above, Ch. 6, pp. 158–61 and Ch. 7, p. 163.

[27] Tabari, II, 1397, 1398, 1411; Crone, 'Qays and Yemen', 27–8.

brought their battle-hardened soldiers against the Muhallabids.[28] Al-ʿAbbas led a smaller force against one of Ibn al-Muhallab's brothers in Basra, where the Syrians put the Iraqis to flight. Shortly afterwards, Maslama and his larger army met Ibn al-Muhallab himself at al-ʿAqr, near Karbala, outside Kufa. The Iraqis were again defeated, Ibn al-Muhallab was killed and his head despatched to Yazid II in Syria. Those of the Muhallabid clan who had not been killed or captured fled to Basra, and from there by boat to southern Iran, where Ibn al-Muhallab's brother al-Mufaddal was able to secure a following among various Iranian and Arabian groups hostile to Marwanid rule, before being chased down by Maslama's commanders in Sind.[29] Initially, Yazid II recognised Maslama as the governor of a reunited Iraq and Iran. However, the caliph quickly thought better of leaving his half-brother with such plenipotentiary power over Iraq's resources and despatched instead ʿUmar b. Hubayra al-Fazari (g. 721–4), a Qaysi commander who had fought on the Roman frontier and against Iraqi rebels under al-Hajjaj. Hence, after a short interlude under Sulayman and ʿUmar II, Iraq and Iran had once more become a single entity, ruled by an occupying Syrian army from Wasit, in Iraq, and governed by an ally who owed his position there to the caliph.[30]

Rome, North Africa and Central Asia

ʿUmar II's decision to remove the Muhallabids from Iraq and the East in 717–18 and then the struggle against them at the beginning of Yazid II's caliphate in 720–1 tied up many of the commanders and soldiers who had formerly carried out the raids on Rome and raids in Anatolia ceased after 718. They resumed in the 720s under Yazid II, but it seems on a much less ambitious scale that has left little trace in the Arabic sources and even less in the Greek ones.[31] Indeed, it is possible that a formal truce may have been agreed

---

[28] Maslama and al-ʿAbbas in Anatolia and the Caucasus: Khalifa, 185, 191, 192, 193, 194, 195, 196, 199, 200, 201–2, 204; Tabari, II, 1181, 1185, 1191–2, 1194, 1197, 1200, 1217, 1235–6, 1255, 1266–8, 1305–6, 1314–17, 1346.

[29] Baladhuri, *Futuh*, 442; al-Tabari, II, 1394–1414.

[30] Khalifa, 208, 210; Baladhuri, *Ansab*, VII, 209, 283–4; Tabari, II, 1416–17, 1432–4, 1436–7; *EI²*, 'Wasit' (M. Sakly). For ʿUmar b. Hubayra on the Roman frontier and in Iran and Iraq, see Baladhuri, *Ansab*, VII, 206–7. On ʿUmar II's entirely Qaysi sub-governors in the East, many from the Syrian frontier, see *SoH*, 47 and n. 337, 143–6; see also Baladhuri, *Ansab*, VII, 210–13.

[31] A raid on Thebasa (Ar. Dabasa) in Cappadocia is recorded for 720–1, and raids are also recorded for 721–2 and 723–4: Khalifa, 210, 211, 212. For fighting in Armenia and Azerbaijan, see Khalifa, 210–12. Theophanes is silent about conflict with the caliphate for the years 718–19 until 723–4, as are the closely related Arabic and Syriac sources: Theophanes, 549–56, s.a. 717–23; *Theophilus*, 215–22.

in c. 718.³² Fighting in the Caucasus seems to match that in Anatolia, with a major Khazar raid in the year of the siege of Constantinople and then a lull until 721–2.³³ However, despite the Muslims' diminished presence on their land borders, the Romans were unable to make gains. Leo III had just taken power in conditions of recurrent civil war and during the crisis of the Muslim and Bulgar attack on Constantinople. The new emperor immediately had to fight a rival who was proclaimed in Sicily in 717–18 and a former emperor who marched on Constantinople with Bulgar support in 718–19. With his rule more secure from 720, Leo III made his son, Constantine, co-emperor and initiated a series of legal, religious, administrative and military reforms, aimed at reinforcing the capacity of the empire to withstand the Muslims' attacks; although the Muslims' siege had failed, it had prompted existential fear of the caliphal forces in the Roman Empire.³⁴

While the Roman frontier was comparatively quiescent after 718, the short caliphates of 715–24 and the unrest in Iraq after 717 contributed to conflict in North Africa and Central Asia. The conquests of the 710s, which had reached beyond the territories formerly directly controlled by the Roman and Sasanian empires, had brought 'Berber', Visigothic and Sogdian groups under Umayyad rule, presenting the novel problem of how to integrate these peoples into the caliphate.³⁵ Somewhat like the Arabic-speaking pastoralist groups of Syria and Iraq, who had transformed the new politics of the 'conquest society' after the 640s, the populations of North Africa, al-Andalus, Khurasan, Sistan and Transoxiana were often militarily capable and organised under local leadership. Also like the tribes of the Syrian steppe, these new frontier groups of the eighth century empire were capable of mounting sustained challenges to existing power structures. However, unlike the Syrian tribes, they were culturally and linguistically quite distinct from the conquerors and they seem sometimes to have been given a less privileged status than the Arabian elements in the armies. Moreover, they were in contact with groups beyond the direct reach of Umayyad military power – other 'Berber' groups in the Sahara, Visigothic

---

[32] A seven-year truce is mentioned in the Greek text about the 'Sixty Martyrs of Jerusalem'; see Christian Sahner, 'Martyrdom and Conversion', in Douglas Pratt and Charles L. Tieszen, *Christian–Muslim Relations: A Bibliographical History. Volume 15, A Thematic History (600–1600)* (Leiden, 2020), 401.

[33] Khalifa, 202, 204, 210, and 211–12. See also Mark Whittow, *The Making of Orthodox Byzantium, 600–1025* (London, 1996), 226. At least one Arabic report counts the six years between the disastrous retreat from Constantinople in 718 and the accession of Hisham in 724 as a pause in the annual campaigns against Rome: Khalifa, 208.

[34] Theophanes, 549–53, s.a. 717–19; *PmBZ*, 'Leon III', no. 4242; Humphreys, 'First Iconoclasm', 328–9, 349–50.

[35] Haug, *Eastern Frontier*, 135.

and Frankish polities in northern Spain and southern France, Turkic groups in Central Asia, and the Tang emperors in China. These connections created a stronger potential for alliances with external powers that rivalled the caliph and his governors. Not only were non-Arabians within the caliphal armies now drawn into local and caliphal politics, bringing with them their distinctive political cultures, but they were also well placed to change allegiance and work with other powers in the region if loyalty to the caliphs' representatives became unattractive.

The governance of Khurasan and Sistan was directly impacted by the short caliphates and the unrest in Iraq, changing hands six times between 717 and 724. This administrative turbulence coincided with the formation, with the support of the Tang Chinese, of the Türgesh federation, to the east of Sogdia and Farghana. The Türgesh had formerly been subordinate to the Western Turks. They occupied territory south and east of Lake Balqash – approximately modern south-east Kazakhstan, east Kyrgyzstan and north-west Xinjiang, in China. This new Turkic power could be brought into alliance by local potentates in Transoxiana against the Arabians, and so much of the ground gained by Qutayba in the 700s and 710s was lost after 715. There was a brief reassertion of Arabian power in 721–2, under Sa'id al-Harashi, who is remembered for the violence of his suppression of resistance. Al-Harashi's governorate was cut short, it seems because his patron in Iraq did not trust him; his replacement faced the ongoing challenge of securing a region against the Türgesh and maintaining the loyalty of the diverse populations of the frontier.[36]

In North Africa, the governorship changed hands four times during the caliphates of Sulayman, 'Umar II and Yazid II: after Sulayman's deposition of North Africa's conqueror, Musa b. Nusayr, in 715, both 'Umar II and Yazid II had also appointed their own men, in 717 and 720, respectively.[37] 'Umar II's appointee is associated with an era of Islamisation among the 'Berbers', which may also reflect processes of social change within the armies in Ifriqiya that were already in train before 'Umar II came to power.[38] The former Roman province had only been brought under stable Arabian rule about twenty years earlier, after 695, and al-Andalus even more recently, after 711. Unusually, the coins to pay the North African and Andalusian armies were struck with Latin slogans until 716–17, when Arabic silver coins in the reformed, 'epigraphic'

---

[36] H. A. R. Gibb, *The Arab Conquests in Central Asia* (London, 1923), 54–64; Bosworth, *Sistan*, 69–70; Haug, *Eastern Frontier*, 122–9, 131–2.

[37] Ibn 'Abd al-Hakam, *Futuh*, 213; Ya'qubi, II, 353, 376; Ibn 'Idhari, *al-Bayan*, I, 47–9.

[38] 'Islamisation': Ibn 'Abd al-Hakam, *Futuh*, 213; Baladhuri, *Futuh*, 231; Ibn 'Idhari, *al-Bayan*, I, 48; Manzano Moreno, 'Conquest and Settlement', 318–19; al-Qadi, 'Non-Muslims', 98.

style began to be issued; Arabic gold issues followed in 720–1.[39] This change may reflect efforts to 'Arabise' and 'Islamise' the payment of the armies of these regions by Muhammad b. Yazid (g. c. 716–17 and c. 721). This latter governor was briefly reappointed in c. 721 after Yazid II's first appointee – a former chief of the *shurṭa* for al-Hajjaj – was rejected by the Berbers in alliance with a former governor of the region. The motives for the North African revolt in c. 721 are variously reported as resentment of the rejected governor's branding the skin of his North African bodyguards or of his imposing taxes associated with the conquered population on Muslim converts. The recent deposition of Musa b. Nusayr, who had close connections with his Berber soldiers, also suggests a local reaction against the impositions and appropriations of outsiders.[40]

---

[39] Walker, *Arab-Byzantine Coins*, 298–305; Marie Legendre, 'Aspects of Umayyad Administration', in Andrew Marsham (ed.), *The Umayyad World* (London and New York, 2021), 136.

[40] Khalifa, 209; Ibn 'Abd al-Hakam, *Futuh*, 213–15; Baladhuri, *Futuh*, 231; Ya'qubi, II, 376; Tabari, II, 1435–6; Ibn 'Idhari, *al-Bayan*, I, 48–9; *EI²*, 'Yazid b. Abi Muslim' (P. Crone); Crone, 'Qays and Yemen', 18, 29. On the *shurṭa*, see below, Ch. 12 pp. 312–16.

8

Hisham b. ʿAbd al-Malik: Renewal and Defeat

When Yazid II died in January 724, after less than four years as caliph, he was succeeded by his half-brother, Hisham b. ʿAbd al-Malik (r. 724–43; see Figure 8.1). Yazid II had nominated Hisham to succeed him before his own son al-Walid b. Yazid (r. 743–4). Hisham's claims on the caliphate had been too strong for Yazid II to ignore: Hisham was a senior son of ʿAbd al-Malik, with powerful allies among his maternal relatives in the Banu Makhzum branch of Quraysh, as well as support from his half-brothers and their sons, all of whom were well connected with the tribes of the Roman–Arabian frontier in northern Syria, eastern Anatolia and the Jazira. As one of the younger sons of ʿAbd al-Malik, born in the 690s, Hisham was in his early thirties when he became caliph. However, unlike his immediate predecessors, who had all died aged about forty, Hisham would live into his mid-fifties and so rule for nineteen years.[1]

The challenges that had confronted ʿUmar II and Yazid II persisted: Rome, Iraq, and economic, religious and social change. Hisham had time to consolidate his grip on the revenues of Egypt and Iraq and to recommit to an existential struggle against the Roman Empire. In so doing, he consciously imitated aspects of the reigns of his father, ʿAbd al-Malik, and his older brothers al-Walid I and Sulayman. Like them, Hisham prioritised military success against Rome, using loyal governors and tax reform to seek more revenue from Egypt and Iraq, and publicly promoting the religious legitimacy of his rule. Hisham's focus on both tax revenues and his own investments in land and commercial infrastructure in the Syrian towns and countryside perhaps led to his image as a 'miser' (*bakhīl*) in more hostile strands of the later tradition.[2] These policies were probably a response to the declining opportunities for

---

[1] Baladhuri, *Ansab*, VII, 310–11; *RoIM*, 120–1; Marsham, 'Kinship', 20, 35–7, 40.
[2] Al-Zubayri, *Nasab*, 164; Baladhuri, *Ansab*, VII, 302, 312–15; Tabari, II, 1730–9; A. Asa Eger, *The Islamic-Byzantine Frontier: Interaction and Exchange among Muslim and Christian Communities* (London, 2015), 212–14. For a particularly negative presentation of these attributes, see Baladhuri, *Ansab*, VII, 627–8; Crone and Hinds, *God's Caliph*, 131–2.

Figure 8.1 Near life-size stucco figure from the palace of Qasr al-Hayr al-Gharbi, between Damascus and al-Rusafa, probably depicting Caliph Hisham, c. 727 CE. Damascus National Museum. Marilyn Jenkins-Madina, courtesy of Aga Khan Documentation Center, MIT Libraries (AKDC@MIT).

tribute and loot to be taken on the frontiers and a recognition that the institutional and economic strength of Umayyad rule needed reinforcement.

For about fifteen years Hisham ruled over a relatively stable and quiescent Iraq and was able to build some pressure against the Roman emperor on the battlefields of Anatolia. However, a push to overcome the Romans in 740 ended in failure. This defeat coincided with a sudden escalation in internal unrest, including the first revolts in Iraq in the name of the family of 'Ali for two generations and a huge revolt in North Africa that permanently ended Umayyad control in the western Maghrib. In both North Africa and western Central Asia, alliances against Umayyad rule were forged between soldiers, or former soldiers, of Arabian heritage and local military actors. In western Central Asia, these challenges were exacerbated by the presence of powerful neighbouring powers – locally, the Türgesh federation and, beyond them, the Tang Empire in East Asia. Connections had also been made between rebel Islamic movements in Iraq and groups on the frontiers. Hisham was alert to the threats posed by forms of Islam that articulated opposition to Umayyad rule and his caliphate witnessed the execution of heretics and efforts to disrupt sedition in the eastern provinces. However, the structural tensions within the empire and the diversity and scale of opposition proved beyond the remedies available to him, leaving the power of the Syrians and the Marwanids more brittle than at any time since the 680s by the time of Hisham's death in February 743.

Hisham's Accession and Appointments

Hisham and his most powerful Marwanid allies, Maslama b. 'Abd al-Malik and the sons of Muhammad b. Marwan, held land in the north and on its frontier marches, where the 'northern' or 'Qaysi' tribes were dominant.[3] These alliances, his own landholdings, the revival of the war with Rome, and the strategic importance of the Caucasus and the Jazira for both the war with Rome and control of Iraq, all probably contributed to Hisham's decision to reside in the northern part of Syria, near the Roman frontier. This was in contrast to earlier caliphs whose itinerary had been further to the south. Hisham created what amounted to a second capital at his estates at al-Rusafa, just south of al-Raqqa (Lat. Callinicum) on the Euphrates, in the Qaysi-dominated *jund* of Qinnasrin. He moved between al-Rusafa and Damascus, stopping at large residential complexes en route between the two.[4] Hisham and his allies are also associated with the consolidation of a fortified forward zone (*thughūr*) in northern Syria and eastern Anatolia.[5] This move north also coincided with closer control of the frontier in Armenia and Azerbaijan, where Hisham is remembered by one Armenian source as levying heavier taxes and by another for his execution of a Muslim Armenian who had apostatised by converting to Christianity.[6]

Hisham's alliances are reflected in his gubernatorial appointments on the frontiers and in the Hijaz. He installed his maternal uncle, Ibrahim b. Hisham al-Makhzumi (g. 724–32), as governor of all the Hijaz, combining the three main governorships of Medina, Mecca and al-Ta'if under his jurisdiction.[7]

---

[3] Baladhuri, *Ansab*, VII, 172; Ya'qubi II, 405; Tabari, II, 1467; *EI*², 'Marwan II' (G. R. Hawting); Denis Genequand, *Les établissements des élites omeyyades en Palmyrène et au Proche-Orient* (Beirut, 2012), 365, 367; Eger, *Islamic–Byzantine Frontier*, 82 n. 27, 89, 99, 141–3, 152, 211–15, 217–18.

[4] Elizabeth Key Fowden, *The Barbarian Plain: Saint Sergius between Rome and Iran* (Berkeley, 1999), 174–82; Genequand, *Établissements*, 95–180, 365.

[5] Baladhuri, *Futuh*, 163–71; Eger, *Islamic–Byzantine Frontier*, 61, 63, 169–70, 176, 180.

[6] Vacca, *Non-Muslim Provinces*, 200. For the *Life* of Vahan of Goghtn, see Christian Sahner, *Christian Martyrs under Islam: Religious Violence and the Making of the Muslim World* (Princeton, 2018), 41–4. See also below, Ch. 11, pp. 274–5.

[7] Tabari, II, 1466, 1471.

Maslama b. ʿAbd al-Malik, after whom Hisham named his son and preferred heir, was reappointed to the governorship of the Caucasian frontier (g. c. 710–15 and c. 725–32, d. 738), while two more of Hisham's half-brothers led campaigns in Asia Minor and the Caucasus; Hisham's sons, who, like their uncles, were also sons by slave women, joined them.[8]

Hisham used the first years after his accession to make statements of intent, promoting his claims to legitimate leadership through the *hajj* and the campaigns against the Romans. In May 725, he led the pilgrimage to Mecca in person – the first caliph to do so since Sulayman b. ʿAbd al-Malik, nine years earlier, and a return to the pattern established by ʿAbd al-Malik and al-Walid. There, he made much of his correct performance of the pilgrimage rites, consulting with a prominent religious scholar beforehand and promulgating the occasion in a letter to be read out in the congregational mosques of all the provinces of the caliphate. He also levied tribesmen from the Hijaz, who were deployed in combination with Syrian troops in a naval raid on Cyprus. Meanwhile, Hisham's son Muʿawiya, his half-brother Maslama b. ʿAbd al-Malik and his maternal uncle Ibrahim b. Hisham led campaigns in Anatolia; Caesarea, the capital of Roman Cappadocia, fell to Maslama in 725 or 726.[9] At about the same time, a large group of Roman envoys were executed.[10] In the later 720s, Hisham sustained this emphasis on the *hajj* and the war with Rome. He invested in the *hajj* route, building aqueducts and cisterns on the route from Syria to the Hijaz, and sought to revive the practice of annual campaigns against the Romans.[11]

Hisham pursued a different appointment policy in Egypt, where he replaced his Egyptian governor nine times during his nineteen years as caliph. Initially, he appointed Umayyad relatives, but then he split the governorship from management of the tax system. Most of his appointees to the former were men of Arabian heritage, often from Egyptian families who had held the governorship under his predecessors. Such men were well placed to manage the Egyptian population and the predominantly 'southern' or 'Yemeni' Egyptian

---

[8] Khalifa, 216, 217; Tabari, II, 1472. For Maslama's dates as commander in the Caucasus, see Khalifa, 217 and 220, and EI², 'Maslama b. ʿAbd al-Malik' (G. Rotter). For Hisham's sons, see al-Zubayri, *Nasab*, 168; Marsham, 'Kinship', 40.

[9] *Theophilus*, 225; Theophanes, 559–62; Khalifa, 217; Tabari, II, 1487–8, 1491–2; Harry Munt, 'The Official Announcement of an Umayyad Caliph's Successful Pilgrimage to Mecca', in Venetia Porter and Liana Saif (eds), *The Hajj: Collected Essays* (London, 2013), 15–20.

[10] Sahner, 'Martyrdom and Conversion', 401; Sahner, *Christian Martyrs*, 18, 231–2, 242–3.

[11] For the *hajj*, see McMillan, *Meaning*, 131. For campaigns in the later 720s, see Theophanes, 562–3, s.a. 726–7; Khalifa, 219, 220; Tabari, II, 1495, 1506–7, 1526–7.

migrant population and army.¹² Meanwhile, Hisham made his former chief scribe, 'Ubayd Allah b. al-Habhab al-Saluli, head of Egyptian taxes, keeping him in post for ten years, during five successive governorships, between *c.* 725 and 734. Ibn al-Habhab is said to have reported directly to Hisham in Syria and to have personally prompted the removal of some of the Egyptian governors. These policies were intended to secure more revenue. Indeed, taxation contributed to a widespread revolt among the tax-paying populations of the Nile Delta in 725–6. In the following year, Ibn al-Habhab requested that 3,000 'northern' Syrian tribespeople be sent to Egypt, to be settled in the Delta to farm uncultivated land and manage the transport of grain to Qulzum on the Red Sea coast. The relocation of these Syrians would have had the triple benefit of providing Ibn al-Habhab and Hisham with loyal forces in Egypt who could balance the power of the local 'Yemeni' forces, deter tax revolts (none are recorded until 739) and control the export of Egyptian grain to the Hijaz.¹³

In Iraq and the East, Hisham appointed another non-Qurashi, Khalid b. 'Abd Allah al-Qasri (g. 724–38). Khalid had long experience in the service of the sons of 'Abd al-Malik, having been governor of Mecca for al-Walid and Sulayman and envoy to Ibn al-Muhallab for Yazid II. He was from the tribe of Bajila, many of whom resided in Kufa, where Khalid was commander of the city's security forces (*shurṭa*) prior to becoming governor, although he also owned property in Damascus.¹⁴ Much like Ibn al-Habhab in Egypt, Khalid is remembered for his concern with the revenues of Iraq and, as with his patron Hisham, for his immense personal wealth. At his accessional speech in Kufa, he is said to have spoken about levying taxes fairly, and during his governorship he is said to have successfully maintained strict control over the quality of the coinage of Iraq, invested in the irrigation system of the Sawad, developed Kufa's mosque, and constructed shops, a palace and a church there, while Khalid's brother Asad built a Kufan market known as Suq Asad.¹⁵

In North Africa, Hisham decided to recognise the man Yazid II had sent there after the rebellion of *c.* 721, replacing him only when he died, in 727.

---

¹² His longest-serving leaders of the prayer were al-Walid b. Rifa'a b. Khalid al-Fahmi (g. 727–35) and Hanzala b. Safwan al-Kalbi (g. 737–42), who had also governed Egypt for Yazid II: Kindi, 71–82.

¹³ Kindi, 72–83; Ibn 'Asakir, XXXVII, 415, §4432. See also Yaacov Lev, 'Coptic Rebellions and the Islamization of Medieval Egypt (8th–10th Century): Medieval and Modern Perceptions', *JSAI* 39 (2012), 309–11. For the Banu Salul and 'Ubayd Allah, see *EI²*, 'Salul' (M. Lecker). For the increase in taxes under Hisham, see Baladhuri, *Futuh*, 223.

¹⁴ Ibn 'Asakir, XVI, 135, 138–9, 140, §1896; For Bajila at Kufa, see *IatMC*, 242. For his role as an envoy, see *EI²*, 'Khalid b. 'Abd Allah al-Kasri' (G. R. Hawting).

¹⁵ Baladhuri, *Futuh*, 277, 286, 290–1, 469; Ibn 'Asakir, XVI, 141, §1896.

Both this new governor and his successor, Ibn al-Habhab (g. 734–40), who was moved to North Africa from Egypt, carried out lucrative slaving raids and launched naval expeditions against Roman Sicily.[16] The mosque, markets and water supply at Qayrawan were also developed.[17] In al-Andalus, the governor appointed by ʿUmar II had already carried out a tax census and launched campaigns north of the Pyrenees in Visigothic Gallia Narbonensis (Septimania, in south-east France). Hisham's governors in al-Andalus continued expansionist warfare against the northern kingdoms and southern Francia and carried out a second tax survey. Defeats in 732 at Poitiers (central France) and at around the same time in Covadonga in Asturias (northern Spain) seem to have shocked the Andalusis, but they were quickly overshadowed by more dramatic events in North Africa at the end of the decade.[18]

Religion and Caliphal Authority

Lengthier and more elaborate public documents about caliphal authority associated, in the later literary sources, with Hisham's caliphate reflect a growth in more formal and public uses of writing.[19] In these publicly promulgated caliphal texts, the ruler asserts his claim to God's favour and the obligation on all the Faithful of obedience to God and the caliph.[20] As with Hisham's predecessors, the claim to be God's representative on earth meant that rival religious ideas proclaimed by others in public could be represented as a treasonous and heretical threat to caliphal authority. However, Hisham and his associates seem to have asserted the claim of the caliph as the defender of right belief and practice more widely and forcefully than many of those who came before them, in part because oppositional movements were increasingly articulated as alternative visions of Islamic belief and practice.[21] At the same time, again like

---

[16] Khalifa, 218, 219, 221, 223, 224–5, 226. For gifts from the first governor in return for keeping his post, see Yaʿqubi, II, 382.

[17] Corisande Fenwick, 'The Umayyads and North Africa: Imperial Rule and Frontier Society', in Andrew Marsham (ed.), *The Umayyad World* (London and New York, 2021), 304–5.

[18] *EI3*, 'Al-Andalus, Political History' (A. García Sanjuán); Eduardo Manzano Moreno, 'The Iberian Peninsula and North Africa', *NCHI*, I, 589.

[19] On writing in caliphal ceremonial, see *RoIM*, 145–67. On writing in general, see Gregor Schoeler, *The Oral and the Writtten in Early Islam*, tr. Uwe Vagelpohl, ed. James E. Montgomery (London and New York, 2006). See also below, Ch. 12 and Box Text, pp. 307–12.

[20] Al-Qadi, 'Religious Foundation'; *RoIM*, 152–3.

[21] There are precedents – for example, under ʿAbd al-Malik and al-Walid I, but these are exclusively Syrian; in one case, highly syncretic, and in the other, a matter of apostasy: Sahner, *Christian Martyrs*, 130–40; Anthony, *Crucifixion*, 55–8; Steven Judd, 'Muslim Persecution of Heretics during the Marwanid Period (64–132/684–750)', *Al-Masaq* 23 (2011), 3–4. For the burning of 'magicians' in Egypt by ʿAbd al-ʿAziz b. Marwan, see B. Evetts (ed. and tr.), *History of the Patriarchs of the Coptic Church of Alexandria* (Paris, 1904–14), I, xvi, 32.

his precursors, Hisham tailored articulations of his legitimacy to his audience. His claims varied between the more thoroughly Islamised older provinces of the empire and the still quite Christian Roman frontier zone, where he sometimes made use of more syncretic symbolism.

In Syria, Hisham is said to have had a former associate of 'Umar II, Ghaylan al-Dimashqi, interrogated and found to be a heretic, before having him and some of his followers executed, probably in the 730s. One of the doctrines which Ghaylan is said to have promoted was that of 'free will' (*qadar*). While some of the leading scholars in the orbit of Hisham's court seem to have been vocal opponents of the idea of free will, many of its proponents were tolerated, and so it is unlikely that this alone was the cause of Ghaylan's demise. Rather, Ghaylan was probably a victim of political intrigue, or was perceived as a threat because of the extent of his following, or because he propounded other unacceptable ideas, or some combination of these things.[22] It is at least possible that he had appealed to resentments in Damascus at the move north by the caliphal court. If so, he would be part of a wider pattern of religious ideas and associated social movements that Hisham and his allies sought to suppress.

The old Iraqi garrisons of Kufa and Basra remained centres of opposition to Marwanid rule. Moreover, both populations had grown fast, from tens of thousands in each city in the mid-seventh century to perhaps well over 250,000 people in each in the middle decades of the eighth century. Migration from surrounding towns and villages, the import of captives and long-distance trading connections had made the cities diverse and volatile places, where religious and political ideas were exchanged and influenced one another.[23] In both places, groups of opponents to the Marwanids formed clandestine networks that sought allies elsewhere in the empire, sending out missions (*da'awāt*, sing. *da'wa*), criticising injustices in Islamic terms and calling for allegiance to their rival interpretations of Islam. The Marwanid authorities in the mid-720s were aware of these secretive movements. Because the idea of leadership by a member of the Prophet's immediate family (defined in various ways) was once again an important focus for many rebels' aspirations, relations with the 'Alids of Medina cooled during Hisham's rule; al-Husayn's grandson, Muhammad al-Baqir (b. *c.* 675–7, d. *c.* 735–8), is said to

---

[22] On Hisham and the suppression of heresy, including the evidence about Ghaylan, see Judd, *Religious Scholars*; Judd, 'Muslim Persecution'; Steven Judd, 'Ghaylan al-Dimashqi: The Isolation of a Heretic in Islamic Historiography', *IJMES* 31 (1999), 161–84.

[23] On the growth of Basra and Kufa, see below, Ch. 10, p. 230. On religion in the garrisons, see Box Text, below, pp. 184–6.

have been viewed with suspicion by Hisham, who called him to Damascus on several occasions.[24]

Less prestigious and more activist religious leaders were dealt with more harshly. In 728 the governor of Khurasan is said to have executed a group of merchants from Kufa who were agitating for the overthrow of the Marwanids and their replacement with a yet unspecified ruler from the Prophet's branch of the Quraysh, the Banu Hashim.[25] The leader of these agents was a non-Arabian client (*mawlā*) of a South Arabian tribe, like many of those who had supported al-Mukhtar at Kufa in the mid-680s.[26] About six years later, in 735, another group were arrested, this time of South Arabians and Tamimis; the protection of kinspeople in Khurasan is said to have prevented their being killed after some of them were tortured.[27] In the following year, a member of the same organisation began to preach in ways that were unacceptable to his fellow conspirators, perhaps because his message owed too much to Iranian religion; that he was arrested and killed by the Umayyad governor may ironically have allowed these fellow conspirators to regain control of the mission in Khurasan.[28] Meanwhile, in Iraq, Khalid al-Qasri was responsible for a series of public executions of rebels, potential rebels and heretics, and the suppression of some small-scale revolts in the vicinity of Kufa and al-Hira, all in or around the year 737. Some of these rebels were burned alive in the courtyard of the congregational mosque, to mark them out as heretics or sorcerers, and to dissuade others from leading resistance.[29] The violence of Khalid's reaction likely also reflects the extent of the threat from insurrectionist movements in Iraq and Khurasan felt by Hisham and his allies by the 730s.[30]

---

[24] *EI²*, 'Muhammad b. Zayn al-'Abidin, Abu Dja'far, called al-Bakir' (E. Kohlberg). See also Box Text, above, pp. 148–50.

[25] Tabari, II, 1501–3. See on this story, Agha, *Revolution*, 13–14.

[26] Agha, *Revolution*, 4–15. See above, Box Text, Ch. 4, pp. 105–8.

[27] Tabari, II, 1586–8. On their tribal affiliations, see Agha, *Revolution*, Appendix One, s.nn.

[28] Tabari, II, 1588–9. On Khidash's ideas, see Agha, *Revolution*, 16–25; Crone, *Nativist Prophets*, 26–7; below, Ch. 11, pp. 291–2.

[29] Gerald Hawting, 'The Case of Ja'd b. Dirham and the Punishment of "Heretics" in the Early Caliphate', in Christian Lange and Maribel Fierro (eds), *Public Violence in Islamic Societies: Power, Discipline, and the Construction of the Public Sphere, 7th–19th Centuries* CE (Edinburgh, 2009), 27–41; Andrew Marsham, 'Attitudes to the Use of Fire in Executions in Late Antiquity and Early Islam: The Burning of Heretics and Rebels in Late Umayyad Iraq', in Robert Gleave and István Kristó-Nagy (eds), *Violence in Islamic Thought from the Qur'an to the Mongols* (Edinburgh, 2015), 106–27.

[30] For Khalid's particular fear of one of the rebels, see Marsham, 'Fire in Executions', 110.

Religious Leaders in Marwanid Basra and Kufa

By the early 700s Marwanid-era Basra and Kufa had growing populations that perhaps already each numbered well over 200,000.[31] They comprised both the descendants of settlers from the Arabian Peninsula and *mawālī* from slave-taking and migration. Consequently, the social backgrounds of the scholars of these garrisons were more diverse than the those of the Medinans, with many more *mawālī* and their descendants among them. Both garrisons were a ferment of political, legal, religious and theological innovation and contention. Many Basran and Kufan scholars were willing to tolerate Marwanid rule, but each garrison was also a centre for religious movements that articulated more militant political aspirations.

In many cases, the most famous religious leaders of this era were claimed by later religious movements and so their own religious and political positions are hard to perceive behind the later polemic. The contradictory traditions about the famous Basran scholar al-Hasan al-Basri (b. *c.* 642?, d. 728) illustrate this point. Al-Hasan al-Basri is said to have been the son of a captive from wars with the Sasanians and to have moved from Medina to Basra in his early youth. He probably served in campaigns in Sistan or Khurasan in the 660s as a scribe or military commander, before returning to Basra, where he is said to have been a legal advisor or judge (*qāḍī*) for 'Umar II. Prior to that, it seems likely that he participated in the revolt of Ibn al-Ash'ath, going into exile from al-Hajjaj afterwards, although his participation in rebellion became a contentious matter in later traditions because many of those who claimed him as an authority were sceptical of revolt in most circumstances.[32]

Certainly, many other Basrans joined the rebellion of Ibn al-Ash'ath against the perceived injustice of al-Hajjaj's regime, and the Azd of Basra were the core of Ibn al-Muhallab's rebellion twenty years later.[33] Moreover, ideas hostile to the Umayyad, 'Alid and Zubayrid caliphs were followed by the North and Central Arabian tribespeople who had settled in Basra and by their kin in the steppes to the south and west. Their so-called 'Kharijite' movements rejected the necessity of Qurashi leadership of the Faithful and could be quick to define sinners as outside the faith – that is, as 'infidels' (*kuffār*, sing. *kāfir*) – who could be killed. The tendency

---

[31] On the populations of the garrison cities, see below, Ch. 10, p. 230.
[32] Suleiman A. Mourad, *Early Islam between Myth and History: Al-Hasan al-Basri (d. 110 H/728 CE) and the Formation of his Legacy in Classical Islamic Scholarship* (Leiden, 2006); *EI3*, 'al-Hasan al-Basri' (S. A. Mourad).
[33] See above, Chs 6 and 7, pp. 135–7 and 170–2.

among the pastoralists of north-eastern Arabia and Iraq to resist external, centralising authority, appears to have contributed to these movements, which recur as a sort of counterpoint to the extension of the Umayyad governors' power and the increasing dominance of Syrian troops in the province.[34]

Kufan society, religion and politics were similarly complex. The careers of 'Amir b. Sharahil al-Sha'bi (b. *c*. 660?, d. *c*. 721–8) and Abu Hanifa (b. *c*. 699?, d. 767) are illustrative. Al-Sha'bi was the son of a South Arabian migrant, who is said to have participated in the revolt of al-Mukhtar in 685–7 before rejecting what he saw as erroneous beliefs among al-Mukhtar's followers. He is said both to have served as a *qāḍī* for al-Hajjaj and – likely because of his southern tribal connections – to have participated in the revolt of Ibn al-Ash'ath, after which he went into exile with the governor of Khurasan before being pardoned and returning to Kufa.[35] In contrast, Abu Hanifa, who studied with al-Sha'bi, was a silk merchant whose father was an emancipated captive from Kabul. Abu Hanifa is said to have avoided most entanglements with both the Umayyad authorities and with rebels, although by the end of the Umayyad period his sympathies are said to have lain with the 'Alids and the wider Hashimite clan. Abu Hanifa seems to have been an influential scholar, who emphasised to the idea of *jamā'a* – the importance of maintaining the political unity of the Faithful – and gave substantial room for personal judgement (*ra'y*) in interpreting the law. After his death, he became a celebrated religious authority, after whom one of the four main schools of legal thought in later Sunni Islam eventually came to be named.[36]

Besides the kind of widespread opposition to Umayyad rule manifested by the rebellions of Ibn al-Ash'ath and Ibn al-Muhallab, which decried the tyranny of Umayyad government and called for 'the Book and the Sunna' (*al-kitāb wa-l-sunna*), religious articulations of opposition at Kufa took two main forms: expectations focused on the claims of 'Ali b. Abi Talib's descendants and close relatives and so-called 'Kharijite' piety that rejected Qurashi leadership. The latter ideas appear to have inspired a wave of small rebellions during Mu'awiya's caliphate and a second wave of stronger opposition to the imposition of Marwanid rule in the 690s and early 700s. They continued to inspire resistance after then, notably in the 740s, often among the tribal groups in the hinterlands of the garrison, as at Basra.[37] However,

---

[34] Hagemann and Verkinderen, 'Kharijism'.
[35] *EI²*, 'al-Sha'bi' (G. H. A. Juynboll).
[36] *EI3*, 'Abu Hanifa' (H. Yanagihashi).
[37] Hagemann and Verkinderen, 'Kharijism'.

the claims of 'Ali's family had more sustained support within the city of Kufa itself, with *mawālī* and members of some of the South Arabian tribes being at the centre of attempts to install an 'Alid as the leader of the empire in the 650s, the 680s and the 740s.[38]

Rome and North Africa

Just as Hisham performed the restoration of 'Abd al-Malik and al-Walid's *ḥajj* and reorganised the revenues of Egypt and Iraq as they had done, he also staked his dynasty's success on victory over the Roman Empire. The campaigns of the first fifteen years of his caliphate built back towards the ambition of capturing Constantinople, which would have been a victory of apocalyptic significance that he could have used to secure his own rule and the prestige of his sons, two of whom led many of the campaigns. The build-up against the Romans was slow because Leo III had responded effectively to Hisham's revival of the annual campaigns in the later 720s. As Justinian II had done before him, Leo III renewed cooperation with the Khazar Khaganate and, in 732, again like his predecessor, Leo III became a son-in-law of the Khagan. The alliance was close; several Khazars were present at Leo III's court and there may also have been Christian bishops in the Khaganate. Khazar attacks in the late 720s and early 730s drew Arab forces into the Caucasus and away from the Anatolian frontier, preventing anything except isolated raids against the Romans.[39]

In 737, Marwan b. Muhammad b. Marwan (g. *c.* 732–44, r. 744–50) temporarily broke the impasse. Marwan carried out a damaging surprise attack on the Khazar Khagan, who is said to have submitted to caliphal authority and adopted Islam. This victory allowed the Muslims to consolidate their power over the smaller polities in the Caucasus and to launch campaigns deep into Asia Minor, led by Hisham's sons – actions which closely follow the build-up to the siege of Constantinople in 717–18. Then, in 740, a naval raid from North Africa against Sicily aimed to capture Syracuse, the strategically important Sicilian capital. Marwan launched further land campaigns in the Caucasus, directed at securing the loyalty of the polities there. Marwan supported Ashot Bagratuni (r. 726 or 732–48) as Prince of Armenia and exiled two of his Mamikonean rivals to Yemen.

Meanwhile, again as in 717–18, a major expedition was sent deep into Anatolia, led by two of Hisham's sons. This attack forced the Romans to make

---

[38] On these episodes, see further above Chs 4 and 5, pp. 88–92, 101–2 and 105–8, and below, pp. 188–91.
[39] Theophanes, 557, 559–60, 562–3, 567–71; Khalifa, 216–25; Whittow, *Making*, 143, 225–6; *PmBZ*, 'Leon III', no. 4242; Vacca, 'Umayyad North', 228.

a stand at Akroinon (Ar. Aqrun), on the very western edge of the Anatolian plateau. Had the Romans been defeated, the way to Constantinople would again have been open. However, led in person by the emperor and his son, the Romans instead inflicted a heavy defeat on the invading Muslim army, while the Muslims' raid on Sicily failed to take Syracuse. The death of Leo III in June the following year precipitated a succession crisis which prevented the Romans' capitalising on these successes, while the defeated Umayyad forces were immediately redeployed against a series of uprisings in North Africa.[40]

Also in 740, revolt had broken out at Tangier. Under the leadership of one Maysara al-Badghari, the Miknasa and Barghawata tribes of western North Africa captured Tangier and killed its governor. An army sent from al-Andalus to recapture the town was also defeated, and the rebels quickly extended their power over the whole region of al-Sus (the interior of modern Morocco). Although they then deposed and killed their leader, replacing him with Khalid b. Humayd al-Zanati, the rebels were nonetheless able to hold on to power: early in 740, they defeated an army sent west from Qayrawan, prompting the recall of the commander of the Sicilian expedition; then, in 741, they defeated and killed Ibn al-Habhab's replacement, sent from Syria with a large contingent of Syrian troops after Ibn al-Habhab himself had fled. Khalid al-Zanati now headed east, towards Qayrawan, drawing other North African groups into his army. The wealthy province of Ifriqiya (modern Tunisia and north-eastern Algeria) was saved only by Hisham despatching his experienced Egyptian governor, Hanzala b. Safwan al-Kalbi, who had just defeated a revolt in Upper Egypt coincident with the beginning of the North African revolt. In 743, Hanzala successfully defended Qayrawan and restored control over the province. However, he abandoned the whole of the western Maghrib (modern Morocco and the bulk of Algeria), where an independent Barghawata emirate was established. Al-Andalus, meanwhile, was drawn into the chaos, first by revolts among North African soldiers and then by conflict between the Syrian fugitives from the defeat in North Africa in 741 and the existing Andalusi elite.[41]

---

[40] Theophanes, 570–2; Khalifa, 226–8, 230; Blankinship, *End of the Jihad*, 175, 195; Whittow, *Making*, 226–8; *PmBZ*, 'Leon III', no. 4242; Vacca, 'Umayyad North', 228–30 and n. 67. Akroinon had previously been attacked by Maslama on his way to Constantinople in c. 716: Theophanes, 540; cf. Khalifa, 201–2.

[41] *EI²*, 'Barghawata' (R. Le Tourneau); 'Maysara' (E. Levi-Provençal), 'Kulthum b. Iyad al-Kushayri' (R. Basset), 'Baldj b. Bishr' (M. Schmitz and A. Huici-Miranda); Manzano Moreno, 'Iberian Peninsula', 590–1. For the revolt in Upper Egypt, see Lev, 'Coptic Rebellions', 311, citing Kindi, 81.

Thus, whereas the North African revolt of c. 721 had simply replaced one governor, regarded as oppressive, with a previous one who was more accepted locally, the revolts of 740 were of a completely different order, involving a coalition of North African tribes and resulting in the complete loss of any control on the part of the Syrian elite and their allies over the western Maghrib. The sources connect both the slaving raids of the Muslims and the oppressive treatment of the North Africans in the Muslim armies with the origins of this insurrection. They also note that the leaders of the revolt, Maysara al-Madghari, and then Khalid b. Humayd al-Zanati, took the pledge of allegiance as 'caliphs'.[42] Missionaries from the vicinity of Basra who followed so-called 'Kharijite' religious traditions that rejected Qurashi leadership and championed the violent correction of sinners had been active in North Africa for about a generation by 740.[43] Whereas earlier revolts within the North African populations had been nativist or syncretic, as in the cases of Kusayla and al-Kahina, or had accepted the principle of Umayyad rule, as in c. 721, the revolt of 740 saw the religious ideas of the Muslim Arab opponents of the caliphs being taken up among non-Arabs on the frontier.

Khurasan and Central Asia

There are similarities between the patterns of unrest on the western frontier during and after the 720s and those on the eastern frontier. In Khurasan as in North Africa, the short caliphates of 715–24 had contributed to instability and, again, the non-Arab population became participants in rebellions articulated in Islamic terms in the 730s and 740s. Further, as in North Africa, missionary movements (da'awāt) from Iraq had found fertile ground among militarised frontier populations that resented their place within the empire. However, whereas it seems that so-called 'Kharijite' ideas took root in North Africa, in Khurasan, ideas that favoured the 'Alids and Hashimites gained more ground. Furthermore, both regions were susceptible to the influence of external powers – the Roman Empire and the pastoralists of the Sahara in North Africa, and the Türgesh and other groups, as well as the more distant Tang Empire, in Khurasan.

In the East, after a brief reassertion of Arab power in the early 720s, the Türgesh inflicted another defeat on the Muslims in 724. This disaster came in the wake of Hisham's accession and the despatch of a new governor, which had exposed rivalries between tribal factions in the army. The defeat of 724 seriously weakened Muslim prestige in the region: during the later 720s and

---

[42] Ibn 'Abd al-Hakam, *Futuh*, 217–19; Tabari, I, 2815–16; *History of the Patriarchs*, I, xvii, 87–8; Ibn 'Idhari, *al-Bayan*, I, 52–4.

[43] For Iraqi religious leaders in North Africa: Tabari, I, 2815; *EI²*, 'Ibadiyya' (T. Lewicki).

early 730s, the Türgesh – viewed by the Sogdians as representatives of Chinese power – consolidated their power in Sogdia and extended it westwards into Tukharistan, so that Balkh and Samarqand were reduced to beleaguered islands of Muslim power east of the Oxus.[44] In 727, Hisham began to appoint governors directly over Khurasan, replacing them three times in the next eight years. These governors brought troops of Syrian heritage with them.[45]

The decline in the power of the caliphs' representatives in Khurasan and points east created space for alternative sources of authority. In 734, a Tamimi leader who had fought in Sogdia alongside local forces, al-Harith b. Surayj, took control of Balkh (in modern northern Afghanistan) and then marched west to target Marw with a growing army drawn from the troops in the region. His support was drawn from among the armies in Juzjan (north-west Afghanistan) and Tukharistan (northern Afghanistan, southern Turkmenistan, Uzbekistan and south-west Tajikistan), and comprised Arabs from Azd, Tamim and Bakr b. Wa'il, as well as local cities' rulers and their soldiers. He is remembered as articulating the grievances of his diverse followers in Islamic terms – calling for 'the Book and Right Custom' – and as having raised 'black banners', in imitation of the Prophet's war banners. The precise grievances and aspirations of his followers are not clear, but groups excluded from power and wealth among the Arab settlers and local populations found common cause under his leadership; as in North Africa, the imposition of taxes on non-Arab Muslims (*mawālī*) is among the resentments mentioned in the sources.[46]

In 735, Hisham restored Khalid al-Qasri's direct authority over Khurasan and re-appointed Khalid's brother Asad (g. 724–7, 735–8) there. Asad's main concerns were defeating al-Harith b. Surayj, restoring control over the province, and expansionist campaigning on the frontier. He is remembered for his ruthlessness: he is said to have doubled the stipends of the troops who campaigned with him, appropriating local resources to pay them, and to have instructed his commanders to carry out enslavement of some rebels and mass public executions of others. Asad's predecessor and then Asad himself bested al-Harith in a series of encounters during 734–6, driving him into

---

[44] Gibb, *Arab Conquests*, 59–76.

[45] The governors were: Ashras b. 'Abd Allah al-Sulami (g. 727–30); al-Junayd b. 'Abd al-Rahman al-Murri (g. 730–4); 'Asim b. 'Abd Allah al-Hilali (g. 734–5). On Syrians in Khurasan in the 730s, see Kennedy, *Armies*, 34, 43.

[46] Tabari, II, 1566–9, 1571–2, 1573–5; Gibb, *Arab Conquests*, 76–9; Haug, *Eastern Frontier*, 139–41; Stuart D. Sears, 'The Revolt of al-Harith b. Surayj and the Countermarking of Umayyad Dirhams in Early Eighth Century CE Khurasan', in Paul M. Cobb (ed.), *The Lineaments of Islam: Studies in Honor of Fred McGraw Donner* (Leiden, 2012), 393–7.

alliance with the Türgesh and then inflicting a rare defeat on the Türgesh at Kharistan 737. Although Asad died of an abcess or tumour early in 738, the ensuing collapse of the Türgesh federation made the reassertion of Marwanid power in the region a possibility for the first time in a quarter of a century.[47]

It may be that the improved prospects in Khurasan and the death of Asad emboldened Hisham to reorganise the government of the eastern provinces. In the spring of 738, Hisham dismissed Asad's surviving brother and long-standing governor of Iraq, Khalid b. 'Abd Allah al-Qasri. Khalid was imprisoned and replaced by Yusuf b. 'Umar b. Muhammad al-Thaqafi (g. 738–44), previously the governor of Yemen. Meanwhile, Khurasan was once more removed from the Iraqi governor's remit, with Hisham appointing the aged but experienced Khurasani commander Nasr b. Sayyar (g. 738–48).

The appointment of Yusuf b. 'Umar, who was a great-nephew of 'Abd al-Malik's former Iraqi governor, al-Hajjaj, marked the return of al-Hajjaj's family to Iraq after twenty-four years. There is much elaboration in the sources on the motives for the removal of Khalid and the appointment of Yusuf. It is possible that Khalid had refused to back a change in the caliphal succession arrangements and was punished with deposition. If so, the appointment of Yusuf amounted to a recognition that the succession would remain as it was, since Yusuf's nephew held the claim to succeed Hisham. Another consideration was probably Hisham's awareness of the growing threat of rebellion in and around Kufa and the need for a governor who could confront the predominantly southern Arabians involved.[48]

If confronting the rebels was the intention, it worked. Yusuf's appointment to Iraq inflamed the factional animosities and resentments of Syrian exploitation of the province that had fuelled the earlier revolts in Iraq: as a Thaqafi, Yusuf was from the 'northern', or 'Qaysi' tribal group, as opposed to the 'southern' or 'Yemeni' background of many of his Iraqi subjects. A revolt was triggered at Kufa almost immediately. Zayd b. 'Ali b. al-Husayn – a great-great-grandson of the Prophet Muhammad – was forced into the open prematurely by Yusuf in January 740. Zayd and a small group of supporters were hunted down and killed by Yusuf's Syrian troops in the streets of Kufa. Zayd's son Yahya b. Zayd then became a fugitive before he was killed in Khurasan by forces loyal to Yusuf b. 'Umar in 743. These revolts were relatively small. Crucially for their later success, the leaders of the pro-Hashimite

---

[47] Tabari, II, 1573–86, 1589–1619, 1638; Haug, *Eastern Frontier*, 141–2; Gibb, *Arab Conquests*, 80–6. On Asad's illness, see Tabari, *History*, XXV, 167, n. 585 (K. Y. Blankinship).

[48] Khalifa, 227; Ya'qubi, II, 387–8; Tabari, II, 1641–67, 1742–3. See further below, Ch. 9, pp. 192–5.

rebel organisation that stemmed from al-Mukhtar's followers dissuaded its adherents in Iraq and Khurasan from joining them.[49] However, the Kufan revolts of the early 740s presaged much greater unrest in the East that would take place in the context of a civil war within Syria over the succession to Hisham.

---

[49] Khalifa, 229; Tabari, II, 1676–88, 1698–1716, 1770–4. Cf. Ya'qubi, II, 391–2, where Zayd's killing is dated to 738–9. On the successors to al-Mukhtar's supporters and Zayd, see Agha, *Revolution*, 26–33.

9

The Collapse of Umayyad Power

The collapse of Umayyad power happened within a decade. The North African revolts of 740 had begun the process, breaking away the western part of the empire from central control, while the failures in Sicily and Anatolia in 740 had also damaged the Syrian armies and weakened Hisham's prestige. When Hisham died, less than three years later, the extent of the rifts within the wider Marwanid clan and their armies were exposed. These fractures were widened by competition between other powerful groups close to the ruling family, among them the Thaqafi relatives of al-Hajjaj, the Makhzumi maternal relatives of Hisham, and the family of Khalid al-Qasri, the deposed governor of Iraq. Because of these conflicts, Hisham's death triggered a succession crisis and civil war in Syria. This breakdown at the imperial centre gave well-established networks of opponents of the Umayyads in Iraq and the East an opening. In the East, as with the 'Berber Revolt' in the West, it was the mass participation of non-Arab forces that gave the rebels an advantage on the battlefield against divided and demoralised Syrian armies.

The End of Marwanid Unity and the Killing of al-Walid II

Towards the end of his life, Hisham had made unsuccessful attempts to nominate his son, Abu Shakir, as his heir. Abu Shakir was to succeed in place of his cousin, al-Walid b. Yazid, who had been named as Hisham's successor by his father, Yazid II, in the early 720s.[1] The tussle over the succession had pitted members of the Marwanid family against one another and had involved other members of the wider ruling elite whose interests were aligned with the succession of one or other candidate. Hisham's sons, his maternal relatives from the Banu Makhzum, his commanders in northern Syria from the Banu 'Abs, and the senior religious scholar at the Marwanid court, Ibn Shihab al-Zuhri, are all said to have been in favour of changing the succession in favour of

---

[1] Baladhuri, *Ansab*, VII, 329–32; al-Zubayri, *Nasab*, 168. Abu Shakir's *ism*, or given name, was Maslama. In al-Zubayri's *Nasab*, he is erroneously Marwan.

Hisham's son. In contrast, al-Walid b. Yazid's place in the succession represented the opposing interests of his maternal uncle, Yusuf b. 'Umar al-Thaqafi, whose appointment to Iraq in 738 presumably marked the end of any ambition to alter the existing arrangements. However, although he had retained the succession, al-Walid II (r. 743–4) took power among a bitterly divided Marwanid elite.[2]

In a relatively open, patrimonial, succession system, the number of viable candidates to be caliph was potentially large. Once the unity of the wider military elite had begun to break down, as it had towards the end of Hisham's caliphate, competition could focus on a range of rival claimants on power. The actions of al-Walid II and his allies after Hisham died at al-Rusafa in early February 743 reflect the insecurity of al-Walid II's position and the extent of the opposition to him among his Marwanid cousins and their allies in the military elite. That a Damascene tribal leader who had opposed his succession plans is said to have been imprisoned on al-Walid II's accession is relatively unsurprising. Much more unusual is that al-Walid II is said to have imprisoned two of Hisham's sons and one of al-Walid I's grandsons. One of them, Sulayman b. Hisham, is said to have been beaten and publicly paraded, in revenge for his father's plan to remove al-Walid from the succession. This would have been a scandalous humiliation for a leading member of the ruling Marwanid dynasty.[3]

Al-Walid II's caliphate also had an unusually narrow base among the military commanders. He depended above all on the backing of his Thaqafi maternal relatives, as well as on some commanders from the Roman frontier, like Yazid b. 'Umar b. Hubayra, and their 'northern' Qaysi troops. These allies immediately moved to secure their position against possible rivals. Competition between Yusuf b. 'Umar al-Thaqafi and the older man Yusuf had replaced in Iraq, Khalid al-Qasri, are the subject of elaboration in the later narrative sources.[4] Whatever the realities of the political manoeuvring before and after al-Walid II's accession, Khalid al-Qasri lost to Yusuf b. 'Umar. The new Thaqafi Iraqi governor is said to have handed over to al-Walid II the huge sum 50,000,000 dirhams. This would have been the equivalent of most of Iraq's

---

[2] Baladhuri, *Ansab*, VII, 329 32; Tabari, II, 1741–50; al-Zubayri, *Nasab*, 168. On al-Zuhri, see al-Tabari, II, 1811 and Box Text, above, pp. 148–9. Cf. Ya'qubi, II, 397.

[3] Tabari, II, 1776; *SoH*, 151, no. 111. For the Damascene tribal leader's father, see Baladhuri, *Ansab*, VI, 560, VII, 25. Date of Hisham's death: Tabari, II, 1728–9.

[4] Baladhuri, *Ansab*, VII, 514–16; Ya'qubi, II, 387–8; Tabari, II, 1777–84, 1812–25. On some of these narratives, see Stefan Leder, 'Features of the Novel in Early Historiography: The Downfall of Xalid al-Qasri', *Oriens* 32 (1990), 72–96; Steven Judd, 'Ibn 'Asakir's Peculiar Biography of Khalid al-Qasri', in Steven Judd and Jens Scheiner (eds), *New Perspectives on Ibn 'Asakir in Islamic Historiography* (Leiden, 2017), 139–56.

annual revenue; even if it is invented or exaggerated, it suggests both the importance of the internal tributary economy of the empire and the pressure on the caliph to gather the resources to pay his Syrian army. In return for his huge payment, Yusuf is said to have received custody of Khalid, who was tortured and killed.[5] Meanwhile, al-Walid II's maternal uncle, Yusuf b. Muhammad al-Thaqafi, replaced Hisham's former Makhzumi governors in the Hijaz. Yusuf b. Muhammad is said to have sent the Makhzumis to Yusuf b. 'Umar, where they met the same fate as Khalid.[6] Yusuf b. 'Umar is also said to have been plotting to remove Hisham's Khurasani governor, Nasr b. Sayyar, but to have been unable to do so before he himself was overtaken by events.[7] In northern Syria, Yazid b. 'Umar b. Hubayra exacted similar revenge on the 'Absi commanders there who had been favoured by Hisham over Ibn Hubayra's family.[8]

While the purges at his accession were unusually widespread and partisan, they were not unprecedented.[9] More exceptional was al-Walid's reported decision to proclaim his young sons as his heirs in terms that emphasised his own claims to absolute divinely sanctioned authority. His haste to do so and his bold language may reflect an awareness of his own narrow base of support and the exceptional precarity brought about by the end of the unity of the Syrian armies: some of the 'southern' tribes in the *jund* of Damascus, many from Kalb, were willing to align themselves with al-Walid II's rivals in the Marwanid family and so to bring about civil war within the Marwanid elite and their military following.[10]

The roots of the grievances of the Damascene Kalbis can be found at the beginning of the eighth century. The defeat of Ibn al-Zubayr and then the exclusion of 'Abd al-'Aziz b. Marwan from the succession had brought Qaysi tribes into alliance with the Marwanids and then displaced the Kalb from their privileged position as the kinspeople by marriage of the caliphs. Since then, the balance of power between the 'southern' Quda'a around Damascus and in the Syrian Desert, of which Kalb were the leading tribe, and

---

[5] On the context for this killing, and Khalid as having plotted against al-Walid II, see Steven Judd, 'Reinterpreting al-Walid b. Yazid', *JAOS* 128 (2008), 450–1.
[6] Khalifa, 235–6; Tabari, II, 1768.
[7] Tabari, II, 1718–25.
[8] Tabari, II, 1783; *SoH*, 105–6, 107. For continuities in Egypt and Sind, see Khalifa, 232–5, 238–9; Kindi, 83–4.
[9] See, for example, the successions of Sulayman, 'Umar II, and Yazid II, above, Ch. 7, pp. 163 and 170–2, and the comments of Judd, 'Reinterpreting', 441.
[10] On the proclamation of his heirs, see Judd, 'Reinterpreting'; *RoIM*, 127–80; Abdulhadi Alajmi, 'Ascribed vs. Popular Legitimacy: The Case of al-Walid II and Umayyad *'ahd'*, *JNES* 72 (2013), 25–34. For the willingness of the Syrians to look to al-Walid II's rivals, see Baladhuri, *Ansab*, VII, 515.

the 'northern' Qaysi groups on the Roman frontier had shifted in favour of the latter. Hisham's foundation of a second capital at al-Rusafa/Sergiopolis in northern Syria reflected the importance of the frontier and the Qaysi armies there; the caliphal court was now among the frontier Qaysi commanders, who benefited from influence, lands and stipends. While Hisham had a close advisor from among the Kalb and still had a chief of 'police' (*shurṭa*) from the 'southern', Damascene, 'Ans, 'southern' troops now tended to be used as reserves, called up as enforcers in Iraq or North Africa, or to enhance larger expeditions against Rome.[11]

Towards the end of Hisham's caliphate, these resentments among the 'southern' Syrians had become entangled with Iraqi politics. The killing of the Damascene governor of Iraq, Khalid al-Qasri, who is placed close to the rebels' plots in the narrative sources, is also said to have particularly angered 'southern' Damascenes. Some of Khalid's associates are named among the rebels, who presumably resented losing Iraq to Yusuf b. 'Umar and his Qaysi soldiers. Poetry associated with the killing of Khalid also emphasises the historical humiliations suffered by 'southern' Arabs across the caliphate at the hands of 'northerners'; the 'northerner–southerner' tribal distinction had begun to carry between provinces. The sources also often describe the 'southern' rebels in Damascus as 'Qadaris', that is, 'proponents of free-will', and as 'Ghaylanis' – followers of Ghaylan al-Dimashqi, who had been executed by Hisham. These labels suggest that Hisham may have had good reason to be wary of Ghaylan, although how widespread or consistently held these theological views were among the rebels is unclear.[12]

Factional Competition in the Umayyad Armies? 'Qays' and 'Yemen'

Tribal identities can be effective and mutable instruments of political organisation. The evidence for the seventh-century conquest society and the Umayyad Empire suggests that this was so in these periods. The conquests and migrations brought together groups from across the Arabian Peninsula

---

[11] On this, cf. the various interpretations of *SoH*, 46; Crone, 'Qays and Yemen', 55; Blankinship, *End of the Jihad*, 223–5. On his advisor, see Box Text below, Ch. 12, p. 311. For his head of the *shurṭa*, see below, Ch. 12, p. 314, n. 47.

[12] Baladhuri, *Ansab*, VII, 515–18; Tabari, II, 1775–8, 1780–5; Blankinship, *End of the Jihad*, 223–4, 226–7; Crone, 'Qays and Yemen', 5; *SoH*, 42, 154–64. See also Ibn 'Asakir, IX, 169, §180, XII, 13, §1179, XV, 305, §1816, XX, 165, §2405, XXV, 6–7, §2970, LX, 311–13, §7660, LXXIII, 137, §9953, LXXIV, 170, §10133. For an associate of Khalid, see *SoH*, 163, no. 40. On the Qays–Yemen divide, see Crone, 'Qays and Yemen' and below Box Text, pp. 195–7. On Ghaylan, see above, Ch. 8, p. 182.

in new combinations, placing them alongside one another and alongside other Arabic-speaking groups from within the conquered territories. New political associations were expressed through the language of shared kinship and hostilities through tribal distinction. The garrisoning of the conquest armies in Kufa, Basra and Fustat, and the formation of new military units in Syria, led to the expansion of groups like Quda'a in Syria and Egypt, and Azd and Rabi'a, in Iraq.[13] The emergence of a stronger notion of a shared 'Arab' identity – the boundaries of which, however, were much contested – was another consequence of these processes of migration, settlement, cooperation and competition. Linguistic evolutions and convergences took place, with the numerous Arabian languages and dialects of the Peninsula being shaped and somewhat homogenised within the concentrations of garrison populations and by the development of trans-regional political networks and scribal norms.[14]

In the Arabic narratives about the politics of the Umayyad era, a distinction between 'southern' and 'northern' tribes is prominent. This distinction was based on the supposed difference between tribes originating in South Arabia ('Yemen'), many of whom began to claim a distant common ancestor in the legendary Qahtan, and tribes originating in the northern part of the Peninsula, many of whom looked back to Qays as their patriarch, and most of whom looked back to Qays' putative grandfather, Mudar.

Some genuine linguistic and cultural differences and long-standing political distinctions informed this division: South and East Arabia were each linguistically and culturally distinct, as were the West and North of the Peninsula. However, these differences took on new political meanings in the Umayyad era, as new kinds of cooperation and competition took place within the provincial armies. One important instance of this is the tension between Quda'a and Qays in Syria. After the battle of Marj Rahit (684), Kalb and the wider grouping of Quda'a came to identify as 'southern' or 'Yemeni' against the 'northern' Qays, who had fought against them. This tension remained a significant factor in Syrian politics thereafter, although the details of specific conflicts show that it was never a simple factionalism – for example, the 'northern', 'Qaysi', Banu 'Abs are found in alliance with the Damascene, 'Yemeni', 'southerners' against al-Walid II for reasons of shared political interest in 743–4.[15]

---

[13] For Rabi'a and Azd, see above, Ch. 3, p. 76, nn. 46 and 47. For the formation of Quda'a, see Crone, 'Qays and Yemen', 44–5 and nn. 235–7.
[14] See Legendre, 'Translation'.
[15] See above, Ch. 5, p. 113 and below, pp. 197–8.

Mutatis mutandis, a similar picture of complex and multi-level tribal identities can be found in other parts of the empire. In Basra, the main tribal groupings were Tamim and Rabi'a, alongside smaller numbers from Qays. These were later joined by migrants from South and East Arabia, known collectively as the Azd. Tamim claimed 'northern' heritage and common ancestry, via Mudar, with Qays. Rabi'a (among whom Bakr b. Wa'il predominated) often, though not always, sided with the Azdis. Because Basrans had contributed most of the troops for the conquest and settlement of Khurasan, similar tribal divisions pertained in the frontier province, too.[16] Thus, across the whole empire, groups came to identify as 'northern' or 'southern' – from either 'Mudar/Qays' or 'Yemen/Qahtan'.

In certain contexts, this 'north–south' distinction could become salient in the rhetoric of political conflict. However, the idea that these groupings amounted to differing political 'parties' within the empire, with differing ideas about political practice has been demonstrated to be false. They have also been described as 'factions', in the sense of a division between similar groups simply competing for power and wealth. While these large-scale tribal identities certainly sometimes functioned in this factional way, it is important not to overstate the consistency of the competition between them, nor the extent of trans-regional coherence in these identities. While the sources sometimes present these things in a schematised fashion, closer scrutiny shows that smaller groups within these wider categories sometimes competed with one another, and sub-groups could also cooperate across the 'north–south' divide. Often, other political interests and associations – such as regional affiliation and local economic interests – help to explain these complexities. For example, Syrians were often resented as a foreign imposition in the provinces where they were increasingly deployed in the eighth century.[17]

Al-Walid II is said to have sought to address the grievances of the Kalbis by raising the stipends of all the Syrians, demanding more revenue from his uncle in Iraq to support the payments. He also recalled Syrian – probably Qaysi – forces from Egypt, perhaps suggesting that he faced both a manpower shortage and

---

[16] Crone, 'Qays and Yemen', esp. 3, 44–9; Kennedy, 'Oral Tradition'; Ulrich, *Arabs*; *EI3*, 'Azd' (P. Webb).

[17] For factions, see Crone and Hinds, 'Qays and Yemen'; Eva Orthmann, *Stamm und Macht: die arabischen Stämme im 2. und 3. Jahrhundert der Hiǧra* (Wiesbaden, 2002). See also Kennedy, *Armies*, 49.

a shortfall in revenue to pay the men.[18] However, these efforts to restore the unity of the Syrians failed. A group predominantly composed of Kalbis from the environs of Damascus was joined by 'Absis from the northern frontier. Both groups had connections with the family of al-Walid I, and they forged an alliance with his son, Yazid b. al-Walid, as well as with another grandson of 'Abd al-Malik, 'Abd al-'Aziz b. al-Hajjaj. Yazid's mother is said to have been a captive member of the Sasanian royal family, which may reflect efforts to augment his status despite his lacking a prestigious mother of Arabian heritage, unlike all his caliphal predecessors.[19]

Yazid b. al-Walid (Yazid III, r. 744) proclaimed his revolt at his father's mosque in Damascus – a location that itself recalled an era when the city and its hinterlands, from where his supporters hailed, were at the centre of power. The speeches and letters to the provinces attributed to Yazid III indicate an attempt to unite the 'southern' Syrians with groups from Kufa and Basra. Criticism of al-Walid II's debauchery and profligacy reflects both the religious language of politics, as well as more material grievances about misuse of the Muslims' wealth. Yazid III is said to have promised an end to lavish caliphal building projects, which might be taken not only as a reference to al-Walid II's well-attested palace-building but also as a criticism of Hisham's move to al-Rusafa and the lucrative estates of the wider Marwanid elite. Equality of stipends for Muslims in all the provinces and an end to the pressures of too frequent campaigning were two further promises. These would have resonated with the Damascene 'southerners', who had seen their pay and prestige decline in favour of the Qaysis on the Roman frontier and who had suffered recent heavy losses in the wars in North Africa and Anatolia. It would also have responded to the long-standing grievances of the Iraqis of Basra and Kufa. Promises to be accessible to all petitioners, and to relinquish the caliphate if called upon to do so, suggest the resentment of groups excluded from the centre of power and recall other late antique depictions of unjust rule as inaccessible, arbitrary and remote. Promises about the proper use of taxes and the retention of revenues in the provinces addressed the grievances of the Iraqis and their hostility to the return of Thaqafi governance after 738.[20]

---

[18] Blankinship, *End of the Jihad*, 223–5. For the increase of payments to the Syrians: al-Tabari, II, 1754–5. For al-Walid II seeking revenue from Iraq: Tabari, II, 1778–81. On the recall of Syrians from Egypt, which provoked a revolt, see Kindi, 83.

[19] His mother's capture is associated with the campaigns of Qutayba in the early 700s: Tabari, II, 1246–7; Cf. Haug, *Eastern Frontier*, 93.

[20] For a thematic summary of Yazid III's speeches, see Blankinship, *End of the Jihad*, 226–30. See also Yazid III's letter to the Iraqis in Tabari, II, 1843–5. For discussion, see Crone, 'Qays

When al-Walid II heard about the revolt, he is said to have been at one of his oasis residences near 'Amman (modern Jordan). He fled north, making for his allies on the Roman frontier, but was surrounded and outnumbered at al-Bakhra', a former Roman fort, about 21km south of Tadmur/Palmyra, in April 744.[21] A pivotal event is said to have been the powerful al-'Abbas b. al-Walid's transfer of loyalty from al-Walid II to his half-brother, Yazid III, after which al-Walid II's forces deserted him.[22] According to one account transmitted by al-Mada'ini (d. c. 840) from one of al-Walid II's grandsons:

> [Al-Walid II] went into the room, sat down, took a copy of the Qur'an, and said, 'This is a day like the day 'Uthman was killed,' and he began to recite. Then the rebels began to scale the wall. The first person over the top was Yazid b. 'Anbasa al-Saksaki. He climbed down and went up to al-Walid, whose sword was at his side. Then Yazid said to him, 'Take off your sword.' Al-Walid replied, 'If I had wanted my sword, the situation between you and me would have been different from this.' Then Yazid took al-Walid's hand, wanting to take him into custody and to have consultations about what should be done with him. At that point ten men came down from the wall; among them were Mansur b. Jumhur, Hibal b. 'Amr al-Kalbi, 'Abd al-Rahman b. 'Ajlan, who was the *mawlā* of Yazid b. 'Abd al-Malik, Humayd b. Nasr al-Lakhmi, al-Sari b. Ziyad b. Abi Kabshah and 'Abd al-Salam al-Lakhmi. 'Abd al-Salam struck al-Walid on the head and al-Sari hit him in the face; then five of them seized him to take him outside. A woman who was with al-Walid in the room screamed, so they let go of al-Walid and did not take him out. Then Abu 'Ilaqa al-Quda'i cut off al-Walid's head.[23]

As the narrative reminds us, al-Walid II was the first Umayyad caliph to be killed since 'Uthman himself, nearly ninety years before, in 656. The killing reflected the failure of shared interest within the Umayyad clan and the failure of solidarity between the Damascene Kalb and the Qays of Qinnasrin and the Jazira; all the named assailants of al-Walid II in the story are from 'southern' tribes.

The regicide further polarised conflict within the Umayyad family, their allies in the wider imperial elite, and in the province of Syria itself. Yazid III

---

and Yemen', 41–2. On building by Hisham and al-Walid II, see above, Ch. 8, p. 178, and below, Ch. 10, pp. 229, 232, 237–42, 244–7.

[21] Tabari, II, 1795–1807. On al-Bakhra', see Genequand, *Établissements*, 70–94. For al-Azraq and al-Aghdaf, near 'Amman, see Tabari, *History*, XXVI, 91–2, n. 465, 148, n. 763 (C. Hillenbrand); Genequand, *Établissements*, 70–1, 309–11, 366. For al-Walid II's death date, see Khalifa, 236; Tabari, II, 1810.

[22] Khalifa, 237; Tabari, II, 1798–9.

[23] Tabari, II, 1800; tr. after C. Hillenbrand, in Tabari, *History*, XXVI, 153–4. Cf. Khalifa, 237; Baladhuri, *Ansab*, VII, 529; Tabari, II, 1809.

deposed Yusuf b. ʿUmar from Iraq, who fled to Syria and was killed there. ʿAbd Allah b. ʿUmar b. ʿAbd al-ʿAziz, a son of ʿUmar II by a Kalbi mother, is said to have been given the task of reconciling the Syrian troops in Iraq to equality of treatment with soldiers from Kufa and Basra. In Syria itself, the military districts of Filastin and al-Urdunn rebelled against their governors and went over to Yazid III, while the district of Hims, nearer the Roman frontier, opposed him. Meanwhile, the commanders of the Qaysi tribes on the frontier itself prepared to oppose Yazid III and his predominantly Kalbi army. Most accounts indicate that the senior commander in the north, ʿAbd al-Malik's nephew Marwan b. Muhammad b. Marwan (g. *c.* 734–44; r. 744–50), initially proclaimed vengeance for the death of al-Walid II, but then entered into negotiations and agreed to pledge allegiance in return for guarantees of his position on the frontier. This volte-face by the most powerful Marwanid and former opponent of Yazid III might have gone some way to healing the rift in the Umayyad family, but the death of Yazid III, aged about forty-six, in the autumn of 744 after a reign of only six months once again threw the empire into turmoil.[24]

The Accession of Marwan II and the Third Civil War

Marwan b. Muhammad now returned to the offensive, putting to flight Yazid III's former ally Sulayman b. Hisham at ʿAyn al-Jarr (ʿAnjar), en route from Hims to Damascus, and then entering the Syrian capital city late in 744 or early in 745, where he was proclaimed caliph. However, Marwan II (r. 744–50) was beset by opponents to his rule. In Syria, Kalb and much of the wider 'southern' federation of Qudaʿa, who had supported Yazid III, opposed him. Marwan II retreated from Damascus to Harran, in the Jaziran Diyar Mudar (on the modern border between Turkey and Syria), which was the centre of his old frontier province and, as its name suggests, was settled by 'northern' Qaysi, or Mudari, tribes. From Harran, he reconquered the military districts of Hims, Damascus and Filastin, carrying out mass public executions after his victories, and demolishing city walls. With most of the Syrian resistance temporarily suppressed, Marwan returned to Damascus, where he gathered the wider Marwanid clan and others to take the pledge of allegiance to two of his sons as his successors, marrying them to daughters of the caliph Hisham in order to tie his own line into that of a son of ʿAbd al-Malik.[25]

---

[24] Tabari, II, 1825–55, 1870–5. For ʿAbd Allah b. ʿUmar's Kalbi mother, see Baladhuri, *Ansab*, VII, 161. For Yusuf's fate, see Baladhuri, *Ansab*, XII, 415. For a rumour that Yazid III was assassinated, possibly by his brother, Ibrahim, who succeeded him, see Yaʿqubi, II, 402.

[25] Tabari, II, 1876–9, 1881–2, 1890–7. On the strategic location of ʿAyn al-Jarr/ʿAnjar, see Aila Santi, "Anjar in the Shadow of the Church? New Insights on an Umayyad Urban Experiment in the Biqaʿ Valley', *Levant* 50 (2019), 1.

Beyond Syria, Marwan II's situation was equally precarious. In Egypt, his attempts to impose a new governor were initially rejected and it was only in late 745 that he successfully imposed a new governor by force, using troops sent from Syria, who then had to contend with incursions into Egypt from Christian Nubia.[26] In South Arabia, a Kindi leader, 'Abd Allah b. Yahya, took the title 'Seeker of the Truth', or 'Seeker of Justice' (*tālib al-ḥaqq*), when he claimed the caliphate in c. 747. By the end of the summer of that year, Talib al-Haqq claimed control not only over South Arabia, but also over Mecca and Medina, as well as winning some support in Iraq and Egypt; he was defeated and killed a year later by forces loyal to Marwan II, in 748.[27] On the Roman frontier the recently united and reorganised Roman forces of Leo III's son Constantine V (r. 741–75) took advantage of the chaos in the Muslims' empire to capture Germanikeia (Ar. Mar'ash) in c. 745 and to destroy the Muslim fleet at Cyprus in c. 747.[28]

In the Jazira, Iraq and western Iran four main groups contested power. First, Yazid III's former governor of Iraq, 'Abd Allah b. 'Umar b. 'Abd al-'Aziz, was still in post, together with his Syrian forces. Second, there were the Banu Shayban and their allies in central and northern Iraq and the Jazira. Third, the Kufan supporters of rule by the Prophet's family were joined by people from the west Iranian highlands. Fourth, Marwan II's forces were led personally by him and by his sons in the Jazira and by al-Walid II's former governor of Qinnasrin, Yazid b. 'Umar b. Hubayra, in Iraq. These four competing groups reflected long-standing conflicts in the wealthiest lands of the empire. The Banu Shayban had a history of resistance to the imposition of Qurashi rule, under local 'Kharijite' leaders, whereas many of the Kufan South Arabians and their *mawālī* formed a network of advocates of rule by relatives of the Prophet and 'Ali. Meanwhile, Syrian and Umayyad interests were now split, between the representatives of Yazid III and his predominantly 'southern' Syrian support and Marwan II and his mostly Qaysi allies.

The Banu Shayban branch of Bakr b. Wa'il had already rebelled at the outbreak of conflict in Syria in 743 and were now led by al-Dahhak b. Qays al-Shaybani (r. 744–6), who proclaimed himself caliph. In 745, al-Dahhak captured Kufa and then accepted the surrender and allegiance of Yazid III's Iraqi governor, 'Abd Allah b. 'Umar b. 'Abd al-'Aziz, at Wasit, together with that of Sulayman b. Hisham, who, having initially been defeated by Marwan II in Syria, had fled to Iraq. Al-Dahhak then returned north to capture Mosul before

---

[26] Kindi, 84–90; *History of the Patriarchs*, I, xviii, 144–5.
[27] *EI*², 'Talib al-Hakk' (E. Francesca); John C. Wilkinson, *Ibadism: Origins and Development in Oman* (Oxford, 2010), 177–83; Egypt: Kindi, 92.
[28] Theophanes, 584–6; Whittow, *Making*, 143, 167–8.

marching west from there against Marwan II's capital at Harran. Al-Dahhak defeated one of Marwan II's sons before Marwan II and his Qaysi allies joined battle with him, at Kafartutha, between Mosul and Harran, where al-Dahhak was defeated and killed. In the summer of 747, Kufa and Wasit were recaptured for Marwan II by Yazid b. 'Umar b. Hubayra and the rebels' new leader, Shayban al-Yashkuri (r. 746–c. 748), was pursued into southern Iran by Yazid b. 'Umar b. Hubayra's allies, dying in in Sistan or Oman later that year or the next.[29]

Shortly after the death of Yazid III, in autumn 744, and before the main victories of al-Dahhak and the Banu Shayban, Ibn Mu'awiya (r. 744–8) had also declared himself caliph at Kufa. Ibn Mu'awiya was a great-grandson of 'Ali b. Abi Talib's full brother Ja'far, and so also a cousin of the Prophet Muhammad. His following in Kufa was said to have been drawn from the South Arabian groups who had supported his third cousin Zayd b. 'Ali four years earlier, as well as Kufan 'slaves' (*'abīd*, sing. *'abd*, which might be taken to indicate not just slaves but also non-Arab 'clients', or *mawālī*). However, he also had a broader range of alliances elsewhere in Iraq and western Iran. Confronted at Kufa by 'Abd Allah b. 'Umar's forces, Ibn Mu'awiya headed east, gathering support at al-Mada'in/Ctesiphon, and then at towns in the highlands of Jibal, Khuzistan and Fars, to the east and south of Iraq, where he appointed his two brothers as governors, collected taxes and minted dirhams to pay his supporters. He was joined by relatives from the Banu Hashim, including, for a time, his cousins, the future Abbasid caliph, Abu Ja'far b. Muhammad (r. 754–75) and Abu Ja'far's uncles 'Abd Allah b. 'Ali (d. 764) and 'Isa b. 'Ali (d. 782). Thus, the core of Ibn Mu'awiya's support was a broadly pro-Hashimite alliance of 'southern' and non-Arab Kufans, alongside some of his own Hashimite relatives. However, most of his military forces were likely drawn from the predominantly 'Persian', and perhaps also 'Kurdish', populations of Jibal, Khuzistan and Fars. Indeed, later sources attribute to Ibn Mu'awiya and his followers religious ideas that were seen as heretical from the point of view of their Muslim authors; probably they reflect the religious traditions of the Aramaean, Persian and Kurdish population of Iraq and Iran. After his defeat by forces loyal to Marwan II in c. 747, Ibn Mu'awiya fled north to Khurasan, where similar alliances between local Khurasanis and southern Arab forces had been forged.[30]

---

[29] Tabari, II, 1897–1916, 1937–41, 1943–9. On previous Shaybani resistance, see above, Ch. 6, pp. 132–3, and Robinson, *Empire*, 121–6, 147–8; Hagemann and Verkinderen, 'Kharijism', 496–7, 503–9.

[30] Tabari, II, 1879–87, 1947–8, 1976–81, III, 4. Cf. Khalifa, 244–5. For the death of 'Isa, see Ya'qubi, II, 480. On Ibn Mu'awiya, see Teresa Bernheimer, 'The Revolt of 'Abd Allah

The 'Abbasid Revolution'

In 745 or 746, Marwan II is said to have sent a letter to the governor of Khurasan, Nasr b. Sayyar. In it, he warns the governor of the danger presented by a rebel movement that had gained widespread support among the non-Arab population of the province.

> The appearance of this 'sprouting-plant' in the territory of Khurasan has been something by which God wishes to humiliate those ungrateful for his blessing and those ignorant of his truth. An evil man brought this about, a man to whom evil men responded. When he saw that the Arabs were preoccupied among themselves he seized the opportunity of their preoccupation with the enmity of some of them towards others of them ... He defamed the Holy Book with lies about it and God's Messenger with a call for loyalty to his descendants ...
>
> Do not abandon decisive action because they have gained the upper hand over you, and because of the greatness of their numbers while you are few ... Remember of what their recent experience comprises: worshipping fires and idols ... They have summoned you to Islam in ignorance of it and call upon you in the name of its truth while abandoning it ...[31]

There are some problems with the authenticity of the letter; it may have been composed after the fact by a historian describing the revolution. Nonetheless, authentic or no, it sets out the situation in Khurasan in the mid-740s. The 'evil man' who has summoned former fire-worshippers to the cause of the Prophet's descendants is never named in the letter but appears to be Abu Muslim al-Khurasani (d. 755). At some point after 744, Abu Muslim had become the leader of the Khurasani rebel movement calling for rule by the Prophet's family. The movement in Khurasan drew much of its support from among the non-Arab population of the province – the letter's former worshippers of fires and idols – but it also drew upon resentment of Marwanid rule among the mixed populations of Marw oasis. Connections between

---

b. Muʿawiya, AH 127–130: A Reconsideration Through the Coinage', *BSOAS* 69 (2006), 381–93; Crone, *Nativist Prophets*, 92–5; *EI3*, "Abd Allah b. Muʿawiya' (A. Borrut); Majied Robinson, 'Qurashi Marriage and the Roots of Revolt: the Rebellion of 'Abd Allah b. Muʿawiya, 744–747', in Andrew Marsham (ed.), *The Umayyad World* (London and New York, 2021), 518–38. On slaves and *mawālī*, see Box Text, pp. 169–70. On Aramaeans, Persians and Kurds, see below, Ch. 11, pp. 277–8.

[31] Ihsan ʿAbbas (ed.), *ʿAbd al-Hamid b. Yahya al-Katib wa-ma tabqa min rasaʾilihi wa-rasaʾil Salim Abi al-ʿAlaʾ* (Amman, 1988), 89–92, 198–201; Wadad al-Qadi, 'The Earliest "Nabita" and the Paradigmatic "Nawabit"', *Studia Islamica* 78 (1993), 32–7; Agha, *Revolution*, 200–6 (the translation partially follows Agha, *Revolution*, 202).

supporters of the claims of the Prophet's family in Kufa and their supporters in Khurasan dated back to at least the 720s, from when sporadic efforts to suppress them are noted in the sources. Marwan II's letter to Nasr suggests a new urgency and an awareness of the danger posed to their rule.[32]

These fears were fully realised in June 747, when Abu Muslim publicly declared rebellion against Marwan II. His timing took advantage of the turmoil across the caliphate and locally in Khurasan. The Marwanids' governor in Khurasan, Nasr b. Sayyar, and his predominantly 'northern', or Mudari, supporters, had been driven out of his capital of Marw by a rebellion by al-Kirmani and his 'southern', Azdi, following. Attempts at a truce between the two groups had ended in failure and Nasr's public execution of al-Kirmani; al-Kirmani's son and his 'southern' supporters then joined the newly declared rebellion. By January 748 at the latest (the sources give various contradictory dates), Abu Muslim had taken control of the capital at Marw and the Marwanids' governor Nasr b. Sayyar was fleeing west, pursued by Abu Muslim's army; Nasr died in December 748, aged eighty-five, at Sawa (near modern Tehran), on the road west towards Iraq.[33]

The Khurasani rebels made rapid progress across the Iranian plateau and into Iraq. Abu Muslim had appointed Qahtaba b. Shabib – the grandson of one of 'Ali's commanders in his conflict with Mu'awiya – as the general in command of the main army that opposed Marwan II's forces. Qahtaba had taken a route west across the north of Iran towards Iraq, using the Iranian desert to the south to protect his left flank. He defeated two armies loyal to Marwan II en route before turning south towards the city of Isfahan, in the highlands above southern Iraq. Near Isfahan, in the winter of 748–9 Qahtaba encountered the Umayyad army of 'Amir b. Dubara. Ibn Dubara had been sent with troops from Syria and the Jazira against Ibn Mu'awiya and then been diverted by Marwan II's commander in Iraq against this new threat from Khurasan. After prolonged manoeuvring for position, the armies met in battle at Jabaliq in March 749. The Umayyad army was routed and Ibn Dubara slain. Qahtaba's army then turned north to besiege Nihawand,

---

[32] For a summary of the events of the 'Abbasid Revolution', with further references, see *EI3*, 'Abbasid Revolution' (E. Daniel). On the unusual demographics of Marw and Khurasan, see de la Vaissière, "Abbasid Revolution'.

[33] On the progress of Abu Muslim's rebellion and the fate of Nasr, see *EI²*, 'Nasr b. Sayyar' (C. E. Bosworth); *EI3*, 'Abbasid Revolution' (E. Daniel). For the details of the failed truce between Nasr and al-Kirmani, see Tabari, II, 1970–6, 1984–5. For the names of some of Nasr's leading allies and supporters, whose mixed ethnic backgrounds reflect the demographics in Khurasan, see Tabari, II, 1690–1, 1920, 1970. Cf. al-Tabari, II, 1544.

capturing the fortress city that guarded the route into Iraq in June of the same year.[34]

News of the defeats of the Umayyad armies in Iran provoked widespread revolts in Iraq against Marwan II's authority. Marwan II's governor there, Yazid b. 'Umar b. Hubayra, was unable to suppress these insurrections as he gathered his forces to oppose Qahtaba at the old Sasanian capital of al-Mada'in/Ctesiphon. However, Qahtaba and the Khurasani army decided to avoid a direct confrontation and instead crossed the waterways of the Tigris and Euphrates and their canals to the north and west, circumventing Ibn Hubayra to make an attack on Kufa, about 100km to the south. Ibn Hubayra pursued him but was defeated in a surprise attack, and Kufa – never a centre of loyalty to Syrian and Umayyad rule – opened its gates to the rebels in August 749.[35]

Shortly before the fall of Kufa, Qahtaba had drowned in a river crossing and so it was his son, Hasan b. Qahtaba who presided over the surrender of the city. There, Hasan contacted activists who had long been preparing for the overthrow of the Umayyad dynasty and the coming of a member of the family of the Prophet. In the negotiations that followed, it seems that the majority of Kufans who favoured a leader directly descended from 'Ali were outmanoeuvred by Abu Muslim and his allies, who were set on an Abbasid cousin of 'Ali and the Prophet. While later Abbasid-era narratives connect the Abbasid family with the Khurasani rebel movement from the 720s, it is likely that in fact Abu Muslim had only engaged with them in the mid-740s. About three or four months after the fall of Kufa, at the end of 749 or the beginning of 750, Abu l-'Abbas b. Muhammad, a great-great-grandson of one of the Prophet's uncles, was publicly proclaimed caliph at the congregational mosque.[36]

Marwan II now prepared to meet the rebel army. Already in August 749, Marwan II had sent forces into northern Iraq, where they had been defeated. Following this defeat, he had resolved to gather all his supporters from Syria and northern Iraq and camp on the river Zab, near Mosul. Meanwhile, his Iraqi governor, Ibn Hubayra, had retreated to the garrison of Wasit, between Kufa and Basra, which he had already prepared for siege, and so the Umayyad forces were split between Mesopotamia and central Iraq. Abu l-'Abbas sent two of

---

[34] On Qahtaba and his military successes in Iran, see *EI*², 'Kahtaba' (M. Sharon); Moshe Sharon, *Revolt: The Social and Military Aspects of the 'Abbasid Revolution* (Jerusalem, 1990), 180–205. But on the composition and ideology of the army and the rebel movement, see *EI3*, 'Abbasid Revolution' (E. Daniel), with further references.

[35] On Qahtaba in Iraq, see Sharon, *Social and Military Aspects*, 205–18.

[36] On Abu Muslim and the Abbasids, see Agha, *Revolution*, 67–75; *EI3*, 'Abu Muslim' (S. Agha).

his Abbasid relatives against these two remaining Umayyad armies; against Marwan II he sent an uncle, ʿAbd Allah b. ʿAli, and – after first sending Hasan b. Qahtaba – he then sent his brother, Abu Jaʿfar, against Ibn Hubayra. On the Zab, at a site called Tal Kashaf, Marwan II's army was routed in January 750 and he fled west, towards Syria. When news of the defeat reached Wasit, Ibn Hubayra sought a guarantee of security from his besiegers and surrendered. The agreement, which was said to have been signed by the new caliph's brother himself was immediately betrayed, and Ibn Hubayra and many of his army and companions were put to death. Meanwhile, Marwan II fled first to his capital of Harran and then through Syria, where he was unable to muster enough support to resist ʿAbd Allah b. ʿAli's army. A series of massacres of the Umayyad family and their allies followed, with the executed corpses publicly displayed; at Damascus the bodies of former Umayyad leaders were even exhumed from their tombs and hung on gibbets. Marwan II himself was overtaken at Busir, near the Fayyum oasis in Upper Egypt, in early August 750; he and his family were killed.[37]

After Marwan II: the Beginning of Abbasid Rule

With the defeat of the Umayyad field armies at Jabaliq, the Zab and Wasit in 749–50, and the killing of Marwan II in the summer of 750, the new Abbasid and Khurasani elite was in a strong position to achieve power over the whole empire. However, the consolidation of the Abbasid victory was a prolonged process, and there was significant resistance from elements of the Umayyad elite in Marwan II's former heartlands in northern Syria, the Jazira and Armenia.[38] Marwan II's governor of Qinnasrin, Abu l-Ward al-Kilabi, joined forces with a great-grandson of Muʿawiya named Abu Muhammad. Abu Muhammad claimed to be the Sufyani – a millenarian figure who would defeat the Abbasids. Troops from Hims and Palmyra joined the revolt and won initial success against the Abbasids before they were defeated and dispersed.

---

[37] Sharon, *Social and Military Aspects*, 207–12. On the battle at the Zab and Tal Kashaf, see Kennedy, *Armies*, 50, citing Abu Zakariyya Yazid b. Muhammad al-Azdi, *Taʾrikh Mawsil*, ed. ʿAli Habiba (Cairo, 1967), 126–31. On the flight of Marwan II and his death, see Tabari, III, 44–51. On the massacres of the Umayyads and their allies, see Chase F. Robinson, 'The Violence of the Abbasid Revolution', in Yasir Suleiman and Adel Al-Abdul Jader (eds), *Living Islamic History: Studies in Honour of Professor Carole Hillenbrand* (Edinburgh, 2010), 226–51. On Ibn Hubayra, the siege of Wasit and the guarantee of security, see Amikam Elad, 'The Siege of Wasit (132/749): Some Aspects of ʿAbbasid and ʿAlid Relations at the Beginning of ʿAbbasid Rule', in Moshe Sharon (ed.), *Studies in Islamic History and Civilisation: in Honour of Professor David Ayalon* (Jerusalem and Leiden, 1986), 59–90.

[38] Paul M. Cobb, *White Banners: Contention in ʿAbbasid Syria, 750–880* (Albany, 2001), 50–1.

A nephew of Abu Muhammad briefly continued the revolt at Aleppo before he himself was defeated. At Harran, Muhammad b. Maslama, a son of the frontier commander Maslama b. 'Abd al-Malik and a grandson of the caliph 'Abd al-Malik, led a revolt before fleeing upon news of the defeat of Abu l-Ward. Further north, Ishaq b. Muslim al-'Uqayli, Marwan II's governor of Armenia, took charge of Umayyad supporters at the frontier town of Sumaysat (modern south-east Turkey). Upon his surrender, he was given a safe conduct and joined the Abbasid army; a grandson of the caliph Hisham, Aban b. Mu'awiya – no doubt conscious that as an Umayyad he would not receive similar favourable treatment – continued to resist until he was captured and killed in 751.[39]

Resistance and revolt by former allies of the Umayyads continued into the 750s but attempts to restore Umayyad rule faded away. Rather, the Syrian revolts of the mid-750s had the character of attempts by former Umayyad troops to negotiate a place within the new Abbasid dispensation. After 755 they were incorporated into the Abbasid armies, and the Syrian revolts ended for more than a generation.[40] The Banu Umayya and their Syrian allies had been deposed from their position at the top of the Muslim empire; in their place was now a family from another branch of Quraysh, the Banu 'Abbas, backed by their armies from Khurasan.

---

[39] On these revolts, see Cobb, *White Banners*, 43–51, 67–82. On Muhammad b. Maslama, see Ya'qubi, II, 425; Robinson, 'Violence', 234. For Abu Muhammad's genealogy, see Ya'qubi, II, 425.

[40] Cobb, *White Banners*, 51, 75–82. For a late example from Egypt, in 783–5, see Kindi, 123–31.

PART III
ECOLOGY, ECONOMY AND SOCIETY IN UMAYYAD TIMES

Part III Introduction

In this third section, the perspective is broadened to look beyond the dynamics of conflict and competition within networks of military and political power. Interactions between the majority of the empire's population and its new ruling classes and other longer-term processes of social and economic change are the concerns of its three chapters. Chapter Ten begins with the environmental context, surveying the 8,000km-wide band of territory between North Africa and al-Andalus in the west and Sogdia and Sind in the east which the Umayyads' armies occupied or contested. From there, it turns to the economic foundations of empire – land use and resources, settlement patterns in the towns and countryside, and commerce and exchange. While there are many deep continuities in the economic and social life of the Mediterranean and the Middle East, the Umayyad era emerges as a turning point, when new and lasting economic and social formations took shape.

Chapter Eleven turns to the social significance of religious community and the impact of the conquests and the formation of the empire on the religious groups among the conquered populations. Religious belief and practice had become crucial markers of belonging and political affiliation in Late Antiquity. This was perpetuated and developed by the Arabian conquerors, whose leaders saw themselves as agents of God's rule on earth on the basis of which they made 'a covenantal pact' (*'ahd* or *bay'a*) with military allies and supporters, while tax-paying populations received covenantal 'guaranteed protection' (*dhimma*). With the end of Roman and Sasanian state power, new relationships were negotiated between religious leaders and the Arabian conquerors. In many cases, this led to competition for patronage by the new rulers as well as an expanded role for religious leaders in the context of the transformation of the structures of state power.

Chapter Twelve addresses structures of governance, organisational power and taxation. The military administration established by the conquering armies concentrated power in the hands of the armies' commanders (*umarā'*, sing. *amīr*), among whom the most senior became the leading political figures in the territories they had conquered (whence the other translation of *amīr*, as 'governor'). Accordingly, the chapter begins with a survey of the geography of the governorships that developed from the conquests, before turning to the governor's role in communication, upholding law and order, and taxation and the payment of the army. The Marwanid era saw recurrent efforts to extract greater revenue from Egypt and Iraq to support the war with Rome and the Syrian troops who were increasingly deployed to control the provinces. At the same time, a trajectory of change from a religiously articulated, but devolved, Arabian 'conquest society' to an empire whose ruling elites asserted their own status in recognisably 'Islamic' terms can be traced. The last decades of Umayyad rule are distinctive for the new uses for Arabic writing at elite levels of governance and the predominance of Muslims in the upper levels of the administration of the core provinces of the empire.

10

Resources, Settlement Patterns and Commerce

While there are many deep continuities in the economic and social life of the Mediterranean and the Middle East, some profound changes began or accelerated in the Umayyad era. A new military class, combining migrants from the Arabian Peninsula and pastoralists from the Syrian steppe reshaped both the landscape and the economy. New towns were founded, and the tax revenues of the urban hinterlands were redirected to new ends. The political unification of the Roman and Sasanian monetary zones and the emergence of Arabic as a lingua franca began to stimulate new commercial activity, just as the demands of the new imperial elites also provoked new patterns of trade or expanded older ones. Some of those same elites became wealthy landowners, and many acquired wealth in bullion, livestock and slaves, taken as loot and tribute on the frontiers. Both these spoils of war and attitudes to slavery, domestic life and inheritance among the new elite prompted high demand for enslaved women, shaping both the frontier economies and demographic patterns in the new cities.[1]

This chapter begins with a brief overview of the physical geography of the lands ruled and contested by the Umayyads. This is followed by an assessment of some of the large-scale climate fluctuations that affected Africa and West Eurasia between the beginning of the sixth and the middle of the eighth century. These climatic effects impacted patterns of disease, agriculture and the economy and so are an important context for the Arabian conquests and subsequent social and economic change. These latter questions of human geography and economic change are the subject of the final parts of the chapter, which begins with the material resources of the empire, before turning to patterns of settlement and commerce.

---

[1] Arezou Azad, 'Living Happily Ever After: Fraternal Polyandry, Taxes and "the House" in Early Islamic Bactria', *BSOAS* 79 (2016), 40; Robinson, *Marriage*, 108–11.

The Physical Geography of the Umayyad Empire

At its greatest extent, in the 720s and 730s, the Umayyad Empire spanned much of the subtropical zone of North Africa and West Eurasia (see Map 10.1). The steppe regions of Arabia, North Africa, southern and eastern Iran were the main corridors of the first conquests, but the Arabian armies extended their control well beyond them, into the neighbouring highland and forest regions. Lowland zones irrigated by the major river systems of the Middle East were the wealthiest arable regions. Some highland and forest zones also supported significant settled agriculture, while in others pastoralism predominated, as it did in the steppes.

In the long strip of territory around the southern Mediterranean, there were a series of three regions with similar climates and ecologies: al-Andalus, the coasts and highlands of the Maghrib and Ifriqiya, the highlands of Syria and the coasts of Anatolia. Their subtropical, Mediterranean climate has been characterised during recent millennia by cooler, wetter weather in the winter, with moisture carried into the region by westerlies from the Atlantic, and hot, dry summers, moderated by the heat capacity of the water in the Mediterranean Sea.

In contrast to the coasts, the inland regions of North Africa, as well as most of Libya, Egypt and the Negev are deserts. They lie to the south of the Atlantic westerlies and are dominated instead by the northern African airmass. Consequently, they are hot and arid, with low rainfall and high summer temperatures, making cultivation difficult or impossible in most places. Further east, the Arabian Peninsula and the Syrian Desert are both part of the same arid zone.[2] In all these regions, extensive steppes between the desert and fertile zones have supported pastoralists, as have some of the highlands. However, the highlands of South Arabia and Oman catch monsoon rains in the summer months, and South Arabia also experiences significant winter rainfall, allowing for settled agriculture on a scale not possible elsewhere in the region.[3]

In the central lands of the empire, the steppes and deserts of Egypt and Iraq are interrupted by the Nile, Euphrates and Tigris. These huge rivers transformed the otherwise arid lands around them into some of the most fertile in the late antique world. All three terminated in swampy marshlands, navigable only by boat – the Nile Delta in Egypt and the Arvand or Shatt al-'Arab, Bata'ih al-Kufa, and other marshlands in southern Iraq.[4]

---

[2] Arie S. Issar, *Climate Changes during the Holocene and their Impact on Hydrological Systems* (Cambridge, 2003), 1–3.
[3] Burns et al., 'A 780-year Annually Resolved Record', 1–2. Cf. Magee, *Archaeology*, 25.
[4] Peter Verkinderen, *Waterways of Iraq and Iran in the Early Islamic Period: Changing Rivers and Landscapes of the Mesopotamian Plain* (London, 2015), 29–109.

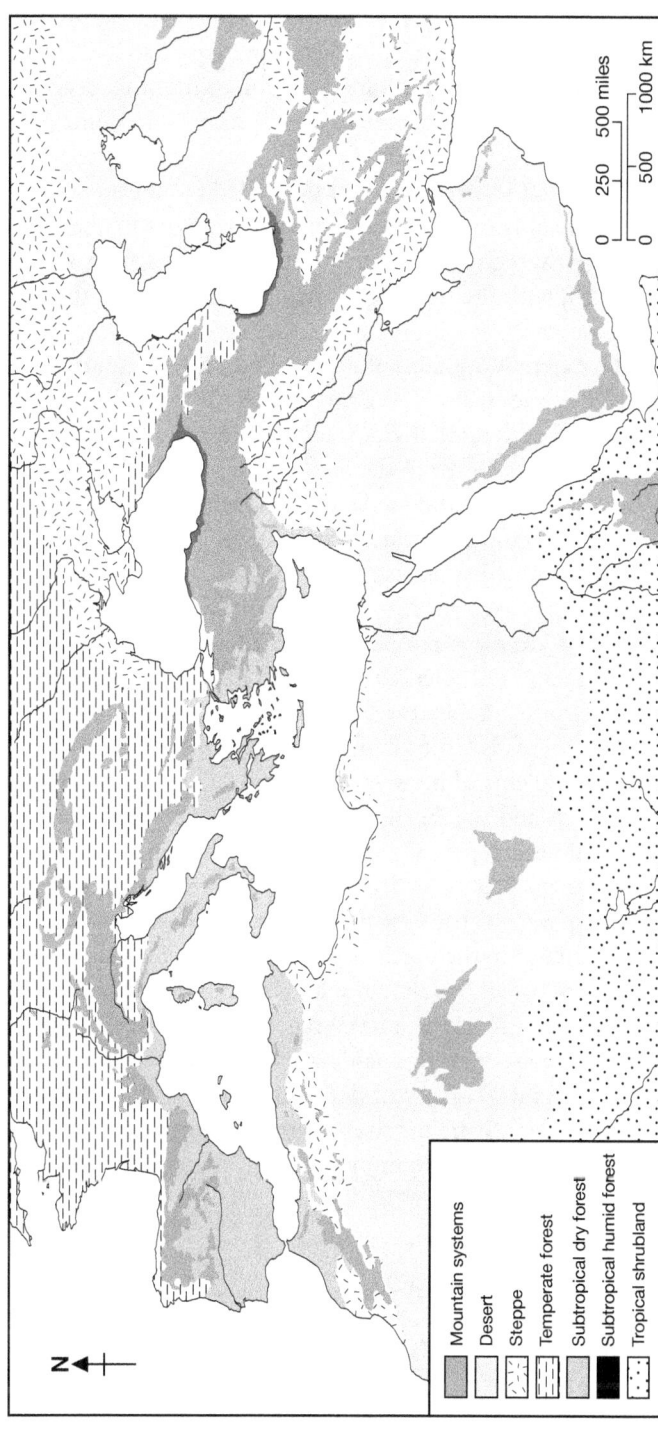

Map 10.1 The main ecological zones of the Mediterranean and West Eurasia. Based on Food and Agriculture Organization of the United Nations, *Global Ecological Zones for FAO Forest Reporting: 2010 Update*, 'Forest Resources Assessment Working Paper 179' (Rome, 2012), 15.

Before the dam-building schemes of the twentieth century, the rains in East Africa from the West African Monsoon caused the Egyptian Nile's water levels to rise suddenly by many metres in the summer months, peaking in August in the south of Egypt and September in the north.[5] In contrast, the Euphrates and Tigris rivers that flow out of Anatolia into Syria, Mesopotamia and Iraq are fed by the steadier rainfall from the Mediterranean westerlies, which fall on the highlands of Anatolia and northern Syria in the winter. Hence, these rivers flow at their fullest in the winter and early spring, between November and March, with the water levels being determined by the tracks of airflow from the west.[6]

East of Iraq, the Zagros mountains of western Iran rise to heights of more than 2,000m above the Iraqi plain. The Zagros catch the westerlies from the Mediterranean, which bring rainfall from autumn to early spring. To the north, the Caspian Sea is cut off from the rest of Iran by the mountains that run along its southern coast, creating a distinctive fertile zone, characterised by higher levels of precipitation. To the north and west are the highlands of the Anatolian Plateau and the mountains of Armenia and Azerbaijan. The Anatolian highlands and western Armenia have a climate influenced by Atlantic westerlies and are more temperate than the northern and eastern highland zones of Armenia and Azerbaijan, though the highlands in all three regions have freezing winter temperatures and high levels of snowfall.[7]

East beyond the Zagros lies the Iranian plateau, which is an arid, semi-desert environment, at heights of between 1,000 and 3,000m, with two large salt deserts in the north and south: the Dasht-i Kavir and the Dasht-i Lut. Where farming is possible, it depends on irrigation which channels the run-off from the mountains at the plateau's edges. Khurasan, in the north-east, has a productive plain fed by water carried by underground tunnels (*qanawāt*, sing. *qanāt*) from the mountains to the north. South-west of the plateau, the highlands of Fars are watered by winter rainfall, and in much of this region productive dry farming is possible. Kirman and Makran, to the south, are more arid. Sistan, in the south-east part of the Iranian plateau, is separated from the rest of the highland zone by the Dasht-i Lut desert and the last highlands of the southern Zagros, in the west. Here the river Helmand carries water out of the mountains of Afghanistan into the swampy inland Helmand Delta, which can

---

[5] *SaMS*, 18–19.
[6] Heidi M. Cullen and Peter B. de Menocal, 'North Atlantic influence on Tigris–Euphrates Streamflow', *International Journal of Climatology* 20 (2000), 853–63.
[7] Reza Modarres and Ali Sarhadi, 'Rainfall Trends Analysis of Iran in the Last Half of the Twentieth Century', *Journal of Geophysical Research: Atmospheres* 114.D3 (2009), 2156–2202; *E.Ir.* 'Climate' (E. Ehlers).

support intensive agriculture. The rest of Sistan is arid, with very high summer temperatures.[8]

To the north and east, the Afghan mountains rise to heights of more than 5,000m north of Kabul. There, the winter temperatures fall well below zero and the summer temperatures can be very high, with twenty-first-century maximums in Kabul at over 30° Celsius. In most of the Afghan highlands, rain and snow fall mainly in winter, although the eastern passes down to the Indus plain receive summer monsoon rains.[9] To the north of Iran and Afghanistan are the southern reaches of the Qara Qum and Qizil Qum ('Black Sand' and 'Red Sand') Deserts, which are divided by the river Oxus. In the southern extensions of these deserts irrigated farming is made possible by the presence of the Marw inland delta. To the east, the river Oxus begins in the Tukharistan valley (ancient Bactria), formed by tributaries that flow south and west out of the steep ravines of the Hindu Kush. These tributaries, as well as rivers flowing north out of Afghanistan, support agriculture in the semi-arid valley, where average summer temperatures have until recently peaked in the mid-to-high thirties, with winter averages at or just below zero. Tukharistan is divided from Sogdia, to its north-west, by the spur of the Buttaman Mountains. In Sogdia, the river Zarafshan flows into inland deltas at the southern end of the Qizil Qum, supporting intensive irrigation agriculture in the otherwise arid plain.

South-east of the Afghan mountains, in Sind (modern Baluchistan), lies the Indus Delta. The Indus is a fourth major Asian river, which floods with the Asian monsoon in the summer months, carrying water from the Karakoram, the Himalayas and the Hindu Kush out to the Arabian Sea. Like the Nile, Tigris and Euphrates, the Indus renders fertile what would otherwise be an arid region, with a modern summer average high temperature in the low forties, and the most recent maximums – inflated by modern anthropogenic global heating – in the low fifties.[10]

---

[8] Modarres and Sarhadi, 'Rainfall'; *E.Ir.* 'Climate' (E. Ehlers).
[9] Qurban Aliyar and Morteza Esmailnejad, 'Assessment of the Change of Trend in Precipitation over Afghanistan in 1979–2019', *IDŐJÁRÁS – Quarterly Journal of the Hungarian Meteorological Service* 126 (2022), 185–201. Anonymous, 'Afghanistan's Climate', *Swedish Committee for Afghanistan*, <https://swedishcommittee.org/afghanistan/climate/> (last accessed 28 June 2023); Anonymous, 'Average Temperature in Kabul', *Weather Spark*, <https://weatherspark.com/y/106802/Average-Weather-in-Kabul-Afghanistan-Year-Round> (last accessed 28 June 2023). (Average maxima and minima elsewhere are also from *Weather Spark*.)
[10] Rahmat Tunio, 'It Seems This Heat Will Take Our Lives', *The Guardian*, 25 May 2022, <https://www.theguardian.com/environment/2022/may/25/it-seems-this-heat-will-take-our-lives-pakistan-city-fearful-jacobabad-after-hitting-51c> (last accessed 27 May 2022).

Large-scale Climate Variation in the Umayyad Period

Three large-scale variations in the climate and weather systems of the Mediterranean and Middle East are thought to have coincided with the Umayyad era. Two were fluctuations in the main weather systems that determine precipitation and river flows in the Mediterranean, East Africa and the Middle East – the North Atlantic Oscillation and the West African Monsoon. The third, and the best understood, is addressed in detail in the Text Box in Chapter Two – the so-called 'Late Antique Little Ice Age', which affected temperatures across the whole region acutely and severely between c. 540 and c. 560 and longer-term and more mildly until c. 750.[11]

The North Atlantic Oscillation, or NAO, is a long-term fluctuation, over decades, in the difference between the low pressure over Iceland and the high pressure over the Azores. When the difference between the two pressure systems is small and the NAO is weak, westerlies from the Atlantic Ocean tend to track south, leading to higher rainfall in North Africa and the Mediterranean. When the difference is great, and the NAO is strong, Central and Northern Europe receives more precipitation, and North Africa and the Mediterranean less. In about 550 CE, the North Atlantic Oscillation began to strengthen, after a fifty-year weak period. It reached a peak in c. 600 but remained strong thereafter, declining slightly only after 750. Thus, the period after 600 probably witnessed more consistently dry conditions on the coasts of North Africa and the Levant.[12]

East African rainfall, some of which feeds the river Nile, is affected by the strength of the West African Monsoon. The evidence from the silt in the lakes of East Africa, records of the Nile flood levels recorded in later Arabic sources, and the evidence of *History of the Patriarchs of Alexandria*, all suggest that the West African Monsoon was weakening after 550 CE and that Nile flood

---

[11] See further on the 'Little Ice Age' Box Text above, Ch. 2, pp. 51–3.
[12] For the shift in the westerlies, see Matthew D. Jones, Neil C. Roberts et al., 'A High-resolution Late Holocene Lake Isotope Record from Turkey and Links to North Atlantic and Monsoon Climate', *Geology* 34 (2006), 361–4; Lee B. Drake, 'Changes in North Atlantic Oscillation Drove Population Migrations and the Collapse of the Western Roman Empire', *Nature: Scientific Reports* 7:1227 (2017), 1–7. For drier conditions in the Zagros, the Levant and the Dead Sea in the early Islamic period, see Issar, *Climate Changes*, 27–8; Michael Decker, *Tilling the Hateful Earth: Agricultural Production and Trade in the Late Antique East* (Oxford, 2009), 9. The historical sources describe high flood levels in the Tigris and the Euphrates in the early seventh century: Hugh Kennedy, 'Feeding the Five Hundred Thousand: Cities and Agriculture in Early Islamic Mesopotamia', *Iraq* 73 (2011), 179. Also on Iraq, see Baladhuri, *Futuh*, 292–3; Verkinderen, *Waterways*, 52–5.

levels were erratic and sometimes unusually low in the first centuries of Islam.[13] Further east, the southern mountains of Afghanistan depend on the Indian Ocean Monsoon, the detailed history of which is not yet well understood. Oman, where there was an acute drought in the early-to-mid sixth century, is also affected by this monsoon.[14]

While it is no longer convincing to see the Arabian conquests and the history of the Umayyad Empire as a simple consequence of environmental change, climatic variations did have economic and social effects.[15] Above all, the conditions that supported the spread of the Justinianic Plague had a major indirect impact.[16] In contrast, the stabler and warmer, albeit still relatively cool, temperatures of the seventh and early eighth century were probably not in themselves of great significance. Conversely, the strengthening of the North Atlantic Oscillation, and the weakening of the West African Monsoon both probably had increasing impacts in the seventh and eighth centuries. In the era of the Arabian conquests and the Umayyad Empire, crop yields in Egypt may have been more erratic than in the periods before and after. It is also possible that southern Syria and northern Arabia, as well as parts of North Africa, would have been drier than in previous and later times.

Demography, Land Use and Resources

The population of the Umayyad Empire in the eighth century may have been similar to that of its contemporary eastern neighbour, Tang China, or the

---

[13] For the West African Monsoon, see Timothy Michael Shanahan, 'West African Monsoon Variability from a High-resolution Paleolimnological Record (Lake Bosumtwi, Ghana)', PhD Dissertation, University of Arizona (2006), esp. 251–2. For the Nile, see Rushdi Said, *The River Nile: Geology, Hydrology and Utilization* (Oxford, 1993), esp. 152, 155, 162; William H. Quinn, 'A Study of Southern Oscillation-related Climatic Activity for AD 622–1900 Incorporating Nile River Flood Data', in Henry F. Diaz and Vera Markgraf (eds), *El Niño: Historical and Paleoclimatic Aspects of the Southern Oscillation* (Cambridge, 1992), 119–49; Klaus Fraedrich, Jianmin Jiang et al., 'Multiscale Detection of Abrupt Climate Changes: Application to River Nile Flood Levels', *International Journal of Climatology* 17 (1997), 1301–15. Cf. *History of the Patriarchs*, I, xviii, 97–8 for three years of drought, followed by plague. See further, on famines and dearths in Egypt, Phil Booth and Andrew Marsham, 'Egyptian Revolts', forthcoming.

[14] For the Indian Ocean Monsoon, see Y. T. Hong, B. Hong et al., 'Inverse Phase Oscillations between the East Asian and Indian Ocean Summer Monsoons during the Last 12000 Years and Paleo-El Niño', *Earth and Planetary Science Letters* 231 (2005), 337–46. For evidence of an acute early sixth-century drought in South Arabia, see Fleitmann et al., 'Droughts'.

[15] See, for example, the sceptical comments of Fred M. Donner about older scholarship in his 'The Islamic Conquests', in Yousef Choueiri (ed.), *A Companion to the History of the Middle East* (Oxford, 2005), 34, with further references.

[16] See above, Box Text, pp. 51–3.

population of the Roman Empire at its peak in the second century, at perhaps around forty or fifty million people. However, such comparative and numerical assessments remain guesswork supported only by limited archaeological and historical data.[17] The distribution of the population followed the availability of water and climatic conditions for farming – the most densely populated regions of North Africa and south-west Asia were around the Tigris and Euphrates in central and southern Iraq, the Nile Valley and Delta in Egypt, Syria, Africa Procunsularis/Ifriqiya and Khurasan. Concentrations of population were also found in Khuzistan, the Jazira, al-Andalus, Fars, Kirman, Sogdia, Tukharistan, Farghana and Sind. As in all pre-modern societies, most people lived in the countryside, with towns and cities accounting for only a small percentage of the total population. In contrast, the highland, steppe and desert regions were much less densely populated, but some of these less fertile spaces were vast and so supported a large total number of people, thinly distributed.

There is some evidence from the Roman Empire that the population of Syria peaked in about 550, or perhaps a little later, before going into decline. Similar patterns may be discernible in Roman North Africa and in Sasanian Iraq. These correlate with the acute phase of the 'Late Antique Little Ice Age' between *c.* 540 and 560, and the onset of the rapid strengthening of the NAO, as well as with the impact of the first waves of the 'Justinianic Plague', which was endemic throughout the Umayyad period.[18] While the mortality figures in the chronicles cannot be taken literally, they are indicative of severity. Michael the Syrian (d. 1199), who preserves mid-eighth century material, says 'a third of the people of the world were wiped off the face of the earth' by

---

[17] McEvedy and Jones, *Atlas*, 126–8, estimated more conservatively, at *c.* thirty million inhabitants of the eighth-century empire; cf. Jean-Noël Biraben, 'Essai sur l'évolution du nombre des hommes', *Population* 34 (1979), 13–25, who arrives at similar estimates. The more recent Blankinship, *End of the Jihad*, 273–4, suggests the population of the Umayyad Empire may have been greater. For a ninth-century source that gives the population of Upper Egypt as over five million, see Zychowicz-Coghill, *First Arabic Annals*, 54 and n. 197.

[18] Jeremy Johns, 'The *Longue Durée*: State and Settlement Strategies in Southern Transjordan across the Islamic Centuries', in E. L. Rogan and T. Tell (eds), *Village, Steppe and State: The Social Origins of Modern Jordan* (London, 1994), 1–31; Jairus Banaji, *Agrarian Change in Late Antiquity: Gold, Labour, and Aristocratic Dominance* (Oxford, 2001), 20–1; Decker, *Tilling*, 21–7. Cf. Jodi Magness, *The Archaeology of the Settlement of Early Islamic Palestine* (Winona Lake, 2003), who is sceptical of population decline. On the plague, see Lawrence I. Conrad, 'Arabic Plague Chronologies and Treatises: Social and Historical Factors in the Formation of a Literary Genre', *Studia Islamica* 54 (1981), 51–93; Lawrence I. Conrad, '*Ta'un* and *Waba'* Conceptions of Plague and Pestilence in Early Islam', *JESHO* 25 (1982), 268–307; Little (ed.), *Plague*. For the pairing of 'fighting and plague' (*al-ṭa'n wa-l-ṭā'ūn*) in an Arabic source, see Baladhuri, *Futuh*, 213.

plague at the turn of the seventh and eighth centuries;[19] a medieval Andalusi source of uncertain date says 'half or more of the population' of al-Andalus died in the plague of 709;[20] Dionysius of Tell Mahre (d. 845) has 100,000 people dying in the Jazira in 743–4, an episode corroborated in the Arabic sources for Syria. Basra, in the marshy lands of southern Iraq, also appears to have been severely impacted.[21] Given the frequency of mentions of plague in the sources and the high mortality rates they describe, plague very likely exacerbated the agricultural labour shortages in the Umayyad period that were also driven by taxation policy.[22]

In most regions, the cycle of the agricultural calendar depended upon winter rainfall, with harvesting in the summer and ploughing and planting in the autumn; in some more arid regions farmers practised 'double-cropping', with two crops in spring and in autumn, using irrigation techniques fed by the winter rains.[23] The major exceptions to this pattern were Egypt, South Arabia and the Indus, where the summer monsoons supported farming. 'Dry farming', that is, farming dependent only on rainfall, was possible only in the few places where rainfall was consistently greater than 400mm per year.[24] In Khuzistan and Khurasan, *qanawāt* carried the run-off from the mountains into agricultural lands.[25] Similar run-off irrigation was needed in much of North Africa, Syria, the Negev, Iran and the more fertile parts of Arabia, where dams, dikes, terracing and other techniques were used to channel water. By far the most agriculturally productive regions were the flood plains and deltas of the Nile, Euphrates and Tigris. These parts of Iraq and Egypt were known in Umayyad times as Sawad – 'black earth' – after their highly fertile alluvial soils. In both regions, farming depended upon specialist, large-scale irrigation engineering. In Iraq, the management of the irrigation system had been undertaken by the Sasanian kings; the wealthiest members of the new Arabian elite took over this role. Whereas major landowners accrued surpluses from their estates, most

---

[19] Michael G. Morony, 'For Whom Does the Writer Write? The First Bubonic Plague Pandemic According to Syriac Sources', in Lester K. Little (ed.), *The Plague and the End of Antiquity: The Pandemic of 541–750* (Cambridge, 2007), 73; *Theophilus*, 193.
[20] James, *History*, 50.
[21] Morony, 'First Bubonic Plague', 73. Cf. *Theophilus*, 231. Arabic sources: Tabari, II, 1789; Ibn 'Asakir, XXXVII, 95. On Basra, see Pierre, 'Can We Flee the Plague', 11–12.
[22] See below, Ch. 12, pp. 323–4.
[23] Brent Shaw, 'Water and Society in the Ancient Maghrib: Technology, Property and Development', *Antiquités africaines* 20 (1984), 163–4; Banning, 'Peasants, Pastoralists'.
[24] Shaw, 'Water and Society', 136; cf. Peregrine Horden and Nicholas Purcell, *The Corrupting Sea: A Study of Mediterranean History* (Oxford, 2000), 13.
[25] John Haldon, 'The Resources of Late Antiquity', *NCHI*, I, 33.

people in Late Antiquity lived a much more precarious existence, with failed harvests and damage to crops being a recurrent feature of many of the sources.[26]

Cereal crops were the mainstay of much of the agricultural economy. Bread made from wheat flour was the staple foodstuff across most of the Roman, Sasanian and early Islamic world. Hard durum wheat was beginning to replace soft wheat in the Mediterranean and points further east. Barley was grown both as animal feed and for human consumption. Rice and rice flour were important in Iraq, Khuzistan, Tukharistan and the Indus Valley, as well, perhaps, as the lowlands south of the Caspian. Some rice was also already cultivated in parts of southern Syria and Egypt before the conquests. Pulses, including lentils, and vegetables were produced alongside cereal crops.[27] Run-off irrigation agriculture allowed the farming of fruit trees alongside winter wheat and barley: the late fifth-century cedarwood legal documents known as the *Tablettes Albertini* describe olive trees, figs, almonds, pistachios and vines being grown at the edge of the cultivable zone in late fifth-century North Africa, while the sixth and seventh-century Nessana papyri show vines, olives, figs, dates, wheat and barley being grown in the late Roman and early Islamic Negev.[28] The Abbasid-era courtier and scholar al-Baladhuri (d. c. 892) lists wheat, date palms and other fruit trees, vines, vegetables, grains and cotton as the products of 'what was watered by the Euphrates' in southern Iraq in the mid-seventh century. Elsewhere in the same text, wheat, barley, beans, vines, clover, sesame, green vegetables, cotton, sugar cane and date palms are listed for the same region.[29] In Roman times, wheat was the key product of the Nile, its Delta and the Fayyum, along with barley, flax and animal fodder; other Egyptian products included green vegetables, lentils and onions.[30]

The people of all these regions farmed animals for food, transport and labour. Specialist stock-farming for cavalry horses is attested in Anatolia, Fars, Khurasan, Egypt and parts of North Africa.[31] Land unsuitable for arable farm-

---

[26] See, for example, Palmer et al., *Seventh Century*, 32, 46, 47, 77; Tabari, II, 1563; James, *History*, 50; *History of the Patriarchs*, I, xvii, 67, I, xviii, 97, 98; Jalal al-Din al-Suyuti, *Ta'rikh*, ed. Ibrahim Salih (Beirut, 1996), 160.

[27] Andrew Watson, *Agricultural Innovation in the Early Islamic World: The Diffusion of Crops and Farming Techniques, 700–1100* (Cambridge, 1983), 15–17, 20; Marius Canard, 'Rice in the Middle East in the First Centuries of Islam', in Michael G. Morony (ed.), *Production and the Exploitation of Resources* (Farnham, 2002), 153–68; Decker, *Tilling*, 97–112; Haldon, 'Resources', 32.

[28] Shaw, 'Water and Society', 142–51, with references for the Negev and the *Tablettes Albertini* at 150–1.

[29] Baladhuri, *Futuh*, 269–71.

[30] *SaMS*, 23–4, 178.

[31] Haldon, 'Resources', 35. For Egypt: Kindi, 77.

ing was given over to grazing and livestock often also grazed arable land after the harvest. In many regions, pastoralists were able to coexist with settled farmers, exploiting different spaces at different times. The same people could also move between nomadic and settled forms of agriculture. However, there were also extensive steppe zones where pastoralism was the only viable economy. Pastoralists herded sheep and goats, alongside camels, horses and cattle; the Arabic noun *al-anʿām* (sing. *al-naʿam*), which features prominently in the Qurʾan, refers to these 'grazing livestock'.[32] With the exception of camels, the same animals were also used by settled farmers. Donkeys and mules were also often used for transport. Some settled communities farmed pigs and chickens; the taboo against the former among the Arabians is maintained in the Qurʾan. Attitudes to dogs also varied, but in most rural regions they were used for herding, guarding and hunting. As for most pre-modern peoples, hunting was a supplement to farming, as well as a prestige sport for aristocrats; human population densities were far lower than in modern times, with concomitantly much larger populations of wild animals. Likewise, fishing from rivers and coasts contributed a key component of the late antique diet, with different attitudes to permitted foods from these sources among different groups.[33]

Building materials, and raw materials for producing tools and weapons, were also vital economic resources. Local sources were used wherever possible for building, but prestige constructions often incorporated materials that were expensive or symbolic in other ways because they had come from further afield, sometimes as part of tribute payments or other diplomatic exchange. Expensive cut stone, including marble, was widely re-used (so-called *spolia* in the modern literature, from Latin). Local building materials could include quarried stone, or dried or baked bricks in regions such as lowland Iraq, where stone was scarce. The timber economy is not yet well understood. The sources mention wood being imported long distances for prestige buildings.[34] A wide range of wood types have been found in Roman and early Islamic era shipwrecks, including tamarisk, teak, cypress, ash, and Turkish pine and oak.

---

[32] There are about thirty occurrences; see ʿAbd al-Baqi, *Muʿjam*, s.v.
[33] For farmed animals in Khurasan and Tukharistan, see Azad, 'Happily Ever After', 39–40; Azad, 'Ecology', 340–1. For an edict decreeing the slaughter of pigs in Syria and elsewhere in c. 693, see *Theophilus*, 189. For dogs, see Roger S. Bagnall, *Egypt in Late Antiquity* (Princeton, 1993), 143. On hunting, see *EI²*, 'Sayd' (F. Viré). For fish and garum paste in Egypt, see *SaMS*, 25–6. On bees in the Qurʾan and in late antique religious thought, see Johan Weststeijn, 'Wine and Impurity in the Sura of the Bees: A Structuralist Interpretation of Qurʾan 16:67', in Josephine van den Bent, Floris van den Eijnde and Johan Weststeijn (eds), *Late Antique Responses to the Arab Conquests* (Leiden, 2021), 56–73.
[34] Palm trunks were requisitioned for the governor's palace in Egypt, but wood for building was also imported: *SaMS*, 25, 79.

There were military shipyards at Tunis and Alexandria, and it is likely that much of the wood for the ships was produced locally, or, in the case of Egypt, also imported from Syria and East Africa. The strategic importance of Rhodes and Cyprus were also in part because of their resources for shipbuilding. Iron, which was vital for shipbuilding and for producing tools and weapons, was mined in eastern Anatolia, Syria, the Arabian Peninsula, East Africa, the Elburz, Azerbaijan, the Zagros and Kirman. Copper was extracted in many of the same regions, while tin was mined in the Arabian Peninsula and the Taurus mountains, as well as imported from as far away as south-west Britain.[35]

Silver and gold were used to mint the high-value coins that were the main units of economic and fiscal measurement and exchange. Consequently, precious metal ores were a vital resource and a focus of military and diplomatic activity, alongside other extremely high-value items, such as slaves, silks, furs and horses. Coins already in circulation were sometimes collected and reminted by the authorities and counterfeiting was punished. Mined precious metal grew in its importance for coin production in the latter decades of Umayyad rule. Silver, which in most cases was extracted from lead ore, was present on the Arabian Peninsula, and was mined in the Maghrib and Ifriqiya, as well as in the eastern Taurus and southern Caucasus, the Elburz Mountains, the Iranian Plateau and Khurasan. Gold was mined in the Caucasus and the Elburz as well as in the Hijaz. Silk production and exchange also tended to be subject to similarly tight controls as gold and silver under both Roman and Sasanian rule and then under the Umayyads, who used garments carrying silk bands (*ṭirāz*) as prestige gifts at their courts and symbols of rank and authority, much like the Roman and Sasanian monarchs (Figure 10.1).[36]

---

[35] Haldon, 'Resources', 34–5. Marcus Rautman, 'The Busy Countryside of Late Roman Cyprus', *Report of the Department of Antiquities, Cyprus* (2000), 323–8. On Rhodes and Cyprus, see also above, Chs 4, 5, 7, 8 and 9, pp. 84, 112, 179 and 201. For late Roman and early Islamic shipwrecks, see Eyal Israeli and Yaacov Kahanov, 'The 7th–9th Century Tantura E Shipwreck, Israel: Construction and Reconstruction', *International Journal of Nautical Archaeology* 43 (2014), 369–88; Ufuk Kocabaş, 'Yenikapı Byzantine-Era Shipwrecks, Istanbul, Turkey: A Preliminary Report and Inventory of the 27 Wrecks Studied by Istanbul University', *International Journal of Nautical Archaeology* 44 (2015), 5–38. For a sword as a valuable and symbolic object, see Baladhuri, *Futuh*, 119–20.

[36] Haldon, 'Resources', 34–5; Jane Kershaw and Stephen W. Merkel, 'Silver Recycling in the Viking Age: Theoretical and Analytical Approaches', *Archaeometry* (2021), 1–18. On silk, see *EI²*, 'Tiraz' (Y. K. Stillman and P. Sanders). For silk production in sixth-century Rome and Iran, see Constantine Zuckerman, 'Silk "Made in Byzantium": A Study of Economic Policies of Emperor Justinian', *Travaux et Mémoires 17: Constructing the Seventh Century* (2013), 323–50. For a silvermine near Qayrawan and the punishment of counterfeiting, see Baladhuri, *Futuh*, 227–8, 469–70. Reminting of silver in the post-Sasanian lands seems to have been rare in Umayyad times, see Stephen W. Merkel, Jani Oravisjärvi, and Jane

figure 10.1 Tiraz embroidered with 'God's Servant Marwan Commander of the Faithful ... in the tiraz of Ifriqiya'. Approximately 65cm × 40cm. Silk, with woven colours on a red background and an inscription embroidered in yellow silk. © Victoria & Albert Museum, London.

Settlement Patterns and Urban Change

The Arabian conquerors' settlements had an urban character from the outset. The Meccans were townspeople, and they recognised the importance of the town for retaining the religious and political identity of their followers and as a base for the exploitation of the resources of the conquered territories. The major provincial garrisons (*amṣār*, sing. *miṣr*) established at or near existing towns were the centres for the administration of tax and the payment of the army, while smaller garrisons were established at strategically or economically important places. The larger garrisons exerted a strong economic pull on the populations in their vicinity, driving demands for goods and services from the surrounding countryside but also acting as magnets for economic migration. In addition to the migration and settlement of tribespeople from the Arabian Peninsula, the migration into the garrisons of non-Arabians, who came as labourers, artisans and service-providers, some as free converts but many as captive slaves, contributed to the rapid growth of some urban populations.[37]

Kershaw, 'Lead Isotopes reveal Silver Sources of the Islamic Golden Age', forthcoming. I would like to thank Jane Kershaw for providing me access to this forthcoming paper.

[37] Hugh Kennedy, 'The Financing of the Military in the Early Islamic State', in Averil Cameron (ed.), *The Byzantine and Islamic Near East III: States, Resources and Armies* (Princeton,

The main garrisons came to be characterised by a nexus of planned monumental governmental buildings at their centre – the 'mosque-palace complex' of the modern literature. The basic form of the pillared (or 'hypostyle') prayer hall, proximate to the residence of the commander and often to other administrative buildings, baths and markets appears to date from the first settlements of the 630s and 640s.[38] However, the Umayyad rulers reshaped this urban core: the placing of the ruler's palace adjacent to the prayer-wall of the mosque may date from the time of Muʿawiya, and this model was followed by al-Hajjaj at Wasit in c. 703–4. Between 705 and 715, al-Walid I built distinctive monumental mosques at Jerusalem, Damascus, Sanaʿa, Fustat and Medina, in the central lands of the empire, imposing an imperial aesthetic on the major cities of Syria, Egypt and Arabia.[39] Similar arrangements of government and public buildings are replicated at numerous smaller Umayyad-era centres across the territory of the empire; the construction of a new centre of government and prayer expressed the loyalty of the buildings' patrons to the new religio-political dispensation and contributed to the assertion of their authority over the migrants settled there. It also stood as an expression of power to others in the urban centre and its hinterland. Where diverse groups settled in one place, their 'cantonments' (*khiṭaṭ*, sing. *khiṭṭa*) usually had their own smaller mosques so that the major garrison cities are said to have had dozens of mosques by the beginning of the eighth century.[40]

The mosque-palace complex was the architectural marker of the new elite's presence, but its relationship to established urban space varied. At largely new settlements, the mosque-palace complex was placed at the centre; this pattern can be seen at Kufa (Figure 10.2) and Wasit, as well as smaller foundations, such

---

1995), 363, 378; Kennedy, 'Feeding', 181. See also Hugh Kennedy, 'From Shahristan to Medina', *Studia Islamica* 102/103 (2006), 22, n. 60.

[38] On the difficult evidence for early Umayyad-era mosques, see Antun, *Architectural Form*, with further references. For 'western and south-western Arabian' culture possibly informing Umayyad urban patterns, see Donald Whitcomb, 'An Urban Structure for the Early Islamic City: An Archaeological Hypothesis', in Amira K. Bennison and Alison L. Gascoigne (eds), *Cities in the Pre-modern Islamic World: The Urban Impact of Religion, State, and Society* (London and New York, 2007), 15–26.

[39] For the suggestion that the location of the palace moved behind the prayer wall in the time of Muʿawiya, see Whitcomb, 'Urban Structure', 24. On the Marwanid monumental mosques, see above, Ch. 6, pp. 153–7.

[40] *EI²*, 'Masdjid. 2. Tribal mosques and sectarian mosques' (J. Pederson); Parvaneh Pourshariati, 'Local Histories of Khurasan and the Pattern of Arab Settlement', *Studia Iranica* 27 (1998), 41–81; Najam Haider, *The Origins of the Shiʿah: Identity, Ritual, and Sacred Space in Eighth-century Kufa* (Cambridge, 2011), 231–5.

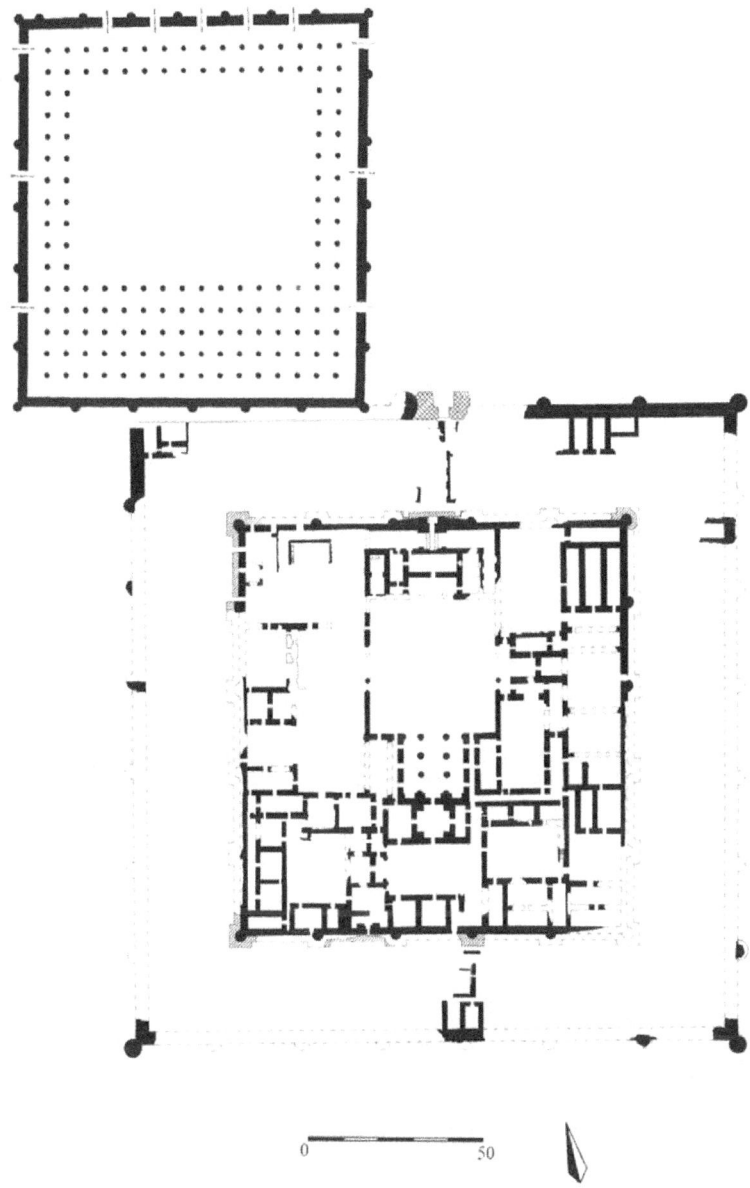

Figure 10.2 Plan of the Umayyad-era mosque-palace complex at Kufa, Iraq. After K. A. C. Creswell, *Early Muslim Architecture: Umayyads AD 622–750* (Oxford, 1969), and A. Santi and G. Labis, in Aila Santi, 'Early Islamic Kufa in Context: A Chronological Reinterpretation of the Palace, with a Note on the Development of the Monumental Language of the Early Muslim Elite', *Annali Sezione Orientale* 78 (2018), fig. 2. Courtesy of Aila Santi.

as 'Anjar, in modern Lebanon.⁴¹ Elsewhere, a new administrative centre was often built just outside an existing town, as at al-'Aqaba on the Red Sea coast, at Hadir Qinnasrin in northern Syria, at Istakhr in the Zagros in Iran, and at Tunis in North Africa.⁴² The claiming of a whole church for an expanded congregational mosque at Damascus after 705 was an exceptional event, related to al-Walid I's development of the imperial capital and rivalry with the Roman Empire.⁴³ Tunis may be another location where a church was completely replaced by a mosque in Umayyad times, but the evidence there is much less definitive.⁴⁴ In other cases, space was found within the existing urban zone: as at Tadmur/Palmyra, al-Rusafa/Sergiopolis, Gerash and Bukhara.⁴⁵ Likewise, at Jerusalem, the deserted Temple Mount and the region to its south were appropriated by the conquerors;⁴⁶ at Sana'a, the congregational mosque is said to have been built in gardens belonging to the former Sasanian governor;⁴⁷ in Marw the first mosque was at the centre of the Sasanian walled city.⁴⁸

As garrisons became towns, palace and government buildings, markets and baths all became widespread features of Islamic urbanism.⁴⁹ In larger settlements, these were replicated at more local levels within the town. The concentration of political, religious and commercial capital in the new buildings of the Umayyad-era cities is striking; palaces, mosques, water supplies and markets were patronised not only for reasons of administration and government, but

---

⁴¹ It has recently been suggested that 'Anjar incorporated existing Christian buildings, which seems plausible. Nonetheless, it has the form of a planned development in which the old buildings were largely erased. See Santi, "Anjar'.

⁴² Hicham Djaït, 'L'Afrique arabe au VIIIe siècle', *Annales: Économies, Sociétés* 28 (1973), 609; Donald Whitcomb, 'The City of Istakhr and the Marvdasht Plain', *Archaeologische Mitteilungen aus Iran* 6 (1979), 363–70; Donald Whitcomb, 'The *Misr* of Ayla: Settlement at al-'Aqaba in the Early Islamic Period', in G. R. D. King and Averil Cameron (eds), *The Byzantine and Early Islamic Near East II: Land Use and Settlement Patterns* (Princeton, 1994), 156–8; *EI²*, 'Tunis' (P. Sebag); Alan Walmsley, *Early Islamic Syria: An Archaeological Assessment* (London, 2007), 79–80, 88–9.

⁴³ See George, *Umayyad Mosque*, and above, Ch. 6, pp. 154–7.

⁴⁴ Corisande Fenwick, 'From Africa to *Ifriqiya*: Settlement and Society in Early Medieval North Africa (650–800)', *Al-Masaq* 25 (2013), 28.

⁴⁵ For Syria: Genequand, *Établissements*, 52–66; Walmsley, *Early Islamic Syria*, 81–7. On Bukhara: Pourshariati, 'Khurasan', 58–9.

⁴⁶ See above, Chs 4 and 6, pp. 92–3 and 142–6 and 153.

⁴⁷ Mikhaïl B. Piotrovsky, 'Late Ancient and Early Mediaeval Yemen: Settlement Traditions and Innovations', in G. R. D. King and Averil Cameron (eds), *The Byzantine and Early Islamic Near East II: Land Use and Settlement Patterns* (Princeton, 1994), 215.

⁴⁸ Hugh Kennedy, 'Medieval Merv: An Historical Overview', in Georgina Herrmann (ed.), *Monuments of Merv: Traditional Buildings of the Karakum* (London, 1999), 28.

⁴⁹ See also on this and what follows, Fanny Bessard, *Caliphs and Merchants: Cities and the Economics of Power in the Near East (700–950)* (Oxford, 2020).

for prestige, piety and commercial gain – markets were often owned by specific individuals and were inherited, along with the rents they generated.[50] Already in the 640s, 'Umar I is said to have built a slave market at Fustat, which attests to the importance of slavery in the new conquest economy. A treasury and public baths were added by the early eighth century. New churches and synagogues are also attested in the literary sources.[51] This has left its traces in the later sources, with the inherited ownership of markets and other urban sites being explicitly noted or being implied by the names given to particular locales: the market of 'Abd Allah b. 'Amir was a source of revenue for the seventh-century governor of Basra and his descendants;[52] 'Abd al-Malik's son, Sa'id, developed the market at Mosul;[53] Athanasius bar Gumoye, the senior scribe in Egypt at the time of 'Abd al-Malik is said to have owned 300 shops in al-Ruha/Edessa, which were managed by his son.[54] There is also some evidence for the concentration of artisanal and industrial production in the Syrian cities, suggesting participation by the new elites in production and industry as well as in commerce. Such patronage of both markets and workshops in Syria, Ifriqiya and Iraq is particularly well attested for the reign of Hisham.[55] From the same period, the archaeology reveals a market at Maslama's estate at Madinat al-Far, and the literary sources refer to 'Khalid al-Qasri's Market' at Kufa. Similarly, inns (*fanādīq*, sing. *funduq*) and other commercial properties were sources of income.[56]

---

[50] Hugh Kennedy, 'From Polis to Madina: Urban Change in Late Antique and Early Islamic Syria', *Past & Present* 106 (1985), 20; Kennedy, 'Shahristan', 24; Nimrod Luz, 'The Construction of an Islamic City in Palestine. The Case of Umayyad al-Ramla', *JRAS* 3 (1997), 36–40. For a bath generating profits, see Baladhuri, *Futuh*, 353–4.

[51] Sijpesteijn, 'Arab Conquest', 451–2; *SaMS*, 79–80.

[52] Michael G. Morony, 'Commerce in Early Islamic Iraq', *Asien, Afrika, Lateinamerika: Zeitschrift des Zantralen Rates für Asien- Afrika- und Lateinamerikawissenschaften in der DDR* 20 (1993), 706.

[53] For the development of the market at Mosul by Sa'id b. 'Abd al-Malik, with references, see Elias Khamis, 'A Bronze Weight of Sa'id b. 'Abd al-Malik from Bet Shean/Baysan', *JRAS* 12 (2002), 146.

[54] Muriel Debié, 'Christians in the Service of the Caliph: Through the Looking Glass of Communal Identities', in Antoine Borrut and Fred M. Donner (eds), *Christians and Others in the Umayyad State* (Chicago, 2016), 55, and see 58–9 on Simeon of the Olives (d. 724) developing churches, gardens, orchards, shops, mills and inns at Nisibis in c. 706.

[55] Fanny Bessard, 'The Politics of *Suqs* in Early Islam', *JESHO* 61 (2018), 499, 503–7; Fenwick, 'Umayyads and North Africa', 304–5.

[56] Hugh Kennedy, 'Elite Incomes in the Early Islamic State', in Lawrence I. Conrad and John Haldon (eds), *The Byzantine and Early Islamic Near East VI: Elites Old and New in the Byzantine and Early Islamic Near East* (Princeton, 2004), 25 for the inns owned by Yahya b. al-Hurr at Mosul in 752–3. On other property belonging to this family (descended from 'Abd al-Malik's grandfather, al-Hakam b. Abi l-'As) and other members of the Marwanid ruling elite at Mosul, see Robinson, *Empire*, 80. For North Africa, see Djaït, 'L'Afrique',

In many places, new centres flourished at the expense of older ones – the destruction at Carthage and the rise of nearby Tunis in Ifriqiya is one example; the growth of inland centres like al-Tabariyya/Tiberias and al-Rusafa/Sergiopolis in contrast to the continued decline of towns like Antioch is another.[57] However, by far the most spectacular new developments were the three garrisons of Fustat, Kufa and Basra, which had become some of the biggest cities in the world within decades of their foundation, dwarfing the smaller Roman and Sasanian settlements nearby. Fustat had begun in c. 643 as a camp, for, it is said, around 4,000 tribesmen, next to the requisitioned Roman fortress of Baylon, just south of the Delta in northern Egypt. One source indicates that the numbers on the register (*dīwān*) entitled to a stipend at Fustat had increased from around 15,000 in the time of its founder, 'Amr, to 40,000 in the time of Mu'awiya, a generation later. Four further updates to Fustat's *dīwān* are mentioned for Marwanid times and the main congregational mosque was also repeatedly expanded. While these numbers may not be reliable, it seems likely that by the eighth century Fustat's population exceeded 100,000 people.[58] Basra and Kufa had been founded in c. 638 and expanded even faster. Using figures for Basran soldiers killed in battle or settled elsewhere in the mid-seventh century, Charles Pellat suggested that already in the 650s its population exceeded 50,000; we should perhaps assume a population of over 250,000 by the mid-eighth century.[59] The army that initially settled at Kufa is said to have numbered 30,000 and one estimate puts Kufa's population already at 140,000 by 670; by the eighth century it may have exceeded 200,000.[60] It is probable that by the mid-eighth century, only a few Chinese cities and perhaps also Constantinople, were larger than Kufa and Basra.[61]

Elsewhere, whether new centres were built adjacent to old ones or existing cities were partially settled by the conquerors, transformation was often

---

[609.] For Syria: Walmsley, *Early Islamic Syria*, 87–8, 97; Genequand, *Établissements*, 170, 362. For Iraq: Baladhuri, *Futuh*, 281, 286 (markets in Kufa).

[57] Walmsley, *Early Islamic Syria*, 111–12; Fenwick, 'Umayyads and North Africa', 296, 304–6.

[58] On Fustat, see George Scanlon, 'Al-Fustat: The Riddle of the Earliest Settlement', in G. R. D. King and Averil Cameron (eds), *The Byzantine and Early Islamic Near East II: Land Use and Settlement Patterns* (Princeton, 1994), 171–80; Sijpesteijn, 'Arab Conquest', 451–2; *SaMS*, 50–1, 80; Bruning, *Rise*.

[59] Estimates vary within the low-to-mid hundreds of thousands for the early eighth century (and are largely guesswork): Pellat, *Milieu*, 5–6; cf. *EI²*, 'Basra' (C. Pellat); *IatMC*, 253; Hugh Kennedy, 'Military Pay and the Economy of the Early Islamic State', *Historical Research* 75 (2002), 156.

[60] *IatMC*, 253.

[61] Christopher Haas, *Alexandria in Late Antiquity: Topography and Social Conflict* (Baltimore, 2006), 45–7; John Haywood, *The New Atlas of World History: Global Events at a Glance* (London, 2011), 76–7.

slower and more organic. In the Roman world, the privatisation of public space and the dominant presence of churches anticipated developments that accelerated under Islam, with mosques joining churches as the main public buildings. In Egypt, it is likely that Arabian soldiers were garrisoned at Aswan, near the southern Nubian frontier, and at strategically important sites. With the consolidation of Muslim rule, especially under 'Abd al-Malik's brother 'Abd al-'Aziz and his successors, there was more extensive Arabian settlement across the whole province.[62] 'Abd al-'Aziz invested extensively in the infrastructure of Upper Egypt, building residences, baths and markets, and founding a new governmental centre at Hulwan, a few kilometres up river from Fustat.[63]

Syria was densely urbanised, with scores of towns and small cities. By the early seventh century, churches had become the pre-eminent public buildings (as opposed to theatres and temples), the broad colonnaded streets had been narrowed by the encroachment of shops and houses, and industrial activities, such as pottery production and glassmaking, which had previously occurred on the outskirts of the cities had moved into their centres. Because of the importance of the existing pastoralist populations of the Syrian steppe in the Umayyads' armies, no new conquest garrison camps developed into major cities. However, Damascus, Tiberias and Jerusalem all appear to have benefited from their status within the new Umayyad dispensation; Damascus and Tiberias were both capitals of military districts (*junds*), and Damascus was also first the provincial and then the imperial capital; Jerusalem was a centre of pilgrimage and ritual, on the itinerary of many of the caliphs. It is likely that Hims/Emesa also benefited from its status as the capital of a military district, but less is known of it archaeologically.[64] In the seventh century, Tadmur/Palmyra gained from its location at the heart of the territory of Kalb, who were the mainstay of the military and political power of Mu'awiya and his son, and who remained a significant element in the later Umayyad armies; a new market was constructed there, probably at the end of the seventh or beginning of the eighth century.[65]

Other Syrian urban centres also continued to be developed, sometimes with new centres adjacent to existing ones: major Umayyad-era buildings are found at Hadir Qinnasrin, Gerash, Baysan/Scythopolis, Pella/Fihl, Hama/

---

[62] *SaMS*, 91–111.
[63] Kindi, 49–50; *History of the Patriarchs*, I, xvi, 42–3; Mabra, *Princely Authority*, 119–41. See also below, Ch. 11, p. 271.
[64] Walmsley, *Early Islamic Syria*, 77–9, 80–1. Filastin's first capital, 'Amwas/Nicopolis was devastated by the plague; the province may have been divided between Lod and Jerusalem, before being reunited under the new foundation of al-Ramla by Sulayman b. 'Abd al-Malik during his father's caliphate, see Luz, 'al-Ramla', 30–1. On *jund*, see below, Ch. 12, p. 298.
[65] Genequand, *Établissements*, 45–67.

Emath, 'Amman/Philadelphia, 'Aqaba/Ayla and Aleppo/Beroea.[66] Sulayman b. 'Abd al-Malik's (later a caliph, r. 715–17) foundation of al-Ramla adjacent to the existing Lod as a new provincial capital for the military district of Filastin, of which he was governor, is another example of this pattern. In the later Umayyad era, the Marwanid elite invested in the agriculture and fortification of the northern frontier, and the small urban centres at al-Rusafa/Sergiopolis in northern Syria and Harran in the Jazira were adopted as capitals by Hisham (r. 724–43) and Marwan II (r. 744–50), respectively.

In Iraq, smaller garrisons were established at 'Ayn Tamr, Anbar, al-Mada'in/Ctesiphon, Sinjar, Hulwan, Haditha and the new town of Mosul, near Nineveh.[67] Besides Kufa and Basra, two further new foundations were al-Hajjaj's Wasit, founded in c. 703–4, adjacent to the existing Sasanian-era Kaskar, and Yazid b. 'Umar b. Hubayra's (g. 744–50) private estate, Qasr Ibn Hubayra, which was on the scale of a small town and survived into the Abbasid period.[68] In Iran, Arabian rule brought a new elite's government, religion and commercial interests into the cities and began to drive the expansion of urban populations beyond their Sasanian-era numbers, especially on the Iranian plateau. In the Zagros, significant garrisons and governorships were established at Hamadhan, Rayy, Isfahan and Istakhr. After 671, the largest Arabian settlement in Iran was at Marw, in Khurasan, when Mu'awiya's governor of Iraq and the East, Ziyad b. Sumayya, sent Rabi' b. Ziyad al-Harithi with 50,000 Basrans and Kufans to settle 'in the lower parts of the river Marw'.[69] Other towns occupied in seventh-century Khurasan included Balkh, Marw-i Rudh, Herat and Nishapur.[70] However, many of these latter centres were not held continuously until the early eighth century, and settlement appears to have been limited. In Sistan, Zaranj was the main settlement, with Bust, on the Helmand river, being used as a forward base for attacks on the Afghan highlands.

Further eastward expansion took place in the context of prolonged warfare, and so fortified urban centres were preferred by the Muslims. When Bukhara was finally subdued in 708, and became the centre of Muslim authority in Sogdia, half the city was requisitioned by its conqueror Qutayba and his army. The congregational mosque was built within the citadel (*quhandiz*) just outside the city, on the site of a temple.[71] At Samarqand a Muslim garrison, said

---

[66] Walmsley, *Early Islamic Syria*, 83–9.
[67] *IatMC*, 251. On Mosul, see further Robinson, *Empire*, 63–89.
[68] *EI²*, 'Wasit' (M. Sakly); *EI²*, 'Kasr ibn Hubayra' (J. Lassner).
[69] See above, Ch. 4, p. 99 and n.55.
[70] Mark David Luce, 'Frontier as Process: Umayyad Khurasan', PhD Dissertation, University of Chicago (2009), 125–6.
[71] Pourshariati, 'Khurasan', 58–9.

to have numbered 4,000, was installed within the city, temples were destroyed and a mosque was built.[72] Further east, the commercial centres of Sogdia and Tukharistan were appropriated as bases for the subjugation of these regions, very often with initial settlement within the walls of conquered cities. Likewise in Sind, although there al-Mansura is an example of a new foundations adjacent to existing settlements.[73]

As in Egypt and Syria, the urban landscape of North Africa was also already changing in late Roman times, with churches becoming the main public buildings, and residential and industrial buildings encroaching on older public spaces.[74] However, in North Africa, the sixth-century Roman reconquest from the Vandals had also led to increased fortification as the Romans sought to re-impose their tax regime.[75] This militarisation of the landscape preceded the prolonged seventh-century conquest period in Ifriqiya, which was more similar to that in Khurasan, Sogdia and Tukharistan than the rapid occupation of Syria and Egypt. Most of the conquering army in North Africa was settled at a single capital (*miṣr*), with smaller garrisons at other strategically or administratively important centres. Elsewhere in North Africa, Muslim garrisons tended to take over existing fortified sites. Besides Qayrawan and Tunis, other important centres included were Béja/Vaga (in northern Tunisia), and Gafsa/Capsa, on the southern desert fringe.[76] Further to the west, there is very limited evidence of a Muslim presence in the archaeology of the Maghrib (modern Algeria and Morocco), although it is likely that Walila/Volubilis was a centre for Muslim rule in the region.[77] In al-Andalus, the Muslim conquerors likewise took over existing Visigothic sites, sometimes also establishing new settlements adjacent to them, as seems to have happened at Cordoba; there is some limited material evidence for the urban Muslim presence in the first decades of the eighth century.[78]

---

[72] *EI²*, 'Samarkand' (H. H. Schaeder-[C. E. Bosworth]); Luce, 'Frontier', 174–5.

[73] On Sind, see Khalifa, 241; cf. Baladhuri, *Futuh*, 439, 444; *EI²*, 'al-Mansura' (Y. Friedmann), 'Multan. 1. History' (Y. Friedmann). On Tukharistan and Sogdia, see Kennedy, 'Shahristan', 31–3; Haug, *Eastern Frontier*, 116–17, 124–5; *EI²*, 'Balkh' (R. N. Frye).

[74] Fenwick, 'From Africa to *Ifriqiya*', 20–3.

[75] Anna Leone, *Changing Townscapes in North Africa from Late Antiquity to the Arab Conquest* (Bari, 2007), 166–279; Corisande Fenwick, 'Early Medieval Urbanism in Ifriqiya and the Emergence of the Islamic City', in L. Callegarin and S. Panzram (eds), *Entre civitas y medina. El mundo de las ciudades en la Península Ibérica y en el norte de África* (Madrid, 2018), 210, with further references.

[76] Fenwick, 'From Africa to Ifriqiya', 15–16. For one new Umayyad fortification, see Fenwick, 'Early Medieval Urbanism', 216.

[77] Corisande Fenwick, *Early Islamic North Africa: A New Perspective* (London, 2020), 72–3.

[78] Javier Martínez Jiménez et al, *The Iberian Peninsula Between 300 and 850: An Archaeological Perspective* (Amsterdam, 2018), 267–76. For burials at Pamplona, in northern Spain, dated

Settlement Patterns in the Countryside

While most Arabian migrants settled in towns, the conquests, and the new structures of power they engendered, impacted rural settlements across the empire. Where defeated enemies fled or were killed, land was expropriated and became the private property of the conquerors. Indeed, the principle that land brought under new cultivation – so called 'dead' land (*mawāt*), which was either desert or deserted – could be claimed as a possession and was liable to much lower rates of tax had empire-wide effects on settlement patterns. Some of the conquering elite became wealthy landowners, with incomes from their estates amounting to tens of thousands of dinars.[79] However, most land remained under the cultivation of its existing tenants and now became the *fay'* – the tax base for the payment of the armies.[80] The demands of this taxation were onerous; after the tax reforms of 'Abd al-Malik (r. 685/692–705), Egypt, Iraq and other provinces saw peasant flight from the land and revolts against the burden of taxation. Meanwhile, the demand from the new settler populations for food had substantial effects, especially in the vicinities of the three great riverine *miṣr*s, Fustat, Kufa and Basra. However, as with urban change, the extent of the impact of the new empire varied greatly, with continuity in rural land use and settlement patterns prevailing across many of the conquered territories.

In Iraq, the destruction of the Sasanian elite opened significant amounts of land to the conquerors in the fertile 'black earth' (Sawad) region of central and southern Iraq. Later sources describe these lands as being seized by 'Umar I (r. 634–44).

> From the Sawad, 'Umar b. al-Khattab took possession of the land of whoever was killed in war or fled, every royal estate (*kull arḍ Kisrā*) and estate of the royal household, every place where water collects, all Dayr Yazid, and every territory of which the Sasanian king (*Kisrā*) had taken possession.[81]

'Umar was understood to have taken these lands so that their revenues would support the Faithful and accounts of 'Uthman and Mu'awiya subsequently

---

715–70, see Manzano Moreno, 'Conquest', 318–20, with further references. For later literary evidence for the taking over of Visigothic centres, see James, *History*, 52, 57.

[79] Hugh Kennedy, 'Landholding and Law in the Early Islamic State', in John Hudson and Ana Rodríguez López (eds), *Diverging Paths? The Shapes of Power and Institutions in Medieval Christendom and Islam* (Leiden, 2014), 165–7, 174–6. See further on the estates, below, pp. 246–7.

[80] *EI3*, 'Fay'' (A. Marsham).

[81] Baladhuri, *Futuh*, 273; see further Jairus Banaji, 'Late Antique Legacies and Muslim Economic Expansion', in John Haldon (ed.), *Money, Power and Politics in Early Islamic Syria: A Review of Current Debates* (Farnham, 2010), 166–8.

distributing them as heritable and alienable 'land grants' (*qaṭīʿa*s) are inflected with criticism, reflecting Iraqi hostility to Umayyad rule.[82] The sources also describe large-scale development of the marshy land around Basra in the mid-seventh century to supply water to its inhabitants and to bring land under cultivation; these developments continued into the eighth century.[83] Similar reclamations of land and irrigation schemes occurred around Kufa, Wasit, al-Anbar and Qasr Ibn Hubayra, and elsewhere in southern and central Iraq in the eighth century.[84] These developments had the potential to deliver huge profits to their owners, often made through the use of agricultural slaves, as well as waged labour.[85]

In contrast, there are no similar reports of the appropriation of land from the conquest period in Egypt, and so it seems likely that the initial Arabian presence there was mostly limited to tribes granted grazing rights in the spring ahead of the campaigning season and small numbers of soldiers supervising a tax system which still depended upon the local elites. One much later source does refer to land seizures in Egypt by Muslims in the wake of rebellions against the heavier fiscal regime of 'Abd al-Malik, as also happened in Iraq at around the same time. Certainly, the Muslim presence in the Egyptian countryside became more extensive: grazing rights sometimes led to more permanent settlement by the tribes; Arabians became more involved in the administration of the tax system, and land surveys facilitated the assignment of deserted and untilled lands to Muslims. Muslims become increasingly evident in the literary sources and in the papyri as a permanent presence in the countryside in the eighth century, involved in agricultural, commercial and administrative activities beyond Fustat.[86]

In Syria, archaeological evidence for the use of 'land grants', and the reclamation of 'dead' land is plentiful. Some of the smaller settlements such as those at 'Anjar, al-Bakhra', Madinat al-Far and Qasr al-Hayr al-Sharqi (Figure 10.3) have the character of aristocratic estates with associated settlements on a scale that might allow them to be considered nascent towns. Other aristocratic

---

[82] Baladhuri, *Futuh*, 273–4, 293; Kennedy, 'Landholding and Law', 176; Banaji, 'Late Antique Legacies', 169–70; Wadad al-Qadi, 'Population Census and Land Surveys under the Umayyads (41–132/661–750)', *Der Islam* 83 (2008), 359–62.
[83] Baladhuri, *Futuh*, 273–4, 359–71, 373; Kennedy, 'Feeding', 182–9.
[84] Baladhuri, *Futuh*, 274, 290–1; Verkinderen, *Waterways*, 31, 34, 39, 45, 55, 252.
[85] Baladhuri, *Futuh*, 293–4; Tabari, II, 156; Michael G. Morony, 'Landholding and Social Change: Lower al-Iraq in the Early Islamic Period', in Tarif Khalidi (ed.), *Land Tenure and Social Transformation in the Middle East* (Beirut, 1984), 210–16.
[86] Kennedy, 'Landholding and Law', 181; *SaMS*, 81–4, 91–111. Cf. Banaji, 'Late Antique Legacies', 167–8, and *Agrarian Change*, 152–9, who argues that significant amounts of Egyptian land were transferred to Muslims at the time of the conquest.

foundations appear to have had less extended settlement associated with them, and so might more properly be considered rural developments. Collectively, these thirty or more new or much-expanded rural elite sites are usually referred to, misleadingly, as the 'Syrian Desert Castles' (see Map 10.2).

In fact, they have few defensive features and are not in the desert, but rather in the steppe zone, where irrigated farming was possible, or occasionally in more fertile regions, and so Denis Genequand has proposed that they

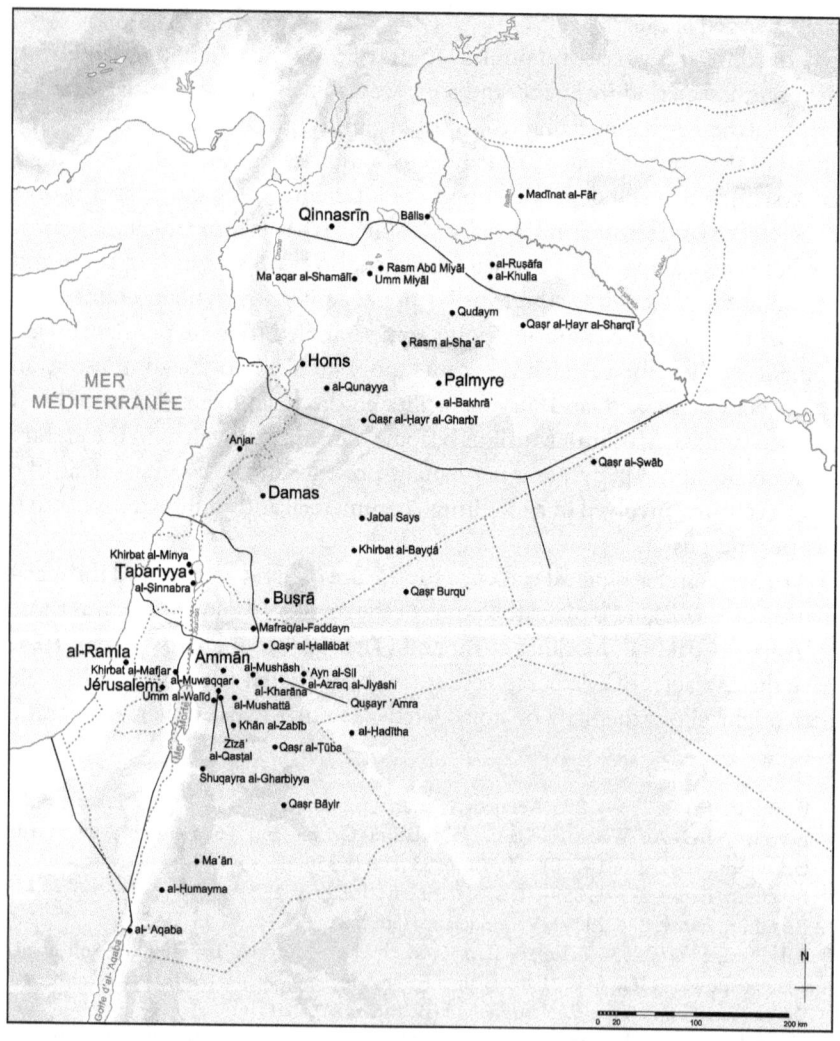

Map 10.2 Umayyad-era 'aristocratic settlements' (or 'desert castles') in Syria. Courtesy of Denis Genequand.

are better considered as 'aristocratic settlements'. Most have archaeologically extant agricultural irrigation associated with them. Many are not attested in the literary sources and are comparatively modest developments, whereas others clearly belonged to the wealthiest members of the ruling elite. Some of the more magnificent developments can attributed to specific members of the Umayyad family or, in at least one case, to other members of the Qurashi elite. Some of the best-preserved and most-discussed examples were constructed by the caliph Hisham (Figure 10.3) and his nephew and nominated heir, al-Walid b. Yazid (later al-Walid II; Figure 10.4).[87]

The impetus for the development of these Syrian estates was both economic and political. The reclamation of unfarmed land allowed for the legitimate acquisition of land by the conquerors, and such lands were liable only to very low levels of taxation. Hence, many of these estates were investments. At the same time,

Figure 10.3 The caliphal palace building at Qasr al-Hayr al-Sharqi, between Tadmur/Palmyra and Raqqa, April 1996. Constructed for the caliph Hisham in 728–9. Photograph by Garth Fowden. Reproduced by kind permission of the Syndics of Cambridge University Library.

[87] On the 'desert castles' (or 'aristocratic establishments'), see Genequand, *Établissements*, with references.

Figure 10.4 Bathhouse reception room floor mosaic at Khirbet al-Mafjar, near Jericho. Approximately 3m × 3m. Probably constructed for al-Walid b. Yazid, c. 724–44 CE. Sean Leatherbury/Manar al-Athar.

they were also prestigious elite buildings. Many are in marginal lands grazed by the flocks of the Syrian nomadic pastoralists, and so also had a political function, as places where their patrons could meet with the leaders of the groups upon which Umayyad military power depended. For example, Qasr al-Hayr al-Gharbi

Figure 10.5 Reconstructed façade of the gateway to the palace at Qasr al-Hayr al-Gharbi at the National Museum, Damascus, January 1993. Photograph by Garth Fowden. Reproduced by kind permission of the Syndics of Cambridge University Library.

is an extended development over nearly 200 hectares (2km²), comprising a large irrigated enclosure of 46 hectares (1050m × 442m), a water mill, reservoir, palace and baths (Figure 10.7). The imposing palace building was elaborately decorated with stucco and murals (Figures 10.5 and 10.6). A (now lost) inscription at the service building or 'khan', midway between the palace and the irrigated enclosure, recorded its construction by Hisham in November 727.

The location of this estate, at the mid-point between Damascus, Hims/ Emesa and Tadmur/Palmyra, suggests a political function for meetings between the caliph and the tribes of the region, notably the Kalb. Its situation in the semi-arid zone where rainfall averages less than 200mm per year would have required the irrigation works to make the settlement habitable. The size of the works suggests some commercial agricultural production beyond what was necessary for subsistence. Another cluster of developments by the Marwanid family are found at the northern end of the migration routes out of the Peninsula, in and around Amman and the al-Azraq oasis.[88]

[88] Genequand, *Établissements*, 161–75, 201, 369, with references.

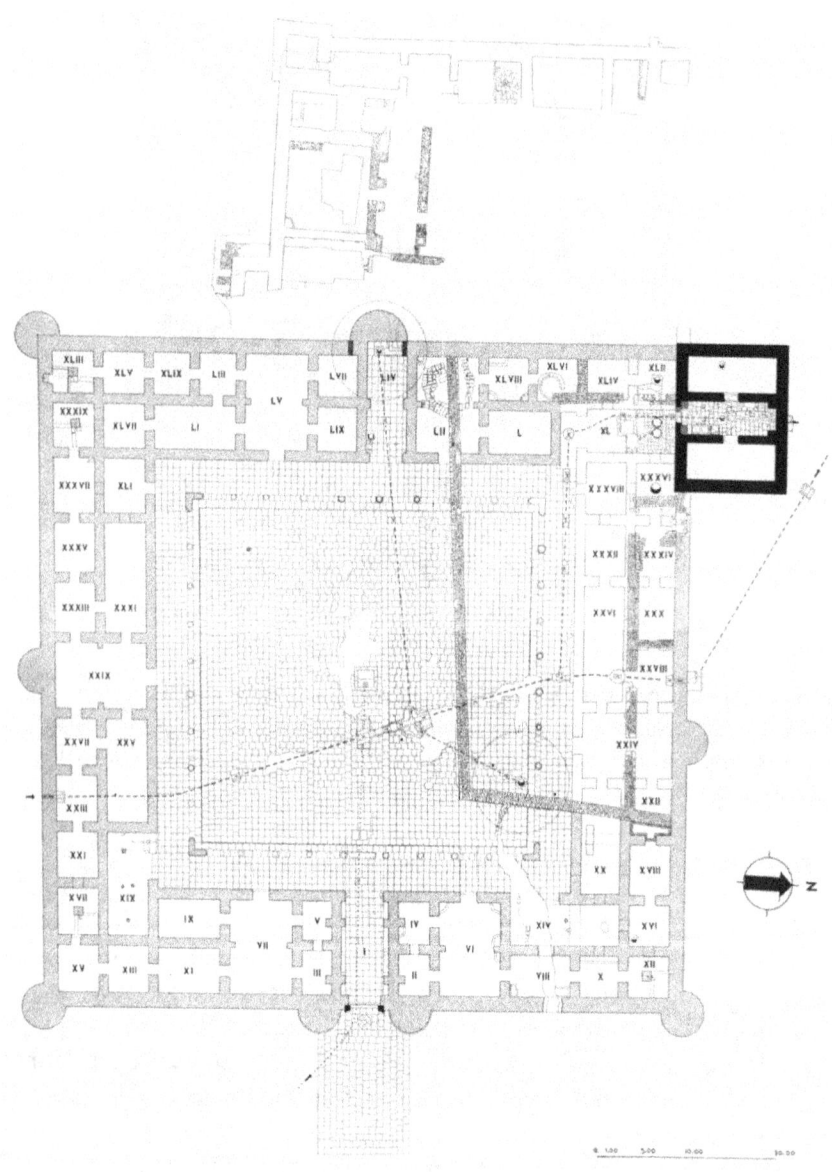

Figure 10.6 Plan of the caliphal palace at Qasr al-Hayr al-Gharbi, between Damascus and Tadmur/Palmyra. After Daniel Schlumberger, *Qasr al-Hayr al-Gharbi* (Paris, 1986). © Presses d'Ifpo, with thanks to Denis Genequand.

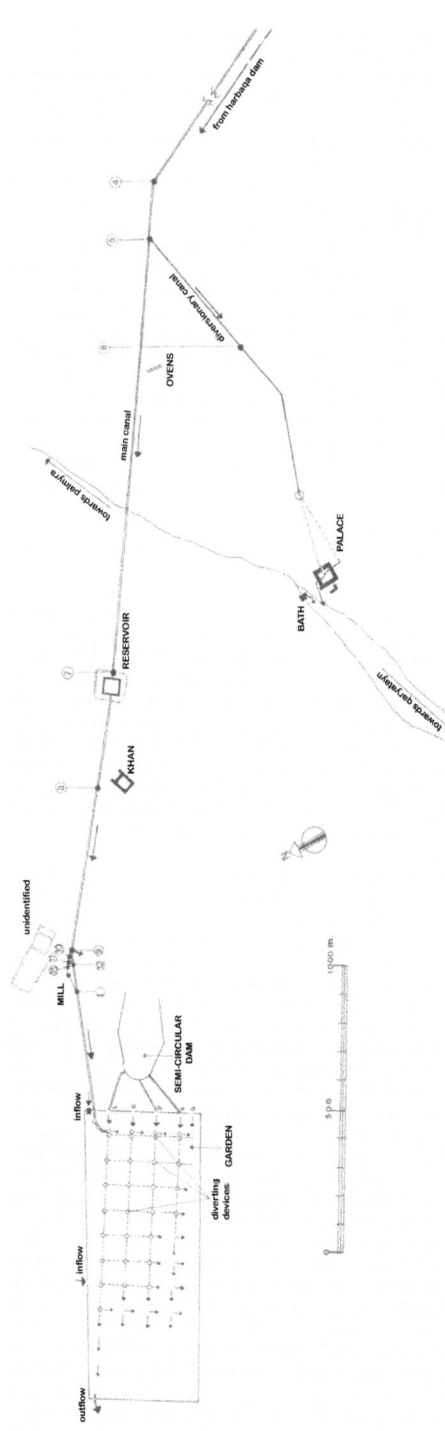

Figure 10.7 Schematic plan of the site of Qasr al-Hayr al-Gharbi. After Schlumberger, *Qasr al-Hayr al-Gharbi*. © Presses d'Ifpo, with thanks to Denis Genequand.

With the growth in the importance of the tribes of the Roman frontier came new elite investment in northern Syria and the frontier zone to the north-west. Hisham and his allies, who held estates on the Euphrates and Balikh rivers, added a second capital at the important Christian pilgrimage centre of al-Rusafa/Sergiopolis, on the Euphrates, just south of al-Raqqa/Callinicim. It expanded accordingly, with mosques, palaces, administrative buildings and associated developments outside its existing Roman walls. Qasr al-Hayr al-Sharqi, on the route south from al-Rusafa to Damascus, was also constructed by Hisham. Madinat al-Far, or Hisn Maslama, in the Balikh Valley, north of al-Raqqa, was developed by the frontier commander Maslama b. 'Abd al-Malik (d. 738), and lands at Balis/Barbalissos, upstream of al-Raqqa to the west, were also developed by him. On the northern edges of the Arabians' territory, a series of fortified centres were developed, controlling the passes on the road between Antioch and Germanikeia (Ar. Mar'ash) – perhaps a response to the dangers presented by the politically independent populations of the Amanus Mountains.[89]

Itinerant Monarchy: The Umayyads and the Syrian Landscape

While not all the so-called 'desert castles' of Greater Syria were built by the Umayyads, many were. They are a physical legacy of Umayyad rule in the landscape of modern Jordan, Syria, Israel and Palestine, and monuments to the patrimonial character of their rule, the importance of their relations with the tribes of the Syrian steppe and the distinctive character of their seasonally itinerant courts. Hunting, bathing, wine-drinking, poetry and music are all associated in the later literary sources with courtly life at the Umayyads' palaces; the implication is often that these activities were luxurious and decadent, with drinking, music and sexual incontinence being attributed to those Umayyad rulers with the most dissolute reputations. However, these were royal and aristocratic pursuits in Late Antiquity and so such luxury was also the exercise of power; it had political and social functions, with the performance of regal generosity, hospitality and munificence binding leading members of the ruling elite together through a shared aristocratic culture.[90]

---

[89] On all these sites, see Walmsley, *Early Islamic Syria*, 81–2, 90–7; Genequand, *Établissements*, 364–7 and *passim*; Eger, *Islamic–Byzantine Frontier*, 61, 63, 169–70, 176, 180.

[90] Genequand, *Établissements*; Denis Genequand, 'Elites in the Countryside: The Economic and Political Factors behind the Umayyad "Desert Castles"', in Andrew Marsham (ed.), *The Umayyad World* (London and New York, 2021), 240–66. On royal and aristocratic culture in Rome and Iran, see Matthew P. Canepa, *The Two Eyes of the Earth: Art and Ritual of Kingship between Rome and Sasanian Iran* (Berkeley, CA and London, 2009), 154–67.

The Umayyad rulers followed seasonal itineraries, moving between Damascus, Jerusalem and residences in the countryside, taking advantage of the varied climate of the different regions of Syria. As leaders in the tradition of tribal chiefs, the Umayyads depended for their military and political power upon personal connections with the heads of the Syrian tribes. Some of the Umayyads' rural residences amounted to stone tents – permanent encampments, around which pastoralists could gather seasonally. Like other late antique and early medieval rulers, the Umayyads had the privilege of requisitioning supplies for their court and entourage. 'Abd al-Malik, we are told, stopped at al-Jabiya, south of Damascus, in the spring, where 'he ordered his companions to camp, and ordered cattle, sheep and goats according to the size of their encampment' (*amara bi-aṣḥābihi bi-inzāl wabaqar wa-aghnām 'alā qadar manāzilihim*). Thus, the Umayyad rulers were mobile monarchs, moving between palaces and estates that stood as physical reminders in the landscape of their authority when they were away.[91] The interiors and exteriors of their palaces, adorned with stucco and stone sculpture, mosaic and painted frescoes were intended to display their wealth, power and authority to visitors, with the decorative schemes combining Roman and Sasanian royal motifs in innovative and distinctive ways.[92]

Mu'awiya's winter palace was at al-Sinnabra, in the temperate climes of the southern shore of Lake Tiberias (the 'Sea of Galilee'). His son Yazid was particularly associated with the rural estate of al-Huwwarin, en route between Damascus and Tadmur/Palmyra, in the heartland of his Kalbi maternal relatives. The likely locations of both al-Sinnabra and al-Huwwarin have been identified, with some low ruins still visible in both locations. This pattern of itinerancy, centred on Damascus but including other residences as well, was followed by the Marwanids. 'Abd al-Malik's itinerary took in al-Sinnabra in winter, al-Jabiya, in the spring, then Damascus, where he stayed at Dayr Murran, then Ba'albak in the height of summer, and finally Damascus again in the autumn.[93]

'Abd al-Malik's son and successor al-Walid I is the last caliph to be associated with al-Sinnabra. Residences in the *jund* of Filastin, near Jerusalem,

---

[91] Borrut, *Mémoire et pouvoir*, 391–5.
[92] There is an extensive literature. See, with further references, Katharina Meinecke, 'Umayyad Visual Culture and Its Models', in Andrew Marsham (ed.), *The Umayyad World* (London and New York, 2021), 103–32; Robert Hillenbrand, 'Hisham's Balancing Act: The Case of Qasr al-Hayr al-Gharbi', in Alain George and Andrew Marsham (eds), *Power, Patronage, and Memory in Early Islam* (Oxford, 2018), 83–132.
[93] For 'Abd al-Malik's itinerary, see Baladhuri, *Ansab*, VI, 343, and the comments in Borrut, *Mémoire et pouvoir*, 396–411.

and in the Balqa', to the south and east of Amman, where there was also an extensive palace complex, appear more frequently in the sources for his reign and that of his brother, Sulayman. Besides al-Sinnabra, al-Walid I is also linked with Qasr Burqu', al-Muwaqqar, al-Qastal and Jabal Says/'Usays; all of the latter are in the north and north-east of modern Jordan, which was the southern part of the military district of Damascus, where it met the Syrian Desert. An inscription from Qasr Burqu' names al-Walid as 'The Son of the Commander of the Faithful' (*ibn amīr al-muʾminīn*), showing that it was a residence he used during 'Abd al-Malik's reign. Sulayman governed Filastin during the reigns of both his father and his brother. During al-Walid I's caliphate, Sulayman resided at his new town, al-Ramla, near Roman Lod/Lydda. Al-Muwaqqar and al-Qastal, just south of Amman, are both linked with Yazid II; these sites and others east of Amman, near al-Azraq, are also linked with his son al-Walid II and his children.[94]

Some of these Umayyad residences were constructed at what appear to have formerly been Christian monastic sites; the role of monasteries as sites of pilgrimage by the pastoralists of post-Roman Syria made them obvious locations for Umayyad gathering places. Indeed, some Christian monasteries were also said to have been stopping places for the early Marwanid caliphs. Dayr Murran, on Mount Qasiyun, above Damascus; Dayr Sim'an, in the foothills of the Limestone Massif, north-west of Aleppo; and Dayr al-Naqira, which may be another name for Dayr Sim'an, are all mentioned in the sources. These stories are suggestive of the continued importance of Christian leaders and sacred sites in the pastoralist political economy of Umayyad-era Syria.[95]

With the accession of Hisham, the pattern of circulation around southern and central Syria was abandoned; instead Hisham created what amounted to a second capital at al-Rusafa, in the *jund* of Qinnasrin in the north of Syria, spending much of his time there, rather than in Damascus; he is also associated with two extensive palace complexes en route between his two capitals, at Qasr al-Hayr al-Sharqi and Qasra al-Hayr al-Gharbi. Hisham's move to northern Syria was part of a gradual shift north in the military and economic focus of the Umayyad rulers. Whereas al-Jabiya, near Damascus, had been a muster-ground for Marwan and 'Abd al-Malik, the meadows of Dabiq, north of Aleppo,

---

[94] Genequand, *Établissemements*, 209, 365–6; Borrut, *Mémoire et pouvoir*, 393–5, 412–35; Robinson, *'Abd al-Malik*, 27–8. On al-Azraq and points east, see also above, Ch. 9, n. 21.

[95] *EI²*, 'Dayr Murran' (D. Sourdel); Garth Fowden and Elizabeth Key Fowden, *Studies on Hellenism, Christianity and the Umayyads* (Athens and Paris, 2004), 149–92; Borrut, *Mémoire et pouvoir*, 304–5, 403.

were the pastures used by Sulayman to gather his armies against the Romans; by the time of Hisham, Dabiq was still in use, but the frontier had moved still further north and west, as is reflected in his allies' holding estates north of the Euphrates river and his association with the further fortification of eastern Anatolia.[96] At the same time, the lands of the upper Euphrates were becoming more important in supplying food and goods to the growing cities of Iraq and so the Umayyad elite profited from these Mesopotamian landholdings.[97]

An aura of sacred power persisted in the landscape not only in the caliphs' absence but also after their deaths. While it is possible that some traditions of pilgrimage to the tomb of ʿUmar II – variously said to have been located at Dayr Murran, Dayr Simʿan or Dayr al-Naqira – may post-date the Umayyad period, there is other evidence that a caliph's tomb was already perceived as sacred. Eighth or early ninth-century reports have some of the Syrian tribes facing the wrath of al-Walid II seek refuge at the tomb of his father Yazid II, or his great-grandfather, Marwan.[98] Such a place of asylum was presumably intended to invoke past alliances and suggests the sacral power of the caliph's tomb. When the Abbasid forces who captured Damascus despoiled the tombs of the Umayyads and crucified their disinterred remains (an act that again recalls medieval and early modern parallels from elsewhere), they were seeking to destroy the Umayyads' numinous power.[99]

The archaeology for other regions of the empire is less well developed than that of Syria. However, literary sources show that the acquisition of landed property and its distribution to supporters was considered an important source of political influence. While al-Yaʿqubi (d. c. 905) is hostile to the Umayyads, his criticism that 'Muʿawiya did in the Jazira and Yemen what he had done in Iraq, setting aside for himself and making his own the estates that had belonged to (former) kings, and he granted them to members of his family and entourage', reflects a well attested practice.[100] Certainly, Muʿawiya also developed extensive agricultural estates in Mecca, Medina and al-Yamama, and his Egyptian

---

[96] Borrut, *Mémoire et pouvoir*, 427–39. See also above, Ch. 8, pp. 178–9.
[97] Kennedy, 'Feeding', and below nn. 105 and 108.
[98] Tabari, II, 1783; *Kitab al-ʿUyun wa-l-hadaʾiq fi akhbar al-haqaʾiq*, in M. J. de Goeje and P. de Jong (eds), *Fragmenta Historicum Arabicorum* (Leiden, 1869). 122.
[99] On these disinterments, see Robinson, 'Violence'.
[100] Yaʿqubi, II, 278 (translation after Matthew Gordon et al. (eds and trs), *The Works of Ibn Wadih al-Yaʿqubi* (Leiden, 2018), III, 914). See also Banaji, 'Late Antique Legacies', 170, with further references.

governor, 'Amr b. al-'As, owned West Arabian lands. Some of Mu'awiya's West Arabian irrigation projects are archaeologically extant, supporting the narratives in the later sources.[101] After the defeat of Ibn al-Zubayr, the Marwanids also sought political control in the Hijaz through land ownership.[102] The literary sources include numerous references to land grants being made in the wake of conquests; in Quhistan in the 640s, around Marw in Khurasan in the 670s, and in North Africa under Hassan b. al-Nu'man and Musa b. Nusayr in the late 690s and 700s.[103] Extensive land grants were also made in al-Andalus in 742, when lands were parcelled out by Abu l-Khattar al-Kalbi.[104] In Mosul in 752–3, a local member of the Marwanid family owned lands on the eastern bank of the Tigris where he went hunting.[105]

The larger estates were sources of huge revenues for the leading members of the new elite.[106] Mu'awiya's estates reclaimed from the marshes of southern Iraq are said to have made five million or fifteen million dirhams per year.[107] Maslama b. 'Abd al-Malik is associated with the northern Syrian estate of Balis/Barbalissos, and another in southern Iraq. In both cases he made agreements in which he invested substantially in the infrastructure of the two locations – an investment of three million dirhams is mentioned for southern Iraq.[108] Hisham's governor of Iraq, Khalid al-Qasri, is said to have had an annual income of variously ten, thirteen or twenty million dirhams. Hisham b. 'Abd al-Malik himself is said to have earned more from his estates than the whole tax revenue of the empire.[109] This is no doubt literary exaggeration, since it would imply an annual personal income of hundreds of millions of dirhams, but it does suggest the vast scale of the landed wealth acquired by

---

[101] Kennedy, 'Landholding and Law', 161–2, 173. Yamama: Tabari, II, 156. On material traces of Mu'awiya, see Donald Whitcomb, 'Notes for an Archaeology of Mu'awiya: Material Culture in the Transitional Period of Believers', in Antoine Borrut and Fred M. Donner (eds), *Christians and Others in the Umayyad State* (Chicago, 2016), 11–28.

[102] Munt, 'Caliphal Estates'.

[103] North Africa: Fenwick, 'From Africa to Ifriqiya', 19; Mohamed Talbi, 'Law and Economy in Ifriqiya (Tunisia) in the Third Islamic Century: Agriculture and the Role of Slaves in the Country's Economy', in Abraham L. Udovitch (ed.), *The Islamic Middle East, 700–1900: Studies in Economic and Social History* (Princeton, 1981), 209–11. Near Kirman: Tabari, II, 2704–5. For Tabas al-Tamr, in Quhistan, see Tabari, *History*, XV, 87, n. 155 (R. S. Humphreys). Khurasan: see above, Ch. 4, p. 99 and n. 55.

[104] *EI*², 'al-Andalus (iii. Outline of the Historical Geography of al-Andalus. 3. Urban toponymy and territorial divisions of *al-Andalus*.)' (E. Lévi-Provençal).

[105] Kennedy, 'Elite Incomes', 25.

[106] See the useful collection of examples in Morony, 'Landholding'.

[107] Al-Qadi, 'Population Census', 361.

[108] Eger, *Islamic–Byzantine Frontier*, 211 n. 31; Kennedy, 'Elite Incomes', 20–2.

[109] Kennedy, 'Elite Incomes', 28; Kennedy, 'Financing', 372; Tabari, II, 1641–2, 1655.

the Umayyad dynasty and their supporters, especially in the latter decades of their rule.[110]

Commerce and Exchange in Rome and Iran

In both the Roman Empire and Sasanian Iran, precious metal coins, controlled by the imperial administrations, were the main units of exchange and taxation. In Roman territories gold was the main precious metal currency, minted into solidi ('solid ones'), which were small, thick, gold coins, about 20mm in diameter and weighing just less than 4.5g.[111] In Iran, the precious metal coinage was struck in silver *drachma*s.[112] These were broad, thin, coins, about 30mm across, which weighed around 4g. The coins were immensely valuable – a goldsmith's assistant in Egypt in 588 CE earned just three solidi per year – and so the main unit of daily exchange for most people in both empires was copper coinage. By the late sixth century the exchange rate between copper and gold coins in the Roman Empire was fluctuating between around 400:1 to 1000:1.[113]

The income gap between the wealthiest Roman aristocrats and merchants and the majority of the population was great. Whereas a goldsmith's assistant in late Roman Egypt earned only three solidi per year, and farm labourers and estate workers earned about twelve, the great landowners and some merchants and bankers were able to accumulate vast reserves of gold; the Apions – a sixth-century Egyptian landowning family whose estate at Oxyrynchus in Egypt is well known from the papyri – had an annual income after tax in excess of 13,000 solidi;[114] a sixth-century banker (Lat. *argentarius*) named Julianus was able to donate 26,000 solidi towards the construction costs of San Vitale

---

[110] As noted by Banaji, 'Late Antique Legacies', 169–70, citing 'Abd al-'Aziz Duri, 'The Origins of Iqta' in Islam', *al-Abhath* 22 (1969), 11.
[111] Luke Treadwell, "Abd al-Malik's Coinage Reform: The Role of the Damascus Mint', *Revue numismatique* 165 (2009), 365.
[112] On coinage levels in the Sasanian economy and their peak between 603 and 635, see Haldon, 'Resources', 68, with further references.
[113] By the early seventh century, both the gold and the copper coinage were centrally controlled, struck mainly at Constantinople: Heidemann, 'Merger', 95, 97. In the same period, the average weight of Roman copper coins was in decline, fluctuating between about 9 and 18 grams, but tending towards lower end of this scale: Banaji, *Agrarian Change*, 66–7, 224–5. For the exchange rate, see Jairus Banaji, 'Discounts, Weight Standards and the Exchange Rate between Gold and Copper: Insights into the Monetary Process of the Sixth Century', in Jairus Banaji, *Exploring the Economy of Late Antiquity: Selected Essays* (Cambridge, 2015), 107.
[114] Todd M. Hickey, 'Aristocratic Landholding and the Economy of Byzantine Egypt', in Roger S. Bagnall (ed.), *Egypt in the Byzantine World* (Cambridge, 2007), 302.

in Ravenna.¹¹⁵ The former figure amounts to more than 4,000 years' wages for the goldsmith's assistant or 1,000 years for an Egyptian labourer, and the latter to double these numbers. In between these polarities, there were lower-level elites, albeit usually nearer to the labourers than the aristocrats and the bankers; the headmen (Gk *meizones*) of the villages in Oxyrynchus could dispose of an inheritance of 360 solidi, and a senior manager on the Apions' estate earned twenty-four solidi.¹¹⁶

In both the Roman and Sasanian empires, the state's management of stable precious metal currencies for tax collection and the payment of their armies encouraged and supported a market economy. Goods were exchanged for cash in order to pay those taxes that were collected in the precious metal coinage (or in copper, to be exchanged for gold or silver). This market exchange occurred at all scales from the very local, to the provincial and the inter-regional.

Assessing the volume of trade in different regions and the relative importance of the imperial state's distribution networks vis-à-vis private commerce has proved difficult and tendentious because of the uneven and partial nature of the evidence.¹¹⁷ So too the question of how patterns of trade and exchange were changing the in the sixth and seventh centuries, and what consequences the Arabian conquests and the formation of the Umayyad Empire had for them. For the Mediterranean world, ceramics have been crucial in these debates. Unlike perishable goods, like grain, oil, cloth or slaves, ceramics leave a sizeable archaeological trace which is often datable and can also reveal the place of the pottery's production. Furthermore, ceramic jars (Lat. *amphorae*) were used to transport some of the most important Mediterranean commodities, olive oil and wine. Fine wares, used as tableware and cookware were also transported alongside other goods, and these too – most notably African Red Slipware (ARS) and Phocean Red Slip Ware (PRS) – have left their trace in the archaeology. This ceramic evidence tends to suggest that the regional trade in the East Mediterranean remained strong into the seventh century, with North Africa and Egypt exporting goods to the northern and Eastern

---

[115] Banaji, *Agrarian Change*, 62.
[116] Hickey, 'Aristocratic landholding', 298 (inheritance); Banaji, *Agrarian Change*, 235 (income).
[117] For trade in the Red Sea, Ethiopia, East Africa and India, see Roberta Tomber, *Indo-Roman Trade: From Pots to Pepper* (London, 2008),161–74. On policing trade, see Haldon, 'Resources', 58, with further references. On the importance of commerce to the Sasanian Empire, and the growth in connectivity in Late Antiquity, see Richard E. Payne, 'The Silk Road and the Iranian Political Economy in Late Antiquity: Iran, the Silk Road, and the Problem of Aristocratic Empire', *BSOAS* 81 (2018), 227–50.

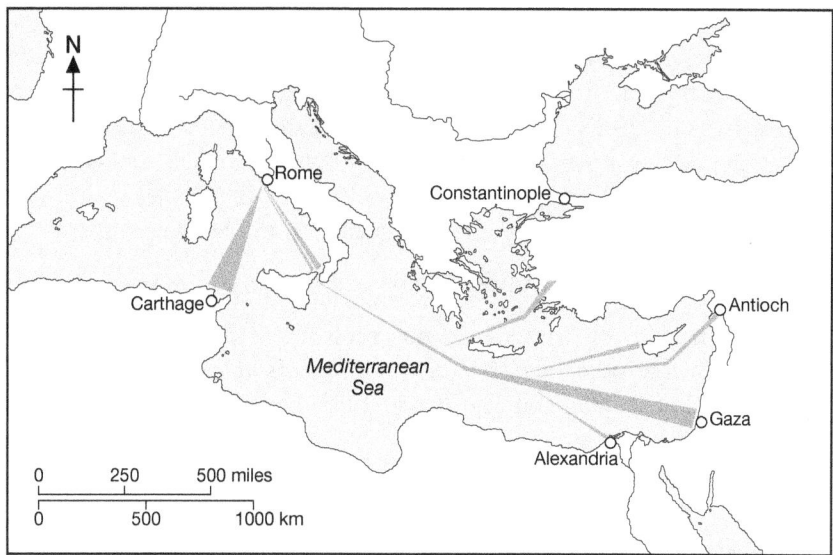

Map 10.3 Map depicting volume of imports in amphorae from a late seventh-century deposit at the Crypta Balbi, Rome. The arrows represent imported volumes calculated on the basis of amphorae capacities. Based on Simon Loseby, 'The Mediterranean Economy' in Paul Fouracre (ed.), *The New Cambridge History Volume 1, c. 500–700* (Cambridge, 2005), map 16.

Mediterranean, and with centres of production in Syria and Gaza exporting their goods westward (see Map 10.3).[118]

Still less is known about trade in Sasanian Iran since overland trade leaves fewer material traces and archaeological investigation of the region has generally been less intensive. Among the better-attested and well-researched trade routes are those along which the long-distance exchange of luxury and high-value goods took place. Overland trade with China, via the so-called 'Silk Road' is the most well-known example of this. Here Sogdian traders (from modern south Uzbekistan and west Tajikistan) acted as the middlemen in trade routes that carried silver and other commodities including slaves east out of Iran and Sogdia, across the mountain passes west of the Tien Shan Mountains and into entrepôts such as Kashghar and Turfan. In return, silk and raw silk for manufacture in Iran were traded west, as well as spices and

---

[118] Useful summaries are Bryan Ward-Perkins, 'Specialized Production and Exchange', *CAH*, XIV, 346–91; Simon T. Loseby, 'The Mediterranean Economy', in Paul Fouracre (ed.), *The New Cambridge Medieval History Volume I, c.500–700* (Cambridge, 2005), 605–38; Simon T. Loseby, 'Post-Roman Economies', in Walter Scheidel (ed.), *The Cambridge Companion to the Roman Economy* (Cambridge, 2012), 334–60.

other commodities.[119] A second route to China was by sea, via the ports of the Gulf and the Indian Ocean but the Arabian Gulf coast appears to have been bypassed, with some trade passing instead through the Iranian shore's ports of Siraf and Hormuz.[120] There is also some evidence of trade and exchange beyond the Caucasus, where late Sasanian (and late Roman) silver vessels have been found near the Ural Mountains.[121] Trade and exchange with the Roman world via northern Iraq became closely regulated by the two empires.[122]

Commerce and Exchange in the Umayyad Empire

The Arabian conquests and the development of the Umayyad Empire had three main impacts on these sixth-century patterns of trade and exchange. First, the end of Roman and Sasanian imperial rule changed the structures supporting state-sponsored exchange of goods. Some were retained in modified forms (notably the tax system) and others ended. Crucially, the two coinage systems were integrated after the 690s, which further facilitated commercial exchange across a huge area of Africa and Eurasia. Second, the political integration of the conquered regions was affected by the manner of the end of the old imperial structures. Whereas regions like Egypt, Syria and southern Iraq were incorporated into the new empire quickly, others, such as Ifriqiya and Khurasan, were contested for prolonged periods. Still others – often those that lay beyond the old empires' military and fiscal domination – such as Mauretania, Sistan, Sogdia, Tukharistan and Farghana, were never fully integrated. The economies of these contested regions, therefore, retained a frontier character, modified by the presence of new Arabian military actors. Indeed, the Umayyad period was characterised by continuous warfare on numerous fronts; the old frontier between Rome and Iran had become the centre of the new empire, while expansionist warfare, and its attendant economic effects – including flows of booty, loot and tribute – took place all around this new core region. The third change, closely connected to conquest and settlement, was the foundation of new urban centres, or the adoption of existing ones, for new military and administrative purposes.

---

[119] Jonathan Karam Skaff, 'Sasanian and Arab-Sasanian Silver Coins from Turfan: Their Relationship to International Trade and the Local Economy', *Asia Major* 11 (1998), 89–90.

[120] Derek Kennet, 'The Decline of Eastern Arabia in the Sasanian Period', *Arabian Archaeology and Epigraphy* 18 (2007), 86–122; James Howard-Johnston, 'The Two Great Powers in Late Antiquity: A Comparison', in Averil Cameron (ed.), *Byzantine and Early Islamic Near East III: States, Resources and Armies* (Princeton, 1995), 204–5. On the Red Sea, which was an alternative route for Indian Ocean trade, see above, n. 117.

[121] Richard N. Frye, 'Byzantine and Sasanian Trade Relations with Northeastern Russia', *DOP* 26 (1972), 263–9.

[122] See above, n. 117.

The extraordinary expansion of some of these towns made them into engines of commerce in their respective regions and trans-regionally, too; the Arabian conquerors and their descendants were important actors in the economy, as purchasers of goods and services, funded by the appropriation of vast amounts of wealth through conquest and taxation, and as participants in commercial and agricultural activity themselves.

The impact of the Arabian conquests on state-supported economic structures often initially amounted to a continuation of modified existing institutions in a decentralised and more localised form. A tax system based upon the collection of much of the revenue in precious metal coinage was maintained, alongside, as in Rome and Iran, taxes collected in kind and corvée labour. However, these revenues were now administered from the new provincial garrison capitals (*miṣr*s), and most of the takings were redistributed within the province to those conquerors named on the register (*dīwān*). ʿAbd al-Malik and his successors sought to intensify the levels of taxation and to have more revenue returned to Damascus. Many of these initiatives may in fact have been counter-productive, leading to flight from the land by peasants and perhaps even to falls in the revenue collected.[123]

For many of the Arabian migrants and their allies and clients, the tax revenues they received at the *miṣr*s were supplemented by income from expansionist warfare. Among the conquerors, as among other peoples in Late Antiquity, convention held that a fifth of moveable wealth seized on the battlefield should be passed to the commander and thence to the caliph. The remainder was distributed by the local commander among his followers.[124] After a victory at Sbeitla (in modern Tunisia) in 647 the portion of each horseman is said to have been 3,000 solidi and each footsoldier 1,000.[125] The payment of tributes to buy off armies was also a widespread practice: in 647, the people of Roman North Africa are said to have paid off ʿAbd Allah b. Saʿd's army with the astonishingly high sum of 2,520,000 solidi;[126] in 716–17, the people of Jurjan (highlands and plains east of the Caspian Sea) were said to have been paying a regular annual tribute of between 100,000 or 200,000 and sometimes even 300,000 drachmas

---

[123] Banaji, 'Late Antique Legacies', 171–3, who sees Egypt at least as returning substantial revenues to Damascus, which indeed seems plausible. But cf. Kennedy, 'Financing', 371–2. For revenues in the Sawad, see Baladhuri, *Futuh*, 270. On flight from the land, see also *SaMS*, 190, 194, 210–12.

[124] *EI3*, 'Fayʾ' (Marsham).

[125] Shihab al-Din Ahmad b. ʿAbd al-Wahhab al-Nuwayri, *Nihayat al-arab fi funun al-adab*, ed. Mufid Qumayhah et al. (Beirut, 2004–5), XIX, 260; tr. M. de Baron de Slane (ed. and tr.), *Histoire des Berbères et des dynasties Musulmanes* (Algiers, 1852–6), I, 322.

[126] Tabari, I, 2818. Cf. Baladhuri, *Futuh*, 227.

to the army of Kufa.[127] The figures from the later sources must treated with scepticism, but that vast amounts of bullion and other valuables passed into the hands of the conquerors in these ways is certain.

Among the commodities acquired through conquest and tribute payment, slaves were some of the most valuable and important. Slavery was a long-standing feature of most ancient and late antique economies, but the conquests created a huge new market and new 'slaving zones' on the new empire's frontiers.[128] Greek inscriptions from Cyprus refer to two raids in the 650s taking 120,000 and 50,000 captives, respectively.[129] In North Africa the campaign of 670 is said to have yielded 80,000 slaves in captives and the regular provision of thousands of slaves often formed part of tribute agreements with groups on the frontiers of the empire.[130] In the 710s and 720s the sources report millions and sometimes tens of millions of dirhams being taken in loot in Sind, as well as tens of thousands of slaves.[131] Slaves were high-value commodities, with the price for a single slave being attested at around thirty dinars, but sometimes far more than that; the revenue from groups of thousands of slaves would be comparable with the annual tax revenues of some provinces.[132]

Some of these slaves were employed on estates in Arabia and Iraq, and perhaps elsewhere.[133] However, the majority probably became domestic servants and sexual partners, with the Arabian Faithful seeing sexual slavery as permitted alongside up to four simultaneous marriages to free women. The wealthiest inhabitants of the empire led huge households. For example, Athanasius Bar Gumoye, the Christian tax official in Egypt under 'Abd al-'Aziz, is said to

---

[127] Kennedy, 'Financing', 367; Tabari, II, 1320–3. Al-Hira is said to have made peace for 80,000 or 100,000 drachmas per year: Baladhuri, *Futuh*, 243. At al-Anbar, terms were either 80,000 or 400,000 drachmas and 1,000 cloaks from Qatawan: Baladhuri, *Futuh*, 246.

[128] For 'slaving zones', see Jeffrey Fynn-Paul, 'Empire, Monotheism and Slavery in the Greater Mediterranean Region from Antiquity to the Early Modern Era', *Past & Present* 205 (2009), 3–40; for interactions between the Umayyad Empire and western Europe, see Michael McCormick, *Origins of the European Economy: Communications and Commerce, AD 300–900* (Cambridge, 2001).

[129] Crone, *Nativist Prophets*, 7.

[130] *Theophilus*, 164; Emily Savage, 'Berbers and Blacks: Ibadi Slave Traffic in Eighth-century North Africa', *The Journal of African History* 33 (1992), 356, n. 37. For a contemporary source on the taking of slaves in Syria and northern Iraq, see Brock, 'North Mesopotamia', 61.

[131] Blankinship, *End of the Jihad*, 65.

[132] McCormick, *Origins*, 754–8; Eliyahu Ashtor, *Histoire des prix et des salaires dans l'Orient medieval* (Paris, 1969), 58–9, 89. For assessments of tax revenues, see Part II Introduction and Ch. 12, pp. 122 and 327.

[133] For 4,000 slaves said to have worked Mu'awiya's estates in al-Yamama, see Tabari, II, 156. See also Munt, 'Caliphal Estates', 442–4. On Iraq, see above, Chs 5 and 6, pp. 105 and 133.

have owned 4,000 slaves. While such numbers usually cannot be taken literally, they are intended to indicate 'very many'.[134] The presence of thousands of slave women in the households of the conquerors and their descendants had a significant demographic impact, with growing numbers of children being born to Muslim fathers and slave mothers. In contrast to most Roman and Asian precedents, these children were free Muslims and did not inherit their mother's slave status.[135]

These flows of wealth into the hands of a small conquering elite are key to explaining the rapid growth of the new garrison towns. On top of the goods and services purchased by the population simply for sustenance and daily life, the garrisons were centres for the recruitment and equipping of the armies, which generated large-scale commerce and exchange. In Iraq, the garrisons of Kufa, Basra and Wasit all had districts known as the 'city of supplies' (*madīnat al-rizq*); when Wasit fell to the Abbasids in 750, its *madīnat al-rizq* was said to have held three million dirhams and a year's food for 30,000 men and 20,000 riding animals.[136] The soldiers' payments were sometimes expected to cover their purchase of riding animals and weapons: in 699, 'al-Hajjaj paid the men their stipends in full, ordering them to equip themselves with excellent horses and full arms', in advance of a campaign in Sistan. Once there (presumably at Zaranj), 'the men all mustered in their camp, markets were set up for them and they began to ready themselves and prepare for battle.' However, in preparation for his campaign in Tukharistan in 693–4, Bukayr b. Wishah 'expended a great amount of money' at Marw, presumably on his retinue and supplies, and al-Hajjaj also supplied an army for the conquest of Sind. When conquests slowed or were temporarily halted, there was pressure to supplement the armies' income from the tax revenue.[137]

High demand and high incomes combined with geography to create new commercial centres in regions where trade was already a significant element of the economy. In the late seventh century, the Armenian geographer now known as Ananias of Shirak wrote that 'Basra is filled with merchants and ships coming from India and all parts of the East.' Later Arabic sources describe long-distance commercial connections, and piracy predating on

---

[134] Palmer et al., *Seventh Century*, 203. On numbers, see Chase F. Robinson, 'Slavery in the Conquest Period', *IJMES* 49 (2017), 158–63; Crone, *Nativist Prophets*, 7–8.
[135] On slave women, see Robinson, *Marriage*.
[136] *IatMC*, 62–3.
[137] Baladhuri, *Futuh*, 436; Tabari, II, 862, 1022, 1043–5, quotations at 862 and 1043–4, tr. after E. Rowson in Tabari, *History*, XXII, 191, 193; Kennedy, 'Financing', 369, 371.

them, in the Indian Ocean in the late seventh or early eighth century.[138] A few sources in Umayyad-era East Asian sources and at least one passing reference in the Umayyad poetry indicate that a trade route linked Iraq with India, China and Sri Lanka, via the Gulf and the Indian Ocean. The archaeological evidence suggests that by the early ninth century, a huge amount of traffic was passing along the Iranian Gulf coast; very likely trade was already expanding in the later seventh and eighth centuries, with increased demand generated by the rapidly growing population of Basra and Kufa.[139] Goods brought to market were said to have been taxed already in the time of 'Umar b. al-Khattab, and certainly by the early eighth century.[140]

The Roman Empire's workshops and the supply lines for its armies, as well as the annual levy of grain from Egypt (Gk *embole*, Lat. *annona*) had been significant elements in the economy, alongside privately funded commerce. Some of this continued under the new Arabian rulers. In Egypt, taxes in kind included food and supplies for officials and for the shipyards of Alexandria.[141] The grain levy from Egypt was continued but redirected, in *c*. 642, to Medina. In the following year, the canal between Fustat/Babil and Qulzum/Clysma, on the Red Sea coast was dredged to improve the transport of the grain, while the port of al-Jar on the Arabian side of the sea was developed by 'Uthman as the reception point for it.[142] Likewise, the shipyards of Alexandria, the silk workshops of Egypt and other strategically critical resources were of particular interest to the new military commanders.[143] As well as tribute payments, exchange of goods could also be organised between caliphs and governors and their counterparts beyond their frontiers. Diplomatic gifts were sent to China.[144] There were also other more commercial arrangements. The Egyptian governor 'Abd Allah b. Abi Sarh is said in some accounts to have agreed an annual payment of food crops to the Nubians equivalent in value to slaves received in exchange. Gold was exchanged for copper coins with the Romans until *c*. 658, when it was perhaps ended as part of the tribute

---

[138] Ananias: Banaji, 'Late Antique Legacies', 174. For the Indian Ocean, see Baladhuri, *Futuh*, 435–6. *Jazīrat al-Yāqūt* ('The Island of Rubies') is perhaps Sri Lanka or Sumatra: *EI*², 'Med' (Y. Friedmann and D. Shulman).

[139] Alain George, 'Direct Sea Trade Between Early Islamic Iraq and Tang China: From the Exchange of Goods to the Transmission of Ideas', *JRAS* 25 (2015), 579–624.

[140] On the *maks* ('custom') tax, see *SaMS*, 180, with further references.

[141] *SaMS*, 174–5.

[142] Baladhuri, *Futuh*, 216; Charles Le Quesne, 'Hajj Ports of the Red Sea: A Historical and Archaeological Overview', in Venetia Porter and Liana Saif (eds), *The Hajj: Collected Essays* (London, 2013), 75–7.

[143] See above, pp. 223–5.

[144] On China, see Gibb, 'Chinese Records', 619–22; Bielenstein, *Diplomacy and Trade*, 356–8.

agreement reached with the Romans.[145] Papyrus was regularly exchanged for gold with the Roman Empire until the 690s, when deteriorating relations interrupted this exchange.[146]

Conclusions

The Arabian conquests and the formation of the Umayyad Empire reshaped the economies of North Africa and the Middle East. Above all, this came about through the redirecting the resources of the old empires' taxation systems to new military groups, who were often settled in new urban centres. The new demand generated at the garrisons redirected flows of commerce and began to alter the demographics and the agricultural economies of the surrounding regions. Attitudes to the taxation of 'dead' land, which incentivised its development, contributed to the acquisition of extensive estates by well-connected members of the military elite. In Syria, the exploitation of marginal lands and the expansion of urban market districts are two of the recurrent patterns of Umayyad-era archaeology and there is some evidence from the literary sources that similar developments were taking place elsewhere in Egypt, Iraq and on the Arabian Peninsula. Control of land was closely connected to political power; by the end of the Umayyad period a wealthy landed imperial elite, benefiting from the ownership of agricultural estates and urban markets, had emerged. Resentment of these disparities contributed to the tensions behind the unrest and conflict of the 740s.

Whereas the military frontiers had advanced fast in these core regions, in the lands beyond them highly militarised, predatory economies developed, as they usually did at the boundaries of military power in the ancient and medieval world. In North Africa and Central Asia thousands of captives were enslaved over many years. Because the children of slave women came to be seen as freeborn, the captives significantly impacted the demographics of the conquerors' settlements. Huge flows of bullion and other prestige goods paid the armies and contributed to the fortunes of their commanders. In Central Asia, the Arabian conquerors competed for control of the valuable trade routes of the so-called 'Silk Road'. Likewise, in the far West, the Arabian conquerors' entanglement with the 'Berber' tribes saw rapid social change and accelerated

---

[145] Martin Hinds and Hamdi Sakkout, 'A Letter from the Governor of Egypt to the King of Nubia and Muqarra concerning Egyptian–Nubian Relations in 141/758', in Wadad al-Qadi (ed.), *Studia Arabica et Islamica: Festschrift for Ihsan 'Abbas on his Sixtieth Birthday* (Beirut, 1981), 209–29; Heidemann, 'Merger', 97–8; Clive Foss, *Arab-Byzantine Coins: An Introduction, with a Catalogue of the Dumbarton Oaks Collection* (Washington, DC, 2008), 20. On the tribute agreement with the Romans, see above, Ch. 4, p. 91.

[146] Baladhuri, *Futuh*, 237, 240.

the rebalancing of trading connections towards the interior and trans-Saharan long-distance commerce.

Finally, while the details will continue to be explored and the picture will change, there is little doubt that environmental disruption contributed to the conditions that brought about the formation of the Umayyad Empire and shaped its subsequent evolution. The bubonic plague probably contributed to the weakening of Rome and Iran in the sixth and early seventh centuries, spread in part by their wars. It remained endemic, perhaps adding to rural labour shortages in the Umayyad period. Pressure on the Egyptian economy caused by reduced Nile flood levels in the later seventh and eighth centuries may have contributed to tax revolts there and increased the challenges facing Marwanid governors as they sought to supply funds to the caliph in Syria. More arid conditions in North Africa and the Levant may also have contributed to conflict over the resources of those regions.

11

Christians, Zoroastrians, Jews and Others in the Umayyad Empire

Among the new political formations of Late Antiquity and the early Middle Ages, the Umayyad Empire is exceptional in the distinctiveness of the new religious tradition that took shape within it. After *c.* 400 CE, new elites in the Latin West had tended to adopt forms of Christianity as a central component of their political culture, while forms of Christianity and Judaism were also adopted by other new elites elsewhere in North Africa and West Eurasia. As with other late antique military associations, pledged allegiance to a leader was understood in religious terms among the Arabians. While this initially seems to have allowed for some latitude in beliefs and practices among the conquering armies led by the Meccans, boundaries between the new religion and other faith traditions tended to harden over the course of the seventh and eighth centuries. At the same time, conflict within the conquerors, migrants and non-Arabian convert populations generated diverse but distinctively Islamic religious traditions and various Muslim populations who were detached from participation in imperial rule, or active rivals to it.

This chapter examines the impact of these processes on the religious communities of the regions of North Africa and Middle East whom the Arabians encountered when they took power. Because religion had such a central place in political identity in Late Antiquity, it is the primary focus of the chapter, although the category of religion has limits; religious leaders exerted only partial influence over those they claimed to lead, and other markers of difference could have equal or greater significance – among them shared language and culture, economic or class interest, and political and military association.[1]

---

[1] On this point, see, for example, Arietta Papaconstantinou, 'Between *Umma* and *Dhimma*: The Christians of the Middle East under the Umayyads', *Annales Islamologiques* 42 (2008), 127–56. See also Nicholas Kyle Longworth, 'Islamic Bureaucrats in Late Antiquity: Administration and Elites during the Umayyad Caliphate (*c.* 661–750 CE)', PhD Dissertation, University of Chicago (2022). I am grateful to Marie Legendre for drawing my attention to the latter, which appeared too late for full inclusion here. On religion in Late Antiquity, see above, Introduction, p. 9 and n. 3.

Because Syrian and Egyptian Christianity were the majority religious traditions in the two most important conquered territories for the Umayyads, the chapter begins with the Christian communities in these provinces, before looking at the experiences of the Jews in the same regions, and then smaller groups such as Samaritans. From there, it turns to the rather different context of post-Sasanian Iraq and western Iran where, before the conquests, Christians and Jews had been large minority communities under the rule of Zoroastrians, alongside many other smaller minority religious communities, including Manichaeans and Mandaeans, as well as various Iranian populations who adhered to local forms of Zoroastrianism.

Beyond these core territories of the new empire, the frontier zones of the Caucasus, North Africa, and Khurasan and Central Asia are treated in turn. In the Caucasus, Christian aristocracies and their military followings became strategically important in the conflict with Rome and the Khazars. North Africa was likewise a zone of conflict with the Romans and was also predominantly Christian, but the presence of the groups labelled collectively by the outsider witnesses who wrote our sources as 'Moors', 'Numidians' or 'Berbers' led to distinctive outcomes. Khurasan and Central Asia were equally complex religious, linguistic and political contexts, where non-Arabian non-Muslims – Zoroastrians, Buddhists, Christians, Manichaeans and others – again participated in warfare and government.

In most of the regions into which the Arabian conquerors migrated, the co-option of local military actors led eventually to the widespread adoption of Islam among those groups. This process began first among some of the Peninsular populations and then among the Arabic-speaking nomadic pastoralists of the Syrian Desert, but something similar happened during and after the next waves of expansion into North Africa and Central Asia, when so-called 'Berber' and 'Persian' groups joined the conquering armies and became Muslim. In contrast, the tax-paying, less militarised, populations of the empire ('the people of the land', Ar. *ahl al-ard*) tended to retain their own beliefs and practices under the military rule of the new Muslim elites.[2] This often led to an expansion in the role of local religious leaders, as they competed for influence in their region and moved to fill the administrative vacuum left by the end of Roman and Sasanian rule. Exceptions to this pattern of distinction between convert militaries and subject non-Muslims were most common among vassal groups who were militarily important to the Arabian conquerors but were beyond their direct control, as in the Caucasus, and parts of North Africa and Central Asia. Conversely, by the latter decades

---

[2] For *ahl al-ard*, see Zychowicz-Coghill, *First Arabic Annals*, 36, 98.

of the Umayyad period, there were also sizeable Muslim populations who were not tax recipients, nor serving members of the army or its associated fiscal administration.

Christianities in the Umayyad Empire

Christianity – or rather the various Christianities – in the Umayyad Empire deserve particular attention. The Umayyad elite in Syria, and their allies in Egypt, ruled majority Christian populations, while their Iraqi governors ruled a significant Christian minority. In Egypt, Syria and the Jazira, Christians were central to the military and organisational power of the Umayyad rulers well into the eighth century. These Christians had diverse connections with one another and connections beyond the frontiers of Umayyad power. Crucially, the Umayyads' main external rivals were the Roman emperors, with whom they contended for control of North Africa, the Mediterranean and the Caucasus. The emperors presented themselves as the rightful leaders of the Christian world, with Romanness (Lat. *romanitas*) and Christianity (*christianitas*) being inextricably intertwined concepts by the seventh century.[3] Moreover, there were also substantial Christian communities across all the conquered territories beyond Egypt, Syria and Iraq, both in former Roman lands and in former Sasanian ones. Many of the other powers in Africa and the Mediterranean were also Christian – the Nubians and Aksumites in East Africa, the Visigoths and Franks in the West, and the Georgians, Armenians and Albanians in the Caucasus.

Sectarian distinctions are prominent in the sources composed by Christian clerics. While the ordinary people whom those clerics led may often not have paid much attention to the niceties of doctrine and theology, nor experienced religion in these abstract terms, church leaders articulated communal boundaries through differences in belief.[4] Doctrine distinguished competing church hierarchies and was entangled with other aspects of social and political organisation. Hence, Christological disputes that can now sometimes seem arcane could take on great religious and political importance. Salvation in this world and the next might depend on choosing sides correctly, with both church politics and efforts by the Roman emperors to assert their authority over the church being expressed in Christological terms.

Roman imperial authorities had tended to promote a 'Chalcedonian' Christology, based on the definition arrived at the Council of Chalcedon

---

[3] Claudia Rapp, 'Hellenic Identity, *Romanitas*, and Christianity in Byzantium', in Katerina Zacharia (ed.), *Hellenisms: Culture, Identity, and Ethnicity from Antiquity to Modernity* (Farnham, 2008), 144–6.

[4] Tannous, *Making*, emphasises the porosity of communal and doctrinal boundaries for the illiterate majority, whom Tannous terms 'simple believers'.

(451 CE), according to which Christ had 'two natures', united in one person and one 'underlying reality' (Gk *hypostasis*). However, in the eastern provinces of the Roman Empire, this Chalcedonian Christology was not widely accepted. By the end of the sixth century, there was a flourishing miaphysite (sometimes, 'monophysite', 'Severan' or 'Jacobite') Christianity in Egypt, East Africa, Syria, Armenia and the highlands of north Mesopotamia. For miaphysites, Christ had 'one nature', of both a divine and human character, which nonetheless remained distinct. In eastern Mesopotamia, Iraq and Iran, the 'Church of the East' adhered to a Christology which was dyophysite like Chalcedonianism but nonetheless usually seen as incompatible with it. All these eastern Christian groups followed traditions established by church leaders who had been anathematised – that is, labelled as schismatic, and in error – by Chalcedonians. Attempts to resolve the sectarian divides in Roman lands with new Christologies had been made by Heraclius in the 620s and 630s, but without success. The third Council of Constantinople in 680–1, convened by Constantine IV (r. c. 669–85), rejected his innovations.[5]

Sectarian divides intersected with distinctions based on ethnicity, language and political affiliation. Greek was the shared language of the educated elites of the eastern Roman world, central to religious discourse in the eastern Roman Empire and its former provinces of Egypt and Syria. However, local vernacular languages had also become important church languages. In Egypt, the local language was Coptic (from the Greek, *Aigyptios*, 'Egyptian'). In its various regional dialects, Coptic had become a written language of the province alongside Greek by the fifth century, spreading rapidly with the conversion of the province to Christianity.[6] In Syria, people in the southern regions of Palestine and the Judaean Desert spoke and wrote Christian Palestinian Aramaic (or CPA, sometimes erroneously called 'Syriac'), while the pastoralist tribespeople of the Syrian Desert spoke, and sometimes wrote, Arabic. In the north, and in the Mesopotamian highlands of Diyarbakir and Tur 'Abdin, the written dialect of Aramaic known more properly as Syriac had become the language of Christian liturgy and literature. In Iraq and Iran, the church used Syriac, too, and there were also Arabic-speaking Christians in al-Hira and its environs. Armenian Christians wrote and worshipped in Armenian, which

---

[5] On sectarian divides in the sixth century, see Pauline Allen, 'The Definition and Enforcement of Orthodoxy', *CAH*, XIV, 820–34. On the same in the seventh century, see Scott Fitzgerald Johnson, 'Introduction: The Social Presence of Greek in Eastern Christianity, 200–1200', in Scott Fitzgerald Johnson, *Languages and Cultures of Eastern Christianity: Greek* (Farnham, 2015), 59–67. On the 'Church of the East' and Chalcedon, see Philip Wood, *The Chronicle of Seert: Christian Historical Imagination in Late Antique Iraq* (Oxford, 2013), 134–42.

[6] Bagnall, *Egypt*, 238–40.

had become a written language with the coming of Christianity in the fourth century. Christians in the western Caucasus used Georgian. In North Africa and the Iberian Peninsula, Latin was the language of the educated elite and of the church and had also spread beyond these circles. In Nubia and Aksum the local languages of Nubian and Geʽez became church languages, alongside Coptic and Greek.[7]

Christian leadership was divided between priesthoods of bishops and their clerics, communities of celibate monks, and solitary hermits. Major towns were the seats, or 'sees' of bishops, and most smaller settlements had their priests. The most prestigious bishoprics in the provinces of Egypt and Syria were at Alexandria, in Egypt, at Jerusalem, in Palestine, and Antioch, in north-west Syria (now in modern Turkey). These were three of the five 'patriarchates' of the Christian church (Constantinople and Rome were the other two). Carthage, in Roman Africa Procunsularis (modern Tunisia), was the most important North African bishopric. The patriarchates claimed authority over the priests in their territories, although in practice their authority could be contested and limited.[8] With the Christological schisms of the fifth and sixth centuries, bishoprics were often contested by rival church organisations. Many of the major sees, including the patriarchates, frequently had two bishops, one Chalcedonian and one non-Chalcedonian, with their attendant rival church hierarchies and flocks.[9]

Monks and hermits played important roles in the lives of the communities they lived alongside and among. Besides being sources of religious and political leadership and teaching, they were significant participants in the economy.[10]

---

[7] For Aramaic, Arabic, Coptic, Greek and Syriac, see Sidney Griffith, 'From Aramaic to Arabic: The Languages of the Monasteries of Palestine in the Byzantine and Early Islamic Periods', *DOP* 51 (1997), 11–31; Fiema et al. '*Provincia Arabia*', 395–433; *ODLA*, 'Armenian literature, language, and alphabet', 'Coptic literature', 'Georgia, languages in', 'Syriac language and literature'. For North Africa, see Susan T. Stevens and Jonathan P. Conant, 'Introduction', in Susan T. Stevens and Jonathan P. Conant (eds), *North Africa under Byzantium and Early Islam* (Washington, DC, 2016), 9; Jonathan P. Conant, 'Literacy and Private Documentation in Late Antique North Africa: The Case of the Albertini Tablets', in Andrew H. Merrills (ed.), *Vandals, Romans and Berbers: New Perspectives on Late Antique North Africa* (London and New York, 2017), 199–224. On Aksum and Nubia, see Munro-Hay, *Aksum*, 202–8, 244–51; Derek A. Welsby, *The Medieval Kingdoms of Nubia: Pagans, Christians and Muslims on the Middle Nile* (London, 2002), 34–8; Adam Łajtar and Grzegorz Ochała, 'Language Use and Literacy in Late Antique and Medieval Nubia', in Geoff Emberling and Bruce Beyer Williams (eds) *The Oxford Handbook of Ancient Nubia* (Oxford, 2021), 787–805.

[8] *ODLA*, 'Patriarch'.

[9] For lists of the various patriarchs, see *ODLA*, 1629–32.

[10] For monasteries around Lake Tiberias and their functions, see Jacob Ashkenazai and Mordechai Aviam, 'Monasteries, Monks, and Villages in Western Galilee in Late Antiquity', *JLA* 5 (2012), 269–97.

In more remote rural regions monks and their solitary counterparts could also take up positions of leadership akin to those of priests.[11] Similarly, the importance of divides between sectarian positions varied according to contexts of patronage and political protection, and other local social and economic factors.[12] Everywhere, the monasteries, like the churches, existed in a symbiotic relationship with political and economic power; in the Roman world, patronage of religious institutions was a means to secure resources' protection from taxation, a means to build prestige and authority, and a source of salvation in the afterlife.[13]

In Syria, the monastery of Mar Saba, which lies above the Kidron Valley, between Jerusalem and the Dead Sea, was a centre of Greek Chalcedonian Christianity, which benefited from imperial patronage. In northern Syria, the monasteries of Gubba Barraya and Qenneshre were centres for miaphysitism, with the latter also being a centre of miaphysite Greek learning.[14] The 'stylite' (pillar) hermits were also important religious leaders in Syria.[15] Further east, the Tur 'Abdin, which are the highlands north of Nisibis (modern south-east Turkey), as well as Mesopotamia and the lands around the Tigris in Iraq, had become flourishing centres of the Church of the East in the later sixth and early seventh centuries, with particularly important monasteries at al-Hira, on the edge of the Syrian Desert, at Mount Izla, near Nisibis, and at Beth Abe, on the edge of the highlands about 80km north-east of Nineveh (near modern Mosul).[16] The Tur 'Abdin were also densely populated with monasteries of the miaphysites, such as Beth Simon and Mor Gabriel.[17] In Egypt, where the Christian monastic movement had originated in the fourth century, there

---

[11] See, for example, above, Ch. 1, pp. 44–5.
[12] See, for example, the observations in Jack Tannous, 'You Are What You Read: Qenneshre and the Miaphysite Church in the Seventh Century', in Philip Wood (ed.), *History and Identity in the Late Antique Near East, 500–1000* (Oxford, 2013), 83–102.
[13] See, for example, Daniel Caner, 'Towards a Miraculous Economy: Christian Gifts and Material "Blessings" in Late Antiquity', *Journal of Early Christian Studies* 14 (2006), 329–77.
[14] Thomas A. Carlson et al., 'Gubba Barraya', in David A. Michelson et al. (eds) *The Syriac Gazetteer*, 'Syriaca.org: The Syriac Reference Portal, 2014'. Entry published 14 January 2014, <http://syriaca.org/place/349> (last accessed 25 August 2022); Tannous, 'You Are What You Read'.
[15] Simon Pierre, 'Le stylite (*estunoro*) et sa *sawma'a* face aux milieux cléricaux islamiques et miaphysites (Ier–IIe/VIIe–VIIIe siècles)', *Al-'Usur al-Wusta* 28 (2020), 174–226.
[16] Dietmar Winkler, *The Church of the East: A Concise History* (London, 2003), 36–7, 44–5.
[17] Thomas A. Carlson et al., 'Mor Gabriel', in David A. Michelson et al. (eds.) *The Syriac Gazetteer*, 'Syriaca.org: The Syriac Reference Portal, 2014'. Entry published 14 January 2014, <http://syriaca.org/place/349> (last accessed 25 August 2022); Tannous, 'You Are What You Read', 96.

Figure 11.1 St Catherine's Monastery at Mount Sinai in 2013. Zoltan Matrahazi/ Manar al-Athar.

were many hundreds of monastic communities, the most famous perhaps being the White Monastery of Upper Egypt, near Panopolis/Ikhmim, which became a centre of Egyptian miaphysitism (often referred to as 'Coptic Christianity'). Other Egyptian monasteries that are prominent in the sources and the archaeology are Kellia and Wadi al-Natrun, in the north-west Nile Delta, Bawit – like the White Monastery, in Upper Egypt – and the unusual subterranean settlement at Esna, in the far south, just north of Edfu and Aswan. In the Sinai Peninsula, the Monastery of Mount Sinai (Figure 11.1) was an important and influential Chalcedonian centre between Egypt and Syria, which had received substantial Roman imperial patronage.[18] South and east of Egypt, monasteries were also established in the kingdoms of Nubia and

---

[18] Bagnall, *Egypt*, 293–303; James E. Goehring, 'Monasticism in Byzantine Egypt: Continuity and Memory', in Roger S. Bagnall (ed.), *Egypt in the Byzantine World, 300–700* (Cambridge, 2007), 390–407.

Aksum, and in post-Roman North Africa.[19] Likewise, hermits and monks were also established in the Caucasus.[20] Monasteries and other religious sites were often the focus of pilgrimage, both local and transregional, with the Monastery of Mount Sinai and, of course, the churches and holy sites in Jerusalem being two notable examples.[21]

The Monastery at Mount Sinai in the Umayyad Era

In late Roman and early Islamic times some Christian sacred places were of trans-regional importance, attracting pilgrims and patrons from across the Mediterranean and the Middle East and beyond. Chief among these sacred sites was Jerusalem, with holy sites that Christians associated with the life of Jesus, as well as with other figures from the Gospels and the Old Testament. One famous late seventh-century text about Jerusalem was composed for the Abbot of Iona, an island off the coast of modern Scotland.[22] The monastery in Sinai now known as St Catherine's (a later association which dates from the eleventh century) was another such place with trans-regional reach. It also produced an early Christian witness to the Arabian conquests.

The southern Sinai is a rugged and mountainous region, with several mountain peaks well over 2,000m high. In Late Antiquity, there were two main settlements in the southern Peninsula, the oasis of Pharan/Wadi Fairan and the port of Rhaithou/Wadi al-Tur/Ra's Raya, on the south-west coast. By the late fourth century, there were monastic communities at both places, as well as at Wadi al-Dayr, near Mount Sinai/Jabal Musa. All three locations were sites for Christian pilgrimage, with many places in their vicinity associated with Old Testament events. Jabal Musa and Jabal Sufsafa were respectively considered the Mount Sinai and Mount Horeb

---

[19] Niall Finneran, 'Hermits, Saints, and Snakes: The Archaeology of the Early Ethiopian Monastery in Wider Context', *The International Journal of African Historical Studies* 45 (2012), 247–71; Władimir Godlewski, 'Monastic Life in Makuria', in Gawdat Gabra and Hany N. Takla (eds), *Christianity and Monasticism in Aswan and Nubia* (Oxford, 2013), 157–74; Anna Leone, *The End of the Pagan City: Religion, Economy, and Urbanism in Late Antique North Africa* (Oxford, 2013), 17, 66.

[20] Nina Garsoïan, 'Introduction to the Problem of Early Armenian Monasticism', *Revue des Études Arméniennes* 30 (2005), 177–236.

[21] See, for example, the Nessana papyri attesting to connections between that Syrian town and Mount Sinai in the mid-680s: Daniel Caner, *History and Hagiography from the Late-Antique Sinai* (Liverpool, 2010), 270.

[22] John Wilkinson, *Jerusalem Pilgrims before the Crusades* (Warminster, 2002), 167–206, 371–86.

of the Old Testament stories about Moses, and both had churches at their tops; a church in Wadi al-Dayr was associated with the burning bush. The monastic sites were largely self-sufficient in agriculture, producing wine, olives and other crops. Like other settled people in the region, their monks navigated a sometimes-difficult relationship with their pastoralist 'Arab' or 'Saracen' neighbours on the Sinai Peninsula.

In the latter part of his reign, the Roman emperor Justinian (r. 527–65) sponsored the construction of a fortified church at the monastic settlement in Wadi al-Dayr. The mosaic in Justinian's basilica depicts the Transfiguration of Christ, which was often associated symbolically with Moses' ascent of Mount Sinai. An image of King David in the same mosaic was likely intended to recall the appearance of Justinian himself. The church and monastery were probably dedicated to Mary, the Mother of God (Gk *theotokos*). Lavish imperial patronage of the site raised the profile of the church and monastery, as did patronage by Pope Gregory the Great (r. 590–604), the bishop of Rome. There is good evidence for much more pilgrimage at Mount Sinai in the later sixth and seventh centuries, with well-established routes into the remote Peninsula from Egypt and Syria. The monastery's monks spoke Latin, Greek, Syriac, Coptic and other languages, which likely included Arabic. The monastery became wealthy, and its library acquired manuscripts from across the Mediterranean and the Middle East. The fame of the church and monastery in this period probably explains the three mentions of 'Mount Sinai' (*ṭūr sayna'* and *ṭūr sīnīn*) in the Qur'an, where it is associated with Moses, olives, agriculture and covenants, and seven other likely mentions as 'the mountain' (*al-ṭūr*).[23]

Documentary evidence from Nessana, in the north of the Sinai Peninsula, near Gaza, shows that by 674, Sinai was part of the Umayyad military district of Filastin, with a governor at Gaza responsible for its taxes. Anastasius of Sinai (d. *c.* 700–1) is an eyewitness to the formation of the new Arabian empire in the mid-to-late seventh century – a development that he hoped might yet be reversed. As with most monasteries and Christian holy sites elsewhere, the monastery was respected by the Arabian conquerors as a sacred place and was able to retain its property, albeit perhaps subject to additional taxation after the mid 690s. Two Greek papyri from Nessana, probably dated to 683 and 684, respectively, describe the governor's wife Ubayya and a freed slave of one of Mu'awiya's uncles making journeys to Mount Sinai. Both were probably Christian members of the new Umayyad

---

[23] On the late antique history and geography, see Caner, *History and Historiography*, 4–69. On the Qur'an, see *EQ*, 'Sinai' (I. Shahid).

ruling elite in Syria and Egypt. Christians from across the Mediterranean and Middle East continued to congregate at Mount Sinai, and manuscripts in multiple languages continued to be collected and copied. In the texts produced by the Christian monks, the 'pagan' Saracens from before the conquests are supplanted by Saracens who have adopted the Arabian monotheist faith – no less in error in the eyes of Anastasius; in practice, relations between the monks and the pastoralists appear to have retained a similar pattern of symbiosis and occasional conflict.[24]

At the time of the conquests of the 630s and 640s, the various Christian church networks of the Middle East were already in turmoil. The past century had witnessed stronger assertion of sectarian boundaries in many regions, while imperial interventions by both Rome and Iran in the sixth and early seventh centuries had drawn the church hierarchies further into the politics of the two empires. Church leaders were also entangled in relations between the empires and their other neighbours. This was because church networks did not map neatly on to Roman imperial administrative boundaries (nor on to the new Arabian governmental structures that began to replace them from the 630s). For example, there were extensive connections between Greek-speaking Christian leaders in Egypt and Syria, as well as close links between the Egyptian church and Christians beyond the Roman frontier to the south, in the kingdoms of Nubia and Aksum. Aksum had been Christian since the fourth century, and the Nubian kingdoms had become predominantly Christian by the end of the sixth century, largely through contact with Egyptians, both miaphysites and Chalcedonians.[25] Both the West Syrian miaphysite and the East Syrian dyophysite churches had concentrations of monasteries and bishops in the north Mesopotamian highland frontier between the Roman and Persian empires – a region that was not controlled closely by the Commander of the Faithful until the Marwanid period.[26]

---

[24] For Anastasius and the papyri, see Caner, *History and Hagiography*, 172–99, 270. On the monks' narratives about 'Arabs' and 'Saracens' and relations with pastoralists, see Caner, *History and Hagiography*, 38–63; Walter D. Ward, *Mirage of the Saracen: Christians and Nomads in the Sinai Peninsula in Late Antiquity* (Berkeley, 2014). For Anastasius' expectations that Arabian power was in decline at the end of the seventh century, see *SIAOSI*, 559 and n. 64. Cf. Caner, *History and Hagiography*, 173.

[25] Ruffini, *Medieval Nubia*, 5; Welsby, *Nubia*, 31–5; Haas, 'Mountain Constantines'. There may also be evidence for contact between Christians in 'Syria' and China in Umayyad times: Bielenstein, *Diplomacy and Trade*, 366–7.

[26] For the history of Diyarbakir and the wider Jazira in the seventh century, see Robinson, *Empire*, 33–62. On the monasteries, see above, p. 262.

Christians in Syria and Egypt

Among the most consequential impacts of the seventh century conquests and the formation of the Umayyad Empire was the incorporation of many of the Arabic-speaking pastoralists of the Syrian Desert into the new military elite. However, pledged allegiance to the Commander of the Faithful did not always entail formally renouncing Christianity, still less fully abandoning Christian beliefs and practices. Many of the Banu Kalb remained Christian at the time of 'Uthman and Mu'awiya, while the Banu Tanukh and Taghlib are major tribal groups who remained Christian throughout the Umayyad period. Indeed, the Taghlibi Christian poet al-Akhtal was a prominent panegyrist at the courts of Yazid I, Marwan I and 'Abd al-Malik.[27] Nonetheless, the Syrian tribes had joined a new political formation that directly challenged the Christian Roman Empire and whose leaders adhered to distinctive religious beliefs and practices.

The decades each side of 700, during which 'Abd al-Malik and al-Walid I and their allies promoted their imperial Islam, were a turning point. By the mid-eighth century, the Tanukh and Taghlib appear to have been exceptions among the tribes of the Syrian Desert and Mesopotamian highlands, and later court poets were much more explicitly Muslim than al-Akhtal had been. At the end of the Umayyad period, those Syrians who defected to the Romans after the defeat at Akroinon were understood to have left their religion and 'become Christian' (Ar. *tanaṣṣarat*).[28] While sites of Christian prayer and pilgrimage remained important to the Arabian Faithful throughout the Umayyad period and long afterwards, distinctions between Christian groups and the Arabian monotheists seem already to have been drawn at these sites from the outset, with separate spaces for prayer and differing traditions about these spaces and their meanings. These distinctions hardened in the eighth century.[29]

The Christian clerics of Syria and Iraq, who wrote in Greek and Syriac, present the perspective of the settled populations on these events. The terms

---

[27] Philip Wood in Fisher et al., 'Arabs and Christianity', 355. On al-Akhtal, see also above, Ch. 5, p. 114, n. 42 and Ch. 6, pp. 128–9.

[28] Agapius, *Kitab al-'Unwan*, ed. and tr. Alexandre Vasiliev (Paris, 1910–15), II, ii, 509; *Theophilus*, 232.

[29] Suliman Bashear, 'Qibla Musharriqa and Early Muslim Prayer in Churches', *The Muslim World* 81 (1991), 267–82; Mattia Guidetti, 'The Contiguity between Churches and Mosques in Early Islamic *Bilad al-Sham*', *BSOAS* 76 (2013), 229–58; Marsham, 'Architecture', 107–10. On the importance of Christian monasteries to the Umayyads and their rivals, see Fowden and Key Fowden, *Studies*, 149–92; Simon Pierre, 'Le rôle de tribus arabes chrétiennes dans l'intégration de l'Orient à l'Église syro-orthodoxe de la mort de Sévère (v. 683–684) à la crise entre Denha II et Julien II (r. 687–709)', *Mélanges de l'École française de Rome: Moyen-Âge* 132 (2020), 255–71.

used by the Christian sources reflect this point of view: the conquerors are 'Arabs', 'Saracens', *tayyaye*, 'Ishmaelites' and 'Hagarenes'.[30] These labels, which refer to culture, language and ethnicity more than religion, predated the events of the seventh century but were now repurposed as labels for the new military elite. Nonetheless, the seventh-century sources do also show awareness of the religious dimension of the conquerors' identity. The new label *magaritai* refers to the Arabians' self-identification as 'emigrants' (Ar. *muhājirūn*).[31] An anonymous Armenian history which was probably composed in the 660s describes the beliefs and practices of the Ishmaelites, mentioning abstention from alcohol and Muhammad's emphasis on Abraham and Moses, among other things.[32] Anastasius of Sinai's *Tales of the Sinai Fathers*, which were also probably composed in the 660s or 670s, refer to the distinctive 'faith' (Gk *pistis*) of 'the Arabs' (*araboi*), including their hostility to images and the cross. Anastasius also contrasts 'Saracens' with 'Christians'; where a 'Saracen' is also a 'Christian' he considers it noteworthy.[33] John of Fenek, writing in the 680s in the Jazira, makes accurate remarks about the beliefs of the 'children of Hagar' and notes the presence of Christians, both dyophysite and miaphysite, in their 'robber bands', implying that most of them were, in contrast, not Christian.[34] Thus, these accounts tend to support the picture of a conquest leadership who adhered to a distinctive religious tradition, while being willing to incorporate Christian, Arabic-speaking pastoralists and other groups into their armies.

Shock at the collapse of the old imperial order and at violent defeat and widespread enslavement feature in much of the seventh-century material.[35] After the initial defeats, further violent resistance to the conquerors by formerly Roman Christian elites was sporadic and limited to a few regions where connections with the Roman Empire were maintained and where the Arabian conquerors were slow, or unable, to establish control because of mountains, marshes or deserts.[36] In this context of military defeat, and with uncertain

---

[30] Fergus Millar, 'Hagar, Ishmael, Josephus and the Origins of Islam', *Journal of Jewish Studies* 44 (1993), 24–43.
[31] See above, Introduction, p. 10 and Ch. 3, Box Text, p. 75.
[32] Thomson and Howard-Johnston, *Armenian History*, 95–6.
[33] Caner, *History and Historiography*, 177, 185, 192.
[34] Brock, 'North Mesopotamia', 61.
[35] See, for example, the destruction described in Egypt by John of Nikiu, *The Chronicle of John, Bishop of Nikiu*, ed. and tr. R. H. Charles (Oxford, 1916), cxii–cxv, cxvii (180–4, 186–7) and *History of the Patriarchs*, I, xiv, 493–5, xv, 258–9, and the view of the coming of Islam in Syria and Iraq from John of Fenek, in Brock, 'North Mespotamia', 57–74.
[36] See, for example, the resistance by the Mardaites in the mountains of Greater Syria (above, Chs 4 and 5, pp. 97, 111 and 112), the resistance that is said to have been put up in the 640s by *al-ḥabash* – perhaps Aksumite or Nubian East Africans – who farmed the part of the Nile

prospects for Roman reconquest, church leaders came to accommodations with the conquerors, while competing with rival faith groups over the opportunities created by the end of Roman rule. From the perspective of Arabian commanders in Syria and Egypt these accommodations were equally necessary because church leaders were crucial sources of expertise and influence in managing the conquered territories. Furthermore, Arabian veneration for the sanctity of Christian holy places and people is evident in the sources. Competition for patronage and protection from the new rulers is a prominent feature of the Christian sources for the seventh century in both provinces.

In Egypt, the Roman emperor Heraclius' (r. 610–41) recent attempts to promote a new doctrine that could reconcile miaphysites and Chalcedonians were cast into doubt by the Arabian victories.[37] Competition between the latter two groups is reflected in narratives of corruption and persecution. For example, in the late compilation of material in Arabic from Egypt known as *The History of the Patriarchs*, the Umayyads govern Alexandria in the 660s or 670s through a Chalcedonian leader named Theodore, who is criticised by the miaphysite author of the text for buying the support of the Umayyads and tyrannising his miaphysite rivals:

> In those days Alexandria was governed by a man whose name was Theodore, who was a chief among a congregation of the Chalcedonians, and was an opponent of the orthodox Theodosians (miaphysites). This man went to Damascus to the leader of the Muslims, whose name was Yazid b. Mu'awiya [at that time in fact the naval commander in the region], and received from him a diploma giving him authority over the people of Alexandria and Maryut and all the neighbouring districts, and declaring that the governor of Egypt had no jurisdiction over him; for he had given Yazid much money. Then Theodore returned and tyrannised over the patriarch, Abba Agathon [r. 661–77], and troubled him; not only demanding of him the money which he was bound to pay, and taking from him 36 denarii [gold coins] as tax every year, on account of his disciples, but that which he spent on the sailors in the fleet he also extracted from him. And whenever he wanted funds he required the patriarchy to supply them.[38]

Delta called al-Bima, in Baladhuri, *Futuh*, 223, and later resistance in the Nile Delta, in Booth and Marsham, 'Egyptian Revolts'.

[37] *History of the Patriarchs*, I, xiv, 489–92. See also Phil Booth, 'The Last Years of Cyrus, Patriarch of Alexandria († 642)', *Travaux et Mémoires 20: Mélanges Jean Gascou* (Paris, 2016), 1–50. I am grateful to Philip Wood for the latter reference.

[38] *History of the Patriarchs*, I, xv, 259. For further intrigues in 685, at the arrival of the governor, see *History of the Patriarchs*, I, xv, 267–71.

Similar machinations are reported in Syria, in the anonymous Syriac, Chalcedonian, 'Maronite Chronicle' (*c.* 680). The chronicle criticises the miaphysites for their agreement to pay annual tribute to Mu'awiya in return for protection:

> In the same month (June 659 CE) the bishops of the Jacobites (miaphysites), Theodore and Sabukht came to Damascus and held an inquiry into the Faith with the Maronites in the presence of Mu'awiya. When the Jacobites were defeated, Mu'awiya ordered them to pay 20,000 denarii (gold coins) and commanded them to be silent. Thus there arose the custom that the Jacobite bishop should pay that sum of gold every year to Mu'awiya, so that he would not withdraw his protection from them and let them be persecuted by the members of the (Chalcedonian) Church. The person called 'patriarch' by the Jacobites fixed the financial burden that all the convents of monks and nuns should contribute each year towards the payment in gold and he did the same with all the adherents of his faith. He bequeathed his estate to Mu'awiya, so that out of fear of that man all the Jacobites would be obedient to him. On the ninth of the same month in which the disputation with the Jacobites took place, on a Sunday at the eighth hour, there was an earthquake.[39]

The disputation in front of Mu'awiya suggests an understandable interest in relations between the Christian communities in his territories on the part of the Syrian commander. The Maronite author interprets events in a manner detrimental to the miaphysites, with what may have been tax payments perceived as bribes, and divine displeasure manifested by an earthquake.[40]

The second civil war (680–92) and its aftermath was a watershed in the relationship between the Umayyads and the Christian churches. After this period there is a growing recognition on the part of Christian sources of the permanence of the new order. As Marwanid power was extended into the Jazira, there was anguish there at the new fiscal regime and heightening differentiation between Muslims and others. The Syriac *Zuqnin Chronicle* remembers 691–2 as a turning point:

> 'Abd al-Malik made a census among the Syrians. He issued a swift decree stating that every person must go to his country, village and paternal house to register his name and that of his father, as well as his vineyards, olive trees,

---

[39] Palmer et al., *Seventh Century*, 30–1.
[40] See the comments in Palmer et al., *Seventh Century*, 29, and the account of conversions to miaphysite Christianity in Syria during Mu'awiya's reign in Brock's translation of John of Fenek: Brock, 'North Mesopotamia', 61–2.

cattle, children and all that he owned. From this time, all the evils were visited upon the Christians. [For] until this time, kings had taken tribute from land, rather than from men. From this time the sons of Hagar began to inflict on the sons of Aram servitude like the servitude of Egypt. But woe unto us! Because we sinned, the slaves ruled over us! This was the first census and survey that the Arabs (*tayyaye*) carried out.[41]

In the following year, 'Abd al-Malik is said to have decreed the slaughter of pigs in Syria, the Jazira and elsewhere and to have ordered the destruction of crosses.[42]

These changes in policy towards the settled, Christian, populations were a consequence of the attempt by 'Abd al-Malik and his allies to consolidate their collective grip on the empire in the wake of the civil war. The challenges presented by the 'Alids, Zubayrids and 'Kharijites', as well as the ongoing competition with the Roman Empire, pushed the Marwanids into publicly asserting their special legitimacy as Islamic rulers. They did this in part by promoting distinctive public symbols of Islam as a religious tradition separate from, and superior to, Christianity, and presenting themselves as victorious warriors against the Christian Roman Empire. It is this political context that explains what can sometimes appear as contradictions in the attitude of the Marwanids to Christianity; as a ruling minority in a Christian world, the Marwanids were obliged to work closely with Christian elites. At the same time, the logic of their place as rulers of the new empire led them to adopt a publicly hostile and superior attitude both to the religion of the defeated peoples and to their main imperial rival, to whom many of their subjects still looked for religious and political authority.

The 680s also witnessed greater intervention in the affairs of the patriarchates of Antioch and Alexandria. Egypt's governor 'Abd al-'Aziz b. Marwan cultivated a close relationship with the miaphysite Church. At his new capital of Hulwan, just south of Fustat, 'Abd al-'Aziz allowed the patriarch to build a new church; it is possible that this is the palace-church complex that is archaeologically extant there.[43] 'Abd al-'Aziz was also directly involved in the appointment of new patriarchs in Egypt in 686 and 689. In 686, he intervened to support the election of Isaac of Shubra (r. 686–9) against a rival, George of Sakha, and again, in 689, Simon the Syrian was appointed with 'Abd al-'Aziz's

---

[41] After al-Qadi, 'Population Census', 366, and Amir Harrak, *The Chronicle of Zuqnin, parts III and IV: AD 488–775* (Toronto, 1999), 147–8. See also al-Qadi, 'Population Census', 368 and n. 90.

[42] *Theophilus*, 189.

[43] *History of the Patriarchs*, I, xvi, 278; Mabra, *Princely Authority*, 120, 143–6.

backing.⁴⁴ Meanwhile, in Syria, 'Abd al-'Aziz's paternal half-brother, the caliph 'Abd al-Malik, intervened directly in the appointment of the miaphysite patriarch at Antioch. The two patriarchs of Antioch and Alexandria were usually in communication, and new appointments prompted correspondence and reaffirmations of shared interest between the two patriarchs under Marwanid rule, perhaps in part facilitated by the closer integration of Egypt under Syrian rule in the 700s.⁴⁵

The new tone of public proclamations by the Marwanids at the end of the seventh century coincided with the revival of the war against Rome in the Mediterranean and with the struggle against rivals for the caliphate in the Hijaz, the Jazira and Iraq. Edicts against the display of crosses were promulgated in both Syria and Egypt, and in Syria the Dome of the Rock was built. The dome dominated the cityscape of old Jerusalem, reinforcing the sacred status of the Umayyad imperial centre of Syria while asserting the prestige of their rule against that of the Romans. The long mosaic inscriptions inside anticipated the anti-Trinitarian message of the coins that would be struck in Iraq and Syria a few years later. At the same time, practical cooperation with Christian elites continued. For example, there is some evidence that 'Abd al-Malik depended upon affinities between miaphysite Christian pastoralists and their Syrian counterparts in securing control of the region from the Zubayrids.⁴⁶

In Egypt, competition between 'Abd al-'Aziz, who governed Egypt, and his paternal half-brother, the caliph 'Abd al-Malik, may also have contributed to attitudes to Christianity there. According to the *History of the Patriarchs*, 'Abd al-'Aziz ordered that public notices echoing the Dome of the Rock's mosaic inscriptions be posted on the doors of Egyptian churches of Fustat and the Delta.⁴⁷ Moreover, Christians in Egypt were not only associated with Roman imperial power, but also with the wider network of Christian elites in East Africa. Egyptian Christians retained connections with Syrian Christians within the Umayyad Empire, and Nubian and Aksumite Christians beyond it, but also with 'Indian' Christians.⁴⁸ A letter from a Nubian king to the miaphysite Patriarch of Alexandria in 690–2 is an indication of important elite-level

---

⁴⁴ *History of the Patriarchs*, I, xvi, 275–8, 281–3.
⁴⁵ For example, in 689, 708 and 724: *History of the Patriarchs*, I, xvi, 27–30, I, xvii, 64–6, 73; Palmer et al., *Seventh Century*, 61, 79. On this see Phil Booth, 'Alexandria and Antioch in the First 'Abbasid Century', *Al-Masaq* 33 (2021), 139–55.
⁴⁶ On the Dome of the Rock, see above, Ch. 6, pp. 142–6. On the Jazira, see Pierre, 'Le rôle des tribus'.
⁴⁷ *History of the Patriarchs*, I, xvi, 279; Palmer et al., *Seventh Century*, 205.
⁴⁸ Terry G. Wilfong, 'The Non-Muslim Communities: Christian Communities', in Carl F. Petry (ed.), *The Cambridge History of Egypt Volume 1: Islamic Egypt, 640–1517* (Cambridge, 1998), 192–5.

contact between Egyptian Christians and the Nubians; it also appears to reflect the adoption of miaphysite Christianity in Nubia in the same period.[49] Such contact with the Nubians is said to have prompted an episode of iconoclasm on the part of 'Abd al-'Aziz, and the miaphysite patriarch is said to have been wary of unsanctioned contact with 'Indians' in the same period.[50]

Fourteen years after the completion of the Dome of the Rock, the beginning of work on the Great Mosque of Damascus was the culmination of this newly assertive proclamation of the power and authority of Islam within and beyond the new empire's borders. It coincided with the escalation of war with Constantinople and what would have seemed at the time as a likely imminent victory over the Roman Empire and its misguided Trinitarian religion. The defeat of 717–18 provoked an inward turn but a continued hardening of boundaries. The edicts attributed to 'Umar II (r. 717–20) and Yazid II (r. 720–4) reflect continued anxieties about relations between Christians and Muslims within the empire. Both caliphs appear to have sought to define communal boundaries more clearly; there are stories of restrictions on the employment of non-Muslims in the imperial administration by 'Umar II, and of edicts against the public display of crosses by Yazid II. The extensive evidence of the destruction of images in churches and synagogues in Greater Syria probably also relate to the new assertion of Islamic norms by the ruling elites; Christians and Jews may have removed figural images in response to edicts by the authorities or may have themselves adopted more iconophobic ideas in the context of the success of Islam.[51]

The success of Muslim converts at the top of the fiscal administration in the first decades of the eighth century, and the growing insistence on the differentiation of Muslims and Christians, were the context for the early career of the Chalcedonian Christian John of Damascus (*fl.* early-to-mid eighth century). John was either a son or a grandson of Sarjun b. Mansur, who had served as chief scribe and tax official in Damascus from the time of Mu'awiya until some point in the reign of 'Abd al-Malik. Unlike his older relatives, John either never served the Umayyad administration in Syria or left in his youth, becoming a monk at Mar Saba near Jerusalem, or at the monastery at the Holy Sepulchre, within the city. John wrote in Greek, composing sermons and liturgical poetry and writing on logic and Chalcedonian Christian theology and in defence of

---

[49] Jakobielski, *History*, 35–6. Cf. *History of the Patriarchs*, I, xvii, 24–5.
[50] *History of the Patriarchs*, I, xvii, 25. 'Indians': *History of the Patriarchs*, I, xvi, 36–7.
[51] Daniel Reynolds, 'Rethinking Palestinian Iconoclasm', *DOP* 71 (2017), 1–64; Basema Hamarneh, 'Christian Art and Visual Culture in Umayyad Bilad al-Sham', in Andrew Marsham (ed.), *The Umayyad World* (London and New York, 2021), 464–85. On 'Umar II and Yazid II, see further above, Ch. 7, pp. 166–8.

the veneration of icons against the iconoclast doctrines supported by Emperor Leo III (r. 717–41) and his son, Constantine V (r. 741–75). From the point of view of the history of relations between Christians and Muslims in the Umayyad era, John's catalogue of Christian heresies is important for including the first extant Christian critique of Islam as a heresy – that is, false teaching leading the faithful astray.[52] *On Heresies* was probably meant more to define the boundaries of Christianity and reinforce Christian solidarity rather than to provide any arguments for use against actual Muslims. As such, it is a testament to the political dominance of the new Arabian monotheism by the latter decades of the Umayyad period.[53] The same impulses are probably reflected in early 'disputation' texts that respond to Muslims' criticisms of Christian theology, which were also composed in the first half of the eighth century.[54]

The last two decades of Marwanid rule was a period when a more thoroughly Islamised and somewhat Arabised imperial administration had developed in many of the core territories of the caliphate and when the threat of Roman reconquest had receded. This administrative integration of the empire had facilitated renewed contacts between some Christians within the empire.[55] However, significant tensions remained. Hisham's resumption of expansionist warfare against Rome prompted the execution of a large group of Roman envoys in c. 725, who are remembered as the 'Sixty Martyrs of Jerusalem' in a Greek source.[56] Moreover, caliphs and governors still had to manage the social tensions between the groups they ruled. Muslims, both of Arabian and non-Arabian heritage, were a much stronger presence in the lower levels of the administration by this time and the urban populations of Muslims in the garrisons now numbered in the hundreds of thousands. In Egypt in 735–6, Hisham's governor had to put down a rebellion by an Arabian leader who had protested at his having permitted Christians to build a new church at Fustat.[57] Hisham's governor in Iraq, Khalid al-Qasri also faced criticism for his willingness to accommodate Christianity.[58] The escalating war with the Romans and

---

[52] Daniel J. Sahas, *John of Damascus on Islam: The "Heresy of the Ishmaelites"* (Leiden, 1972); *ODLA*, 'John of Damascus'; Sean W. Anthony, 'Fixing John Damascene's Biography: Historical Notes on His Family Background', *Journal of Early Christian Studies* 23 (2015), 607–27. Cf. George, *Umayyad Mosque*, 90–1, 209.

[53] Cf. Sahas, *John of Damascus*, 94–5. See also the useful discussion of the purposes of heresiology: Averil Cameron, 'How to Read Heresiology', *Journal of Medieval and Early Modern Studies* 33 (2003), 471–92.

[54] *SIAOSI*, 454–72.

[55] See above, n. 45.

[56] Sahner, 'Martyrdom and Conversion', 401; Sahner, *Christian Martyrs*, 18, 231–2, 242–3.

[57] Kindi, 77–8.

[58] *EI²*, 'Khalid b. 'Abd Allah al-Qasri' (G. Hawting).

Khazars in the 730s seems to have led to violence against Christians within the empire. The Armenian *Life of Vahan* describes the execution in 737 of a Muslim Armenian who had converted to Christianity.[59] Theophanes records Hisham's massacre of Christian prisoners in the wake of the Muslims' defeat at Akroinon in 740.[60]

The Umayyad elite nonetheless remained dependent for the administration of the empire upon non-Muslim groups, as well as upon some Christian military groups. While Hisham worked at reviving the Islamic leadership model of 'Abd al-Malik, with its emphasis on war against the Roman Empire and on pilgrimage to Mecca, he also developed Rusafat Hisham, near al-Rusafa/ Sergiopolis, in the hills above the Euphrates outside al-Raqqa/Callinicum, as his main residence after his accession as caliph. This palace centre was in the frontier *jund* of Qinnasrin, from where many of the tribes that prosecuted his war against Rome were drawn, and where the landholdings of his paternal half-brother and supporter, Maslama b. 'Abd al-Malik were also found. Harran, in the highlands further to the north, was the base from which his cousin, Marwan b. Muhammad, maintained his alliances with Christian Armenian vassals and the tribes of northern Syria and Mesopotamia. The continued importance of Christianity in the 'Umayyad North' is reflected in the construction of the congregational mosque in the courtyard of the basilical church within the city walls at al-Rusafa/Sergiopolis. This was an arrangement that recalled the division of the Church of St John the Baptist in Damascus before it was appropriated by al-Walid I in 706 and would appear to reflect similar political circumstances to those that had pertained in Damascus a generation earlier; it was a pragmatic acknowledgement of the power of the Christian holy places among the populations upon whom the caliph depended for his political and military influence.[61]

Jews in Syria and Egypt

Syria was the centre of Judaism in the eastern Roman Empire in the sixth and seventh centuries. There were large Jewish communities in and around Lake Tiberias (the 'Sea of Galilee') and in the Golan. There were also communities in and around Jerusalem and Jericho and scattered across the rest of Greater Syria. Tiberias, on the western shore of Lake Tiberias was the major centre

---

[59] Sahner, *Christian Martyrs*, 41–4. See above, Ch. 8, pp. 178 and 181–3.
[60] Theophanes, 573, s.a. 739–40.
[61] Key Fowden, *Barbarian Plain*, 175–183. See also on al-Rusafa, above, Chs 8, 9 and 10, pp. 178, 195, 242 and 244–5. On Damascus, see George, *Umayyad Mosque*, and above, Ch. 6, pp. 154–7. For the 'Umayyad North', see above, Ch. 6, pp. 129–30.

of Jewish learning in the eastern Roman world.[62] In Egypt there were many thousands of Jews living in Alexandria and in many of the other towns and villages. These Egyptian Jews maintained close contact with Syrian Judaism.[63] The religious leaders most of the Jews of Syria and Egypt were the rabbis. They interpreted the Palestinian Talmud, which is the collection of commentary on the law compiled in Palestine in the fifth century CE.[64]

Syrian and Egyptian Jewish communities had been under pressure during the fourth, fifth and sixth centuries as Roman political ideology became more assertively Christian and Christian communities became emboldened against their neighbours.[65] The crisis of the early seventh-century war between Rome and Iran triggered a wave of violence between Jewish and Christian communities in Syria and Egypt, with Jews accused of having sided with the Sasanian occupiers in the 610s and 620, and Christian reprisals against them in the wake of the Roman victory of 628, including an edict ordering the expulsion of the Jews from Jerusalem. In 630 there was a state-sponsored campaign of forced baptism of Jews across Roman territories.[66]

The Arabian conquests of the mid-630s seem to have ended the violent persecutions of the years after 628, and there is some evidence of cooperative interaction between the Jews and the Arabian migrants. The archaeology of Syria shows that synagogues remained in use throughout the seventh and eighth centuries, and the later Arabic historical tradition remembers a large population of Jews in seventh-century Alexandria, with the later versions of the surrender treaties for the city including special clauses relating to the rights of the Jews there.[67] While the legal and poetic material produced by the Jews of Syria in Late Antiquity can be difficult to date, early Abbasid-era Hebrew eschatological texts preserve material that dates to the time of the seventh-century conquests. Moreover, some fragmentary materials were clearly produced in Umayyad times. These texts depict the Arabian conquerors as deliverance from Roman oppression and see Umayyad building work on the Temple Mount under Muʿawiya and ʿAbd al-Malik as a sign of the

---

[62] Walmsley, *Early Islamic Syria*, 121–4.
[63] Bagnall, *Egypt*, 275–8; Haas, *Alexandria*, 127.
[64] *ODLA*, 'Jews and Judaism'.
[65] For these processes in Roman Syria, see Walmsley, *Early Islamic Syria*, 122–3, and more generally, Nicholas de Lange, 'Jews in the Age of Justinian', in Michael Maas (ed.), *The Cambridge Companion to the Age of Justinian* (Cambridge, 2005), 401–26.
[66] *History of the Patriarchs*, I, xiv, 492; Alfred J. Butler, *The Arab Conquest of Egypt and the Last Thirty Years of the Roman Dominion* (Oxford, 1978), 82–3, 133–4; *WtaWC*, 174, 203, 231, 335, 337.
[67] Walmsley, *Early Islamic Syria*, 123; *SaMS*, 39; Haas, *Alexandria*, 127.

coming apocalypse.[68] Another response to Islamic rule was a syncretic and messianic movement recorded in northern Syria in the 720s which was quickly suppressed by the Muslim authorities.[69]

Other Religious Groups in Syria and Egypt

Besides the rabbinic Jews, the smaller religious minorities in Egypt and Syria had also suffered Roman persecutions, especially in the fifth and sixth centuries. The Samaritans were a Judaic group who lived in the lands around Sebaste (Ar. Nablus), as well as in some other towns in Syria. Although a cycle of persecution and revolt had diminished their wealth and numbers, they were still a significant community in the lands north of Jerusalem and in some coastal towns. Later accounts have the inland communities surrendering to the Arabian conquerors on particularly favourable terms, with their tax status only later coming to resemble that of other conquered Syrian groups, towards the end of the seventh century.[70] How far other non-Christian religious groups survived in Roman territories is unclear. The most well-known example comes from the highland border zone between Rome and Iran, at Harran (Lat. Carrhae), in western Mesopotamia rather than Syria proper. There, traditional 'pagan' beliefs and practices had survived, perhaps in part both because the town often lay beyond the reach of the Roman authorities, under occasional Sasanian rule and because the population was strategically important in conflict with the Sasanians.[71] Elsewhere in Egypt and Syria, church leaders often lamented the 'pagan' and non-Christian beliefs and practices of their flocks, especially in rural and steppe regions, but non-Christian institutional leadership beyond that of the Jews and Samaritans seems to have ended by the later sixth century.[72]

Iraq and Western Iran after the Conquests: Zoroastrians, Christians, Jews and Others

Whereas Egypt and Syria were overwhelmingly Christianised by the early seventh century, with Jewish populations in some of their towns and cities, Iraq was far more religiously diverse. Christians were probably a large minority of mostly Aramaic speakers, but also some more recent converts whose

---

[68] *SIAOSI*, 237–40, 307–21.
[69] Theophanes, 554, s.a. 720–1; *Theophilus*, 220. Cf. Harrak, *Chronicle*, 162–4, where a similar event is dated to the mid-730s and ends in the execution of the heretic by Hisham.
[70] Baladhuri, *Futuh*, 158; Milka Levy-Rubin, 'New Evidence Relating to the Process of Islamization in Palestine in the Early Muslim Period: The Case of Samaria', *JESHO* 43 (2000), 257–76; *ODLA*, 'Samaria and Samaritans'.
[71] *ODLA*, 'Harran'.
[72] See the discussions in *ODLA*, 'Paganism' and Tannous, *Making*, 151–4, 473.

first language was Persian. There was also a large Aramaic-speaking Jewish population. Mandaeans were another Aramaic-speaking group, as well as Manichaeans, who were probably linguistically more mixed. Most of the wealthiest ruling elite of Iraq were Persian-speaking Zoroastrians, and the populations of the highlands of western Iran were predominantly Persian-speaking and Zoroastrian, alongside some Christians and Jews and other smaller religious groups. Iranian pastoralist groups in the Iraqi, Jaziran and western Iranian highlands are often called 'Kurds' (Ar. *akrād*) in the sources; some were Christian, while others probably followed local Iranian religious traditions.[73]

So-called 'Gnostic' traditions were prevalent in Iraq, notably in the Manichaean and Mandaean traditions, but also among some Jews, Christians and Zoroastrians. The label Gnostic, which derives from the Greek *gnosis* ('knowledge'), has been criticised as excessively schematising but it remains a useful shorthand for often esoteric religious ideas that emphasised the idea of the material world as an error, or even evil, and a hierarchy of supernatural beings, one of whom may have mistaken himself for God. Sparks of the divine were thought to be imprisoned within each human being, ready to be returned to God through the intervention of a saviour figure.[74] Certainly, as in the predominantly Jewish and Christian formerly Roman lands, there is good evidence for syncretic and hybrid religious beliefs and practices, as well as for efforts by priests to assert boundaries between their communities. Also as in the former Roman lands, the end of the old imperial administration threw relations between religious communities into turmoil, with old patterns of patronage being replaced by new relationships between priests and the ruling Arabian elite.

Zoroastrians in Iraq and Western Iran

Zoroastrianism was primarily, though not exclusively, the religion of the Iranians as a specific ruling ethnic group and was a religion of temples, ritual and law, in contrast to the more cross-cultural, participatory and congregational late antique Christianity. A priest (Middle Persian *mobed*) carried out Zoroastrianism's sacrificial fire ritual (*yasna*) on behalf of the laypeople, and

---

[73] *EI²*, 'Kurds. B. The Islamic Period up to 1920' (V. Minorsky); *IatMC*, 265–6, 277–430. On Manichaeans, see *EI²*, 'Zindīk' (F. de Blois); Samuel N. C. Lieu, 'Manichaeism', in Susan Ashbrook Harvey and David G. Hunter (eds) *The Oxford Handbook of Early Christian Studies* (Oxford, 2009), 221–36. For Christians, see Payne, *State of Mixture*, 11 *et passim*.
[74] See the useful summary and discussion, with further references, in Crone, *Nativist Prophets*, 215–20.

with their patronage.⁷⁵ The sacred fire temples of Zoroastrianism were four-pillared structures supporting a dome (*gombad*). They were built on hilltops, often near water. Some were within villages and towns, while others, such as the Sasanian royal pilgrimage site at Takht-e Soleyman, in modern Iranian Azerbaijan, were in remote rural locations. Unlike Christianity, Sasanian Zoroastrianism does not seem to have had codified scriptures; this was a process that largely post-dated the coming of Islam.⁷⁶

Whereas Judaism and Christianity appear to have been afforded a privileged status as part of a shared monotheist tradition, there is little indication that the Hijazi monotheists thought of Zoroastrianism in this way. However, pragmatism led to Zoroastrians being accorded a similar protected status to that of Jews and Christians, leaving behind traces of disputes about the legitimacy of this decision. In later Islamic law Zoroastrians held an ambivalent status; their women and meat were forbidden to Muslims for all that they could be protected and taxed in the same way as Christians and Jews. Moreover, as a state-sponsored religion of the aristocracy, the fate of Zoroastrianism was closely bound up with that of the Sasanian ruling class. Zoroastrianism was made vulnerable by the collapse of the Sasanian armies in the 640s, the flight and killing of the last Sasanian king, Yazdgird III, in 651, and the subsequent exile of the remnants of his family in Central Asia. Many of the lands controlled by the priesthood were expropriated in the conquests alongside Sasanian royal lands.

In such circumstances, conversion to Christianity or Islam may have seemed attractive to secure a more favoured status within the new empire. This is indeed what seems to have happened, with Zoroastrianism becoming predominantly a religion of the peoples of Khuzistan, the Zagros, Fars and points north and east by the later eighth century, while the conformity of practice which had been imposed by the Sasanian-era priesthood fell away.⁷⁷ Anguish at the Arabians' defeat of the Sasanians and the end of the power of the Zoroastrian priests is reflected in a Middle Persian apocalyptic literature, which was written down in the centuries after the Umayyad period but appears to preserve seventh and eighth-century materials.⁷⁸

---

⁷⁵ Crone, *Nativist Prophets*, 375–9; *ODLA*, 'Zoroastrianism'.
⁷⁶ Mary Boyce, 'On the Zoroastrian Temple Cult of Fire', *JAOS* 95 (1975), 454–65; Soroor Ghanimati, 'Kuh-E Khwaja and the Religious Architecture of Sasanian Iran', in Daniel T. Potts (ed.) *The Oxford Handbook of Ancient Iran* (Oxford, 2013), 878–908.
⁷⁷ Crone, *Nativist Prophets*, 388; *IatMC, passim*, and esp. 300–2.
⁷⁸ *SIAOSI*, 321–8.

Christians in Iraq and Western Iran

Although Christianity in Iraq may have benefited in some respects from the collapse of the Sasanian elite and the end of state support for Zoroastrianism, the Church of the East nonetheless had to adapt to a dramatically altered situation. The Church had enjoyed some success in the sixth and early seventh centuries, with conversions among the Sasanian aristocracy, as well as protection from the Sasanian kings. The Catholicos (senior bishop) at Ctesiphon had been recognised by the Sasanian monarch as the leader of Christians in the Sasanian Empire. Proselytising and the advantage of royal protection had contributed to a revival of monasticism in Sasanian lands, as well as the success of missionary activities in regions populated by Christian merchant communities, notably on the Indian Malabar coast and, far beyond the Sasanian frontiers, at Chang'an in Tang China.[79] The Arabian conquests brought about both an end to the frontier between Rome and Iran and the end of close imperial control.

These new circumstances created instabilities in aristocratic patronage and the influence of the church, with competition with the West Syrian miaphysites in the highlands of Diyarbakir being a prominent feature of the sources.[80] Indeed, the East Syriac sources from Iraq and northern Mesopotamia (the Jazira) represent the conquest era, the first civil war and its immediate aftermath (c. 635–c. 664), as a period of chaos and insecurity.[81] The Christian institutions in Iraq that weathered the conquests and the formation of the Islamic empire most successfully were the monasteries.[82] The monasteries' dependence on local patrons, as opposed to the Sasanian ruling family, and their inextricable links with their local region may all have helped their survival. They also benefited from conversions by former Zoroastrians, who sought to protect their property by donating to the church and avoiding taxes by becoming monks and priests.[83]

The collapse of the Sasanian and Zoroastrian elites also generated other opportunities for church institutions – that coins were struck by Iraqi

---

[79] Winkler, *Church of the East*, 36–7, 44–5, 46–7, 53–4. See also Lee E. Patterson, 'Minority Religions in the Sasanian Empire: Suppression, Integration, and Relations with Rome', in Eberhard W. Sauer (ed.), *Sasanian Persia: Between Rome and the Steppes of Eurasia* (Edinburgh, 2017), 188–93; Philip Wood, 'Christians in Umayyad Iraq: Decentralization and Expansion', in Alain George and Andrew Marsham (eds), *Power, Patronage, and Memory in Early Islam: Perspectives on Umayyad Elites* (Oxford, 2018), 255–9.

[80] Thomas of Marga, *The Book of Governors*, ed. and tr. E. A. Wallis Budge (London, 1893), II, xviii, 211–2; Wood, 'Christians in Umayyad Iraq'.

[81] See the account of John of Fenek, translated in Brock, 'North Mesopotamia'.

[82] Wood, 'Christians in Umayyad Iraq'.

[83] *IatMC*, 302.

Christians for the first time during the conquest period suggests an expansion of the social and economic role of the church; so too does the extension of the role of bishops as sources of legal judgement and mediation for their flocks.[84] In the 680s, the Zubayrid opponents of the Umayyads appear to have cultivated a relationship with the dyophysite pastoralist groups of northern Iraq and Diyarbakir, while the Umayyads backed predominantly miaphysite groups.[85] It is probably not a coincidence that Mus'ab b. al-Zubayr's last stand was as 'the Monastery of the Catholicos' in the Jazira.[86]

These associations may help to explain why there seems to have been a comparatively distant relationship between the Umayyads' governors and the leadership of the Church of the East in the seventh and early eighth centuries. The Catholicos Hnanisho I (r. 686–98) was said to have been deposed after intrigues by a rival and shortly afterwards al-Hajjaj (g. 694–714) abolished the Catholicate, which was not restored until 715, after al-Hajjaj died.[87] Unlike 'Abd al-'Aziz and 'Abd al-Malik, in Egypt and Syria, al-Hajjaj did not need the church hierarchy to manage his province. Whereas Egypt and Syria were Umayyad political heartlands, with a predominantly Christian population, the Church of the East in Iraq represented only one group among many. The former association between dyophysite pastoralists and the Zubayrids in the Jazira probably made him wary of the Church of the East as he sought to consolidate the Marwanids' grip on the Jazira with the backing of miaphysite groups. When the Zubayrid threat had subsided after 715, subsequent Marwanid governors did see fit to restore the Catholicate.

Judaism in Iraq and Western Iran

The rabbinic Jewish community of Iraq perhaps numbered in the hundreds of thousands, with the main Jewish settlements being concentrated on the Euphrates in central and southern Iraq. Until the mid-fifth century CE, the rabbinic Jews of Iraq were led by the Exilarch (Aramaic *resh galutha*), who was a member of an aristocratic family who traced their ancestry to the Biblical King David. This hereditary leader was recognised by the Sasanian king, as the basis for indirect rule of the rabbinic Jewish community in Iraq. However, during the fifth and sixth centuries, the rabbinic Jews had suffered intermittent persecutions, with synagogues and schools being closed, forced conversions and interruptions in the Exilarchate. In 590–1 the Jews had joined in the failed

---

[84] Wood, 'Christians in Umayyad Iraq', 258; Richard E. Payne, 'East Syrian Bishops, Elite Households, and Iranian Law after the Muslim Conquest', *Iranian Studies* 48 (2015), 5–32.
[85] Pierre, 'Le rôle de tribus'.
[86] See above, Ch. 5, p. 114.
[87] Wood, 'Christians in Umayyad Iraq', 267.

revolt of Bahram Chubin, prompting the final abolition of the Exilarchate. After a hiatus of about fifty years, in the 640s, the Exilarch was restored by the Arabian conquerors of Iraq. However, the Exilarch's authority was diminished in the eyes of the rabbis, who portrayed his authority as depleted by corrupt acquisition of the office. By 730, the Exilarchs had become figureheads, with responsibility for tax revenues allocated to them by the Muslim authorities, while more everyday religious leadership of the rabbinical Jews was in the hands of the Geonim, the heads of the religious schools of Iraq. Jewish judges were appointed jointly by the Exilarch and the Geonim.[88]

The turmoil of the later sixth century, the war between Rome and Iran of 602–28, and the Arabian conquests and their aftermath contributed to the success of messianic ideas and movements among the Iraqi Jews, as they did in other religious communities. In 644–7, there was a rebellion in the name of the Messiah of about 400 Jewish weavers, carpet makers and linen bleachers at Falluja, in the Sawad of Kufa. They burned three churches and killed the local governor before Kufan troops suppressed the revolt. Another Jewish rebel movement was led by Abu 'Isa al-Isfahani. The chronology of Abu 'Isa's revolt is unclear; it probably started in the time of 'Abd al-Malik and was followed by various similar Jewish syncretic and messianic movements in the eighth century. Abu 'Isa's rebellion suggests a local response to the greater religious and political assertiveness of the Marwanid rulers; Abu 'Isa proclaimed himself as a prophet, announcing the coming Messiah, and advocated that Jews read the Gospels and the Qur'an. On his defeat and death some his followers claimed he had in fact merely disappeared into a mountain; one of his followers, Yudghan, led a movement awaiting his return at Isfahan.[89]

Manichaeans, Mandaeans and Others in Iraq and Western Iran

The prophet Mani (c. 216–74 or 277) had been influential at the court of the Sasanian king Shapur I but died in prison under Shapur's successor, Bahram I. Mani came from a Jewish-Christian Iraqi community and the scriptures associated with him reflect this background, as well as Gnostic ideas, alongside elements of Buddhism and Zoroastrianism. His followers preferred terms such as the 'Holy Church' to 'Manichaeans', but Manichaean remains the standard label in modern scholarship. Manichaeans were often persecuted by the Sasanians and later by the Christian Romans. Nonetheless, Mani's ideas flourished briefly in third and fourth-century Roman Egypt and North Africa

---

[88] *IatMC*, 319–31.
[89] *IatMC*, 327–8; *EI3*, 'Abu 'Isa al-Isfahani' (Y. Erder). On other apocalyptic materials, see *SIAOSI*, 257–330.

and, more lastingly, in Iraq, Iran and Sogdia.[90] The leader of the Manichaeans of Iraq in Marwanid times seems to have had a similar relationship with the authorities as the Iraqi Jewish and Christian leaders. As with some of them, the Manichaean leader's close relationship with the Marwanid governor – possibly Khalid al-Qasri – seems to have been used against him by sectarian rivals within Iraqi Manichaeism.[91]

The Mandaeans were an Iraqi religious group who spoke a dialect of Aramaic, known as Mandaic. Many of their extant scriptures were compiled later in the Islamic era, but there is some evidence that a distinctive Mandaean tradition predated the Arabian conquests, perhaps developing in the fifth century CE. Like Manichaeism, Mandaeism was a Gnostic religion, with esoteric beliefs and practices. Mandaeans practised baptismal purification rites and adhered to distinctive, sometimes inverted, versions of Jewish and Christian stories and beliefs about astral entities. Their ideas about light and darkness resembled Manichaeism and Zoroastrianism. Evidence for the Mandaean experience of Umayyad rule is very limited, but traces of apocalyptic ideas about the coming of the Arabs in their scriptures resemble similar materials in other religious traditions from the period. The Mandaeans' survival in Iraq as 'Sabians' – a Quranic label used to classify religious groups as worthy of protected status under Islamic rule – also suggests that their experiences of Umayyad rule were not unlike those of Iraqi Jews, Christians and Manichaeans.[92]

Religion and Identity beyond Egypt, Syria and Iraq

The Arabian conquerors of the 630s and 640s took power over a substantially demilitarised settled population in Egypt, Syria and Iraq, and co-opted the remnants of the Roman and Sasanian forces that had not fled. Hence, they were able to rule over relatively quiescent subject populations in the settled regions. The militarily capable Arabic-speaking pastoralists of the Syrian Desert were quickly brought into alliance with the new rulers. Where these pastoralists came into conflict with others within the imperial elites,

---

[90] Lieu, 'Manichaeism'; *ODLA*, 'Mani, Manichaeism, and the Manichaeans'.
[91] Abu l-Faraj Muḥammad b. al-Nadim (= Ibn al-Nadim), *Kitab al-Fihrist li-l-Nadim*, ed. R. Tajaddud (Tehran, 1971), 397–8, where the chronology and Umayyad personalities seem confused. Cf. Melhem Chokr, *Zandaqa et zindiqs en islam au second siècle de l'hégire* (Damascus, 1993), 43–50; *EI²*, 'Zindik' (F. de Blois).
[92] *SIAOSI*, 264, n. 17; Michael G. Morony, 'Magic and Society in Late Sasanian Iraq', in Scott B. Noegel et al. (eds), *Prayer, Magic, and the Stars in the Ancient and Late Antique World* (Philadelphia, 2003), 83–107; Kevin van Bladel, *From Sasanian Mandaeans to Sabians of the Marshes* (Leiden, 2017).

it was in the context of war between Qurashi commanders, or as 'Kharijite' rebels. Rebellions in the name of pre-conquest faith traditions were rare. The most significant exception was that of the Mardaites (Ar. *al-jarājima*), in the Cilician and Lebanese highlands, whose Christian identity seems to have been important to them and who sometimes acted in coordination with the Roman Empire. The Egyptian Desert and the marshes of the Egyptian Delta and the Iraqi Sawad also occasionally proved difficult to control. But these were exceptions – most of Egypt, Syria and southern Iraq swiftly came under Arabian rule, and the Jazira was more fully integrated into the empire after the 690s.

In contrast, on the other former frontiers of Rome and Iran, there were no pre-existing Arabic-speaking populations. Furthermore, power continued to be violently contested by a variety of actors for prolonged periods. Three such zones were particularly significant for the history of the Umayyad Empire – the Caucasus, North Africa and Khurasan. All three were only brought under direct rule in the second and third waves of conquest, in the later seventh and early eighth centuries, and in all three the Arabian conquerors depended upon bringing local, non-Arabian, military actors into their armies. Consequently, all three regions witnessed some adoption of Islam by the non-Arabian populations. In the Caucasus, conversion seems to have been limited and of little long-term consequence for the region, which remained predominantly Christian. However, in North Africa and Khurasan, Islam became a vehicle for the formation of successful new religio-political identities. In North Africa, this took the form of so-called 'Kharijite' Islam, where the Commander of the Faithful did not need to be from Quraysh. In the East, the Shi'i idea that the Prophet's Hashimite relatives had a right to rule the empire gained significant ground. In both regions these ideas combined with local cultures and political structures, although the character of these syncretisms can only be partially glimpsed.

The Caucasus

The highlands of the Caucasus are a frontier zone by virtue of their geography. Difficult mountain terrain fills the space between the Anatolian highlands and the Black Sea in the west, the hills of northern Syria and Iraq in the south, the Caspian Sea to the east, and the plains of western Central Asia to the north. The mountains are hard for an external power to control directly, so the peoples of the Caucasus were often able to maintain a degree of political independence from the empires that surrounded them by navigating great power politics, using alliances with the empires against their local rivals. With the collapse of Sasanian power, and the flight of the Roman army from Syria, the Umayyads became the major power to the south and east, contesting Roman attempts to make use of their connections with many groups in the region, and the growing power of the Khazar Turks in the plains to the north.

Christianity in the Caucasus was entangled in these wider conflicts and in the complex local politics of the region itself. Armenian Christianity was predominantly miaphysite in orientation and had split formally from the Chalcedonian Church at the Council of Dvin in 607, which had been convened with Sasanian support. In response, the Roman emperors of the seventh century often sought to bring Armenia back into communion with the imperial church.[93] Caucasian Albania (modern north Azerbaijan and Dagestan), which became part of Umayyad Azerbaijan, was Chalcedonian until the eighth century, when its church, with its senior bishopric at Partaw/Bardhaʿa, adopted miaphysite Christianity, in line with the Armenian church to the west – perhaps a reflection of Marwanid patronage of miaphysites and a recognition of Roman defeat.[94] Lazica (modern western Georgia), in the far west, largely remained outside the reach of Umayyad power, and was ruled by a Roman governor. Lazica was populated by Georgian-speaking Christians, who held to a Chalcedonian Christology, in line with their Roman rulers.[95]

With greater direct involvement in the Caucasus by Marwanid commanders from about 695, the Umayyads also became interested in church affairs, and are represented in Albanian and Armenian sources as supporters of the miaphysites against Chalcedonianism; encounters between Umar II and Hisham and Armenian Christians are also remembered in the Armenian sources.[96] In the middle decades of the Marwanid era, the Armenian Catholicos Yovhannes Ojnecʿi (r. 717–28) led efforts to reconcile Armenian Christianity with the West Syrian Christians, reaching an accord with them in 725–6. The Umayyad frontier commander's anxiety about connections between Syrian and Armenian Christians is suggested by his refusal to allow the Armenian Catholicos to travel to Syria itself.[97]

During the Marwanid period, large numbers of Armenians served in the caliphs' frontier armies. However, the leading Armenian families, the Mamikoneans and Bagratunids, supplied troops in their capacity as independent vassals, using the title 'Prince of Armenia', and the Christian Armenian troops do not seem to have been integrated with the Arabian Muslim soldiers.

---

[93] Garsoïan, *Interregnum*, 57–63.
[94] *ODLA*, 'Albania, Caucasian'.
[95] *ODLA*, 'Lazica'; Claudia Rapp, 'Georgian Christianity', in Ken Parry (ed.), *The Blackwell Companion to Eastern Christianity* (Oxford, 2007), 142–4.
[96] Vacca, 'Umayyad North'.
[97] Garsoïan, *Interregnum*, 91.

The Arabian Muslim presence was confined to the garrisons at Dvin and Bardhaʻa. As a result, there is no evidence for large numbers of converts to Islamic beliefs and practices in Armenia and Azerbaijan. Where the sources mention conversions, they are comparatively isolated anecdotes about individuals.[98] The distinctive shape of frontier politics in the Caucasus allowed for the continued dominance of Christianity in the region in later centuries, making it unique among the lands that had formed part of the Umayyad Empire.

The same military and political context helps to explain why two rare early examples of converts from Arabian monotheism to Christianity come from Umayyad Armenia. Dawit of Dvin was executed by the Umayyad governor in *c.* 703 when the Marwanids imposed more direct rule in the region. It seems likely that Dawit was an Arabian soldier who had converted to Christianity during the civil war period, when the Caucasus fell out of the direct control of the new empire.[99] In contrast, Vahan of Goght'n was the Muslim convert son of an Armenian nobleman, who had been captured during the same imposition of Marwanid rule, and who in adulthood seems to have served as an Umayyad vassal in his ancestral lands. In 737, Hisham is said to have executed Vahan for apostasy from Islam after Vahan had journeyed from Armenia to Rusafa and publicly proclaimed his Christian faith.[100] While the date of Vahan's death matches that of many so-called apostates or heretics executed by Hisham in Iraq and Syria, it is also the year of victories against the Khazars and the extension of Marwanid power in the Caucasus; this local context is probably significant.[101]

North Africa

The huge expanse of North Africa west of Egypt had fallen out of Roman control in the fifth century before the core urban centres were reconquered in the sixth. These prolonged conflicts had contributed to the complex politics of the seventh century. In Africa Proconsularis, Byzacena and points east (modern Tunisia and Libya), the urban centres and their hinterlands were under Roman control, although the extent of the fortification of these towns suggest a highly militarised environment. Beyond these regions were independent political groups, some in alliance with the Romans. Some were highly Romanised; others were more rooted in the culture of the pastoralists of the

---

[98] Vacca, *Non-Muslim Provinces*, 21–2, 35.
[99] Sahner, *Christian Martyrs*, 93–6. But cf. Garsoïan, *Interregnum*, 30, n. 21, who counts him as an Armenian who had been brought up a Muslim.
[100] Sahner, *Christian Martyrs*, 41–4; Vacca, *Non-Muslim Provinces*, 178.
[101] See above, Ch. 8, p. 178.

steppes and deserts. The terms 'Moors' (Lat. *Mauri*, Gk *Maurousioi*) and 'barbarians' (Lat. *barbari*, Gk *barbaroi*) can be used in the Roman sources simply to refer to political independence or to real or perceived cultural difference, or both.[102] Likewise, the later Arabic sources often distinguish between 'Romans' (*al-rūm*) and 'barbarians', or 'Berbers' (*al-barbar*).[103] Again, these categories may be political or cultural or both, and conceal much about the complexities of seventh and eighth-century North African politics and culture.

Much of the population of the cities, towns and villages of Africa Procunsularis, Byzacena and Tripolitania were Latin-speaking. The reintegration of much of the region into the Roman Empire after the 540s had also brought immigrant Greek-speaking populations from the eastern Mediterranean. More Greeks as well as Coptic-speakers arrived from Egypt in the wake of the conquests there in the 640s. Alongside Latin, Greek and Coptic, the various local Afro-Asiatic languages of North Africa were spoken, especially in the rural hinterlands of the towns and in steppe and mountain regions. Most of the settled population of North Africa were Christian, but there was also a significant Jewish population at Carthage and in other coastal cities.[104] Christianity had also spread among the pastoralist populations, in combination with local religious and cultural practices.[105] North African Christians were usually in communion with Chalcedonian Constantinople, although the region was also well known for its schismatic movements and heresies.[106]

The settled and nomadic pastoralist populations of the North African countryside have left almost no written records of their own and so the Roman and Islamic sources, as well as the linguistic evidence of place names, and some archaeology of settlement patterns, are the main indications of their

---

[102] On Late Roman North Africa, see Jonathan P. Conant, *Staying Roman: Conquest and Identity in Africa and the Mediterranean, 439–700* (Cambridge, 2012). On fortifications, see Denys Pringle, *The Defence of Byzantine Africa from Justinian to the Arab Conquest: An Account of the Military History and Archaeology of the African Provinces in the Sixth and Seventh Centuries* (Oxford, 1981).

[103] For example, Ibn 'Abd al-Hakam, *Futuh*, 170; Baladhuri, *Futuh*, 229. That the term 'Berber' appears in Arabic early is suggested by its presence in late Umayyad materials: Zychowicz-Coghill, *First Arabic Annals*, 33–4, 40, 74, 108.

[104] These communities had come under pressure from Christians in the sixth and early seventh centuries, see Shira L. Lander, 'Inventing Synagogue Conversion: The Case of Late Roman North Africa', *Journal of Ancient Judaism* 4 (2013), 401–16.

[105] For example, the archaeology of the Jebel Nafusa in Tripolitania suggests that the Berbers of this region were Christian: Yves Modéran, *Les Maures et l'Afrique romaine (IVe–VIIe siècle)* (Rome, 2003), 783. On 'paganism' among the 'Moors' in the sixth century, the spread of Christianity, and problems with the sources, see also Conant, *Staying Roman*, 267–9.

[106] Averil Cameron, 'Vandal and Byzantine Africa', *CAH*, XIV, 561–6. See also the comments in Conant, *Staying Roman*, 214–16, 306–61.

social and political identities. The sixth-century Roman sources mention about thirty 'Moorish' groups, while the early Arabic sources, extant from the ninth century, mention far fewer 'Berber' ones – perhaps about ten in total. The informants of the earliest Arabic materials may have been more remote from events and so more schematic in their ethnic labels. However, the overall decline in numbers of tribes named in the written sources from late Roman to early Islamic times probably also reflects some political realities, with larger-scale political organisations being prompted in part by interactions with a new empire whose military commanders fostered closer connections with pastoralist groups than had their Roman predecessors.[107]

This cooperation with settled and pastoralist groups impacted religious belief and practice. Although Christianity persisted as the majority religion in the settled regions of North Africa long after the Umayyad period, there is little detailed evidence after about 700. Carthage was damaged by the Umayyad conquest of 698, but it nonetheless remained an important regional bishopric into medieval times, with some of its churches continuing in use and being renovated.[108] In other towns, many of which were not sacked by the Arabian conquerors, it is likely that the majority of the churches remained in use throughout the Umayyad era.[109] The evidence for the countryside is even weaker. However, the literary sources remember the 720s as the era of the conversion to Islam of those 'Berber' populations allied with the Muslims. Certainly, that populations with Latin and Greek Christian affiliations were important to the Muslim commanders in North Africa in the first years of the eighth century is strongly suggested by their unusual decision to strike aniconic dinars with simplified and less anti-Trinitarian affirmations of the faith in Latin on them, as opposed to the direct attacks on the Trinity in Arabic that began to be used in Syria, Egypt and points east after 696–7.[110]

---

[107] Modéran, *Les Maures*, 699–702, 776; Mohamed Benabbès, 'The Contribution of Medieval Arabic Sources to the Historical Geography of Byzantine Africa', in Susan T. Stevens and Jonathan P. Conant (eds), *North Africa under Byzantium and Early Islam* (Washington, DC, 2016), 124–5.

[108] Heinz Halm, *The Empire of the Mahdi: The Rise of the Fatimids*, tr. Michael Bonner (Leiden, 1996), 99; Susan T. Stevens, 'Carthage in Transition', in Susan T. Stevens and Jonathan P. Conant (eds), *North Africa under Byzantium and Early Islam* (Washington, DC, 2016), 89–104; Fenwick, 'From Africa to *Ifriqiya*', 27.

[109] Philipp von Rummel, 'The Transformation of Ancient Land- and Cityscapes in Early Medieval North Africa', in Susan T. Stevens and Jonathan P. Conant (eds), *North Africa under Byzantium and Early Islam* (Washington, DC, 2016), 112.

[110] On the coins, see Trent Jonson, 'A Numismatic History of the Early Islamic Precious Metal Coinage of North Africa and the Iberian Peninsula', DPhil Dissertation, University of Oxford (2014). See also Ch. 7, pp. 174–5.

With conversion came the potential for forms of resistance to Umayyad rule articulated in Islamic terms. The potential for political independence within the framework of the new empire had already been demonstrated by the foundation of the emirate of Nakur, near Tangier, from about 710, and then by the revolt of *c.* 721.[111] The so-called Great Berber Revolt in 740 is remembered in the later Arabic sources for the proclamation of a new caliphate and the taking of pledges of allegiance to its leaders, both of whom had Arabised names – Maysara al-Badghari and Khalid b. Humayd al-Zanati.[112] In some accounts the revolt's leaders were influenced by emigrants from Iraq whose Kharijite religious ideas were in opposition to the Umayyads.[113] The revolt led to the foundation of the emirate of Barghawata, in the far west of North Africa, under the leadership of Tarif, variously said to have been an outsider leader, from Spain or from further east in North Africa. The emirate is said in later sources to have maintained elements of the Kharijite inspiration of the revolt, in combination with local North African beliefs and practices.[114] This was a frontier region of the empire where the non-Arabian populations responded to the presence of the Arabian conquerors with the formation of new political identities that fused the new Arabian religious and political customs with local North African ones.

Khurasan and Transoxiana

The Arabian settlement of Khurasan began in earnest in 671, with migrations to the Marw oasis. Marw remained the base for further eastward expansion, which tended to have the character of raiding for tribute down to the 700s. In the 700s, Herat, in northern Afghanistan, became another base for raids and conquests further to the south and east, and across the Oxus in Transoxiana (Ar. *mā warā' al-nahr*) – territories contested by Turks, Hephthalites and Sogdians. Further south, the highlands of Afghanistan proved resistant to Arabian expansion: the two Turkic kingdoms of Kabul and, after 680, Zabulistan remained independent into the ninth century. In Sogdia and points east, a new Turkic federation, that of the Türgesh, emerged at the end of the seventh century and presented an ongoing challenge to Arabian power until its collapse in the 740s.[115]

---

[111] *EI*², 'Nakur' (C. Pellat) and above, Ch. 7, pp. 174–5.
[112] See above, Ch. 8, pp. 187–8.
[113] Tabari, II, 2815.
[114] *EI*², 'Barghawata' (R. Le Tourneau).
[115] See above, Chs 4, 5, 6, 7 and 8, pp. 98–9, 104, 134–6, 158–61, 173–4 and 188–90. On the Turkic kingdoms, see also Minoru Inaba, 'The Identity of the Turkish Ruler to the South of Hindukush from the 7th to the 9th Centuries AD', *ZINBUN* 38 (2005), 2.

In the territories that had formed the north-east frontier province of the Sasanian Empire, the Arabic sources refer to negotiations with *marzbān*s ('marcher lords', 'high nobility') and sometimes *dihqān*s ('masters of villages', 'minor landowners').[116] Many of the Iranian nobility retained their position in return for tax payments and military service. Hence, in Khurasan, as on the other frontiers in the north and west, non-Arabians were armed and somewhat politically independent. This Khurasani population had a distinctive political culture, based on aristocracy and landownership. They were Persian-speaking, and predominantly Zoroastrian in religion, although the Church of the East also had a significant presence in the former Sasanian capital of Merv (Ar. Marw) and there were two Buddhist temples there.[117] There were also Buddhists at Balkh (in the northern highlands of modern Afghanistan), and points south and east which had rarely been under the direct control of the Sasanians.[118] These same regions of Badhghis, Tukharistan, Kabul and Zabulistan also had local religious traditions.[119]

In the late sixth century, the Eastern Turkic Khaganate had controlled much of the territory east of the Oxus river but, by the early seventh century, the Turks were politically fragmented.[120] The Turks had ruled the region as an occupying tributary military elite, much as the Arabians would in the seventh century, and so most of the population of Transoxiana had other ethnic and religious identities. In the northern Afghan highlands – Badghis and Tukharistan – the Hephthalites were one of the populations who had served as vassals to the Turks. The Turkic and Hephthalite peoples had their own languages and their own religious traditions.

In the northern Afghan highlands of Badghis and Tukharistan, the settled population were Bactrian, with their own language and culture. The best evidence of Bactrian in the Umayyad era comes from Rob and other towns in the vicinity of Balkh.[121] Local deities from this region included 'Wakhsh, the king of gods' and 'Kamird, the king of gods'. Balkh itself was a centre of Bactrian Buddhism, and it is likely that Buddhism was prevalent elsewhere in the same region, alongside other religions.[122] Further to the

---

[116] Elton Daniel, *The Political and Social History of Khurasan under Abbasid Rule 747–820* (Minneapolis and Chicago, 1979), 17.
[117] Kennedy, 'Merv', 27; de la Vaissière, 'Abbasid Revolution', 112–13.
[118] For Buddhists at Balkh, see Kevin van Bladel, 'The Bactrian Background of the Barmakids', in Anna Akasoy et al. (eds), *Islam and Tibet: Interactions along the Musk Routes* (Farnham, 2011), 47–58.
[119] Azad, 'Happily Ever After', 41.
[120] Inaba, 'Identity'.
[121] Nicolas Sims-Williams, *Bactrian Documents from Northern Afghanistan* (London, 2012).
[122] Azad, 'Happily Ever After', 41–2.

north, in Paykand, Bukhara and Samarqand, the settled populations were predominantly Sogdian. The urban centres of Sogdia were often independent polities, ruled by Sogdian 'kings'. Like Bactrian, Sogdian was an Iranian language with its own script, the documentary evidence for which is quite extensive. Sogdian traders dominated the trade networks of the 'Silk Road' that linked Iran and China and there was a significant Sogdian presence in Tang China itself, too. Sogdians were Buddhist, Zoroastrian, Manichaean and Eastern Christians.[123]

The Arabian conquerors became another military and political actor in this complicated geographical and political environment and their presence further reshaped religious and political identities in the Khurasan and points east. As elsewhere in the late antique world, religious and political identities were intimately connected. As on the western frontier, and elsewhere in the new empire, pledged agreements were made between the Arabian conquerors and non-Arabian military elites, such as the *dihqāns* and *marzbāns* of Khurasan and the Tarkhan Nizak and the Sogdian kings of Transoxiana. Other groups made agreements to pay tribute or tax but not to offer military service and so remained outside the new ruling military class. The consequences of some of these surrender terms can be seen in the eighth-century Sogdian and Bactrian documents from the region, including the persistence of local religious and cultural practices.[124]

As in Iraq and western Iran, the defeat of the Sasanian Empire had removed Sasanian royal claims over Zoroastrianism in Khurasan and its frontiers, and so Zoroastrian religion tended to develop a local and syncretic character. Beginning with Khurasan and Jurjan in the 720s and 730s, the later Arabic sources refer to 'Khurramism' (*al-khurramiyya*) as an important religious tradition in the former Sasanian territories. Patricia Crone argues that this was a schematising label used to refer to these diverse, regional, 'non-Sasanian' Iranian religious traditions. Such traditions were prevalent among those Khurasanis and Sogdians who joined the rebel movement that brought about Abbasid rule. The revolutionary leader Khidash, who was executed in 736, is said to have been a 'Khurrami' who advocated sharing women. This latter accusation could reflect his tolerance of fraternal polyandry among his eastern supporters but is also commonly directed against those labelled as 'heretics'. After the execution of the successful revolutionary commander

---

[123] Valerie Hansen, 'Review: New Work on the Sogdians, the Most Important Traders on the Silk Road, AD 500–1000' *T'oung Pao* 89 (2003), 149–61; Geoffrey Khan, *Arabic Documents from Early Islamic Khurasan* (London, 2007); Étienne de la Vaissière, *Sogdian Traders: A History* (Leiden, 2005).
[124] Azad, 'Happily Ever After'.

Abu Muslim by his Abbasid caliph in 755, many of the rebellions across the Iranian plateau are said to have been 'Khurrami', which probably reflects the fragility of the coalition of Arab Muslim and Iranian non-Muslim groups in the revolutionary coalition; eastern Iranians had converted en masse as they joined movements resisting Umayyad rule. Among some of those who became the core of the Abbasids' army and administration, this conversion was followed by the adoption of an Islam acceptable to the wider imperial elite; among others, 'heretical' religious movements expressed dissatisfaction with Abbasid rule.[125]

Conclusions

Across the former territories of the Roman and Sasanian empires, the military success of the Arabian Faithful dramatically reshaped the religious landscape. Religious leaders among the conquered peoples had to come to an accommodation with their new rulers. The loss of the privileged status of the Chalcedonian Christians and the state-sponsored Zoroastrian priesthood mirror one another in the West and the East; by the time of John of Damascus, in the early-to-mid eighth century, the old Roman Christian elites had been marginalised at the top levels of the Umayyad administration; similarly, in the same period in Iraq and parts of Iran, the state-sponsored Zoroastrianism of the Sasanians was in decline, while more local forms of Iranian religion had persisted. However, the parallels cannot be pushed too far; congregational, somewhat vertically socially integrated, Christian institutions may have had greater resilience after the conquests than the Zoroastrian religion of the Sasanian aristocracy. Moreover, the presence of a surviving Roman Empire and other Christian ruling elites allowed some Christians to look beyond Arabian dominions for institutional religious authority, while the acceptance of much of the Christian tradition by the conquerors helped sustain Christian institutions. Where Zoroastrianism did persist, often in more local and diverse forms than the old religion of the Sasanian monarchs, it benefited from the absence of Arabian conquest and settlement from many parts of the Iranian plateau.

Parallels can also be seen where the Arabian conquerors reached the old Roman and Sasanian frontiers in the Caucasus, North Africa and Central Asia. Here, the presence of independent, militarily effective, non-Arabian groups who had viable political choices besides loyalty to Umayyad commanders generated new political and religious formations. In the Caucasus, the vassal status of aristocratic elites and their armies and the small and

---

[125] For all this, see Crone, *Nativist Prophets*.

geographically confined Arabian presence led to the widespread persistence of Caucasian forms of Christianity, albeit reshaped by the new religious and political context. In contrast, syncretic forms of North African and Central Asian Islam emerged in parallel in the first half of the eighth century and became the ideological platforms for spectacular military successes against the Umayyads in the 740s.

12

The Provinces, Government and Taxation

The structures of organisational power are the subject of this chapter. As a tributary empire, founded upon military conquest, the distinction between 'conqueror' and 'conquered' was among the most important forms of social differentiation. Membership of the former group implied an elevated social status, often physical separation from the conquered majority in garrisons or on the steppe, and a separate legal status, under the jurisdiction of the command hierarchy of the conquest polity – the Commander of the Faithful (*amīr al-mu'minīn*) and his sub-commanders (the *amīr*s). Moreover, the conquerors were the recipients of payments made to them by the conquered. Security and some degree of communal self-governance was the offer in return. The conquered populations retained their own local legal jurisdictions but were governed by the conquerors' laws where the two groups interacted. Interactions on the empire's frontiers were more violent, unstable and predatory than those in the stable core provinces.

If 'conqueror' and 'conquered' was a fundamental social distinction, a fundamental social process was its complication over the course of the Umayyad century. In the decades leading up to the crisis of the 'Abbasid Revolution' of 747–50, the conquering elite had begun to diversify, with some remaining military specialists, paid from taxation and tribute, and others abandoning military activity for other occupations. The distinction between 'soldier' and 'civilian' was far from absolute, and individuals could move between activities or combine them.[1] Likewise, from the outset some of the population of conquered lands had found places within the new imperial structures and could undergo processes of religious conversion and cultural or linguistic Arabisation, or both, as they joined, or attempted to join, the new elite. These processes accelerated

---

[1] This process is sometimes described as the 'professionalisation' of the military, with analogues in the 'professionalisation' of the administration. See, for example, Robinson, *'Abd al-Malik*, 68–70; *SaMS*, 210. However, these men were often also landowners and merchants, see Michael Ebstein, 'Shurṭa Chiefs in Basra in the Umayyad Period: A Prosopographical Study', *Al-Qantara* 31 (2010), 129.

in the latter part of the Umayyad period in the transition from a monotheist Arabian 'conquest society' to more fully articulated 'Islamic empire'.[2]

These processes had four main phases under Umayyad rule. The first is 'Uthman's Medinan government of 644–56. 'Uthman had inherited the structures of the 'conquest society'. He presided over continued territorial expansion and the transfer of the leading commands and some valuable lands to 'Abshami allies. Then, under Mu'awiya (r. c. 661–80), the Syrian frontier became the new political and military centre of the empire and the close administrative relationship between Syria and Egypt was further developed. Third, in the aftermath of the second civil war of 680–92, came some of the most dramatic changes after the conquests themselves. 'Abd al-Malik's struggle against his Zubayrid and other rivals, and against the Roman Empire, prompted administrative changes, with a greater insistence on salary payments only for serving soldiers, changes to the provincial taxation systems and the precious metal coinage, and the greater public articulation of Islamic religion by the ruler and his representatives.

'Abd al-Malik's reign coincided with the beginning of a generational shift in senior scribal and fiscal roles, with non-Arabian converts to Islam beginning to compete with non-Arabian non-Muslims at the upper levels of the administration. Changes to the taxation system and its extension into new regions continued during the next two generations of Umayyad rule, while demographic change continued apace. A fourth horizon can be seen at c. 725, by which time Muslims predominated in the upper echelons of the administration in the central lands of the empire and the use of Arabic writing by these leading scribes had become more widespread and diverse. Egypt had been brought under the close control of the caliphs in Syria, while the wealthy but restive province of Iraq remained more administratively separate. Beyond the core territories of the empire, the extent and character of administrative power still varied greatly; swathes of Iran and western North Africa lay beyond the reach of the Umayyads' representatives.

This chapter begins with the geography of imperial power – reviewing the locations where commanders loyal to the Umayyads were consistently present and those that were more contested or ambiguous. From there, it turns to the personnel themselves. 'Commander' or 'governor' (*amīr*, pl. *umarā'*) was the title held by the leaders of the major garrisons and armies, as well as by many of his subordinates in the territories for which he was responsible. Besides the *amīrs*' military role, their organisational responsibilities included communications and record-keeping, law and order, and taxation. These three main

---

[2] *SoH*, 29, 61–2. See also Robinson, *Empire*, 33–4.

governmental roles are addressed in turn. The best evidence comes from Egypt and the Negev, where the survival of administrative documents on papyrus gives direct insight into the administration. Elsewhere, written documents are almost completely absent for the Umayyad period, but the survival of many thousands of coins, as well as lead seals and glass and lead weights do provide documentary evidence for aspects of government and administration across the empire.[3] The later literary sources in Arabic preserve substantial information on the people in the highest levels of the administration, while chronicles composed in Syriac provide insights into the conquered peoples' experiences of taxation.

The Empire and its Provinces

In this first section of the chapter, the administrative geography of the empire is outlined, with an eye both to questions of continuity and change and the extent of control exerted by the Umayyads and their allies. Lowland Syria, the Nile Valley and western Delta in Egypt, together with the Hijaz and South Arabia were core territories, where the caliph was often able to appoint and remove governors and where both governors and their armies were usually loyal to the caliph. Southern Iraq, and its dependent territories to the east, were critically important to Umayyad power, but Iraq's garrisons and pastoralist tribes tended to be hostile to Umayyad rule, and so its governor was crucial to protecting the Umayyads against rivals and rebels. From the early Marwanid period, the Jazira (North Mesopotamia), Armenia and Azerbaijan became a combined frontier command, usually given to a senior member of the Marwanid clan by a slave mother. Qayrawan and Tunis in Ifriqiya, and Marw in Khurasan, were important centres by the beginning of the eighth century. Both tended to be subordinate to governors in Egypt and Iraq, respectively. Beyond these regions, control was much more uneven, with much of the Maghrib and Sind untouched by Arabian settlement, and much of the Iranian plateau and points north and east also remaining independent or contested terrain.

The swift replacement of Roman and Sasanian military power in Iraq, Egypt and Syria led to continuities in the administrative structures of these provinces. What became the province of Iraq corresponded approximately to the late Sasanian provinces of Ard Jukha, Ard Babil, Ard Kaskar, Maysan and Khuzistan, with their urban centres respectively at Ctesiphon (Ar. al-Mada'in), al-Hira and Babil, Kaskar, al-Ubulla and al-Ahwaz (see Map 12.1).

Al-Hira, Maysan and Kaskar were all supplanted by nearby garrisons – Kufa near al-Hira, Basra near al-Ubulla, and then, much later, Wasit near Kaskar. After the death of 'Ali b. Abi Talib in c. 661, the former Sasanian

---

[3] For other documentary sources, see above, Box Text, Ch. 3, n. 34?.

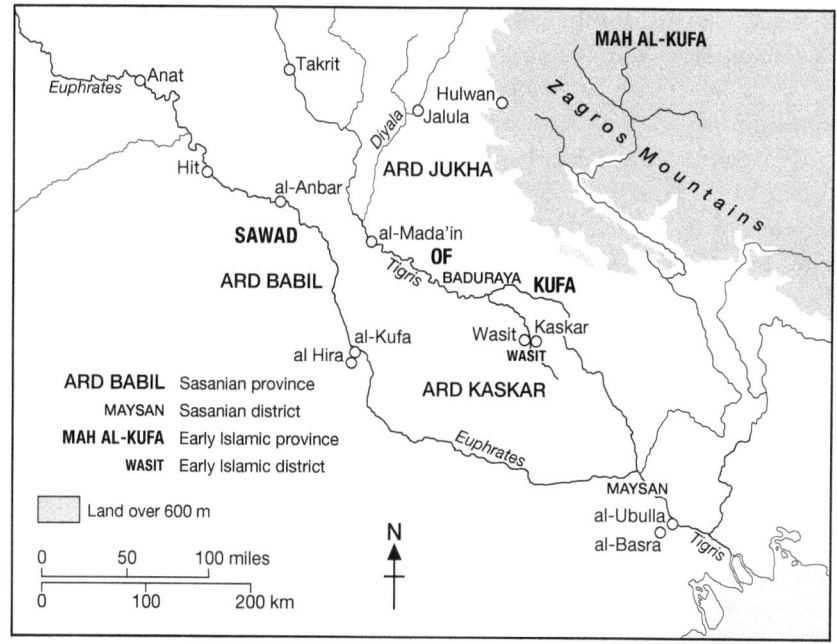

Map 12.1 Late Sasanian and early Islamic Iraq. Based on Michael G. Morony, *Iraq after the Muslim Conquest* (Princeton, 1984), 127.

imperial capital of Ctesiphon/al-Mada'in became a merely local centre, while al-Ahwaz retained its local importance as the capital of Khuzistan. Below the level of these former provinces, the Sasanian districts (Ar. *kuwar*, sing. *kūra*), and their sub-divisions at the level of small towns or villages, exhibit a greater degree of continuity, although the latter often changed with the movement of rivers' courses, changes to canals and expansion of irrigated land.[4]

As in post-Sasanian Iraq, in post-Roman Egypt and Syria, the organisational structures of the former empire shaped Umayyad ones. In Egypt, the former diocesan capital of Alexandria was subordinated to the new camp at Fustat, adjacent to the former Roman fortress at Babylon, just south of the Nile Delta. However, the seventh-century Roman administrative structure of

---

[4] Michael G. Morony, 'Continuity and Change in the Administrative Geography of Late Sasanian and Early Islamic al-'Iraq', *Iran* 20 (1982), 1–49; *IatMC*, 125–64; Touraj Daryaee, 'The Effect of the Arab Muslim Conquest on the Administrative Division of Sasanian Persis', *Iran* 41 (2003), 193–204.

four main provincial sub-divisions (sometimes, anachronistically, 'eparchies') was retained (see Map 12.2).[5]

Syria was initially organised as four 'military districts' (*junds*), based on the four zones that had been controlled by the four senior Roman commanders (Gk *douxoi*, sing. *doux*, Lat. *duces*, sing. *dux*) in the region. Most likely, the use of the term *jund* for Syria and northern Iraq relates somehow to the presence of Arabic-speaking tribes that were co-opted into the new ruling elite.[6] From about 640, Damascus, a former seat of one of the *douxoi*, was the administrative capital of the whole of Syria. At some point between the 660s and the early 680s, a fifth *jund* at Qinnasrin controlling the Euphrates and the northern frontier with the Romans was created in the frontier zone north of Hims/Emesa (see Map 12.3).[7]

In both Egypt and Syria, the smaller Roman sub-divisions of the territories governed by *douxoi* were retained. These *kūra*s (Gk *chora*, often referred to as 'pagarchies' in the literature on Egypt), and, below, that *iklīm*s (Gk *klema*) were reorganised in Syria the middle years of Mu'awiya's caliphate.[8] Under Mu'awiya and Yazid I, the militarily crucial commands of the *jund*s in Syria went predominantly to men from Kalb and Kinda, although a Medinan and a Qurashi also held commands there. Under the Marwanids, these commands went predominantly to members of the ruling Marwanid clan.[9]

The Arabian Peninsula was an exception in two important respects. It had never been part of the Roman or Sasanian empires, nor had it ever formed part of a single, centralised polity, divided as it was by its geography. In the west, there was the Hijaz, whose oasis settlement at Yathrib/Medina was the centre of the nascent empire until 656, and whose shrine at Mecca achieved trans-regional significance with the success of Islam, and briefly had metropolitan status, between 683 and 692, under Ibn al-Zubayr. The key seats of government in the Hijaz were Medina, Mecca and al-Ta'if.[10] In the south, the former Himyarite capital

---

[5] *SaMS*, 33–6; Bernhard Palme, 'The Imperial Presence: Government and Army', in Roger Bagnall (ed.), *Egypt in the Byzantine World, 300–700* (Cambridge, 2007), 248.

[6] John Haldon, 'Seventh Century Continuitues: The *Ajnad* and the Thematic Myth', in Averil Cameron and Lawrence I. Conrad (eds), *The Byzantine and Early Islamic Near East III: States, Resources and Armies* (Princeton, 1995), 379–423; Blankinship, *End of the Jihad*, 47–50. Legendre, 'Aspects', 135, notes that there are no securely datable Umayyad-era usages.

[7] Haldon, '*Ajnad*'; Blankinship, *End of the Jihad*, 47–50.

[8] Clive Foss, 'Mu'awiya's State', in John Haldon (ed.), *Money, Power and Politics in Early Islamic Syria: A Review of Current Debates* (Farnham, 2010), 84–5.

[9] Gundelfinger and Verkinderen, 'Governors'.

[10] See, for example, Khalifa, 65, 88, 124, 186, 213–14, 232, 238, 241. For the combination of the three under one governor during the caliphates of Mu'awiya, 'Abd al-Malik, Hisham and

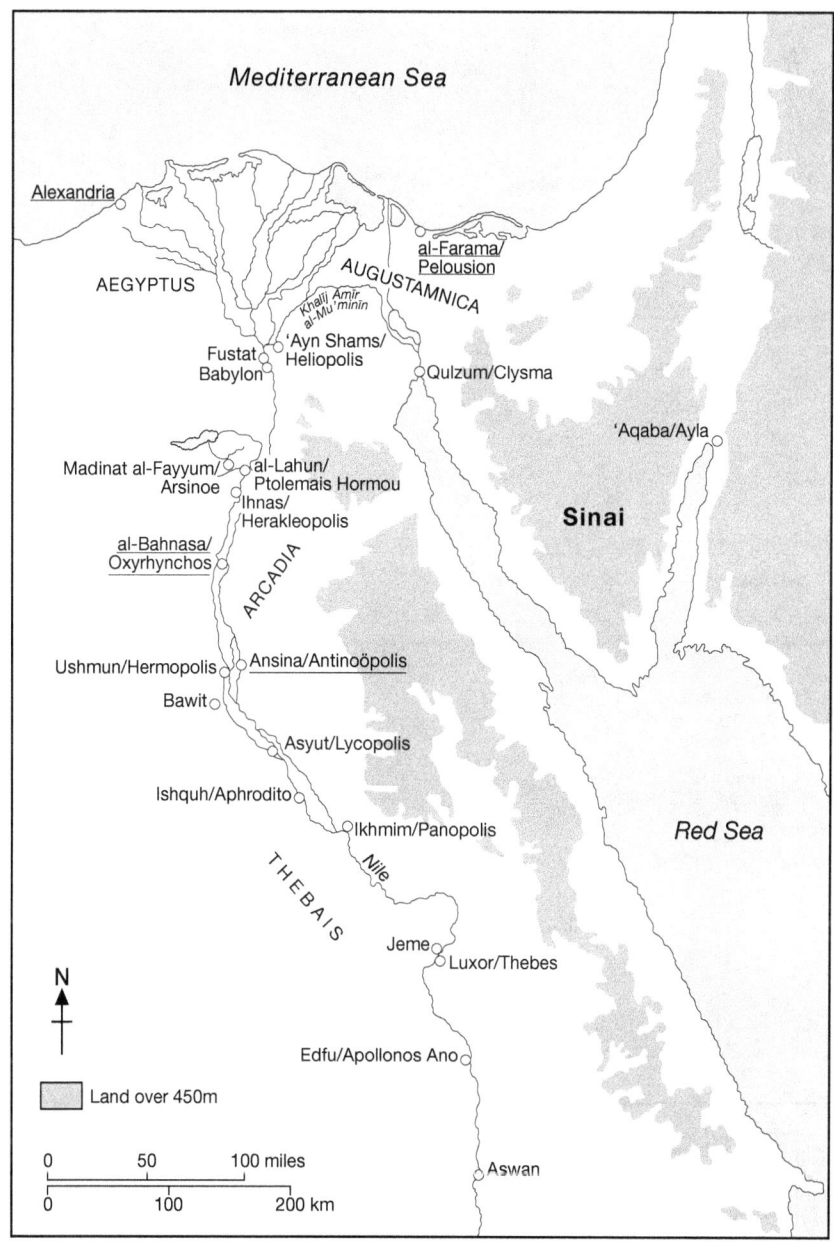

Map 12.2 Late Roman and early Islamic Egypt. The four main former seats of the Roman *douxoi* are underlined and names of their territories are in capitals. Based on Petra Sijpesteijn, *Shaping a Muslim State: The World of a Mid-Eighth-Century Egyptian Official* (Oxford, 2013), xvi.

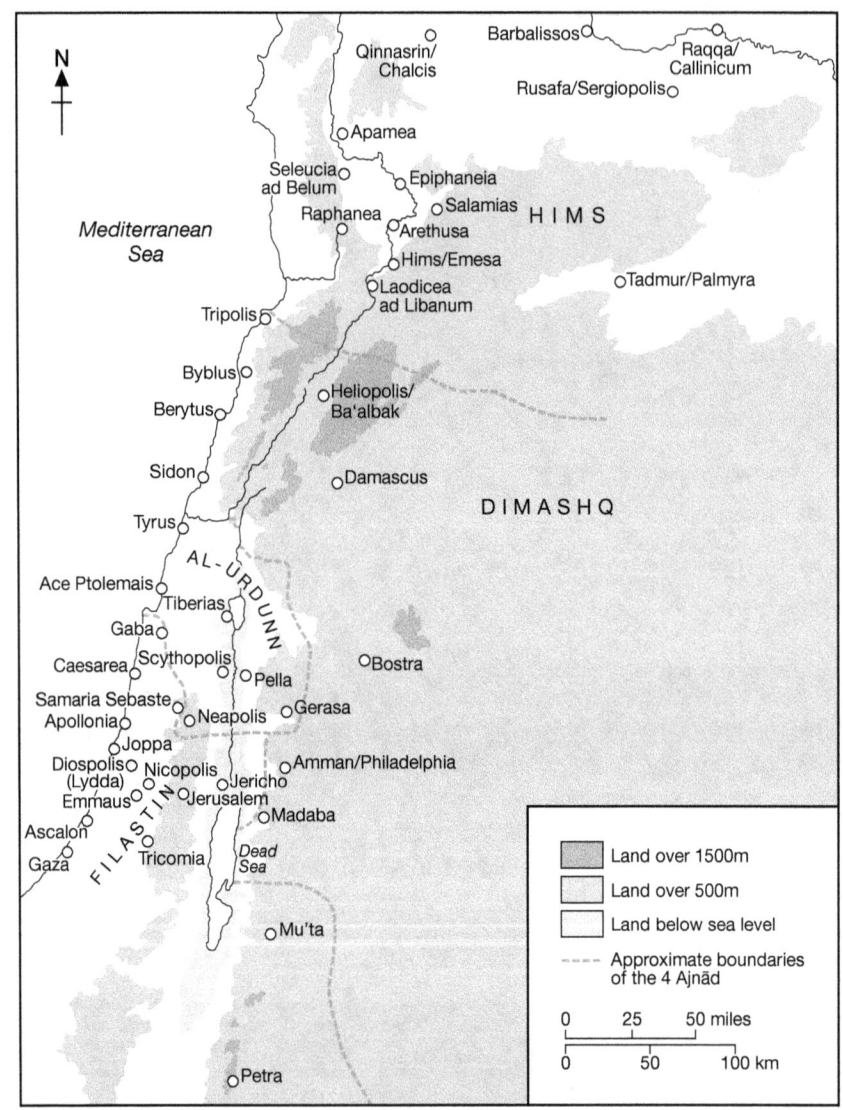

Map 12.3 The military districts (*ajnād*) of Syria after the conquests. Based on John Haldon, 'Seventh-Century Continuities: The *Ajnad* and the "Thematic Myth"', in Averil Cameron (ed.), *The Byzantine and Early Islamic Near East III: States, Resources and Armies* (Princeton, 1995), xiii.

of Sanʿa became the centre of Hijazi rule, with additional governors sometimes appointed to al-Janad in the south-west and Hadramawt in the east.[11]

Beyond the Hijaz and Himyar, direct government was more tenuous. In Oman, there was significant settlement at Sohar. North along the Gulf coast, there were several small settlements, including Dibba (an enclave of modern Oman, in the United Arab Emirates), and, on the northern section of the coast, al-Qatif, in the region which was referred to in its entirety as Bahrayn. Oman and Bahrayn were initially ruled together from Dibba, before both being placed under Basran jurisdiction after 644.[12] Al-Yamama, a region in the eastern central part of the Arabian Peninsula, is also consistently mentioned as a separate governorship, sometimes together with Bahrayn. Both regions were frequently independent of centralised rule, with their pastoralist inhabitants able to evade and resist the impositions of settled state structures.[13]

Among the most important developments in the Marwanid era was the extension of Umayyad organisational power into northern Mesopotamia, known in Arabic as al-Jazira, and into the Caucasus, known as Armenia and Azerbaijan. These regions, which formed one governorship, have been described as the 'Umayyad North' (see Map 12.4). Mosul, in the Jazira, had been founded by Kufan tribesmen next to Nineveh in the late 630s or early 640s, but appears to have been largely independent of Umayyad control until after the second civil war of 680–92.[14] The Kufan rebel al-Mukhtar's governor had used Mosul as a base from which to rule much of al-Jazira in the mid-680s; the same arrangement was adopted by Musʿab b. al-Zubayr (g. 686–91) and then by the Marwanids. The latter began to impose direct rule on Mosul, settling Basran tribesmen there to break the link with Kufa and establishing the town as the major garrison in the province of al-Jazira,

---

Yazid III, see Khalifa, 124, 186, 232, 241. On the governorship of Medina and the leadership of the *ḥajj*, see McMillan, *Meaning*.

[11] G. Rex Smith, 'The Early and Medieval History of Sanʿa' ca. 622–1382/1515', in R. B. Serjeant and Ronald B. Lewcock (eds), *Sanʿaʾ: An Arabian Islamic City* (London, 1983), 51–3; G. Rex Smith, 'The Political History of the Islamic Yemen down to the First Turkish Invasion (1–945/622–1538)', in Werner Daum, *Yemen: 3000 Years of Art and Civilisation in Arabia Felix* (Innsbruck, 1987), 129–30. For a governor at al-Janad in 655–6, see Tabari, I, 3057.

[12] Isam Al-Rawas, *Oman in Early Islamic History* (Reading, 2000), 49–67.

[13] Khalifa, 65, 88, 189, 198, 204, 207, 214, 233, 239; *EI²*, 'al-Yamama' (G. R. Smith). For al-Yamama as joined with Bahrayn under Yazid II, see Khalifa, 214. See also above, Ch. 3, p. 65, n.4 (Yamama), and Chs 4 and 6, p. 133 (Bahrayn).

[14] Robinson, *Empire*, esp. 36–9, 50–1, 77–8. Cf. al-Qadi, 'Population Census', 364.

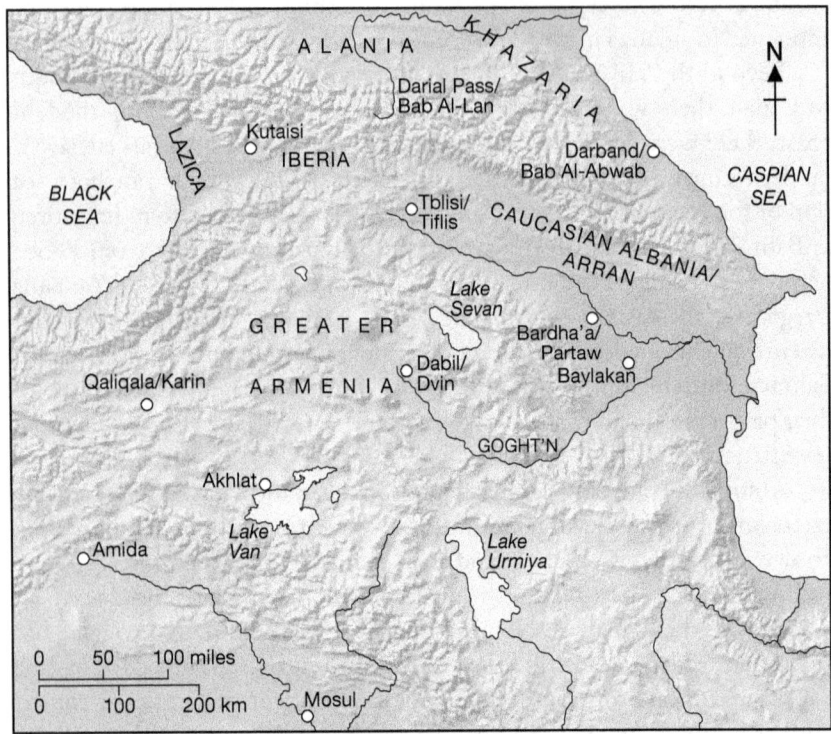

Map 12.4 The 'Umayyad North' (the Caucasus and Mesopotamia). Based on Alison Vacca, 'The Umayyad North (or: How Umayyad was the Umayyad Caliphate?)', in Andrew Marsham (ed.), *The Umayyad World* (London and New York, 2021), 220.

alongside Edessa and Harran.[15] Thereafter the frontiers in Armenia and Azerbaijan tended to be the responsibility of the governor of al-Jazira.[16]

Umayyad 'Armenia' comprised the lands of the Armenian-speaking peoples, which had been divided between Roman and Sasanian influence, as well as eastern parts of Georgian-speaking Iberia. Caucasian Albania (modern Azerbaijan) is called Azerbaijan in the Arabic sources. In these highland provinces, the Umayyads were unable to impose direct rule but instead developed alliances with local elites. Under Muʿawiya, diplomacy was used to seek to undermine the loyalty to the Romans of various actors in the region, and then after the second civil war, a policy of more direct intervention began, but one

[15] Robinson, *Empire*, 50–3, 77–8.
[16] Khalifa, 198, 207, 214, 234–5; Tabari, II, 1562.

that nonetheless still depended heavily upon the devolution of governance to local notables who maintained a vassal status, similar to that they had held in the Sasanian Empire. The largest Marwanid garrisons were at Qaliqala/Karin, at Dvin (near Yerevan, in modern Armenia), and at Bardhaʿa/Partaw (modern Barda, in Azerbaijan). There were also frontier posts on the borders with the Khazars, at Bab al-Abwab (Derbend, in modern Dagestan, in southern Russia) and the Darial Pass (in modern Georgia). The 'Umayyad North' became a single province for the purposes of military administration and pay, with a mint issuing coins and weights for its troops. In contrast, the Iberian kingdom of Lazica, in the lowland zone on the eastern coast of the Black Sea, remained under Roman rule during most of the Umayyad period.[17]

In lands of the southern Mediterranean, to the south and west of Syria, the Egyptian governor at the garrison of Fustat (founded *c.* 643) presided, at least officially, over further expansion westwards (see Map 12.5).[18] Raids into Roman Libya in the 640s had led to the establishment of a garrison near the coast at Barqa (Lat. Barca), in what had been Roman Libya Superior (modern north Libya).[19] Then, in the 670s, Qayrawan was first established as a new garrison in Roman Africa, about 1,000km to the west of Barqa. Qayrawan and Barqa were abandoned and then re-established during the crises of the 680s and 690s; thereafter Qayrawan remained the major administrative centre of Ifriqiya (Roman Africa Procunsularis, or modern northern Tunisia and eastern Algeria). By about 708, a garrison subordinate to Qayrawan had been set up at Tangier (Ar. Tanja, Lat. Tingis) on the Atlantic Coast, at the western entrance to the Strait of Gibralter, a further 1,400km to the west. Tangier was the base from which the conquest of Visigothic Spain took place; in 711 Cordoba was captured and became the main garrison in Umayyad Spain.[20]

In the East, the new garrisons of Kufa and Basra, founded near al-Hira and al-Ubulla, respectively, in the late 630s, were the main centres until

---

[17] Vacca, *Non-Muslim Provinces*; Vacca, 'Umayyad North'. On the Darial Pass, see Eberhard Sauer et al., 'Northern Outpost of the Caliphate: Maintaining Military Forces in a Hostile Environment (the Dariali Gorge in the Central Caucasus in Georgia)', *Antiquity* 89 (2015), 885–904. For sub-governors in the Caucasus under Muhammad b. Marwan, see Khalifa, 189. See also above, Ch. 11, pp. 284–6 and Ch. 6, pp. 129–31.

[18] Tabari, II, 94, says that the government and further conquest of 'Egypt, Barqa, Ifriqiyya and Tripoli' was first united under one governor, based in Egypt, with a deputy in Ifriqiya, by Muʿawiya, in 670–1. But cf., for example, Zychowicz-Coghill, *First Arabic Annals*, 76–9, where things look more complex.

[19] Kennedy, *Conquests*, 206–8. For the administrative geography of this part of what had once been the Roman diocese of Egypt, see James G. Keenan, 'Egypt', *CAH*, XIV, 613.

[20] Kennedy, *Conquests*, 209–11, 223–4, 310–14. See also Martínez Jiménez et al., *Iberian Peninsula*, 267–76.

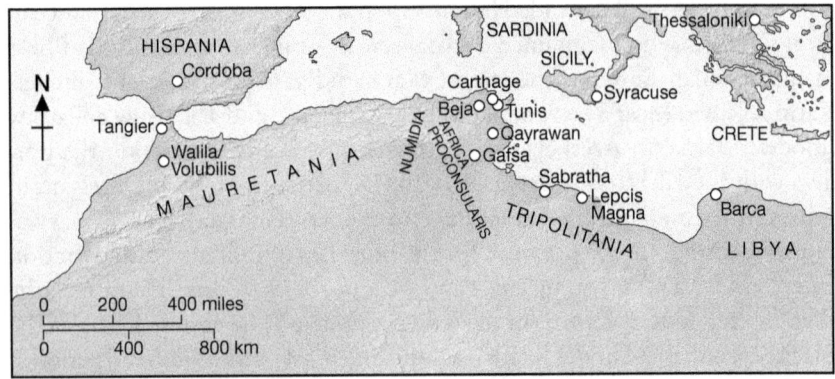

Map 12.5 Late Roman and early Islamic South Mediterranean and North Africa.

the building of Wasit in 703 or 704. The former Sasanian capital of al-Mada'in was also garrisoned and was briefly an imperial capital under 'Ali (r. 656–61). Basra briefly become the capital of the whole of the East under Ziyad b. Sumayya (g. c. 670–3). With the restoration of Umayyad power after the second civil war, the whole of the eastern part of the empire was again handed to a single governor, based in Iraq, between 697 and 717 and between 720 and 730. The new foundation at Wasit replaced Kaskar after 703–4 and was the capital from then until 715 and for part of the period 720–30, when Kufa and al-Hira were also occasionally capitals.[21]

Already by the 640s, armies from Kufa had taken Nihawand, on the route north into the Zagros, and the strategic centres of Hamadhan and Isfahan in the same highlands (see Map 12.6). From Hamadhan, raids had been conducted east, along the road to Khurasan, taking Rayy (near modern Tehran), and reaching as far as Bistam, just to the south-east of the Caspian Sea.[22] This region became the frontier province of Jibal, with its administrative centre at Rayy.[23] Raids were also made north from here into Azerbaijan and Armenia.[24] The same period also saw the subjugation by the Basrans of Khuzistan – the Dujayl river valley below the Zagros, in southern Iraq. There, the existing Sasanian centre of al-Ahwaz remained the local capital.[25] Fars, in the southern

[21] See above, Chs 3, 4, 6, 7 and 8, pp. 70–2, 97–8, 131–8, 151, 170–2, 180.
[22] Kennedy, *Conquests*, 176–9.
[23] Bertold Spuler, *Iran in the Early Islamic Period: Politics, Culture, Administration and Public Life between the Arab and the Seljuk Conquests, 633–1055*, ed. Robert G. Hoyland and tr. Gwendolin Goldbloom and Berenike Walburg (Leiden, 2015), 292.
[24] Kennedy, *Conquests*, 179–80.
[25] Chase F. Robinson, 'The Conquest of Khuzistan: A Historiographical Reassessment', *BSOAS* 67 (2004), 21–5. On al-Ahwaz, see Spuler, *Iran*, 292 and, for example, Tabari, II, 1034.

Zagros highlands, was brought under the authority of the Basran governor in Iraq, who presided over the conquest of Istakhr, the capital of Fars, in about 649, and then, to the south, the province of Kirman, with its capital at Sirjan (or later, perhaps Jiruft).[26] From there, further raids were made into Sistan and Khurasan. Zaranj, on Lake Zirih, became the garrison in Sistan from *c*. 652 onwards. This was the base from which raids were made into Afghanistan, as well as north, into Khurasan.[27] In 671 Marw became the main garrison in Khurasan, supplanting Zaranj as the most important outpost on the eastern frontiers of the empire.[28] The provinces of southern and eastern Iran – Fars and Kirman – remained volatile and difficult to govern.[29]

The Marwanid period also saw the further extension of Muslim rule on the Iranian plateau and its peripheries (see Map 12.6). Quhistan, which lay between Sistan and Khurasan in the centre of the plateau, was initially the main route between the two provinces. However, Quhistan was only partially subdued in the seventh and early eighth centuries; the first mention of an Arabian Muslim governor there, subordinate to Khurasan, is as late as 744.[30] The hills and grasslands of Jurjan, north of the plateau and to the east of the Caspian, controlled the eastern end of the route between Rayy and Khurasan. These were impassable to the Muslims until 716–17, when Jurjan was conquered and garrisoned. The lowlands around the southern Caspian – Gilan and Tabaristan – remained in a tributary relationship, ruled by local Iranian leaders.[31] Makran and the Indus Valley beyond it were invaded in 710–12, where the existing town of Multan and then a foundation named al-Mansura became important centres.[32] In Sogdia, Bukhara was garrisoned at about the same time and was made subordinate to the Khurasani commander in Marw.[33]

Governors

Just as the garrison, or *miṣr*, was the key geographical element in the administration of the conquered territories beyond Syria and the Jazira, the commander at the head of each garrison – the *amīr* – was the key person in the administration.

---

[26] Martin Hinds, 'The First Arab Conquests in Fars', *Iran* 22 (1984), 39–53; Kennedy, *Conquests*, 180–5. For the date of the fall of Istakhr, see *EI*², 'Istakhr' (M. Streck-[G. C. Miles]). On Sirjan, see Spuler, *Iran*, 295. For Jiruft as the capital of southern Kirman, see Tabari, II, 1003; Tabari, *History*, xiv, 74, n. 323 (G. Rex Smith).
[27] Kennedy, *Conquests*, 185–92; Bosworth, *Sistan*, 13–21.
[28] See above, Ch. 4, n. 56?.
[29] Gundelfinger and Verkinderen, 'Governors'; Legendre, 'Translation'.
[30] *EI*², 'Kuhistan' (J. H. Kramers); Spuler, *Iran*, 297; Tabari, II, 1224, 1847, 1860–1.
[31] Tabari, II, 1320–35. On the settlement of Jurjan, see Pourshariati, 'Khurasan'.
[32] Khalifa, 241; cf. Baladhuri, *Futuh*, 439, 444; *EI*², 'al-Mansura' (Y. Friedmann).
[33] Haug, *Eastern Frontier*, 116–17; *EI*², 'Bukhara' (W. Barthold [R. N. Frye]).

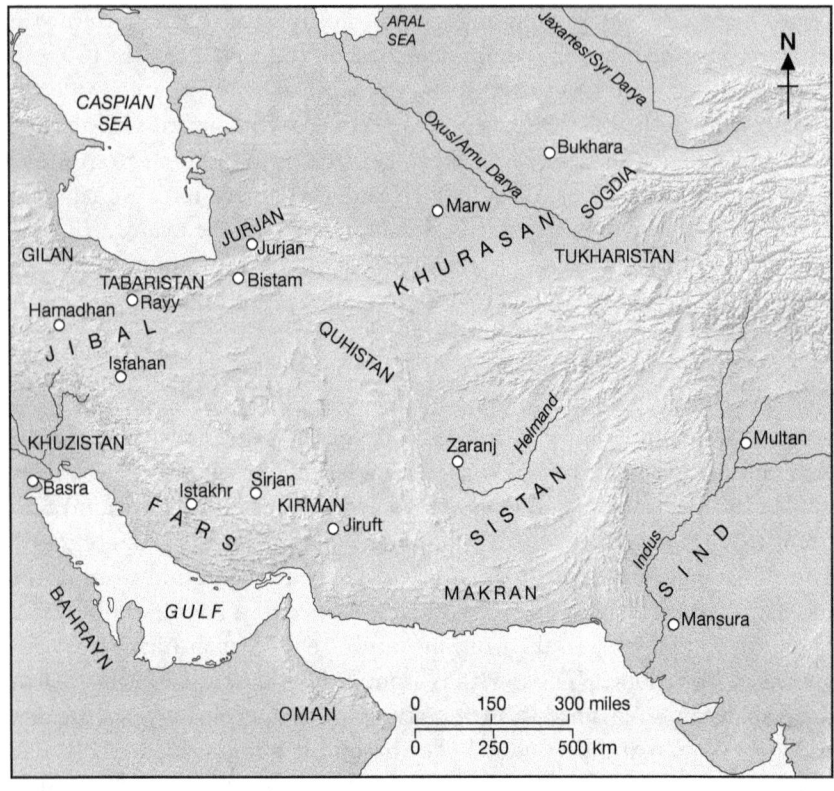

Map 12.6 The eastern lands of the Umayyad Empire in Marwanid times.

The *amīr*s took responsibility for the distribution of tax and tribute to their armies, for law, order and justice within the new garrisons, and for the leadership of congregational prayer. In some cases, leadership of the prayer was separated from responsibility for taxation. Sub-commanders, also often simply called *amīr*s, were in turn appointed to head the smaller garrisons in the territories under their control. The *amīr*s of the main garrisons were direct appointees of the caliph, notionally at least. In practice, some commanders would have been difficult to remove, and some held power for many years. Nonetheless, the caliphs did replace governors and substantial additional payments were often said to have been demanded of governors by the caliphs.[34] *Amīr*s often acted with autonomy on the frontiers, where expansionist warfare allowed for de

[34] Baladhuri, *Futuh*, 231, 232; Ya'qubi, II, 382. Other terms for *amir* include *walī* and *'āmil*. The latter became associated with fiscal and scribal responsibilities. See Gundelfinger and Verkinderen, 'Governors', 256 and n. 2.

facto positions of power to be achieved and granted retrospective recognition, as happened with North Africa and al-Andalus.

During the eighth century, a distinction between Muslim members of the military and Muslim settlers more involved in commerce, agriculture or other activities began to emerge; at the same time, growing numbers of peoples of non-Arabian heritage had joined the new religion, via enslavement, military service and migration. These social developments coincided with the expansion of the cities, greater settlement by Arabian monotheists in the countryside, and wider deployment of Syrian soldiers in the provinces. Meanwhile, nomadic pastoralists continued to negotiate their relationships with the new settled elites, increasingly as Muslims themselves. The basic administrative structure established during the conquests remained in place during these changes, but it expanded and changed in response to the new circumstances. In what follows, each of the main activities of the government in the provincial garrisons is surveyed – communications and record-keeping, law and order, and taxation.

Communications and Record-keeping

All empires depend on effective communications. The use of scribal specialists and expert messenger systems, such as postal relays, were long-established instruments of empire, upon which the Arabian conquerors also depended from the outset, bringing their own distinctive versions of these practices with them.[35] The public promulgation of messages from the ruling elite to relevant groups was another crucial aspect of imperial power. Among the West Arabian conquerors the spoken word had distinctive formal genres, including a variety of poetic styles and a tradition of formal public speech, sometimes delivered in an incantatory rhyming prose (*saj'*). The publishing of decrees and other formal texts by temporary or permanent display in public places was also widespread in Late Antiquity, including in Himyar before Islam, and it remained a widespread practice in the Umayyad Empire.[36]

The *amīr*s of the garrisons were critical nodal points for these communications. Friday prayers at the main congregational mosque were usually led

---

[35] On pre-Islamic precedents for Umayyad-era Arabic scribal practices, see Geoffrey Khan, 'The Opening Formula and Witness Clauses in Arabic Legal Documents from the Early Islamic Period', *JAOS* 139 (2019), 23–40. For the same for postal relays, see Adam J. Silverstein, *Postal Systems in the Pre-modern Islamic World* (Cambridge, 2007), 42–51. See also *SaMS*, 65, and *EIC*, 78, 81, on the administrative sophistication of the Arabians.

[36] Legendre, 'Aspects', 142–3; Khan, 'Opening Formula', 29; Robert G. Hoyland, 'Khanasira and Andarin (Northern Syria) in the Umayyad Period and a New Arabic Tax Document', in Alain George and Andrew Marsham (eds), *Power, Patronage, and Memory in Early Islam* (Oxford, 2018), 137.

by the *amīr*. This was the occasion for the *khuṭba*, or Friday sermon, which was an important forum for public, formal, communication between the commander and the garrison. Versions of famous speeches by governors are recorded in the later sources, and it is quite possible that echoes of the original content are indeed preserved in them, since such occasions were remembered and recited.[37] Written communications were sent from the caliph to the provincial commanders by postal riders (Ar. *barīd*), who were in the service of the caliph and his commanders. At the death of a caliph, the *barīd* carried the news of the accession of the new ruler to the governors, who had to respond with pledged allegiance (*bayʿa*) to him. The same network is also said sometimes to have been used to transport troops and was often how a new governor was said to reach his province. By the later Umayyad period, the *barīd* was a sophisticated infrastructure of milestones, waystations and professional riders, which contributed both to the symbolism of imperial power and its actual exercise (Figure 12.1).[38] By the same period, written caliphal communications were managed by the *ṣāḥib dīwān al-rasāʾil* ('chief of the letter-writing office'), whose output had a distinctive, formal style, which served the same combination of symbolic and practical functions (Figure 12.2).[39]

The later Arabic tradition says that Arabic was already being used for contracts and treaties in the Hijaz in the sixth and early seventh centuries. Arabic graffiti from the same region is documentary evidence for the use of written Arabic there, just as official inscriptions and graffiti suggest the use of Arabic by the Romans' sixth-century allies.[40] With the conquests, Arabic continued to be used for these and other purposes by the Arabic speakers who predominated among the conquest armies. It is notable that a well-developed Arabic scribal practice appears immediately in the unique Egyptian documentary record with the conquest of that province in the early 640s. However, the administration of the conquered territories was by necessity multilingual, with the old languages of Roman and Sasanian imperial rule retaining prestige,

---

[37] See, for example, the famous *khuṭba* of al-Hajjaj on his accession: Tabari, II, 863–71. For references to sermons denouncing the rebel al-Harith at the garrison of Marw, Tabari, II, 1566. See further on sermons, Qutbuddin, *Orations*.

[38] Silverstein, *Postal Systems*, 54–87. For the transport of troops, see Tabari, II, 1060. For governors arriving with *barīd* horses, see Tabari, II, 1527; Kindi, 62. On pledges of allegiance, see *RoIM*.

[39] Al-Qadi, 'Religious Foundation'; *RoIM*, 145–80.

[40] See above, Ch. 2, pp. 47–50; Al-Jallad, 'Palaeo-Arabic'; *RoIM*, 26–37, with further references.

Figure 12.1 Milestone inscribed in Arabic in the name of 'Abd al-Malik, Commander of the Faithful, from Khan al-Hathrura, between Jerusalem and Damascus, 685–705 CE. 41cm × 40cm. Istanbul, Türk ve Islam Eserleri Müzesi, no. 2511. Photograph by Andrew Marsham.

and scribes and leaders from the populations of the conquered territories contributing to the new Arabian dispensation.[41]

Chief Scribes and Tax Officials at the Syrian Umayyad Court

With Mu'awiya's victory in the first civil war in 661, the position of chief scribe (*kātib*) of the commander of the province in Damascus became scribe to the Commander of the Faithful, responsible for record-keeping and communications between the ruler and the *amīr*s elsewhere. Likewise, the position of head of the Syrian *dīwān*s ('army registers') or head of *al-kharāj* ('tax'), as the later sources describe his position, became the finance official for the ruling Syrian armies. After 'Abd al-Malik's victory in the second civil war, in 692, the latter official is more often referred to in the sources as 'head of tax and the army' (*ṣāḥib al-kharāj wa-l-jund*), which may reflect wider-ranging responsibilities beyond Syria as greater administrative influence was

[41] See Stroumsa, 'Greek and Arabic'; Legendre, 'Aspects', 141–3; Legendre, 'Translation'.

sought over the tax systems and army registers in the provinces. Both the chief scribe and tax official appear in later lists alongside the heads of the *shurṭa* ('militia' or 'police') and the *ḥaras* ('bodyguards'), the *ḥājib* ('gatekeeper') and the keeper of the *khātam* ('seal'), as well as courtiers with less defined offices, who are said to have been leading advisors to the ruler.[42] While the sources are not detailed and are at times confused about offices and their holders, changes in the backgrounds of these leading personalities at the Umayyad court reflect religious and demographic change. In what follows, the intertwined histories of the two offices of chief scribe and chief of tax and army pay are outlined.

Muʿāwiya's chief scribe and gatekeeper was ʿUbayd Allah b. ʿAws al-Ghassani, who is said to have remained as the chief scribe for for Yazid I (r. 680–3) and Marwan I (r. 684–5). ʿUbayd is described as 'a Syrian tribal leader' (*sayyid ahl al-Shām*), which suggests the importance of affinity with the Arabic-speaking post-Roman tribes for the role of scribe and gatekeeper in seventh-century Syria. Muʿāwiya's 'head of the registers and all of his government' (*ṣāḥib al-dawāwīn wa-amrihi kullihi*), or alternatively, 'head of tax' (*ṣāḥib al-kharāj*) was Sarjun b. Mansur al-Rumi ('Sergius, son of Mansur, the Roman'), who retained a similar role during Yazid I's rule and for the first part of ʿAbd al-Malik's. Sarjun was from a prominent Chalcedonian Christian Damascene family; his father likely served in the Roman administration, and his son – or more likely – grandson, was the famous Christian scholar, St John of Damascus, who may have briefly worked for the Umayyads in the early eighth century.[43] Sarjun's urban and clerical background is suggestive of the importance of continuity in fiscal administration after the conquests. Apart from one isolated report that Sarjun became Muslim, he is widely described as a Christian, whereas his successors as head of tax and the army do appear to have been Muslims.

Marwan I's *mawlā* and scribe, Salim Abu l-Zuʿayziʿa, is said to have become ʿAbd al-Malik's chief scribe. Abu l-Zuʿayziʿa is also said to have

---

[42] Three important lists are: Khalifa, where the occupants of these positions are listed at the end of most caliphal reigns; al-Tabari, *Taʾrikh*, II, 835–40; Abu ʿAbd Allah Muhammad al-Jahshiyari, *Kitab al-Wuzaraʾ wa-l-Kuttab*, eds Mustafa al-Saqa et al. (Cairo, 1938), 21–88. For biographies of individuals, see Ibn ʿAsakir, s.nn. See also David White Biddle, 'The Development of the Bureaucracy of the Islamic Empire during the late Umayyad and early Abbasid Period', PhD Dissertation, University of Texas, Austin (1972); Longworth, 'Islamic Bureaucrats'.

[43] On Sarjun, see Anthony, 'Fixing'; Sidney Griffith, 'The Mansur Family and Saint John of Damascus: Christians and Muslims in Umayyad Times', in Antoine Borrut and Fred M. Donner (eds), *Christians and Others in the Umayyad State* (Chicago, 2016), 29–53. On John of Damascus, see above, Ch. 11, pp. 273–4.

temporarily held the post of head of 'Abd al-Malik's bodyguard (*ḥaras*). The Medinan religious scholar Qabisa b. Dhuʿayb al-Khuzaʿi is also mentioned as a 'scribe' (*kātib*) of his brother-in-law 'Abd al-Malik, in the sense of a close confidante and advisor. At some point during 'Abd al-Malik's reign, Sarjun b. Mansur was replaced as 'head of tax and the army' (*ṣāḥib al-kharāj wa-l-jund*) by Sulayman b. Saʿd al-Khushani, a *mawlā* from a branch of the Syrian tribal group Qudaʿa. Sulayman b. Saʿd remained in this post under both al-Walid I and Sulayman. Sulayman b. Saʿd is associated in the later Arabic tradition with innovation of using Arabic, as opposed to Greek, in the *dīwān*s. While the papyri show that the transition to using Arabic in the administration was nothing like as sudden or complete as the literary evidence has often been understood to imply, his era does coincide with the shift towards the greater use of Arabic in the upper levels of the administration.[44] Al-Walid I's scribe and keeper of his seal is said in some sources to have been his *mawlā*, Janah Abu Marwan, while his maternal cousin, al-Qaʿqaʿ b. Khulayd al-ʿAbsi is mentioned as one of his 'scribes' in the sense of leading intimate and advisor. Sulayman and 'Umar II are said to have had the same scribe, al-Layth b. Abi Ruqayya, who was a *mawlā* of a paternal half-sister of Muʿawiya and her Thaqafi husband; the religious scholar Rajaʾ b. Haywa al-Kindi, the son of *mawlā* who had moved from Iraq to Syria, is said to have been an influential presence at both of their courts.

'Umar II's head of tax and the army was Salih b. Jubayr al-Ghassani (or al-Ghudani or al-Sadaʾi), who was either from al-Tabariyya/Tiberias, in al-Urdunn, or from Filastin. Salih combined this office with the position of scribe under Yazid II, before he was replaced by Usama b. Zayd, a *mawlā* of Tanukh or Kalb, who had formerly been head of Damascus' army register and then head of Egyptian tax, for al-Walid I and Sulayman. Usama is said to have remained head of tax at the very beginning of Hisham's reign, before Hisham appointed ʿUbayd Allah b. al-Habhab, a *mawlā* of the Banu Salul, and then, after ʿUbayd Allah's appointment to Egypt in 725, Saʿid b. ʿUqba, a *mawlā* of Banu al-Harith b. Kaʿb, also from al-Tabariyya. A leading influence at Hisham's court was al-Abrash ('the Freckled One'), Abu Mujashiʿ Saʿid b. al-Walid al-Kalbi, while his chief scribe is said to have been Salim Abu l-ʿAlaʾ, a client (*mawlā*) of one of the Marwanid family. One of al-Walid II's heads of tax is said to have been a grandson of al-Hajjaj, 'Abd al-Malik b. Muhammad b. al-Hajjaj; if so, he is unusual for being a member of the tribal elite and a relative of the caliph, rather than one of his clients (*mawālī*). Salim Abu l-ʿAlaʾ and his son 'Abd Allah are named as heads of

---

[44] Legendre, 'Aspects', 141–2.

the writing office under al-Walid II; his son-in-law, the grandson of a freed slave from Iraq, 'Abd al-Hamid b. Yahya (c. 688–750), became Marwan II's scribe. Yazid III's scribe was Thabit b. Sulayman b. Saʻd, reflecting his support among the Syrian Qudaʻa.

By the 730s, the office of 'chief scribe' was very different from what it had been in earlier decades; references to an 'office of public lettters' (*dīwān al-rasāʼil*) in the literary sources for the period after 'Abd al-Malik probably reflect organisational changes in response to the new scale and importance of written communication. The heads of the writing office for much of the time of Hisham and after (724–50), Salim Abu l-'Ala' and 'Abd al-Hamid, are notable for the volume of their writing that is recorded in later sources; this appears to reflect a genuine change in the public use of Arabic prose in the last decades of the Umayyad caliphate, with long texts in a new and distinctive style becoming the basis for public readings of proclamations from the caliph. This shift from orality to writing in caliphal communications after *c*. 725 forms part of a wider cultural shift in the balance between the two, with longer written compilations of religious material also beginning in the same period.[45]

Law and Order

Law and order in the garrisons was maintained by a military unit known as the *shurṭa*. *Shurṭa* probably derives from the Latin *cohors*, which can refer simply to a military unit, or to the paramilitary force responsible for security in late Roman cities. *Shurṭa* is often translated as 'police', which tends to disguise the combined military, religious and judicial functions of the *shurṭa*, as well as the extent of their power. The *ṣāḥib al-shurṭa* ('chief of the *shurṭa*') was a senior position within the administration, appointed by the *amīr* and often deputising for him in his absence. The post often led to advancement to a senior military command or the governorship of a province. The *ṣāḥib al-shurṭa* was usually drawn from among the leaders of the Arabian tribespeople of the garrison (*ashrāf*, sing. *sharīf*), and so was an important link between the governor and the settlers. Consequently, it could also be a flashpoint for competition between interest groups, as seems to have happened at the arrival of Qurra b. Sharik as governor in Egypt in 709.[46]

The *shurṭa*'s primary role was the enforcement of law and order, suppressing violent crime and feuds, and enforcing of other legal and moral

---

[45] *RoIM*, 145–80. On writing and the *ḥadīth*, see Schoeler, 'Oral Torah'.
[46] Kindi, 64–5.

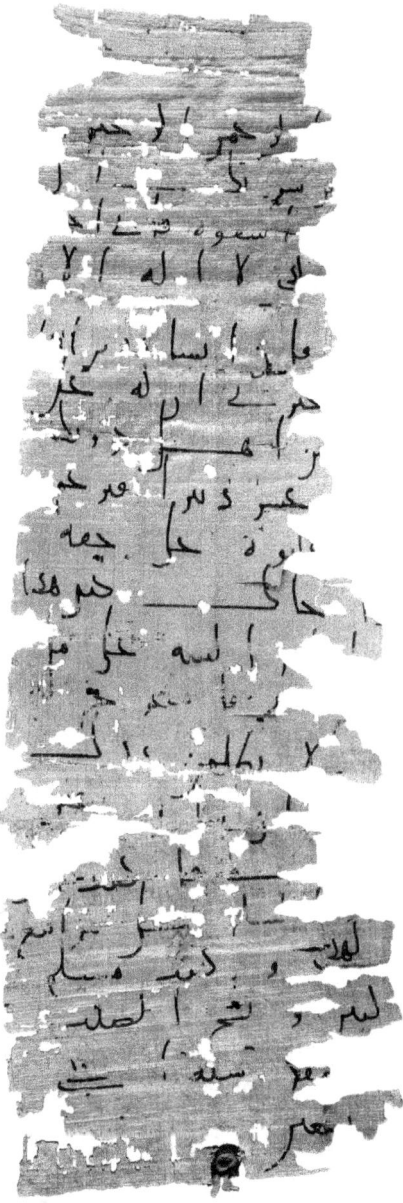

Figure 12.2 Papyrus document in Arabic about a tax debt, dated Safar AH 91/ December 709–January 710 CE. In the name of Qurra b. Sharik, al-Walid I's governor in Egypt (g. 709–14 CE). 20cm × 53.7cm (much of the right side missing). Oriental Institute, Chicago, E13756. © Oriental Institute, Chicago. See Nabia Abbott, *The Qurra Papyri from Aphrodito in the Oriental Institute* (Chicago, 1938), 47–9.

norms, including the imprisoning of debtors and the stoning of adulterers. The *shurṭa* sometimes appear to have acted independently in matters of law, without recourse to the *amīr*, or, in later periods, the *qāḍī* ('judge' or, better for the Umayyad period, 'legal advisor'). However, there are also instances of the *shurṭa* enforcing decisions made by others in the administration. Beyond the suppression of criminal activity, the chief of the *shurṭa* and his men are also often found suppressing more organised violence, banditry and rebellion, as an elite military element in the garrison. The *ṣāḥib al-shurṭa*'s status was also reflected in ceremonial; for example, in formal processions at Basra and Marw, the chief of the *shurṭa* would parade in front of the *amīr*, bearing a short spear called the *ḥarba*.[47]

While the chief of the *shurṭa* seems to have taken much of the responsibility for the criminal law and the enforcement of moral and religious practice in the garrisons, the *amīr* was also assisted in adjudication and administration by the *qāḍī*, often translated – again, rather inaccurately – as 'judge'. As with so much of the administrative apparatus of the empire, the position of *qāḍī* appears in the later literary sources from the time of the foundation of the garrisons in the conquered territories under 'Umar b. al-Khattab (r. 634–44) and so seems to reflect the need to establish new administrative structures to manage the tribal armies. However, the *qāḍī* in Umayyad times acted as an assistant to the governor in administering justice and was not an independent 'judge'; his position has been variously described as that of a 'lieutenant' or 'secretary'. The evidence of the documentary sources from Egypt shows that the *amīr* acted as the senior arbitrator and judge in his province and that the chief of the *shurṭa* usually also exercised judicial authority. The *qāḍī* was a specialist advisor in religion and law, to whom legal decisions may sometimes have been delegated. Sometimes the offices of *ṣāḥib al-shurṭa* and *qāḍī* were combined in one person.[48]

---

[47] On the *shurṭa*, see Arssan Mussa Rashid, 'The Role of the *Shurṭa* in Early Islam', PhD Thesis, University of Edinburgh (1983); *IatMC*, 93–6; Fred M. Donner, 'The Shurta in Early Umayyad Syria', in Adnan Muhammad Bakhit and Robert Schick (eds), *The Fourth International Conference on the History of Bilad al-Sham during the Umayyad Period: Proceedings of the Third Symposium, 24–29 October 1987* (Amman, 1989), II, 247–62; Ebstein, '*Shurta* Chiefs'. For the *ḥarba* at Marw, see Tabari, II, 862. Al-Hajjaj was the head of the *shurṭa* in Filastin, and Hisham's *shurṭa* chief was later governor of Armenia: Baladhuri, *Ansab*, V, 343, VII, 311. Al-Hajjaj's *shurṭa* chief was later governor of Ifriqiya for Yazid II: Ibn 'Idhari, *al-Bayan*, I, 48. Khalid al-Qasri was head of the *shurṭa* in Kufa for 'Umar b. Hubayra before becoming governor of Iraq himself under Hisham: Ibn 'Asakir, XVI, 140, §1896.

[48] On the *qāḍī* in early Islamic and Umayyad times, see Mathieu Tillier, *Les cadis d'Iraq et l'état abbasside, 132/750–334/945* (Damascus, 2009), 66–97; Mathieu Tillier, *L'Invention*

A letter of advice to an Umayyad prince composed in the 740s says that the *qāḍī* should be 'a man of integrity, good manners, intelligence, virtue, piety ... he must have the wisdom of age, be helped by his long experience and be versed in public affairs'. The status accorded to the *qāḍī* in this late Umayyad text tends to suggest that the position had become more important over the century since the first conquests; this would seem plausible in the context of rapidly expanding populations in the garrisons and evolving ideas about Islamic law and justice among them. There is also some evidence that the caliphs began to intervene more directly in the appointment of *qāḍī*s, especially from the 710s. These attempts at central control also suggest that a greater importance was being accorded to specialists in law.[49]

Management of the marketplace was another specialist office which appears in the sources for the very early period. The prominence of this position in the sources suggests the importance of commerce for the Hijazi elite, something which also seems to be reflected in the language and ethical concerns of the Qur'an. There are references in the later sources to people appointed in charge of the *sūq* at Mecca and Medina in the time of Muhammad and Abu Bakr, but it is only for the time of 'Umar b. al-Khattab and the foundation of the garrisons that the title '*āmil al-sūq* ('market official', often translated, 'market inspector') first appears in these sources; the same title is then used of individuals under 'Uthman and Ibn al-Zubayr. There are also a very small number of references to the position in the first half of the eighth century in the Hijaz and in Iraq.[50]

---

du cadi: la justice des musulmans, des juifs et des chrétiens aux premiers siècles de l'Islam (Paris, 2017); cf. Hannah-Lena Hagemann, 'Muslim Elites in the Early Islamic Jazira: The Qadis of Harran, al-Raqqa, and al-Mawsil', in Hannah-Lena Hagemann and Stefan Heidemann (eds), *Transregional and Regional Elites: Connecting the Early Islamic Empire* (Berlin, 2020), 331–58. For the documentary evidence, see Lucian Reinfandt, 'Judicial Practice in Umayyad Egypt (661–750 AD). 'Version 01 | Imperium and Officium Working Papers (IOWP)' (2013), <http://iowp.univie.ac.at/?q=node/259> (last accessed 10 March 2015), 3–4 and n. 11. For *qāḍī*s in Umayyad Iraq, see *IatMC*, 437–42. For the combination of *ṣāḥib al-shurṭa* and *qāḍī* in one person, see *SaMS*, 85, n. 266; Tabari, II, 1526. For the delegation of arbitration and justice to the *qāḍī*, see also *SaMS*, 204 and n. 467.

[49] On the centralisation of appointments, see Wael Hallaq, *The Origins and Evolution of Islamic Law* (Cambridge, 2005), 57–8. Tillier, *Les cadis*, 83–6, is more circumspect. Cf. Hagemann, 'Muslim Elites', 351–2. For the quotation, see Tillier, *Les cadis*, 88.

[50] *EI*², 'Hisba. i. General Sources, Origins, Duties (Cl. Cahen and M. Talbi); Ronald P. Buckley, 'The Muhtasib', *Arabica* 39 (1992), 59–65. For the *agoranomos* in late Roman Egypt, see Bagnall, *Egypt*, 58. See further, Bessard, *Caliphs and Merchants*, 208–12. On the Qur'an, see Andrew Marsham, 'Some Observations on Commerce and Covenant in the Qur'an', in George Brook et al. (eds), *Near Eastern and Arabian Essays: Studies in Honour of John F. Healey* (Oxford, 2018), 303–13.

The *ʿāmil al-sūq* appears to have had authority over the proper running of the market, and especially over weights, measures and scales. With the establishment of garrisons in Roman and Sasanian territory, local weights and measures (and presumably some local commercial customs) were adopted. Then, from the mid-690s, the reforms instituted under ʿAbd al-Malik saw the development of a new Arabic-language system of weights based on the new weight standards of the reformed coinage; edicts such as that associated with ʿUmar II indicate that subsequent caliphs sought to impose standard weights and measures across the caliphate, although both the existence of such edicts and the evidence of surviving weights indicate that these efforts were uneven in their success, and the reformed, Arabic, system existed in parallel with Roman and Sasanian ones.[51]

Like the *amīr*s themselves, the three officials appointed by the *amīr* for the maintenance of law and order in the garrisons – the *ṣāḥib al-shurṭa*, the *qāḍī* and the *ʿāmil al-sūq* – tended to be drawn from among the leading Arabian tribal groups.[52] This was a consequence of the political, cultural and religious basis of their position – they were charged with judging and ruling according to the customs accepted by the Arabian settlers and their pastoralist allies in Syria and Iraq. Indeed, one of the earliest names of the new calendar used by the settlers (now called the *hijrī* calendar) was the era of 'the jurisdiction of the faithful' (*qaḍāʾ al-muʾminīn*), which suggests the importance that justice and the law had for the new Hijazi elite.[53] The personal connections of these administrators to the tribespeople whom they had to govern would also have been a necessity, without which they would have lacked both status and influence. Likewise, connections of kinship, alliance or patronage to the governor would also have been a factor in their appointment; for example, al-Hajjaj's *ṣāḥib al-shurṭa* was both his *mawlā* and his adopted brother.[54]

The administration of justice and the maintenance of order within the conquered communities were largely delegated to the conquered populations themselves, although the governor could be called upon to intervene. Local structures of power and authority inherited from Roman and Sasanian times were often maintained. In Egypt, the *douxoi* of the four provinces, or

---

[51] Khamis, 'Bronze Weight', 148–54; Buckley, 'Muhtasib', 64.
[52] See above in this chapter, pp. 312–16, with references. See also, for Egypt, *SaMS*, 86.
[53] Yusuf Ragib, 'Une ère inconnue d'Égypte musulmane: l'ère de la juridiction des croyants', *Annales islamologiques: Hawliyat Islamiyah* 41 (2007), 187–207. For the idea that this *qaḍāʾ al-muʾminīn* may have dated from *c*. 628 and not 622, see Tillier and Vanthieghem, 'Recording Debts'.
[54] Yazid b. Abi Muslim: *SoH*, 56, n. 420. The ʿAns of Damascus supplied the *ṣāḥib al-shurṭa* of the Marwanid caliphs: *SoH*, 163; Kennedy, *Armies*, 35.

eparchies, continued to be drawn from the local elite during the mid-seventh century, but shorn of any military authority and with Arabian military commanders (*amīr*s) installed alongside them. The sixty pagarchies and numerous towns and villages into which the provinces were sub-divided continued to be led by members of the native population. Bishops also appear in the papyri as enforcers of law and order in their communities.[55] In Iraq and Iran, an Arabian military presence and administration was also established in some of the major urban centres outside the garrisons in the 650s, and there was also significant rural settlement in the Sawad in the same period. Nonetheless, in Iraq and Iran as in Egypt, the internal affairs of the conquered communities remained in the hands of the minor landed elite and village headmen (Ar. *dihqān*s) and in some cases the former Sasanian frontier commanders (Ar. *marzbān*s).[56]

Taxation

The first conquests of the 630s had brought the very wealthiest territories in the Mediterranean and the Middle East under Arabian rule – the Sawad ('Black Earth') of Iraq and Egypt, the fertile hills and plains of Fars, in southern Iran, and the highlands and plains of western and northern Syria. A second wave of expansion in the 670s brought Khurasan into the empire, while North Africa was more fully incorporated after 698. These were productive agricultural zones, as well as important sources of mineral wealth.[57] Like the Roman and Sasanian empires before them, Arabian power depended substantially upon the exploitation of these places in the service of the ruling elite; it was with the wealth of the conquered lands that the loyalty of the armies was purchased. Iraq and Egypt are by far the best understood regions of the empire because of the quality of the source material – the later literary sources for Iraq and both the literary tradition and the many papyrus documents for Egypt. In Egypt and Iraq, the last decade of the seventh century and the first decades of the eighth were transformative, with concerted efforts to extract higher revenues, alongside reforms in the administration and the coinage. The subsequent decades of Marwanid rule, down to the 740s, saw recurrent reform directed at maintaining or increasing income and at attempting to manage the consequences of migration, conversion and social change. The evidence for other provinces is much thinner. In more remote regions, and

---

[55] *SaMS*, 64, 70–2, 91–3. For the bishops, see above, Ch. 11, p. 281 and n. 84.
[56] Herat is said to have been ruled by an *amīr* and a *dihqān* in 737: Tabari, II, 1635–6. See further *IatMC*, 251–3; *E.Ir.* 'Dehqan' (A. Tafazzoli); Kennedy, 'Merv', 27–8.
[57] Blankinship, *End of the Jihad*, 47–75.

those that were less densely settled by the conquerors, much greater local autonomy persisted.[58]

Most taxation and tribute was distributed to the armies. At around the time of the foundation of the garrisons in the conquered provinces, *dīwān*s, or 'registers', of tribesmen eligible for payments (*'aṭā*) from the revenue of the conquered territories were composed by the provincial governors. A similar register was also compiled at Medina, listing all the members of the new community settled there and the incomes that they were allocated. These payments seem to have been conceived initially as compensation for migration (*hijra*) to the new garrisons or, in the case of the Medinan tribes, for assisting the emigrants. The majority of those on the *dīwān* at Medina are said to have received between 500 and 1,000 dirhams, which would have amounted to sizeable, but not enormous, incomes – much higher than the incomes of the wealthier peasantry in Roman Egypt, but nonetheless far short of the incomes of the major landowners there. About forty years later, there were said to have been 40,000 men on the *dīwān* in Egypt, of whom a select 4,000 were receiving 200 dinars annually – a much larger income, which would have been equivalent to the annual tax revenue of a whole village for each elite soldier.[59] Under the Marwanids, the diversion of tax revenue away from provincial armies and towards Syrian troops posted in the provinces prompted resentment and conflict, above all in Iraq.[60]

From the Conquests to the Beginning of the Second Civil War

The old image of unsophisticated Arab conquerors, lacking in administrative and economic knowledge and leaving the administration of the conquered territories to the defeated populations is a misrepresentation. The conquerors took a close interest in taxation from the outset, bringing scribal and administrative traditions from the Peninsula with them. Arabic administrative documents appear immediately upon the conquests, from the very early 640s; their

---

[58] See above, Box Text, Ch. 3, pp. 72–5, and n. 57, above in this chapter. For administrative similarities between Khurasan and Egypt in early Abbasid times, see Khan, *Arabic Documents*, 92–136.

[59] Tabari, I, 2412–4; *EI*², 'Diwan' (Cl. Cahen); Kosei Morimoto, 'The Diwans as Registers of the Arab Stipendiaries in Early Islamic Egypt', in Raoul Curiel and Rika Gyselen (eds), *Itinéraires d'Orient: Hommages à Claude Cahen* (Bures-sur-Yvette, 1994), 353–66. For comparisons with sixth-century incomes in Egypt, see Banaji, *Agrarian Change*, 227–9, 235–7. For the *'aṭā* and the *hijra*, see Kennedy, 'Military Pay', 162. For the later Egyptian *dīwān*, see Ibn 'Abd al-Hakam, *Futuh*, 102, 316; Kennedy, 'Military Pay', 162; cf. Bagnall, *Agrarian Change*, 230.

[60] See above, Chs 6, 7, 8 and 9, pp. 136–8, 161, 163, 167–8, 170–2, 180, 182–7, 189–91 and 195–8.

content reflects an Arabic scribal tradition brought to Egypt by the conquerors themselves.[61] Also during ʿUmar I's rule, a survey of the lands of Iraq south of Hulwan is said to have formed the basis for a modified version of the existing Sasanian land tax. Estimates of local population numbers formed the basis for a poll tax, imposed collectively and gathered by the local notables (*dihqāns*), again, as in Sasanian times. In Egypt, similar assessments were also made – most likely based on existing population counts and assessments of the productivity of the land, supplied by representatives from the conquered population.[62] The seventh-century papyri and the literary sources also indicate that a new poll tax (Ar. *jizya*, Gk *diagraphon* or *andrismos*) was introduced in Egypt alongside the existing land tax, by the early 680s at the latest. The latter was assessed per adult male but gathered collectively through local Egyptian tax collectors.[63]

As in Rome and Iran, taxes were assessed in coin, using money as a unit of account, but collected in both coin and kind.[64] The late Roman practice of redistributing food via state-sponsored grain distribution (Gk *embole*, Lat. *annona*), also continued under Arabian rule. The canal from Fustat to Qulzum (Clysma), on the Red Sea, was restored in order to supply the Hijaz with food in the conquest period, and this form of distribution of taxation continued under the Umayyads.[65] As in Roman and Sasanian times, there were also levies on labour, animals and resources: building materials for Fustat were requisitioned from the pagarchies; the shipyards at Alexandria constructed the ships which were deployed against Roman forces in the Mediterranean, crewed by Egyptian sailors and soldiers.[66] Tolls and market taxes were also levied.[67] An increase in the volume of the surviving Egyptian papyri from the first decades of Arabian rule in comparison to the late Roman period may reflect the existing administrative personnel's struggle to adapt to the new, and generally greater, demands, as well as the problems of communication and interaction with the occupying forces.[68]

---

[61] *SaMS*, 66–72. See also above, Box Text, Ch. 3, pp. 72–5.
[62] *IatMC*, 99–101, 106–10; al-Qadi, 'Population Census', 347–52.
[63] *SaMS*, 72–4; cf. Arietta Papaconstantinou, 'Administering the Early Islamic Empire: Insights from the Papyri', in John Haldon (ed.), *Money, Power and Politics in Early Islamic Syria: A Review of Current Debates* (Farnham, 2010), 58–65; Legendre, 'Aspects', 138. On tax levels in Egypt, see *SaMS*, 72–3; Kosei Morimoto, *The Fiscal Administration of Egypt in the Early Islamic Period* (Kyoto, 1981), 37–8, 41–2, 113–14.
[64] Legendre, 'Aspects', 137. On Iraq, see *IatMC*, 61–3.
[65] Le Quesne, 'Hajj Ports', 75; *SaMS*, 76–7; Foss, 'Muʿawiya's State', 90. For the *embole* in 706–7, see al-Qadi, 'Population Census', 387.
[66] Foss, 'Muʿawiya's State', 87–8; *SaMS*, 70–1, 76, 79.
[67] Morimoto, *Fiscal Administration*, 128; *IatMC*, 117–18.
[68] *SaMS*, 75–6.

The coinage used in this period was a decentralised and disrupted continuation of the Roman and Persian systems. Copper coins struck in the remaining Roman territories continued to arrive in Syria and Egypt and other former Roman territories in large quantities until 658. This suggests that the Arabian rulers of these provinces were exchanging gold for copper coins in the 640s and 650s. Existing Roman gold also continued to circulate under Arabian rule and new Roman gold issues would have entered Arabian territories through trade and tribute payments.[69] In Iran, the silver currency of the defeated empire continued to circulate. New coins in gold, silver and copper were also struck. The variation in their resemblance to their Roman and Sasanian prototypes in both design and weight, as well as the proliferation of minting locations, suggests a decline in centralised control over all three metals in the mid-seventh century, with local elites taking control of coinage issues in both the post-Roman and post-Sasanian zones.[70]

Continuity of personnel at the level of the district and village is reflected in linguistic continuity in the documentary evidence: the papyri from the Fayyum and various other sites in Egypt and from Nessana in the Negev show that Greek remained in use. The local Coptic language, which had already grown in importance under Roman rule, became an administrative language. However, Arabic borrowings immediately appeared in Greek and Coptic. Several new Greek or Coptic terms were also introduced, and other words changed their meanings in response to the changing circumstances. For example, *diagraphon* was a term introduced in Greek to describe the new poll tax, while *symboulos* and *protosymboulos* appear for the first time in the papyri as terms for the *amīr* and the caliph, respectively. It seems likely that similar things happened in Iraq and Iran, with similar continuities in Aramaic and Pahlavi (Middle Persian), but equivalent evidence is lacking.[71]

Mu'awiya's rule (c. 661–80) saw the further consolidation of the provincial control of the taxation systems established after the conquests. The two key provinces were ruled by three long-reigning governors, Maslama b. Mukhallad al-Ansari (g. 667–82) in Egypt and Ziyad b. Sumayya (g. Basra 665–73; Basra and Kufa c. 670–3) and his son 'Ubayd Allah (g. 675–83), in

---

[69] Heidemann, 'Merger', 97–8, 107; cf. Foss, *Arab-Byzantine Coins*, 20. On tribute, see above, Ch. 6, pp. 151–2, 154–5, 158.

[70] E.Ir., 'Arab-Sasanian Coins' (M. Bates); Rika Gyselen, *Arab-Sasanian Copper Coinage* (Vienna, 2000); Foss, *Arab-Byzantine Coins*, 22–57; Alan Walmsley, 'Coinage and the Economy of Syria-Palestine in the Seventh and Eighth Centuries CE', in John Haldon (ed.), *Money, Power and Politics in Early Islamic Syria: A Review of Current Debates* (Farnham, 2010), 21–8.

[71] *SaMS*, 66–71.

Iraq. Ziyad had worked as a scribe for the former governor of Basra, al-Mughira, and so had probably been involved in the original establishment of the *dīwān* there. Likewise, Maslama b. Mukhallad had been a scribe for 'Amr b. al-'As in Egypt.[72] Alongside these long-serving Arabians were influential members of the former empires' scribal classes. In Iraq, Zadhanfarrukh (*fl. c.* 665–97) served first Ziyad and then 'Ubayd Allah.[73] In Egypt, one Theodore (*fl.* 660s and 670s) was given authority in Alexandria.[74] In Mu'awiya's own province of Syria, Sarjun b. Mansur al-Rumi ('Sergius the Roman', *fl. c.* 660–700) and 'Ubayd Allah b. 'Aws al-Ghassani ('the Ghassanid', *fl. c.* 660–83) served as head of tax and chief scribe.[75] The prominence of these members of the former Roman and Sasanian elites at the heart of the new Arabian administration is indicative of the importance that co-opting leading members of local elites had for the success of the new empire. Nonetheless, some changes in the onomastics of administration – and so by inference, of the social and cultural identity of the officials and scribes – can be perceived. In the Egyptian papyri, the four senior officials with the Roman title of *doux*, who would formerly have had Greek or Coptic names, begin to have Arabic names, and there are increasing numbers of mentions of administrators with Arabic names carrying out functions in the sixty or so rural districts of Egypt.[76]

At the same time as Mu'awiya and his governors sought to impose their control over taxation, they also began to intervene more in the coinage system. The rise of Syria as the centre of the new empire under Mu'awiya coincides with the end of imports of Roman copper coins.[77] Mu'awiya attempted to issue a gold and silver coinage in Syria, on which the Roman cross was modified into a sort of pole on steps. However, a near-contemporary literary source suggests that these coins did not gain widespread acceptance.[78] There is also some evidence for an attempt to assert some centralised control over the striking and circulation of Syrian copper coins.[79] Meanwhile, in post-Sasanian Iraq and Iran, the name of the Sasanian king was removed from the coins and replaced by Mu'awiya or – much more often – one of his governors. Nonetheless, despite these indications of some efforts at centralisation, the number of locations in

---

[72] See above, Ch. 4, p. 98.
[73] M. Sprengling, 'From Persian to Arabic', *The American Journal of Semitic Languages and Literatures* 56–7 (1939–40), 184–8.
[74] *SaMS*, 102; Bruning, *Rise*, 45–6, 162–4.
[75] See Box Text, above, pp. 309–12.
[76] *SaMS*, 87–92, 102–3.
[77] See above, p. 320 and n. 69.
[78] Foss, 'A Syrian Coinage'. See also above, Ch. 4, pp. 92–3.
[79] Foss, *Arab-Byzantine Coins*, 38–55.

which coins were struck and their great diversity continued; this likely reflects the co-option of local Iranian elites by the new Arabian rulers.[80]

The Second Civil War and the Early Marwanids

Taken together, the evidence from the late 680s and early 690s reveals the reorganisation of Umayyad territory in Syria, the Jazira and Egypt, with taxation being imposed as territory was secured during the war with the Zubayrids. A papyrus from Nessana in the Negev refers to 'the land survey of the Saracens' in Syria in about 689, most likely conducted after the reconquest of most of the province and the peace treaty with the Romans. With the fall of Iraq in 691, a poll tax was imposed in Mosul and the wider Jazira, for the first time. In 693–4, which was the year after the defeat of Ibn al-Zubayr, 'Abd al-Malik's half-brother and governor in Egypt, 'Abd al-'Aziz, imposed a poll tax on Egyptian monks and made an assessment of new taxes in the province. In both Egypt and the Jazira, the new taxes were made proportional to the productivity of the land. There is also papyrological evidence from Egypt for more detailed accounts of individual taxpayers and their tax liabilities being made at this time.[81] These changes do appear to have succeeded in extracting more revenue, at least in the short term. A late eighth-century Syriac chronicle from the Jazira preserves local traditions about the burdensome impositions of the 690s and after.[82] The year after the 693–4 reform of the Egyptian tax system is said to have seen the departure of Egypt's governor, 'Abd al-'Aziz, for Damascus with a caravan of 20,000 camels laden with tribute.[83]

In all these provinces, there appear to have been further attempts to maintain and develop the tax structures. In Syria, a census in 697–8 followed a reform of the coinage. After the accession of 'Abd al-Malik's son al-Walid to the caliphate in 705 there were more surveys and assessments: two further censuses in the Jazira are mentioned for 708–9 and 710–11; likewise, in Egypt, various forms of more partial survey and assessment are recorded for 706 and 708–9. The surveys in Egypt and the Jazira 708–9 and 710–11 coincided with the arrival of al-Walid's new governors in Egypt and Syria respectively.[84] Governors

---

[80] *E.Ir.*, 'Arab-Sasanian Coins' (M. Bates); Gyselen, *Arab-Sasanian Copper Coinage*, 28–9; Touraj Daryaee, 'Persian Lords and the Umayyads: Cooperation and Coexistence in a Turbulent Time', in Antoine Borrut and Fred M. Donner (eds), *Christians and Others in the Umayyad State* (Chicago, 2016), 73–81. Cf. Foss, 'Mu'awiya's State', 81–2.

[81] Al-Qadi, 'Population Census', 366–9, 373–6, 381–6. See also Robinson, *'Abd al-Malik*, 71–7. For the context of the war with Ibn al-Zubayr, see above, Ch. 6, pp. 127–8.

[82] See above, Ch. 11, pp. 270–1.

[83] Al-Qadi, 'Population Census', 383. The number of camels should probably not be taken literally.

[84] On these, see al-Qadi, 'Population Census', 370–2, 379–81, 385–98.

elsewhere were also making efforts to increase revenues. In Khurasan, the land tax was imposed on all landowners, both the Muslim settlers and the native population during the governorship of Umayya b. ʿAbd Allah (g. c. 693–7/8).[85]

There are no references to comprehensive land surveys and censuses in Iraq in this period. Circumstantial evidence suggests that none took place. Effective control over Iraq, and dependent territories to the east, had proved much harder to secure, with violent conflict persisting into the years immediately prior to ʿAbd al-Malik's death in 705. Second, the adaptation of the Sasanian tax system, imposed initially under ʿUmar and modified by Ziyad under Muʿawiya, had already led to a proportional system of taxation combining both a land tax and a poll tax, alongside other forms of taxation. Furthermore, eastward expansion in Iran, Khurasan, Transoxiana and India was still yielding massive revenues in tribute and war booty.[86] Rather, al-Hajjaj (g. 694–714) is remembered primarily for changes to expenditure and organisation – for his reform of the coinage, for the reduction of some military pay, for the foundation of the new Syrian garrison at Wasit, and for the reform of the *dīwān* and the *ʿaṭā*, so that the *ʿaṭā* became a salary only for serving soldiers.[87] He also sought to secure revenue by imposing the existing system of taxation more effectively, notably by pursuing Iraqi fugitives from the land and converts to Islam who were attempting to evade taxation.[88]

Similar social consequences are also visible in the papyri from Egypt and the Negev, as well as in the evidence of the literary sources. The Syriac sources refer to a 'census of the foreigners' (that is, fugitives from taxation) in Syria in 697–8, with many of them being sent back to pay taxes in their places of origin. The Egyptian papyri show that by 705 local tax registers were very detailed records for each village and pagarchy of each tax-paying individual and their landholdings, very likely also with the land's size and productivity.[89] The tax-paying peasant populations now had to obtain permission from the ruling authorities to leave their place of residence. Egyptian papyrus 'passports' or 'safe conducts' (Ar. *amānāt*, sing. *amān*) are extant from 717–20. It is possible that the use of lead seals to mark those who had paid their taxes,

---

[85] This is said to have entailed local non-Muslim tax collectors taking taxes from Muslim settlers, Tabari, II, 1029. Umayya was the son of a governor of Fars and the son-in-law of Ziyad b. Sumayya, see Baladhuri, *Ansab*, V, 49–52; Bosworth, *Sistan*, 49–50; Crone, 'Qays and Yemen', 12.
[86] On all this, see above, Chs 4 and 6 pp. 70–2, 131–8 and 158–61.
[87] See above, Ch. 6, p. 132.
[88] *SaMS*, 193.
[89] Al-Qadi, 'Population Census', 379–80, 385–6. On other occasions fugitives were allowed to remain in their new abode on condition that they worked the land there and paid tax on it, see *SaMS*, 102.

as described in various later literary sources, may also date from about 720, although this is more likely to be a literary trope than a widespread practice.[90] Certainly, flight from the land and the losses incurred by abandoned farmland appear as a concern of tax officials in the first decades of the eighth century.[91] It is likely that the depletion of the rural population by war and plague had contributed to these labour shortages and that they were exacerbated by demands for labour by the Umayyad authorities.[92]

The same period also saw the replacement of non-Muslims by Muslims at the top of the taxation system in Egypt, Syria and Iraq. This change reflects the increasing importance of adherence to Islam as a defining feature of the ruling elite, including for a new generation drawn from among the conquered populations.[93] In Egypt, where the evidence is best, the Muslim administrators tended not to be landowners, but rather administrative specialists appointed by Fustat and moving between different administrative positions. This change from local Christian landed leadership to a specialist Muslim governing class (some convert *mawālī* and some of Arabian heritage) is also reflected in administrative terminology – an indigenous local leader of a rural region, or pagarchy, is referred to as its *ṣāḥib* ('chief') in the early eighth century, but the Muslim equivalent is called *'āmil al-amīr* ('agent of the amir').[94]

The reforms to the tax system coincided with changes to the coinage and weights and measures. Efforts were made to impose control over all three currencies, to unify the two precious metal coinages within a mutually exchangeable system, and to establish a new system of weights and measures, replacing the old Roman and Sasanian systems. In 696–7 the two precious metal currencies were reformed so that their weight standards differed markedly from their Roman and Sasanian antecedents. The new dinar weighed 4.25g, as opposed to the old Roman weight of just under 4.5g; the new dirham was supposed to weigh just short of 3g, but existing examples often weigh more. These smaller

---

[90] Chase F. Robinson, 'Neck-sealing in Early Islam', *JESHO* 48 (2005), 402–36; *SaMS*, 96; cf. Legendre, 'Aspects', 143–5. For efforts to levy taxes from relatives of dead debtors, see Morimoto, *Fiscal Administration*, 120; *IatMC*, 114.

[91] *SaMS*, 94–5, 102, 190.

[92] See above, Ch. 10, pp. 220–1.

[93] In Syria, Sarjun b. Mansur al-Rumi was replaced by Sulayman b. Sa'd al-Khushani, a *mawlā* of Quda'a, during the caliphate of 'Abd al-Malik: al-Jahshiyari, *al-Wuzara'*, 40; Biddle, *Bureaucracy*, 147. In Iraq in c. 701, Zadhanfarrukh was replaced by his deputy, Salih b. 'Abd al-Rahman, the Arabic-speaking son of a Sistani captive: Baladhuri, *Futuh*, 300; *IatMC*, 53–4. In Egypt, the Edessan Christian, Athanasios, was replaced in 704: Palmer, *Seventh Century*, 202–4; *History of the Patriarchs*, I.xvii, 54–5; Morimoto, *Fiscal Administration*, 114, 119.

[94] *SaMS*, 103–4, 201–2.

coins would have begun to drive the higher-value old coins out of circulation: in Syria, the Marwanid regime seems to have controlled the coinage closely and this led to a fairly uniform Islamic precious metal coinage; in Iraq and Iran, much more old Sasanian-style coinage, which was closer in weight to its replacement, remained in use.[95] The designs of these new coins also began to be standardised. Between 692 and 697 there had been a series of experiments at the Damascus mint with images that directly challenged Roman imperial imagery. In 696–7, an entirely new, purely 'epigraphic' coinage was introduced, together with the new, lower weight standard. The Arabic inscriptions included Quranic citations and assertions of God's unity and Muhammad's status as a Prophet.

From 698, this new 'reform' coinage became the standard issue from Marwanid-controlled mints. In the post-Roman regions of the empire east of Qayrawan, Damascus became the single mint from which gold coins were issued.[96] Copper minting remained in the hands of local authorities, but there were also some efforts to promote a standardised copper currency.[97] In the East, the reformed coins were issued by about forty mints across the central and eastern lands of the empire. There, a further refinement of the script used on the coins took place in 705 – a development which followed shortly after the foundation of the new garrison of Wasit in Iraq by al-Hajjaj. At the same time, coin production was suddenly limited to just three mints: Wasit itself, the imperial capital at Damascus, and the peripatetic frontier mint controlled by 'Abd al-Malik's brother, Muhammad b. Marwan. However, from about 708–9, minting once again resumed in mints across the eastern provinces. (In Syria, Damascus remained the sole mint for the precious metal coins.[98])

The coins of the provinces west of Egypt were rather different. With the conquest of Carthage in 698, 'Uqba b. Nafi' began minting gold coins for the North African garrison, but while their slogans echoed those on the eastern coins to some extent, they were inscribed in the Latin language and script. This likely reflects both the expectations of the army in the region, which comprised many locals, many of whom were Latin-speaking and Christian, as well as the independence of North African governors appointed from 'Abd al-'Aziz's Egypt and not from Damascus. Further west, after 711 in al-Andalus and by 723 4 at the latest in the Maghrib, commanders were striking their

---

[95] Heidemann, 'Merger', 97, 99–107; Bacharach, 'Signs', 19–22.
[96] Heidemann, 'Merger', 97.
[97] Lutz Ilisch, "Abd al-Malik's Monetary Reform in Copper and the Failure of Centralization', in John Haldon (ed.), *Money, Power and Politics in Early Islamic Syria: A Review of Current Debates* (Farnham, 2010), 125–46.
[98] See above, Ch. 6, n. 10?

own gold coins. The eastern-style, aniconic Arabic coins were struck in silver in al-Andalus and Ifriqiya from 716–17 and in gold and silver from 720–1. This probably reflects the accession of a new governor, who brought with him the more emphatically anti-Trinitarian coinage design.[99]

The Later Marwanid Period: 'Umar II, Yazid II and Hisham

As for earlier periods, the best evidence for the last decades of Marwanid rule comes from Egypt, where the papyri provide unique documentary evidence. An important change was a shift in the demography of the countryside. In the first decades of the eighth century people with Muslim names begin to appear in growing numbers, as a result both of settlement by the conquering population and conversion among the conquered. These changes put new strains on a taxation system that depended upon the distinction between tax-paying conquered non-Muslims in the countryside and tax-receiving Muslim conquerors in the new garrisons. The conquered populations paid a land-tax, a poll-tax, the grain tax, levies for administration and various tolls and customs, as well as corvée labour. In contrast, the Muslim conquerors paid only alms-taxes on their property and capital. The later sources attribute an edict to 'Umar II (r. 717–20) which is said to have attempted to address shortfalls generated by conversion to Islam and the acquisition of land (and so the loss of its tax revenue) by the Muslim conquerors.[100]

The caliphates of Yazid II (r. 720–4) and Hisham (r. 724–43) saw further interventions in the tax system.[101] Iraq had passed through the hands of a number of governors after al-Hajjaj's death in 714. It was only in 723–4, following the reunification of the East in 721, that a major land survey was carried out there, 'causing hardship to the taxpayers'.[102] There is also anecdotal evidence that Hisham's first governor in Iraq, Khalid al-Qasri (g. 724–38) was appointing Arabs as senior taxation officials for what was the first time in some regions of Iran.[103] Khalid and his successors in Iraq are also associated in the later texts with much tighter control of the quality of the precious metal coinage there.[104] This change in the coinage appears to be reflected in the material evidence,

---

[99] Legendre, 'Aspects', 136 and above, Ch. 7, pp. 174–5.
[100] H. A. R. Gibb, 'The Fiscal Rescript of 'Umar II', *Arabica* 2 (1955), 1–16; *SaMS*, 105–9, 173, 190–8.
[101] Al-Qadi, 'Population Census', 402–10; Robinson, 'Neck-sealing', 423–32.
[102] On Iraq and the East from 714 until 720, see above, Ch. 7, pp. 163 and 167–72. For the land survey of 723–4, see Ya'qubi, II, 376; al-Qadi, 'Population Census', 365. See also Blankinship, *End of the Jihad*, 88.
[103] Tabari, II, 1470–1.
[104] Baladhuri, *Futuh*, 469.

with larger amounts of newly mined silver being used in addition to recycled Sasanian coins from around this time.[105] In Egypt, the first years of Hisham's governorship saw both a land survey and a census; the former prompted rebellions among the tax-paying Egyptian population in al-Hawf al-Sharqi (the eastern part of the Delta) in 725–6. The papyri show that by 732–3, the tax quota (Gk *epizetumena*) had been increased for the first time since the 690s, and the literary sources refer to the total revenue of Egypt returning to the four million dinars that it is said to have yielded under 'Umar. A further tax revolt in Upper Egypt (al-Sa'id) in 739 seems also to be related to this more onerous tax regime in the last decades of Umayyad rule.[106]

The Egyptian evidence for the 720s and after shows that the tax system now had more Muslim personnel, among whom senior figures used Arabic more in their work. By about 725 the non-Muslim Egyptian pagarchs, drawn from the local population, had been completely replaced by Muslim career scribes, who moved between different appointments. Also, after *c*. 725, administrative letters in Arabic between senior tax officials first appear in the papyrological record, while Greek appears to have been abandoned. However, lower-level administration often continued to be in Greek and Coptic, and officials at the level of the village, within the pagarchies, were usually still Egyptian. By same period, the post of *doux*, previously sitting alongside the *amīr*s in the four subdivisions of Egypt, had been abolished; Muslim governors now ruled them directly and reported to Fustat.[107] Elsewhere, things were probably quite different. One later history of the scribes describes Zoroastrians writing in Persian in the administration of Khurasan at the end of Hisham's caliphate.[108] By the time of Hisham's caliphate, the top layers of imperial government in the core lands of the empire had a clearly Arab and Islamic character; elsewhere Islam was the idiom of imperial authority, but administration frequently retained local forms.

---

[105] Jane Kershaw, personal communication, 15 March 2022. See also Merkel et al., 'Lead Isotopes'.
[106] Al-Qadi, 'Population Census', 404–9; Lev, 'Coptic Rebellions', 309–12.
[107] *SaMS*, 109–10, 116, 202–3.
[108] Al-Jahshiyari, *al-Wuzara'*, 67.

Afterword

The life and writings of the celebrated scribe Ibn al-Muqaffaʿ (d. c. 756) encapsulate some important changes in religious and political culture that had been wrought during the century of Umayyad rule. Ibn al-Muqaffaʿ was born Rozbih, to one of the scribal families of Fars, in south-west Iran. His father is said to have served as a scribe for the Umayyad administration in the early-to-mid eighth century and Ibn al-Muqaffaʿ himself worked for the Umayyad governor of Kirman, before entering the service of the Abbasids. Thus, he was a Persian-speaking native of Iran, who had converted to Islam at some point in his service of the Muslim imperial elite, and who wrote mostly in Arabic for his patrons. Like his Iraqi contemporary, ʿAbd al-Hamid (d. 750), who also served as a scribe under the last Umayyads, Ibn al-Muqaffaʿ is remembered as one of the first exponents of long-form, literary, Arabic prose.[1]

Among the many works attributed to Ibn al-Muqaffaʿ is his 'Treatise about the Caliph's Entourage' (*Al-Risala fi l-Sahaba*), which is a work of political advice for the second Abbasid caliph, al-Mansur (r. 754–75). The *Risala* was composed in about 755, at the outset of al-Mansur's reign. One of its main concerns is the diversity of legal practice among the Muslims of the empire's cities. The Abbasids had made Kufa their capital and so Ibn al-Muqaffaʿ begins the relevant part of the treatise there, with Kufa and neighbouring al-Hira.

> Among what the Commander of the Faithful must investigate is the matter of the contradictory legal judgements in these two Iraqi garrisons, and in other garrisons and regions. Their divergences amount to a serious matter when they concern the shedding of blood, sex, and property. At al-Hira, blood feud and fornication (*al-dam wa-l-farj*) are considered lawful, whereas at Kufa they are forbidden; a similar variation exists within Kufa, where what is lawful in one region is forbidden in another. Despite their variety, the

---

[1] *EI²*, 'Ibn al-Mukaffaʿ' (Ch. Pellat); J. D. Latham, 'The Beginning of Arabic Prose Literature: The Epistolary Genre', in A. F. L. Beeston et al. (eds), *Arabic Literature to the End of the Umayyad Period* (Cambridge, 1983), 154–79.

commands and judgement of legitimate judges about them are legally binding upon Muslims concerning their blood or their women. Although there is a difference among those Iraqis and Hijazis who have examined that, each of them stubbornly persists in pride in what is his own and disparaging what is not. That drives them to rulings which shock those reasoning men who hear of them.[2]

He goes on to propose that the caliph himself intervene, having the rightful *sunna* ('proper practice') set down in writing.[3] However, Ibn al-Muqaffaʿ was killed, on the wrong side of Abbasid palace intrigue, shortly after writing his treatise and no such law code was composed.

Ibn al-Muqaffaʿ's exasperation with the diversity of legal decisions being made in the cities of the empire is revealing of how an Islamic legal tradition had developed by the end of the Umayyad period. Beliefs and practices varied, and there were numerous local religious authorities with contradictory opinions about proper practice. Nonetheless, the idea of the law, based upon scripture and the precedents established by Muhammad and his associates and their successors, had become prevalent, for all that how these things should be known and applied remained contested. Although Ibn al-Muqaffaʿ laments contradictions and diversity, in retrospect some of the first lineaments of later Islamic orthodoxies can be seen to have been taking shape. The two eldest of the four men who would eventually come to lend their names to the four main schools of medieval Sunni legal thought, Abu Hanifa (d. 767) and Malik b. Anas (d. 796) were teaching in Kufa and Medina, respectively. The same period was also within the lifetime of Jaʿfar al-Sadiq (d. 765), a Medinan scholar who became a key figure in later Shiʿism, and the Basran Abu ʿUbayda (d. c. 767), who was a founding figure in Ibadi Islam. Syrian scholars, such as al-Awzaʿi (d. 774), had ideas that were influential but did not become the basis of lasting schools of thought, perhaps in part because of the failure of Umayyad rule.

The conditions for these developments had come about during the long century when the Umayyad family had successfully held their position at the top of a new empire. Their alliances with the pastoralist tribes of the Syrian steppe and the western Jazira had been critical to their retaining power, with the large expanse of grazing land between the Red Sea in the south and the highlands beyond the Euphrates in the north furnishing them with loyal military manpower. Until the disasters of the 740s, these tribes had seen off

---

[2] Charles Pellat, *Ibn al-Muqaffaʿ mort vers 140/757 <<conseilleur>> du calife* (Paris, 1976), 41-3 (§34).
[3] Pellat, *Ibn al-Muqaffaʿ*, 42-3 (§36).

challengers and extended Umayyad control of the empire. However, the first, crucial, conquests had been led not just by Umayyads, but by other members of Quraysh, as well as the Ansar, and their other Arabian allies. The Meccans had successfully parlayed their status as the guardians of a West Arabian shrine into imperial authority, with leadership of the *ḥajj* intimately associated with political leadership of the new polity. When the Syrians lost control, it was to more frontiersmen – but this time from the empire's eastern edges. Nonetheless, such was the sacred status of the Prophet's clan that another branch of Quraysh, the Abbasids, were installed as imperial rulers in the Umayyads' place.

Because the Prophet and then his caliphal successors combined religious and political leadership, it is often said that the connection between political power and religious authority in Islam is much closer than in other major religious traditions. This is something of a truism, which partially breaks down with the emergence of networks of religious scholars. Nonetheless, the development of imperial power and religious authority were indeed profoundly intertwined; moreover, the emergent Islamic religious tradition both reflected and responded to the religiously inflected articulations of the Christian Roman emperors and other late antique monotheist leaders. Because the Umayyads ruled from the frontier with Rome, an era of head-on conflict between Roman Christian and Arabian Muslim elites further shaped the emergent Islamic tradition – in the salience given to critiques of the Trinity, in chiliastic traditions about Jerusalem, Constantinople and Rome, and in some of the narratives about the life of the Prophet that resemble Christian saints' lives.[4] However, the defeat of the Umayyads' attacks on Constantinople, and the success of Muslim rule in the former lands of the Sasanians, meant that in future centuries it was the culture of Ibn al-Muqaffaʿ's Iran that came to exert a greater influence on Islamic-era culture and civilisation than the legacy of Rome.

Hence, the Umayyad century can be seen as a unique moment between the era of Roman and Sasanian domination of the Middle East and the era of 'classical' Islam, centred on Iraq and Iran. In the space between Rome and Iran, the Syrian pastoralists came to the fore, supplying the military force that underpinned Umayyad leadership of a vast empire and the Umayyads' capacity to shape its aesthetic and ideological articulations. Probably, these military resources became depleted by the export of Syrian troops to control the provinces from the early eighth century and then by the defeats and losses in the 730s and 740s. Failures against the Roman capital in 717–18 and 740

---

[4] On the saints' lives, see Andrew Marsham, 'Bede, Ibn Ishaq, and the Idols: Narratives of Conversion at Late Antique Edges', in Phil Booth and Mary Whitby (eds), *Travaux et Mémoires 26: Mélanges James Howard-Johnston* (Paris, 2022), 335.

also dealt serious blows to Umayyad prestige. A deeper underlying weakness in the empire was that the Umayyads sought to rule the wealthy province of Iraq from the Syrian frontier, provoking repeated resistance in the former. It was the coincidence of this ongoing unrest with division within the tribes of Syria and the Jazira, internecine strife within third and fourth generations of the Marwanid clan and their allies, and the rise of new Islamic movements in North Africa and Khurasan that combined to bring about the downfall of both the Umayyads and the Syrian tribes. The Islamic empires of subsequent centuries would draw their military resources from other groups – very often from the new steppe frontiers of the expanding Islamic world.

Bibliography

Primary Sources

'Abbās, Iḥsān (ed.), *'Abd al-Hamīd b. Yaḥyā al-Kātib wa-mā tabqā min rasā'ilihi wa-rasā'il Sālim Abī al-'Alā'* (Amman, 1988).
Agapius, *Kitāb al-'Unwān*, ed. and tr. Alexandre Vasiliev (Paris, 1910–15).
al-Azdī, Abu Zakariyya Yazīd b. Muḥammad, *Ta'rīkh al-Mawsil*, ed. 'Alī Habība (Cairo, 1967).
al-Azraqī, Abu l-Walīd Muḥammad b. 'Abd Allāh, *Kitāb Akhbār Makka*, ed. Ferdinand Wüstenfeld (Leipzig, 1858).
al-Balādhurī, Aḥmad b. Yaḥyā, *Futūḥ al-Buldān*, ed. M. J. de Goeje (Leiden, 1866).
al-Balādhurī, Aḥmad b. Yaḥyā, *Ansāb al-Ashrāf*, ed. M. Fardūs al-Aẓm (Damascus, 1997–2004).
Brock, Sebastian, 'North Mesopotamia in the Late Seventh Century: Book XV of John Bar Penkaye's *Rīš Mellē*', *JSAI* 9 (1987), 51–75.
Caner, Daniel, *History and Hagiography from the Late-Antique Sinai* (Liverpool, 2010).
de Baron de Slane, M. (ed. and tr.), *Histoire des Berbères et des dynasties Musulmanes* (Algiers, 1852–6).
Evagrius, *The Ecclesiastical History of Evagrius Scholasticus*, tr. Michael Whitby (Liverpool, 2000).
Evetts, B. (ed. and tr.), *History of the Patriarchs of the Coptic Church of Alexandria* (Paris, 1904–14).
al-Farazdaq, Abū Firās Tammām b. Ghālib, *Dīwān al-Farazdaq*, ed. and tr. R. Boucher (Paris, 1870).
Gold, Milton, *Tarikh-e Sistan* (Rome, 1976).
Gordon, Matthew, Chase F. Robinson, Everett K. Rowson and Michael Fishbein (eds and trs), *The Works of Ibn Wadih al-Ya'qubi* (Leiden, 2018).
Harrak, Amir, *The Chronicle of Zuqnin, parts III and IV: AD 488–775* (Toronto, 1999).
Hoyland, Robert G., *Theophilus of Edessa's Chronicle and the Circulation of Historical Knowledge in Late Antiquity and Early Islam* (Liverpool, 2011).
Humbach, Helmet and Prods O. Skjaervo, *The Sassanian Inscription of Paikuli Part 3.1: Restored Text and Translation by Prods Skjaervo* (Wiesbaden, 1983).
Ibn 'Abd al-Ḥakam, Abu l-Qāsim, *Kitāb Futūḥ Miṣr wa-Akhbāriha (= The History of the Conquest of Egypt, North Africa and Spain)*, ed. Charles C. Torrey (New Haven, 1922).

Ibn ʿAbd Rabbihi, *al-ʿIqd al-Farīd*, eds Aḥmad Amīn, Aḥmad al-Zayn and Ibrāhīm al-Abyārī (Cairo, 1940–53).
Ibn ʿAsākir, ʿAlī b. al-Ḥasan, *Taʾrīkh Madīnat Dimashq*, ed. ʿUmar Gharāma al-ʿAmrawī (Beirut, 1995–2000).
Ibn Aʿtham al-Kūfī, Aḥmad, *Kitāb al-Futūḥ*, ed. Muḥammad ʿAbd al-Muʿīd (Hyderabad, 1968–75).
Ibn al-Athīr, ʿIzz al-Dīn, *Al-Kāmil fī Taʾrīkh*, ed. C. J. Tornberg (Leiden, 1853–71).
Ibn Hishām, Abū Muḥammad ʿAbd al-Malik, *Kitāb Sīrat Rasūl Allāh: Das Leben Muhammed's nach Muhammad Ibn Ishak*, ed. Ferdinand Wüstenfeld (Göttingen, 1859–60).
Ibn ʿIdharī al-Marrakashī, Muḥammad, *Al-Bayān al-Mughrib fī Akhbār al-Andalus wa-l-Maghrib*, eds G. S. Colin and E. Lévi-Provençal (Beirut, 2009).
Ibn al-Nadīm, Abu l-Faraj Muḥammad, *Kitāb al-Fihrist li-l-Nadīm*, ed. R. Tajaddud (Tehran, 1971).
Ibn Saʿd, *Kitāb al-Ṭabaqāt al-Kabīr = Ibn Saad Biographien Muhammads, seiner Gefährten und der späteren Träger des Islams bis zum Jahre 230 der Flucht*, ed. Eduard Sachau et al. (Leiden, 1904–40).
al-Jahshiyārī, Abū ʿAbd Allāh Muḥammad, *Kitāb al-Wuzarāʾ wa-l-Kuttāb*, eds Muṣṭafā al-Saqā, Ibrāhīm al-Abyārī and ʿAbd al-Ḥāfiẓ Shalabī (Cairo, 1938).
James, David, *A History of Early al-Andalus: The Akhbar Majmuʿa* (London, 2012).
Jarīr b. ʿAṭiyya b. al-Khaṭafa, *Sharḥ Dīwān Jarīr*, ed. Muḥammad I. ʿA. al-Ṣāwī (Beirut, n.d.).
John of Nikiu, *The Chronicle of John, Bishop of Nikiu*, ed. and tr. R. H. Charles (Oxford, 1916).
Khalīfa b. Khayyāṭ al-ʿUṣfurī, *Taʾrīkh Khalīfa b. Khayyāṭ*, eds Muṣṭafā Najīb Fawwāz and Ḥikma Kashlī Fawwāz (Beirut, 1995).
al-Kindī, Abū ʿUmar Muḥammad b. Yūsuf, *The Governors and Judges of Egypt* (= *Kitāb Wulāt Miṣr wa-Quḍātihā*), ed. Rhuvon Guest (Leiden, 1912).
Kitāb al-ʿUyūn wa-l-ḥadāʾiq fī akhbār al-ḥaqāʾiq in M. J. de Goeje and P. de Jong (eds), *Fragmenta Historicum Arabicorum* (Leiden, 1869).
Mango, Cyril and Roger Scott (eds and trs), *The Chronicle of Theophanes Confessor: Byzantine and Near Eastern History AD 284–813* (Oxford, 1997).
al-Muqaddasī, Shams al-Dīn Abū ʿAbd Allāh Muḥammad b. Aḥmad, *Kitāb Aḥsan al-Taqāsīm fī Maʿrifat al-Aqālīm*, ed. M. J. de Goeje (Leiden, 1906).
Mustawfi, Hamd-Allah, *The Geographical Part of the* Nuzhat al-Qulub, tr. Guy Le Strange (Leiden, 1919).
al-Nuwayrī, Shihāb al-Dīn Aḥmad b. ʿAbd al-Wahhāb, *Nihāyat al-arab fī funūn al-adab*, ed. Ḥasan Nūr al-Dīn, Mufīd Qumayḥah, Yaḥyā al-Shāmī et al. (Beirut, 2004–5).
Palmer, Andrew, Sebastian Brock and Robert Hoyland, *The Seventh Century in the West Syrian Chronicles* (Liverpool, 1993).
Pellat, Charles, *Ibn al-Muqaffaʿ 'mort vers 140/757 <<conseilleur>> du calife* (Paris, 1976).
Photius, *Epitome of the Ecclesiastical History of Philostorgius*, tr. Edward Walford (Oxford, 1855).
Procopius, *History of the Wars*, ed. and tr. H. B. Dewing (Cambridge, MA, 1914–28).
Rufinus, *The Church History of Rufinus of Aquileia: Books 10 and 11*, tr. Philip R. Amidon (Oxford, 1997).
al-Suyūṭī, Jalāl al-Dīn, *Taʾrīkh al-Khulafāʾ*, ed. Ibrāhīm Ṣāliḥ (Beirut, 1996).

al-Ṭabarī, Abū Jaʿfar Muḥammad b. Jarīr, *Taʾrīkh al-Rusul wa-l-Mulūk*, eds M. J. de Goeje et al. (Leiden 1879–1901).
al-Tabari, Abu Jaʿfar Muhammad b. Jarir, *The History of al-Tabari*, eds and trs Ehsan Yar-Shater et al. (Albany, NY, 1985–2007).
Thomas of Marga, *The Book of Governors*, ed. and tr. E. A. Wallis Budge (London, 1893).
Thomson, R. W. and James Howard-Johnston, *The Armenian History Attributed to Sebeos* (Liverpool, 1999).
al-Yaʿqūbī, Aḥmad b. Abī Yaʿqūb, *Historiae* (= *Taʾrīkh al-Yaʿqūbī*), ed. M. J. Houtsma (Leiden, 1883).
al-Zubayrī, Abu ʿAbd Allāh al-Muṣʿab b. ʿAbd Allāh, *Kitāb Nasab Quraysh* (Cairo, 1953).

Secondary Literature

ʿAbd al-Bāqī, Muḥammad Fuʾād, *Muʿjam al-Mufahras li-alfāẓ al-Qurʾān al-Karīm* (Cairo, 1945).
Abbott, Nabia, *The Qurra Papyri from Aphrodito in the Oriental Institute* (Chicago, 1938).
Agha, Saleh S., 'The Arab Population in Hurasan during the Umayyad Period: Some Demographic Computations', *Arabica* 46 (1999), 211–29.
Agha, Saleh S., *The Revolution Which Toppled the Umayyads: Neither Arab nor ʿAbbasid* (Leiden, 2003).
Akpınar, Mehmetcan, 'Medinan Scholars on the Move: Professional Mobility at the Umayyad Court', in Mohamad El-Merheb and Mehdi Berriah (eds), *Professional Mobility in Islamic Societies (700–1750): New Concepts and Approaches* (Leiden, 2021), 15–39.
Alajmi, Abdulhadi, 'Ascribed vs. Popular Legitimacy: The Case of al-Walid II and Umayyad *ʿahd*', *JNES* 72 (2013), 25–34.
El-Ali, Saleh, 'Muslim Estates in Hidjaz in the First Century AH', *JESHO* 2 (1959), 247–61.
Aliyar, Qurban and Morteza Esmailnejad, 'Assessment of the Change of Trend in Precipitation over Afghanistan in 1979–2019', *IDŐJÁRÁS – Quarterly Journal of the Hungarian Meteorological Service* 126 (2022), 185–201.
Allen, Pauline, 'The Definition and Enforcement of Orthodoxy', *CAH*, XIV, 820–34.
Andersson, Tobias, *Early Sunni Historiography: A Study of the Tarikh of Khalifa b. Khayyat* (Leiden, 2019).
Anonymous, 'Afghanistan's Climate', *Swedish Committee for Afghanistan*, <https://swedishcommittee.org/afghanistan/climate/> (last accessed 28 June 2023).
Anonymous, 'Average Temperature in Kabul', *Weather Spark*, <https://weatherspark.com/y/106802/Average-Weather-in-Kabul-Afghanistan-Year-Round> (last accessed 28 June 2023).
Anthony, Sean W., 'The Syriac Account of Dionysius of Tell Mahre Concerning the Assassination of ʿUmar b. al-Khattab', *JNES* 69 (2010), 209–24.
Anthony, Sean W., *Crucifixion and Death as Spectacle: Umayyad Crucifixion in Its Late Antique Context* (New Haven, 2014).
Anthony, Sean W., 'Fixing John Damascene's Biography: Historical Notes on His Family Background', *Journal of Early Christian Studies* 23 (2015), 607–27.
Anthony, Sean W., *Muhammad and the Empires of Faith: The Making of the Prophet of Islam* (Oakland, 2020).

Anthony, Sean W., 'Prophetic Dominion, Umayyad Kingship: Varieties of *Mulk* in the Early Islamic Period', in Andrew Marsham (ed.), *The Umayyad World* (London and New York, 2021), 39–64.

Antun, Thallein M., *The Architectural Form of the Mosque* (Oxford, 2016).

Arce, Ignacio, 'Romans, Ghassanids and Umayyads. The Transformation of The *Limes Arabicus*: From Coercive and Deterrent Diplomacy towards Religious Proselytism and Political Clientelarism', in Guido Vannini and Michele Nuccioti (eds), *La Transgiordania nei secoli XII–XIII e le 'frontiere' del Mediterraneo medieval* (Oxford, 2012), 53–72.

Ashkenazai, Jacob and Mordechai Aviam, 'Monasteries, Monks, and Villages in Western Galilee in Late Antiquity', *JLA* 5 (2012), 269–97.

Ashtor, Eliyahu, *Histoire des prix et des salaires dans l'Orient medieval* (Paris, 1969).

Athamina, Khalil, 'Non-Arab Regiments and Private Militias during the Umayyad Period', *Arabica* 45 (1998), 347–78.

Azad, Arezou, 'Living Happily Ever After: Fraternal Polyandry, Taxes and "the House" in Early Islamic Bactria', *BSOAS* 79 (2016), 33–56.

Azad, Arezou, 'Ecology, Economy, and the Conquest of Khurasan', in Andrew Marsham (ed.), *The Umayyad World* (London and New York, 2021), 332–54.

Al-Azmeh, Aziz, *The Emergence of Islam in Late Antiquity: Allah and His People* (Cambridge, 2014).

Bacharach, Jere L., 'Signs of Sovereignty: The Shahada, Qur'anic Verses, and the Coinage of 'Abd al-Malik', *Muqarnas* 27 (2011), 1–30.

El-Badawi, Emran Eqbal, *The Qur'an and the Aramaic Gospel Traditions* (London and New York, 2014).

Bagnall, Roger S., *Egypt in Late Antiquity* (Princeton, 1993).

Banaji, Jairus, *Agrarian Change in Late Antiquity: Gold, Labour, and Aristocratic Dominance* (Oxford, 2001).

Banaji, Jairus, 'Late Antique Legacies and Muslim Economic Expansion', in John Haldon (ed.), *Money, Power and Politics in Early Islamic Syria: A Review of Current Debates* (Farnham, 2010), 165–79.

Banaji, Jairus, 'Discounts, Weight Standards and the Exchange Rate between Gold and Copper: Insights into the Monetary Process of the Sixth Century', in Jairus Banaji, *Exploring the Economy of Late Antiquity: Selected Essays* (Cambridge, 2015), 91–109.

Bang, Peter F., 'Empire – A World History: Anatomy and Concept, Theory and Synthesis', in Peter F. Bang, C. A. Bayly and Walter Scheidel (eds), *The Oxford World History of Empire: Volume One: The Imperial Experience* (Oxford, 2021), 1–88.

Bang, Peter F., 'The Roman Empire', in Peter F. Bang, C. A. Bayly and Walter Scheidel (eds), *The Oxford World History of Empire Volume Two: The History of Empires* (Oxford, 2021), 240–89.

Bang, Peter F., C. A. Bayly and Walter Scheidel (eds), *The Oxford World History of Empire Volume Two: The History of Empires* (Oxford, 2021).

Banning, E. B., 'Peasants, Pastoralists and "Pax Romana": Mutualism in the Southern Highlands of Jordan', *Bulletin of the American Schools of Oriental Research* 261 (1986), 25–50.

Bashear, Suliman, 'The Title "Faruq" and Its Association with 'Umar I', *Studia Islamica* 72 (1990), 47–70.

Bashear, Suliman, 'Qibla Musharriqa and Early Muslim Prayer in Churches', *The Muslim World* 81 (1991), 267–82.
Bates, Michael and Mehdy Shaddel, 'Note on a Peculiar Arab-Sasanian Coinage of Ibn al-Ash'ath', *JRAS* (2022), 1–10.
Bemmann, Jan, and Michael Schmauder (eds), *Complexity of Interaction along the Eurasian Steppe Zone in the First Millennium CE* (Bonn, 2015).
Benabbès, Mohamed, 'The Contribution of Medieval Arabic Sources to the Historical Geography of Byzantine Africa', in Susan T. Stevens and Jonathan P. Conant (eds), *North Africa under Byzantium and Early Islam* (Washington, DC, 2016), 119–28.
Bernheimer, Teresa, 'The Revolt of 'Abd Allah b. Mu'awiya, AH 127–130: A Reconsideration Through the Coinage', *BSOAS* 69 (2006), 381–93.
Bessard, Fanny, 'The Politics of *Suq*s in Early Islam', *JESHO* 61 (2018), 491–518.
Bessard, Fanny, *Caliphs and Merchants: Cities and the Economics of Power in the Near East (700–950)* (Oxford, 2020).
Biddle, David White, 'The Development of the Bureaucracy of the Islamic Empire during the Late Umayyad and Early Abbasid Period', PhD Dissertation, University of Texas, Austin (1972).
Bielenstein, Hans, *Diplomacy and Trade in the Chinese World, 589–1276* (Leiden, 2005).
Biraben, Jean-Noël, 'Essai sur l'évolution du nombre des hommes', *Population* 34 (1979), 13–25.
Blair, Sheila, 'What Is the Date of the Dome of the Rock?', in Jeremy Johns (ed.), *Bayt al-Maqdis: Jerusalem and Early Islam* (Oxford, 1999), 59–87.
Blankinship, Yahya K., *The End of the Jihad State: The Reign of Hisham Ibn 'Abd al-Malik and the Collapse of the Umayyads* (Albany, 1994).
Booth, Phil, 'The Last Years of Cyrus, Patriarch of Alexandria († 642)', *Travaux et Mémoires 20: Mélanges Jean Gascou* (Paris, 2016), 1–50.
Booth, Phil, 'Alexandria and Antioch in the First 'Abbasid Century', *Al-Masaq* 33 (2021), 139–55.
Booth, Phil and Andrew Marsham, 'Egyptian Revolts', forthcoming.
Borrut, Antoine, 'L'espace maritime syrien au cours des premiers siècles de l'Islam (VIIe–Xe siècle): le cas de la région entre Acre et Tripoli', *Tempora* 10–11 (1999–2000), 1–34.
Borrut, Antoine, *Entre mémoire et pouvoir: L'éspace syrien sous les derniers Omeyyades et les premiers Abbasides (v. 72–193/692–809)* (Leiden, 2011).
Borrut, Antoine, 'The Future of the Past: Historical Writing in Early Islamic Syria', in Alain George and Andrew Marsham (eds), *Power, Patronage, and Memory in Early Islam: Perspectives on Umayyad Elites* (Oxford, 2018), 275–300.
Bosworth, Clifford E., *Sistan Under the Arabs, from the Islamic Conquest to the Rise of the Saffarids (30–250/651–854)* (Rome, 1968).
Bosworth, Clifford E., 'A Note on *Ta'arrub* in Early Islam', *JSS* 34 (1989), 355–62.
Bowersock, Glen W., 'Mavia, Queen of the Saracens', in Werner Eck, Hartmut Galsterer and Hartmut Wolff (eds), *Studien zur antiken Sozialgeschichte. Festschrift Friedrich Vittinghoff* (Vienna, 1980), 477–95.
Boyce, Mary, 'On the Zoroastrian Temple Cult of Fire', *JAOS* 95 (1975), 454–65.
Brooks, E. W., 'The Arabs in Asia Minor (641–750), from Arabic Sources', *The Journal of Hellenic Studies* 18 (1898), 182–208.

Brown, Peter, *The World of Late Antiquity: From Marcus Aurelius to Muhammad* (London, 1971).
Bruning, Jelle, *The Rise of a Capital: Al-Fustat and Its Hinterland, 18/639–132/750* (Leiden, 2018).
Buckley, Ronald P., 'The Muhtasib', *Arabica* 39 (1992), 59–117.
Bulliet, Richard W., *Conversion to Islam in the Medieval Period: An Essay in Quantitative History* (Cambridge, MA and London, 1979).
Burbank, Jane and Frederick Cooper, *Empires in World History: Power and the Politics of Difference* (Princeton, 2010).
Burns, Stephen J., Dominik Fleitmann, Manfred Mudelsee, Ulrich Neff, Albert Matter and Augusto Mangini, 'A 780-year Annually Resolved Record of Indian Ocean Monsoon Precipitation from a Speleothem from South Oman', *Journal of Geophysical Research: Atmospheres* 107, D20 (2002), ACL 9-1–ACL 9-9.
Butler, Alfred J., *The Arab Conquest of Egypt and the Last Thirty Years of the Roman Dominion* (Oxford, 1978).
Cameron, Averil, 'Vandal and Byzantine Africa', *CAH*, XIV, 552–69.
Cameron, Averil, 'How to Read Heresiology', *Journal of Medieval and Early Modern Studies* 33 (2003), 471–92.
Canard, Marius, 'Rice in the Middle East in the First Centuries of Islam', in Michael G. Morony (ed.), *Production and the Exploitation of Resources* (Farnham, 2002), 153–68.
Canepa, Matthew P., *The Two Eyes of the Earth: Art and Ritual of Kingship between Rome and Sasanian Iran* (Berkeley, CA and London, 2009).
Canepa, Matthew P., 'The Parthian and Sasanian Empires', in Peter F. Bang, C. A. Bayly and Walter Scheidel (eds), *The Oxford World History of Empire Volume Two: The History of Empires* (Oxford, 2021), 290–324.
Caner, Daniel, 'Towards a Miraculous Economy: Christian Gifts and Material "Blessings" in Late Antiquity', *Journal of Early Christian Studies* 14 (2006), 329–77.
Carlson, Thomas A. et al., 'Gubba Barraya', in David A. Michelson et al. (eds) *The Syriac Gazeteer*, 'Syriaca.org: The Syriac Reference Portal, 2014'. Entry published 14 January 2014, <http://syriaca.org/place/349> (last accessed 25 August 2022).
Carlson, Thomas A. et al., 'Mor Gabriel', in David A. Michelson et al. (eds) *The Syriac Gazeteer*, 'Syriaca.org: The Syriac Reference Portal, 2014'. Entry published 14 January 2014, <http://syriaca.org/place/349> (last accessed 25 August 2022).
Chokr, Melhem, *Zandaqa et zindiqs en islam au second siècle de l'hégire* (Damascus, 1993).
Clarke, Nicola, *The Muslim Conquest of Iberia: Medieval Arabic Narratives* (London and New York, 2012).
Cobb, Paul M., *White Banners: Contention in 'Abbasid Syria, 750–880* (Albany, 2001).
Cole, Juan, '*Paradosis* and Monotheism: A Late Antique Approach to the Meaning of Islam in the Quran', *BSOAS* 82 (2019), 405–25.
Conant, Jonathan P., *Staying Roman: Conquest and Identity in Africa and the Mediterranean, 439–700* (Cambridge, 2012).
Conant, Jonathan P., 'Literacy and Private Documentation in Late Antique North Africa: The Case of the Albertini Tablets', in Andrew H. Merrills (ed.), *Vandals, Romans and Berbers: New Perspectives on Late Antique North Africa* (London and New York, 2017), 199–224.

Conrad, Lawrence I., 'Arabic Plague Chronologies and Treatises: Social and Historical Factors in the Formation of a Literary Genre', *Studia Islamica* 54 (1981), 51–93.
Conrad, Lawrence I., '*Ta'un* and *Waba*' Conceptions of Plague and Pestilence in Early Islam', *JESHO* 25 (1982), 268–307.
Conrad, Lawrence I., 'Abraha and Muhammad: Some Observations apropos of Chronology and Literary Topoi in the Early Arabic Historical Tradition', *BSOAS* 50 (1987), 225–40.
Cook, David, *Studies in Muslim Apocalyptic* (Princeton, 2002).
Creswell, K. A. C., *Early Muslim Architecture: Umayyads* AD *622–750* (Oxford, 1969).
Crone, Patricia, *Slaves on Horses: The Evolution of the Islamic Polity* (Cambridge, 1980).
Crone, Patricia, *Meccan Trade and the Rise of Islam* (Cambridge, 1987).
Crone, Patricia, 'The First-century Concept of *Higra*', *Arabica* 41 (1994), 352–87.
Crone, Patricia, 'Were the Qays and Yemen of the Umayyad Period Political Parties?', *Der Islam* 71 (1994), 1–57.
Crone, Patricia, 'The Significance of Wooden Weapons in al-Mukhtar's Revolt and the Abbasid Revolution', in Ian R. Netton (ed.), *Studies in Honour of Clifford Edmund Bosworth Volume I: Hunter of the East: Arabic and Semitic Studies* (Leiden, 2000), 174–87.
Crone, Patricia, '*Shura* as an Elective Institution', *Quaderni di Studi Arabi* 19 (2001), 3–39.
Crone, Patricia, 'Quraysh and the Roman Army: Making Sense of the Meccan Leather Trade', *BSOAS* 70 (2007), 63–88.
Crone, Patricia, *The Nativist Prophets of Early Islamic Iran* (Cambridge, 2012).
Crone, Patricia and Martin Hinds, *God's Caliph: Religious Authority in the First Centuries of Islam* (Cambridge, 1986).
Cullen, Heidi M. and Peter B. de Menocal, 'North Atlantic Influence on Tigris-Euphrates Streamflow', *International Journal of Climatology* 20 (2000), 853–63.
Daniel, Elton, *The Political and Social History of Khurasan under Abbasid Rule 747–820* (Minneapolis and Chicago, 1979).
Daryaee, Touraj, 'The Effect of the Arab Muslim Conquest on the Administrative Division of Sasanian Persis', *Iran* 41 (2003), 193–204.
Daryaee, Touraj, 'Persian Lords and the Umayyads: Cooperation and Coexistence in a Turbulent Time', in Antoine Borrut and Fred M. Donner (eds), *Christians and Others in the Umayyad State* (Chicago, 2016), 73–81.
de Jong, Albert, 'Religion in Iran: The Parthian and Sasanian Periods (247 BCE–654 CE)', in Michele Renee Salzman and Marvin A. Sweeney (eds), *The Cambridge History of Religions in the Ancient World* (Cambridge, 2013), 23–53.
de la Vaissière, Étienne, *Sogdian Traders: A History* (Leiden, 2005).
de la Vaissière, Étienne, 'The 'Abbasid Revolution in Marw: New Data', *Der Islam* 95 (2018), 110–46.
de Lange, Nicholas, 'Jews in the Age of Justinian', in Michael Maas (ed.), *The Cambridge Companion to the Age of Justinian* (Cambridge, 2005), 401–26.
Debié, Muriel, 'Christians in the Service of the Caliph: Through the Looking Glass of Communal Identities', in Antoine Borrut and Fred M. Donner (eds), *Christians and Others in the Umayyad State* (Chicago, 2016), 53–71.
Decker, Michael, *Tilling the Hateful Earth: Agricultural Production and Trade in the Late Antique East* (Oxford, 2009).

Déroche, François, *Qur'ans of the Umayyads: A First Overview* (Leiden, 2013).
Di Cosmo, Nicola, 'Ancient Inner Asian Nomads: Their Economic Basis and Its Significance in Chinese History', *Journal of Asian Studies* 53 (1994), 1092–1126.
Di Cosmo, Nicola, 'China–Steppe Relations in Historical Perspective', in Jan Bemmann and Michael Schmauder (eds), *Complexity of Interaction along the Eurasian Steppe Zone in the First Millennium* CE (Bonn, 2015), 49–72.
Dixon, Abd Al-Ameer, *The Umayyad Caliphate 65–86/684–705* (London, 1971).
Djaït, Hicham, 'L'Afrique arabe au VIIIe siècle', *Annales: Économies, Sociétés* 28 (1973), 601–21.
Donner, Fred M., *The Early Islamic Conquests* (Princeton, 1981).
Donner, Fred M., 'The Shurta in Early Umayyad Syria', in Adnan Muhammad Bakhit and Robert Schick (eds), *The Fourth International Conference on the History of Bilad al-Sham during the Umayyad Period: Proceedings of the Third Symposium, 24–29 October 1987* (Amman, 1989), II, 247–62.
Donner, Fred M., 'Centralized Authority and Military Autonomy in the Early Islamic Conquests', in Averil Cameron (ed.), *The Byzantine and Early Islamic Near East III: States, Resources and Armies* (Princeton, 1995), 337–60.
Donner, Fred M., *Narratives of Islamic Origins: The Beginnings of Islamic Historical Writing* (Princeton, 1998).
Donner, Fred M., 'The Islamic Conquests', in Yousef Choueiri (ed.), *A Companion to the History of the Middle East* (Oxford, 2005), 28–51.
Donner, Fred M., *Muhammad and the Believers: At the Origins of Islam* (Cambridge, MA, 2010).
Donner, Fred M., 'Qur'anicization of Religio-Political Discourse in the Umayyad Period', *Revue des mondes musulmans et de la Méditerranée* 129 (2011), 79–92.
Drake, Lee B., 'Changes in North Atlantic Oscillation Drove Population Migrations and the Collapse of the Western Roman Empire', *Nature: Scientific Reports* 7:1227 (2017), 1–7.
Duri, 'Abd al-'Aziz, 'The Origins of Iqta' in Islam', *al-Abhath* 22 (1969), 3–24.
Ebstein, Michael, 'Shurta Chiefs in Basra in the Umayyad Period: A Prosopographical Study', *Al-Qantara* 31 (2010), 103–47.
Eger, A. Asa, *The Islamic–Byzantine Frontier: Interaction and Exchange among Muslim and Christian Communities* (London, 2015).
Elad, Amikam, 'The Siege of Wasit (132/749): Some Aspects of 'Abbasid and 'Alid Relations at the Beginning of 'Abbasid Rule', in Moshe Sharon (ed.), *Studies in Islamic History and Civilisation: in Honour of Professor David Ayalon* (Jerusalem and Leiden, 1986), 59–90.
Elad, Amikam, *Medieval Jerusalem and Islamic Worship: Holy Places, Ceremonies, Pilgrimage* (Leiden, 1995).
Elad, Amikam, "'Abd al-Malik and the Dome of the Rock: A Further Examination of the Muslim Sources', *JSAI* 35 (2008), 167–226.
Encyclopaedia Iranica, online edition, 2023, <https://www.iranicaonline.org/> (last accessed 28 June 2023).
Encyclopaedia of Islam, First Edition, eds M. Th. Houtsma, T. W. Arnold, R. Basset and R. Hartmann, A. J. Wensinck, W. Heffening, E. Lévi-Provençal and H. A. R. Gibb (Leiden, 1913–38).
Encyclopaedia of Islam, Second Edition, eds P. Bearman, Th. Bianquis, C. E. Bosworth, E. van Donzel and W. P. Heinrichs (first published online 2012), <https://refer

enceworks.brillonline.com/browse/encyclopaedia-of-islam-2> (last accessed 28 June 2023).
Encyclopaedia of Islam, THREE, eds Kate Fleet, Gudrun Krämer, Denis Matringe, John Nawas and Devin J. Stewart, <https://referenceworks.brillonline.com/browse/encyclopaedia-of-islam-3> (last accessed 28 June 2023).
Encyclopaedia of the Qur'an, ed. Johanna Pink, <https://referenceworks.brillonline.com/browse/encyclopaedia-of-the-quran> (last accessed 28 June 2023).
Faruque, Muhammad, 'The Revolt of 'Abd al-Rahman ibn al-Ash'ath: Its Nature and Causes', *Islamic Studies* 25 (1986), 289–304.
Fenwick, Corisande, 'From Africa to *Ifriqiya*: Settlement and Society in Early Medieval North Africa (650–800)', *Al-Masaq* 25 (2013), 9–33.
Fenwick, Corisande, 'Early Medieval Urbanism in Ifriqiya and the Emergence of the Islamic City', in L. Callegarin and S. Panzram (eds), *Entre civitas y medina. El mundo de las ciudades en la Península Ibérica y en el norte de África* (Madrid, 2018), 203–19.
Fenwick, Corisande, *Early Islamic North Africa: A New Perspective* (London, 2020).
Fenwick, Corisande, 'The Umayyads and North Africa: Imperial Rule and Frontier Society', in Andrew Marsham (ed.), *The Umayyad World* (London and New York, 2021), 293–313.
Fiema, Zbigniew T., 'The Byzantine Military in the Petra Papyri – a Summary', in Ariel S. Lewin and Pietrina Pellegrini (eds), *The Late Roman Army in the Near East from Diocletian to the Arab Conquest* (Oxford 2007), 313–19.
Fiema, Zbigniew T., Ahmad Al-Jallad, Michael C. A. Macdonald and Laïla Nehmé, '*Provincia Arabia*: Nabataea, the Emergence of Arabic as a Written Language, and Graeco-Arabica', in Greg Fisher (ed.), *Arabs and Empires before Islam* (Oxford, 2015), 373–433.
Finneran, Niall, 'Hermits, Saints, and Snakes: The Archaeology of the Early Ethiopian Monastery in Wider Context', *The International Journal of African Historical Studies* 45 (2012), 247–71.
Fisher, Greg, *Between Empires: Arabs, Romans, and Sasanians in Late Antiquity* (Oxford, 2011).
Fisher, Greg, 'Emperors, Politics, and the Plague: Rome and the Jafnids 570–585', in Denis Genequand and Christian Robin (eds), *Les Jafnides: des rois arabes au service de Byzance* (Paris, 2015), 223–37.
Fisher, Greg, 'From Mavia to al-Mundhir: Arab Christians and Arab Tribes in the Late Roman Near East', in Kirill Dimitriev and Isabel Toral-Niehoff (eds), *Religious Culture in Late Antique Arabia* (Piscataway, NJ, 2017), 165–218.
Fisher, Greg, Philip Wood, George Bevan, Geoffrey Greatrex, Basema Hamarneh, Peter Schadler and Walter Ward, 'Arabs and Christianity', in Greg Fisher (ed.), *Arabs and Empires before Islam* (Oxford, 2015), 276–372.
Fleitmann, Dominik, John Haldon, Raymond S Bradley, Stephen J. Burns, Hai Cheng, R. Lawrence Edwards, Christoph C. Raible, Matthew Jacobson and Albert Matter, 'Droughts and Societal Change: The Environmental Context for the Emergence of Islam in Late Antique Arabia', *Science* 376 (2022), 1317–21.
Food and Agriculture Organization of the United Nations, *Global Ecological Zones for FAO Forest Reporting: 2010 Update*, 'Forest Resources Assessment Working Paper 179' (Rome, 2012).

Foss, Clive, *Arab-Byzantine Coins: An Introduction, with a Catalogue of the Dumbarton Oaks Collection* (Washington, DC, 2008).
Foss, Clive, 'Mu'awiya's State', in John Haldon (ed.), *Money, Power and Politics in Early Islamic Syria: A Review of Current Debates* (Farnham, 2010), 75–96.
Fowden, Garth and Elizabeth Key Fowden, *Studies on Hellenism, Christianity and the Umayyads* (Athens and Paris, 2004).
Fraedrich, Klaus, Jianmin Jiang, Friedrich-Wilhelm Gerstengarbe and Peter C. Werner, 'Multiscale Detection of Abrupt Climate Changes: Application to River Nile Flood Levels', *International Journal of Climatology* 17 (1997), 1301–15.
Frye, Richard N., 'Byzantine and Sasanian Trade Relations with Northeastern Russia', *DOP* 26 (1972), 263–9.
Fynn-Paul, Jeffrey, 'Empire, Monotheism and Slavery in the Greater Mediterranean Region from Antiquity to the Early Modern Era', *Past & Present* 205 (2009), 3–40.
Gabrieli, Francesco, 'Muhammad ibn Qasim ath-Thaqafi and the Arab Conquest of Sind', *East and West* 15 (1965), 281–95.
Gajda, Iwona, 'L'Arabie du Sud unifiée par Himyar', in Vogt Burkhard and Christian Robin (eds), *Yémen: au pays de la reine de Saba': exposition présentée à l'Institut du monde arabe du 25 octobre 1997 au 28 février 1998* (Paris, 1997), 188–96.
Garsoïan, Nina, 'Introduction to the Problem of Early Armenian Monasticism', *Revue des Études Arméniennes* 30 (2005), 177–236.
Garsoïan, Nina, *Interregnum: Introduction to a Study on the Formation of Armenian Identity (ca 600–750)* (Leuven, 2012).
Gebre Selassie, Yohannes, 'Plague as a Possible Factor for the Decline and Collapse of the Aksumite Empire: A New Interpretation', *ITYOPIS* 1 (2011), 36–61.
Genequand, Denis, *Les établissements des élites omeyyades en Palmyrène et au Proche-Orient* (Beirut, 2012).
Genequand, Denis, 'Elites in the Countryside: The Economic and Political Factors behind the Umayyad "Desert Castles"', in Andrew Marsham (ed.), *The Umayyad World* (London and New York, 2021), 240–66.
George, Alain, *The Rise of Islamic Calligraphy* (London, 2010).
George, Alain, 'Direct Sea Trade Between Early Islamic Iraq and Tang China: From the Exchange of Goods to the Transmission of Ideas', *JRAS* 25 (2015), 579–624.
George, Alain, *The Umayyad Mosque of Damascus: Art, Faith and Empire in Early Islam* (London, 2021).
George, Alain, 'A Builder of Mosques: The Projects of al-Walid I, from Sanaa to Homs', in Melanie Gibson (Ed.), *Fruit of Knowledge, Wheel of Learning: Essays in Honour of Robert Hillenbrand* (London, 2022), 16–49.
Ghanimati, Soroor, 'Kuh-E Khwaja and the Religious Architecture of Sasanian Iran', in Daniel T. Potts (ed.) *The Oxford Handbook of Ancient Iran* (Oxford, 2013), 878–908.
Gibb, H. A. R., *The Arab Conquests in Central Asia* (London, 1923).
Gibb, H. A. R., 'Chinese Records of the Arabs in Central Asia', *BSOAS* 2 (1923), 613–22.
Gibb, H. A. R., 'The Fiscal Rescript of 'Umar II', *Arabica* 2 (1955), 1–16.
Gibbons, Ann, 'Why 536 Was "the Worst Year to Be Alive"', *Science: News: Archaeology*, 15 November 2018, <doi: 10.1126/science.aaw0632>.

Godlewski, Władimir, 'Monastic Life in Makuria', in Gawdat Gabra and Hany N. Takla (eds), *Christianity and Monasticism in Aswan and Nubia* (Oxford, 2013), 157–74.
Goehring, James E., 'Monasticism in Byzantine Egypt: Continuity and Memory', in Roger S. Bagnall (ed.), *Egypt in the Byzantine World, 300–700* (Cambridge, 2007), 390–407.
Grabar, Oleg, *The Shape of the Holy: Early Islamic Jerusalem* (Princeton, 1996).
Grabar, Oleg and Said Nuseibeh, *The Dome of the Rock* (London, 1996).
Griffith, Sidney, 'From Aramaic to Arabic: The Languages of the Monasteries of Palestine in the Byzantine and Early Islamic Periods', *DOP* 51 (1997), 11–31.
Griffith, Sidney, 'The Mansur Family and Saint John of Damascus: Christians and Muslims in Umayyad Times', in Antoine Borrut and Fred M. Donner (eds), *Christians and Others in the Umayyad State* (Chicago, 2016), 29–53.
Grohmann, Adolf, *From the World of Arabic Papyri* (Cairo, 1952).
Guest, A. R., 'The Foundation of Fustat and the *Khittah*s of That Town', *JRAS* (1907), 49–83.
Guidetti, Mattia, 'The Contiguity between Churches and Mosques in Early Islamic Bilad al-Sham', *BSOAS* 76 (2013), 229–58.
Guilland, Rodolphe, 'L'Expédition de Maslama contre Constantinople (717–718)', in Rodolphe Guilland, *Études Byzantines* (Paris, 1959), 109–33.
Gundelfinger, Simon, and Peter Verkinderen, 'The Governors of al-Sham and Fars in the Early Islamic Empire – A Comparative Regional Perspective', in Hannah-Lena Hagemann and Stefan Heidemann (eds), *The Early Islamic Empire at Work. Volume 1, Transregional and Regional Elites – Connecting the Early Islamic Empire* (Berlin, 2020), 255–329.
Gyselen, Rika, *Arab-Sasanian Copper Coinage* (Vienna, 2000).
Haas, Christopher, *Alexandria in Late Antiquity: Topography and Social Conflict* (Baltimore, 2006).
Haas, Christopher, 'Mountain Constantines: The Christianization of Aksum and Iberia', *JLA* 1 (2008), 101–26.
Hagemann, Hannah-Lena, 'Muslim Elites in the Early Islamic Jazira: The Qadis of Harran, al-Raqqa, and al-Mawsil', in Hannah-Lena Hagemann and Stefan Heidemann (eds), *Transregional and Regional Elites: Connecting the Early Islamic Empire* (Berlin, 2020), 331–58.
Hagemann, Hannah-Lena, *The Kharijites in Early Islamic Historical Tradition: Heroes and Villains* (Edinburgh, 2021).
Hagemann, Hannah-Lena and Peter Verkinderen, 'Kharijism in the Umayyad Period', in Andrew Marsham (ed.), *The Umayyad World* (London and New York, 2021), 489–517.
Haider, Najam, *The Origins of the Shi'ah: Identity, Ritual, and Sacred Space in Eighth-century Kufa* (Cambridge, 2011).
Haider, Najam, *The Rebel and the Imam: Explorations in Muslim Historiography* (Cambridge, 2019).
Haldon, John, 'The Resources of Late Antiquity', *NCHI*, I, 17–71.
Haldon, John, 'Military Service, Military Lands, and the Status of Soldiers: Current Problems and Interpretations', *DOP* 47 (1993), 1–67.
Haldon, John, 'Seventh Century Continuitues: The *Ajnad* and the Thematic Myth', in Averil Cameron and Lawrence I. Conrad (eds), *The Byzantine and*

Early Islamic Near East III: States, Resources and Armies (Princeton, 1995), 379–423.

Haldon, John, *The Empire That Would Not Die: The Paradox of Eastern Roman Survival, 640–740* (Cambridge, MA, 2016).

Hallaq, Wael, *The Origins and Evolution of Islamic Law* (Cambridge, 2005).

Halm, Heinz, *The Empire of the Mahdi: The Rise of the Fatimids*, tr. Michael Bonner (Leiden, 1996).

Hamarneh, Basema, 'Christian Art and Visual Culture in Umayyad Bilad al-Sham', in Andrew Marsham (ed.), *The Umayyad World* (London and New York, 2021), 464–85.

Hansen, Valerie, 'Review: New Work on the Sogdians, the Most Important Traders on the Silk Road, AD 500–1000' *T'oung Pao* 89 (2003), 149–61.

Haug, Robert, *The Eastern Frontier: Limits of Empire in Late Antique and Early Medieval Central Asia* (London and New York, 2019).

Hawting, Gerald, *The First Dynasty of Islam: The Umayyad Caliphate, AD. 661–750* (London, 2000).

Hawting, Gerald, 'The Case of Ja'd b. Dirham and the Punishment of "Heretics" in the Early Caliphate', in Christian Lange and Maribel Fierro (eds), *Public Violence in Islamic Societies: Power, Discipline, and the Construction of the Public Sphere, 7th–19th Centuries* CE (Edinburgh, 2009), 27–41.

Hawting, Gerald, 'Ibn al-Zubayr, the Ka'ba and the Dome of the Rock', in Andrew Marsham (ed.), *The Umayyad World* (London and New York, 2021), 374–392.

Haywood, John, *The New Atlas of World History: Global Events at a Glance* (London, 2011).

Heck, Paul, '"Arabia without Spices": An Alternate Hypothesis', *JAOS* 123 (2003), 547–76.

Heidemann, Stefan, 'The Merger of Two Currency Zones in Early Islam: The Byzantine and Sasanian Impact on the Circulation in Former Byzantine Syria and Northern Mesopotamia', *Iran* 36 (1998), 95–112.

Hickey, Todd M., 'Aristocratic Landholding and the Economy of Byzantine Egypt', in R. Bagnall (ed.), *Egypt in the Byzantine World* (Cambridge, 2007), 288–308.

Hillenbrand, Robert, 'Hisham's Balancing Act: The Case of Qasr al-Hayr al-Gharbi', in Alain George and Andrew Marsham (eds), *Power, Patronage, and Memory in Early Islam* (Oxford, 2018), 83–132.

Hinds, Martin, 'Kufan Political Alignments and their Background in the Mid-seventh Century AD', *IJMES* 2 (1971), 346–67.

Hinds, Martin, 'The Murder of the Caliph 'Uthman', *IJMES* 3 (1972), 450–69.

Hinds, Martin, 'The Siffin Arbitration Agreement', *JSS* 17 (1972), 93–113.

Hinds, Martin, 'The First Arab Conquests in Fars', *Iran* 22 (1984), 39–53.

Hinds, Martin and Hamdi Sakkout, 'A Letter from the Governor of Egypt to the King of Nubia and Muqarra Concerning Egyptian–Nubian Relations in 141/758', in Wadad al-Qadi (ed.), *Studia Arabica et Islamica: Festschrift for Ihsan 'Abbas on his Sixtieth Birthday* (Beirut, 1981), 209–29.

Hirschfeld, Yizhar, *The Roman Baths of Hammat Gader: Final Report* (Jerusalem, 1997).

Hodgson, Marshall G. S., *The Venture of Islam: Conscience and History in a World Civilization* (Chicago, 1974).

Hong, Y. T., B. Hong, Q. H. Lin, Yasuyuki Shibata, Masahi Hirota, Y. X. Zhu, X. T. Leng, Y. Wang, H. Wang and L. Yi, 'Inverse Phase Oscillations between the

East Asian and Indian Ocean Summer Monsoons during the Last 12000 Years and Paleo-El Niño', *Earth and Planetary Science Letters* 231 (2005), 337–46.

Horden, Peregrine, 'Climate and Social Change at the Start of the Late Antique Little Ice Age', *The Holocene* 30 (2020), 1643–8.

Horden, Peregrine and Nicholas Purcell, *The Corrupting Sea: A Study of Mediterranean History* (Oxford, 2000).

Hornborg, Alf, Brett Clark and Kenneth Hermele (eds), *Ecology and Power: Struggles over Land and Material Resources in the Past, Present, and Future* (Abingdon and New York, 2012).

Hosein, Rasheed, 'Tribal Alliance Formations and Power Structures in the Jahiliyah and Early Islamic Periods: Quraysh and Thaqif (530–750 CE)', PhD Dissertation, University of Chicago (2010).

Howard-Johnston, James, 'The Two Great Powers in Late Antiquity: A Comparison', in Averil Cameron (ed.), *The Byzantine and Early Islamic Near East III: States, Resources and Armies* (Princeton, 1995), 157–226.

Howard-Johnston, James, *Witnesses to a World Crisis: Historians and Histories of the Middle East in the Seventh Century* (Oxford, 2010).

Hoyland, Robert G., *Seeing Islam As Others Saw It: A Survey and Evaluation of Christian, Jewish and Zoroastrian Writings on Early Islam* (Princeton, 1997).

Hoyland, Robert G., *Arabia and the Arabs: From the Bronze Age to the Coming of Islam* (London and New York, 2001).

Hoyland, Robert G., 'Late Roman Provincia Arabia, Monophysite Monks and Arab Tribes: A Problem of Centre and Periphery', *Semitica et Classica* 2 (2009), 117–39.

Hoyland, Robert G., *In God's Path: The Arab Conquests and the Creation of an Islamic Empire* (Oxford, 2015).

Hoyland, Robert G., 'Khanasira and Andarin (Northern Syria) in the Umayyad Period and a New Arabic Tax Document', in Alain George and Andrew Marsham (eds), *Power, Patronage, and Memory in Early Islam* (Oxford, 2018), 133–46.

Humphreys, Mike, 'The "War of Images" Revisited. Justinian II's Coinage Reform and the Caliphate', *Numismatic Chronicle* 173 (2013), 229–44.

Humphreys, Mike, *Law, Power, and Imperial Ideology in the Iconoclast Era, 680–850* (Oxford, 2014).

Humphreys, Mike, 'First Iconoclasm, ca. 700–780', in Mike Humphreys (ed.), *A Companion to Byzantine Iconoclasm* (Leiden, 2021), 325–67.

Ilisch, Lutz, "'Abd al-Malik's Monetary Reform in Copper and the Failure of Centralization', in John Haldon (ed.), *Money, Power and Politics in Early Islamic Syria: A Review of Current Debates* (Farnham, 2010), 125–46.

Inaba, Minoru, 'The Identity of the Turkish Ruler to the South of Hindukush from the 7th to the 9th Centuries AD', *ZINBUN* 38 (2005), 1–19.

Israeli, Eyal and Yaacov Kahanov, 'The 7th–9th Century Tantura E Shipwreck, Israel: Construction and Reconstruction', *International Journal of Nautical Archaeology* 43 (2014), 369–88.

Issar, Arie S., *Climate Changes during the Holocene and Their Impact on Hydrological Systems* (Cambridge, 2003).

Jagher, Reto, Hani Elsuede and Jean-Marie Le Tensorer, 'El Kown Oasis, Human Settlement in the Syrian Desert during the Pleistocene', *L'Anthropologie* 119 (2015), 542–80.

Jakobielski, Stefan, *A History of the Bishopric of Pachoras on the Basis of Coptic Inscriptions* (Warsaw, 1972).
Al-Jallad, Ahmad, *The Religion and Rituals of the Nomads of Pre-Islamic Arabia: A Reconstruction based on the Safaitic Inscriptions* (Leiden, 2022).
Al-Jallad, Ahmad and Hythem Sidky, 'A Paleo-Arabic Inscription on a Route North of Ta'if', *Arabian Archaeology and Epigraphy: Early View* (2021), 1–14.
Jamil, Nadia, *Ethics and Poetry in Sixth Century Arabia* (Cambridge, 2017).
Jankowiak, Marek, 'The First Arab Siege of Constantinople', *Travaux et Mémoires 17: Constructing the Seventh Century* (Paris, 2013), 237–320.
Jankowiak, Marek, 'P.Lond. I 113.10, the Exile of Patriarch Kyros of Alexandria, and the Arab Conquest of Egypt', in Phil Booth and Mary Whitby (eds), *Travaux et Mémoires 26: Mélanges James Howard-Johnston* (Paris, 2022), 287–314.
Johns, Jeremy, 'The *Longue Durée*: State and Settlement Strategies in Southern Transjordan across the Islamic Centuries', in E. L. Rogan and T. Tell (eds), *Village, Steppe and State: The Social Origins of Modern Jordan* (London, 1994), 1–31.
Johns, Jeremy (ed.), *Bayt al-Maqdis: Jerusalem and Early Islam* (Oxford, 1999).
Johns, Jeremy and Julian Raby (eds), *Bayt al-Maqdis: 'Abd al-Malik's Jerusalem* (Oxford, 1992).
Johnson, Scott Fitzgerald, 'Introduction: The Social Presence of Greek in Eastern Christianity, 200–1200', in Scott Fitzgerald Johnson, *Languages and Cultures of Eastern Christianity: Greek* (Farnham, 2015), 1–122.
Jones, Matthew D., Neil C. Roberts, Melanie J. Leng and Murat Türkeş, 'A High-resolution Late Holocene Lake Isotope Record from Turkey and Links to North Atlantic and Monsoon Climate', *Geology* 34 (2006), 361–4.
Jonson, Trent, 'A Numismatic History of the Early Islamic Precious Metal Coinage of North Africa and the Iberian Peninsula', DPhil Dissertation, University of Oxford (2014).
Judd, Steven, 'Ghaylan al-Dimashqi: The Isolation of a Heretic in Islamic Historiography', *IJMES* 31 (1999), 161–84.
Judd, Steven, 'Reinterpreting al-Walid b. Yazid', *JAOS* 128 (2008), 439–58.
Judd, Steven, 'Muslim Persecution of Heretics during the Marwanid Period (64–132/684–750)', *Al-Masaq* 23 (2011), 1–14.
Judd, Steven, *Religious Scholars and the Umayyads: Piety-minded Supporters of the Marwanid Caliphate* (London and New York, 2014).
Judd, Steven, 'Ibn 'Asakir's Peculiar Biography of Khalid al-Qasri', in Steven Judd and Jens Scheiner (eds), *New Perspectives on Ibn 'Asakir in Islamic Historiography* (Leiden, 2017), 139–56.
Keenan, James G., 'Egypt', *CAH*, XIV, 612–37.
Kennedy, Hugh, 'The Umayyad Caliphate circa 132/750', in Hugh Kennedy (ed.), *Historical Atlas of Islam*. First published online in 2012, <http://dx.doi.org/10.1163/1573-3912_hai_HAI_9> (last accessed 25 April 2020).
Kennedy, Hugh, 'From Polis to Madina: Urban Change in Late Antique and Early Islamic Syria', *Past & Present* 106 (1985), 3–27.
Kennedy, Hugh, 'The Financing of the Military in the Early Islamic State', in Averil Cameron (ed.), *The Byzantine and Islamic Near East III: States, Resources and Armies* (Princeton, 1995), 361–78.

Kennedy, Hugh, 'From Oral Tradition to Written Record in Arabic Genealogy', *Arabica* 44 (1997), 531–44.
Kennedy, Hugh, 'Medieval Merv: An Historical Overview', in Georgina Herrmann (ed.), *Monuments of Merv: Traditional Buildings of the Karakum* (London, 1999), 27–44.
Kennedy, Hugh, *The Armies of the Caliphs: Military and Society in the Early Islamic State* (London, 2001).
Kennedy, Hugh, 'Military Pay and the Economy of the Early Islamic State', *Historical Research* 75 (2002), 155–69.
Kennedy, Hugh, 'The Decline and Fall of the First Muslim Empire', *Der Islam* 81 (2004), 3–30.
Kennedy, Hugh, 'Elite Incomes in the Early Islamic State', in Lawrence I. Conrad and John Haldon (eds), *The Byzantine and Early Islamic Near East VI: Elites Old and New in the Byzantine and Early Islamic Near East* (Princeton, 2004), 13–28.
Kennedy, Hugh, 'From Shahristan to Medina', *Studia Islamica* 102/103 (2006), 5–34.
Kennedy, Hugh, *The Great Arab Conquests: How the Spread of Islam Changed the World We Live In* (London, 2007).
Kennedy, Hugh, 'The Justinianic Plague in Syria and the Archaeological Evidence', in Lester K. Little (ed.), *The Plague and the End of Antiquity: The Pandemic of 541–750* (Cambridge, 2007), 87–96.
Kennedy, Hugh, 'Feeding the Five Hundred Thousand: Cities and Agriculture in Early Islamic Mesopotamia', *Iraq* 73 (2011), 177–99.
Kennedy, Hugh, 'Landholding and Law in the Early Islamic State', in John Hudson and Ana Rodríguez López (eds), *Diverging Paths? The Shapes of Power and Institutions in Medieval Christendom and Islam* (Leiden, 2014), 159–81.
Kennet, Derek, 'The Decline of Eastern Arabia in the Sasanian Period', *Arabian Archaeology and Epigraphy* 18 (2007), 86–122.
Kershaw, Jane and Stephen W. Merkel, 'Silver Recycling in the Viking Age: Theoretical and Analytical Approaches', *Archaeometry* (2021), 1–18.
Key Fowden, Elizabeth, *The Barbarian Plain: Saint Sergius between Rome and Iran* (Berkeley, 1999).
Key Fowden, Elizabeth, 'Shrines and Banners: Paleo-Muslims and their Material Inheritance', in Lorenz Korn and Ivrem Çiğden (eds), *Encompassing the Sacred in Islamic Art* (Wiesbaden, 2020), 5–24.
Khamis, Elias, 'A Bronze Weight of Sa'id b. 'Abd al-Malik from Bet Shean/Baysan', *JRAS* 12 (2002), 143–54.
Khan, Geoffrey, *Arabic Documents from Early Islamic Khurasan* (London, 2007).
Khan, Geoffrey, 'The Opening Formula and Witness Clauses in Arabic Legal Documents from the Early Islamic Period', *JAOS* 139 (2019), 23–40.
Al-Khoee, Hasan, 'Functions of Arabic Public Speeches in Early Islam: The Evidence from the Second Civil War (64–70/683–689)', PhD Dissertation, SOAS, University of London (2020).
Kister, M. J., 'Al-Hira: Some Notes on Its Relations with Arabia', *Arabica* 15 (1968), 143–69.
Kister, M. J., 'Some Reports Concerning Mecca from Jahiliyya to Islam', *JESHO* 15 (1972), 61–93.

Kister, M. J., 'The Struggle against Musaylima and the Conquest of Yamama', *JSAI* 27 (2002), 1–56.
Klat, Michel G., *Catalogue of the Post-reform Dirhams: The Umayyad Dynasty* (London, 2002).
Kocabaş, Ufuk, 'Yenikapı Byzantine-Era Shipwrecks, Istanbul, Turkey: A Preliminary Report and Inventory of the 27 Wrecks Studied by Istanbul University', *International Journal of Nautical Archaeology* 44 (2015), 5–38.
Kradin, Nicolai N., 'Nomadic Empires in Inner Asia', in Jan Bemmann and Michael Schmauder (eds), *Complexity of Interaction along the Eurasian Steppe Zone in the First Millennium CE* (Bonn, 2015), 11–48.
Łajtar, Adam and Grzegorz Ochała, 'Language Use and Literacy in Late Antique and Medieval Nubia', in Geoff Emberling and Bruce Beyer Williams (eds) *The Oxford Handbook of Ancient Nubia* (Oxford, 2021), 787–805.
Lander, Shira L., 'Inventing Synagogue Conversion: The Case of Late Roman North Africa', *Journal of Ancient Judaism* 4 (2013), 401–16.
Landau-Tasseron, Ella, 'Alliances among the Arabs', *Al-Qantara* 26 (2005), 141–73.
Latham, J. D., 'The Beginning of Arabic Prose Literature: The Epistolary Genre', in A. F. L. Beeston, T. M. Johnstone, R. B. Serjeant and G. Rex Smith (eds), *Arabic Literature to the End of the Umayyad Period* (Cambridge, 1983), 154–79.
Le Quesne, Charles, 'Hajj Ports of the Red Sea: A Historical and Archaeological Overview', in Venetia Porter and Liana Saif (eds), *The Hajj: Collected Essays* (London, 2013), 74–83.
Le Strange, Guy, *Palestine under the Moslems: A Description of Syria and the Holy Land from AD 650 to 1500* (London, 1890).
Lecker, Michael, 'Judaism among Kinda and the Ridda of Kinda', *JAOS* 115 (1995), 635–50.
Lecker, Michael, *Muslims, Jews and Pagans: Studies on Early Islamic Medina* (Leiden, 1995).
Lecker, Michael, 'Biographical Notes on Ibn Shihab al-Zuhri', *JSS* 41 (1996), 21–63.
Lecker, Michael, 'Were Customs Dues Levied at the Time of the Prophet Muhammad?', *Al-Qantara* 22 (2001), 19–43.
Lecker, Michael, 'The Levying of Taxes for the Sassanians in Pre-Islamic Medina', *JSAI* 27 (2002), 109–26.
Leder, Stefan, 'Features of the Novel in Early Historiography: The Downfall of Xalid al-Qasri', *Oriens* 32 (1990), 72–96.
Legendre, Marie, 'Aspects of Umayyad Administration', in Andrew Marsham (ed.), *The Umayyad World* (London and New York, 2021), 133–57.
Legendre, Marie, 'The Translation of the *Diwan* and the Making of the Marwanid "Language Reform": Secretarial Agency, Economic Incentives, and Regional Dynamics in the Umayyad State', in Antoine Borrut, Manuela Ceballos and Alison Vacca (eds), *Navigating Language in the Early Islamic World: Multilingualism and Language Change in the First Centuries of Islam* (Turnhout, forthcoming).
Leone, Anna, *Changing Townscapes in North Africa from Late Antiquity to the Arab Conquest* (Bari, 2007).
Leone, Anna, *The End of the Pagan City: Religion, Economy, and Urbanism in Late Antique North Africa* (Oxford, 2013).

Lev, Yaacov, 'Coptic Rebellions and the Islamization of Medieval Egypt (8th–10th Century): Medieval and Modern Perceptions', *JSAI* 39 (2012), 303–44.
Levy-Rubin, Milka, 'New Evidence Relating to the Process of Islamization in Palestine in the Early Muslim Period: The Case of Samaria', *JESHO* 43 (2000), 257–76.
Levy-Rubin, Milka, *Non-Muslims in the Early Islamic Empire: From Surrender to Coexistence* (Cambridge, 2011).
Levy-Rubin, Milka, '"Umar II's *Ghiyar* Edict: Between Ideology and Practice', in Antoine Borrut and Fred M. Donner (eds), *Christians and Others in the Umayyad State* (Chicago, 2016), 157–72.
Lewis, Norman E., *Nomads and Settlers in Syria and Jordan, 1800–1980* (Cambridge, 1987).
Lieu, Samuel N. C., 'Manichaeism', in Susan Ashbrook Harvey and David G. Hunter (eds) *The Oxford Handbook of Early Christian Studies* (Oxford, 2009), 221–36.
Lindstedt, Ilkka, '*Muhajirun* as a Name for the First/Seventh Century Muslims', *JNES* 74 (2015), 67–73.
Lindstedt, Ilkka, 'Arabic Rock Inscriptions up to 750', in Andrew Marsham (ed.), *The Umayyad World* (London and New York, 2021), 411–37.
Little, Lester K. (ed.), *The Plague and the End of Antiquity: The Pandemic of 541–750* (Cambridge, 2007).
Longworth, Nicholas Kyle, 'Islamic Bureaucrats in Late Antiquity: Administration and Elites during the Umayyad Caliphate (*c*. 661–750 CE)', PhD Dissertation, University of Chicago (2022).
Loseby, Simon T., 'The Mediterranean Economy', in Paul Fouracre (ed.), *The New Cambridge Medieval History Volume I, c. 500–700* (Cambridge, 2005), 605–38.
Loseby, Simon T., 'Post-Roman Economies', in Walter Scheidel (ed.), *The Cambridge Companion to the Roman Economy* (Cambridge, 2012), 334–60.
Luce, Mark David, 'Frontier as Process: Umayyad Khurasan', PhD Dissertation, University of Chicago (2009).
Luz, Nimrod, 'The Construction of an Islamic City in Palestine: The Case of Umayyad al-Ramla', *JRAS* 3 (1997), 27–54.
Mabra, Joshua, *Princely Authority in the Early Marwanid State: The Life of 'Abd al-'Aziz ibn Marwan* (Piscataway, 2017).
Macdonald, Michael C. A., 'Arabs, Arabias and Arabic before Late Antiquity', *Topoi* 1 (2009), 277–32.
Macdonald, Michael C. A., Aldo Corcella, Touraj Daryaee, Greg Fisher, Matt Gibbs, Ariel Lewin, Donata Violante and Conor Whately, 'Arabs and Empires before the Sixth Century', in Greg Fisher (ed.) *Arabs and Empires before Islam* (Oxford, 2015), 11–89.
Madelung, Wilferd, *The Succession to Muhammad: A Study of the Early Caliphate* (Cambridge, 1997).
Magee, Peter, *The Archaeology of Prehistoric Arabia: Adaptation and Social Formation from the Neolithic to the Iron Age* (Cambridge, 2014).
Magness, Jodi, *The Archaeology of the Settlement of Early Islamic Palestine* (Winona Lake, 2003).
Mann, Michael, *The Sources of Social Power Volume 1: A History of Power from the Beginning to AD 1760* (Cambridge, 1986).
Manzano Moreno, Eduardo, 'The Iberian Peninsula and North Africa', *NCHI*, I, 581–621.

Manzano-Moreno, Eduardo, 'Conquest and Settlement: What al-Andalus Can Tell Us about the Arab Expansion at the Time of the Umayyad Caliphate', in Andrew Marsham (ed.), *The Umayyad World* (London and New York, 2021), 314–31.
Marsham, Andrew, *Rituals of Islamic Monarchy: Accession and Succession in the First Muslim Empire* (Edinburgh, 2009).
Marsham, Andrew, 'Public Execution in the Umayyad Period: Early Islamic Punitive Practice and Its Late Antique Context', *Journal of Arabic and Islamic Studies* 11 (2011), 101–36.
Marsham, Andrew, 'The Pact (*amana*) Between Muʻawiya Ibn Abi Sufyan and ʻAmr Ibn Al-ʻAs (656 or 658 CE): "Documents" and the Islamic Historical Tradition', *JSS* 57 (2012), 69–96.
Marsham, Andrew, 'The Architecture of Allegiance in Early Islamic Late Antiquity: The Accession of Muʻāwiya in Jerusalem, ca. 661 CE', in Alexander Beihammer, Stavroula Constantinou and Maria Parani (eds), *Court Ceremonies and Rituals of Power in Byzantium and the Medieval Mediterranean: Comparative Perspectives* (Leiden, 2013), 87–112.
Marsham, Andrew, 'Attitudes to the Use of Fire in Executions in Late Antiquity and Early Islam: The Burning of Heretics and Rebels in Late Umayyad Iraq', in Robert Gleave and István Kristó-Nagy (eds), *Violence in Islamic Thought from the Qur'an to the Mongols* (Edinburgh, 2015), 106–27.
Marsham, Andrew, '"God's Caliph" Revisited: Umayyad Political Thought in Its Late Antique Context', in Alain George and Andrew Marsham (eds), *Power, Patronage, and Memory in Early Islam: Perspectives on Umayyad Elites* (Oxford, 2018), 3–37.
Marsham, Andrew, 'Some Observations on Commerce and Covenant in the Qur'an', in George Brook, Adrian H. W. Curtis, Muntasir al-Hamad and G. Rex Smith (eds), *Near Eastern and Arabian Essays: Studies in Honour of John F. Healey* (Oxford, 2018), 303–13.
Marsham, Andrew, 'Bede, Ibn Ishaq, and the Idols: Narratives of Conversion at Late Antique Edges', in Phil Booth and Mary Whitby (eds), *Travaux et Mémoires 26: Mélanges James Howard-Johnston* (Paris, 2022), 315–39.
Marsham, Andrew, 'Kinship, Dynasty, and the Umayyads', in Maaike van Berkel and Letizia Osti (eds), *The Historian of Islam at Work: Essays in Honor of Hugh Kennedy* (Leiden, 2022), 12–45.
Martínez Jiménez, Javier, Isaac Sastre de Diego, and Carlos Tejerizo García, *The Iberian Peninsula Between 300 and 850: An Archaeological Perspective* (Amsterdam, 2018).
Mattingly, D. J., 'The Laguatan: A Libyan Tribal Confederation in the Late Roman Empire', *Libyan Studies* 14 (1983), 96–108.
McCormick, Michael, *Origins of the European Economy: Communications and Commerce, AD 300–900* (Cambridge, 2001).
McEvedy, Colin, and Richard Jones, *Atlas of World Population History* (London, 1978).
McMahon, Lucas, 'The Foederati, the Phoideratoi, and the Symmachoi of the Late Antique East (ca. AD 400–650)', Masters Dissertation, University of Ottawa (2014).
McMillan, Margaret E., *The Meaning of Mecca: The Politics of Pilgrimage in Early Islam* (London, 2011).

Meinecke, Katharina, 'Umayyad Visual Culture and Its Models', in Andrew Marsham (ed.), *The Umayyad World* (London and New York, 2021), 103–32.
Merkel, Stephen W., Jani Oravisjärvi and Jane Kershaw, 'Lead Isotopes Reveal Silver Sources of the Islamic Golden Age', forthcoming.
Millar, Fergus, 'Hagar, Ishmael, Josephus and the Origins of Islam', *Journal of Jewish Studies* 44 (1993), 24–43.
Millar, Fergus, *The Roman Near East, 31 BC–AD 337* (Cambridge, MA and London, 1993).
Millar, Fergus, 'Christian Monasticism in Roman Arabia at the Birth of Mahomet', *Semitica et Classica* 2 (2009), 97–115.
Miller, Nathaniel, 'Seasonal Poetics: The Dry Season and Autumn Rains among Pre-Islamic Nagdi and Higazi Tribes', *Arabica* 64 (2017), 1–27.
Miller, Nathaniel, 'Dear Muʿawiya: An "Epistolary" Poem on a Major Muslim Military Defeat during the Mediterranean Campaigns of AH 28–35/649–56 CE', *Al-Usur al-Wusta* 31 (2023), 45–76.
Mitter, Ulrike, 'Origin and Development of the Islamic Patronate', in Monique Bernards and John Nawas, *Patronate and Patronage in Early and Classical Islam* (Leiden, 2005), 70–133.
Modarres, Reza, and Ali Sarhadi, 'Rainfall Trends Analysis of Iran in the Last Half of the Twentieth Century', *Journal of Geophysical Research: Atmospheres* 114.D3 (2009), 2156–2202.
Modéran, Yves, *Les Maures et l'Afrique romaine (IVe–VIIe siècle)* (Rome, 2003).
Mohammad, Zakaria, 'The Holy Sepulcher and the Garbage Dump: An Etymology', *Jerusalem Quarterly* 50 (2012), 108–12.
Morimoto, Kosei, *The Fiscal Administration of Egypt in the Early Islamic Period* (Kyoto, 1981).
Morimoto, Kosei, 'The Diwans as Registers of the Arab Stipendiaries in Early Islamic Egypt', in Raoul Curiel and Rika Gyselen (eds), *Itinéraires d'Orient: Hommages à Claude Cahen* (Bures-sur-Yvette, 1994), 353–66.
Morony, Michael G., 'Continuity and Change in the Administrative Geography of Late Sasanian and Early Islamic al-ʿIraq', *Iran* 20 (1982), 1–49.
Morony, Michael G., *Iraq after the Muslim Conquest* (Princeton, 1984).
Morony, Michael G., 'Landholding and Social Change: Lower al-Iraq in the Early Islamic Period', in Tarif Khalidi (ed.), *Land Tenure and Social Transformation in the Middle East* (Beirut, 1984), 209–22.
Morony, Michael G., 'Commerce in Early Islamic Iraq', *Asien, Afrika, Lateinamerika: Zeitschrift des Zantralen Rates für Asien- Afrika- und Lateinamerikawissenschaften in der DDR* 20 (1993), 699–720.
Morony, Michael G., 'Magic and Society in Late Sasanian Iraq', in Scott B. Noegel, Joel Walker and Brandon Wheeler (eds), *Prayer, Magic, and the Stars in the Ancient and Late Antique World* (Philadelphia, 2003), 83–107.
Morony, Michael G., 'Economic Boundaries? Late Antiquity and Early Islam', *JESHO* 47 (2004), 166–94.
Morony, Michael G., 'For Whom Does the Writer Write? The First Bubonic Plague Pandemic According to Syriac Sources', in Lester K. Little (ed.), *The Plague and the End of Antiquity: The Pandemic of 541–750* (Cambridge, 2007), 59–86.
Motzki, Harald, 'The Collection of the Qurʾan: A Reconsideration of Western Views in Light of Recent Methodological Developments', *Der Islam* 78 (2001), 1–34.

Mourad, Suleiman A., *Early Islam between Myth and History: Al-Hasan al-Basri (d. 110 H/728 CE) and the Formation of his Legacy in Classical Islamic Scholarship* (Leiden, 2006).
Mulder, Stephennie, *The Shrines of the 'Alids in Medieval Syria: Sunnis, Shi'is and the Architecture of Coexistence* (Edinburgh, 2014).
Munro-Hay, Stuart C., *Aksum: An African Civilisation of Late Antiquity* (Edinburgh, 1991).
Munt, Harry, 'The Official Announcement of an Umayyad Caliph's Successful Pilgrimage to Mecca', in Venetia Porter and Liana Saif (eds), *The Hajj: Collected Essays* (London, 2013), 15–20.
Munt, Harry, *The Holy City of Medina: Sacred Space in Early Islamic Arabia* (Cambridge, 2014).
Munt, Harry, 'Caliphal Estates and Properties around Medina in the Umayyad Period', in Alain Delattre, Marie Legendre, and Petra Sijpesteijn (eds) *Authority and Control in the Countryside: From Antiquity to Islam in the Mediterranean and Near East (6th–10th Century)* (Leiden, 2019), 432–63.
Munt, Harry, 'The Transition from Late Antiquity to Early Islam in Western Arabia', in Andrew Marsham (Ed.), *The Umayyad World* (London and New York, 2021), 357–73.
Munt, Harry, Touraj Daryaee, Omar Edaibat, Robert Hoyland and Isabel Toral-Niehoff, 'Arabic and Persian Sources for Pre-Islamic Arabia', in Greg Fisher (ed.), *Arabs and Empires before Islam* (Oxford, 2015), 434–500.
Neuwirth, Angelika, *The Qur'an and Late Antiquity: A Shared Heritage*, tr. Samuel Wilder (Oxford, 2019).
Newby, Gordon D., *A History of the Jews of Arabia: From Ancient Times to their Eclipse under Islam* (Columbia, SC, 1988).
Noth, Albrecht, and Lawrence I. Conrad, *The Early Arabic Historical Tradition: A Source-critical Study* (Princeton, 1994).
Orthmann, Eva, *Stamm und Macht: die arabischen Stämme im 2. und 3. Jahrhundert der Hiğra* (Wiesbaden, 2002).
Oxford Dictionary of Late Antiquity, ed. Oliver Nicholson (Oxford, 2018).
Palme, Bernhard, 'The Imperial Presence: Government and Army', in Roger S. Bagnall (ed.), *Egypt in the Byzantine World, 300–700* (Cambridge, 2007), 244–70.
Papaconstantinou, Arietta, 'Between *Umma* and *Dhimma*: The Christians of the Middle East under the Umayyads', *Annales Islamologiques* 42 (2008), 127–56.
Papaconstantinou, Arietta, 'Administering the Early Islamic Empire: Insights from the Papyri', in John Haldon (ed.), *Money, Power and Politics in Early Islamic Syria: A Review of Current Debates* (Farnham, 2010), 57–74.
Patterson, Lee E., 'Minority Religions in the Sasanian Empire: Suppression, Integration, and Relations with Rome', in Eberhard W. Sauer (ed.), *Sasanian Persia: Between Rome and the Steppes of Eurasia* (Edinburgh, 2017), 181–98.
Payne, Richard E., 'East Syrian Bishops, Elite Households, and Iranian Law after the Muslim Conquest', *Iranian Studies* 48 (2015), 5–32.
Payne, Richard E., *A State of Mixture: Christians, Zoroastrians, and Iranian Political Culture in Late Antiquity* (Oakland, CA, 2016).
Payne, Richard E., 'The Silk Road and the Iranian Political Economy in Late Antiquity: Iran, the Silk Road, and the Problem of Aristocratic Empire', *BSOAS* 81 (2018), 227–50.

Pellat, Charles, *Le Milieu basrien et la formation de Jahiz* (Paris, 1953).
Penn, Michael Philip, 'Monks, Manuscripts, and Muslims: Syriac Textual Changes in Reaction to the Rise of Islam', *Hugoye: Journal of Syriac Studies* 12 (2009), 235–57.
Petrie, Cameron, *Resistance at the Edge of Empires: The Archaeology and History of the Bannu Basin (Pakistan) from 1000 BC to AD 1200* (Oxford, 2017).
Pierre, Simon, 'Le rôle de tribus arabes chrétiennes dans l'intégration de l'Orient à l'Église syro-orthodoxe de la mort de Sévère (v. 683–684) à la crise entre Denha II et Julien II (r. 687–709)', *Mélanges de l'École française de Rome: Moyen-Âge* 132 (2020), 255–71.
Pierre, Simon, 'Le stylite (*estunoro*) et sa *sawma'a* face aux milieux cléricaux islamiques et miaphysites (Ier–IIe/VIIe–VIIIe siècles)', *Al-'Usur al-Wusta* 28 (2020), 174–226.
Pierre, Simon, 'Can We Flee the Plague? A Theological, Moral and Practical Issue in the Early Islamicate World', *Journal of Islamic Ethics* 5 (2021), 1–16.
Piotrovsky, Mikhaïl B., 'Late Ancient and Early Mediaeval Yemen: Settlement Traditions and Innovations', in G. R. D. King and Averil Cameron (eds), *The Byzantine and Early Islamic Near East II: Land Use and Settlement Patterns* (Princeton, 1994), 213–20.
Piotrovsky, Mikhaïl B., 'Les causes d'une disparation', in Vogt Burkhard and Christian Robin (eds), *Yémen: au pays de la reine de Saba': exposition présentée à l'Institut du monde arabe du 25 octobre 1997 au 28 février 1998* (Paris, 1997), 218–19.
Popovic, Alexandre, *La Révolte des esclaves en Iraq au IIIe, IXe siècle* (Paris, 1976).
Potts, Daniel T., 'Trans-Arabian Routes of the Pre-Islamic Period', in F. E. Peters (ed.), *The Arabs and Arabia on the Eve of Islam* (Aldershot, 1999), 45–80.
Pourshariati, Parvaneh, 'Local Histories of Khurasan and the Pattern of Arab Settlement', *Studia Iranica* 27 (1998), 41–81.
Pringle, Denys, *The Defence of Byzantine Africa from Justinian to the Arab Conquest: An Account of the Military History and Archaeology of the African Provinces in the Sixth and Seventh Centuries* (Oxford, 1981).
Prosopographie der mittelbyzantinischen Zeit Online, eds Ralph-Johannes Lilie, Claudia Ludwig, Beate Zielke and Thomas Pratsch (Berlin, 2013), <https://doi.org/10.1515/pmbz> (last accessed 28 June 2023).
al-Qadi, Wadad, 'Islamic State Letters: The Question of Authenticity', in Averil Cameron and Lawrence I. Conrad (eds), *The Byzantine and Early Islamic Near East I: Problems in the Literary Source Material* (Princeton, 1992), 215–76.
al-Qadi, Wadad, 'The Earliest "Nabita" and the Paradigmatic "Nawabit"', *Studia Islamica* 78 (1993), 27–61.
al-Qadi, Wadad, 'The Religious Foundation of Late Umayyad Ideology and Practice', in Manuela Marín and Mercedes García-Arendal (eds), *Saber religioso y poder político en el Islam: Actas del Simposio Internacional…1991* (Madrid, 1994), 231–73.
al-Qadi, Wadad, 'Population Census and Land Surveys under the Umayyads (41–132/661–750)', *Der Islam* 83 (2008), 341–416.
al-Qadi, Wadad, 'Non-Muslims in the Muslim Conquest Army in Early Islam', in Antoine Borrut and Fred M. Donner (eds), *Christians and Others in the Umayyad State* (Chicago, 2016), 83–128.
Quinn, William H., 'A Study of Southern Oscillation-related Climatic Activity for AD 622–1900 Incorporating Nile River Flood Data', in Henry F. Diaz and Vera

Markgraf (eds), *El Niño: Historical and Paleoclimatic Aspects of the Southern Oscillation* (Cambridge, 1992), 119–49.
Qutbuddin, Tahera, '*Khutba*: The Evolution of Early Arabic Oration', in B. Gruendler and M. Cooperson (eds), *Classical Arabic Humanities in Their Own Terms: Festschrift for Wolfhart Heinrichs* (Leiden, 2008), 176–273.
Qutbuddin, Tahera, *Arabic Oration: Art and Function* (Leiden, 2019).
Ragib, Yusuf, 'Une ère inconnue d'Égypte musulmane: l'ère de la juridiction des croyants', *Annales islamologiques: Hawliyat Islamiyah* 41 (2007), 187–207.
Rapp, Claudia, 'Georgian Christianity', in Ken Parry (ed.), *The Blackwell Companion to Eastern Christianity* (Oxford, 2007), 137–55.
Rapp, Claudia, 'Hellenic Identity, *Romanitas*, and Christianity in Byzantium', in Katerina Zacharia (ed.), *Hellenisms: Culture, Identity, and Ethnicity from Antiquity to Modernity* (Farnham, 2008), 127–47.
Rashid, Arssan Mussa, 'The Role of the *Shurta* in Early Islam', PhD Dissertation, University of Edinburgh (1983).
Rautman, Marcus, 'The Busy Countryside of Late Roman Cyprus', *Report of the Department of Antiquities, Cyprus* (2000), 323–8.
Al-Rawas, Isam, *Oman in Early Islamic History* (Reading, 2000).
Reinfandt, Lucian, 'Judicial Practice in Umayyad Egypt (661–750 AD). 'Version 01 | Imperium and Officium Working Papers (IOWP)' (2013), <http://iowp.univie.ac.at/?q=node/259> (last accessed 10 March 2015).
Retsø, Jan, 'The Road to Yarmuk: The Arabs and the Fall of Roman Power in the Middle East', in L. Rydén and J. O. Rosenqvist (eds), *Aspects of Late Antiquity and Early Byzantium* (Istanbul, 1993), 31–41.
Reynolds, Daniel, 'Rethinking Palestinian Iconoclasm', *DOP* 71 (2017), 1–64.
Robin, Christian, 'Le royaume hujride, dit «royaume de Kinda», entre Himyar et Byzance', *Comptes-rendus des séances de l'Académie des Inscriptions et Belles-Lettres* 140 (1996), 665–714.
Robin, Christian, 'Himyar et Israël', *Comptes-rendus des séances de l'Académie des Inscriptions et Belles-Lettres* 148 (2004), 831–908.
Robin, Christian, 'Himyar, Aksum, and *Arabia Deserta* in Late Antiquity: The Epigraphic Evidence', in Greg Fisher (ed.), *Arabs and Empires before Islam* (Oxford, 2015), 127–71.
Robinson, Chase F., *Empire and Elites after the Muslim Conquest: The Transformation of Northern Mesopotamia* (Cambridge, 2000).
Robinson, Chase F., 'The Conquest of Khuzistan: A Historiographical Reassessment', *BSOAS* 67 (2004), 14–39.
Robinson, Chase F., *'Abd al-Malik* (Oxford, 2005).
Robinson, Chase F., 'Neck-sealing in Early Islam', *JESHO* 48 (2005), 402–36.
Robinson, Chase F., 'The Violence of the Abbasid Revolution', in Yasir Suleiman and Adel Al-Abdul Jader (eds), *Living Islamic History: Studies in Honour of Professor Carole Hillenbrand* (Edinburgh, 2010), 226–51.
Robinson, Chase F., 'Slavery in the Conquest Period', *IJMES* 49 (2017), 158–63.
Robinson, Majied, *Marriage in the Tribe of Muhammad: A Statistical Study of Early Arabic Genealogical Literature* (Berlin and Boston, 2019).
Robinson, Majied, 'Qurashi Marriage and the Roots of Revolt: the Rebellion of 'Abd Allah b. Mu'awiya, 744–747', in Andrew Marsham (ed.), *The Umayyad World* (London and New York, 2021), 518–38.

Robinson, Majied, 'The Population Size of Muhammad's Mecca and the Creation of the Quraysh', *Der Islam* 99 (2022), 10–37.
Rosen-Ayalon, Myriam, *The Early Islamic Monuments of al-Haram al-Sharif: An Iconographic Study* (Jerusalem, 1989).
Rubin, Aaron, *A Brief Introduction to Semitic Languages* (Piscataway, NJ, 2010).
Rubin, Uri, *Between Bible and Qur'an: The Children of Israel and the Islamic Self-image* (Princeton, 1999).
Ruffini, Giovanni R., *Medieval Nubia: A Social and Economic History* (Oxford, 2012).
Safar, Fu'ad, *Wasit: The Sixth Season's Excavations* (Cairo, 1945).
Sahas, Daniel J., *John of Damascus on Islam: The "Heresy of the Ishmaelites"* (Leiden, 1972).
Sahner, Christian, 'The First Iconoclasm in Islam: A New History of the Edict of Yazid II (AH 104/ AD 723)', *Der Islam* 94 (2017), 5–56.
Sahner, Christian, *Christian Martyrs under Islam: Religious Violence and the Making of the Muslim World* (Princeton, 2018).
Sahner, Christian, 'Martyrdom and Conversion', in Douglas Pratt and Charles L. Tieszen, *Christian–Muslim Relations: A Bibliographical History. Volume 15, A Thematic History (600–1600)* (Leiden, 2020), 389–412.
Said, Rushdi, *The River Nile: Geology, Hydrology and Utilization* (Oxford, 1993).
Santi, Aila, 'Earlt Islamic Kufa in Context: A Chronological Reinterpretation of the Palace, with a Note on the Development of the Monumental Language of the Early Muslim Elite', *Annali Sezione Orientale* 78 (2018), 69–103.
Santi, Aila, '"Anjar in the Shadow of the Church? New Insights on an Umayyad Urban Experiment in the Biqa' Valley', *Levant* 50 (2019), 1–14.
Sarris, Peter, *Empires of Faith: The Fall of Rome to the Rise of Islam* (Oxford, 2011).
Sarris, Peter, 'Viewpoint: New Approaches to the "Plague of Justinian"', *Past & Present* 254 (2022), 315–46.
Sauer, Eberhard, Konstantin Pitskhelauri, Kristen Hopper, Anthi Tiliakou, Catriona Pickard, Dan Lawrence, Annamaria Diana, Elena Kranioti and Cathering Shupe, 'Northern Outpost of the Caliphate: Maintaining Military Forces in a Hostile Environment (the Dariali Gorge in the Central Caucasus in Georgia)', *Antiquity* 89 (2015), 885–904.
Savage, Emily, 'Berbers and Blacks: Ibadi Slave Traffic in Eighth-century North Africa', *The Journal of African History* 33 (1992), 351–68.
Sayed, Redwan, *Die Revolte des Ibn al-Aš'at und die Koranleser: Ein Beitrag zur Religions- und Sozialgeschichte der frühen Umayyadenzeit* (Freiburg, 1977).
Scanlon, George, 'Al-Fustat: The Riddle of the Earliest Settlement', in G. R. D. King and Averil Cameron (eds), *The Byzantine and Early Islamic Near East II: Land Use and Settlement Patterns* (Princeton, 1994), 171–80.
Schlumberger, Daniel, *Qasr el-Heir el-Gharbi* (Paris, 1986).
Schoeler, Gregor, 'Oral Torah and *Hadit*: Transmission, Prohibition of Writing, Redaction', in Gregor Schoeler, *The Oral and the Writtten in Early Islam*, tr. Uwe Vagelpohl, ed. James E. Montgomery (London and New York, 2006), 111–41.
Schoeler, Gregor, *The Oral and the Writtten in Early Islam*, tr. Uwe Vagelpohl, ed. James E. Montgomery (London and New York, 2006).
Sears, Stuart D., 'The Revolt of al-Harith b. Surayj and the Countermarking of Umayyad Dirhams in Early Eighth Century CE Khurasan', in Paul M. Cobb (ed.),

The Lineaments of Islam: Studies in Honor of Fred McGraw Donner (Leiden, 2012), 379–405.
Sells, Michael, 'The *Muʿallaqa* of Tarafa', *Journal of Arabic Literature* 17 (1986), 21–33.
Sen Nag, Oshimaya et al. (eds), *WorldAtlas*, <https://www.worldatlas.com/> (last accessed 22 August 2022).
Shaddel, Mehdy, 'Periodisation and the *futuh*: Making Sense of Muhammad's Leadership of the Conquests in Non-Muslim Sources', *Arabica* 69 (2022), 96–145.
Shahid, Irfan, *Byzantium and the Arabs in the Fourth Century* (Washington, DC, 1984).
Shahid, Irfan, *Byzantium and the Arabs in the Sixth Century* (Washington, DC, 1995).
Shanahan, Timothy Michael, 'West African Monsoon Variability from a High-resolution Paleolimnological Record (Lake Bosumtwi, Ghana)', PhD Dissertation, University of Arizona (2006).
Sharon, Moshe, *Revolt: The Social and Military Aspects of the ʿAbbasid Revolution* (Jerusalem, 1990).
Shaw, Brent, 'Water and Society in the Ancient Maghrib: Technology, Property and Development', *Antiquités africaines* 20 (1984), 121–73.
Shoemaker, Stephen J., '"The Reign of God Has Come": Eschatology and Empire in Late Antiquity and Early Islam', *Arabica* 61 (2014), 514–58.
Shoemaker, Stephen J., *Creating the Qurʾan: A Historical–Critical Study* (Oakland, 2022).
Sijpesteijn, Petra, 'The Arab Conquest of Egypt and the Beginning of Muslim Rule', in Roger S. Bagnall (ed.), *Egypt in the Byzantine World, 300–700* (Cambridge, 2007), 437–55.
Sijpesteijn, Petra, *Shaping a Muslim State: The World of a Mid-Eighth-Century Egyptian Official* (Oxford, 2013).
Silverstein, Adam J., *Postal Systems in the Pre-modern Islamic World* (Cambridge, 2007).
Silverstein, Adam J., 'Q 30: 2–5 in Near Eastern Context', *Der Islam* 97 (2020), 11–42.
Sims-Williams, Nicolas, *Bactrian Documents from Northern Afghanistan* (London, 2012).
Sinai, Nicolai, 'When Did the Consonantal Skeleton of the Quran Reach Closure?', *BSOAS* 77 (2014), 273–92, 509–21.
Sinai, Nicolai, *Rain-giver, Bone-breaker, Score-settler: Allah in Pre-Quranic Poetry* (New Haven, 2019).
Skaff, Jonathan Karam, 'Sasanian and Arab-Sasanian Silver Coins from Turfan: Their Relationship to International Trade and the Local Economy', *Asia Major* 11 (1998), 67–115.
Smith, G. Rex, 'The Early and Medieval History of Sanʿaʾ ca. 622–1382/1515', in R. B. Serjeant and Ronald B. Lewcock (eds), *Sanʿaʾ: An Arabian Islamic City* (London, 1983), 49–67.
Smith, G. Rex, 'The Political History of the Islamic Yemen down to the First Turkish Invasion (1–945/622–1538)', in Werner Daum, *Yemen: 3000 Years of Art and Civilisation in Arabia Felix* (Innsbruck, 1987), 129–39.
Sneath, David, *The Headless State: Aristocratic Orders, Kinship Society, and Misrepresentations of Nomadic Inner Asia* (New York, 2007).

Spellberg, D. A., 'The Umayyad North: Numismatic Evidence for Frontier Administration', *American Numismatic Society Museum Notes* 33 (1988), 119–27.

Sprengling, M., 'From Persian to Arabic', *The American Journal of Semitic Languages and Literatures* 56–7 (1939–40), 175–224.

Spuler, Bertold, *Iran in the Early Islamic Period: Politics, Culture, Administration and Public Life between the Arab and the Seljuk Conquests, 633–1055*, ed. Robert G. Hoyland, tr. Gwendolin Goldbloom and Berenike Walburg (Leiden, 2015).

Stetkevych, Suzanne Pinckney, 'Umayyad Panegyric and the Poetics of Islamic Hegemony: Al-Akhtal's *Khaffa al-Qatinu* ("Those that dwelt with you have left in haste")', *Journal of Arabic Literature* 28 (1997), 89–122.

Stevens, Susan T., 'Carthage in Transition', in Susan T. Stevens and Jonathan P. Conant (eds), *North Africa under Byzantium and Early Islam* (Washington, DC, 2016), 89–104.

Stevens, Susan T. and Jonathan P. Conant, 'Introduction', in Susan T. Stevens and Jonathan P. Conant (eds), *North Africa under Byzantium and Early Islam* (Washington, DC, 2016), 1–9.

Stroumsa, Guy, *The End of Sacrifice: Religious Transformations in Late Antiquity* (Chicago, 2012).

Stroumsa, Guy, *The Making of the Abrahamic Religions in Late Antiquity* (Oxford, 2015).

Stroumsa, Rachel, 'Greek and Arabic in Nessana', in Alexander Schubert and Petra Sijpesteijn (eds), *Documents and the History of the Early Islamic World* (Leiden, 2014), 143–57.

Su, I-Wen, 'Writing History under the Patronage: The Representation of Sulayman b. 'Abd al-Malik in the *Ansab al-ashraf* and Its Relation to the 'Abbasid Court Culture', *Foreign Language Studies* 24 (2016), 1–25.

Su, I-Wen, 'The Early Shi'i Kufan Traditionists' Perspective on the Rightly Guided Caliphs', *JAOS* 141 (2021), 27–47.

Talbi, Mohamed, 'Law and Economy in Ifriqiya (Tunisia) in the Third Islamic Century: Agriculture and the Role of Slaves in the Country's Economy', in Abraham L. Udovitch (ed.), *The Islamic Middle East, 700–1900: Studies in Economic and Social History* (Princeton, 1981), 209–49.

Tannous, Jack, 'You Are What You Read: Qenneshre and the Miaphysite Church in the Seventh Century', in Philip Wood (ed.), *History and Identity in the Late Antique Near East, 500–1000* (Oxford, 2013), 83–102.

Tannous, Jack, *The Making of the Medieval Middle East: Religion, Society, and Simple Believers* (Princeton, 2018).

Tannous, Jack, 'Arabic as a Christian Language and Arabic as a Language of Christians', in A. S. Ibrahim (ed.), *Medieval Encounters: Arabic-speaking Christians and Islam* (Piscataway, NJ, 2022), 1–93.

Tesei, Tommaso, 'Heraclius' War Propaganda and the Qur'an's Promise of Reward for Dying in Battle', *Studia Islamica* 114 (2019), 219–47.

Tillier, Mathieu, *Les cadis d'Iraq et l'état abbasside, 132/750–334/945* (Damascus, 2009).

Tillier, Mathieu, *L'Invention du cadi: la justice des musulmans, des juifs et des chrétiens aux premiers siècles de l'Islam* (Paris, 2017).

Tillier Mathieu and Naïm Vanthieghem, 'Recording Debts in Sufyanid Fustat: A Reexamination of the Procedures and Calendar in Use in the First/Seventh

Century', in John Tolan (Ed.), *Geneses: A Comparative Study of the Historiographies of the Rise of Christianity, Rabbinic Judaism and Islam* (London and New York, 2019), 148–88.
Tomber, Roberta, *Indo-Roman Trade: From Pots to Pepper* (London, 2008).
Toral-Niehoff, Isabel, 'Late Antique Iran and the Arabs: The Case of al-Hira', *Journal of Persianate Studies* 6 (2013), 115–26.
Treadwell, Luke, "Abd al-Malik's Coinage Reform: The Role of the Damascus Mint', *Revue numismatique* 165 (2009), 357–81.
Tunio, Rahmat, 'It Seems This Heat Will Take Our Lives', *The Guardian*, 25 May 2022, <https://www.theguardian.com/environment/2022/may/25/it-seems-this-heat-will-take-our-lives-pakistan-city-fearful-jacobabad-after-hitting-51c> (last accessed 27 May 2022).
Ulrich, Brian, *Arabs in the Early Islamic Empire: Exploring al-Azd Tribal Identity* (Edinburgh, 2019).
Vacca, Alison, *Non-Muslim Provinces under Early Islam: Islamic Rule and Iranian Legitimacy in Armenia and Caucasian Albania* (Cambridge, 2017).
Vacca, Alison, 'The Umayyad North (Or: How Umayyad was the Umayyad Caliphate?)', in Andrew Marsham (ed.), *The Umayyad World* (London and New York, 2021), 219–39.
van Bladel, Kevin, 'The Bactrian Background of the Barmakids', in Anna Akasoy, Charles Burnett and Ronit Yoeli-Tlalim (eds), *Islam and Tibet: Interactions along the Musk Routes* (Farnham, 2011), 43–88.
van Bladel, Kevin, *From Sasanian Mandaeans to Sabians of the Marshes* (Leiden, 2017).
van Ess, Josef, *Theology and Society in the Second and Third Centuries of the Hijra: A History of Religious Thought in Early Islam*, tr. John O'Kane and Gwendolin Goldbloom (Leiden, 2017–20).
van Putten, Marijn, '"The Grace of God" as Evidence for a Written Uthmanic Archetype: The Importance of Shared Orthographic Idiosyncrasies', *BSOAS* 82 (2019), 271–88.
Verkinderen, Peter, *Waterways of Iraq and Iran in the Early Islamic Period: Changing Rivers and Landscapes of the Mesopotamian Plain* (London, 2015).
von Rummel, Philipp, 'The Transformation of Ancient Land- and Cityscapes in Early Medieval North Africa', in Susan T. Stevens and Jonathan P. Conant (eds), *North Africa under Byzantium and Early Islam* (Washington, DC, 2016), 105–17.
Walker, John, *A Catalogue of the Arab-Sassanian Coins (Umaiyad Governors in the East, Arab-Ephthalites, 'Abbasid Governors in Tabaristan and Bukhara)* (London, 1941).
Walker, John, *A Catalogue of the Arab-Byzantine and Post-reform Umaiyad Coins* (London, 1956).
Walmsley, Alan, *Early Islamic Syria: An Archaeological Assessment* (London, 2007).
Walmsley, Alan, 'Coinage and the Economy of Syria-Palestine in the Seventh and Eighth Centuries CE', in John Haldon (ed.), *Money, Power and Politics in Early Islamic Syria: A Review of Current Debates* (Farnham, 2010), 21–44.
Wander, Steven H., 'The Cyprus Plates and the "Chronicle" of Fredegar', *DOP* 29 (1975), 345–6.
Ward, Walter D., *Mirage of the Saracen: Christians and Nomads in the Sinai Peninsula in Late Antiquity* (Berkeley, 2014).

Ward-Perkins, Bryan, 'Specialized Production and Exchange', *CAH*, XIV, 346–91.
Watson, Andrew, *Agricultural Innovation in the Early Islamic World: The Diffusion of Crops and Farming Techniques, 700–1100* (Cambridge, 1983).
Watt, John W., 'The Portrayal of Heraclius in Syriac Historical Sources', in B. H. Stolte (ed.) *The Reign of Heraclius (610–641): Crisis and Confrontation* (Leuven, Paris and Dudley, MA, 2002), 63–79.
Watt, W. Montgomery, *Muhammad at Mecca* (Oxford, 1953).
Watt, W. Montgomery, *Muhammad at Medina* (Oxford, 1956).
Webb, Peter, *Imagining the Arabs: Arab Identity and the Rise of Islam* (Edinburgh, 2016).
Webb, Peter, 'Ethnicity, Power and Umayyad Society: The Rise and Fall of the People of Ma'add', in Andrew Marsham (ed.), *The Umayyad World* (London and New York, 2021), 65–102.
Wellhausen, Julius, *The Arab Kingdom and Its Fall*, tr. M. G. Weir (Calcutta, 1927).
Welsby, Derek A., *The Medieval Kingdoms of Nubia: Pagans, Christians and Muslims on the Middle Nile* (London, 2002).
Weststeijn, Johan, 'Wine and Impurity in the Sura of the Bees: A Structuralist Interpretation of Qur'an 16:67', in Josephine van den Bent, Floris van den Eijnde and Johan Weststeijn (eds), *Late Antique Responses to the Arab Conquests* (Leiden, 2021), 56–73.
Whitcomb, Donald, 'The City of Istakhr and the Marvdasht Plain', *Archaeologische Mitteilungen aus Iran* 6 (1979), 363–70.
Whitcomb, Donald, '*Amsar* in Syria? Syrian Cities after the Conquest', *ARAM* 6 (1994), 13–33.
Whitcomb, Donald, 'The *Misr* of Ayla: Settlement at al-'Aqaba in the Early Islamic Period', in G. R. D. King and Averil Cameron (eds), *The Byzantine and Early Islamic Near East II: Land Use and Settlement Patterns* (Princeton, 1994), 155–79.
Whitcomb, Donald, 'An Urban Structure for the Early Islamic City: An Archaeological Hypothesis', in Amira K. Bennison and Alison L. Gascoigne (eds), *Cities in the Pre-modern Islamic World: The Urban Impact of Religion, State, and Society* (London and New York, 2007), 15–26.
Whitcomb, Donald, 'Notes for an Archaeology of Mu'awiya: Material Culture in the Transitional Period of Believers', in Antoine Borrut and Fred M. Donner (eds), *Christians and Others in the Umayyad State* (Chicago, 2016), 11–28.
Whittow, Mark, *The Making of Orthodox Byzantium, 600–1025* (London, 1996).
Wilfong, Terry G., 'The Non-Muslim Communities: Christian Communities', in Carl F. Petry (ed.), *The Cambridge History of Egypt Volume 1: Islamic Egypt, 640–1517* (Cambridge, 1998), 175–97.
Wilkinson, John, *Jerusalem Pilgrims before the Crusades* (Warminster, 2002).
Wilkinson, John C., *Ibadism: Origins and Development in Oman* (Oxford, 2010).
Wink, André, *Al-Hind, the Making of the Indo-Islamic World* (Leiden, 1991).
Winkler, Dietmar, *The Church of the East: A Concise History* (London, 2003).
Wood, Philip, *The Chronicle of Seert: Christian Historical Imagination in Late Antique Iraq* (Oxford, 2013).
Wood, Philip, 'Christians in Umayyad Iraq: Decentralization and Expansion', in Alain George and Andrew Marsham (eds), *Power, Patronage, and Memory in Early Islam: Perspectives on Umayyad Elites* (Oxford, 2018), 255–74.

Wüstenfeld, Heinrich Ferdinand, *Genealogische Tabellen der arabischen Stämme und Familien. In zwei Abtheilungen.* (Göttingen, 1852–3).
Yarbrough, Luke, 'Did 'Umar b. 'Abd al-'Aziz Issue an Edict Concerning Non-Muslim Officials?', in Antoine Borrut and Fred M. Donner (eds), *Christians and Others in the Umayyad State* (Chicago, 2016), 173–206.
Zellentin, Holger, *The Qur'an's Reformation of Judaism and Christianity: Return to the Origins* (London and New York, 2019).
Zellentin, Holger, *Law beyond Israel: From the Bible to the Qur'an* (Oxford, 2022).
Zuckerman, Constantin, 'Heraclius and the Return of the Holy Cross', in Constantin Zuckerman (ed.), *Travaux et Mémoires 17: Constructing the Seventh Century* (Paris, 2013), 197–218.
Zuckerman, Constantine, 'Silk "Made in Byzantium": A Study of Economic Policies of Emperor Justinian', *Travaux et Mémoires 17: Constructing the Seventh Century* (2013), 323–50.
Zychowicz-Coghill, Edward, *The First Arabic Annals: Fragments of Umayyad History* (Berlin and Boston, 2021).

Index

Note: italic indicates illustration, n indicates notes, m indicates maps, c indicates charts

Aban b. Muʿawiya, 207
Aban b. ʿUthman, 147
ʿAbbas, Banu *see* Abbasids
al-ʿAbbas b. al-Walid, 156, 171–2, 199
Abbasid Revolution, 24–5, 105, 203–6, 294
Abbasids, 6c, 206–7, 245
  Abu Hashim, 108
  Abu Jaʿfar b. Muhammad al-Mansur, 202, 206, 328–9
  administration 292, 328–9
  Arabic historical tradition, 18, 20
  army, 292
  Hashim, Banu, 119, 149
  Hebrew texts, 276
  Khurramism, 291–2
  Kufa, 328–9
  Muhammad, Prophet, 330
  Sunni Islam, 7–8
ʿAbd al-ʿAziz b. al-Hajjaj, 198
ʿAbd al-ʿAziz b. Marwan, 16c, 83, 109c, 110, 112, 120c, 130, 149, 150, 151
  Athanasius bar Gumoye, 252–3
  building projects, 231
  caliphal succession, 110, 150
  Christianity, 271–3
  Kalbi relatives, 130, 166
  mother, 83, 87c, 109c, 110, 122, 130, 166
  North African governors, 158, 325
  Qaysi tribes, 194
  taxation and tribute, 322
ʿAbd al-ʿAziz b. al-Walid, 120c, 152, 156–7, 161

ʿAbd al-Hamid b. Yahya, 312, 328
ʿAbd Allah b. Abi Hashim/ʿAsim, 94–95
ʿAbd Allah b. Abi Sarh, 254
ʿAbd Allah b. ʿAli, 202, 206
ʿAbd Allah b. ʿAmir b. Kurayz, 83, 85, 88, 148, 229
ʿAbd Allah b. Jabir, 73–5
ʿAbd Allah b. Saʿd, 82, 88, 251
ʿAbd Allah b. ʿUmar b. ʿAbd al-ʿAziz, 200, 201, 202
ʿAbd Allah b. Yahya, 201
ʿAbd Allah b. al-Zubayr *see* Ibn al-Zubayr
ʿAbd al-Malik b. Marwan 15–16, 16m, 110–50, *129*, 162
  administration, 295, 309–12, *309*
  Christianity, 144–6, 270–2
  coinage, 128–9, *129*, 138–42, *140*, 250, 324–5
  Dome of the Rock, Jerusalem, 138, 142, *143–5*, 144–6
  dynastic succession, 119, 120c, 121–2, 150
  governors, 83, 110, 114, 123, 129–30, 131–2, 134–5, 147–8
  hajj, 145–7, 179
  Ibn al-Zubayr, 110–14
  Iraq, 123, 131–4, 323
  Islam, 138–50, 267, 271, 275, 295
  itinerant monarchy, 242–3
  Medinan scholars, 148–50
  milestone, *309*
  poetry, 128–9
  Qurʾan, 19, 86
  Roman Empire, 127–31, 162

360

Sarjun b. Mansur al-Rumi, 273, 311
succession, 110, 119, 120c, 150
taxation, 234–5, 251, 270–1
Wasit, 123, 137
weights, measures and scales, 316
'Abd al-Malik b. Muhammad b. al-Hajjaj, 311
'Abd Shams, 56, 66–7, 82, 83–4, 98, 109c, 295
Abraha, 51
Abraham, 57, 146, 268
al-Abrash, Abu Mujashi' Said b. Al-Walid al-Kalbi, 311
'Abs, Banu, 150, 151, 192, 194, 196, 198, 311
Abu l-'Abbas b. Muhammad, 205–6
Abu l-'As b. Umayya, 82, 108, 109c, 110
Abu Bakr, 7, 58–9, 67, 68, 154
  markets, 315
  Qur'an, 86
  Zubayrids, 80, 90, 104, 119, 149
Abu Hanifa, 185, 329
Abu Hashim, 108
Abu 'Isa al-Isfahani, 282
Abu Ja'far b. Muhammad al-Mansur, 202, 206, 328–9
Abu l-Khattar al-Kalbi, 246
Abu l-Muhajir, 100
Abu Muhammad, 206–7
Abu Musa al-Ash'ari, 69, 70, 88, 89
Abu Muslim al-Khurasani, 203–5, 292
Abu Shakir b. Hisham, 192
Abu Sufyan b. Harb, 16c, 29–30, 56–8, 66, 67, 82, 109c
Abu 'Ubayda b. al-Jarrah, 67, 69, 329
Abu l-Ward al-Kilabi, 206
administration, 211–12, 294–327
  'Abbasid, 292
  amṣār (sing. *miṣr*), 225, 228, 296–305
  Arabians, 235, 274
  Arabic language, 274, 311, 312
  Muslims in, 155, 235, 273, 274
  non-Arabians in, 12, 168, 274, 292, 295, 310
  non-Muslims in, 121, 259, 275, 292, 295, 310
  sources, 21, 72–5, 296, 311, 312
  see also law and order; scribes; taxation

administrative geography, 296–305
Afghanistan, 84, 99, 124, 135, 159, 216–17, 219, 289, 305 *see also* Helmand; Sistan; Zabulistan
Africa Proconsularis, 124, 304m *see also* Ifriqiya; North Africa
agriculture, 105, 133, 221–2, 237, 239, 245–6, 307, 317
al-Ahwaz, 69, 91, 133, 136, 296–7, 304
'A'isha bt. Abi Bakr, 81c, 90, 103, 107, 147, 149
al-Akhtal, 128–9, 267
Akroinon, 187, 267, 275
Aksum, 46, 49, 51, 56, 60, 61, 84, 259, 261, 264, 266, 272
al-'Ala' b. al-Hadrami, 66–7
Albania, Caucasian 96, 259, 285, 302, 302m
alcohol *see* wine
Aleppo (Lat. Beroea), 122, 207, 232
Alexandria, 54, 74, 121, 297, 299m
  Judaism, 276
  patriarchs, 261, 271–3
  shipyards, 84, 122, 223–4, 254, 319
  Theodore, 321
  tribal groups, 76–7
  'Uthman, 89, 91
'Ali b. Abi Talib, 5–8, 6c, 15, 80, 81c, 89–93, 101–8, 131, 154, 185, 202, 296–7
'Ali b. al-Husayn, Zayn al-'Abidin, 150
'Alids, 106, 111, 148, 182–8, 271
Amaseia, 152
'Amir b. Dubara, 204
'Amir b. Sharahil al-Sha'bi, 185
*amīr*s, 305–9, 312, 314, 316, 317, 320, 327
'Amman (Gk, Philadelphia), 199, 232, 236m, 239, 244, 300m
'Amr b. al-'As al-Sahmi, 69–70, 82, 90–1, 98–9, 159, 161, 230, 245, 321
'Amr b. Sa'id al Ashdaq *see* al-Ashdaq
'Amru, king of the Lakhmids', 43
Ananias of Shirak, 253
Anastasius of Sinai, 265–6
  Tales of the Sinai Fathers, 268
Anatolia, 54, 129, 145, 152, 155, 158, 164, 171–3, 198
  climate and ecology, 214
  geography and resources, 216, 222, 224

Anatolia (cont.)
  Hisham b. 'Abd al-Malik, 125, 176–9, 186–7, 192, 245
  Qaysi tribe, 122, 150
  see also Asia Minor
al-Anbar, 28m, 232, 235, 297m
al-Andalus, 173, 174, 181, 187, 214, 220–1, 233, 307, 325–6 see also Spain
animal sacrifice, 63
animals, 37, 63, 222–3, *238*
  buffaloes, 161
  camels 37, 223, 322
  cattle 223, 243, 271
  dogs, 223
  elephants, 161
  goats 223, 243
  horses, 34, 74, 91, 112, 222, 223, 224, 253, 308n
  sheep, 37, *39*, *73*, 74, 75, 156, 223, 243
  wild animals, 223, *238*
'Anjar, 200, 228, 235, 236m
'Ans, 195
Ansar, 58, 67, 71, 86–9, 93, 98, 100, 330
Anthony, Sean, 149
Antioch, 38m, 97, 121, 230, 242, 261, 271–2
apocalypse, 54–5, 55, 121, 163, 186, 330
  Jewish, 276–7
  Mandaean, 283
  al-Mukhtar, 105
  Qahtan, 136–7
  Sufyani, 206
  Zoroastrian, 279
al-'Aqaba/Ayla, 38m, 228, 232, 236m, 299m
al-'Aqr, 172
'Arabians', 12–13
Arabian Peninsula, 10–11, 31–53, 36m, 79m, 298–301
  climate and ecology, 214
  geography and ecology, 35–40
  Ibn al-Zubayr, 104
  migration to Iraq, 184
  mining, 224
  Najadat 'Kharijites', 133
Arabic language, 86, 137–8, 196, 295, 308–9, *309*, *313*
  in administration, 307–9, *309*, 311, 312, *313*, 327, 328

administrative papyri, 72–5, *73*, *313*
coinage, 128, *129*, 137, *140*, 141
*dīwān*s, 311
Ibn al-Muqaffa', 328
inscriptions, 42, 48, 94–5, *309*, 325
'Old Arabic', 41, 42
sources, 18–21, 24, 63, 97, 221, 253–4, 289, 302
Syrian pastoralists, 260, 267, 283–4, 298, 310
weights, measures and scales, 316
Arabs, 12–13, 22, 40–4, 162, 168, 170, 175, 188, 196, 265, 268, 283
Aramaeans, 202
Aramaic language, 260, 277–8, 283, 320
Ard Babil, 297m
Ard Jukha, 296, 297m
Ard Kaskar, 296, 297m
aristocratic estates *see* 'desert castles'
Armenia, 112, 131, 150, 296, 301–4
  Abbasids, 206–7
  Bagratunids, 186, 285–6
  Christianity, 84, 259–61, 275, 285–6
  chronicles, 21, 268
  Heraclius, 54
  language, 178, 260–1, 302
  Mamikoneans, 186, 285–6
  mountains, 216
  Mu'awiya b. Abi Sufyan, 83–4
  Muhammad b. Marwan, 129–30
  al-Mukhtar al-Thaqafi, 107
  'Prince of Armenia', title, 285–6
  'Umayyad North', 296, 301–4
  see also Caucasus
Arwa bt. Kurayz, 82
Asad clan of Quraysh, 57c, 149, 180, 189–90
al-Ashdaq, 'Amr b. Sa'id, 109c, 110, 112–13, 122, 127
Ashot Bagratuni, 186
Asia Minor, 68, 91, 96–7, 101, 130–1, 164, 179, 186; *see also* Anatolia
Asma' bt. Abi Bakr, 81c, 103, 149
Asturias, 3m, 181
Aswan, 231, 299m
Athanasius bar Gumoye, 229, 252–3
Attila the Hun, 34
Avars, 3m, 54, 79m

Awraba federation, 100, 104
al-Awzaʿi, 329
Ayla *see* al-ʿAqaba
ʿAyn al-Jarr *see* ʿAnjar
ʿAyn Tamr, 232
Azariqa 'Kharijites', 133–6, 141
Azd, 171, 184, 189, 196, 197, 204
Azerbaijan, Umayyad,
   Christianity, 285–6
   Hisham b. ʿAbd al-Malik, 178
   mining, 224
   mountains, 216
   Muhammad b. Marwan, 129
   al-Mukhtar al-Thaqafi, 107
   'Umayyad North', 296, 301–4
   ʿUthman, 88
   see also Caucasus
al-Azraq, 236m, 239

Baʿalbak *see* Heliopolis
Bab al-Abwab/Darband, 302m, 303
Bab al-Mandab straits, 35, 36m
Bab al-Saghir Cemetery, 1, 5
Babil, Egypt, *see* Babylon
Babil, Iraq, 296
Babil, Sasanian province *see* Ard Babil
Babylon (Ar. Babil), Egypt, 70, 74, 230, 254, 299m
Bactrian language, 290, 291
Badghis, 290
Bagratunids, 186, 285–6
Bahram I, 282
Bahram Chubin, 282
Bahrayn, 67, 133, 301, 306m
Bajila, 180
al-Bakhraʾ, 199, 235, 236m
Bakr b. Waʾil, 41, 50, 105, 189, 197, 201
al-Baladhuri, 222
Balis *see* Barbalissos
Balkh, 99, 159, 160m, 189, 232, 290
Balqaʾ, 56, 244
Barbalissos (Ar. Balis), 236m, 242, 246, 300m
'barbarians', 43–4, 287
Bardhaʿa (Partaw), 285, 286, 302m, 303
Barghawata tribe, 187, 289
barīd, 308
Barqa (Lat. Barca), 303, 304m

Basra, 70, 79m, 84, 98–9, 122–3, 171, 182, 230, 232, 234, 235, 253, 296, 297m, 303–4, 306m, 314
   ʿAbd Allah b. ʿAmir b. Kurayz, 83, 88, 229
   ʿAbd Allah b. ʿUmar b. ʿAbd al-ʿAziz, 200
   ʿAbd al-Malik, 114
   African agricultural slaves, 105, 133
   ʿAli b. Abi Talib, 89–91
   Bishr b. Marwan, 131–2
   commerce, 253–4
   *dīwān*s, 321
   al-Hajjaj b. Yusuf al-Thaqafi, 123, 132, 135–7
   Ibn al-Muhallab, 171–2
   'Kharijites', 133, 188
   Muʿawiya b. Abi Sufyan, 93
   plague, 221
   religious leaders, 184–6
   shurṭa, 314
   tribal groups, 76, 79–80, 196–7, 198
   ʿUbayd Allah b. Ziyad, 97–8, 102, 320–1
   Yazid b. ʿUmar b. Hubayra, 205
   Ziyad b. Sumayya, 97–8, 320
bathing, baths, *94*, 94–5, 226, 228, 229, 231, *238*, 239, 242
Battle of the Bridge, 69
Battle of the Camel, 90, 102–4, 107
Battle of the Harra, 103
Battle of Jabaliq, 204
Battle of the Khazir, 107
Battle of al-Qadisiyya, 69
Battle of Siffin, 107
Battle of Yarmuk, 68–9
Battle of the Zab, 205–6
Bawit monastery, 263, 299m
bayʿa see pledge of allegiance
Baysan *see* Scythopolis
Beja/Vaga, 233, 304m
'Berbers', 104, 124–5, 158, 173–5, 192, 287–9; *see also* North Africa
Beroea *see* Aleppo
Beth Abe monastery, 262
Bible, 40, 63
Bihkuban, 107
bishops, 186, 261, 271–2, 280–1, 288, 317

Bishr b. Marwan, 131–2
Bistam, 304, 306m
Bostra (Ar. Busra), 50, 67, 236m, 300m
Buddhism, 282, 290–1
building materials, 223–4, 319
Bukayr b. Wishah, 253
Bukhara, 99, 160m, 228, 232, 291, 305
Bulgars, 111, 165, 173
al-Burj, 48
Busir, 206
Bust, 135, 136, 160m, 232

Caesarea, Anatolia, 179
Caliph, Caliphate, 2, 4, 5–8, 6c, 14–16, 16c, 71–2, 120c, *177*, 188, 330
   authority, 138, 157, 163–4, 181–2, 245, 306, 315, 316, 328–9, 330
   coins, 128–9, 138
   hajj, 156–7, 179
   poetry, 128–9, 138, 163–4
   see also Commander of the Faithful
Callinicum *see* Raqqa
camels *see* animals
capital punishment *see* execution
Capsa/Gafsa, 233, 304m
Carthage, 100, 130, 131, 230, 261, 287, 288, 304m, 325
Catholicos of the Church of the East, 280, 285
Caucasus, 54, 111–12, 302m
   'Abd al-Malik, 129–31
   Christianity, 261, 264, 284–6
   Heraclius, 95
   Hisham b. 'Abd al-Malik, 178–9
   Ibn al-Zubayr, 104
   Khazars, 173, 186
   Mu'awiya b. Abi Sufyan, 96
   silver, 224
   'Umayyad North', 301–2, 302m
   see also Albania, Caucasian; Armenia; Azerbaijan; Khazars; Lazica
Caucasian Albania *see* Albania, Caucasian
census, 181, 270–1, 322, 323, 327
Central Asia, 32–5, 72, 78, 84, 124–5, 172–5, 177, 188–91, 279
ceramics, 248–9, 249m
cereal crops, 222 *see also* taxation, *embole*
Chalcedon, Asia Minor, 96, 259

Chalcedonian Christianity, 49, 93, 259–62, 263, 266, 269, 270, 273–4, 285, 287, 310
charisma, 64–5
Chang'an, 280
chief scribe *see* scribes, chief
China
   Central Asian steppes, 34
   Christianity, 280
   plague, 52
   Tang Empire, 21, 85, 124, 127n, 159–61, 160–1n, 174, 177, 188, 219–20, 230
   trade routes, 84, 99, 249–50, 254, 280, 291
   Türgesh, 174, 188–9
   Yazdgird III, 159
Christian Palestinian Aramaic (CPA), 260
Christianity, 45, 47, 50–1, 61, 154–6, 168, 169–70, 257–93, 324
   Aksum, 272
   Arabic texts, Christian, 20
   Armenian, 84, 260–1, 275, 285–6
   bishops, 186, 261, 271–2, 280–1, 288, 317
   Heraclius, 54–5, 62–3
   Hisham b. 'Abd al-Malik, 178
   icons, 107
   Indian, 272
   Jafnids, 49
   Jerusalem, 144–6
   Maronite, 97, 270
   missionaries, 280
   monasteries, 244, 261–66
   Mu'awiya b. Abi Sufyan, 93
   Nicene Christian tradition, 45, 49
   North Africa, 287–8
   Nubian, 201, 259, 272–3
   persecution of Jews, 276
   pilgrimage, 242, 244, 264–6
   relics, 48, 54
   Roman Empire, 9, 14, 32, 44–5, 95, 121, 138, 182, 259, 267, 271, 330
   scripture, 19–20, 55, 60, 63
   Syrian, 267–75, 285
   see also Chalcedonian Christianity; Church of the East; dyophysites; miaphysites; monks

Christology, 128, 259–60, 269
Church of the East, 49, 260, 262, 280, 281, 290, 291; *see also* dyophysites
Cilicia, 130
climate and ecology, 38m, 51–3, 215m, 217, 218–19
Clysma (Ar. Qulzum), 254, 319
coinage,
   ʿAbd al-Malik, 128, *129,* 137–42
   circulation, 70, 112, 254–5, 255, 320, 324–5
   Damascus, *129*
   Egypt, 325–6
   epigraphic, *140*, 174–5, 325
   al-Hajjaj b. Yusuf, 137–42
   Ibn al-Zubayr, 141
   incomes in Roman Egypt, 247–8
   Iraqi Christians, 280–1
   Justinian II, Emperor, *129*
   Khalid b. ʿAbd Allah al-Qasri, 180, 326–7
   Marwanids, 138–42, 317
   minting, 131, 133, 137, 141, 174–5, 280–1, 303, 320–2, 325–6
   Muʿawiya b. Abi Sufyan, 202, 321–2
   payments to the army, 70, 71, 131, 141, 225, 234, 253, 295, 318
   precious metals, 131, 224, 251, 254–5, 320
   Qatari b. Fujaʿa, 133, *134*
   taxation, 251, 319
   'Umayyad North', 303
   unification of, 324–5
   see also taxation; tribute
Commander of the Faithful (Ar. *amīr al-muʾminīn*), 13–14, *94,* 94–5, *225,* 244, 267, 294, 320
   ʿAbd al-Malik, 128, *309*
   and Christianity, 267
   'Kharijite' Islam, 284
   al-Mansur, 328
   Muʿawiya b. Abi Sufyan, 13, *94*
   Qatari b. Fujaʿa, 133, *134*
   ʿUmar (I) b. al-Khattab, 71–2
   see also Caliphs, Caliphate
commerce and exchange, 55–6, 247–55, 307 *see also* trade routes

communications and record-keeping, 307–9
Companions of the Prophet, 1, 5, 7, 8, 82, 166
'conquest society', 23, 64–77, 173
Constans II, Emperor, 78, 95–7, 99, 125
Constantine, Emperor, 32, 45, 173
Constantine IV, Emperor, 96–7, 260
Constantine V, Emperor, 201, 274
Constantinople, 3m, 16, 33m, 54–5, 68, 78, 79m, 88, 121, 162–75, *165*, 230, 261
   ʿAbd al-Malik, 128, 130–1, 330
   in apocalyptic, 121, 163
   Bulgars, 173
   campaigns of 653–4 ce, 84, 88, 95
   campaigns of 668–74 ce, 96–7, 99–100
   campaigns of 700s ce, 121, 130, 152, 155, 162–4, 273
   campaigns of 720s, 730s and 740 ce, 125, 186–7
   Council of, Third, 260
   Council of, Quinisext/in Trullo, 128
   Hisham b. ʿAbd al-Malik, 125, 186–7
   Maslama b. ʿAbd al-Malik, 152, 164–5
   Muʿawiya b. Abi Sufyan, 95–7
   siege of 626 ce, Sasanian, 54
   siege of 717–18 ce, 24, 121, 162–75, 273
   Sulayman, 163–6
   ʿUmar II, 167
   al-Walid I, 155
Constantius, Emperor, 46
conversion to Islam 11, 71, 169–70, 174–5, 258–9, 267, 273, 275, 279, 284, 288, 292–3, 324, 326, 328
copper, 224, 247–8, 254–5, 320–1, 325
Coptic language, 260, 261, 287, 320, 327
Cordoba, 233, 303, 304m
Councils, Church
   Bostra, 569 ce, 50
   Chalcedon, 451 ce, 49, 259–60
   Constantinople, Third, 680–1 ce, 260
   Constantinople, Quinisext/in Trullo, 691–2 ce, 128
   Dvin, 607 ce, 285
court culture, Umayyad, 224, 242–3, 309–12; *see also* poetry
Covadonga, 181

Crone, Patricia, 291
crucifixion *see* execution
Crypta Balbi, 249m
Ctesiphon (Ar. al-Mada'in), 33m, 54, 69, 78, 106–7, 199, 202, 232, 296–7, 297m, 304
   Catholicos, 280
   Mutarrif b. al-Mughira al-Thaqafi, 132
   'Umar b. Hubayra al-Fazari, 205
Cyprus, 84, 112, 179, 201, 224, 252
Cyzicus Peninsula, 96

Dabiq, 244–5
al-Dahhak b. Qays al-Fihri, 108–10
al-Dahhak b. Qays al-Shaybani, 201–2
Dahir, King, 161
Damascus, 38m, 68, 108, 152, 231, 243, 244, 245, 298, 300m, 311
   'Abd al-Malik, 112
   Christianity, 275
   coinage, *129*, 131
   Hisham b. 'Abd al-Malik, 178, 182–3
   Khalid b. 'Abd Allah al-Qasri, 180
   monasteries, 244
   Mosque, Umayyad, 153, *155*, 157, 226, 228, 273
   Mu'awiya b. Abi Sufyan, 1, 69, 82, 86–92, 309
   Mu'awiya (II) b. Yazid, 103
   tribal groups, 194–6
   al-Walid I, 154–7
   Yazid III, 198–200
Damascus, 'military district' or *jund*, 194, 244, 300m
Darband *see* Bab al-Abwab
Darial Pass, 302m, 303
David, King, 55, 156, 164, 265, 281
Dawit of Dvin, 286
Dayr Murran, 243, 244, 245
Dayr al-Naqira, 244, 245
Dayr Sim'an, 244, 245
demography, 219–25
'desert castles', *177*, 178, 235–9 236m, *237–41*, 242–4, 244
Dibba, 301
Diocletian, Emperor, 32
Dionysius of Tell Mahre, 221

diplomacy, 60, 96, 154, 155, 159, 167, 223, 224, 254, 302
   Roman 51, 125
   Sasanian, 51, 60, 224
   see also gifts; tribute
*dīwān*s, 71, 230, 251, 308, 309–12, 318, 321, 323; *see also* administration; taxation
Diyar Mudar, 200; *see also* al-Jazira; Mesopotamia
Diyarbakir, 260, 280, 281; *see also* al-Jazira; Mesopotamia
Dome of the Rock, Jerusalem, 137, 138, 142–7, *143*, *144*, *145*, 153, 272, 273
Dvin, 285, 286, 302m, 303
dyophysites, 49, 50, 61, 260, 266, 268, 281; *see also* 'Church of the East'

earthquakes, 95, 270
East Africa, 51, 60, 61, 224, 260; *see also* Aksum; Nubia
ecology, 35–40, 210–327, 215m
Edessa (Ar. al-Ruha), 229, 302
Edfu, 263, 299m
Egypt, 4, 67–77, 110, 112, 123–4, 158, 180, 181, 206, 230–5, 282, 299m, 303
   'Abd al-'Aziz b. Marwan, 83, 110, 130
   'Abd al-Malik b. Marwan, 110, 127
   administration, 74, 295–6, 298, 299m, 311, 314, 316–27
   agriculture, 79, 219, 221–2, 245
   'Amr b. al-'As, 30, 69–70, 82, 90–1
   Arabic language, 308
   Christianity, 49, 121, 259–66, 269, 271–7, 281
   climate and ecology, 219–22
   commerce and exchange, 247–8
   douxoi, 316–17
   geography, 214, 284, 296–8
   governors, 69–70, 82, 83, 88, 98, 103, 110, 123–4, 130, 151, 163, 179, 180, 201
   Hisham b. 'Abd al-Malik, 176, 179–80, 187, 274
   Ibn al-Zubayr, 102, 103, 127
   Jews and Judaism, 275–7
   languages, 72–5, 260–1, 287
   monasteries, 262–6

mosques, 153, 226
Mu'awiya b. Abi Sufyan, 90–1, 97–9, 295
Nubian incursions, 201
papyri, 65, 72–5, *73*, 128, *313*, 317, 321–4, 327
plague, 52
Quraysh, connections with, 56, 60
resources, 79, 110, 111, 122, 176, 212, 224, 254
revolt of 739 ce, 187
Sasanian conquest, 54
settlement, 72, 76, 79, 180, 196, 231, 235
slaves, 252–3
strategic importance, 122
Talib al-Haqq, 201
taxation, 79, 122, 152, 176, 212, 234, 254, 311, 317–27
'Uthman, 88–90
al-Walid I, 151–3, 163
al-Walid II, 197–8
see also Alexandria; Fustat; Nile, River
Elburz mountains, 224
Emesa (Ar. Hims) *see* Hims/Homs
'emigrants' *see* migrants, Arabian; *muhajirun*
empire, comparison, 2–4, 13–14, 23, 331
empire, definition, 13–14
Empty Quarter, 37–9
Esna monastery, 263
Ethiopia *see* Aksum
Euphrates river, 31, 36m, 205, 214, 281, 297m, 298, 329
  agriculture in Iraq, 122, 220, 221, 222
  Hisham b. 'Abd al-Malik, 178, 242, 245, 275
  hydrology, 216, 218n
  Roman Sasanian war, 54
  Siffin, 90
execution, 107, 112, 115, 159, 178, 183, 189, 200, 204, 274, 275, 291–2

'Faithful' (Ar. *mu'min*, pl. *mu'minīn*), 4–5, 10, 11, 12, 13–14, 17, 61–7, 75, 76, 78, 141, 162, 168, 316
  Christianity, 267
  coinage, 128, 141
  'Commander of the Faithful' (Ar. *amīr al-mu'minīn*), 13–14, 71–2, *94*, 94–5, 128, 133, *134*, 225, 267, 294, *309*
  'Helper of the Faithful' (Ar. *nāsir al-mu'minīn*), 136–7
  'jurisdiction of the faithful' (Ar. *qaḍā' al-mu'minīn*), 316
  'Kharijites', 133, 184
  'Muslims', 10, 12, 162
  Qur'an, 19–20, 61–2
  'Son of the Commander of the Faithful' (Ar. *ibn amīr al-mu'minīn*), 244
Falluja, 282
al-Farazdaq, 156, 164
Farghana, 3m, 124, 160m, 174, 220, 250
farming *see* agriculture
Fars, 3m, 31, 83, 84, 91, 124, 220, 222, 304–5, 306m, 317
  Ibn Mu'awiya, 202
  Ibn al-Muqaffa', 328
  irrigation, 216
  'Kharijites', 133
  Zoroastrianism, 279
Fatima bt. al-Husayn, 1
Fatima bt. Muhammad, 5, 6c, 80, 81c, 101
Fayyum, 74, 299m, 320
Fertile Crescent, 37, 38m, 41, 45, 47, 76
Fihl (Gk. Pella), 231
Filastin ('military district' or *jund*), 200, 232, 243–4, 265, 300m
Fisher, Greg, 50
fishing, 223
food distribution, 319
Franks, Francia, 174, 181, 259
free will, 182, 195
fruit trees, 222, *238*
Fustat, 70, 76–7, 158, 196, 229, 230, 234, 297m, 299m, 303, 319
  Christianity, 271, 272, 274
  grain, 254
  Hulwan, 231
  mosque, 153, 226
'Fustat Umayyad codex', *139*

Gabitha, 68
Gafsa/Capsa *see* Capsa/Gafsa
Gallia Narbonensis, 181

garrisons, 225–6, 232–3, 253, 305–7
  coinage, 325–6
  dīwāns, 318, 323
  shurṭa, 312
  'Umayyad North', 301–3
  weights, measures and scales, 316
Gaza, 249, 249m, 265, 300m
Geʻez language, 261
genealogy *see* kinship; maternal kinship
Genequand, Denis, 236–7
Genghis Khan, 2
geography, 35–40, 214–17
Geonim, 282
George, Alain, 153
George of Sakha, 271–2
Georgia, 112; *see also* Iberia; Lazica
Georgian Christians, 259
Georgian language, 261, 285, 302
Gerash/Gerasa, 228, 231, 300m
Germanikeia (Ar. Marʻash), 130, 164, 201, 242
Ghassan, Banu *see* Ghassanids
Ghassanids, 47, 68, 93; *see also* Jafnids
Ghaylan al-Dimashqi, 182, 195
Ghaylanis, 195
Ghurak, 159
gifts, 181, 224, 254; *see also* tribute
Gilan, 305
Gnosticism, 278, 282, 283
Goght'n, 286, 302m
Golan Heights, 68, 97, 275
gold, 224, 247, 254–5, 320, 321, 325, 326
governance, 294–327
graffiti, 14, 48, 308
grain levy *see* taxation, *embole*
grasslands *see* pasture
grazing *see* pasture
Greek language
  in administration, 72–5, 311, 320, 321, 327
  Chalcedonian Christianity, 262, 265, 273
  inscriptions, 48, 94–5, 252
  language, 48, 72–5, 93–5, 260–1, 265, 266, 267–8, 273, 287, 320, 327
  papyri, 72–5, 265–6
  sources, 21, 128, 172, 273, 274
Greek Fire, 97

Gregory the Great, Pope, 265
Grigor Mamikonean, 84
Gubba Barraya monastery, 262
Gurgan *see* Jurjan

Hadir Qinnasrin, 228, 231
Haditha, 232
Hadramawt, 45–6, 55, 66–7, 301; *see also* South Arabia; Yemen
Hagar, 268, 271
Hagarenes, 268
Hajar mountains, 36
ḥajj, 88, 91, 100–1, 146–8, 152–3, 156–7, 179, 330; *see also*, pilgrimage
al-Hajjaj b. Yusuf al-Thaqafi, 114–15, 123, 132–8, 147, 150–2, 158–9, 163, 175, 190, 226, 316, 323
  ʻAbd al-Malik b. Muhammad b. al-Hajjaj, 311
  ʻAmir b. Sharahil al-Shaʻbi, 185
  Basra, 123, 132–3, 253
  Catholicos of the Church of the East, 281
  coinage, 137–41, 323, 325
  al-Hasan al-Basri, 184
  Hijaz, 114–15, 147
  Ibn al-Muhallab, 171–2
  Iran, 134–6, 152, 158–9, 253
  Iraq, governor, 123, 132–38, 316, 323
  Kufa, 123, 132–3, 253
  Muhallabids, 134, 159, 168, 171
  Qur'an, 137–8
  Sind, 161, 253
  succession, caliphal, 152, 158–9, 161
  al-Walid I, 150–2, 158–61
  Wasit, 136–8, 226, 232, 253, 325
  Yazid II, 166, 175
al-Hakam b. Abi l-ʻAs, 16c, 58, 82, 83, 109c
Hama, 231
Hamadhan, 232, 304
Hammat Gader, inscription, 94–5, *94*
Hanifa, Banu, 66, 104–5, 133
Hanzala b. Safwan al-Kalbi, 187
ḥaram, at Mecca, 56, 67, 85, 114
Harb b. Umayya, 108, 109c
al-Harith b. al-Hakam, 83
al-Harith b. Jabala, 47–8, 50
al-Harith b. Kaʻb, Banu, 311

al-Harith b. Surayj, 189–90
Harran (Lat. Carrhae), North Mesopotamia, 38m, 200, 202, 206–7, 232, 275, 277, 302
Harran, Syria, inscription, 48, *49*
Haruris, 91; *see also* Kharijites
al-Hasan al-Basri, 80, 184
Hasan b. Qahtaba, 205, 206
Hashim, Banu, 56, 57, 80, 81c, 119, 149 183, 185, 188, 190–1, 202, 284
Hassan b. Malik b. Bahdal, 87c, 104
Hassan b. al-Nu'man, 130, 131, 246
Hawazin, 66
al-Hawf al-Sharqi, 327; *see also* Egypt; Nile, Delta
Hebrew language, 21, 276–7
Heliopolis (Ar. Ba'albak), 68, 243, 300m
Helmand river, 99, 135, 160m, 216–17, 232, 306m
Hephthalites, 78, 84, 99, 104, 159, 289, 290
Heraclius, Emperor, 54–5, 58, 63, 93, 95, 97, 260, 269
Herakleopolis/Ihnas *see* Ihnas/Herakleopolis
Herat, 159, 160m, 232, 289
heresy
 in Christianity, 64, 274, 287
 in Islam, 182, 277n, 286, 291–2
hermits, 45, 261–2, 264
Hijaz, 17, 36m, 55–60, 76, 272, 298–301
 'Abd al-Malik, 127, 147
 'Ali b. Abi Talib, 90–1
 'Alids, 101
 Arabic language, 74, 308
 estates, Umayyad, 93, 246
 geography, 35, 36m, 214, 215m, 296, 298
 grain supply, 180, 319
 gold mining, 224
 governors, 100, 114, 132, 147–8, 151, 178–9, 194
 al-Hajjaj b. Yusuf al-Thaqafi, 114–15, 132
 Hisham b. 'Abd al-Malik, 178–80
 Ibn al-Zubayr, 103–4, 110–11, 114, 146–8
 Mu'awiya b. Abi Sufyan, 93, 96, 100, 101

'Umar II, 166
al-Walid I, 151
writing, 74, 308
Yazid (I) b. Mu'awiya, 101, 104
see also West Arabian
Hims/Homs (Gk. Emesa), 38m, 68, 200, 206, 231, 236m, 298, 300m
 mosque, 153, 156
Hims ('military district' or *jund*), 200, 300m
Himyar, Himyarites, 42, 43, 45–7, 51, 53, 61, 89, 298, 301, 303–4, 307, 328–9; *see also*, South Arabia; Yemen
al-Hira, 38m, 67, 69, 296, 297m, 303–4, 328–9
 Arabic language, 260
 Christianity, 50, 260, 262
 Khalid b. 'Abd Allah al-Qasri, 183
 Nasrids, 47, 70
Hisham b. 'Abd al-Malik, 120c, 176–95, *177*, 275, 326–7
 administration, 181, 311, 312, 326–7
 Christianity, 182, 275, 285
 daughters, 200
 estates, 237, 237–42, 238–41, 246, 275
 governors, 178–81
 heresy, 181–3, 195, 286
 markets and workshops, 229
 al-Rusafa, 198, 232, 242, 244, 245, 275
 succession, 192–3
 war with Rome, 125, 176–7
Hisham b. Isma'il al-Makhzumi, 147, 151
Hisn Maslama, 242
Hispania *see* Spain
historiography, 8–11, 16–21, 24
The History of the Patriarchs of Alexandria, 218–19, 269, 272
Hnanisho I, 281
Hormuz, Straits of, 35
horses *see* animals
Hujr b. 'Adi al-Kindi, 101
Hujrids, 46; *see also* Kinda
Hulwan, Egypt, 231, 271
Hulwan, Iraq, 107, 232, 297m, 319
hunting, 223, 242, 246,
al-Husayn b. 'Ali, 80, 101–2, 105–7, 119, 148–50, 182–3
al-Huwwarin, 243

Ibadi Islam, 329
Iberia, in the Caucasus, 302, 302m
Iberian Peninsula *see* al-Andalus; Spain
Ibn al-Ashʿath, 135–8, 159, 171, 184, 185
Ibn Dubara *see* ʿAmir b. Dubara
Ibn al-Habhab, 180–1, 187, 311
Ibn Hadidu, 72–5
Ibn Hubayra *see* Yazid b. ʿUmar b. Hubayra
Ibn Muʿawiya *see* ʿAbd Allah b. Muʿawiya
Ibn al-Muhallab, 163, 170–2, 180, 184, 185
Ibn al-Muqaffaʿ, 328–30
Ibn Shihab al-Zuhri *see* al-Zuhri, Ibn Shihab Muhammad b. Muslim
Ibn al-Zubayr, 102–15, 127–8, 135, 148–50, 194, 246, 322
  ʿAbd al-Malik, 144, 146–48, 271
  coinage, 141
  ḥajj, 146–7
  Kaʿba, 146–7
  markets, 315
  mother 81c, 103, 149
Ibrahim b. Hisham al-Makhzumi, 178, 179
iconoclasm, 168, 273, 274
Ifriqiya, 124, 151–2, 220, 230, 233, 296, 303
  climate and ecology, 214
  commerce and exchange, 250
  conversion, 174
  Hanzala b. Safwan al-Kalbi, 187
  languages, 287
  markets, 229
  silver, 224
  see also North Africa
Ihnas/Herakleopolis, 72–5, 299m
ʿIkrima b. Abi l-Hakam, 66
Imruʾ al-Qays, 42
India, 39, 84, 161, 254, 280, 323; *see also* Sind
Indian Christians, 272
Indian Ocean, 37, 39, 250, 253–4
Indus, 84, 98, 160m, 161, 217, 221, 222, 305, 306m
Iran, 24, 31–2, 33m, 43–53, 84–5, 88, 91, 111, 124, 133, 163, 201–2, 228, 232, 295, 296, 305, 330
  ʿAbbasid Revolution', 203–5
  and the Arabian Peninsula, 37, 39
  geography, 216–17
  al-Hajjaj b. Yusuf al-Thaqafi, 133–6

Ibn al-Ashʿath, 136
irrigation, 221
mining, 224
religions, 183, 260, 277–83, 290–1
settlement, 99, 228, 232–3
taxation, 317, 320–1, 326
trade routes, 84, 249–50, 253–4
Yazid b. al-Muhallab, 163, 170–2
see also Sasanian Empire
Iraq, 23–4, 54, 67–77, 83–4, 97–9, 122–4, 131–5, 158, 176–8, 182–3, 190–1, 196, 229, 232, 234–5, 253–4, 296, 297m, 298, 330
  ʿAbbasid Revolution, 204–6
  ʿAbd Allah b. ʿUmar, 200–2
  ʿAbd al-Malik, 110–14, 127, 131
  agriculture, 221–3
  ʿAli b. Abi Talib, 80, 90–2, 93
  building materials, 223
  Christianity, 50, 61, 259–60, 262, 272, 274, 277–83
  coinage, 138–41
  geography, 214, 216
  governors, 69–70, 82–3, 88, 97–8, 131–2, 151, 161, 163, 170–1, 180, 190, 192–3, 195, 303–5
  al-Hajjaj b. Yusuf al-Thaqafi, 131–4, 150–1, 158–61
  Ibn al-Ashʿath, 135–7
  Judaism, 277–83
  Khalid b. ʿAbd Allah al-Qasri, 180, 183, 192, 195
  law and order, 315–17
  Mandaeism, 282–3
  Manichaeism, 282–3
  Marwan II, 200–5
  Muʿawiya b. Abi Sufyan, 93, 96–8, 245–6
  Muhallabids, 163, 166–8, 170–2
  al-Mukhtar, 105–8
  plague, 52, 220–1
  settlement, 232, 234–5, 246
  taxation, 79, 138, 167–8, 198, 212, 234, 317–26
  tribal groups, 84, 195–6
  ʿUmar II, 172–3
  ʿUthman, 82–3, 88–9
  Yazid II, 170–2
  Yusuf b. ʿUmar al-Thaqafi, 193

Zoroastrianism, 277–83
Zubayrids, 80, 90, 93, 103–6, 110–11, 113–14
iron, 224
irrigation, 180, 216, 217, 221–2, 235, 237, 239, 246, 297
'Isa b. 'Ali, 202
Isaac of Shubra, 271–2
Isfahan, 122, 204, 232, 304
Ishaq b. Muslim al-'Uqayli, 207
Ishmaelites, 268
Islam, 10, 11–14, 59–63, 62, 121, 170, 182, 257, 267–8, 273–4, 330
   'Abd al-Malik, 138–50, 267, 271, 295
   administration and taxation, 274, 295, 323, 324, 326–7
   'Berbers', 125, 288–9
   conversion to, 11, 169–70, 174, 258–9, 267, 279, 284, 288, 292–3, 324, 326, 328
   Hisham b. 'Abd al-Malik, 178, 286
   historiography, modern, 9–10, 17–19
   historiography, medieval, 11, 18–21, 59
   Ibadi, 329
   Ibn al-Muqaffa', 328
   Ibn al-Zubayr, 102–3, 127, 141, 146, 148–9, 271, 298
   Islamic movements, anti-Umayyad, 24, 124, 177–8, 181–3, 184–5
   Kharijite, 184–5, 271, 284
   Khazars, 186
   law, 279, 315, 329
   Marwanids, 181–3, 271
   and political power, 330
   Shi'i, 5–8, 10, 102, 182–3, 185–6, 271, 284
   Sunni, 7–8, 10, 185
   'Umar II, 167
   Umayyads, 8 13, 23–24, 121, 138–50, 153–7
   al-Walid I, 153–7, 267
Israel, 4, 242
Istakhr, 84, 122, 228, 232, 305
Istanbul, *165*
Italy, 95

Jabal Musa, 264–5
Jabaliq, 204, 206

al-Jabiya, 243, 244
Jacobites *see* miaphysites
Ja'far al-Sadiq, 150, 202, 329
Jafnids, 47–50, 51, 53, 61, 68
Jalula, 69, 297m
al-Janad, 301
Janah Abu Marwan, 311
al-Jar, 254
jarajima see Mardaites
Jarir, 155–6, 163–4
Jaxartes river, 160, 160m, 306m
al-Jazira, 84, 220, 232, 245, 266, 267, 272, 284, 296, 301, 329–31
   Christianity, 259, 268, 270–1, 280, 281
   al-Hajjaj b. Yusuf al-Thaqafi, 133
   Hisham b. 'Abd al-Malik, 176, 178
   Ibn al-Zubayr, 281
   Marwan II, 200–1, 204, 206
   Marwanids, 129, 296, 301–2
   'Monastery of the Catholicos', 281
   plague, 221
   Qays, 122, 199
   religion, 278
   taxation, 152–3, 270–1, 322
   'Umayyad North', 129
   see also Diyar Mudar, Diyarbakir, Mesopotamia
Jerusalem, 38m, 68, 121, *143*, 228, 236m, 261, 300m
   'Abd al-Malik, 142–6
   Dome of the Rock, 142–6, *143*, *144*, *145*
   Heraclius, 54–5
   and Islam, 330
   itinerant monarchy, 243
   Jews, 276
   Mu'awiya b. Abi Sufyan, 69, 92–3
   pilgrimage, 146, 231, 264
   al-Walid I, 153
   al-Walid II, 226
Jesus, 7, 49, 57, 138, 264
Jews *see* Judaism
Jibal, 91, 124, 133, 163, 202, 304
Jiruft, 133–4
John (Yohannnes), 72–5
John of Damascus, 273–4, 310
   On Heresies, 274
John of Ephesus, 49–50

John of Fenek, 268
Jordan, 4, 35, 37, 47, 56, 242, 244
Juansher, 96
Judaism, 13–14, 19–21, 46–51, 58, 60, 61, 63, 273, 275–283, 287
'judge' see qāḍī
jund, 298, 300m
Jurjan, 163, 251, 291, 305, 306m
Justinian, Emperor, 47, 265
Justinian II, Emperor, 128, *129*, 131, 152, 155–6, 186
Justinianic Plague, 51–3, 69, 219–21
Juzjan, 189

Ka'ba, 56, 66, 85, 114, 138, 145–7, 153–4, 156
Kabul, 135, 160m, 185, 217, 289, 290
Kabulistan, 159
Kafartutha, 202
al-Kahina, 131, 188
Kalb, Banu, 30, 86, 87c, 103–4, 311
  'Abd al-'Aziz b. Marwan, 110, 130
  'Abd al-'Aziz b. al-Walid, 161
  'Abd al-Malik, 111–12, 150
  Christianity, 267
  Marwan (I) b. al-Hakam, 108
  Marwan (II) b. Muhammad, 110
  Mu'awiya b. Abi Sufyan, 86–9, 92, 298
  Qasr al-Hayr al-Gharbi, 239
  'southern' tribes, 113, 150, 194–200
  Syrian Desert, 122
  Tadmur/Palmyra, 231
  'Umar II, 166
  al-Urdunn, 104
  Yazid (I) b. Mu'awiya, 101, 243
Karbala, 102, 105, 172
Karin/Qaliqala, 303
Kaskar, 137, 232, 296, 297m, 304
Kaysaniyya movement, 106–8, 190–1
Kellia monastery, 263
Khalid b. 'Abd Allah al-Qasri, 183, 229, 246–7, 190, 192
  Christianity, 274
  coinage, 326–7
  executions, 183
  Iraq, 180
  Ka'ba, 154
  Khurasan, 189

Manichaeism, 283
taxation, 326
Yusuf b.'Umar al-Thaqafi, 193–5
Khalid b. Humayd al-Zanati, 187–8, 289
Khalid b. al-Walid, 66
Kharijite Islam, 184–5, 284
  'Ali b. Abi Talib, 91–3
  Azariqa, 133
  Bakr b. Wa'il, 105
  Hanifa, Banu, 104–5
  Marwanids, 149, 184–5, 271
  Najadat, 133
  North Africa, 188, 284, 289
  Shayban, Banu, 201
  Tamim, 105
  Zubayrids, 149
Kharistan, 190
Khaybar, 50
Khazars, 3m, 84, 79m, 88, 96, 104, 111, 131, 152, 173, 186, 275, 285, 286, 302m, 303
Khazir river, 107
Khidash, 291–2
Khirbet al-Mafjar, near Jericho, 236m, *238*
Khirbet al-Mird, 72
al-Khirrit b. Rashid al-Naji, 91
Khurasan, 84, 124, 151–2, 173, 174, 206–7, 220, 232–3, 250, 284, 296, 304–5, 306m, 317
  Abbasid Revolution, 183, 188, 190–1, 203–5, 207, 284, 331
  Abu Muslim al-Khurasani, 203–5
  agriculture, 221–2
  'Ali b. Abi Talib, 91
  climate and ecology, 216
  frontier, 151–2, 159–61, 163, 173–4, 184, 188–90, 232–3, 250, 258, 284, 289–90, 291–2
  governors, 158–9, 163, 174, 188–90, 194, 204, 296, 232, 323
  al-Hajjaj b. Yusuf al-Thaqafi, 134–6, 158–63
  Hisham b. 'Abd al-Malik, 188–91
  Ibn Mu'awiya, 202
  Islam, 188, 203, 284, 331
  land grants, 246
  non-Muslims, 258, 289–90, 291–2, 327
  Persian language, 327

religion and identity, 289–92
settlement and tribal groups, 197, 232, 246, 289–90
Shi'i Islam, 284
silver, 224
taxation, 98–9, 323
Khurramism, 291–2
Khusro II Parvez, 53–4, 95
Khuzistan, 124, 202, 220–2, 279, 296–7, 304, 306m
Khwarazm, 160, 160m
Kinda, 46, 56, 66, 113, 123, 136, 201, 298; *see also* Hujrids
kinship, 6c, 16c, 15, 24, 81c, 87c, 109c, 120c, 113, 192, 196, 316
  'Abd al-'Aziz, 130
  'Abd al-Malik, 119
  'Alids, 81c, 119
  conquests, 78, 113, 196, 316
  al-Hajjaj b. Yusuf al-Thaqafi, 114, 132, 135, 151, 159, 161, 166, 168, 171, 190, 311, 316
  Ibn al-Zubayr, 81c, 102–3
  leadership, 67
  Quraysh, 6c, 57c, 79, 119
  see also maternal kinship
Kirman, 91, 133, 159, 216, 220, 224, 305, 328
al-Kirmani, 204
Kish, 135
Kufa, 70, 79m, 122–4, 182, 196, 230, 232, 234–5, 253, 254, 296, 297m, 303–4
  Abbasid Revolution, 108, 183, 185–6, 190, 202, 204–5
  'Abd Allah b. 'Umar b. 'Abd al-'Aziz, 200–1
  'Abd al-Malik, 114, 131–2
  'Ali b. Abi Talib, 93
  governors, 82–3, 88–9, 97, 99, 131, 180, 190, 202, 303–4, 320
  Hisham b. 'Abd al-Malik, 190–1
  al-Husayn b. 'Ali, 101–2
  Ibn al-Ash'ath, 135–7
  Ibn al-Muhallab, 171–2
  Ibn Mu'awiya, 202
  Ibn al-Muqaffa', 328–9
  Khalid b. 'Abd Allah al-Qasri, 180, 229

mosque-palace complex, 226–8, *227*
Mosul, 301–2
Mu'awiya b. Abi Sufyan, 97–9
al-Mukhtar al-Thaqafi, 105–7, 111
'Penitents' movement, 105
religious leaders, 184–6
settlement and tribal groups, 76, 79, 198
'Uthman, 82–3, 88–90
Yusuf b. 'Umar, 190–1
Zayd b. 'Ali, 190–1
'Kufic' Arabic script, 141
'Kurds', 202, 278
Kusayla, 104, 188

Lake Balqash, 174
Lake Sistan *see* Lake Zirih
Lake Tiberias, 68, 92, 94, 97, 104, 243, 275–6
Lake Zirih, 99, 160m, 305
Lakhm, 43, 68; *see also* Nasrids
land grants, 235–6, 246
land survey, 152–3, 181, 235, 271, 319, 322–3, 326–7
land tax, 319, 323, 326
land use, 219–24
'Late Antique Little Ice Age' *see* climate and ecology
Latin language, 174–5, 261, 265, 287–8, 312, 325
law and order, 312–17, 328–9
Layla bt. Zabban b. al-Asbagh 87c, 109c, 110, 122, 130, 166n
al-Layth b. Abi Ruqayya, 311
Lazica, 285, 302m, 303
Lebanon, 4, 97, 228
Leo III, Emperor, 125, 164–7, 173, 186, 187, 201, 274
Leontius, Emperor, 131
Libya, 100, 214, 303, 286, 304m
Life of Vahan, 275
Lod/Lydda, 231n, 232, 244, 300m
Lombards, 3m, 95
Luwata nomads, 100

Ma'add, 41, 42
al-Mada'in *see* Ctesiphon
Madhhij, 42

Madinat al-Far, 229, 235, 236m, 242
Maghrib *see* North Africa
mahdī, 105, 108, 121, 156, 163–4
Makhzum, Banu, 56, 57c, 66, 108, 122, 176, 192, 194
Makran, 160m, 161, 216, 305
Malabar, 280
Malik b. Anas, 329
Mamikoneans, 186, 285–6
Mandaean religion, 278, 282–3
Mandaic language, 283
Mani, 282–283
Manichaeism, 278, 282–3, 291
al-Mansur *see* Abu Ja'far b. Muhammad al-Mansur
al-Mansura, 233, 305
Mar Saba monastery, 262, 273
Mara'-l-Qays, 42
Mar'ash *see* Germanikeia
marble, *94*, 142–3, 153, 154, 223
Marcian, Emperor, 49
Mardaites, 97, 111, 112, 284
Ma'rib dam, 51
Marj Rahit, 110, 113, 114, 196
markets, 180, 228–9, 231, 315, 319
Maronite Christians, 97
'Maronite Chronicle', 92, 270
marshes, 214–16, 246, 268, 284
Marw, 33m, 85, 99, 158, 160m, 232, 289, 290, 296, 305
   Abu Muslim al-Khurasani, 203–4
   Bukayr b. Wishah, 253
   al-Harith b. Surayj, 189
   irrigation, 217
   land grants, 246
   mosque, 228
   shurṭa, 314
Marwan (I) b. al-Hakam, 16c, 23, 83, 85, 100, 108–11, 109c, 112, 119, 120c, 132, 267, 310–11
Marwan (II) b. Muhammad b. Marwan, 109c, 120c, 178, 186, 200–7, *225*, 232, 244, 245, 275, 312
Marwanids, 3m, 108c, 120c, 306m
Marw-i Rudh, 232
Mary, 54, 92, 265
Masjid al-Haram, 154; *see also ḥaram*, at Mecca; Ka'ba; Mecca, sanctuary

Maslama b. 'Abd al-Malik, 151–2, 157, 163–5, 171–2, 246, 275
   Hisham b. 'Abd al-Malik, 178–9
   Madinat al-Far, 229, 242
Maslama b. Hisham *see* Abu Shakir b. Hisham
Maslama b. Mukhallad al-Ansari, 98, 320–1
maternal kinship, 81c, 87c, 109c, 130, 198, 253, 296
   'Abd Allah b. 'Umar b. 'Abd-'Aziz, 200
   'Abd al-'Aziz b. Marwan, 83, 109c, 110, 122, 130
   'Abd al-'Aziz b. al-Walid, 156, 161
   'Abd al-Malik, 83, 109c, 122
   'Abd al-Malik, sons, 122
   al-Ashdaq, 'Amr b. Sa'id, 109c, 112, 122
   al-Hasan b. 'Ali, 80
   Hisham b. 'Abd al-Malik, 176, 178, 179, 192
   al-Husayn b. 'Ali, 80
   Maslama b. 'Abd al-Malik, 151
   Muhammad b. Marwan, 130
   Muhammad, Prophet, 70, 80
   Sulayman b. 'Abd al-Malik, 122
   'Umar II, 151, 166
   'Uthman, 82, 83, 88
   al-Walid I, 122, 151, 311
   al-Walid II, 193–4
   Yazid (I) b. Mu'awiya, 109c, 104, 243
   Yazid II, 166
   Yazid III, 198
   Zubayrids, 70, 80, 90, 102–3, 146, 149
Mauretania, 250, 304m
mawālī, 12, 106, 108, 169–70, 184–6, 189, 201, 202, 234, 309–11, 324
Mawia, 44–5, 49
Maysan, 296, 297m
Maysara al-Badghari, 187–8, 289
Maysun bt. Bahdal, 86–8, 87c
Mecca, 3m, 13, 22, 55, 65–7, 79m, 93, 102–3, 225–6, 298
   'Abd al-Malik, 145–6, 153
   'Ali b. Abi Talib, 89–91, 102–3, 108
   governors, 132, 153, 170, 178, 180, 275
   al-Hajjaj b. Yusuf al-Thaqafi, 114–15, 132

al-Husayn b. ʻAli, 102
Hisham b. ʻAbd al-Malik, 178–80, 275
Ibn al-Zubayr, 102–3, 114–15, 146–7
Khalid b. ʻAbd Allah al-Qasri, 154, 178, 180
markets, 56, 315
Muʻawiya b. Abi Sufyan, 93, 101, 245
Muhammad, Prophet, 57–60
al-Mukhtar al-Thaqafi, 106–7
pilgrimage, 13, 56, 63, 146, 152, 157, 275, 330
Quraysh, 55–6, 63, 66–7, 79, 82, 89–90, 93, 108, 330
sanctuary, 13, 79, 85, 147, 153, 330; see also *ḥaram*, at Mecca; Kaʻba
Talib al-Haqq, 201
ʻUmar II, 170
and urban change, 225
ʻUthman, 82, 89–91
al-Walid I, 153, 180
Medina, 4, 3m, 57–60, 66–7, 76, 79m, 82, 88–9, 100, 146, 148–50, 184, 254, 298, 318
ʻAbd al-Malik, 30, 147, 148–50
governors 108, 100, 112, 147, 154, 170, 178, 298
Hisham b. ʻAbd al-Malik, 149, 178, 182
al-Husayn b. ʻAli, 102
Ibn al-Zubayr, 103–4, 110–11, 114–15
Jews, 50, 58
markets, 83, 315
Marwan II, 108, 111
mosque, Prophet's, 85–6, 153–7, 226
Muʻawiya b. Abi Sufyan, 92–3, 100, 245
Qabisa b. Dhuʻayb al-Khuzaʻi, 311
religious scholars, 148–50, 151, 329
Talib al-Haqq, 201
ʻUmar b. ʻAbd al ʻAziz, 151, 154, 166–7, 170, 315
ʻUthman, 83, 85–9
al-Walid I, 156–7, 163, 226
Yazid (I) b. Muʻawiya, 112, 146
Yazid II, 146
Merv *see* Marw
Mesopotamia, 23, 42, 52, 84, 205, 216, 245, 260, 262, 266, 277, 301; *see also* Diyar Mudar; Diyarbakir; al-Jazira

miaphysites, 49–50, 61, 260, 262–3, 266, 268–273, 280–1, 285
Michael the Syrian, 220–1
Middle Persian *see* Persian language
migrants, Arabian 11, 14, 23, 70–1, 76–7, 78–9, 257; *see also muhajirun*
ʻAli b. Abi Talib, 89–91
demographic change, 162, 225, 307
economic and social change, 168, 213, 225, 251, 307
Egypt, 179
Iraq, 182, 196–7
and Jews, 276
Khurasan, 99, 124
al-Mukhtar, 107
settlement patterns, 213, 226, 234, 307
Syria, 77
tribal identities, 113, 195–6
Miknasa, 18
milestones of ʻAbd al-Malik, *309*
'military district' *see jund*
millenarianism *see* apocalypse
mining, 224, 317, 327
missionaries, Christian, 46
missionaries, Islamic (*daʻawāt*), 182, 183, 188, 203
monasteries, 243–5, 261–5, 273, 280
'Monastery of the Catholicos', 114
Mount Sinai, 263–4, *263*, 264–6
Mongols, 2, 7, 13
monks, 261–2, 265, 273, 280, 322
monophysites *see* miaphysites
monotheism, 61, 62, 97, 121, 156, 162, 169–70, 266–7, 274, 279, 286, 330
coinage, 141
Judaeo-monotheism, South Arabian, 46
monsoon *see* precipitation
'Moors', 34, 287, 288; *see also* 'Berbers', North Africa
mosaic, 143, *145*, 153, 243, *238*, 265, 272
Moses [Biblical and Quranic prophet], 57, 265, 268
Moses, bishop, 45
mosque-palace complex, 226–8, *227*
mosques, 179, 226–8, 230–3, 275, 307–8; *see also* under specific cities
Mosul, 38m, 107, 122, 201–2, 205, 229, 232, 246, 301–2, 302m, 322

Mount Amanus, 97
Mount Horeb, 264-5
Mount Izla, 262
Mount Sinai *see* Sinai
mountains, 216-17, 268
Mu'awiya b. Abi Sufyan, 1-5, 7-8, 10, 15,
  6c, 16c, 23-4, 30, 90-104, 144
  'Abd al-Malik, 111-12, 121, 127, 132,
    141-2, 144, 147-8
  'Ali b. Abi Talib, 90-2, 204
  Armenia, 84, 302-3
  chief scribes, 273, 309-11
  Christianity, 94-5, 267, 269-70
  coinage, 92-3, 321-2
  'Commander of the Faithful', 14-15, *94*
  estates, 245-6
  governors, 23, 97-9, 320-1
  hajj, 147-8
  Hammat Gader inscription, *94*
  Jerusalem, 92, 142, 276-7
  Kalb, Banu, 30, 83, 86-7, 87c, 89, 150,
    231, 267
  'Kharijites', 185
  land grants, 234-5, 245
  marriages, 83, 86-7, 87c
  mosque-palace complex, 226
  Sarjun b. Mansur al-Rumi, 273
  al-Sinnabra, 243
  succession to Mu'awiya, 101-4, 108,
    109c, 110, 146, 206-7
  Syria, 67, 69-71, 77, 82, 88, 90, 295, 298
  taxation, 23, 320-3
  Temple Mount, Jerusalem, 142, 276-7
  'Uthman, 86-90
  war with Rome, 22-3, 29-30, 67, 69, 82,
    84, 91, 95-7, 99-100, 121, 295
Mu'awiya b. Yazid, 16c, 103
Mudar, 136, 196, 197, 200, 204
al-Mufaddal b. al-Muhallab, 172
al-Mughira b. Shu'ba al-Thaqafi, 69-70,
  97, 132, 321
Muhajirun [migrants from Mecca], 58
muhajirun, [as term for migrant
  conquerors], 10, 65-7, 70-1, 73-5,
  92, 162, 268; *see also* migrants
al-Muhallab b. Abi Sufra, 134-5, 159
Muhallabids, 159, 161, 163, 167-8,
  170-2

Muhammad, Prophet, 6c, 47, 57-68, 76,
  79, 82, 93, 101, 119, 315
  on Marwanid coinage, 140-1
  memorialisation, 17, 24, 64, 146, 149,
    154
  tomb, 154
  al-Zuhri, 149
Muhammad al-Baqir, 150, 182-3
Muhammad b. al-Hanafiyya, 105-8, 119
Muhammad b. al-Qasim al-Thaqafi, 161,
  163
Muhammad b. Marwan, 129-31, 151, 178,
  325
Muhammad b. Maslama b. 'Abd al-Malik,
  207
Muhammad b. Yazid, 175
al-Mukhtar al-Thaqafi, 105-8, 111, 119,
  183, 185, 191, 301
Multan, 160m, 305, 306m
mu'min/mu'minin see 'Faithful'
Musa b. Nusayr, 130, 158, 174, 175, 246
Mus'ab al-Zubayr, 104, 105, 110, 112,
  114, 281, 301-2
music, 242
'Muslims' (*muslimun*),
  in the administration, 295, 310, 327
  as group identity, 10, 62, 121, 162, 168,
    235, 273-5, 286, 307, 326
  demographics, 11, 253
  in the historiography, 10-11
  in the Qur'an, 62
  taxation, 323-4
Mutarrif b. al-Mughira al-Thaqafi,
  132-3
al-Muwaqqar, 244

Nabataea, 37, 41, 43
Nafi' b. al-Azraq, 104-5, 133
Nafud, 37
Na'ila bt. al-Farafisa, 87c, 88, 90
Na'ila bt. 'Umara, 87c, 88
Najadat, 133
Najda b. 'Amir, 104-5, 133
Najran, 42, 61, 66
Nakur, 289
Namara inscription, 41-3, *42*, 45-6
Narseh, 43, 159
Nasr b. Sayyar, 190, 194, 203-4

Nasrids, 45, 47, 50, 51, 53, 60, 67, 70; see also Lakhm
Negev, 72, 214, 221, 320, 322, 323
Nessana, 72
Nessana papyri, 222, 265–6, 320, 322
Nestorians see Church of the East; dyophysites
Nicene Christian tradition, 45, 49
Nihawand, 204–5, 304
Nile river, 31, 74, 256, 299m
  agriculture, 122, 214, 221–2
  Delta, 180, 214, 263, 297, 299m
  hydrology, 218–19
Nineveh, 38m, 54, 262, 301
Nishapur, 160m, 232
Nisibis, 262
nomads, 32–4, 37–40, 44; see also Avar nomad federation; Luwata nomads; pastoralist groups
non-Arabians, 11–13, 102, 105, 106, 124, 162, 168, 169–70, 174, 192, 225, 289, 307
  administration, 274, 295
  Ibn al-Ash'ath, 137
  Ibn Mu'awiya, 202
  Khurasan, 188, 203, 290–1
  sources, 21
  taxation, 168, 175, 189
non-Muslims in administration, 162, 170, 275, 295
non-Muslims and taxation, 326
North Africa, 172–175, 177, 187–8, 214, 220, 224, 228, 233, 295, 296, 304m, 317, 325–6
  'Abd al-Malik, 129–31
  agriculture, 221, 222–3
  'Berber' revolts, 124, 162, 175, 177, 187–8, 331
  Christianity, 261, 284, 286–9
  coinage, 325–6
  frontier, 24, 83, 124–5, 129, 131, 158, 173–4, 188
  geography, 214, 218–19, 220
  governors, 83, 158, 170, 174–5, 180–1, 306–7
  Hisham b. 'Abd al-Malik, 180–1, 186–8, 192, 195
  irrigation, 221

al-Kahina, 131, 188
Kusayla, 104, 188
language and identity, 287
Manichaeism, 282–3
monasteries, 264
Mu'awiya b. Abi Sufyan, 96
non-Arabians, 124–5, 189
religion and identity, 124, 284, 286–9, 331
settlement patterns, 233, 246
slaves, 100, 124, 131, 151–2, 158, 252
trade and exchange, 248–9, 249m
see also 'Berbers'
North Atlantic Oscillation (NAO), 218–19, 220
Northumbria, 21
Nubian kingdoms, 83–4, 231, 254, 261, 263–4, 266
Nubian Christians, 201, 259, 272–73
Numidia, 34, 304m

olives, 222, 265
Oman, 35, 36, 36m, 53, 60, 202, 214, 301
On Heresies, 274
orality/oral tradition, 17, 21, 312
Oxus river, 78, 99, 135, 159, 160m, 189, 217, 289, 290, 306m
Oxyrhynchus 247, 248, 299m

'pagans', 266, 277
Pahlavi see Persian language
Paikuli, 43
Palestine, 'military district'/jund see Filastin
Palestine, modern, 4, 242
Palestine, Roman 42, 44, 260, 261, 276
Palmyra (Ar. Tadmur), 37, 43, 206, 228, 231, 236m, 243, 300m
papyri, 47–8, 311, 313, 317, 319–20
  export to Roman Empire, 255
parchment, 24, 72, 138, 139
Partaw see Bardha'a
Parthian Empire, 31
pastoralist groups, 68, 78, 188, 287–8, 316, 329–30
  animals, 223, 238–9
  Arabic language, 80, 173, 260, 267
  'Arabs', 40–1

pastoralist groups (cont.)
  Christianity, 268
  dyophysitism, 281
  geography, 214
  Iraq, 296
  'Kharijites', 283–4
  miaphysitism, 272
  monks and, 265
  pasture, 29, 32, 34, 35, 37, 38, *39*, 66, 215m, 223, 235, 245, 305, 329
  patriarchates, 261, 271–2
  Paykand, 99, 291
  Pella (Ar. Fihl), 231, 300m
  Pellat, Charles, 230
  Penitents (Ar. *tawwābūn*), 106, 119
  Pergamom, Asia Minor, 164
  Persian language, 43, *134*, 141, 202, 278, 279, 290, 320, 327, 328
  Petra, 37, 38m, 47–8, 300m
  Philadelphia *see* 'Amman
  Philippikos Bardanes, Emperor, 152
  Philostorgius, 46
  Phoenice Libanensis, 68
  Phoinix, near Rhodes, 164
  pilgrimage
    Christian sites and the Arabian Faithful, 242, 244, 267, 275
    Heraclius, 54–5, 93
    Jerusalem, 54–5, 93, 142, 231, 264
    Mecca, 55–6, 63
    monasteries, 244, 264–6
    Mount Sinai, 264–6
    Penitents, 105
    al-Rusafa, 242
    Takht-e Soleyman, 279
    'Umar II's tomb, 245
    see also hajj
  piracy, 253–4
  Piruz, 91, 99
  plague, 51–3, 69, 219–21
  pledge of allegiance (*bay'a*), 92–3, 100, 101, 102n, 103, 142, 146, 188, 200, 205, 211, 267, 289, 308
  poetry, 20, 49, 121, 166n, 307
    al-Akhtal, 128–9, 267
    'Arabs', 162
    al-Farazdaq, 155, 164
    Jarir, 155–6, 163–4

John of Damascus, 273–4
'southern' and 'northern' tribes, 195
Sulayman b. 'Abd al-Malik, 163–4
trade routes, 254
Turanda, 157
Umayyad Mosque at Damascus, 154–6
Poitiers, 181
poll tax, 319, 320, 322, 326
polytheism, 61; *see also* 'pagans'
postal riders *see barīd*
precious metals, 224, 247–8, 251
precipitation 36, 38m, 216, 218
  dew, 164
  monsoon, 36, 214, 216, 217, 218, 219, 221
  rainfall, 35, 36, 36, 38m, 128, 214, 216, 217, 218, 221, 239
  snowfall, 216, 217
prophecy, 64–5

Qabisa b. Dhu'ayb al-Khuza'i, 311
Qadaris, 195
qāḍī, 314–16
al-Qadisiyya, 69
Qahtaba b. Shabib, 204–5
Qahtan, 196
Qahtani, 136–7
Qaliqala/Karin, 302m, 303
al-Qa'qa' b. Khulayd al-'Absi, 311
Qarqisiya (Lat. Circesium), 38m, 113–14
Qaryat al-Faw, 46
Qasr al-Hayr al-Gharbi, *177*, 178, 236m, 238–9, *239–41*, 244
Qasr al-Hayr al-Sharqi, 178, 235, 236m, *237*, 242, 244
Qasr Burqu', 236m, 244
Qasr Ibn Hubayra, 232, 235
al-Qastal, 236m, 244
Qatari b. Fuja'a, 133–5
qatī'a see land grants
al-Qatif, 301
Qayrawan, 99, 104, 158, 181, 187, 233, 296, 303, 304m, 325
Qays, Qaysis, 113, 122, 193–202
  al-'Abs, 150
  Maslama b. 'Abd al-Malik, 163
  Muhammad b. Marwan, 130
Qinnasrin, 178

Qurra b. Sharik al-'Absi, 151
'Umar b. Hubayra al-Fazari, 164, 172
'Umar II, 166, 170–1
Yusuf b. 'Umar al-Thaqafi, 190
Zubayrids, 113–14
see also Syria, 'northern' tribes
Qenneshre monastery, 262
Qinnasrin (Gk, Chalcis), 38m, 178, 199, 201, 206, 236m, 244, 275, 298, 300m
Quba', Medina, mosque, 153
Qubbash, al-Balqa', 56
Quda'a, 68, 70, 113, 194, 196, 200, 311, 312; see also Syria, 'southern' tribes
Quhistan, 99, 160m, 246, 305
Qulzum (Gk, Clysma), 180, 254, 299m, 319
Qur'an, *139*, 223
   'Abd al-Malik, 86, 137–8
   Abu 'Isa al-Isfahani, 282
   animal sacrifice, 63
   basmala, 74–5
   codex, 19–20, *139*
   coinage, 138, 140–1, 325
   compilation, 19–20, 59–60, 86, 138
   Dome of the Rock, Jerusalem, 143
   Egyptian papyri, 74
   'Faithful' (Ar. *mu'minīn*), 61–3, 65–6
   al-Hajjaj b. Yusuf al-Thaqafi, 137–8
   and Hijazi polity, 59–60
   Judaism and Christianity, 63
   markets, 315
   martyrdom, 62–3
   Mount Sinai, 265
   Muhammad, Prophet, 64
   al-Mukhtar al-Thaqafi, 106–7
   Muslims, 62
   pilgrimage, 63
   poetry, 163
   Surat al-Hijr (Q. 15), *139*
   Surat al-Ikhlas (Q. 112), *140*
   Surat al-Nahl (Q. 16), *139*, 223n
   Surat al-Nisa' (Q. 4), 143
   Surat al-Tawba/al-Bara'a (Q. 9), *140*, 141
   as Umayyad document, 19–20
   'Uthman, 85–6
Quraysh, 55–6, 57c, 58, 60, 65–7, 76, 78–9, 80, 89, 100, 119, 136, 330
   Abbasids, 207, 330
   'Amr b. al-'As, 69–70, 98

   commerce, 55–6
   Egypt, 69–70, 98
   ḥajj, 55–6, 63, 330
   Hashim, Banu, 57c, 119, 183
   Ibn al-Ash'ath, 136
   Ibn al-Zubayr, 102–3
   'Kharijites', 124, 133, 184–5, 188, 201, 284
   Makhzum, 56, 57c, 108, 147, 176
   Mecca, 58, 63, 76, 93
   Sa'd b. Abi Waqqas, 69
   Syria, 56, 67, 77, 80, 237, 298
   Thaqif, 56, 106, 132
   'Uthman, 86, 89
Qurra b. Sharik al-'Absi, 151, 153, 163, 312, *313*
quṣūr see 'desert castles'
Qutayba b. Muslim al-Bahili, 159–61, 160m, 174, 232

Rabah Shir Zanji, 133
Rabi' b. Ziyad al-Harithi, 232
Rabi'a, 196, 197
rain *see* precipitation
Raja' b. Haywa al-Kindi, 311
al-Ramla, 232, 236m, 244
Raqqa (Lat. Callinicum), 38m, 178, 236m, 242, 300m
Rashidun, *see* 'Rightly Guided Caliphs'
Rayy, 122, 159, 232, 304, 305, 306m
relics 48, 54, 90, 107
religious scholars, 137, 147, 151, 154, 166, 167, 192, 311
Rhodes, 224
'Ridda Wars' *see* 'Wars of Apostasy'
'Rightly Guided Caliphs', 7–8, 15
rivers
   agriculture, 220–22
   physical geography 214–16, 217
Roman Empire, 3m, 13, 16–17, 31–35, 33m, 42–53, 78, 95, 162, 166–7, 172–3, 230, 233, 261, 271, 273
   'Abd al-Malik, 142, 144–6, 295
   administration, 296–8, 316–17, 321
   Africa, 83–4, 99, 100, 122, 124, 233, 251, 303, 304m
   Arabian Peninsula, 37–9, 41–6, 47–51, 53

Roman Empire (*cont.*)
   Armenia, 131, 302
   armies and navies, 68–9, 104, 107, 111–12, 152
   Asia Minor, 83–4, 179
   Christianity, 9, 32, 121, 153–4, 167, 259–60, 268–9, 330
   coinage, 140–1, 320, 324
   commerce and exchange, 247–50, 254–5
   demography, 219–20
   Egypt, 49, 54, 56, 60, 70, 76, 82, 89, 90, 282–3, 318
   frontier with Umayyad Empire, 122, 163, 167–8, 172, 173, 176, 178, 188, 193, 195, 198–201, 242, 330
   Hammat Gader inscription, 94–5
   Hisham b. 'Abd al-Malik, 176, 177, 179, 186–8, 275
   Judaism, 275–6
   Mardaites, 284
   Parthian Empire, 31
   Sasanian Empire, 13–14, 22, 29, 31–5, 33m, 42–3, 45–6, 47–8, 50–1, 53–5
   silk, 224
   sources, 16–18, 287–8
   Syria, 39, 44–5, 49, 54, 56, 59, 60, 67–9, 77
   taxation, 319, 322
   tribute from, 154, 155, 251, 320
   tribute to, 91, 128, 254–5
   truces with Arabians, 91, 97, 111, 128, 145, 167, 172–3
   'Uthman, 88
   al-Walid I, 150–1, 228
Rufinus, 45
al-Ruha *see* Edessa
al-Rusafa, 178, 193, 195, 198, 228, 230, 232, 236m, 242, 244, 275, 286

Sabians, 283
sacrifice, animal *see* animal sacrifice
Sa'd b. Abi Waqqas al-Zuhri, 69
Sa'd al-Harashi, 174
Sahara, 32–5, 173–4, 188
Sa'id b. 'Abd al-Malik, 229
Sa'id b. al-'As, 83, 87c, 88, 109c
Sa'id b. 'Uqba, 311
Salih b. Jubayr al-Ghassani, 311

Salih b. Kaysan, 154
Salim Abu l-'Ala', 311–12
Salim Abu l-Zu'ayzi'a, 310–11
Salul, Banu, 311
Samaritans, 277
Samarqand, 99, 159, 160m, 161, 189, 206, 232–3, 291, 325
Sana'a, 51, 89, 153, 226, 228, 301
   mosque, 153
Saracens, 44, 45, 73, 75, 265, 266, 268, 322
Sardinia, 152, 304m
Sardis, Asia Minor, 164
Sarjun b. Mansur al-Rumi, 92–3, 273, 310, 321
Sasanian Empire, 4, 11, 13–14, 16–17, 31–2, 33m, 34, 43, 60, 78, 98–9, 220, 290–1, 296–7, 321
   administration, 308–9, 316–17, 320–1
   agriculture, 221–2
   and Arabia, 50–3, 55
   and Armenia, 302–3
   Christianity, 49–51, 259, 280–1
   coinage, 133, 140–1, 320, 327
   commerce and exchange, 247–50
   Council of Dvin, 285
   Iraq, 59, 67, 69, 234–5
   Judaism, 50, 276
   Khusro II Parvez, 53–4
   monasticism, 280
   Narseh, 159
   Nasrids, 47, 53
   Piruz, 91
   plague, 52–3
   religions, 277–83, 289–92
   Shapur I, 31–2
   silk, 224
   Takht-e Soleyman, 279
   Yazdgird III, 78, 85, 279
   Yazid (III) b. al-Walid, 198
Sawad, 180, 221, 234–5, 282, 284, 317
Sayf ibn Dhi Yaz'an, 51
Sbeitla (Sufetela/Subaytila), 84, 251
scribes, 72–5, 309–12
   'Abd al-Hamid, 312
   Athanasius bar Gumoye, 229
   chief, 309–12
   al-Hasan al-Basri, 184
   Ibn al-Muqaffa', 328

Marwan b. al-Hakam, 83, 100, 108
Sarjun b. Mansur al-Rumi, 92–3, 273
'Ubayd Allah b. 'Aws al-Ghassani, 321
'Ubayd Allah b. al-Habhab al-Saluli, 180
Ziyad b. Sumayya, 321
Scythopolis (Ar. Baysan), 231, 300m
Sebaste (Ar. Nablus), 277, 300m
Sebasteia, Anatolia, 152
Sebastopolis, Anatolia, 130
Semitic languages, 41
Sergiopolis *see* al-Rusafa
sex,
  laws and customs, 252, 328
  Umayyads' reputations, 167, 242
Shabib b. Yazid al-Shaybani, 132
Shammar Yuhar'ish, 42, 45–6
Shapur I, 32, 282
Sharahil b. Zalim, 48
Shayban, Banu, 201–2
Shayban al-Yashkuri, 202
sheep *see* animals
Shi'i Islam, 4–8, 6c, 102, 150, 284, 329
shipyards, 223–4, 254, 319
Shurahbil b. Hasana, 66
shurṭa, 175, 180, 195, 310, 312–14
Sicily, 95–6, 125, 173, 181, 186, 187, 192, 304m
Siffin, 90, 107
silk, 224, *225*, 247, 249–50, 321
'Silk Road', 249–50, 291
silver, 224, 320, 326, 327
Simon the Syrian, patriarch, 271–2
Sinai,
  Monastery at Mount, 263–4, *263*, 264–6
  Peninsula, 36m, 37, 263–6, 268, 299m
Sind, 124, 160m, 161, 163, 172, 217, 220, 233, 252, 253, 296
Sinjar, 232
al-Sinnabra, 243–4
Sirjan, 305
Sistan, 124, 160m, 232, 253, 306m
  climate and ecology, 216–17
  al-Hajjaj b. Yusuf al-Thaqafi, 134–7
  Piruz, 91
  Qutayba b. Muslim al-Bahili, 159, 161
  Shayban al-Yashkuri, 202
  Sulayman b. 'Abd al-Malik, 163
  trade routes, 84, 98–9

'Umar II, 173–4
Yazid (I) b. Mu'awiya, 104
'Sixty Martyrs of Jerusalem', 274
slaves, 91, 202, 213, 224, 225, 248, 249, 252–4, 271, 307
  agricultural, 105, 133, 235, 252
  concubines, 167, 252
  domestic, 252
  freed slaves (*mawālī*), 106, 107, 169, 202
  gifts, 157
  Ibn Mu'awiya, 202
  Jurjan and Tabaristan, 163
  Khurasan, 151–2
  Mardaites, 97
  North Africa, 100, 124, 131, 151–2, 158, 252
  al-Mukhtar, 106, 107
  Musa b. Nusayr, 158
  non-Arabians, 225, 307
  prices, 252
  Sind, 161, 252
  Sistan, 135, 159
  'slaving zones', 252
Sogdia, 99, 124, 160m, 173, 220, 232–3, 283, 289, 291, 305
  mountains, 217
  Qutayba b. Muslim al-Bahili, 159–60
  trade routes, 249–50
  tribute, 135
  Türgesh federation, 174, 189
Sogdian language, 291
Sohar, 301
Solomon, King, 55, 142, 156, 163, 164
sources, 16–21
South Arabia, 35–40, 36m, 60–1, 76–7, 80, 196, 214, 298–301
  agriculture, 221
  governors, 66, 89, 151, 170, 190, 298–301
  al-Husayn b. 'Ali, 102
  Ibn Mu'awiya, 202
  languages, 41, 46, 51
  al-Mukhtar al-Thaqafi, 105
  plague, 52
  Quraysh, 55–6
  religion and identity, 51
  Talib al-Haqq, 201
  see also Himyar, Yemen

'southern' and 'northern' tribes, 194–7
Spain, 124, 158, 174, 181, 289, 303, 304m;
    see also al-Andalus
Sri Lanka, 254
stucco, 85, *177*, *239*, 243
Sufyani, 206
Sulayman b. 'Abd al-Malik, 150–1, 162–75
    chief scribes and tax officials, 311
    Dabiq, 245
    Filastin, 244
    governors, 163
    al-Hajjaj b. Yusuf al-Thaqafi, 159, 161
    Hisham b. 'Abd al-Malik, 176
    Khalid b. 'Abd Allah al-Qasri, 180
    mother, 150; see also Wallada bt.
        al-'Abbas
    Muhallabids, 161, 163
    pilgrimage, 148, 179
    poetry, 164
    al-Ramla, 232, 244
    succession to Sulayman, 166
Sulayman b. Hisham, 193, 200, 201
Sulayman b. Sa'd al-Khushani, 311
Sulayman b. Surad, 106
Sumaysat, 207
Sunni Islam, 4–8, 167, 185, 329
suq see markets
swamps *see* marshes
Syracuse, 95, 187, 304m
Syria, 67–77, 93, 108–14, 133, 180, 220–1,
    228–9, 231–3, 235–7, 242–5, 295–8,
    300m, 316, 330
    'Abd al-Malik, 114, 119, 127, 129–30,
        144, 309
    agriculture, 221–3
    Christianity, 155, 167, 259–62, 266,
        269–73, 281, 285
    coinage, 138–42
    geography, 214, 216
    al-Hajjaj b. Yusuf al-Thaqafi, 123, 132,
        136
    Hisham b. 'Abd al-Malik, 176, 178–9,
        182
    Ibn al-Zubayr, 103–4, 108–9, 127
    iron mining, 224
    itinerant monarchy, 243–5
    Judaism, 275–7
    Kalbi group identity, 86–8, 87c, 122

Marwan II, 200, 204–7
Maslama b. 'Abd al-Malik, 246
Mu'awiya b. Abi Sufyan, 92, 94–5,
    96–7, 101, 309
Muhallabids, 171–2
Quraysh, 55–6
taxation, 317–18, 320–5
trade routes, 249
tribal groups, 76–7, 79–80, 150, 166,
    190–2, 194–6
'Uthman, 82–4, 86–92
wood for ships, 224
see also Syrian armies; Syrian Desert
Syriac language, 21, 41, 68, 93, 97, 128,
    260, 267–8, 270–1, 322, 323
Syrian armies, 103, 121, 123, 125, 132, 136,
    161, 163, 179, 185, 189, 192, 194,
    200, 201
Wasit, 137
Syrian Desert 33m, 35, 36m, 38m, *39*,
    215m
    alliances, 47
    Arabic language, 48–9, 76, 260
    Christianity, 49–50, 93
    geography, 35, 37, 214, 244
    Kalb, 122, 194–5
    Mawia, 44–5
    pastoralist groups, 11, 13, 22–3, 60,
        67, 78, 231, 260, 267, 283–4,
        329–30
    Romans, 43, 47–8
    Sasanians, 43, 47
Syrian steppe *see* Syrian Desert

Tabaristan, 133, 134, 163, 305, 306m
al-Tabariyya *see* Tiberias
Tablettes Albertini, 222
Tadmur *see* Palmyra
Taghlib, Banu, 40–1, 267
al-Ta'if, 56, 66, 69, 76, 82, 106, 107, 114,
    178, 298
Takht-e Soleyman, 279
Tal Kashaf, 206
Talha b. 'Ubayd Allah, 90, 93
Talib al-Haqq, 201
talisman *see* relics
Tamim, 105, 133, 155–6, 183, 189
    Basra, 197

Tang Empire *see* China
Tangier, 158, 187, 289, 303, 304m
Tanukh, Banu, 44–5, 267, 311
Tarif [Barghawata leader], 289
Tariq b. Ziyad, 158
Tarkhan Nizak, 159, 291
tax officials, 121, 309–12
taxation, 162, 168, 175, 189, 234–7, 248, 290–1, 306, 317–27
   census, 181, 270–1, 322, 323, 327
   Egypt and Iraq, 79, 122–3, 137, 254, 324
   embole, 254
   Hisham b. 'Abd al-Malik, 176, 179–81, 246
   Ibn Mu'awiya, 202
   in kind, 254, 319, 326
   labour service, 319, 324, 326
   and labour shortages, 221, 256, 324
   monasteries, 265, 280
   revenue, 122, 180, 193–4, 246, 251, 252, 317–18, 322–4, 326–7
   surveys, 152–3, 319, 323
   tolls, 254, 319, 326
   'tributary empires', 31
   Zoroastrianism, 279
Tayma', 50
tayyaye, 44, 92–3, 268, 271
Temple Mount, Jerusalem, 142, *143*, 228, 276–7
Thabit b. Sulayman b. Sa'd, 312
Thaqif, Banu, 56, 66, 122, 132, 136, 190, 192–3, 194, 311
   al-Hajjaj b. Yusuf al-Thaqafi, 114, 132, 135, 137, 161, 171
   Mu'awiya b. Abi Sufyan, 98, 132, 311
   al-Mughira b. Shu'ba al-Thaqafi, 69, 98, 132
   Muhammad b. al-Qasim al-Thaqafi, 161
   al-Mukhtar al-Thaqafi, 106
   Mutarrif b. al-Mughira al-Thaqafi, 132
   al-Walid (II) b. Yazid, 192–3
   Yazid (I) b. Mu'awiya, 132
   Yazid (III) b. al-Walid, 198
   Yusuf b. Muhammad al-Thaqafi, 194
   Yusuf b. 'Umar al-Thaqafi, 190, 193
Theodore (appointed in Alexandria), 269, 321
Theodore Rshtuni, 84

Theophanes, 275
Tiberias (Ar. al-Tabariyya), 38m, 230, 231, 236m, 311, 275, 300m, 311
Tiflis, 54, 302m
Tigris river, 31, 122, 133, 205, 214, 216, 218n, 220, 221, 246, 262, 297m
tin, 224
tirāz see silk
tolls, 254, 319, 326
trade routes, 31, 37, 84, 247–50, 249m, 253–4 *see also* commerce and exchange
Transoxiana, 159–60, 173, 174, 289–92
tribute, 12, 71, 91, 154, 155, 251, 291, 320, 323
   'Abd al-'Aziz b. Marwan, 322
   'Abd al-Malik, 112, 128, 152
   amīrs, 181n, 193–4, 306
   building materials, 223
   Caucasus, 111
   commerce and exchange, 250–2, 254–5
   dīwāns, 318
   gold, 320
   al-Hajjaj b. Yusuf al-Thaqafi, 323
   Hisham b. 'Abd al-Malik, 177
   Iraq, 167
   Khurasan, 85
   'Maronite Chronicle', 270
   Marwanids, 134–5, 158–61
   Mecca, 59
   Mu'awiya b. Abi Sufyan, 91
   North Africa, 124
   'tributary empires', 31
   al-Walid I, 154–5
   Yazid b. al-Muhallab, 163
Trinitarianism, 93, 129, 138, 141, 272, 273, 288, 326
Tripolitania, 287, 304m
Tukharistan, 99, 160m, 189, 217, 220, 222, 233, 253, 290
Tunis, 223–4, 228, 230, 233, 296
Tunisia, 84, 99
Tur 'Abdin, 260, 262
Turanda, 157
Türgesh, 174, 177, 188–90, 289
Turks, 3m, 54, 84, 174, 289, 290
Tustar, 136
Twelver Shi'i tradition, 5–7

Tyana, 152
Tyre, 96, 300m

'Ubayd Allah b. 'Aws al-Ghassani, 310, 321
'Ubayd Allah b. al-Habhab *see* Ibn al-Habhab
'Ubayd Allah b. Ziyad, 97–8, 102, 107, 110, 111, 320–1
al-Ubulla, 70, 296, 297m, 303–4
'Umar (I) b. al-Khattab, 68, 71–2, 234–5, 254, 295
   calendar, 74
   commanders and governors, 69–70, 98
   markets, 229, 315
   Medinan mosque, 85
   Muhammad, Prophet, 67
   al-Mukhtar al-Thaqafi, 106
   plague, 69–70
   qāḍī, 314
   Qur'an, 86
   taxation, 254, 319, 323
   tomb, 154
'Umar (II) b. 'Abd al-'Aziz, 151, 154, 162–75, 184
   Christians, 168, 285
   Ghaylan al-Dimashqi, 182
   governors, 170–1, 172, 181
   image in the later sources, 166–7
   marriages, 166
   maternal ancestry, 166
   Muslims and Christians, 273
   taxation, 181, 311, 326–7
   tomb, 245
   weights, measures and scales, 316
'Umar b. Hubayra al-Fazari, 164–5, 172, 193
'Umayr b. Sa'd al-Ansari, 69–70
Umayya b. 'Abd Allah, 323
Umayyad dynasty, 15–16, 16c, 120c
'Umayyad North', 129, 301, 302m, 303; *see also* Armenia, Azerbaijan, Caucasus, Jazira, Mesopotamia
'Uqba b. Nafi', 99–100, 325
urban change, 225–33
al-Urdunn, 92n, 104, 200, 300m, 311
'Urwa b. al-Zubayr, 148–9
Usama b. Zayd, 311
'Usays (Jabal Says), 236m, 244

'Uthman b. 'Affan, 7, 15–16, 16c, 80–92, 87c, 98, 109c 166, 267, 295, 315
   Christianity 267
   civil war (*fitna*), 88–9
   descendants, 100
   governors, 82–4
   land grants 234–5
   marriages, 64n2, 86–8, 87c
   and Marwanid legitimation, 86, 100, 108, 147–8, 166, 199
   Mecca and Medina, 85–6, 100, 254
   Qur'an, 86, 138
   war with Rome, 84–5, 88
'Uthmanic Codex, 19, 86, 138

Vaga/Beja *see* Beja/Vaga
Vahan of Goght'n, 286
Valens, Emperor, 44–5
Vandals, 96, 233
Visigoths, 124, 158, 173–4, 181, 233, 259, 303
Volubilis (Ar. Walila), 233, 304m

Wadi al-Dayr monastery, 264–5
Wadi al-Natrun monastery, 263
walā', 169–70
al-Walid (I) b. 'Abd al-Malik, 150–7, 176, 180, 198, 311
   Constantinople, 162, 163
   Damascus, 228, 275
   governors, 151, 154, 157, 158–61
   ḥajj, 148, 179
   Islam, 267
   land survey, 322
   al-Sinnabra, 243–4
al-Walid b. 'Uqba, 83
al-Walid b. 'Utba b. Abi Sufyan, 100
al-Walid (II) b. Yazid, 176, 192–201, 226, 237, 244, 245, 311
Walila (Lat. Volubilis), 233, 304m
Wallada bt. al-'Abbas, 150
'Wars of Apostasy', 59, 104
Wasit, 123, 135–8, 151, 163, 171, 172, 201, 202, 205–6, 232, 253, 296, 297m, 304, 323
   coinage, 325
   irrigation, 235
   mosque-palace complex, 226–8

weights, measures and scales, 296, 303, 316, 324–5
West African Monsoon, 216, 218–19
West Arabian
  federation, 47, 60, 61–3
  irrigation projects, 245–6
  pastoralist groups, 58
  religion, 62–3, 106
  see also Hijaz
White Monastery of Upper Egypt, 263
wine, 167, 242, 248, 249m, 265, 268
'world crisis', 22, 47–63

Yahya b. Zayd, 190
al-Yamama, 245, 301
Yamanat, 46
al-Ya'qubi, 147, 245
Yarmuk, 68
Yathrib (later Medina), 50, 57–8, 60, 66–7, 76, 82, 92, 298
Yazdgird III, 85, 91, 159, 279
Yazid (II) b. 'Abd al-Malik, 120c, 162–76, 180, 192, 311
  image in the later sources 166–7
  maternal ancestry and marriages, 166
  Muhallabids, 171–2
  Muslims and Christians, 273
  North Africa, 175, 181
  palaces near Amman, 244
  taxation, 326–7
  tomb, 245
Yazid b. Abi Sufyan, 67, 69
Yazid (I) b. Mu'awiya, 87c, 96, 101–4, 310
  Christianity, 267
  al-Huwwarin, 243
  mother, 86–8, 87c
  Syrian 'military districts' (*jund*s), 108, 298
  Thaqif, Banu, 132
Yazid b. al-Muhallab *see* Ibn al-Muhallab
Yazid b. 'Umar b. Hubayra, 193, 201, 202, 205–6, 232

Yazid (III) b. al-Walid, 198–202, 312
Yemen, 35, 36m, 37, 51, 89, 151, 153, 186, 190, 196, 245; *see also* Himyar; South Arabia
Yemenis (tribal group), 89, 113, 136, 179–80, 190, 195–7, 199, 200, 201, 202, 204; *see also* Quda'a; Syria
Yovhannes Ojnec'i, Armenian Catholicos 285
Yusuf b. 'Umar al-Thaqafi, 190, 193–5, 200

Zab, 205–6
Zabulistan, 289, 290
Zadhanfarrukh, 321, 324n
Zagros Mountains, 216, 224, 232, 279, 297m, 304–5
zandaqa see heresy, in Islam
Zaranj, 3m, 84, 99, 135, 160m, 232, 305, 306m
Zayd b. 'Ali b. al-Husayn, 190, 202
'Zayn al-'Abidin', 'Ali b. al-Husayn, 150
Ziyad b. Sumayya, 97–9, 232, 304, 320–1, 323
Zoroastrianism, 14, 21, 32, 50, 258, 277–83, 290–1, 292, 327
al-Zubayr b. al-'Awwam, 70, 81c, 90, 93
Zubayrids, 81c, 103, 111, 322
  'Abd al-Malik, 112–14, 271, 295
  Abu Bakr, 80, 119
  dyophysitism, 281
  'Kharijites', 133, 184
  Khurasan, 134
  Medina, 148–50
  al-Mukhtar al-Thaqafi, 106–8
Zufar b. al-Harith al-Kilabi, 113–14
Zuhra, Banu, 57c, 66, 149
al-Zuhri, Ibn Shihab Muhammad b. Muslim, 148, 149, 192
Zunbil, 135, 136, 159
Zuqnin Chronicle, 270–1

EU representative:
Easy Access System Europe
Mustamäe tee 50, 10621 Tallinn, Estonia
Gpsr.requests@easproject.com

www.ingramcontent.com/pod-product-compliance
Lightning Source LLC
Chambersburg PA
CBHW052139300426
44115CB00011B/1444